The
PORTUGUESE
MAKING
OF
AMERICA

MANUEL MIRA

P.A.H.R. FOUNDATION, INC.
FRANKLIN, NC 28734 - USA

Follow the Colorful and Revealing History
of The Early Settlers in North-America.
The Melungeons and other Groups

Portuguese presence in the United States of America has a long history much of which has yet to be unfolded. Unless courageous researchers take the bull by the horns our past will fade into obscurity thereby forever shadowing the untold truth. Fortunately, because of Manuel Mira's remarkable thirst for knowledge coupled with a tremendous appetite for historical revelation, we are now blessed with his English version of The Portuguese Making of America — a very important contribution to Appalachia's Melungeon population. The powerful book is not only a tribute to the many whose Portuguese roots have been lost in the annals of time, but equally a historical instrument which serves to trigger further study by researchers at the local, national and international levels.

Manuel Mira is to be congratulated for finally bringing to fruition The Portuguese Making of America. It is, indeed, a most significant entry into the everlasting annals of Portuguese-American and Canadian history.

**Adalino Cabral, Ph.D. Portuguese, Hispanic and American
Cultures and Languages Educator Boston area**

"Manuel has good informal style of his own.The inclusion of many facts about the development of the Portuguese background, with the careful research he has done, and carefully footnoted, adds a good deal to the book, and makes a welcome addition, particularly to those researchers with some background of Melungeon reading, or study, or an interest in European history."

**Jean Patterson Bible
Historian, researcher, author
Dandridge, Tennessee**

This book brings together a great diversity of historical resources and oral accounts of Iberian exploration and settlement since the 1500's of what would become the United States. [and]... provides detailed timelines and numerous citations that will be helpful for future researchers and genealogists.

(The Forgotten Portuguese book review, Portuguese Studies Review, ICGP, University of New Hampshire)

**Thaddeus C. Guldbrandsen University of
North Carolina at Chapel Hill**

"No library on Americana will be complete without this valuable book. It brings together all the Portuguese discoveries and explorations"

Manuel Luciano da Silva, M.D. - Physician & Historian

* * *

Manuel Mira also wrote "The Forgotten Portuguese" and "Os Portugueses na Formação da America" in Portuguese.

Front cover illustration: The mythical giant and monster Adamastor serves as a theme the whole cover. It was described by Camões, the Portuguese national poet in his epic book "Os Lusíadas" in Canto V, 49-50-51 as shown below.

The fearsome monster was proceeding with its prophecies of the fates in store for us...

I'm that mighty hidden cape, called by you Portuguese the cape of the Storms, that neither Ptolomy, Pomponius, Strabo, Pliny...

Until now it has remained unknown: your daring offends it deeply.
Adamastor is my name.
I was one of the giant sons of the earth, btrother to Enceladus, Briareus, and the others.

With them I took part in the war against Jupiter, not indeed piling
mountain upon mountain but as a sea-captain, disputing Neptune's suqadrons of the deep.

Cover of the epic poem book "Os Lusíadas" written by Camões in late 16th century and showing a contemporary engraving.

Our young people is proud of their history and also working to preserve our proud Heritage.

Ana Mafalda Costa

Ana Mafalda Costa was born in Oporto, Portugal, on June 6th, 1973 and she has lived all her life in Oliveira de Azeméis, district of Aveiro. She received a Bachelor's degree in International Relations and a Master of Arts (Teaching of English and German) by the University of Minho, in Braga.

She has always shown a keen interest in languages and her strong curiosity on the subject has taken her to attend several courses related to language teaching. From her translation and retranslation pieces of work, one should mention the English version of the poetry book "Perfect Simplicity", bilingual edition, by Armindo Magalhães; "Resurrection Man" by Eoin McNamee, in cooperation with Ana Maria Chaves; and "Cold Mountain" by Charles Frazier. This last piece of work, extraordinarily demanding due to the richness of specific vocabulary, such as the flora of the states of Virginia, North Carolina and Tennessee, has enabled Ana Mafalda Costa to get acquainted with the American Culture and History.

Ana Mafalda translated this book to the Portuguese language.

Nancy Portugal

Nancy Portugal is the daughter of Marcia and Tony Portugal from the Madeira Island. Nancy was born in New York and lives in Jupiter, Florida. She is 24 years old and graduated from the University of Central Florida in 1999 with a Bachelor of Fine Arts Degree, specialized in drawing. Nancy is the author of the paint used to illustrate the cover of this book.

Her artistic imagination has put together the mythical monster Adamastor and the Portuguese shipwrecks in an imaginary American shore, with the American Indian woman welcoming the Portuguese with open arms.

* * *

Also published by the P.A.H.R. Foundation: The Forgotten Portuguese in hard cover and "Os Portugueses na Formação da América" in Portuguese, by the same author.

About the Author

Manuel Mira, who was born in Portugal and lives in the Appalachians, has been able to identify with these forgotten groups.

His research has brought to light for the first time some of the missing pieces in the Melungeon puzzle. His work also presents several aspects of American and Portuguese history.

The author has lived for extensive periods of time in three continents. This has given him considerable knowledge of the different groups of people with whom the Portuguese have integrated.

His love for history and deep interest in social and community affairs gave him an opportunity to compile many years of experience and research into a book that will be a welcome addition to any library.

Manuel Mira is married to Lurdes, has a son and a daughter, and six grandchildren.

Manuel is the chairman of an electronic manufacturing firm, and writes for the *Luso-Americano*, a Portuguese-American newspaper in Newark, New Jersey and the *Lusa,* a Portuguese national news agency.

He has been awarded the Portuguese Community Medal of Merit by the Portuguese Government for his outstanding services on behalf of the Portuguese Communities throughout the world.

His first book has been placed in the Portuguese Embassies in many countries by Secretary of State of the Portuguese Department of Foreign Affairs.

This same book has also been placed in most major Universities throughout North-America with the cooperation of the F.L.A.D. of Lisbon, Portugal.
Luso-American Development Foundation.

With the help of many members, the P.A.H.R. Foundation has placed it in some of the major Libraries in the USA. It is also part of the Library of Congress and the Portuguese National Library collections.

Manuel Mira has donated all proceeds to the Foundation.

Publisher's Cataloging-in-Publication
(Provided by Quality Books, Inc.)
Mira, Manuel, 1933-   .
The Portuguese Making of America / by Manuel Mira. -- 1st ed. p. cm.
    Includes bibliographical references and index.
    LCCN: 00-091243
    ISBN: 0-9658927-1-9

    1. Portuguese Americans--Genealogy. 2. Melungeons--
History. 3. Portugal--History. 4. Portugal--Genealogy.
    5. Cherokee Indians. 6. Lumbee Indians.   I. Title.

    E184.P8M57 200   973'.04691   QBI00-792

Early North-American History with 424 pages, 119 illustrations, 1028 footnotes
and an extensive complete bibliography. Over 1000 names with their origins.
    Proceeds of the sale of this book will be donated to the Portuguese-American
Historical Research Foundation, a North Carolina non-profit corporation
dedicated to the research of early American history and the Portuguese people's
contribution to the making of America.
    History and the subject of this book is an ongoing research. The author invites
the reader to submit any corrections, omissions or suggestions to be inserted in
the next edition. Contributions are welcome and authorship acknowledged.

Write to: The Portuguese-American Historical
Research Foundation, Inc. (PAHR Foundation, Inc.)
277 Industrial Park Road—Franklin, NC 28734—USA
email: portugal@dnet.net
http://www.PortugueseFoundation.org

The paper used in this book meets the minimum requirements of American
National Standard for Information Sciences—Permanence of Paper
for Printed Library Materials, ANSI Z39.48—1984.

Contents and Reference Details

Part I—Contents and Reference Detail (Cont.)

Chapter IV

The 20th Century

Part II

Part II—Contents and Reference Detail (Cont.)

Part II—Contents and Reference Detail (Cont.)

Table of Illustrations

Table of Illustrations (Cont.)

Dedication

To all authors whose books and papers have been quoted in this work.
Without their prior research, this book would have been almost impossible.
Also to my wife Lurdes, my family, and friends who went without my company during the many long hours of research.

Preface

In 1998, Manuel Mira presented me with the distinct honor of writing the Preface to the first edition of this book. Now, in 2001, I have been asked to write a preface to the second edition. I accept that offer without hesitation and with great pride.

Manuel Mira is a meticulous researcher who leaves no stone unturned and, refreshingly, is also open minded to the theories and educated conjecture of others. It is this broad-mindedness that makes Manuel such a joy to work with, and likewise makes his own assertions well worth pondering.

The answer to the Melungeon origins riddle is undoubtedly a complex, multi-ethnic one, with the mystery being in how we eventually seam together the Mediterranean, Native American, African, Asian, and European strains that undeniably contributed to our gene pool. This updated edition of Manuel's book will offer even more food for thought as we explore the various origin scenarios, and especially as we consider a number of possible Portuguese origins. In my opinion, there is no doubt that the earliest Melungeon populations carried "Portuguese" heritage, probably from a variety of both traditional and non-traditional Portuguese sources. I also suspect that at least some of our seemingly non-Portuguese traditions of origin (e.g., Turkish, Jewish, African, etc.) may well have come via the early Portuguese settlements, where people of many ethnic, racial, and religious backgrounds were brought. In short, Mr. Mira's work is important far beyond the simple Portuguese elements that may be involved. His book contains information and records and theoretical rationales that can be useful to Americans of all creeds and colors searching for their full identities, or simply interested in better understanding the hidden ethnic diversity that makes America the great nation that she is.

Let me again congratulate Manuel Mira on a job well done!

N. Brent Kennedy, Ph.D.
Vice Chancellor
The University of Virginia's College at Wise

Author of
The Melungeons:
The Resurrection of a Proud People
Mercer University Press

Acknowledgments and Credits

I am most grateful to many persons who helped and furnished material, permitting me to use and quote from it. They are too many to mention here. To the following P.A.H.R. Foundation's Advisory Council Members for their support and advice: Eduardo Mayone Dias, Ph.D.; N. Brent Kennedy, Ph.D.; Evelyn McKinley Orr; Geoffrey Gomes, M.A.; and Dr. Manuel Luciano da Silva, M.D. Also to New Jersey's Luso-Americano newspaper, Antonio Matinho and Fernando dos Santos, of Newark. I should not forget the many participants who graciously provided personal interviews. To one and all, my sincere thanks.

Last but not least, to Adalino Cabral, Ph.D., instructor of Portuguese, Spanish and English bilingual education for his careful and detailed analysis of this work, his constructive criticism and suggestions.

How this Book is Organized

In order for the reader to obtain the most benefit, a few steps should be followed. The first nine pages, starting with page iii, show the table of contents. This is very important and has a detailed description of the many items discussed. Pages xiii to xxiv are of an introductory nature and also describe some of the research done about the Melungeons, a group who claims Portuguese ancestry.

Part I starts with Chapter I and ends on Chapter IV covering early American History and possible connections between Melungeons, Native Americans and other groups of early settlers. Part II contains Chapter V through X is mostly dedicated to the history of the Portuguese people and their presence in North America since the 15th century. In both parts, an effort was made to present the study and research in a chronological sequence, to enable the reader to follow the events and understand the social changes in the different time periods.

The Appendix section provides substantial reference material with thousands of surnames which will be most useful for genealogists. It also presents several informative tables with 16th century shipwrecks, weddings between Portuguese men and native women, language analysis, and many other bits of information the reader can refer to anytime. The index is mostly patronymic in nature, but also toponymic showing the most important names and geographic places.

Prologue

Why am I doing this research? The question may arise as to why this research has been undertaken. In his excellent, well written and well documented book, *The Portuguese Americans,*[1] Professor Emeritus Leo Pap, himself an immigrant from Switzerland and a distinguished linguist of the State University of New York at New Paltz, defends the Portuguese Community from an absurd remark made over 70 years ago. In Pap's preface, he cites a demeaning comment made by a bibliographer after a sociological study of the 1920's. It reads: *The study shows that the Portuguese are, by all accepted standards, a low grade people...* In response, Pap maintains that the Portuguese are neither high-grade or low-grade, but that: *...on their overwhelming majority* [they] *consist of ordinary laboring people with their distinct traditions.*[2] This research is in tune with Dr. Leo Pap's sense of justice to the Portuguese who have helped, and continue to help, build a strong America

I have heard it said many times, *I don't know what my ancestors did for America.* Even one more reason to get involved. If I don't know, does anyone else care to know? I would like to call this project *We are America's Portuguese.* The Portuguese people are one of the oldest European groups of settlers, if not the oldest in the U.S., and its presence is recorded since Colonial times. However it is one of the most ignored, and the researcher M. Estellie Smith is absolutely correct when she classified them as the *invisible minority.*

The Portuguese saw what happened to the more militant Irish and Italians when they were discriminated against and signs read *No Irish need apply* and *No Micks, Dagos...* thus invisibility was their best protection.[3]

Douglas Wheeler in his *Historical Dictionary of Portugal* also writes: *For a small country perched on the edge of Western Europe but with an early history which began more than 2,000 years ago, there is a vast bibliography extant in many languages.*[4] Family unit is still the best survival means for mankind, and I believe that strong family ties account for the survival of the Melungeons and other groups. Unfortunately, the future is not so bright for families throughout the world. Doug Levy wrote in *USA Today* that families are declining worldwide. Developing nations are seeing the breakdown of traditional families in much the same way as the United States and other industrial nations. Rising divorce rates, childbirth outside of marriage, and migration are among the reasons cited.[5]

This book may not be able to prove that the Portuguese are the ancestors of the Melungeons and other groups, although it may come very close. Also, it does not criticize any of the research or work done in the past by very qualified persons. By all means, they helped me and will help others who would like to pursue this subject any further. I will try to focus on the fact that the *Melungeons and other groups* may have several genetic mixtures, with the possibility of one stronger component, and if it seems that I am placing a stronger emphasis on the Portuguese, it is mostly because I can relate to what has been written about them, and at the same time try to fill the ever present knowledge vacuum about the history of Portugal.

I have merely compiled the facts as recorded by others. If they seem speculative, others have made them so. My work only asks questions that someone else with more expertise may be able to answer. In certain instances, I may also have doubts about fact authenticity. If so, it will be up to the reader to be the final judge based on the information presented. My aim is not to convince you, but to **inform** you.

Introduction

In today's age of easy transportation and communication, most of us believe that 1,000 or even 500 years ago, humans traveled very little or not at all. This is a misconception. Just because they did not have cars or airplanes does not mean that they did not go anywhere. By doing a surface history study, we quickly discover that people and goods moved from one place to another, carrying with them their culture in all its aspects.

During the reign of Portugal's King João II (1471-1495) the total distance traveled by the crew of the discovering vessels totaled fifty million miles.[6]

Wherever I go in my travels, I always wonder if the Portuguese were there or if they had any impact on the locale I happen to be visiting. The Appalachian Mountains had a special attraction for my wife and me. In 1987 when we visited western North Carolina, we liked it and decided to stay.

As time went on, I kept wondering if the Portuguese had been there or not. Near Franklin, N.C., I noticed a historical plaque honoring Juan Pardo for having passed through while commanding a Spanish expedition in 1567. Barbara McRae, a local writer and historian, told me about the Melungeons, other groups, and the Portuguese. That was the start of my research. Since then I have made contact with Mrs. Jean Patterson Bible and Dr. N. Brent Kennedy. These two fine persons have written and published books about the Melungeons. Since the start, I was fascinated with their story, and so was Antonio Matinho, the editor of the Luso-Americano of Newark, New Jersey, which is the largest Portuguese-American newspaper, published twice a week in the United States and distributed to all fifty states. I wrote a series of seven articles for that newspaper, and publication started on March 14, 1995. The interest was overwhelming on the part of the readers, who made numerous calls and showed an interest in knowing more about the Melungeons who, like them, also emigrated to this continent in search of a better life and freedom, and equally suffered discrimination in one form or other.

Finding myself living in the area where the Melungeons lived—and some still live—an opportunity presented itself to do research with a personal feeling and involvement with the local people.

Discrimination? The Melungeons suffered discrimination and prejudice. I am no stranger to that; just like them, I have been a victim of it since I was born, and did not stop until much later. At 18, tired of living in a country that was not offering the space and opportunity I needed to build my future as a free person, I left Portugal and immigrated to Brazil where I lived for five years.

Although the language is the same, I was discriminated against and recognized that I was not one of them because I had lighter skin. Most Brazilians have a darker olive skin—and the natural treatment was derogatory.

My Portuguese accent gave me away. That prompted me to learn the local lingo and mimic their pronunciation, so much so that in two years, it was hard for anyone to detect my Portuguese ancestry through my daily speech.

Five years later when I visited Portugal, my own mother did not recognize my voice. Why did I learn to speak like the Brazilians? The answer is very simple. It was a means of survival, and when you are alone and many thousands of miles from the place you used to call home, you will do anything to survive and gain acceptance.

After five years in Brazil, I came to the United States in 1957 and then to Toronto, Canada, where I lived for the next 16 years. Again, I felt discrimination because of the language difference and the color of my skin. I was not blonde; I had dark brown hair and brown eyes. In Brazil, I stood out because I was lighter, and in Canada, I stood out because I was darker.

Discrimination does not choose places. Again, as a means of survival, I tried to learn the language and eliminate my foreign accent. Unfortunately I was not able to do it totally; I was already 24 years old.

In the process of learning the best way to get accepted, I also learned quickly that if you are valuable and productive to the society and the system, discrimination slowly disappears. Still, many persons anglicized my name to Manny, which I did not mind, and shifted the pronunciation of my last name—Mira—from a Portuguese sound to an American sound, and in the process, misspelling it.

I also proved to myself that one can overcome discrimination, and that I did, when I was able to have my son admitted to Upper Canada College. That was a place one could not be admitted to if one's great-grandmother spoke broken English. That was a truly WASP type college (White Anglo-Saxon Protestant). Why am I expressing all this? The Melungeons had to do the same and more, as the reader will see after reading any of the books about these proud people.

As the reader will later read, the Melungeons did change their names, culture, religion, and language to survive in a strange and dangerous environment, where discrimination and prejudice were prevalent.

One thing they did not change was their origin. More than 200 years ago, when asked by John Sevier (he attempted to organize the State of Franklin (1784), forerunner of Tennessee, and later became governor) who they were, they said with pride, "We are Portuguese", they *proudly called themselves Portuguese.*[7]

Today they still know that their ancestors were *Portuguese,* although that word does not have the same meaning for them as it does for me.

Unfortunately, many of them avoided, and wanted to forget, the past, as well as the names Melungeon and Portuguese, because of the hardships that were brought upon them. My goal is to wipe that sad memory out of their minds and to say, be proud of your ancestors no matter who they were. If this work can accomplish that in just a single Melungeon, my effort was not in vain. It has been very difficult to trace the many Melungeon families. There are many who left their villages and went in search of a better life in the different parts of this country, which they did successfully. Many immigrants identify with their plight, as they also have been there before. I bring up some points on the books written by Bonnie Ball, Jean Patterson Bible and Dr. N. Brent Kennedy, first to reinforce their theory on the Portuguese Melungeons, and second to question others.

Fig. 1—The author, Manuel Mira, overlooking the Appalachian Mountains

Because this is a Portuguese point of view, I have to admit my own strong emphasis on anything connected with the Portuguese. However, I will also look into possibilities of other nationalities, races and ethnic groups, to compare, strengthen or weaken the Portuguese theory.

I acknowledge and emphasize that I am not a professional writer or historian. Therefore criticism or corrections that may help this book's message to be better understood, are welcome. Also it is not my intention to criticize, glorify or vilify any races or nationalities.

The reader must be warned beforehand that the events should be taken in the context of the time or epoch in which they occurred. Also, keep in mind that the world of the 15th and 16th centuries was a totally different one from that of the 20th century. What was accepted as normal behavior by the society then is unthinkable in terms of the last quarter of the 20th century.

Throughout the book, skin colors or races are mentioned, such as *Black, White, Negro, Mulatto*, etc. These words must be taken in the context of this research. There is no intended derogatory connotation whatsoever.

As far as the word *Negro* is concerned, it is a fact that in Portugal it is not derogatory. On the contrary, derogatory is using the name Black or *Preto* in Portuguese. Also what is common and politically correct in the USA, such as the usage of the name African-American to denote a *Black* person of African ancestry is not proper in Portugal where the term African-Portuguese describes not only a Black person of African ancestry, but also the many White persons born in Africa. We also must remember that just because a person is of a very dark color, he/she is not necessarily from Africa, he/she could be from Australia or from one of the many Far East areas.

This book in many instances is arranged chronologically, and may have the appearance of a history of Portugal in certain chapters. This it is not intended to be, but I will focus heavily on the Portuguese during the 15th and 16th centuries and afterwards. Whenever a Portuguese or other nationality name is shown, the Portuguese or one of that particular nationality spelling is kept, or as known. I strongly object to the use of Portuguese names translated from Portuguese to Spanish and then using the Spanish name to describe an original Portuguese name in an English book. I can also check the facts much easier from a dual cultural point of view, as a Portuguese and as an American, plus with a good share of Appalachian Mountain feeling. In any event, it is believed that the Melungeons or other groups— Portuguese or not—should have their place in the historical making of America, and if this work can help accomplish that, then all the time spent will have been worth while.

The Spanish and the Portuguese

This is not a book about the governments of Portugal, Spain or any other country. It is about their people, who gave their contributions to the making of America. While most of the navigation and exploration done by the Portuguese in America was done under the Spanish flag and paid for by the Spanish crown, it was their individual work and pioneering spirit that contributed to the making of this nation.

The Spaniards and Portuguese are like two brothers. They may look alike; however they are very different in many respects. The first Spanish discovery was made when the grandchildren of the first Portuguese navigators were already adults.

The Melungeons, an Endless Subject of Study and an Old Story

As soon as I started researching the Melungeon people, I found out that this was not something new. Their claim of being Portuguese as well as the name Melungeon was always there. Looking at the several books and articles already written on the subject, they had proven their existence in the 1700's in remote western regions, including Arkansas, as early as 1810.

For more than a century, much has been written about these people: theses, dissertations for masters' and Ph.D. degrees, articles in daily newspapers, magazines, historical reviews and books.

Many authors, scientists, and scholars have studied the mystery of the Melungeons with varied results, but with no definite conclusions.

Books about Melungeons

The Melungeons by Bonnie Ball. Miss Bonnie was a teacher and historian, and taught elementary school in Virginia to the Melungeon offspring. She was the author of numerous articles, poems and small books. Her parents were well acquainted with the Melungeons from their generation. She was also the author of the book, *The Melungeons*—the first major work written about the Melungeons. It provides considerable information for anyone who intends to study this subject. While doing the research, Jean Patterson Bible provided me with one copy.

It can be acquired from Over Mountain Press, Johnson City, Tennessee.

***The Melungeons, Yesterday and Today* by Jean Patterson Bible.** Mrs. Bible is a historical, travel, and feature writer whose articles have been published in *The New York Times, Baltimore Sun, Atlanta Journal, The American Home, Historical Review and Antique Digest.* A lecturer and former history, modern language, and English teacher, Mrs. Bible also writes historical articles for regional newspapers.

She became interested in the Melungeons in the early 1970's. Her extensive research on their history in the Southeast culminated in the writing of *above named book.* This was one of the first books I consulted. It was written in 1975, and is a very valuable resource. Additionally, Jean loaned some photos and provided further important information. The title again of her book is *The Melungeons, Yesterday and Today,* and it may

Fig. 2—Bonnie Ball, author of the book **The Melungeons.**

be ordered through Jean Patterson Bible, P.O. Box 886, Dandridge, Tennessee 37725. It is a hardcover book, easy to read, and with many illustrations. Dr. Kennedy did refer to these two books, as well as others, quite often, and the author will be doing the same.

***Melungeons and other Mestee Groups* by Mike (McGlothlen) Nassau.** This book was originally prepared in 1993, then revised and enlarged in 1994, as a class handout for an anthropology course at the University of Florida in Gainesville. It contains much information about the different mixed race groups and their possible origins. It does not treat the Melungeons in detail as other books do. It has been distributed to University libraries, and may be requested through interlibrary loan.

The text of the book in small print, without the reprinted articles, is posted on the Internet, (www.geocities.com/mikenassau) ou write to Mike Nassau, 4130 NW 64th Street, Gainesville, FL 32601.

With his background as a population geneticist working in cattle breeding, he believes strongly in heterosis (alteration) and that hybridization is advantageous. Thus he prefers to be viewed as mixed, and not a member of any one racial classification.

Fig. 3—Jean Patterson Bible

The book provides information on another group of Melungeons that may or may not be connected with the Melungeons from the Appalachians. Nassau's book also contains copies of Melungeon related articles which make for a good research package for anyone interested in researching that or other groups. The book seems to be a personal crusade favoring the recognition of all unofficially recognized groups of mixed races into one class, the Mestee race. It also gives some of the data previously published by Pollitzer and Gilbert, as well as a description of all separate groups, and a table showing the Melungeon name frequency in northwest Florida.

Nassau's book ends with a postscript written in a July 1994 insert: *I now accept that it may be easier to be Indian and fit into one of the already established categories than it is to get a new category like Mestee recognized. This accords well with my preference to not proliferate human taxonomy any further.* [8]

It is commendable that Mr. Nassau thinks in that manner. People have enough labels as it is. Another one would not help make us better human beings.

As for the word Mestee, it does not matter how it is written. In the end it will always sound like mestizo. This word is not necessarily well accepted. As for the French word *mestis* or *mêtis*, it is not necessarily very well accepted in France since a large North-African population, mainly Algeria, emigrated into France.

In Brazil, the word *mestiço* in Portuguese should not be used loosely. There, the word *mulatto* is well accepted and seldom used in a derogatory manner. However, *mulatos* refer to themselves as *caboclos*. In Brazil originally *criolo* meant a home-born slave; now it also means a native of Rio Grande do Sul, and, again it is not taken in a derogatory sense.

The Portuguese word *caboclo* also is often used to describe in an affectionate manner a person from the countryside (*sertão, sertanejo*) which is usually a Brazilian of European, Indian and Black ancestry. The dictionary describes it as born of African and Indian. Gilberto Freyre, the Brazilian writer, teacher, politician, and great humanist, wrote of the Portuguese: *God created the White and Black men, but the Portuguese made the mulatto.* [9]

Mr. Nassau points out that there are other groups which may call themselves Melungeons but are not connected with the Appalachian Melungeon community, such as the Dead Lake people from the Florida panhandle, the Redbones from Louisiana, and others. [10]

According to Brewton Berry, Dead Lake people of West Florida have no connection with the Melungeons of Tennessee, whereas the Redbones from Louisiana do. Let us keep in mind that there was a large community of Portuguese in Louisiana, of which there are still signs today, such as a tombstone marking with a Portuguese name in the early 1800's. See Portuguese in Louisiana.

The Melungeons' own explanation of their origin is that they descended from Portuguese sailors... Newman's Ridge on the Tennessee-Virginia border, is a long way from the sea-going people... [11]

That did not stop the early Spanish and Portuguese explorers—Hernando de Soto, Juan Pardo and others before them—from reaching the same area in the early 1500's, and later when our American pioneers went west.

However, Mike Nassau, in a reply to Kennedy's objection to this statement, conceded that, after settling on the coast and mixing with the Indians, their descendants might well have moved to the mountains.

What has not yet been fully researched is other communities much closer to the coast that also call themselves Portuguese and have been there at least since the early 1800's. See Chapter VIII.

The Melungeons—The Resurrection of a Proud People by **N. Brent Kennedy, Ph.D.** Kennedy's book was published in 1994, and is fascinating reading especially for Portuguese-Americans, as well as for others who wish to appreciate the odyssey of early Spanish and Portuguese explorers

Fig. 4—The book by Dr. N.Brent Kennedy, published by Mercer University Press

who arrived in the New World long before other Europeans. His book is very important for anyone interested in researching Melungeon family genealogy.

It provides many names and their family trees. It is full of pictures of many Melungeons of the past.

Brent Kennedy ends his book with the following invitation: *You are invited to participate in ongoing research regarding all aspects of Melungeon history.* The author not only accepted the invitation and reinforced some points in his book, but also added some comments on some of the possible theories presented.

Fig. 5—Brent Kennedy, author of the book , **The Melungeons—The Resurrection of a Proud People.** *Background shows a river where he used to play as a child.*

Kennedy's book will be cited very often, to the point that it may look like a study, which is not the case. He is the first (Melungeon) writer to look into different aspects of the mystery and has taken a genuine interest in solving it. Certain aspects presented in these books may not be relevant for the Portuguese point of view, but are still important enough for the reader to became familiar with the Melungeons and their odyssey. The reader is directed to their importance. By reading them, it will help in better understanding what follows in this book.

The Portuguese Making of America

Who are they? Where did they really come from? and... Why?

The following are questions by those who have seen and observed the Melungeons. The author also has other questions to add:

1. What is the reason for their Mediterranean appearance?
2. Why did they choose the area in the states of North Carolina, Virginia, Tennessee and Kentucky?
3. Why did they live most of the time in the mountain ridges?
4. Why, in 1958, did another group classified as Portuguese have their children segregated, and not allowed in white schools?
5. Why did they use names with Portuguese roots?
6. Why did most of them always answer *We're Portuguese*?
7. Why was the classification of Portuguese able to survive to date (1997)?
8. Why was it necessary to enact specific laws for the Portuguese, the Melungeons and other groups?
9. Why is there evidence of Portuguese-style food and folklore in Melungeon locales?
10. Why do we find little houses over the graves in the cemeteries, much like those in Portugal?
11. Why have the Melungeon looks of an East Indian survived to this century and in the middle of the mountains, away from seaports? See Chapter VIII.
12. Why was the name Canará used by Melungeons, a name all the way from India? See Chapters IV and IX.
13. Why were the Melungeons able to survive in the early beginnings of America, and the English only after several attempts much later?
14. Why is the Melungeon name so similar to the name of an Angolan province, a former Portuguese colony?
15. Why is the name Melungeon so similar to a name used by the Blacks in the African East Coast, where many Portuguese ships stopped on their way to India or returning to Portugal?
16. What people, besides the Portuguese, would have the means to come to the Americas in those early days?
17. Why did the name Gois or Goa find so many derivatives used by countless numbers of Melungeon descendants?

The Gowen Research Foundation out of Lubbock, Texas 79413 was created to research the Goins family genealogy. Email: gowen@llano.net.

See Appendix A for common surnames. Many more questions may arise as the reader proceeds. Please feel free to forward them to the Foundation.

The author will address these questions, or at least provide additional information in the attempt to decipher the Melungeon mystery, and other so-called Portuguese groups of unknown origin. Also the author has no intention of removing or demeaning other possible heritages that the Melungeons may have, nor is it his intention to criticize or judge the action or actions taken by previous individuals or governments. Societies change, and facts taking place in a particular time frame must be judged in the context of that same period. Moreover it is clearly not the author's intention to demean any race, ethnic group or religion. It is a fact that the Portuguese people mixed with different races and ethnic groups in many different parts of the world, without a major problem.

To reiterate, this book will describe several coincidences and hypotheses that may or may not be related to the Portuguese. The reader will need to arrive at his own conclusions. This book is an attempt to research some of the early settlers of America from the 15th to the 17th centuries. It may benefit those who are trying to trace their origins, in the same way that many are able to trace their family origins to England or Ireland. The descendants of the Melungeons or other groups should also be able to trace the origin of their ancestors with some logic.

Melungeons and Human Ethnic Heritage

Socrates wrote 2500 years ago that:... *the perfect human being is a mixture of all human beings.*

The Melungeons may be another human vestige of the Portuguese presence in the Americas of the 15th and 16th centuries.

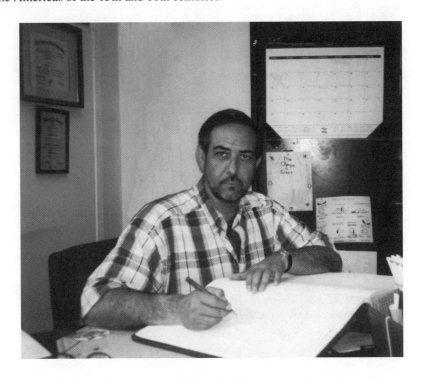

Fig. 6—Scott Collins, Hancock County Clerk Master.
A Melungeon descendant.

Each group, nationality or race should be proud of their past achievements. Whatever ethnic background one comes from, one should be able to find many contributions that their ancestors made for America.

Hancock and Sneedville the Last Stand

Fig. 7—Hancock Courthouse in Sneedville, Tennessee, which until recently had one of the largest Melungeon populations.

Notes

[1] The book is still in print. Order it from Luso-Americano in Newark, NJ.
[2] *The Portuguese-Americans* by Leo Pap, preface.
[3] *Portuguese Enclaves: The* Invisible Minority by M. Estellie Smith, pp. 83, 88.
[4] *Historical Dictionary of Portugal* by Douglas L. Wheeler, p. 184.
[5] *USA Today* newspaper, 5/28/95.
[6] *O Roteiro da Flandres e D. João II* by Joaquim Bensaude, p. 20.
[7] Note on the Melungeons by Swan M. Burnett, p. 347 (*American Anthropologist*, V. II, 1889) See Chapter I for more detailed information about John Sevier, his letters and the author's extensive research.
   Also see The Melungeons by McDonald Furman.
[8] *Melungeons and other Mestee Groups* by Mike Nassau, p. 167.
[9] *Os Pioneiros Portugueses* by Dr. Manuel Luciano da Silva, p. 159.
[10] *Melungeons and other Mestee Groups* by Mike Nassau, p. 30.
[11] Ibid, p. 38.

Chapter I—Part I
Possibly the first European settlers of the USA

Melungeon – Melungo – Melunjão – Malungo (u) – Mulango
Malange – Malanje – Mazungu – Muzungo – Melungen
Mu alungo – Melan – Mélange – Melun-cãn – Melongena

Is a knowledge of the Melungeons really necessary? The historian John Parker wrote about the four year cruise of the oceans in the late 1800's by H.M.S. *Challenger*, considered one of *the truly great discovery voyages of all time.*[1] Although no new lands were discovered, a broader and deeper knowledge was acquired. History should be a constant voyage of discovery.

Possible Origins of the Name Melungeon

What's a "Melungeon": The earliest date the word was defined by a dictionary was in 1892 as written by Dr. Isaac K. Funk.[2] Melungeon—*"One of a very dark people living in the Mountains of Tennessee."* We caution the reader to understand the definition as someone who was not black, but was not white either. In those days you were either black or white, therefore a very dark person meant not being white and blonde. Also from the Dictionary of Americanisms, Vol. II, p. 1004 (1951): *A member of a group of people of mixed Indian, white, and Negro blood found in some parts of the mountainous portions of Tennessee and western North Carolina.* Similar descriptions can be found in the Dictionary of American English of 1942. This research will also show that the year 1813 as the first time that the Melungeons were actually mentioned and recorded. See the actual transcripts as registered in 1813 and 1840 at the end of this chapter.

The Melungeon name may not be a mystery after all, as we shall discuss later. It is possible that the Melungeons knew the word, and used it among themselves to such an extent that others heard it and associated it with them. *Others had discovered the Afro-Portuguese word Melungo or Mulango, supposedly translated Shipmate or Comrade, but could draw no direct correlation to Melungeon.*[3] Malungo means comrade, companion or friend.[4] David Henige, Ph.D. agrees that a modified form of the name *mu alungo* had a similar meaning of "shipmate" or "in the same boat."[5] However Henige states that the term is African according to any Portuguese historical dictionary, which may not necessarily be correct since the name is also related to the white people.

Two Portuguese dictionaries—recent editions available at the (Biblioteca Nacional) Portuguese National Library in Lisbon, Portugal—confirm that the name Melungo means *white person* insofar as the Blacks are concerned. It is a title given to Europeans by the natives of East Africa on the Indian Ocean. It is also the same as Mazungo or Mazungu.[6] Melungo was also a term used by the Changane tribe, a branch of the Zulus in Mozambique and South Africa, with the meanings of *white* or *boss.*[7] The Portuguese visited the African East coast in 1498, and that's what they were called. Mike Nassau, who spent six and a half years teaching Bantu-speaking people in Zambia, notes a possible Bantu origin of the word Melungeon, later changed to Melungo in Portuguese. *Hence the word for white person is Muzungu but the Swahili word is Mzungu.*[8]

Recently, Professors John Thornton and Linda Heywood have stated that the word *Malungu* may have derived from the Kimbundu, Kikongo languages or even Umbundun. They do not necessarily agree that the province Malange in Angola may be the source for the word Melungeon. Malang(j)e was first visited in 1483 by the Portuguese explorer Diogo Cão and according to an Angola Embassy in Washington official, the name Malanje or similar sounding word was spoken to Portuguese explorers, however he believes the word was not connected to a geographical name. Tim Hashaw is also researching the Portuguese connection through Angola. He has written a series of articles about the origin of the Melungeons, which were published by the Gowen Research Foundation.

The first ten names shown above are connected to the Portuguese people. There are several explanations for the name Melungeon. Some writers contend that the name Melungeon originates from *the French word mélange. The word Melungeon probably derives from melange and was the name given to these people by French traders...*[9] This theory is being perpetuated by other authors. However, the chronology does not seem right, since it has been said that the Melungeons came in the late 1700's to the mountains already inhabited by people other than the French. They were fur traders passing through, and did not stay long enough to coin a name. There were no French settlements in the Appalachians to speak of, and the few that were present would hardly give them a name that would stick for a long period.

Why would the French name the Melungeons from the French word *mélange?* Because they were darker? The French are not on the average fair skinned or blonde people. Also the name is spelled with an "a", not "u", as in *Mel̲u̲ngeon.* Although it has been misspelled many times, the letter "u" always remained.

One other question comes to mind: Why did the French apply the name *mélange* to a certain group of people only in the U.S.? The name could also have been applied in Brazil, because the French arrived in Rio de Janeiro in 1555.

The mixture of races in Rio was similar to that in the British Colonies in North America. There were Indians, Blacks, and Whites in Brazil, at about the same time. No record of such a name has been found or attributed to the French.

The French activity started with the project of establishing colonies of French Protestants (Huguenots) in 1555.[10] However, they arrived in Florida in 1562, with Jean (Ribaut) Ribault as their leader, but stayed only until 1565. After the French civil wars in 1598, colonizing efforts were renewed, mostly in Acadia (Nova Scotia), Canada. Fur traders had earlier reached Lake Superior, traveled the Fox and Wisconsin rivers to the Mississippi in 1673, and descended to Arkansas.

In Louisiana, the French explorer Robert Cavelier de La Salle descended the Mississippi River in 1682, and claimed the entire river basin for France.

A later consequence was the founding of New Orleans (Nouvelle-Orléans) in 1718 by Jean-Baptiste Lemoyne. Although in Louisiana the French left considerable influence—with most of the people there having darker skin—the name Melungeon was never used. Another term, *Cane River Mulattos,* was applied to dark skinned people in Louisiana. In that part of the country, where the French stayed for quite some time, they did not call the *mixed* or *mélange* people *Melungeon.* Why would they do so in Tennessee where the French merely passed through, mostly as fur traders? Dr. Celestin Pierre Cambiaire, an *Officier d'Academie* in France, makes a good case for the French word *mélange* in his 1933 book about East Tennessee and West Virginia. He even changes the word Melungeons to *Melangeons.* Bonnie Ball repeated it by quoting the same name from his book.

Cambiaire also justifies the French connection by stating that *in 1714, Charleville had already a store where Nashville stands now.* Also that *some French traders or trappers must have given the name Melangeons.*[11] Nashville is almost 400 miles away from the Appalachian Mountains, and even farther from Charleston, West Virginia. Cambiaire writes that the Melungeons arrived in Tennessee between 1810 and 1815, which is not correct. The dates that connect them with John Sevier are in the late 1700's. The established *store* in 1714 and the French in Nashville could not have had anything to do with the name Melungeon. When the first settlers arrived they found the Melungeons, but there are no reports of finding any French settlement, except in 1699 where a colony of French Huguenots settled in Virginia in the Indian Town of Monacan.[12]

By then there were communications between the English and the French, and no report of the name Melungeon to anyone with dark skin or mixed ancestry. By the late 16th century and early 17th century, the Southeast was heavily traveled. Finally, no French document was ever found with the word Melungeon written on it.

Another possible origin for the name Melungeon is the Greek word *Melan.* However Dr. Edward T. Price wrote in 1951 that the possibility of the word deriving from the French *mélange* or even the Greek *Melan* seems remote.[13] These groups of settlers probably knew no Greek, so why would they choose a Greek-derived term to coin such a name.

The next term is *Melun-cãn*, a Turkish word from the old Ottoman language, which when pronounced, sounds the same as Melungeon. It means *cursed soul* or *one whose luck has run out.*[14] It is possible to consider that origin, but harder to justify, unless there was a small group of Turkish slaves—not necessarily from Turkey but from areas under the Ottoman Empire—that may have been left by Sir Francis Drake on the coast of North Carolina or Virginia. It is also possible that the word Melungeon and the word *Melun-cãn* may have been accepted by both Portuguese and Turks due to the similarity of sounds. Later in this book there will be a discussion on that aspect of the Melungeons. The modern expression of Melungeon may have originated at the time of Portuguese discoverers to mean "shipmate" or "companion," derived from an old Portuguese pronounced *Melunjão.* *A clever suggestion is that it is derived from the Afro-Portuguese melungo (melõongo), meaning shipmate, the term by which Portuguese sailors were said to call one another.*[15] It may also have been derived from the Portuguese word Melungo, which has two meanings, depending on the area where it is used. For the present, we may accept the definition of white man. And, according to officials at the Embassy of Portugal, in sixteenth-century Portuguese, "mulango" probably was pronounced very similarly, if not identically, to our present-day word Melungeon.

These people later resented the name Melungeon, when it started to be used in a discriminatory manner. Eventually the same happened when they considered themselves Portuguese, which meant the same as Melungeon. What they really wanted was to erase from their memories anything that would not look like English or British origin; they just wanted to assure their survival. Similar situations occurred with other groups that were not necessarily identified as Melungeons but as Portuguese. This did not help either. Discrimination was there because of skin color. As for Melongena, this is an interesting hypothesis (see page 68).

Melungo or Melungeon, Possibly Brought by English Explorers in Africa

In an interview with a Portuguese from Mozambique (East Africa), the author was told that the name Melungo is still being used today.

The letter "G" has the sound of "J" as in JET and also the sound as in GET. In Portugal during the early 1940's, children were taught in the early grades of school to pronounce the letter G as in JET, however, later generations were taught to pronounce it as in GET. Also the pronunciation varies: it is either *melon Jon* or *melon go*.

Both British and Dutch traders followed in the wake of 15ᵗʰ century Portuguese explorers. English navigator Frobisher went on voyages to the Guinea coast of Africa in 1553 and 1554. It is possible that when the English arrived in Africa, they were also called Melungos by the natives in the same manner that they were calling the Portuguese already living there. The English carried the name to England, and later when they found similar looking people (the Portuguese) in America, naturally they called them Melungos or Melungeons.

It is a fact that the English had a great influence in Mozambique, a former Portuguese colony. Some tribes still pronounce English words ending with a Portuguese sound or vowel, e.g., spoon as "spoona", fork as "forka", etc. They also drive on the left as in England, contrary to the other former Portuguese West African colony, Angola, where driving is on the right. Recently (1995), Mozambique joined the British Commonwealth, and they are talking about the possibility of changing the national language from Portuguese to English— to which a government official replied, "not so," but it is considered a second language.

There is another fact which is very often ignored. Quite a number of people from India and Asia settled on the East Coast of Africa, due to the stopover by the navigators going to or returning from India. It is not unusual to see a person born in Mozambique with an Asian appearance.

The expedition of Diogo Cão, ordered by King João II, discovered the major part of Angola in 1482-83, including the area of Malange or Malanje.[16] This name may be connected or associated with the Melungeons, due to the possible contact with the Portuguese people living in the Angolan north-central province of Malanje, and/or the city of Malanje on the country's principal plateau, West Africa. Portuguese navigators reached the Kongo kingdom in the northwest and parts of the Malanje highlands by the 1480's, and converted the king of Kongo, together with many Bakongo, to Christianity.

This may be one of the reasons why the Melungeons accepted this name in the beginning, as it had a familiar and dear sound, although they did not like it later, as it would be mentioned in a derogatory manner.

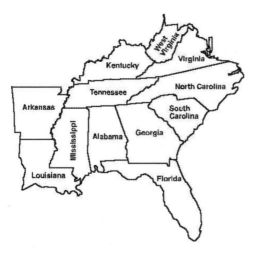

Fig. 8— Map of the States, showing where the Portuguese and Spanish explored in the 1500's and where the Melungeons and other groups settled.

Geographical Regions

The Melungeon people and their descendants have lived for many years in the Appalachian mountain region, particularly in the Blue Ridge and the Smoky Mountains.

The Melungeons were sometimes considered an Indian group. *Indian, White, and specially Portuguese blood are said to be* prominent, according to Gilbert.[17]

Most of them have left the security of the mountain ridges for the valleys and cities, to take advantage of the progress that has bypassed them. The Melungeons and other groups lived in the following sizable communities: Counties in North Carolina: Jackson, Swain, Robeson, Allegheny, Surry, Macon, Cherokee, Northampton and Buford. In South Carolina: Lancaster. In Tennessee: Hancock, Ashe, Yancey, Hawkins, Tazewell, Claiborne, Hamblen, Rhea, Roane, Loudon, Cocke, Davidson, Franklin, Grundy, Hamilton, Knox, Marion, Meigs, Morgan, Overton, Rhea, Roane, Sullivan, White, Wilson, Bledsoe, and Van Buren. In Virginia: Lee, Blackwater, Scott, Wise, Dickenson. In Kentucky: Letcher, Dickerson, Magoffin. In southwestern Virginia: Giles, Russell, and Washington.[18]

These were the safe places known, but they were not the only ones. Thousands of Melungeons migrated to the West, most to Arkansas, Oklahoma, Indiana, Texas and California. Still others went to Rockville, Maryland, Ohio, and to Blountstown, Florida, just west of Tallahassee. Generally, the ones that stayed were the ones with fair skin, who were able to prosper and did not feel the—FPC free persons of color—discriminatory laws as much. These were put into place by the English settlers in the mountains.

Melungeons before Roanoke and Jamestown

There are enough reasons to believe that the Melungeons arrived in America before the English settlers of Roanoke and Jamestown, Virginia. One fact no one can dispute is that they were able to establish a colony and survive on their own to date, probably since the early 1500's. Therefore, by the time the English settlers arrived in Jamestown, there were already at least one or more generations of Melungeons established. So far, all the research points to that.

Santa Elena and the Carolina coast—1526

There are many theories about the origin of the Melungeons, and one of them is the Santa Elena theory. This Colony was inhabited by thousands of men, women and children from the Iberian Peninsula. That gave the Spaniards a base of operations for their explorations of the Carolinas, Georgia, Alabama and Tennessee.

In July 1526, a fleet with 500 men, women and children, soldiers and priests, along with the first Black slaves, sailed from Spain to American shores. Later in that year, after disease, Indian attacks and many other problems, the Colony was abandoned, and only 150 made it back home.

That was the first attempt to establish a colonial town in the territory of the United States, with the first landings in the south Santee river and the second in the Sapelo Sound area of Georgia.[19] Joseph Judge wrote in the *National Geographic Magazine*: *From Santo Domingo—Dominican Republic—a wealthy lawyer, Lucas Vásquez de Ayllón, led the first settlement attempt to the Carolina coast in 1526.* And in the west coast of Florida near *Tampa Bay was also the site of Hernando de Soto's landing with 600 men in ten ships.* [Among them were many Portuguese noblemen along with the writer of the first book about the Southeast, Álvaro Fernandes, a native of Elvas. Hernando de Soto] *...wandered for three years through the Southeast, discovering the Mississippi River, in which he was buried.*

[Again on the east coast of Florida] *Pedro Menéndez de Aviles founded St. Augustine in 1565 along with a town on modern Parris Island—Santa Elena—from which expeditions reached the Tennessee Valley and Chesapeake Bay. ...Excavations at Santa Elena, St. Augustine, and St. Catherines—South Carolina—along with recent scholarly work on 16th century documents in Spain, have shed light on this long-neglected epoch.*[20]

Lost Soldiers of Hernando de Soto—1540

Louisa Davis writes about a letter that was postmarked 1907 and had been sent to Miss Collins of Sneedville, Tennessee by J. H. Rhea, one of her uncles. The letter mentions *a legend that persists to explain the presence of the dark/skinned people in the area; they are descendants of the Spaniards and perhaps Portuguese men in* [Hernando] *De Soto's party who ventured from Florida into parts of North Carolina and Tennessee in search of gold in 1540...became lost... were captured or befriended by the Cherokees.* After reading it, Davis made the following remarks: *There is nothing of the backwardness of the traditional mountaineer in the letter, and it is obvious that Hancock County has—and for generations has had—its aristocracy, some of whom take pride in their Spanish and Portuguese ancestry...*[21]

That legend talks only of men. If the Mediterranean European looks were to survive for 400 years, complete families from Southern Europe would be needed. The Hernando de Soto exploratory trip was narrated in a book by a Portuguese member of the expedition, the Gentleman of Elvas. There is no mention of any lost soldiers, except for the many deaths—including Hernando de Soto himself—that occurred during the expedition due to the extremely harsh living conditions. (See Chapter VII for more on Hernando de Soto and the Elvas book.)

Pardo and Caravels with Emigrants—1566

In July (1566) *a troop of 250 men under Capt. Juan Pardo arrived from Spain and built a more substantial fort and a number of houses.*[22] Later in the year he reached the Tennessee Valley, after having passed near Asheville and Franklin, where there is an historic plaque commemorating his passage in the area. *On his way home—to Santa Elena—drove in a series of manned forts across the Southeast from Tennessee to South Carolina, and on March 2, 1568, he reached Santa Elena, bringing sacks filled with corn and tales of the wild west. Pardo describes the interior as good for bread and wine and all kinds of livestock.*[23]

This same good news most likely would have arrived in Portugal, even if Pardo was not Portuguese. In either case, it would not have been difficult to recruit some or most of the emigrants from Portugal, which at the time was suffering a serious economic and social crisis due to famine and plagues, as well as religious persecution from the recently installed Inquisition, and if that was not enough, also the perspective of Portugal's crown being united with that of Spain. All that made it easier for many families to leave and look for a better life or just a means to survive in a promised land.

That hope soon brought settlers to Santa Elena. Two caravels unloaded 193 immigrants, farmers and their families, who formed a town government... By October 1569, the little capital numbered 327 souls. Around the fort clustered 40 houses...[24] If some of these families survived together with other earlier arrivals, a population of just 200 could very well be the Melungeons' ancestors, according to Kennedy: *...given a known Melungeon population in the late 1700's of a minimum of 1,000 people, possibly as high as 2,000, coupled with a possible arrival date during the Elizabethan period, an average of four surviving children per couple, and the death of older members, I backtracked to an original population in the range of minimally 200 people, including both men and women.*[25] This is very interesting, but research has shown that they also had other physical traits besides Mediterranean.

This may possibly be new information about America's lost century. *In 1566, Captain Juan Pardo, a Spanish officer most likely of Portuguese origin, recruited some two hundred soldiers, probably from the mountains of northern Spain and Portugal that is, the Galician Mountains, and brought them to the Santa Elena Colony... What is of great interest here is that if these soldiers were indeed recruited from either the Galician Mountains or southern Spain, then there is every likelihood that they and their families were of mixed Berber, Jewish, and Basque heritage.*[26]

The mixture of these three heritages is likely, but with the Berber element in a much smaller proportion, since they settled in the north of the Iberian Peninsula during the 8th century. Let us keep in mind that Galicia and the Basque region were later overwhelmed by the Visigoths, a Germanic people. If so, they should not be darker. The people of the northeast Iberian Peninsula are usually of a fair complexion, and those found in America in the 18th century are of darker skin. It is easier to find fair skin and blond haired people in the north of Portugal, than in the south, where the Moorish influence was greatest.

Pardo's Forgotten Soldiers—1567

Another theory is that Juan Pardo set up forts as a means of support for the explorers during their expeditions, and then the soldiers and the forts were forgotten. The theory about the origin of the Melungeons may be connected with Juan Pardo. *The historian and writer Eloy Gallegos, when doing research in the Archives of Seville for his upcoming book about the American Southeast, discovered that Juan Pardo's name was signed as Joao Pardo as it was written in Portuguese according to original records of the XVI century.*[27] This explorer, who may be the key to the Melungeon mystery, had Portuguese men working for him.

David J. Weber, in his book, *The Spanish Frontier,* poses a question: *Unlike* [Hernando] *de Soto, Pardo planted settlements along the way. He built a chain of five small fortifications with a detachment assigned to each one. Pardo returned safely to Santa Elena, but his path of garrisons disappeared, their few defenders either killed by Indians or absorbed into Indian tribes.*[28] If they were absorbed by the Indians, the group would be too small to make any noticeable difference—but the Melungeons kept their physical characteristics to the present.

Historian J. G. Hollingsworth writes an account of Pardo who, in 1566, left *Spaniards at Joara, but soon after his departure the Indians became hostile and forced the Spanish force... to flee to the lands of the Creeks.*[29] Another story states: *the soldiers in the interior forts became reckless and unruly... the red men revolted and drove them out.* The name Joara is also called Xula or Cofitachequi, and is located near Marion in North Carolina, near present McDowell Bottom. Archaeological excavations are planned for that site, according to the archaeologist David More.

Fig. 9—Sign near Franklin, N.C honoring Juan Pardo.

Pardo went on to the foothills of the Appalachians...he built a fort and left behind a company under Sgt. Hernando Moyano de Morales....During the spring of 1567 a letter from Sergeant Moyano in the faraway foothills reached Santa Elena. He was up to his neck in Indian trouble.[30] After we read Joseph Judge's article, *letter from Sergeant Moyano... reached Santa Elena,* and Pardo received *news of the French.* We know that they had communications, so they could not be lost or forgotten.

It is also a fact that the policy of King Felipe I of Spain, in order to colonize the vast American territories of the Southeast—known then as La Florida—was to recruit only married men to go to the New World. But in the same fleet of which Pardo was part, in total were sent *1200 soldiers, 500 sailors and 14 women.*[31] The proportion of man/woman is somewhat unexplainable.

The Arrival of the Melungeons—Before 1558 or 1584?

Sir Walter Raleigh's first expedition departed England on April 27, 1584 and arrived at the Carolina coast on July 4. Included in this expedition were Captain Master Philip Amadas, Master Arthur Barlowe, and as Master Pilot, the Portuguese Simão Fernandes from Terceira Island, Azores, who discovered the inlet that later would be called Port Ferdinand. Master Arthur Barlowe, who discovered part of the country now called Virginia, gave to Sir Walter Raleigh a narrative of the voyage. After having had contact with the natives, he writes the following description: *They are of colour yellowish, and their haire blacke for the most part, and yet we sawe children that had very fine auburn and chestnut colour haire....and few early descriptions mention hair of other colours, except with the assumption that it represents admixture with the Europeans....reddish hair is often found in children whose hair later becomes, to all appearances, black.*[32]

If in 1584 the English found European looking children, we have to assume that their ancestors must have arrived long before that. You can easily find brown and auburn hair among the Portuguese, from the center to the north of Portugal. They could not have been English, as that was their first trip there.

Also worth considering is the story told by the Indians about a shipwreck 20 years before...*it seems they had twentie yeers since, which as those two men*

*Fig. 10—Juan Pardo, explorer, reaches the Tennessee Valley
and meets the ancestors of the Creek and Cherokee Indians*[33]

declared, was out of a wracke which happened upon their coast of some Christian shippe, being beaten that way by some storme, and outrageous weather, whereof none of the people saved.[34] That date would be about 1564, making it possible for the ship to be either French, Spanish or Portuguese.

A similar story is told after Master Barlowe traveled inland near a town called Sequotan, where Wingina appears to be the chief of all the villages from the Pamlico River to Roanoke Island...*neere unto which, six and twentie yeers past,* (1558) *there was a shippe castaway, whereof some of the people were saved, and those were white people, whom the Countrey people preserved. After ten daies, remaining in an out Island uninhabited, called Wococan,* (an island in the Carolina Outer Banks) *they with the help of some of the dwellers of Sequotan, fastened two boates of the Countrey together, and made mastes unto them, and sailes of their shirtes, and having taken into them such victuals as the Countrey yeelded, they departed after they had remained in this out Island three weeks: but shortly after, it seemed they were cast away, for the boates were found upon the coast, cast aland in another Island adioyning:* These shipwrecks prove that they were common in these parts of the east coast. They may not have survived, but why not others? ...*other than these, there was never any people apparelled, or white of colour, either seen, or heard amongst these people.*[35] These natives in particular may not have seen any other white men, but it is known that other explorers and navigators were traveling along the east coast since the early 1500's, starting with the Portuguese, and the Spaniards with their early settlement in South Carolina as well as the French in Port Royal (all prior to the English). However, it was important for England to justify to the world that taking possession of the land in the name of Her Majesty Queen Elizabeth was right, since no other country had claimed it.

Santa Elena Settlers Left Behind and the End of the Colony—1587

For twenty years Spanish and Portuguese settlers and their families lived intermittently in Santa Elena. During that time, there were Indian attacks and hungry soldiers. Then, in 1587, *a year after Drake's attack, orders were issued* [by King of Spain Felipe II] *to the 33 families at Santa Elena to tear down their fort and move to St. Augustine, where defenses would be concentrated.* The *English freebooter, Sir Francis Drake,* had sacked and burned it in the previous year. *Despite their vigorous protests, it was done, and Santa Elena was no more.*[36] *All of the Santa Elena colonists, however, did not make this last journey. There is strong evidence that large numbers of the settlers abandoned the Colony and escaped into the hinterland.*[37] This is possible, but again they could not be the main element of the Melungeons, since most of the 33 families must have made it to Florida. Did they all go to St. Augustine? *The American History*—written by the English—states that there were no survivors, which is not possible. The same historians did not have any problem in accepting the survival of the English settlers when attacked by the Indians, so why not the settlers of Santa Elena? *I contend that the remnants of João "Juan" Pardo's forts, joined by refugees from Santa Elena, and possibly a few stray Dominicans and Jesuits, exiled Moorish French Huguenots, and escaped Acadians, along with Drake's and perhaps other freed Moorish and Iberian captives, survived on these shores, combined forces over the ensuing years, moved to the hinterlands, intermarried with various Carolina and Virginia Native Americans, and eventually became the reclusive Melungeons.*[38]

These conclusions may be valid; however a strong component is needed to complete the equation. Although it may be possible, it does not explain the Asian features and skin color darker than the average Portuguese.

The greatest conflicts in Melungeon research have resulted from those well-meaning individuals who have latched onto a single component of our multifaceted origins and incorrectly pushed that lone "explanation" as the only one. Such narrow interpretations are not only in serious error, but damaging to the credibility of all those seeking to establish our true roots.[39]

Although sometimes it may appear that this book is latching on to the Portuguese origin theory, this is not the case. However, it is difficult to believe that so many different races, nationalities and cultures would have been able to live together for a long period of time under stressful conditions. What may be possible is that if all these different groups of people landed on this continent, they would have gone on their separate ways and formed separate groups; but staying together and calling themselves Portuguese would not have been logical.

Meanwhile, further north, the English were trying to establish a settlement at Roanoke. Is it a coincidence that both Santa Elena and Roanoke were lost colonies, or did some of the settlers survive? Apparently John White was confident the settlers were alive, and had gone to live with the Hatteras Tribe of Manteo.[40]

Drake and the Lost Roanoke Colony
Sir Francis Drake the Knight, Privateer and Pirate

This section is largely dedicated to bringing together the important details of Sir Francis Drake's voyages that may be connected with the Lost Roanoke Colony, and/or the possibility of Drake having left Moors, Turks or South American Indians in South Carolina.

Drake was born between 1540 and 1543 in Devonshire, England. He became an admiral in the English navy and circumnavigated the globe (1577-80), playing an important role in defeating the Spanish Armada (1588). He was one of the most famous seamen of the Elizabethan Age. In 1572—having obtained a privateering commission from the Queen, which amounted to a license to plunder the King of Spain's lands—Drake set sail for America in command of two small ships, the *Pasha*, of 70 tons, and the *Swan*, of 25 tons. In 1577, he was chosen as the leader of an expedition intended to pass around South America through the Strait of Magellan, and to explore the South American east coast. He set sail in December with five small ships, manned by fewer than 200 men, and reached the Brazilian coast in the spring of 1578. Two years later, Drake and his ship *The Golden Hind* came back into the Atlantic with only 56 of the original crew of 100. On Sept. 26, 1580, Drake brought his ship into Plymouth Harbor. She was laden with treasure and spices, and Drake's fortune was permanently made. Despite Spanish protests about his piratical conduct in their imperial waters, Queen Elizabeth herself came aboard *The Golden Hind*, which was lying at Deptford in the Thames Estuary, and personally bestowed knighthood on Drake.

The Queen's trust in him was shown in 1585, when Elizabeth placed him in command of a fleet of 25 ships. Hostilities with Spain had broken out once more, and he was ordered to cause as much damage as possible to the Spaniards' overseas empire. Drake fulfilled his commission, capturing Santiago in the Portuguese Cape Verde Islands, taking and plundering the cities of Cartagena in Colombia, St. Augustine in Florida, and San Domingo (Santo Domingo, Hispaniola). The effect of his triumph in the West Indies was cataclysmic. Spanish credit, both moral and material, almost foundered under the losses. The Bank of Spain broke, the Bank of Venice (to which Felipe II was principal debtor) nearly collapsed, and the great German Bank of Augsburg refused to extend the Spanish monarch any further credit. Even Lord Burghley, Elizabeth's principal minister, who had never approved of Drake or his methods, was forced to concede that *Sir Francis Drake is a fearful man to the King of Spain*. Drake's later years were not happy, however. An expedition that he led against Portugal proved abortive, and his last voyage, in 1596 against the Spanish possessions in the West Indies, was a failure, largely because the fleet was decimated by fever, killing Drake, who was buried at sea off the town of Puerto Bello (modern Portobelo, Panama).[41]

English Navigation and the Portuguese

Official piracy was by no means an English monopoly. Already in the 15th century it had reached large proportions. During France's reign of King Louis XI, French pirates and corsairs attacked Portuguese caravels to the point that, in 1458, Portuguese King Afonso V prepared a fleet to exterminate the pirates near the coast.[42] *There was a strong feeling, which Drake shared, that English navigation lagged behind that of Spain and Portugal in that there were no training institutions for pilots and masters.*[43]

Drake used the Portuguese chronicler Lopes Vaz, a native of Elvas, to write about the voyage to Nombre de Dios on the Gulf of Darien in 1572. He also wrote the account of John Oxnam of Plymouth to the West Indies and the South Seas in 1575.[44] Nuno da Silva, another Portuguese from Oporto, was taken by Drake in the Cape Verde Islands during his famous voyage around the world in 1577, when he captured a Portuguese cargo boat. A pilot, he guided Drake to Brazil[45] and later he was released in Acapulco, Mexico.

Before Drake set off across the world, he acquired a map in Lisbon, the best he could find. Thomas Cavendish, following Drake's courses, captured a Portuguese by the name of Diogo (last name unknown) on the coast of Mexico and another, Nicolas Rodrigo, off the California coast. Nicolas had been in Canton and Japan.

On that same trip, Drake picked up useful information ...*from a Portuguese pilot, faithless to the Spaniards as were so many of his kind.*[46] Certainly the writer reflects here the difference between Portuguese and Spaniards.

Drake in Brazil and the Mulangos

Kennedy dedicates a number of pages to other Melungeons, and alludes to the possibility of Muslim or Christian converts transported to South America in the 16th century. ...*They referred to themselves as "mulango," or, as pronounced in Portuguese "Muh-lun-zhawn." However, connecting these South American "Mulangos," or Melungeons, with their possible North American counterparts seemed a daunting if not impossible task.*[47]

As earlier discussed, the word *mulango* does not seem to be connected with South America or the Portuguese in Brazil, however Professors John Thornton and Linda Heywood did connect a similar word *malungu* — and meanings as previously stated, such as boat and shipmate — in Brazil, according to a letter published by the Gowen Research Foundation. In this chapter, the meaning of *mulango* was presented. It is the name of a plant from which a reddish oil is extracted, and used in East Africa as well as in India. Dr. Bob Gilmer, a Melungeon research committee member, brought to Kennedy's attention that Sir Francis Drake may have dropped off *South American Muslims on Roanoke Island, just off the coast of present-day North Carolina* .[48] That story is repeated throughout David Quinn's books and is based on Irene Wright's translation of the original documents, written as a result of depositions taken by a Spanish official. ...*and a number of Negros, and Central American Indians he had rescued from the Spaniards with Lane. Lane had been involved in fighting with the Indians.*[49] (See other pages in this same chapter for more on these depositions.)

Kennedy cites Thomson: ...*Drake's numerous excursions into Portuguese Brazil as well as other parts of South America, and of his collusion* (conspiracy) *with the Portuguese and the "Cimarrons" (a South American mixed-race people) against the Spanish.*[50] Cimarrón is a Spanish name and means runaway slave or domestic animal, and also lazy sailor.[51]

There are no references in the Portuguese-Brazilian dictionary or the *Grande Enciclopedia Luso-Brasileira*. In English it means wild and unruly. It is also the name of a river flowing from northeast New Mexico to the Arkansas River near Tulsa, Oklahoma. The connection between Cimarrón and the Portuguese does not seem to be there. Drake's brother John made contact with Cimarrons, but it seems that this people lived in the Caribbean islands occupied by the Spaniards.[52]

It did not make sense that they would try to colonize Brazil with Muslims—converted or not to Catholicism. Also, history records show that Portugal did not need any labor, forced or voluntary, in Brazil during the early 16th century. The slave trade to Brazil did not start until the 17th century.

It is also important to consider the fact that in April 1569, the English captured 11 ships of a Portuguese fleet going to Antwerp. How many seamen did they take as prisoners to England or elsewhere? Prior to that, the city of Funchal, on Madeira Island, was raided by a fleet of Frenchmen led by the corsair Pierre de Monluc. For a detailed story of this raid that killed hundreds of Madeirans, sacked all churches, and captured 300 black slaves, read *Saudades da Terra* by Gaspar Frutuoso.

Drake Deposited Moorish Slaves and Indians in Roanoke

Boxer stated in his book *Portuguese Seaborne Empire* that *People engaged in oceanic trade did not travel with their families, least of all the Muslim men with ideas about the seclusion of women.*[53] This agrees with Kennedy's assumption of the Moors men, only with the possible exception of Indian women also released by Drake.

Certainly if Drake's Moors were primarily men, as we know they were, the tendency for their children to adopt the father's heritage would be (1) strong, given the patrilineal tradition of the Moors, and (2) as a result of this tendency, would better explain the widespread dissemination of the so-called "Melungeon" heritage. Several hundred Moorish men could leave quite a genetic and cultural heritage after but one generation, to say nothing of the estimated fourteen generations since their arrival. Additionally, the accompanying claim to be "Portyghee" fits with both the South American Moors and the Pardo Santa Elena components as well.[54]

For only the male population to survive and be accepted by the Indian community is rather difficult, if not impossible. Surely the Indians must have been very protective, and seeing only males coming to their villages to take their women, would not put them in a very welcoming mood, to say the least. However, the possibility that a very small number could be accepted—if they did not pose any danger—should not be ruled out.

Kennedy presents an explanation: *He* (Drake) *arrived at Roanoke Island, just off the North Carolina shores, where large numbers of English soldiers implored him to take them home to England. In order to make room on his ships for the English garrison on Roanoke Island, it is believed that Drake may (and I emphasize the word may) have deposited most of these captives on the island or the nearby coast.*[55] This is a very important possibility, and particular attention should be given since it would answer some of the questions related to the Melungeons. However, records do not confirm Drake's passenger drop-off.

Preliminaries of the 1584 Voyage

The following is a summary of the voyages made by the English to establish a base of operations on the east coast closer to the West Indies. There are some controversies about what Drake did or did not do, depending on which writings one believes. Therefore both narrations are being presented, one by the English and the other by the Spanish. If one were to take what follows into consideration, Kennedy's possible assumption above is rather weak. But he does say *may*.

Drake, a few years earlier, was in the slave business with John Hawkins, and doing raids off the coast of Africa, capturing or buying slaves. Would he give up such a valuable cargo?

In 1584, Sir Walter Raleigh obtained a charter from Queen Elizabeth I giving him the right to possess lands in the New World not already under Christian control.

A voyage was planned with Arthur Barlowe and Philip Amadas in charge, and the Portuguese Simão Fernandes was the pilot. They departed on April 27 and arrived on July 13 at Roanoke, Virginia. [56]

Irene Wright's book describes Simão Fernandes as having been in Florida in 1576. He is also described by Quinn as having *ambiguities in an obscure text* in reference to the Spanish narration.[57] Also: ...*the deponent says that when the Portuguese* [Fernandes] *discovered this port he wished to land on one promontory, but the wild Indians ate 38 Englishman... The Portuguese* [Simão Fernandes] *took with him to England two wild Indians, leaving two Englishmen as hostages* [to make sure] *that he would return later.*[58]

The 1584 voyage was just to discover or to look for a base where the English could raid the Spaniards returning from the Caribbean.

Grenville's First Trip—1585

This trip was under Grenville, who departed England on April 9 arriving in Port Ferdinand—Carolina Outer Banks—on July 21. Lane was left there with 108 men in August 1585. They stayed until the summer of 1586, and most were later picked up by Drake. The building of a fort and houses was started later. On August 25, Grenville returned to England after capturing a Spanish ship off Bermuda. Aboard was Henrique Lopes, a Portuguese merchant who said that according to the ship's manifest, at least 40,000 ducats in gold, silver and pearls was on board. All of that was handed over to Grenville, and more treasure was obtained from the passengers. Grenville denied that there: ...*was any treasure registered at all.*[59] He proceeded to the Azores where he arrived in early October, landed the captured Spaniards, took in supplies and sailed home, arriving at Plymouth on October 18. [60]

Drake's Voyage of 1585-86 as Narrated by the English

Drake departed England on September 14, and headed to Spanish America with an armada of 25 vessels and 2,300 men. He started out by plundering some vessels at the Vigo River, sailed to the West Indies via the Canaries and the Portuguese Cape Verde Islands, plundered and burned the town of São Tiago, crossed the Atlantic in 18 days and landed in Española or Hispaniola—what is today Haiti and the Dominican Republic—on New Year's Day, 1586. Before arriving in Dominica, and acording to Biggs' between and two three hundred men died at sea. Captain Walter Biggs' narrative, which he wrote while sailing with Drake gives a detailed account of this particular trip. Biggs died before completion, but someone else completed it for him. There is no account of capturing any slaves.

While attacking Santo Domingo according to Biggs:...*Somewhat after midnight, they who had guard of the Castle, abandoned same;* **some being taken prisoners** [author's emphasis] ...*and some fleeing away.* Before leaving Santo Domingo, Biggs tells us that: ...*we were contented to accept of 25,000 ducats... for the ransom of the rest of town.* The next event describes the killing by the Spaniards of a Negro messenger boy sent by the general. In revenge, a couple of friar prisoners were hanged. There, some of Drake's men were attacked and killed by Indians—fighting alongside the Spaniards—armed with poison arrows. Drake went on to Carthagena and again his crew was plagued with sickness and death. On February 25, 1585, [this date is wrong it should be 1586] Drake's log shows in a resolution that he only has *not above 700* men and *some 150... sick.* After accepting: *...The ransom of 110,000 ducats... we do therefore consider, since all these cities, with their goods and prisoners taken in them... being all put together, are found far short to satisfy that expectation which by the generality of the enterprises was first conceived;* Gibbs states further that also due to the: *...slenderness of our strength...small number of able bodies.* [61]

They decided to proceed to the Florida coast arriving in St. Augustine May 28. No quantity or kind of prisoners were mentioned in this rather detailed and lengthy narrative by Captain Walter Biggs. It is logical to conclude that Drake had some prisoners and a limited number of good able men, not near the 2300 that he started out with.

After St. Augustine the next intended attack was St. Helena however *...we came thwart St. Helena, the shoals appearing dangerous, and we having no pilot to undertake the entry... The ninth of June upon sight of a special great fire...found some of our English countrymen that had been sent by thiter the year before by Sir Walter Raleigh.* Gibbs, describes next the events that took place and resulted with Drake departing to England on June 18. But before that he gave Master Ralph Lane: *...choice of two offers...leave a ship with...month's victual...being one hundred and three persons...or return into England.* Lane accepted the first offer but *...there arose a great storm...brake many cables, and lost many anchors... Master Lane and his company were driven to put to sea in great danger, in avoiding the coast, and could never see us until we met in England.* Unfortunately Gibbs is rather vague describing the following events that took place. *...after all this, the General offered them* [The Roanoke Colonists] *...passage into England, although he knew he should perform it with greater difficulty than he might have done before...the which being granted, and the rest sent for out of the country and shipped, we departed from that coast 18 June. abandoned same;* [62]

Gibbs does not tell us how many colonists came with Drake and how many prisoners and what nationality were left in Roanoke island. We know that three men were left behind, either by desertion or because they could not find their way back to the ship in time. Walter Spearman, in the American History Illustrated, [63] attests that Drake left Roanoke in 1586 with Governor Lane, his group, and the entire fleet of ships laden with spoils from the Spanish West Indies.

There is no mention of slaves or captives, Indians or blacks, but if Drake in fact took the slaves from Santo Domingo and Cartagena, what did he do with them? Did he leave them ashore on Roanoke Island? Did he take them to England? How many? Biggs mentions that they took *some* [64] in Santo Domingo. He was already hard pressed for space and provisions for his own men, which he had to share with Lane and his men.

The only other information related to this is the deposition made by Pedro Sanchez made much later at Havana where he states that Drake carried off 200 Moors and 150 *negros and negresses.* [65] It is believed that these numbers were exaggerated specifically to impress the king of Spain. Irene Wright describes Pedro Diaz' answers to a questioning session which took place in Cuba. Who was he? We came across him when he was in custody in Bidford after his return with Grenville in 1586. *His name appears to be Pedro (Pero) Diaz but also Franco or Pimenta, and he was the pilot of the Santa Maria when captured by Grenville in 1585 off Bermuda.* [66]

It is necessary to proceed with caution regarding Pedro Díaz' narration. He at one point says that he was taken—while with the English—twice to an English settlement, and that at that time there were some 320 men, and as many women there.[67] That would make a total of 640 people. The number was nowhere close to that. At some other point he also states that 210 people were recruited in London for the settlement in Virginia.[68] According to White, the number is 150. The number who remained in Virginia was 110.[69]

Drake in the West Indies, as Narrated by David B. Quinn

Among others, Quinn uses Irene Wright's translation of the Spanish papers in the Archives of Seville.

Arrived in S. Domingo Jan. 1, 1586...*Sir Francis Drake,...a major fleet under Drake...terrorized...Vigo, Santiago in the Cape Verde Islands....*[70] Also written is:...*he carried off 150 negroes and negresses from Santo Domingo and Cape Verde—more from Santo Domingo.* [71] This could not be confirmed by Portuguese sources, although the Cape Verde Islands had many Portuguese officials at the time. In *Santo Domingo...Cartagena Drake had released many European and Turkish galley slaves at these two last ports and at one point was said to have been carrying with him some three hundred of South American Indians who helped him at Cartagena as well as a number of black, predial slaves.*[72] If they were Indians from Cartagena, they could not be South American Indians. Quinn quotes Mary Frear Keeler as writing, *Indians of Cartagena* [73] *...he also captured several vulnerable Portuguese "sugarmen" coming from Brazil. The Portuguese were forced to pay heavily for having been invaded by Spain in 1580.* [74] *...Sir Francis Drake, it was very different in 1586. Sir Francis Drake in his sweep through the West Indies, had released from the galleys at Santo Domingo and Cartagena hundreds of slaves of many nationalities—French blacks, a large number of subjects of the Turkish sultan, and members of other European nations...Whether any of them got ashore on the Outer Banks and were deserted when Drake sailed away we cannot say, but it is not unlikely that a few saved their lives that way, though nothing has been heard of what became of any who may have done so. We know only that Drake brought Europeans and Moors back to England and, perhaps, a handful of blacks but no considerable number.*[75] *At Santo Domingo and Cartagena he had also been collecting men—galley slaves (mainly Moors, but including some Europeans), a few soldiers (again mainly Moors), Negro domestic slaves to whom* *he promised their freedom, and a substantial number of South American Indians (about 300 including women).*[76]

David Quinn also wrote: *We have no confirmation of this one report about the removal of the Indians from Cartagena.*[77] He adds a footnote that: *An early report to reach England said he had rescued no less than 1200 English, French, Flemings and Dutch from the galleys at Santo Domingo and took, besides 800* [78]—other English sources state only 80—*people of the country with him...the numbers being, of course,* ***exaggerated*** [79] (author's emphasis). England was trying to win European allies against Spain, and that would be good propaganda. The numbers are certainly exaggerated. They could add up to more than 2,000. With his original crew of 2,300, how would Drake feed and house them? The only French mentioned was the one they met in St. Augustine.

As counter propaganda, the English Ambassador in Paris wrote that there was a Negro in that town who ran away from Drake after he landed in England. He confessed that Drake brought home little or nothing, and the taking of Cartagena as well as the rest was false.[80]

During the same time frame, there was much speculation about the English activity in Virginia. A deposition document of a Spanish sailor was translated by Irene Wright, which reads that:

No less than forty English vessels had set out for the settlement of Virginia by way of the Indies. Four of them were bringing women settlers...And in 1591 a grand assault by 150 vessels would be made on the Indies. [Quinn adds his own remarks] *This picture of the Virginia settlement, painted to illustrate English hopes and to colour Spanish fears, had little relation to reality, and raises suspicion that the information was 'planted' for Spanish consumption.* [81]

Quinn continues: *Whether these motley passengers were responsible for the outbreaks of sickness and disease among his own men we cannot say, nor can we tell how many of them succumbed, but he had not set any of them on shore when he turned back from Carthagena...on the 11th they met.* [Drake and Lane] *Drake had much to offer—his motley crew of passengers, the small boats he had seized at San Augustín...* ***He did not have much food to spare*** [82] [author's emphasis]. Again, what did he do with 300 South American Indians and 100 Negro slaves? If he did not have much food to spare, would he risk the lives of his men, many of them sick, to take the slaves and feed them? *...sickness had depleted their ranks...potable water was not very easy to find...estimates of Drake's strength varied from 1200 to fewer than 500...*[83] What about the mixture of Indians and Blacks?

Could that be considered an easy task? *...at Cartagena there had been disagreement among the English officers.* [84] Quinn further questions: *Were some lost in the storm? Were they all set on shore...? If not, did they die or were they killed on the way to England or were they landed at Portsmouth?*[85] Quinn's words are very interesting: *It is ironical, however, that the whole sequence of colonization was destroyed, inadvertently, by Drake.*[86]

Further English Voyages, by Irene Wright, contains a wealth of information about Drake. The following are some interesting passages:*...galley slaves whom the*

Spaniards had unchained.[87] This is different from what has been written, crediting Drake with freeing prisoners.

CF Primrose Log. P. 16 and A. de I., 147-6-5 Santo Domingo 49—Don Diego de Osorio to the Crown, Santo Domingo, June 30, 1586. Also Acts Privy Council, New Series, XIV, p. 205 mention of Turks, galley slaves, Drake took to England upon his return. Other remained at large in the Island or made off with French Corsairs. The author continues: *...they carried with them everything they cared to take...galley slaves, negroes...from Santo Domingo to Cartagena.*[88] Did Drake leave the slaves at Cartagena? Again, Irene Wright relates that *...he obtained further amounts from their masters for the return of the slaves...*[89] A word of caution by the author: *...they should be compared with Bigg's discourse and the Primrose log.*[90] Which narration are we going to accept, the detailed one by Captain Walter Gibbs or the results of an interrogation done in Cuba by a Spanish official as translated by Irene Wright? It is hard to believe that the English narration so full of details, would miss entirely such an important occurrence as the coming aboard of hundreds of slaves as free passengers. About the deposition Ms. Wright adds *...deposition made at Havana on June 26, 1586 by an Aragonese seaman...this person must have made another probable early deposition...Although it is difficult to give much credence to a man who asserted that Drake was a Portuguese... Drake's address to his prisoners, presumably to his Moorish prisoners...(his assurance that he would return them to their own country...).*[91] Were they Turkish or Moorish from South Spain, and to which country would he take them? The vessels were not necessarily equipped to rescue and house large quantities of people for long periods. By then Portugal was being governed by a Spanish King.

Kennedy writes: *...Given the desperate circumstances of these people, it makes exceedingly good sense that they would have abandoned the island as quickly as feasible. Why would they wait for either the English or, worse still, pursuing Spanish or Portuguese ships to come recapture them?*[92]

A possible answer may be given by historian George Malcom Thompson who writes: *It had released many galley slaves, a hundred of whom, Turks, the Queen sent to Grand Seignior....*[93] This may indicate that Drake brought 100 Turk galley slaves to England. The expedition was commercial not humanitarian, and the only reason he brought the Turks was because they had a value. If so, why would he leave any on Roanoke?

There is still the question of Turk slaves returned to Turkey via England, an event which some writers may be connecting with Drake's freed slaves in Santo Domingo or Cartagena. Charles Boxer shows the reader what may be a partial explanation: *By the last quarter of the 16th century, the sugar trade of Brazil was very profitable, and between 1589 and 1591, Elizabethan privateers captured 69 ships.*[94] Would it be possible that the captured people were sent to London and were sold as slaves?

When looking into the possibility of Muslim slaves brought to America by Spaniards, a question arises. Under the terms of the contract dated March 20, 1565, the king of Spain directed Pedro Menéndez to bring: *...four members of the Society of Jesus, and ten or twelve religious of any other order he desired to preserve his* *colonists from the contamination of heresy and see that there were no Jews, Moors or Marranos among them.*[95] The King did allow Menéndez to import 500 *negro* slaves.[96] The Moors and Turks would have arrived before 1585, at Pardo's time, and 20 years before Drake. Would the Spaniards bring them to Santo Domingo? With the Inquisition firmly in place, would they allow Muslims to come to America? If they were *conversos*, why would they be sent as slaves after being converted? Now let us examine the naval activity.

From the chart of English voyages [Fig. 11], it can be seen that the area was quite busy with sailing ships. If Drake had put ashore his motley passengers, what happened to them? Even if they were in a hurry to leave, they would not have gone very far. Not much later, Grenville did quite a bit of exploring. He received information from the Indians that Drake and Lane had gone, but no word of anyone else in the area. According to David Quinn, Drake had perhaps 300 South American Indians and 100 Negro slaves to dispose of as a free labor for the Roanoke settlers.[97] Either these numbers were exaggerated or Drake never picked up any large number of slaves or Indians. If Drake took them, were they lost in the storm? Did they die or were they killed on the way to England? This is doubtful. Drake was already low on provisions. Most likely, the crew would have a hard time accepting them on board since they blamed them for the many who died due to sickness brought on board previously. They were so anxious to leave that they did not even wait for their three lost countrymen.

The only trace found was relative to the shipping of approximately 100 ex-galley slaves from England to the Turkish dominions. This may have nothing to do with Drake. They also could have been captured by the English somewhere else, or from the Spaniards on their return trip.

Grenville and Raleigh Voyages—1586

With Grenville in charge, the second trip departed Bideford, England on April 9, arrived at the Canaries on April 14, and on May 2 he encountered a ship from Spain belonging to Breton merchants. He took wine and oil, and on Cape Finisterre boarded two more vessels, one of them a Norman, took their goods, and sent them to England.[98] On May 8, Grenville captured a Dutch fly boat with cargo bound for Spain. He kept the cargo and the boat. Next he stopped at Porto Santo, Madeira for water. However, the islanders fought so bravely that the English returned to their ships, according to Diaz, the Spanish narrator, and left the islands without getting any fresh water.[99]

Grenville sailed for Virginia, arriving at Port Ferdinand at the end of the second week or into the third week of July. By then, another ship sent by Raleigh with supplies had already left Roanoke. Although this date is very important, apparently it is not possible to know it exactly. However, Hakluyt tells us [100] that this supply ship arrived *immediately* after Lane's men left with Drake. It may have arrived between the 20th and 25th of June and left by the end of the month or the first week of July. [See Chart at the end of the Chapter] They finally arrived at Port Ferdinand on July 21.

Grenville would have arrived sometime in the middle of July, and departed by the end of August after having made some explorations leaving 15 or 18 men, which along with the three early ones were the first lost colonists. Obviously his priority was in piracy, and picking off prizes, not colonizing or establishing any settlement.

Another interesting fact in the Grenville voyage is that on the way to England he stopped in the Azores, headed for a trip to Newfoundland for fresh supplies, and returned to the Azores Islands, where he overtook a barque with passengers and a cargo of hides at Vila Franca do Campo, São Miguel Island, and another ship off Terceira Island.[101] That indicates how easy it was for the Portuguese to go from the Azores to the North American east coast.

John White Voyages and the Rescue Voyages—1587-1590

On May 8, 1587, John White sailed with Captain William and the Portuguese pilot Simão Fernandes, together with women and children. They arrived in Virginia on July 22, and on August 18, his granddaughter (Virginia Dare) was born. On August 27, he left to get supplies, never to see his family again.

In the Roanoke Colony were left 83 men, 17 women, 11 children, plus two that were born there, less one dead, George Howe, killed on arrival, for a total of 112 human beings.[102] John White and Simão Fernandes—the Portuguese pilot—returned to England with the Indians Manteo and Towaye.[103]

John White was employed by Raleigh as an artist on the North American voyages.[104] His tale is a piece of autobiography. As such, it is not necessarily history. It tells what he experienced. It does not relate fully in any sense what happened.[105]

On April 22, 1588, John White departed with Captain Facy. He was a seaman whose mind was wholly set on prize taking, without being too careful whether or not he overstepped the delicate line between privateering and piracy.[106]

Because of the priority placed on prize catching, first they boarded a Scottish ship, then a Breton. They stole what they could, then chased a Flushing ship. After that, they were the ones being chased by the French, who engaged them in a fierce battle resulting in many casualties. They returned to England and arrived on May 22. That was the end of the Roanoke Colony, and of the 1588 rescue trip.

John White was sent back in 1590 to look for the English settlers left there in 1587, and found Roanoke Island deserted. The story of this trip begins with John Watts, the greatest of privateering entrepreneurs, and his partners in the Thames in January 1590.

After several problems, John White left on March 20.[107]

He chased and captured a number of Spanish vessels, and finally arrived in Virginia on August 15 to find out that all the colonists had vanished, leaving only the letters *CRO* carved on a tree, and on one post the word *CROATOAN*.[108] That was the last communication from the colonists. No one was ever found.

Another aspect is the fact that due to hardships throughout the rest of Europe, and the rising of English power under Queen Elizabeth I, many continental Europeans emigrated to England. England employed Venetians, Portuguese and Genovese mariners in their early sea exploration. It is therefore possible that many of the first settlers of the Roanoke Colony may have been foreigners. Some of the names of the Roanoke colonists certainly are not typically English as shown on the list of Colonists at the end of this chapter.

Ruth Wetmore, an experienced archaeologist that has worked in the Southeast for many years, is of the opinion that at least a few of the Roanoke Colony settlers were Portuguese.[109] At least one of them, Simão Fernandes, was. Some of the other names could very easily be considered of Portuguese roots. Also, Simão Fernandes, being Portuguese, probably had Portuguese servants or friends that he referred to as being part of the group while in England. It is also interesting to note that on Santo Domingo Island, a place practically destroyed by Drake, more than half of the population was Portuguese, according to the high court or *Audiencia*.[110]

Fig. 11—Map of the Roanoke voyages 1584-1590. The Roanoke Voyages by David B. Quinn, Vol. I, inside front cover, Hakluyt Society of London.

List of the Colonists who arrived at Roanoke

John White *
Christopher Cooper
Dyonis Harvie *
Cutbert White
William Sole
George Howe
Thomas Warner
John Tydway *
Thomas Topan
John Spendlove *
Edward Powell
Thomas Gramme
John Stilman *
Brian Wyles
John Farre *
Richard Shaberdge
Thomas Ellis
Thomas Smith
Richard Taverner *
John Starte *
Arnold Archard
John Cheven *
William Dutton
Richard Arthur
Robert Little
Lewes Wotton
Henry Rufoote
Charles Florrie
Thomas Harris

Ananias Dare
Thomas Steuens
William Willes
John Bright *
John Cotsmur *
Simão Fernandes
Anthony Cage
Ambrose Viccars
Henry Berrye
John Hemmington *
Humfrey Newton
Marke Bennet
Peter Little
Geroge Martyn
John Bridger *
John Burden *
William Browne
Richard Kemme
John Earnest *
Richard Darige
John Wright *
Thomas Hewet
Morris Allen
John Chapman *
Hugh Tayler
Michael Bishop
Richard Tomkins
Henry Milton
William Nicholes

Roger Baille
John Sampson *
John Brooke *
Clement Taylor
Roger Pratt
Nicholas Johnnson *
John Jones *
Edmond English
Richard Berrye
Thomas Butler
Thomas Colman
John Gibles *
John Wyles *
Hugh Pattenson
Griffen Jones *
James Hynde *
Michael Myllet
Thomas Harris
Henry Johnson *
William Lucas
James Lassie *
William Berde (Verde)
William Waters
William Clement
Richard Wildeye
Henry Browne
Henry Dorrell
Henry Payne
Thomas Pheuens

Women:

Elyoner Dare
Wenefrid Powell
Elizabeth Glane
Alis Chapman
Margaret Lawrence
Rose Payne

Margery Harvie
Joyce Archard
Jane Pierce
Emme Merrimoth
Joan Warren *
Elizabeth Viccars

Agnes Wood
Jane Jones *
Audry Tappan
Colman
Jane Mannering *

Children:

John Sampson *
Thomas Archard
George Howe

Robert Ellis
Thomas Humfrey
John Pratt *

Ambrose Viccars
Thomas Smart
William Wythers

The previous list does not include Virginia Dare, the first English child born in Virginia, and Harvie.

* The letters I and u were used in the 16th century. For the benefit of the reader they were substituted by the letters J and v to denote modern spelling.

The 16th Century Virginia-Roanoke Voyages Chronology Chart

April 27, 1584	Barlowe/Amadas/Fernandes leaves England
July 13, 1584	Arrival in Roanoke to explore area
September 15, 1584	Return to England with two Indians
April 19, 1585	Leave England with 100 colonists
July 27, 1585	Arrive at the Roanoke Island
August 25, 1585	Grenville leaves for England, arrives October
Sept.14, 1585	Drake leaves England
Jan. 1, 1586	Drake arrives in Española
May 2, 1586	Grenville leaves England
May 26, 1586	Drake in Santo Domingo
May 27, 1586	Drake in St. Augustine
June 9, 1586 *	Drake arrives in Roanoke
June 18, 1586 *	Drake and Lane departed with colonists
June 20/25, 1586 *	Raleigh's supply ship arrived
June 30/July 7, 1586 *	Raleigh's supply ship departed
July 15, 1586 *	Grenville ship arrives in Roanoke, leaves 15 men
July 28, 1586 *	Drake arrives in England, after Lane
August 8/18, 1586 *	Eight ships sighted off Santa Elena
August 25, 1586 *	Grenville departed Roanoke
April 26, 1587 *	John White leaves England with 126 colonists
July 22, 1587 *	John White arrives at Port Ferdinand
August 18, 1587 *	First English child is born in Virginia
August 27, 1587 *	John White returns to England
September 17, 1587	John White in Azores
October 18, 1587	Pilot Simão Fernandes arrives in England
November 8, 1587	John White arrives in Southampton
April 22, 1588	White leaves England with 7 men and 4 women
May 22, 1588	White returns without ever reaching Virginia
March 20, 1590	White departs England on the *Hopewell*
May 26, 1590	*Hopewell* attacks Spanish ships
August 15, 1590	White arrives in Virginia, no one at Roanoke
October 30, 1590	White returns to England, no colonists found

* Voyages related to the Lost Roanoke Colony

See Fig. 11 for the Map of Roanoke Voyages

New England in 1602 and Jamestown Colony—1607

After the Roanoke Colony failed, an effort was made by 32 Englishmen to establish another colony in 1602. They reached Cape Cod about May 15. A letter to Sir Walter Raleigh describes their encounters with the natives: *These people, as they are exceeding courteous, gentle of disposition...of complexion or colour much like a dark olive...black hair...Some of them are black, thin bearded...They pronounce our language with great facility...*[111]

Is it possible that they could have been descendants of early 16th century arrivals on the U.S. East coast? No colony was established in New England, but as soon as Jamestown was founded, attempts were made to find the missing settlers of Roanoke Island: *Captain John Smith records...information obtained from Indians in the Jamestown vicinity told about men...who dressed like Englishmen.*[112] It is unlikely that the Indians could tell the difference between English dressing and other Europeans, since there were Germans and Poles beside English, according to John Smith.

In 1700, John Lawson wrote: *...some Indians, that are more civilized than the rest, which wear Hats, Shooes, Stockings, and Breeches...will often buy the English-made coats, which they wear on Festivals and other days of visiting.*[113]

It did not take long for different Indian nations to acquire the dressing habits of the English, which was already happening for some time in 1700.

In the October 30, 1966 issue of the *Baltimore Sun*, Mary Conelly wrote about the Lumbees and quoted one of the original settlers, George Percy: *...a savage boy about the age of ten years, which had a head of perfect yellow hair and a reasonable white skin, which is a miracle amongst the savages.*[114] The Lumbees have just recently been recognized as an Indian tribe, and the same encounters with white people have been attributed to them and the Melungeons as a sign of their presence in the early days of English settlement. The Lumbees claim to be direct descendants of the Lost Roanoke Colony settlers; however, their complexions vary from very dark to very fair, which leads us to believe that they intermixed with others besides the English and the Indians. In any case, George Percy's statement indicates a presence of white people, besides the English, in the early 1500's.

First Africans from Angola to Virginia—1619

Early American history as we know it is not complete. Thanks to historians and researchers like Engel Sluiter, John Thornton, William Thorndale, and others, new information is being uncovered. William and Mary Quarterly Magazine has published related articles in their issues of April 1997 and July 1998. The researchers just mentioned have consulted numerous sources used in their research, which are cited in the magazine. Mark St. John of the Newport News Daily Press also published an excellent article about these revolutionary findings.[115] The following are a few facts written by contemporary writers at the beginning of the 17th century:

Captain John Smith wrote in his *Generall History of Virginia*: *About the last of August came in a dutch man of warre that sold us twenty Negars.*

John Rolfe wrote: *About the latter end of August, a Dutch man of Warr...arrived at Point-Comfort...He brought anything but 20. and odd Negroes.*

This is the only statement related to the importation of Blacks into Virginia after the Jamestown settlement in 1607. The origin of these Africans has not been established, but we now know for sure where the *20 and odd Negroes* came from. Let us keep in mind that Portugal was at that time governed by a Spanish king, so most of the slaves from Africa were being sent to the West Indies and Brazil. Slavery as an institution did not exist in Virginia at that time, and it was not until December 1641 (1661?) that statutory recognition of slavery took place. Also at the time, King James had made peace with Spain, and legal privateering came to an end.

The question is, what part of Africa did this group of Blacks come from, and what do the Portuguese or Melungeons have to do with them? The answer was found when California historian Engel Sluiter sifted through Portuguese Colonial shipping records, and came across a Portuguese merchant-slaver that lost its human cargo to English and Dutch privateers in the West Indies. The timing and description of the attack almost certainly ties that ship, known as the San Juan Bautista, to the Dutch adventurers who brought the first blacks to Virginia. The records also link that human cargo to the Angolan port town of Luanda, and to Africans originating in the central highlands of Angola, today known as the Province of Malanje.

This revolutionized the field by pinpointing the name, nationality, and port of origin of the ship that carried the Blacks from Africa to the New World. However, no one knew if they were slaves.

Then in 1998, Pennsylvania historian John Thornton examined the Portuguese colony of Angola during the early 17th century, and turned up not only the region in Angola from which the Blacks came, but also the military campaign in which they were probably captured. Since Portuguese law required that all African slaves be baptized and made Christian before their arrival in America, it is appropriate to assume that these unwilling immigrants were likely to have been Christians.

Thornton also established that Mendes de Vasconcellos' military forces got far out of hand and captured 4,000 Christians, prompting Bishop Manuel Bautista Soares and Portuguese settlers to protest vigorously, but to no avail. Thornton also found that the Dutch were the only ones involved in the capture of the Portuguese ship. The Dutch traded the captured prisoners for much-needed supplies. These Africans were likely to have been Christians in that they had years of experience in trading and dealing with Europeans, spoke a common language, and probably knew how to raise crops and domestic animals.

Such traits would have made them better able to adapt to their lot in Vrginia than the ethnically and linguistically diverse groups of Blacks that began to arrive from West Africa later in the 1600's. Continued trading with Portuguese Angola may help explain why the first generations of Africans were so much more successful at working their way out of servitude than those who followed. It may also help scholars understand why attitudes about race hardened in the late 1600's, when the concept of limited-term indenture began to mutate into the institution of lifelong slavery.

According to the information supplied by contemporary writers, it was thought that these Blacks were the first ones to arrive in Virginia, until 1995 when historian William Thorndale uncovered the 1619 Virginia census which shows 32 *Negroes* (15 men and 17 women) at the service of the planters. A word of caution, English explorers had been in Africa since the 1550's, did they bring these or other *Negroes* to America before?

Now we should ask: Why were contemporary historians silent about these facts? Two reasons—one is obvious, the attack on the Portuguese ship was made against the King's orders, so English and Dutch corsairs were engaged in illegal privateering by attacking ships from a nation which England was at peace with.

The other is that the settlers quickly found out that these Africans had been introduced to the Christian faith. The Virginian slaveholders, with their fear that Christianity would make them free, would have been reluctant to admit it.

There are still many questions as to the composition of these Africans from the Portuguese colony. Were they all Black? The Portuguese had been in Angola for more than one hundred years, so most likely mixed marriages took place. There were only 20—what happened to the rest? The ship left Angola with 350, and the same Captain was reported later with 147, but no ship? What happen to the crew? Was the crew all Black? Keep in mind that for centuries after that, dark complexioned people were considered *Negro* or *Mulatto* on the Census.

What happened to these African-Portuguese? They worked their way out of servitude and were successful. John Thornton ends his article with a profound statement: *These new captives perhaps gave a certain Angolan touch to the early Chesapeake. Significantly, the grandson of one of their contemporaries, who had arrived in 1621, in 1677 named his Eastern Shore estate "Angola."* [116] This is not the only case of success, many more were recorded. Also Portuguese names were found early in Virginia, such as Big Manuel, Rodriggus, Anthony Portuguese, John Pedro, Paul d'Angola, etc. Tim Hashaw wrote a series of articles for the Gowen Research Foundation on his research about the Malange origin of the Melungeons and the Portuguese connection. Another fact: There are at least 12 locations in the U.S. named Angola. The author wrote in his book *The Forgotten Portuguese,* (1998) before the above research was done, about a possible connection with the Angola province Malang(j)e, which is possible but the story is far more complex than that. One final question: Should the name Melungeon be connected to just Angola? According to the researchers 50,000 or more Blacks came out of Malange in the 17th century, but most went to Spanish Latin America. If so, why only in the Southeast was the name Melungeon able to survive?

Blacks and Whites Living Together in Virginia

When discussing the first several groups that populated America after its discovery by the Europeans in the 15th century, we must note the presence of black people at an early period. In Abraham Wood's letter, there is a story told by an Indian who was able to escape the white people after killing ten of them. These people had a bell and spoke in an unknown language: *They have many blacks among them...many swine and cattle...they have two mulatto women.* [The letter adds that the Indians, since their men were killed] *...all ye white and black people they take they put to death.* [Wood's letter adds] *...all this I presented to ye Grand Assembly of Virginia.* [117]

The letter goes on to describe Gabriel Arthur's travels: *...they travelled eight days west and by south, as he guest, and came to a town of negroes, spatious and* *great, but all wooden buildings...they marched...and about five or six miles...came within sight of a Spanish town...brick buildings.... Hung ye bell which Mr. Needham gives relation of and harde it ring in ye evening.* [118]

We have learned of a bell ringing and some sort of praying in a language the English could not understand. Now we are told of the same bell in the evening which is when Catholics pause to pray. What is puzzling is the Spanish town. Is it really Spanish, or possibly Portuguese that look and dress like them? The letter further reads that: *Ye 7th day a Spaniard in a gentille habitt, accoutered with gunn, sword and pistol...one of the Tomahittans...shot him to death...In his pockets were two pieces of gold and a small gold chain...* [Notice that the writer does not say that he was a soldier] *...they hasted to ye negro town.* [119] After that, they went to Port Royal in what is today South Carolina, which in earlier years was the Santa Elena of the Spaniards.

We could safely conclude that the town was not Spanish, or at least not controlled by the Spanish government. The Spaniards had left the area almost one hundred years before. The fact that nearby was a town of *negros* hardly demonstrates that the Spaniards would let *negros* live free when in Florida and in the Caribbean they were importing and holding black slaves.

If they were Black and apparently living free, what would they have in common with the *white bearded men*? Is it possible that not all Black people that came to this country were slaves, but came of their own free will? It is doubtful, unless they were not aware of slavery in America, or came before slavery was legal.

David Beers Quinn wrote about Drake's captured slaves: *...when free coloured labour was Drake's intended gift...it is curious and ironic commentary on the later history of this and other plantation colonies.* [120]

In 1564, John Sparke, who accompanied John Hawkins, wrote a description of Florida's natives: *There is one thing to be marveled at, for the making of their* [Indians'] *fire, and not only they but also the Negroes do the same...* [121] Are these *Negroes* slaves? If so, to whom do they belong? Or are they free Blacks living with the Indians from whom they learned their ways, having arrived before the Spaniards? Let us keep in mind that the Portuguese knew the location and existence of Florida prior to 1502.

There is still another question. When *Black* or *Negro* was mentioned in the 17th century, did they know the difference between Blacks from Arabia, or the dark skinned Moors from North Africa (Berbers), and the Blacks from West Africa?

Victor Marques, President of the Portuguese-American Southeast Chamber of Commerce, uncovered additional information about the presence of blacks in Virginia, within the time frame of the early settlement of Jamestown. Bill Hendrick of the Atlanta Journal tells the story: *The four sets of bones, first unearthed 50 years ago, are thought to date between 1620 and 1680... One of the skeletons was that of a Black man thought to be age 26...The four are among 21 sets of skeletons dug up on the coast of southeastern Virginia at the site of historic Jamestown, the first permanent English settlement in the New World.* [122]

History is constantly changing, so it is always a good idea to keep an open mind. The above information was based on declarations by Smithsonian forensic anthropologist Douglas W. Owsley. Prior to that discovery, scientists knew of only one other native of Africa who lived and died in the early colonial period.

This also proves that Africans came to America very early, and also that they were free. Whatever Blacks the Spaniards brought were slaves. What other nation was trading on both coasts of Africa, and had the capability of transporting people to the New World, both slave and free? At that time not all Blacks were slaves, and not all Whites—mainly from the Far East—were free.

Search in 1624—First Encounters in 1654

The earliest encounter by Europeans with non-native people is registered in Spanish archives, which show that several unsuccessful expeditions to the Georgia-Carolina interior were sent to find *Gente Blanca* (White People) in 1624. Apparently there was a belief in Spain that white people were already in the southeast before Spanish forces arrived. These rumors continued as late as 1661. This has been one of the arguments used by Welsh people advocates. The lack of success of the Spanish expeditions may mean one of two things: either the search party did not go sufficiently north and west, or they were looking for fair skinned people only.[123]

If they *(gente blanca)* were the ancestors of the Melungeons or other groups of early settlers, most likely they would be darker, having blended with the Indian population in similar settlements. Later in 1654, Cole adds a footnote to Abraham Wood's letter: *...Spaniards were in intercourse with the Cherokees from an early date. They were in the gold regions of the southern Alleghenies in 1654.*[124] It is not logical that a settlement of Spaniards would live in the midst of the English, unless they were not Spanish but Portuguese, a common error made by many historians, due to the fact that Portugal was governed by Spanish kings from 1580 to 1640. It is also possible that some of the settlers brought in by the Spaniards may have survived. However, non-Spanish could be the main element. In order not to sound overwhelming on the Portuguese side, here is what Yeardley wrote: *...he told them was one Spaniard residing, who had been seven years with them, a man very rich, having about thirty in family, seven whereof are negroes...*[125]

This was in Tuskarorawes Indian country, and may not prove much but it tells us something about Spanish living with Indians and having slaves.

...[B]efore the year 1700 French explorers reported finding them...One theory of their origin is that a band of ship wrecked Portuguese sailors wandered from the North Carolina coast.[126]

Why Portuguese? Why not the French, English or the Spaniards? They all sailed along the east coast. There is no record of any other nation sailing on the open Atlantic Ocean. The only other power in the 15th and 16th centuries was the Ottoman Empire, and they were confined to the east Mediterranean Sea and the Indian Ocean. Therefore, we have to assume that they must have been people of one of these four nationalities, and that it should have happened in the early part of the 1500's or not much later than the middle of the 1500's. By the late 1500's, there was much activity by the Spaniards, the English, and the French, who attempted to colonize the Southeast coast.

With the exception of the English Roanoke lost colony, neither Spain nor France claimed having lost any colony. It is also known that there was trading activity, according to the following account from Francis Yeardley, in South Virginia and Carolina: *In September last,* (1653) *a young man, a trader for beavers...with three more...went to Rhoanoke Island...found the great commander of those parts with his Indians...who received them civilly, and shewed them the ruins of Sir Walter Ralegh's fort...*[127] There is no mention of the English colonists or the survivors 66 years later. Yeardley, a minister, was shown the ruins of the fort in Roanoke Island by local Indians, and met an Indian trader who upon seeing children reading and writing, gave up his son in order that he be taught how to read and write:

...[H]*earing and seeing the children read and write...he asked me...whether I would take his only son...and teach him to do as our children, namely in his terms, to speak out of the book, and to make a writing.*[128] This did not turn out so simply, since the rest of the colonists were not ready to accept Indians in their community. Yeardley later describes their attitude in his narrative when the Indian brought in his child: *...and carried themselves* (the colonists) *uncivilly towards them, forbidding their* (Indian and his child) *coming in any more.*[129]

Spanish Fort and a Mine after Santa Elena—1670

Historian Hollingsworth wrote that: *...1670 is the earliest date of which there is any probability of a trader from the English settlements traversing this section of the state* [Surry County, VA] *although the Spaniards seeking gold...on some expedition from their fort and mine near Lincolnton, N. Carolina.*[130] Were they really Spanish? This is in the western portion of North Carolina, and the Spaniards were in Florida by then. Kennedy mentions the possibility of these being: *...new arrivals or Pardo's descendants.*[131]

It is rather difficult to believe that the Spaniards would forget or leave their men—after all, they were in St. Augustine, which is not too far away, and stayed there for a long time. According to Juan de Ribas, a soldier:*...by 1600 the only Spaniards left in the Indian Fields were a fifer with his wife and children.*[132]

We just have to remember that Hernando de Soto's men had found their way to Mexico more than 20 years before. If so, why not Florida, which is much closer? The other possibility is that the Spaniards did not care, because these settlers were not Spanish but instead were descendants of Pardo's original settlers, either Portuguese or another nationality.

John Lederer in 1670

On May 20, 1670, there was another German adventurer named John Lederer, who wrote the following based on information given to him by local Indians (Santee and Cheraw): *...that two days journey and half from hence to the Southwest, a powerful nation of bearded men were seated, which I suppose to be Spaniards, because the Indians never have any...*[133] This is definitely a sign that either the Portuguese or the Spaniards were there in some form at those early times. Again the question, why would the Spaniards stay so far away from their secure settlement in Florida? This also may make a case for these people being the descendants of the lost Roanoke Colony. More than 50 years had passed since the Jamestown settlement, and its existence would be known, mainly to anyone who spoke English. As John Lederer traveled to this area, so had other people. John Watson also mentions the Keyauwee Indians: *...who wore beards and mustaches, an unprecedent custom among Indians.*[134] This narration is from 1700, and it is possible that these Indians mixed with Europeans who arrived in the early 1500's

Abraham Wood Letter, Catholic Mass and the Bell—1673

Samuel Cole Williams, a historian from Tennessee, transcribed from the letter of Abraham Wood to John Richards in London what could be considered a religious ceremony of a Catholic nature: *...that ye white people have a bell which is six foot over which they ring morning and evening and att that time a great number of people congregate togather and talkes he knowes not what....*[135] The ringing of church bells, called the *Trindade* or Trinity hour at sundown, was, and probably still is, a common occurrence in the villages in Portugal, as well as the use of beads of the rosary for praying. The usage of beads for religious purposes is still present today. The archeological finds of any beads could be related to this. This is also a Catholic ritual in Portugal, and one which the author can remember in the little village where he was born. The local church would ring the bell at sundown, which they called in Portuguese *toque da Avé Maria* or Holy Mary toll, to remind everyone to pause and pray on the beads of the Rosary—*terço* or *rosário* in Portuguese— which most older women did and still do on their knees. By the 15th century, the Moors had for the most part been converted to Catholicism. The bell ringing—and bow—is part of the Catholic mass ritual, during the Eucharistic Prayer and the Breaking of the Bread. The author remembers as a young boy being told that when the bell rang, it was extremely important to be silent and bow; failure to do so would be considered a sin.

Wood's letter also mentions what we can safely assume that they were not English and spoke a foreign language:*...and talkes he knowes not what*. If they could not understand, what language was it? The Catholic church always celebrated mass in Latin, and not until recently authorized the use of vernacular languages. Is it possible that the language they could not understand was Latin? Recently the author spoke with an old lady living in the mountains, and she mentioned that a friend of hers was a Melungeon, and that her friend's grandmother said her prayers in a strange or unknown language. Kennedy writes that:*...The mere existence of a bell at that time period would seem to indicate a Catholic origin. And the fact that these English- speaking Indians did not understand the language of these mysterious, apparent*

Europeans is also an intriguing piece of evidence. These "hairy people" worshipping at a bell were obviously not English.[136]

They could not be Spanish either, since the English speaking Indians could recognize Spaniards and had mentioned them in other writings of the same period. As for *hairy people,* the Portuguese have that dubious honor.

On the same note, we should not overlook the possibility that elements of the lost Roanoke Colony joined an already established colony of Europeans that may have arrived there much earlier and later taught them the English language. John Lawson, considered the first North Carolinian historian, writes in his journal in 1700 as he approaches the coast of North Carolina: *...he was given two chickens by friendly Indians, a clear indication of contact with Europeans because the eastern Indians had no domestic fowl prior to the coming of whites.*[137]

There is also another claim: *they frequently communicate with spirit world.*[138] This is true, not only in Portugal but also in Brazil on a larger scale, where spiritual sessions called "Macumba" are practiced.

April 1673 Journey—White, Long Beards and Whiskers

Some chroniclers left an account of what they saw back in the 17th century. The following are some of what has been recorded: *...Eight dayes journy down this river, lives a white people which have long beardes and whiskers and weares clothing, and on some of ye other rivers lives a hairy people.*[139] Chapman J. Milling wrote about old chronicles that described the Indians: *To appearance the men* [Carolina Indians] *have no beards nor hair on their head except a round turf on its crown.*[140] Gilbert confirms in his thesis in 1934 that beards and mustaches in the Cherokee were rare.[141]

This early report indicates that they were not Indians wearing clothing. They were white to the Indians and had hair on their bodies, besides the head or the face. An interesting fact, if they were Moors or Turks—Muslims—the clothing would be different from traditional European, and if they were different, the Indians would have mentioned that. Another much earlier report comes from Hernando de Soto's expedition in 1540: *The natives were a friendly people, appearing well dressed and more civilized than any people seen in all the territories of Florida, wearing clothes and shoes.*[142] Based on the above, it is possible that they might be referring to people that were connected in some way with the Portuguese.

Shipwrecked Sailors, Pirates—1685

Bonnie Ball in her book presents another story: *James Aswell, a Tennessee history expert...possible explanation for the Melungeons is an old story that Portuguese ships were plying the Caribbean as pirates at the time of the Portuguese revolt against Spain in 1685.* On the same book: *...a band of ship-wrecked sailors... Portugal, after revolting successfully against Spain, dispatched a ship to sieze Cuba in 1685.*[143]

That paragraph has to be imaginative, as the revolt against Spain was in 1640 and not in 1685. By 1685, if there were any spare Portuguese sailors or ships, they would have been better recompensed if they chased the Spaniards near the Portuguese coast, when they would be returning home from the Caribbean loaded with gold and silver. King João IV of Portugal was the Duke of Braganza before he led the restoration of the independence of his country in 1640.

When he took over the government, the Portuguese treasury was depleted, and when he died in 1656, there was a war still going on. In 1665, his son Afonso VI was the king.[144]

While Portugal's crown was united with Spain, Portugal lost many overseas colonies and trade facilities. It does not make sense that Portugal would embark on such an expensive venture at a time when the national defense interests demanded all resources and attention.[145]

Not until 1668 did Spain sign the peace treaty with Portugal. Most of the overseas time and resources after the separation from Spain were spent in removing the Dutch from Brazil,[146] and the Caribbean was of little interest to Portugal. In none of the Portuguese sources consulted are there any references to such an expedition to the Caribbean against Spain.

Also, there is the tradition of a Portuguese ship and a mutiny:... *A letter...from Mr. L. Gibson, a resident of Scotland County...refers to a dark skinned people...The old man who told me about their ancestry more than fifty years ago...called them something to me like Mongolians...No doubt the name he called was Melungeons...in another paragraph...local legend that the people were descendants of Portuguese pirates or sailors...and anglicized their Portuguese names...whether they were pirates or shipwrecked sailors would have made little difference—their safety lay in changing their names. With the passage in 1699 of the stringent anti-piracy laws, rope happy citizens were apt to act first and think afterwards.*[147] Piracy was common in the 16th century. Even countries at peace with each other allowed piracy for their own benefit.

As for there being Portuguese pirates or pirates of any other nationality, it is unlikely. The presence of families or women aboard pirate ships could hardly be considered. This again points to a presence of Portuguese before the 17th century. As for the name "Mongolian," let us keep our minds open, remembering that it has been written that the Melungeons had an occasional Asiatic appearance.

Pirates, shipwrecked sailors...it is possible, but most likely they would all be men, with no provisions and plans for a long stay. That does not explain the surviving of the Melungeons to this century as a group. Perhaps they were part of a boat full of would-be settlers, bound for another part of the world, with complete families, provisions and plans for a long stay.

The Huguenots Found White People in 1708

Bonnie Ball writes: *...the legend of a white people found on the Lumber River in Robeson County in North Carolina, by the French Huguenots in 1708, and were* *said to have owned farms and living like Europeans. They also reputed to have spoken an older form of English.*[148] The author has not been able to find the source for that information. Is it possible that the French Huguenots would be traveling so close to the English when they were at war? Is it possible that an older form of English would be recognized by French speaking people?

After all, only 100 years had passed since Elizabethan English was spoken in England. The language did not change that much to be considered an old form of English. If these white people were the survivors of the Lost Roanoke Colony, would there be that many who would be able to keep the language for 120 years, while living with the natives? If there were just a few, that would not be possible. If there were many, and they knew the language and English culture, why not look for them? Lawson writes in 1700 that a second settlement was made in 1650: *A second settlement of this Country was made about fifty years ago...by several substantial Planters, from Virginia and other Plantations.* This is about 60 years after the settlers were left in Roanoke. The first two European children—Virginia Dare and Harvie—born in the United States (1587) shortly after their arrival, would have a good chance of still being alive and would have received from their parents or other English survivors some culture they could remember.

In the same manner as we today are able to get some information of what was happening then, I am sure that they or any other group of people would know that the English were in Jamestown with a growing settlement and ships coming or going to and from England: *...[T]he Fame of this new discovery Summer-Country spread thro' the neighbouring Colonies, and in a few Years, drew a considerable Number of Families thereto, who all found Land enough to settle themselves in.*[149] Even then it was hard to keep a secret.

Let us not forget the Indian traders who traveled over long distances for as long as one year or more. The traders and the Indians would move often and carry with them information found along the way: *...and to this day, they are a shifting wandering people; for I know some Indian Nations, that have chang'd their settlements, many hundred miles; sometimes no less than a thousand....*[50] [Also] *they are expert Travelers, and they have not the use of...our Compass.*[151]

Dress and language may be characteristic of more than one group, not to just any one in particular. Is it possible that the Huguenots did not recognize the language and assumed that it was an older form of English?

Possible Route to the Mountains—1740-50

The early history of the pioneers is a long way from being completed. Swanton gave us a very good glimpse of what North Carolina was like in the early colonial days. Many documents are still to be uncovered. Samuel Cole Williams, in his *Early Travels in the Tennessee Country*, may give us a clue to which direction the early unknown group of settlers was traveling.

Pioneers trading with Indians passed through the area as early as 1740, and in 1747 Dr. Thomas Walker led an expedition. On March 31, 1750, Walker made a puzzling entry into the journal: *In the Fork between Holston's and the North River, are five Indian Houses built with logs and covered with bark.*[152]

Allegedly, Indians did not have log cabins in 1750. If these log cabins were not made by Indians, who built them? Another entry on April 9: *We travelled to a river...hunters call Clinch's River...*near what is now Sneedville in Hancock County. *...we rode four miles to Beargrass River.* This river was later renamed Powell for Ambrose Powell of Walker's party.[153]

...On the top of the Ridge are Laurel Trees marked with Crosses, and other blazed figures on them....in 1779...going to the spot they found it as related.[154] Since the natural gateway from north to south was through this gap, and it was one of the routes followed by later Melungeons to the East Tennessee mountains, it is possible that the crosses and the figures may have been made by a group of them on their way to Clinch Mountain, since they traditionally used the cross as a religious symbol. However, it is more probable that the crosses were made by trappers or explorers in the vicinity. Pollitzer and Brown's 1969 survey:...*strongly suggests that they migrated west* [from Virginia and North Carolina] *to form the nucleus of the present Melungeons.*[155] For a complete text of Thomas Walker's expedition see *Annals of SW Virginia.*

The North Carolina Tax Lists of 1755

Jean Patterson Bible brings to our attention that most of the Melungeons may have originated in North Carolina.

The Orange County tax lists and censuses of 1755 shows a number of Melungeon family names, including John Collins, Samuel Colens... all noted as "mulatto." Since Negroes are recorded as such, it is probable that the tax officials simply used the word "mulatto" to indicate darker coloring...and then enumerators knew of no other way to classify them.[156]

Henry Price also mentions: *The dark complexion characteristics among Melungeon family names...records a settlement of mullatoes including Thomas Gibson...Thomas Collins...*[157]

See Chapter VIII of this book for the findings of other groups that claim Portuguese ancestry but may not be connected with the Melungeons.

John Sevier in 1782-84

Prior to 1769, and according to John Stuart in a letter to Governor Botecourt:... *none of his majesty's subjects were settled westward of the point where the Virginia-North Carolina line intersects the Holston River.*[158] John Sevier stated in a letter, presumably to Major Stoddard,[159] about a conversation he had with the great warrior Oconostota, and related to the Welsh while on his campaign against the Indians in 1782: *...Sevier observed traces of ancient though regular fortifications...inquired of Oconostota...the reply was that it had been handed down by the forefathers...a period when the Cherokees resided in the South Carolina region, a race of white*

Fig. 12—John Sevier portrait by Charles Wilson Peale. Courtesy Tennessee Historical Society

people had inhabited the country...were called Welsh.[160] If Madoc had arrived in the 1100's, more than 600 years would have passed.

Could the Indians have kept this information for that long? If so, there should be plenty of other information about this continent, which apparently has yet to surface. Let us keep in mind, that was almost 300 years after a possible arrival of the first Europeans on the coast of South Carolina. No one really knows when the Melungeons were first discovered, although by the time Tennessee Governor John Sevier had a possible encounter with them in August 1784, their numbers were apparently substantial.

Sevier's original family name was *Xavier,* a very common name in Spain and Portugal—St. Francis of Xavier is an example. However, the French writer Cambiaire claims that the name is French.

About the Melungeons and the State of Franklin, Louise Davies wrote: *When* [in 1784] *John Sevier attempted to organize the State of Franklin* [forerunner of Tennessee], *there was living in the mountains of Eastern Tennessee a Colony of dark-skinned, reddish-brown complexioned people, supposedly of Moorish descent, who called themselves Malungeons, and claimed to be of Portuguese descent. They lived to themselves exclusively, and were looked upon neither as negroes or Indians.*[161] Why Moorish descent? By then the Moors had been in Portugal for over 800 years, 400 of those as Portuguese citizens. Naturally the Portuguese inherit some of their appearance. There is, however:... *the reddish brown complexion* [this adds to the puzzle, because the Portuguese from Portugal do not have a reddish brown complexion] ...[O]*lder Melungeons always claimed positively that they were Portuguese.*[162]

Louise Davies adds that John Sevier: *...found, in the high ridges of Hancock and Rhea counties...Colony of...people...who...had fine European features and claimed to be Portuguese.*[163] This was also quoted by Swan M. Burnett in the *American Anthropologist*, V. II, 1889, as well as Dromgoole in 1891 in the *Boston Arena* and many other writers after that. It may be possible that Will Allen Dromgoole's relationship to Major Dromgoole who worked with Sevier is the best angle for the "original" description quote cited to Louis Davis.

It is therefore assumed that at least a few generations had already been living there: *A yellowish document addressed to the Governor of North Carolina locked in a box in the State Archives, which contain the first official notice taken of the Melungeons. The report written with a quill on now-brittle foolscap by John Sevier, later the first Governor of Tennessee, described the large, mysterious Colony of bronze-skinned people he found in northeastern Tennessee. Sevier crossed the Appalachians in 1774, and 5 years before settlers discovered the Melungeons who had been there for 200 years, according to the estimate of Mary Sue Going of the Watauga Association of Genealogists.*[164] Sevier's reports written about 1782-84, describe some of the mysterious dark-skinned people as having straight black hair and dark blue eyes.

The author has done extensive research in trying to locate the original letter or document that has been quoted for more than 100 years without result. The only original Sevier letters were found in the Newberry Library in Chicago. It is strange that only two letters were found written by Sevier and these were related to the Welsh people supposedly brought in by Madoc. One of the clerks at the Newberry Library mentioned that there is still a possibility of finding other documents since not every paper has been catalogued in the computer. One other source investigated was the Wisconsin Historical Society where the so called Draper papers are kept. Lyman Copeland Draper wrote extensively about Sevier and had an interview with one of his sons. Again there is no mention of the early Sevier trips made into what is known today as the State of Tennessee. Other manuscripts by Draper were found, but with no connection with any particular group except Indians.

Pioneers of Pure English Strain—1769

Cambiaire writes about the early settlers in East Tennessee and Western Virginia: *...we find, almost exclusively, descendants of pioneers of pure English strain, who in 1769 began to settle this part of the country, then peopled by Indians, and almost inaccessible. These mountaineers have a distinct physical type, speak the English of the 18th century without any slang and modernisms.*[165]

This situation may also be applied to the Melungeons living in the same inaccessible area, their language may have remain unchanged for long periods. Therefore, the Elizabethan English which no longer was spoken in the 18th century might not apply. Dromgoole describes their speech or dialect as:*...a cross between mountaineer and the negro...Their dialect is difficult to write.*[166] *...They spoke in broken English, a dialect distinct from anything ever heard...*[in the area][167]. Could we consider this anything close to Elizabethan English?

The Indians of Robeson County have been connected with the lost Roanoke Colony, and in 1769 James Lowrie settled in Robeson. Among the family names was found an Allen Lowrie, son of William, married to Polly Cumba, or Cumbo, said to be of Portuguese extraction.[168]

* * *

Moors in South Carolina and FPC—1790-95

In her book *The Arabs in America,* Beverlee Mehdi wrote that in 1790, The House of Representatives in South Carolina provided that:....*sundry Moors, Subjects of the Emperor of Morocco be tried in court according to the laws for South Carolina and not under Negro codes.*[169] Also, the South Carolina State Statute V1431 of 1792 banned Moors from entering the state for a period of two years.[170] This time period is much later than the one expected to be the time that the Melungeons arrived in North America. By the late 1700's it would have been possible for written records to survive to our days. Moors could be considered recent arrivals. Let us keep in mind that by then, there was more communication between settlers and natives. It is logical to assume that the original Melungeons did not have any contact with other people except the natives for at least a generation, and by the time they made contact, they were out of step with the rest of the world.

As we shall see later in this book, the term Moor is generic and applied mostly to Muslims and others from North Africa to the Indian Ocean, except the Turks. Also, the term *Moor* was not used by the Moors themselves. Should we consider all subjects of the Emperor of Morocco as Moors? I do not think so. Many Jews and other nationals fleeing political and religious persecution went to Morocco and other North African regions.

Moors living in late 18th century America may have originated in southern Europe, Mediterranean North African countries, or others, bordering the Indian Ocean half way around the world.

These sundry Moors most likely may have joined people that would have something in common, such as skin color or appearance, or even discrimination.

These possible connections with the Melungeons or any other group may not be too difficult to research as census records were already in place.

Anyone interested in pursuing genealogy roots on *"sundry Moors, subjects of the Emperor of Morocco"* should be encouraged to do so, and may establish a possible connection. However, if the research goes before the 1700's, then it is an enormous task.

In this same year (1790) a guide for census takers ordered them to identify all free whites over the age of 16 and Blacks. This may have been the beginning of the term FPC—Free Persons of Color—as they tried to identify people like the Melungeons and other groups not seen as White Anglo-Saxon.[171]

It seems that whenever a person could not be classified as Black, Indian or White the term FPC was used. Naturally, the term was not designed to describe any one particular group of people, such as the Melungeons, although Kennedy does state that... *North Carolina declared Melungeons to be free persons of color.*[172] However it does not say that applied exclusively to the Melungeons.

Dr. Virginia DeMarce, in her review essay on the National Genealogical Society, does not think the same way. *North Carolina never "declared Melungeons" to be free persons of color; nor did a Tennessee statute single out Melungeons for persecution.*[173] North Carolina did, however, pass laws applicable to a specific group, the Portuguese, in this century.

Discriminatory laws may have been made in the past, but were always disguised or justifiable by the makers of such laws.

It is remarkable that Tennessee history is silent on the subject since by the census taken in 1795 the Melungeons must have been numbered with the 973 "free persons" other than whites. There could hardly have been so many free negroes within the bounds of the present state only about 25 years after the first settlement.[174] This may be due to the coming of the Melungeon population, which did not happen until later, and/or may not have been so obvious.

According to Kennedy, the book by Dr. Horace R. Rice, *The Buffalo Ridge Cherokee*, shares that, because some people had a black component in their gene pool, they could not be Indian.[175] If one converses with some old timers still living in the western mountains of North Carolina, near Cherokee, they will say that in the beginning of this century, many claims were denied to people—who would have liked to be considered Cherokee—on the basis of even the slightest chance of being Black, Mulatto or dark skinned.

Elizabethan and Broken English—Anglo Surnames

Is a manner of speaking a clue? : *They reportedly spoke an Elizabethan English... since their English was broken and not fluent as one would expect for a "mother tongue," I assumed they were not English, but instead had picked up the language and the surnames for survival's sake.*[176]

The Melungeons must have arrived in the early 1500's. The English spoken by them was of that time frame, and had to be learned from someone speaking a similar language from that period. By the time they were found, a few generations could have passed. The English were already settling in Virginia and other parts of the East Coast. Let us not forget that some Indians had been to England, learned the language and returned to America, spreading their knowledge among the different tribes.

Finally, these encounters with a people that spoke old English were reported by a Frenchman, not necessarily an authority on the language. These people, living in isolation, keep up with neither the changing language nor the colloquial speech patterns of country and mountain people.

This is not surprising, and surely many American surnames are not necessarily written the same way as when their ancestors first arrived in America. There are a number of stories—sometimes more like anecdotes—of immigrants arriving at the immigration officer's desk on New York's Ellis Island. Before they left the desk, they would unwittingly allow their names to be changed forever due to their illiteracy or inability to speak English.

This is not the case with the Melungeons. There were no immigration officers to greet them, but once they established that the English were in charge, they did whatever was necessary to get along. (See Appendix A for the most famous name change in the world, which remains a mystery.)

Many immigrants change their names today, to make their lives easier. Others spend the rest of their lives correcting the spelling. On the other hand, there was the possibility that some of them already had English names.

As for speaking broken English, it is quite natural. By the time the first English settlers met them, and put it on record, it is possible that they might have had contact with other English-speaking people, thereby picking up the language from them, but not necessarily writing it down in such a way as to reach our present day. Again Kennedy's analyses are correct on the survival conclusion.

...[B]y the 1750's—when the first great waves of English and Scot-Irish settlers came down the Valley of Virginia—the Melungeons were speaking a broken form of Elizabethan (that is, sixteenth-century) English and carrying English surnames as well....and given England's heavy trade with Portuguese during the Elizabethan period, we would expect many Portuguese to speak at least some English.[177]

A language can disappear in just one generation, and with no books, it would probably happen more quickly. Illiteracy was quite common in those days. However, in 1850, 40% of the Goinses Melungeons were registered in the census as literate. That was remarkable for the time.[178]

An explanation from a Portuguese point of view is easy, due to the fact that Portugal had at that time, and still has, very close ties with England. Edmund of Langley, the first Duke of York and son of King Edward III of England, headed the Lisbon expedition of 1381-82 to aid King Fernando of Portugal against Castille, which unfortunately was a failure. However, this points out the early ties that Portugal had with England, and with the English language:...*as far back as there are records, an English dialect has been spoken by the Melungeons, and they have been Christians....they are similar to mountaineers in dialect....*[179] The term Elizabethan and/or broken English created some questions, and to clear them, further research was done to find out when these terms were first mentioned in connection with the Melungeons—as well as interviews with local and long time residents of the Appalachian Mountains.

In Western North Carolina, a more logical explanation was discovered. During an interview with several of the older folks, it was learned that it was common for mountain people to speak older English. This was confirmed by Benita Howell, Ph.D., an anthropology professor at the University of Tennessee in Knoxville, who stated: *"I've never heard this said of Melungeons in particular; rather of all "isolated" Appalachians. It turns up in the local color travel literature of the late 19th century and was related to WASPs obsession with British racial purity at a time when non-British immigration to the Northeast was increasing dramatically. Sometimes it is Elizabethan English, sometimes Anglo-Saxon even is referenced. The speech contains some archaic forms but certainly isn't and never has been frozen into Elizabethan or any other earlier form; that would be an impossibility from the standpoint of everything that is known about languages and language generally."*

It is well known that the southeastern states constitute the Bible belt, where religion is a very important facet of daily life. It is also common to hear the pastors in church quoting Bible passages from the original King James version, which is closer to Elizabethan English. It was learned through a local minister that the Pilgrims and the Puritans, when they first arrived in New England, preferred the German version of Martin Luther's Bible. Bonnie Ball writes about their speech: *Old Jack Bowling was the progenitor of the Scott County Bollings, and his people were strong, and spoke broken English* (1820).[180] Dromgoole also mentions that they: *...spoke a broken English, a dialect distinct from anything I ever heard* (1890).[181] Had Miss Dromgoole visited some Indian town or reservation in the same area, it would have been interesting to learn what she would have said about the Indians' speech.

Anglo-Norman and speaking 18th Century English

Dr. Cambiaire in 1933 writes about the mountaineers of East Tennessee and West Virginia as:...*a race of people who represent what is left of the pure...Anglo-Norman race in America.* [A Norman is a native of Normandy in the north of France] *...descendants of pioneers of pure English strain, who in 1769, began to settle this part of the country...These mountaineers have a distinct physical type, speak the English of the 18th century without any slang or modernisms....*[182] It is not known exactly what Dr. Cambiaire meant by *distinct physical type.* Anglo-Saxons or Anglo-Normans have the looks of most English. He could have actually been referring to the Melungeons. The description of their lifestyle (Anglo-Normans) is the same as described by other writers about the Melungeons, and when describing the Melungeons, he states that: *Their language is the English of two centuries ago* which makes it also the 18th century as the rest of the mountaineers.

The Earliest Accounting of the Melungeons—1813/1840

With the help of Kevin Mull, we were able to find a couple of recordings of the Melungeons. We caution the reader of the following transcriptions as they may be considered in poor taste. Although some may find it offensive, it has to be taken in the context of the time period. For those who find it offensive, we apologize. Hollywood often portrays similar situations in films of many other people, thus the behavior can't be considered derogatory to the Melungeons. We're talking about the early 1800's before the Civil War. The first reference was made in the Stoney Creek Baptist Church (Scott Co., VA) Minutes of 1813, which may be the earliest proven reference to Melungeons. On page 20, dated Sept. 26, 1813, is written: *"Church sat in love. Brother Kilgore, Moderator. Then came forward Sister Kitchen and complained to the church against Susanna Stallard for saying she harbored them Melungins. Sister Sook said she was hurt with her for believing her child and not believing her, and she won't talk to her to get satisfaction, and both is "pigedish,"* [prejudiced?] *one against the other. Sister Sook lays it down and the church forgives her. Then came forward Cox and relates to the church that he went to the Association and took the letter and they received the letter in fellowship Dismissed."*

The second reference was published in the (Jonesborough, TN) Whig, on Oct.7, 1840. Editor Parson Brownlow (who was anti-slavery, but known to hate blacks) referred to a person as:...*an impudent Melungeon from Washington City, a scoundrel who is half Negro and half Indian.*

The Melungens in 1848

The next account of Melungeons appeared in the Knoxville Register of Tennessee on September 6th, 1848, as an article titled, "THE MELUNGENS," and reprinted in Littell's Living Age in March 1849. It is being presented in its entirety for the many readers who have showed interest in it.

You must know that within some ten miles of this owl's nest, there is a watering-place, known hereabouts as "Blackwater Springs."

It is situated in a narrow gorge, scarcely one half a mile wide, between Powell's Mountain and the Copper Ridge, and is, as you may suppose, almost inaccessible. A hundred men could defend the pass against even a Xerxian army. Now this gorge and the tops and sides of the adjoining mountains are inhabited by a singular species of the human animal called Melungens. The legend of their history, which they carefully preserve, is this: A great many years ago, these mountains were settled by a society of Portugese adventurers, men and women —who came from the long shore parts of Virginia, that they may be freed from the restraints and drawbacks imposed upon them by any form of government. These people made themselves friendly with Indians, and freed, as they were, from any kind of social government, they uprooted all conventional forms of society, and lived in a delightful Utopia of their own creation, trampling upon the marriage relation, despising all forms of religion, and subsisting on corn (the only possible product of the soil) and the game of the woods. These intermixed with the Indians, and subsequently their descendants (after the first advances of the whites into this part of the state) with the negroes and the whites, thus forming the present race of Melungens. They are tall, straight, well-formed people, of a dark copper color, with Circassian features, but wooly heads and similar appendages of our negro. They are priviledged voters in the state in which they live, and thus, you will perceive, are accredited citizens of the commonwealth. They are brave, but quarrelsome; and are hospitable and generous to strangers. They have no preachers among them, and are almost without knowledge of a Supreme Being.

They are married by the established forms, but husband and wife seperate at pleasure, without meeting with any reproach or disgrace from their friends. They are remarkably unchaste, and want of chastity on the part of the females is no bar to their marrying. They have but little association with their neighbors, carefully preserving their identity as a race, or class, or whatever you may call it; and are in every respect, save that they are under the state government, a seperate and distinct people. Now this is no traveller's story. They are really what I tell you, without abating or setting down aught in malice.

They are behind their neighbors in the arts. They use oxen instead of horses in their agricultural attempts, and their implements of husbandry are chiefly made by themselves of wood. They are, without exception, poor and ignorant, but apparently happy.

Having thus given you a correct geographical and scientific history of the people, I will proceed with my own adventures. The doctor was, as usual, my compagnon de voyage, and we stopped at "Old Vardy's," the hostelrie of the vicinage. Old Vardy is the "chief cook and bottle-washer" of the Melungens, and is really a very clever fellow; but his hotel savors strongly of that peculiar perfume that one may find in the sleeping-rooms of our negro servants, especially on a close, warm, summer's evening. We arrived at Vardy's in time for supper, and, that dispatched, we went to the spring, where were assembled several rude log huts, and a small sprinkling of "the natives," together with a fiddle and other preperations for a dance. Shoes, stockings, and coats were unknown luxuries among them—at least we saw them not.

The dance was engaged in with the right hearty good will, and would have put to the blush the tame steppings of our beaux. Among the participants was a very tall, raw-boned damsel, with her two garments fluttering readily in the amorous night breeze, whose black eyes were lit up with an unusual fire, either from repeated visits to the nearest hut, behind the door of which was placed an open-mouthed stone jar of new-made corn whiskey, and in which was a gourd, with a "deuce a bit" of sugar at all, and no water nearer than the spring.

Nearest her on the right was a lank, lantern-jawed, high-cheeked, long-legged fellow, who seemed similarly elevated. Now these two, Jord Bilson (that was he), and Syl Varmin (that was she), were destined to afford the amusement of the evening; for Jord, in cutting the pigeon-wing, chanced to light from one of his aerial flights right upon the ponderous pedal appendage of Syl, a compliment which this amiable lady seemed in no way disposed to accept kindly.

"Jord Bilson," said the tender Syl, "I'll thank you to keep your darned hoofs off my feet." "Oh, Jord's feet are so tarnal big he can't manage 'em all by hisself," suggested some pacificator near by. "He'll have to keep 'em off me," suggested Syl, "or I'll shorten 'em for him." "Now look here, Syl Varmin," answered Jord, somewhat nettled at both remarks, "I didn't go to tread on your feet, but I don't want you to be cutting up any rusties about. You're nothing but a cross-grained critter, anyhow." "And you're a darned Melungen." "Well, if I am, I ain't nigger-Melungen, anyhow—I'm Indian-Melungen, and that's more 'an you is." "See here, Jord," said Syl, now highly nettled, "I'll give you a dollar ef you'll go out on the grass and right it out." Jord smiled faintly and demurred, adding—"Go home, Syl, and look under you puncheons and see if you can't fill a bed outen the hair of them hogs you stole from Vardy."

"And you go to Sow's Cave, Jord Bilson, ef it comes to that, and see how many shucks you got offen that corn you tuck from Pete Jomen. Will you take the dollar?" Jord now seemed about to consent, and Syl reduced the premium by one half, and finally came down to a quarter, and then Jord began to offer a quarter, a half, and finally a dollar; but Syl's prudence equalled his and seeing that neither was likely to accept, we returned to our hotel, and were informed by old Vardy that the sight we had witnessed was no "onusual one. The boys and gals was jist having a little fun." And so it proved, for about midnight we were wakened by a loud noise of contending parties in fierce combat, and, rising and looking out from the chinks of our hut, we saw the whole party engaged in a grand melee; rising above the din of all which, was the harsh voice of Syl Varmin, calling out—"Stand back here, Sal Frazer, and let me do the rest of the beaten of Jord Bilson; I hain't forgot his hoofs yit." The melee closed, and we retired again, and by breakfast next morning all

hands were reconciled, and the stone jar was replenished out of mutual pocket, and peace and quiet ruled where so lately all had been recriminations and blows. After breakfast, just such as the supper had been at old Jack's save only that here we had a table, we started for Clinch River for a day's fishing, where other and yet more amusing incidents awaited us.

But as I have dwelt upon this early part of the journey longer than I intended, you must wait until the next letter for the concluding incidents.

Melongena

Melongena/Solanaceae, is the scientific name for the eggplant, which is also called aubergine, guinea squash, solanum melongena. It is a great substitute for meat, high in fiber and low in sodium and is native of Asia where it is an important food crop and grown extensively in the eastern and southern areas, including India. Keep that in mind as it may provide a very good clue for the origin.

Notes

[1] Original Sources... Historiography... by John Parker, p. 31
   (Terrae Incognitae 13, 1981).
[2] Funk & Wagnalls, New Standard Dictionary of the
   English Language, 1913,   p. 1548.
[3] The Melungeons by N. Brent Kennedy, p. 94.
[4] Dicionario da Lingua Portuguesa by Candido de Figueiredo, p. 1611,
   Bertrand, 1996.
[5] The Melungeons Become a Race by David Henige,
   Appalachian Journal, Vol. 25, S. 3, p. 280.
[6] Dicionario da Lingua Portuguesa by Candido de Figueiredo, p. 1611,
   Bertrand, 1996.
[7] Dicionario da Lingua Portuguesa by Antonio Morais Silva
   (1954), Vol. VI, p. 666,
   and José Pedro Machado (1981), Vol. VII, p. 1; Ibid, p. 57.
[8] Mike Nassau letter of March 1997 to author.
[9] Melungeons and other Mestee Groups by Mike Nassau, p. 36.
[10] History of Huguenot Emigration to America, by Charles W. Baird DD, p. 21.
[11] East Tennessee and Western Virginia by Celestin Pierre Cambiaire, p. ix.
[12] Virginia Frontier by F. B. Kegley, p. 15.
[13] The Melungeons... by Edward T. Price, p. 269.
[14] The Melungeons by Brent Kennedy, p. xviii; [15] Ibid.
[16] Historia de Portugal by Oliveira Marques, p. 5, Vol. II.
[17] Surviving Indian Groups by William Harlen Gilbert, Jr., p. 426.
[18] The Melungeons by Bonnie Ball, p. 61.
[19] The Forgotten Centuries, by Charles Hudson, p. 4.
[20] National Geographic Magazine, March 1988, p. 335.

Notes (Cont.)

[21] The Mystery of the Melungeons by Louise Davis, p. 11 (Nashville Tennesseean 9/29/1963).

[22] National Geographic Magazine, March 1988, p. 351.

[23] Ibid, March 1988, p. 354.

[24] Ibid, p. 354.

[25] The Melungeons by N. Brent Kennedy, p. 94.

[26] Ibid, pp. 104, 105 ; [27] Ibid p. 133.

[28] Spanish Frontier by David J. Weber, p. 71.

[29] History of Surry Country by J.G. Hollingsworth, p. 5.

[30] National Geographic Magazine, March 1988, p. 353.

[31] Catholic Historical Review, Vol. LI, No. 3, by Michael V. Gannon, p. 340.

[32] The Roanoke Voyages by David Beers Quinn, Vol. I, pp. 102, 103.

[33] National Geographic Society, March 1988 issue, p. 330 (Painting by John Berkey).

[34] Ibid, p. 104.

[35] Ibid, p. 111.

[36] National Geographic Magazine by Joseph Judge, p. 362.

[37] The Melungeons by Brent Kennedy, p. 108; [38] Ibid, p. 119; [39] Ibid, p. 125.

[40] The only land I know by Adolph Dial, p. 4.

[41] Encyclopedia Britannica, 1993.

[42] As Berlengas e os Piratas by José de Almeida Santos, p. 1994.

[43] Set Fair for Roanoke by David Quinn, p. 20.

[44] The Portuguese in America by Manoel da Silveira Cardozo, p. 10.

[45] Sir Francis Drake by George Malcom Thompson, pp. 105-106; [46] Ibid, p. 191.

[47] The Melungeons by N. Brent Kennedy, p. 110; [48] Ibid, p. 110.

[49] North America Discovery by David Beers Quinn, p. 202.

[50] The Melungeons by N. Brent Kennedy, p. 111.

[51] Espanhol-Português Dicionario, p. 269, Porto Editora.

[52] Sir Francis Drake by George Malcom Thompson, p. 75.

[53] The Portuguese Seaborne Empire by Charles R. Boxer, p. 45.

[54] The Melungeons by N. Brent Kennedy, p. 120; [55] Ibid , p. 111.

[56] The Roanoke Voyages by David B. Quinn, Vol. I, p. 79; [57] Ibid, p. 80;

[58] Ibid, p. 81.

[59] The Roanoke Voyages by David B. Quinn, Vol. 1, pp. 169.

[60] Ibid, p. 170

[61] Harvard Classics, Vol. 33, narrative by Captain Walter Biggs, pp. 250-264

[62] Ibid, pp. 265-267

[63] American History Illustrated, May 1969, pp. 22-27, by Walter Spearman.

[64] Harvard Classics, Vol. 33, narrative by Captain Walter Biggs, p. 250

[65] Further English Voyages... by Irene Wright, p. 212

[66] The Roanoke Voyages by David B. Quinn, Vol. II, p. 786.

[67] Ibid, p. 812.

[68] Ibid, p. 793.

Notes (Cont.)

[69] Ibid, p. 498.

[70] Set Fair for Roanoke by David Quinn, p. 132.

[71] Turks, Moors, Blacks… by David B. Quinn (Terrae Incognitae 14, 1982, p. 98).

[72] Set Fair for Roanoke by David Quinn, p. 132.

[73] Turks, Moors, Blacks… by David B. Quinn (Terrae Incognitae 14, 1982, p. 97).

[74] Set Fair for Roanoke by David Quinn, p. 132, p. 131.

[75] Ibid, pp. 343-4.

[76] The Roanoke Voyages by David B. Quinn, Vol. I, p. 251.

[77] Turks, Moors, Blacks… by David B. Quinn (Terrae Incognitae 14, 1982, p. 99).

[78] Ibid, p. 98.

[79] The Roanoke Voyages by David B. Quinn, Vol. I, p. 251.

[80] Turks, Moors, Blacks… by David B. Quinn (Terrae Incognitae 14, 1982, p. 104).

[81] The Roanoke Voyages by David B. Quinn, Vol. II, p. 588.

[82] Ibid, Vol. I, pp. 252-253.

[83] Further English Voyages by Irene Wright, p. lvii; [84] Ibid, p. lvii.

[85] The Roanoke Voyages by David B. Quinn, Vol. I, p. 254; [86] Ibid, Vol. I, p. 466.

[87] Further English Voyages by Irene Wright, p. xl.

[88] Ibid, p. xli;

[89] Ibid, p. lvii;

[90] Ibid, p. xlii;

[91] Ibid, p. lvii.

[92] The Melungeons by N. Brent Kennedy, p. 112.

[93] Sir Francis Drake by George Malcom Thompson, p. 193.

[94] The Portuguese Seaborne Empire by Charles Boxer, p. 105.

[95] The Catholic Historical Review, Vol. LI, No. 3, Oct. 1965, by Mathew J. Connolly, p. 308.

[96] Ibid, p. 307.

[97] The Roanoke Voyages by David B. Quinn, Vol. I, pp. 254-255.

[98] Ibid, Vol. I, p. 465.

[99] Ibid, Vol. II, p. 789.

[100] Ibid, Vol. I, p. 479, note 4.

[101] The Roanoke Voyages by David B. Quinn, Vol. I, p. 470.

[102] Ibid, Vol. II, p. 499-506.

[103] Ibid, Vol. II, pp. 539-541.

[104] Set Fair for Roanoke by David Quinn, p. 24.

[105] Ibid, p. 273.

[106] The Roanoke Voyages by David B. Quinn, Vol. II, pp. 555-556.

[107] Ibid, pp. 579, 580.

[108] Ibid, Vol. II, pp. 579, 593.

[109] Ruth Wetmore while on a Cherokee excavation site in Macon County, Oct. 1995.

Notes (Cont.)

[110] The Portuguese in America by Manoel da Silveira Cardozo, p. 13.

[111] The Elizabethan's America by Louis B. Wright, p. 143.

[112] The Only Land I Know by Adolph Dial, p. 4.

[113] A New Voyage to Carolina by John Lawson (Hugh Lefler), p. 200.

[114] The Melungeons by Bonnie Ball, p. 38.

[115] William and Mary Quarterly, April 1997 and July 1998 by Engel Sluiter and John Thornton.

[116] First African in Virginia by Mark St. John Erickson. The Roanoke Times, Virginia, January 24, 1999.

[117] Early Travels in the Tennessee Country by Samuel Cole Williams, pp. 29-30.

[118] Ibid, p. 34.

[119] Ibid.

[120] The Roanoke Voyages by David Beers Quinn, Vol. 1, p. 255.

[121] Makers of America by Wayne Moquin, p. 67.

[122] Native Africans' bones by Bill Hendrick, Atlanta Journal, p. C7, May 11th 1997.

[123] Who Discovered…by Zella Armstrong, pp. 94-95 (Herbert E. Bolton, Spain's Title to Georgia).

[124] Early Travels in Tennessee Country by Samuel C. Williams, pp. 28-29.

[125] Narratives of Early Carolina by Alexander S. Salley, Jr. , p. 27.

[126] The Melungeons by Bonnie Ball, p. vi (Knoxville News Sentinel Oct. 10, 1958).

[127] Narratives of Early Carolina by Alexander S. Salley, Jr. , pp. 25-26.

[128] Ibid, p. 26.

[129] Ibid.

[130] History of Surry County by J.G. Hollingsworth, p. 12.

[131] The Melungeons by Brent Kennedy, p. 105.

[132] Catholic Historical Review, Vol. LI, No. 3, by Michael V. Gannon, p. 352.

[133] The Discoveries of John Lederer by William P. Cumming, pp. 31-32.

[134] Red Carolinians by Chapman J. Milling, p. 218.

[135] Early Travels in the Tennessee Country by Samuel Cole Williams, pp. 28-29.

[136] The Melungeons by N. Brent Kennedy p. 11.

[137] The Only Land I Know by Adolph L. Dial, p. 6.

[138] The Mystery of the Melungeons by Louise Davis, p. 11 (Nashville Tennesseean, 9/29/1963).

[139] Early Travels in the Tennessee Country by Samuel Cole Williams, pp. 28-29.

[140] Red Carolinians by Chapman J. Milling, p. 5.

[141] The Eastern Cherokees by William Harlen Gilbert Jr., p. 196; [142] Ibid, p. 66.

[143] The Melungeons by Bonnie Ball, pp. vi, 73.

[144] Historia de Portugal by José Mattoso, Vol. 8, p. 320.

[145] Ibid;

[146] Ibid, pp. 320-321.

[147] Arkansas Gazette, January 14, 1914, by Eliza N. Heiskell.

[148] The Melungeons by Bonnie Ball, p. 37.

Notes (Cont.)

[149] A New Voyage to Carolina by John Lawson (Hugh Lefler), p. 70.

[150] Ibid, p. 173.

[152] Ibid, p. 200.

[152] Early Travels in the Tennessee Country by Samuel Cole Williams, p. 171.

[153] Ibid, pp. 172-173.

[154] Ibid, p. 174.

[155] Survey of Demography… by Pollitzer and Brown, pp. 389-399
      (Human Biology, Sept. 1969).

[156] The Melungeons by Jean Patterson Bible, p. 20, The North Carolinian,
      Vol. 1, 1955-56, pp. 107-108.

[157] Melungeons: The Vanishing Colony of Newman's Ridge
      by Henry R. Price, p. 10.

[158] Ibid, p. 6.

[159] The Melungeons by Jean P. Bible, p. 83
      (Who Discovered America by Zella Armstrong, p. 8).

[160] Tennessee Valley and Tennessee History by Samuel Cole Williams, pp. 1-2.

[161] The Malungeons by Will Allen Dromgoole, p. 469 (Boston Arena, 1891).

[162] Early Travels in the Tennessee Country by Samuel Cole Williams, p. viii.

[163] The Mystery of the Melungeons by Louise Davis, p. 11.
      (Nashville Tennesseean 9/29/1963).

[164] The Gowen Research Foundation newsletter, Vol. I, p. 4, December 1989.

[165] East Tennessee and Western Virginia Ballads by Celestin Cambiaire, p. v.

[166] The Malungeons by Will Allen Dromgoole, p. 475 (Boston Arena, 1891).

[167] Ibid, p. 745.

[168] The American Indian in North Carolina by Douglas L. Rights, p. 146.

[169] Arabs in America by Beverlee Mehdi, p. 1.

[170] Gowens Research Foundation, letter from Evelyn McKinley Orr.

[171] Letter by Evelyn Orr of the Melungeon Research Committee.

[172] The Melungeons by N. Brent Kennedy, p. 46.

[173] The Melungeons, Review Essay by Dr. Virginia DeMarce, p. 138
      (National Genealogical Society, June 1996).

[174] History of Tennessee and the Tennesseeans Hale and Merritt, p. 180.

[175] The Melungeons by N. Brent Kennedy, p. 14.

[176] Ibid, p. 94.

[177] Ibid, p. 121.

[178] The Melungeons by Jean Patterson Bible, p. 57.

[179] The Treatment of the Melungeon by Jacqueline Daniel Burks, p. 15
      (Zuber p. 2, 4).

[180] The Melungeons by Bonnie Ball, p. 76.

[181] The Malungeons by Will Allen Dromgoole, p. 745 (Boston Arena, 1891).

[182] East Tennessee and Western Virginia by Celestin Pierre Cambiaire, p. v.

Chapter II
The Native American Indian and The Melungeon Connection

Long before the Europeans discovered Florida, the southeastern United States was settled by native Americans. Actually, there is a ten thousand year period of occupation in the Southeast that precedes the earliest European arrivals.

The 1950 census identified over twenty Native American Indian groups in the South, each with a size between a few hundred and a few thousand.

Red Bones, Turks, Brass Ankles of South Carolina; Issues of Virginia; Lumbees, Haliwa and the so-called Cubans of North Carolina; and the Cajans of Alabama are just some of them.[1]

The origins of these groups are somewhat uncertain; however the Melungeon group is the only one who may present a connection with the past.

When the Europeans arrived in the 16th century, it is estimated that more than 20,000 natives from fifty tribes lived in the Souteast.

Cherokee Indians

When the Cherokee Indians in Virginia were encountered by white settlers in the 17th century, they occupied the Appalachian Mountains, mostly the Southeastern territory. However, archaeological studies have been made and reveal their existence around A.D. 1000. Other studies also revealed that the Lee-Pisgah ceramics date from around the same time, concluding that the Pisgah people were the Cherokee ancestors.[2]

The Cherokee at one time controlled a territory of about 40,000 square miles, from the north of Georgia to the Allegheny region. The area included what is known today as the states of Virginia, Tennessee, North Carolina, and South Carolina.

The Portuguese chronicler travelling with Hernando de Soto in 1540 wrote *CHALAQUE,* naming the Cherokee for the first time as shown in the book published in Portugal in 1557.[3] A French document written in 1699 has also been found, with the word *CHARAQUI* (Cherokee). The name Cherokee was first written in 1708 as the English name for that Indian nation.

The proper name by which the Cherokee call themselves is Yûñwiyă signifying real people.[4]

It is known that when the Trail of Tears occurred in 1838, the Melungeons were living in the same area occupied by the Cherokees. It is also known that the Melungeons intermarried with them. Many Melungeons were known to have suffered the same fate as the Cherokees when they were moved west to the reservations, and many died along the way. Although the Melungeon-Cherokee is not officially recognized, research points to a definite association.

There is a similarity between early Christians and the Cherokees in the interpretation of Creation and Paradise: *Although the early Cherokees did not worship personages...They viewed earth as a great island floating in a sea of water...On this island the Cherokees were the principal people. The similarities*

Fig. 13—Lawanda Myers, a   *Fig. 14—Jim Myers, a possible*
member of the Cherokee Tribe.   *Melungeon descendant.*

between early Christian beliefs and those of the aboriginal Cherokees are interesting. It was only in the early 1500's that the Christian concept of heaven and earth met with serious opposition....Prior to the "Enlightenment" and the period of exploration, the Catholic Church assumed that the earth was flat and surrounded by water. [5]

The Cherokee had been established in the Southern mountains for at least two or three centuries before their first contact with Western civilization during the incursions of Hernando de Soto in 1540 and Juan Pardo in 1566.[6] It is also possible that they may have been there much earlier. John Lawson was intrigued by the Indians he encountered: *...that these People might come from some Eastern Country; for when you ask them whence their fathers came, that first inhabited the Country, they will point Westward and say, where the Sun sleeps....*[7] Mooney is inclined to think that the early Spanish contacts made a considerably permanent impression on the Cherokee.[8]

Their housing is described by Timberlake in 1760 when he:... *noted that the Overhill Cherokee built rectangular houses...about 16 feet abroad, were sometimes 2 stories, and were often as long as 60 or 70 feet.*[9]

At least one linguistic remnant of the Spanish incursion is evident today. The Cherokee word for cow, *waca,* is unmistakably derived from the Latin word *vacca.*[10] The word *vaca* is the same for Spanish and Portuguese, with one exception, in Spanish it is pronounced with a "*b*" sound and in Portuguese with a "*v*" sound as in English. The Creeks, another nearby tribe, also uses a similar word: *...waga.*

Another coincidence is that the Spaniards—during Soto's 1540's expedition—were shown European articles which they were told had been obtained from white men who had entered the river's mouth many years before.[11] Other tribes were evidently encountered by Pardo and Soto expeditions.[12]

It is also possible that Portuguese as well as Spanish may have been in the area prior to 1540 and traded with the Indians. In practically all Spanish expeditions, Portuguese were among the troops, and the above indicates a possible Portuguese connection.

During this research, Jim Myers, who owns the Log Cabin Gift Shop in Saunokee

Village, within the Cherokee reservation, was interviewed. Presently he is searching his genealogical family tree. Based on what he has found so far, he believes that he may be a Melungeon descendant. His wife Lawanda is a Cherokee Indian, but her maiden name is French. Jim's father's name was Harmon Myers. He told the author that about 20 years ago when he tried to search his roots, he got tremendous opposition on the part of his cousins. They did not want the past to be known, possibly due to possible illegitimacy and having been registered in the U.S. Census as Mulattos. Jim is of a medium-heavy stature, with brown eyes and light complexion. His grandmother was an English lady, a possible descendant of Sam Houston. She was a teacher and, when he started to ask her questions about the past, she started to cry and asked him not to do it.

Apparently, what Jim has been able to find out is that some of his ancestors were registered as Mulattos and, based on the area where they lived, they could not be black, because the blacks registered lived in a totally different area. His great-grandparents worked in iron foundries, which is where a lot of Melungeons worked. Jim and his wife certainly have fine European features, as can be seen on the pictures. Jimmy's name was given to the author by the office of Charles Taylor, Federal Congressman for the Franklin area, who is also interested in this research.

Charles Frazier, who was raised in North Carolina and is the author of the best seller book *Cold Mountain,* describes a boy as *black-headed, brown skinned...Some Cherokee blood, or may be Creek...* and a child as a comparison: *I've seen white children darker complexed... Octoroon or quadroon, makes no difference. She's a nigaroon.*[13]

The story takes place in the mountains of western North Carolina. What people do you think the author is talking about? He said white children. Not black.

The Trail of Tears and President Andrew Jackson, a Spanish Citizen

Like the Melungeons, the Cherokees have suffered tremendously. One example is the Trail of Tears engineered by President Andrew Jackson.[14] It was part of the Great Removal, in 1838, when most Indian tribes in the east were taken to what is now northeastern Oklahoma, there they formed the Western Cherokees of Oklahoma. Before the 20th century this was one of the most massive and historical relocations of human population.[15] President Jackson was retaliating against the Indians for their service to Great Britain during the war of 1812. As part of that relocation, a large number of Melungeons may have gone west.

At the time of removal in 1838, a few hundred Cherokees escaped to the mountains, thereby serving as the nucleus for the 3,000 Eastern Cherokees who in the 20th century lived in western North Carolina. Most still live there. It is believed that some Melungeons and others may have joined them and gone west to Tennessee.

In his book, Kennedy discusses a possible relationship between the Melungeons and President Jackson,[16] an issue which may deserve further study for the interested reader. His life was very interesting, especially when searching the archives of the Indias in Seville. There, one of the archivists shared that some research had recently been done regarding President Andrew Jackson's biography. Some documents were found proving that he pledged the oath of allegiance to Spain. This was rather strange, and further research in the Library of Congress under the author Robert Remini, Jackson's biographer, proved that the archivist was right. Remini had already published a lengthy article in the 1995 Spring issue of the magazine *Tennessee Historical Quarterly*. [17]

Apparently, in order to establish his law practice, he needed fast money. The quickest way was to become a Spanish citizen, thereby enabling him to trade, use the Mississippi and other rivers, own land, and do business in Natchez. On July 15, 1789, Andrew Jackson and 17 other prominent Americans signed a three-page oath of allegiance to Spain. Later, he forgot about the document and went on to become a national hero in several battles.

Remini's story is fascinating, and gives us an insight into what life was like at the turn of the 18th century when the Melungeons first started to become visible. Jackson, just:...*like hundreds of others before him who took the oath, did what necessity dictated.* [18]

When discussing early settlers such as the Melungeons, one needs to be mindful that, at about the same time, North Carolina was reluctant to give up the western lands. During a discussion in the Senate, the characteristics of these western settlers were mentioned in a very descriptive manner: ...*And these westerners were a tough, mean, and independent breed. Some of them were later described as "North Carolina blue beards, who are rugged, dirty, brawling, browbeating monsters, six feet high, whose vocation is robbing, drinking, fighting and terrifying every peaceable man in the community.* [19]

Some of those characteristics sound familiar to Melungeons but also to frontier mountain men.

Machapunga Indians

In 1700, Lawson wrote a rather strange piece of information about Indian customs found in some families: ...*two Families of the Machapunga Indians, use the Jewish Custom of Circumcision, and the rest do not.* [20]

There is also a reference based on the records of the London-based Society for the Propagation of the Gospel, founded at the beginning of the 18th-century, which contains references (written by South Carolina-based ministers) to native Americans who:...*practiced (male) circumcision to many Indian, mulatto, and Portuguese among the colony's slaves, and to "nonbelievers" in the backcountry that included both "heathens and infidels."* [21]

Why such a custom among the Indians? Did some Jews actually arrive at an early period and settle with the Indians? It is a known fact that Sephardic Jews came to North-America quite early, starting with Columbus' first voyage, which they also indirectly financed.

Portuguese and American Indian Descent

John Shelton Reed wrote an article titled "Mixing in the Mountains," for the magazine *Southern Cultures*. He visited Hancock County, and while looking for *typical hillbilly-stereotype story* his attention was diverted when he was told: *Many families here belong to a hundred or so Melungeon clans of Portuguese and American descent.* [22]

The Melungeons and the Saponi-Tutelo Indians

Nassau (McGlothlen) writes that the Melungeons were founded by free mulattos and mestees (Indian/Black mix with or without white) from North Carolina. Also, they were in Hancock County before whites arrived there. From the time and location of their origin, the Indian element is probably Saponi and Tutelo, but it:... *is usually incorrectly thought to be Cherokee by the Melungeons.* [On the other hand] *approximately 2,000 Saponi and Haliwa Indians still live in the Warren and Halifax Counties* [The same area where until recently a group claiming Portuguese descent also lived] *in Northeast North Carolina.* [23] Another report revealing the Saponi and Tutelo Indians is the one from:...*Governor Spotswood in 1715, in which he states that the Indians of Fort Christanna, including the Tutelo, Saponi...numbered 300.*[24] Also, Mooney mentions in his book *Siouan Tribes of the East*: ...*Evidently the tribe...was in decline, as it was about to join the Saponi and Tutelo.*[25]

At that time, these Indians were still an identifiable group, and in order to survive until the 20th century the Melungeons would also be a group in itself. The Melungeons are not likely to be a creation of the 19th century! All immigrant groups arriving in the 19th century are traceable.

The Indian component of the Melungeons was identified by Jack Forbes as Saponi, which may be possible, but in J. Anthony Paredes' latest book *Indians of the Southeastern United States in the late 20th Century,* there does not seem to be any connection cited.

The Southern range includes the Redbones, Brass Ankles, and Turks. This last group is speculated by some outsiders as having Indian ancestry, such as the Sumter Turks. These, however, have said that they do not concur that they are Indians.

They consider themselves to be:...*white Turk Americans.*[26] They also have common Melungeon surnames. According to a story, the name Turk was given to them by General Sumter, who presented an affidavit to the authorities stating that they were indeed Turks imported personally from the Ottoman Empire as contract labor.[27] Turk groups may play an interesting part in the mystery of the Melungeons.

Kennedy seems to believe that the decimated Indian tribes in Virginia would present a:...*legitimate source of Moorish-Indian-European...*[28] to form the Melungeons. That is doubtful. If they were Turks from the Ottoman Empire, how did they get here? Also, the blacks as a fourth element for being a part of some Melungeons cannot be ignored.

Both the Melungeons and the Redbones have spoken only English since they were first noted, even though the Redbones are surrounded by French.[29] Why would the French name them *mélange* if they were speaking English?

Henry Price questions the disenfranchising of the Melungeons in 1834 and states that the Melungeons arrived [in Tennessee] from North Carolina along with the whites, not long before them: *...some of their leaders, got good land and quite a lot of it.*[30] Could it be that they left, or were pushed out of North Carolina and some acquired large tracts of land, which were no good for agriculture? As for arriving there in 1834, it is likely to have been a much earlier date. One needs to be mindful of the ongoing problems that the Government had with the Indians, and the eventual removal in 1838.

Nassau (McGlothlen) gives a table showing the frequency of Melungeon names in Northwest Florida to a total of 362, which is interesting.[31] *Some Indians groups absorbed so many Blacks that some of them became a separate entity, like the Black Seminoles in Florida.*[32] Also in the Florida panhandle (Wewahitchka-Blountstown), the Dead Lake People have been called Melungeons and identified with them.[33] Jack Goins in his book Melungeons, page 85 also poses a question: *Were they* [Melungeons] *related to the Saponi Indians?*

The Indian Tribes of Croatoan, Hatteras and Lumbees

There is a strong belief that some of the Roanoke colonists may have joined these tribes and passed along the English language as spoken in 1587. In his 1971 book *European Discovery of America,* Morison writes the following: *...and the existence of blue-eyed and fair haired types among them, as well as the incorporation of Elizabethan words in their language and their using surnames from John White's colonists bears this out.*[34]

This may be possible, but the incorporation of some Elizabethan words may also indicate that the number of colonists was extremely small. Let us not forget the Indians who have been in England.

Lawson also writes about the type of English spoken in 1700: *...yet those that speak English, learn to swear the first thing they talk of.*[35] As for the surnames, some of them were also common in the later English colonies. They, like the slaves and many other people in this country, used the most common names of the time. It is important to keep in mind that the information about these tribes was not found until much later. It was not until 1891—with Alexander Brown's publication of *Genesis of the United States*—that a general interest was shown.

The blue eyes and fair hair could have come from some other early settlers: *The Croatan Indians was the legal description in North Carolina for a people of a mixed Indian and white blood, found in various E.*[eastern] *sections of the state, chiefly in Robeson County, and numbering approximately 5,000....Across the line in South Carolina are found a people, evidently of similar origin, designated the "Redbones." In portions of w.* [western] *N.C. and E.*[east] *Tenn. are found the so-called "Melungeons"...or Portuguese.*[36] This was written in 1912, and Robeson County was traditionally also a Melungeon place.

Dial states that: *When Scottish immigrants began to settle the upper reaches of North Carolina's Cape Fear Valley in the early 1730's, they were amazed to find a group of English-speaking people already living near the Lumbee River.*[37]

This area is less than 100 miles from the coast, where shipwrecks were common. Weather patterns were not known, and no warnings of any kind existed. As a result, many vessels, when going to or coming from Europe or South America, met with tragedy on the sea coast of North Carolina.

The fact that they spoke English for more than 100 years with continuous English settlement is hardly surprising:*...mid-twentieth century...spoke a pure Old English.*[36] This is a similar situation with the mountain people of Western North Carolina and East Tennessee. Is there a connection? Dial states:*...the oral tradition of Cherokee blood is so strong among the Lumbees...that it is impossible to dismiss the claim.*[39]

John Lawson in 1700/45 and the Hatteras Indians

On December 28, 1700, John Lawson began a voyage to Carolina from Charles Town and wrote about the Hatteras while describing the first colony of Carolina: *A farther Confirmation of this we have from the Hatteras Indians, who either then lived on Roanoke-Island, or much frequented it. These tell us that several of their Ancestors were white People, and could talk in a book, as we do; the Truth of which is confirm'd by gray Eyes being found frequently amongst these Indians, and no others.*[40] Just before Lawson arrived in Virginia, a law was passed providing for the offense of stealing or setting adrift a boat or canoe. *Whereas white persons violating this law were only fined, Indians received 39 lashes on their naked backs for the first offense and suffered the amputation of an ear for the second. Many years before these acts were passed by the white colonist the Cusabo* [Indians] *had been forced to sell their best lands to the invading race.*[41]

With this type of discrimination and justice—only one of many instances—the Melungeons, Indians or any other group not readily identified with whites would seek a safer place away from the English colonies near the coast. Chapman also tells us that:*...Here and there...are small groups of people who are plainly not of pure white ancestry...The hereditary prejudice of these people is demonstrated by the fact that...their children are not allowed to attend white schools, they habitually refuse to send them to colored schools.*[42]

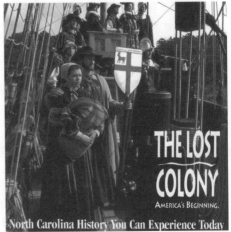

Fig. 15—The "Lost Colony" replays the tale of the Roanoke Island Colony.[44]

Lumbees, Lost Roanoke Colony Mystery

According to an English story, Roanoke is an interesting traditional name. Apparently, when an English-man saw an Indian rowing his canoe with oaken oars on the Moratuck River (original name of the Roanoke River, and an Algonquin Indian name), he asked him: *What are you doing there?* The Indian replied in ill-tutored English, *Rowin' Oak.* [43]

The Indian tribe *The Lumbees... were found by the Huguenots* [Lutherans] *in 1708, and were said to have owned farms and lived in a "civilized manner" (like Europeans). They are also reputed to have spoken an older form of English...Their complexions vary from dark to very fair; it is not unusual to see blue eyes and blond among them.* [45]

If they were English, why not looking for their countrymen instead of living isolated? A permanent English settlement was already in place by the early 1600's.

Kennedy adds: *The "Mediterranean appearance" of so many Melungeons, as well as their original denial of either an English or Indian heritage, argue against a purely Lost Colony and/or English hypothesis.* [46]

After so many years and mixed marriages, their Mediterranean appearance is still present: *Captain John Smith, is giving an account of a conversation he had with the Powatan Indians. Apparently the Lost Colony was massacred, but some escaped.* [47]

That report may shed light on some later findings. It is possible that some Melungeons, mixed with different Indian tribes, may have brought with them some names. *"Allen Lowrie, son of William, married Polly Cumba, or Cumbo, said to be of Portuguese extraction.* [48] However, Lumbee historian Adolph L. Dial, professor at Pembroke State University, N.C., does not mention any possible connection with the Portuguese in the books he wrote about the Lumbees. He does not explain why the Lumbees have a: *...dark-skinned mixed-heritage population who, in the mid 1800's were also called Melungeons.* [49] If they had a strong component of the white English settlers, they would be lighter-skinned rather than dark, unless part of the English settlers were southern European. The Senate and the House of Representatives enacted a law designating this group of Indians as Lumbees in 1956, stating also that they may be connected with the Lost Roanoke Colony, and found by the first white settlers on the Lumber River and Robeson County. [50] They were also called the Cherokee Indians of Robeson County.

This same writer asserts that:*... parts of this book are based on logical supposition and oral history.* [51] Although historians generally do not accept oral history, many history books are partly based on written memoirs or edited documents. The surnames found among the Melungeon families are also found in the *Association Regional Lumbee Development*, such as Moore, Bell, etc. [52]

Many books have been written about this mystery, and no verifiable explanation has been found. Since there is a strong possibility that Drake left Moors, South American Indians and black slaves at Roanoke—when he rescued the English colonists—research on several books and documents available has been undertaken, in an effort to analyze the trips made by the English who journeyed to America. See Chapter I for these findings in chronological order.

Powatan Indian People

The Powatan people that once occupied most of what is now the eastern shore of the Chesapeake Bay in Virginia became better known because the Powatan Chief was the father of Pocahontas.

They were involved in wars with the first English settlers of Jamestown. The conflict lasted until 1644 when most of the Indian power was destroyed.

The Melungeons may have had some relations with these Indians prior to the English settlers' arrival. Prior to the conflicts, they may have taken the way west towards the mountains.

Rev. Morgan Jones—Welsh Speaking Indians and Fables—1669

Admiral and historian Samuel Elliot Morison describes the following encounters as tales: *When Rev. Morgan Jones, traveling through the Carolinas in 1669, fell with the Tuscaroran tribe called the Doeg, who understood his native Cymric, and among them he happily lived for months, preaching the Gospel in Welsh. There are several eighteenth century travelers' tales to the same effect, only it is always a different Indian tribe who speaks Welsh, exhibits a relatively fair complexion, and cherishes Welsh relics such as a printed Bible in that language.* Morison also describes John Evans' trip in search of Welsh-speaking Indians. During one year of living with Indians from latitude N 35° to N 49° (North Carolina to Newfoundland) he responded to the London Literary Society that: *I think you may with safety inform my friends that they* [Welsh Indians] *have no existence.* Morison ends the Madoc Welsh story with: *...We may dismiss the Welsh Indians myth with the authoritative words of the Bureau of American Ethnology: "There is no provable trace of Welsh, Gaelic or any other European language in any native American language."* [53]

Morison also wrote that when Columbus sailed, he already knew that the only way to cross the Atlantic was by way of the Canary Islands, to find the westerly winds and currents. Did Madoc know? What school of navigation did he attend? What scientific information was available at that time? Admiral Morison adds: *...fable that...despite all proofs that it is not and could not be true.*[54] Then the question of why they would be called Welsh reappears after 400-500 years. A few people speaking a language amongst strangers would not survive, and if they were many, why did they practically disappear?

In Europe during this same period, entire nations were born out of very small counties, and in 400 years, even with plagues and wars, their population grew. John Sevier's letter dated October 9, 1810, states that according to his source: *...they* *are no more white people; they are now all become Indians, and look like other red people of the country.*[55] This letter is kept in the Newberry Library in Chicago, that also holds the Greenlee collection of more than 10,000 Portuguese history works and rare maps.[56]

What population growth can Madoc and the Welsh account for, even with the help of the Indians? Surely in the same period in Wales, the growth was phenomenal compared to the size of a small kingdom. Much more is needed even to consider such a possibility. While doing research about the Welsh, the author came across a story that adds more confusion. Captain Wynne wrote a letter in 1608 to Sir John Egerton from Jamestown that: *The people of Monacan speak a far differing language from the subjects of Powatan, their pronunciation being very like Welsh, so that the gentlemen in our company desired me to be their interpreter.*[57]

Was it really Welsh, or did it just sound similar? Did he really become their interpreter? Cambiaire, a French writer, points out another instance of confusion— about French Bretons that sounded like Welsh: *...in 1622 when some English settlers attacked by the Indians fled from Virginia into Carolina, they met some French Bretons, descendants of French people left in the vicinity of Fort Caroline in 1565. As these Bretons were still speaking their native language, which resembles that of the Welsh, those among English settlers who had come from Wales thought that these Frenchmen were the descendants of an ancient Welsh Colony.*[58] With all the Spanish activity, it is hard to believe that many French would still be around, and if so that would be another lost colony, this time the Fort Caroline lost colony.

There is a letter written by John Sevier in 1810, replying to a request for information about the Welsh. It relied heavily on oral information from the Indian Chief Oconostota, but it is rather confusing. It connects the supposed Welsh with the French, and the chronology does not seem to fit.[59]

There is also the Irish fable of the sea-going monks. St. Brendan the Navigator, who was born in the last quarter of the 5th century, set out with 17 others to search for an island of monks, called the Promised Island of Saints. The medieval conception of St. Brendan's isles also shows a western Antilla Island.

The Portuguese also have a story of seven bishops and other Christians—men and women from Porto, Portugal—who sailed with cattle, provisions and goods when the Iberian peninsula was conquered by the Moors and Rodrigo was the last Visigothic king. These people from Porto occupied the same Antilla island, also called Seven Cities.[60] This land or group of islands was located far to the west of Portugal, supposedly Newfoundland. At the time of Henry the Navigator, a Portuguese storm-driven ship landed at this place, was welcomed in Portuguese and urged to remain, but declined. When the sailors returned, they told the story to Henry. He told them to return, but they refused to go.

According to Dr. Luciano da Silva, author of *The True Antilles* which describes his discoveries about the proper location of the Antilles, the Portuguese name for this island is *Antilhas* and was perpetuated as the Antilles, which is the name for the West Indies.[61] Did Madoc, Brendan's monks, or Portuguese Christians arrive in

America hundreds of years before Columbus? Nothing was ever found. What is left are fables. Morison also writes about the early boats: *This type could not sail to windward like the Portuguese caravels.*[62]

Indian or Melungeon came from Portugal—1834

From the following, it is evident that the Melungeons would not easily give up their heritage. Even at a high cost, they kept their pride: *...the Lumbees embraced the official designation of "Indian"...Most of the Melungeons held out, never taking advantage of this classification. Instead, they continued in their struggle to preserve their Old World customs while insisting on their southern Europeanism.*[63] There is one factor of which many persons are aware: Portuguese immigrants are known to be hard workers, and do not necessarily look for welfare. *But hints at the truth come from changing "facts" surrounding certain ancestors, sometimes reflected in a single individual who was "Portuguese at birth," "Portuguese-Indian" as an adult, and at death, simply "Indian."* [64]

The theory of Portuguese ancestry persists: *His wife Betty Reeves was possibly a full Melungeon, the daughter of Ashe Countians George Reeves, Sr. and Jane Burton. As Mary Killen Hollyfield, a descendant of Betty Reeves recalled in 1929: The Reeves are said to have come from Portugal. They had brown eyes and black hair. I've heard it said they were part Indian too. Betty Reeves herself claimed to be "Portuguese Indian," a term used by many Melungeons to explain their heritage.*

The Portuguese portion of the term was eventually dropped, most likely because (1) no one believed it, (2) the Melungeons had no proof to back it up, and (3) it had become synonymous with Melungeon anyway. Being "Indian" was increasingly considered preferable to "Melungeon" or Portuguese." [65]

Although this situation may make researching into the past difficult, there are still numerous documents awaiting expert eyes.

Portugee Indian Tribe—1926

A book by Arthur H. Estabrook and Ivan E. McDougle, published in 1926, discusses several tribes, such as the Wins, and also the so-called Portuguese Indian tribe. *Geraldine Hall, a sister of Andrew, dark in color... considered herself a Portugee Indian.*[66] This book goes into detail describing the possible problems of marrying within their own group, which may have caused mental retardation. However it also explains the Virginia law at the time whereby marriages between races were forbidden by statute, and goes on to explain the need for recording the color of the persons. The Wins were also classified as *free persons of color* by the federal census.[67] It is also interesting that Virginia passed a law in 1924 describing the term: *...white person shall apply only to the person who has no trace of blood other than Caucasian.*[68]

Redbones, Redsticks, Sabines and the Natchitoches

It has been said that the French named the *Redbones* of Louisiana, apparently derived from the French *Os Rouge* which was used to describe persons of mixed Indian blood.

We have to question that, because it appears that the *Redbones* name went with the groups. Perhaps the name *Os Rouge* was applied to descendants of the *Redbones*.[69] Redsticks, Sabines and the Natchitoches are also important. McDonald Furman's late 1800 work on the Redbones, and *The Cherry Winche Country* written in the 1930's by Webster Talmadge Crawford in which he concludes: *They appear to bear the stamp of Mediterranean stock.*[70] Red Stick or Baton Rouge in French was first recorded by the French, and can be traced back to 1686.[71]

Brass Ankles

Louise Pound from the University of Nebraska in *"American Speech"* Magazine April 1943, pp. 152-53 wrote a note about the Brass Ankles : *"...of Professor Farr's list of Tennessee Expressions, several are quite common in South Carolina: Brass Ankle for mulatto— is very often used by the older generation, though less often used by younger speakers. My father thinks that the term originated in the neighborhood of Monck's Corner, South Carolina where the descendants of a Portuguese colony who had intermarried with negros and afterwards married largely within their own group were noted for their brass bracelets and anklets. To this group the white and the negro settlers in the neighborhood applied the name brass ankle, which was later extended to any mulatto."* Brass Ankle is also a term used to identify a mixed mulatto who has a lower ankle that glistens in the sun, showing some white among a negro. Many descendants of these *Brass Ankles* today are considered white.

Anthropology, Archaeology and the Archaeologists

The National Geographic Magazine story published in March 1988 and written by Joseph Judge describes the daily life of the settlers in the 16th century. His report along with photographs by Bill Ballenberg and paintings by John Berkey brings to life the work of the archaeologists, such as David Hurst Thomas. According to Kennedy, Dr. Chester DePratter of the University of South Carolina's Institute of Archaeology and Anthropology, and Dr. Stanley South are key members of the research team excavating Santa Elena.

During excavations at a Cherokee pre-historic village and burial ground site located in the Industrial Park of Macon County, The archaeologist Ruth Y. Wetmore, spoke about the Melungeons and the possible Turkish connection, she mentioned that the word Turk in those days, meant anyone that did not speak English properly. Also, of one reasons to come to the mountains was the possibility of the sailors, hearing about gold and precious stones in the mountains, would jump ship. One, would now ask, what good the gold will do, if they could not get back to their country ?

America has a very short history in comparison to Europe. However, if we look into the many Indian nations' histories before the Europeans arrived, then we have a much longer history. As findings by archaeologists surfaced, they caused the following recent newspaper headline: *Cherokee remains, relics found at Macon Industrial Park.*[70] Due to economic reasons, no further study or even a preservation of the site was done, and American history was lost forever. Dave Moore, who was the archaeologist heading the excavation in Macon County, stated in an interview that another excavation is planned for a possible site where Pardo may have had a fort built, also in North Carolina, near Morgantown, by the foothills. Pardo entered the interior with 125 soldiers on December 1, 1566:....*established a fort at Joara...same town as Hernando de Soto's Xuala...forts with garrisons of fifteen to thirty men were built at Chiaha, Cauchi, and Joara.*[73] This town was part of the chiefdom of Cofitachequi. Xuala, or Joara, is located near the foothills of Appalachia, close to Marion or McDowell Bottom in North Carolina.

David Moore is the same archaeologist who presented a paper titled *New Evidence of the 16th Century Spanish Artifacts in the Catawba River Valley*, also in North Carolina.

See Appendix "B" in Part II for the latest discoveries in prehistoric America by two renowned Archaeologists who claim European settlers from Portugal may have arrived in North-America 18,000 years ago.

Indian Tribes that may be connected with Portuguese early settlers

Tribe	**Location**
Black-Waters	East Tennessee
Black-Dutch	
Black-Irish, Brown People	
Blue-Skin	Kentucky, Melungeons
Brass Ankles, Red Legs	Indians w/Portuguese surnames , named because of metal bracelets and jewelry they wore.
Bushwhackers	New England
Carmels	Ohio and Kentucky
Cajans and Creoles	Alabama and Louisiana
Catawba	North and South Carolina
Cheraw	South Carolina
Cherokees	North Carolina
Chickahominy	Virginia
Creeks	Alabama
Croatans	Virginia, North Carolina
Cubans	North Carolina

Indian Tribes that may be connected with Portuguese early settlers

Tribe	Location
Dead Lake	Dead Lake People, Florida Panhandle
Dominickers, Free Jack	West Virginia
Guineas	West Virginia
Haliwa	Warren and Halifax Counties, Northeast NC
Jackson Whites	New York and New Jersey
Keating Mountain	New York
Lumbees or Rivers	Indians w/Portuguese surnames, Virginia Valleys
Issues	Virginia
Jackson Whites	Morris and Passaic Counties in New Jersey and Orange and Rockland Counties in New York
Machapunga	South Carolina
Mashpee	Cape Cod, Indians w/Portuguese surnames, Nunes, Gomes, Pereira, Macedo
Mattaponi	
Moors	Maryland and New Jersey
Nansemond	
Nanticokes	Sussex County in Delaware and Bridgeton in Cumberland County, New Jersey
Pool Tribe	Pennsylvania
Portugee	Virginia
Powatans	Virginia North Carolina
Ramps	Virginia
Redbones	Florida panhandle, Wewahtchka-Blountstown, Louisiana.
Ridgemanites	East Tennessee
Saponi//Tutelo	Hilsboro, North Carolina
Savanoe	Savannah River
Shawnee	Ohio, Kentucky
Slaughters	New England
Turks	Sumter County
Tuscarora	North Carolina
Wesorts	Maryland
Yuchi (Chisca)	Children of the Sun Appalachian Highlands

The above information was the result of researching many books, magazines, documents and newspapers mentioned in the Bibliography section.

Notes

1 Southern Cultures, Vol. 3, No. 4, "Mixing in the Mountains" by
   John Shelton Reed, p. 27.
2 The Buffalo Ridge Cherokee by Horace R. Rice, p. 14.
3 Annals of Northwest North Carolina by J.G. Hollingsworth, p. 4.
4 History, Myths... of the the Cherokees by James Mooney, p. 15.
5 The Cherokee Perspective by Lawrence French and Jim Hornbuckle, p. 4.
6 Acculturation of the Eastern Cherokees by Leonard Bloom, N.H.R., Vol. 19,
   1942, p. 331.
7 A New Voyage to Carolina by John Lawson (Hugh Lefler), p. 173.
8 Ibid, p. 332.
9 Red Carolinians by Chapman J. Milling, p. 12.
10 A New Voyage to Carolina by John Lawson (Hugh Lefler), p. 332.
11 Myths of the Cherokee by James Mooney, p. 193.
12 Catawba Nation and its neighbors by Frank G. Speck, N.H.R. Vol. 16, 1939,
   pp. 405-406.
13 Cold Mountain by Charles Frazier, pp. 167, 284.
14 The Red Carolinians by Chapman J. Milling, p. 332.
15 Indians of the Southeastern U.S. by J. Anthony Paredes, pp. 2, 30.
16 The Melungeons by N. Brent Kennedy, p. 27.
17 Andrew Jackson takes an Oath of Allegiance to Spain by Robert V. Remini.
18 Tennessee Historical Quarterly by Robert V. Remini, p. 10 (Spring 1995 issue).
19 Ibid, p. 4.
20 A New Voyage to Carolina by John Lawson (Hugh T. Lefler), p. 219.
21 Appalachian Journal, Vol. 25, No. 3, Spring 1998, "Response to Henige" by
   Darlene Wilson, pp. 292-3.
22 Southern Cultures, Vol. 3, No. 4, "Mixing in the Mountains" by
   John Shelton Reed, p. 27.
23 The Indians of the Southeastern U.S., by J. Anthony Paredes, pp. 46, 73.
24 Indians in 17th century Virginia by Ben McCary, p. 78.
25 Red Carolinians by Chapman J. Milling, p. 218.
26 The Indians of Southeastern U.S. by J. Anthony Paredes, p. 73.
27 Melungeons and Other Mestee Groups by Mike McGlothlen, p. 62.
28 The Melungeons by N. Brent Kennedy, p. 137.
29 The Melungeons and Mestee Groups by Mike McGlothlen, p. 40.
30 Ibid, p. 41.
31 Ibid, p. 64.
32 Ibid, p. 9.
33 Ibid, p. 30.
34 The European Discovery of America by Samuel Eliot Morison, p. 677.
35 A New Voyage to Carolina by John Lawson (Hugh Lefler), p. 240.

Notes (Cont.)

[36] Ibid.
[37] The Only Land I Know by Adolph Dial, p. 1.
[38] Ibid, p. 11.
[39] Ibid, p. 16.
[40] A New Voyage to Carolina by John Lawson (Hugh Lefler), p. 69.
[41] Red Carolinians by Chapman J. Milling, pp. 56-58.
[42] Ibid, p. 64.
[43] The Roanoke Canal by Peggy Jo Cobb Braswell, p. 9.
[44] Photo by Outer Banks Photographer, Ray Mathews, cover of Sprint Carolina Phone Co.
[45] The Melungeons by Bonnie Ball, p. 37.
[46] The Melungeons by N. Brent Kennedy, p. 81.
[47] The Melungeons by Bonnie Ball, p. 12.
[48] The American Indian in N.C. by Douglas L. Rights, p. 146.
[49] The Melungeons by N. Brent Kennedy, p. 26.
[50] The Only Land I Know by Adolph L. Dial and David K. Eliades, p. 187.
[51] Ibid, p. ix.
[52] The Indians of Southeastern U.S. by J. Anthony Paredes, p. 49.
[53] The European Discovery of America by Samuel Eliot Morison, pp. 85-86.
[54] Ibid, p. 85.
[55] Who Discovered America by Zella Armstrong, p. 169-170.
[56] Luso-Americano by Henrique Mano, April 2, 1997.
[57] The Elizabethan's America by Louis B. Wright, p. 186.
[58] East Tennessee and West Virginia by Celestin Pierre Cambiaire, p. xiv.
[59] The Melungeons by Jean Patterson Bible, p. 83, 85.
[60] La Busqueda del Paraiso y las Legendarias islas del Atlantico by Louis-Andre Vigneras, p. 45.
[61] The True Antilles by Dr. Manuel Luciano da Silva, 1987.
[62] European Discovery of America by Samuel Eliot Morison, p. 16.
[63] The Melungeons by N. Brent Kennedy, p.15.
[64] Ibid, p. 20.
[65] Ibid, pp.56-57.
[66] The Mongrel Virginias by Arthur Estabrook, p. 132.
[67] Ibid, pp.174, 175.
[68] Ibid, p. 180.
[69] Gowens Research Foundation Dec. 1996 Newsletter by Evelyn McKinley Orr.
[70] Ibid.
[71] Ibid, February 1997.
[72] Asheville Citizen-Times, p. 3B, Dec. 29, 1995.
[73] The Forgotten Centuries by Charles Hudson, p. 202, 203.

Chapter III

Besides Portuguese, Other Possible Origins

Besides being Mediterranean looking, there are other origins discussed. However, if the Mediterranean looks survived 400 years even with miscegenation, other origins should also have been able to survive more readily, because the interracial marriages would have been minimal. Kennedy, emphasizes that:...*given the surviving Mediterranean characteristics, further hypothesized that both genders of the original settling group must have possessed Melungeon genes, whatever their ethnic nature. Otherwise, over a four-hundred-year period the Melungeon's dominating Mediterranean physical characteristics would have most likely been "bred out" through successive intermarriage with Native Americans.*[1]

Armando Cortesão, a Portuguese historian on assignment at *UNESCO* in the early 1950's, said:...*he was convinced that ancient peoples, Phoenicians and Greeks sailed far into the Atlantic.*[2]

Since we are looking into other groups, it is worthwhile noting that there was a group of *red skinned people* living in the Blue Ridge Mountains, who considered themselves white folks. *The general light color of the skin indicates the presence of some white blood.*[3] Why do we find isolated groups that clearly show white ancestry, who were also moonshiners?

In Robeson County, North Carolina, another group called *The Rivers* (Lumbees) is mentioned. They also claim to be descended from the Lost Roanoke Colony.

Interestingly, Estabrook in his book *The Mongrel Virginians* mentions that:... *French emigrants, as early as 1690, had settled in Licking County, where they came in contact with the mixed race to whom they gave the name "Mero."* [4] Why not Melungeon, since early writers mention that the name originated with the French word *mélange*? One more reason to question the French naming of the Melungeons.

Another interesting fact, why *Mero?* Well it just happens that the name *Mero* is the name of a Mountain in India.

Native Iberians

Kennedy states: ...*simply because one considered himself or herself to be Spanish or Portuguese, this did not in any way translate to being truly native Iberian (whatever that would mean, since the native Iberians were themselves a mixture of Phoenician, Sea Peoples, Roman, Celt, and so on).*[5] Spain was made up of many small kingdoms. It originated with Leon, and later Castile—the strongest kingdom—which gave its people the Castilian or Spanish language. Some Spanish provinces still have their own languages and use them, e.g. Basques, Catalonians, Galicians. Because of the importance of Spain as a much larger country and population, the tendency is to amalgamate Spain and Portugal into a single nation. However, Portugal is a separate and totally different country, in both language and culture.

A misconception by many people is that the Spanish and Portuguese languages are one and the same. This is not so. William J. Entwistle, an Oxford University professor, wrote that the difference in the Portuguese and Spanish languages may be appreciated by reading the Lord's prayer in these two languages.[6]

The name Iberian is not commonly used in Portugal. One is either Spanish or Portuguese. Also, the name Iberian is used exclusively by Spain. Even their national airlines is called Iberian Air Lines. There's a possibility that some of the Melungeon ancestry originated in Spain, but only a very small number. Even that is questionable.

Eloy Gallegos in his book makes a comment usually made by someone who knows very little about Portugal and its people, its culture and language, when he states: *To attempt to distinguish between Portuguese and Spanish, except for the dialect, it is like attempting to distinguished between a Tennessean and a Virginian. The division is a political subdivision, not a genetic one.*[7]

Well, first of all the Portuguese do not speak a dialect, they actually speak Portuguese, a language spoken by more than 200 million people all over the world. The Portuguese language is the only language spoken in Portugal, which is more than Spain can say, where several are spoken, such as the Catalan, Basque, and Galician, plus dialects from Aragon, Navarre, Leon, Asturias, and Santander.

Second, in the same manner that you can't distinguish between a Virginian and a Tennessean, there are similarities between the Portuguese, Spanish, Italian and many other Mediterranean people. Spain, the country as we know it today, only became Spain after Columbus made his first voyage, while Portugal is the oldest country in the world that has unchanged geographical borders.

Mr. Gallegos is right when he says that Portugal is a political division of Spain, but is also divided geographically, culturally and genetically—except for the same reason that we all are genetically connected in one form or another.

This author very strongly disagrees with Mr. Gallegos' statement, as do all Portuguese who have cherished their differences for more than eight centuries.

Why would the Spaniards remain in Virginia and the Carolinas, when they had all the protection in their own province, Florida, which remained in their possession until the 19th century? Most Spaniards went to the Caribbean and to Central and South America, because they heard that everyone was getting rich with gold and silver. Also, immigration from Spain to the United States has always been extremely low, except between the 16th and 17th centuries. By 1650, a total of 440,000 Spaniards had emigrated to the New World, primarily to Mexico and South America, unlike the English and the French. North America was their only option in the New World.

Spaniards had the opportunity to make their fortunes in the fabulous mining regions of Mexico, Central America, and in the Andean regions of South America. Taking into consideration that Spain had four times the population,[8] Spaniards emigrated much less than the Portuguese. They were either Portuguese or Spanish, but not Iberians, as a race or as a nationality.

Nassau (McGlothlen) comments about a community of Portuguese and Spanish ancestry being in the Appalachians before the 1700's, probably referring to a very small part of Melungeon ancestry at best. It does not take many to grow into a large community if they started in the 1500's. It is understood, however, that they went into the mountains only after being pushed out by the other English-speaking immigrants. The writer also accepts the possibility that Moors and Iberians were incorporated into the Indians and with others.

This is just a start. Although it may not have happened, it is a positive note to look into other possibilities besides a mixed race of Indians, Blacks, and English-speaking Europeans. In Florida, there is plenty of material to be researched if one keeps an open mind. What has been found so far is that many scholars are ready to accept any exotic explanation for the origin of the Melungeon ancestry, and will discount immediately the possibility that they have Portuguese ancestors. This could be correct. Again, an open mind is necessary, however.

Eloy Gallegos wrote a book about the Melungeons, in which he makes a case for the Spanish being the ancestors of the Melungeons. He mentions an inscription engraved on the side of a mountain near Highlands in North Carolina that reads *T.T. UN LUEGO SANTA A LA MEMORIA* and a possible connection between the Spaniards and the Melungeons.[9]

Robert Zahner wrote a book about Whiteside Mountain, where those words were engraved, and has known this place since 1930.

In his book he describes what he saw: *...the grammar is not classic Spanish, and not ready translatable, the letters, all capitals about two inches high, are well formed and chiseled with care...An array of evidence in the inscription itself, however, establishes that the carving is of modern origin.*[10] This is a fact due to the style of the modern straight type of letters, used only after the 18th century. Zahner goes on to say that the *Asheville Citizen-Times* in 1966 and the *Cashiers Chronicle* in 1987 published a letter revealing the mystery of the inscription, and pointing to several authors who may have made the engravings at the beginning of this century.

Lost Tribe of Israel, Phoenicians, Vikings, Welsh

The theories of ancient peoples being the direct ancestors of the Melungeons are difficult to consider, due mainly to the span of time in which they may have occurred. In a period of only 500 years, civilizations are created and destroyed, and if any of these people did indeed arrive in America, then a civilization would have been created in the same manner as in Europe. As for the Lost Tribe of Israel, Kennedy writes: *...and although there may be a Jewish ethnic component within the Melungeon population, there is scant evidence to suggest that this component arrived on these shores thousands of years ago.*[11] Cyrus Gordon, professor of Mediterranean studies, said that fleeing Jews discovered America 1,000 years before Columbus, based on evidence found in a burial mound at Bat Creek, Tennessee in 1885.[12] That may be possible, but connecting them to the Melungeons or another group is a rather difficult task. It is hardly possible that a group would survive thousands of years and vanish as a group in a mere 400 years. A Jewish community would not live in isolation, and signs of their faith would not disappear. *Descendants of early Carthaginian, or perhaps Phoenician, seamen who may have discovered the New World some 2,000 years before the birth of Christ.*[13] *Melungeons look*

Mediterranean...John Fetterman...paints a graphic...image...great ship, such as...Phoenician used, shipwreck on Carolina coast...[14] Although it may be somewhat difficult, it is not impossible to cross the ocean with the right wind and currents. But what about supplies for at least a month of crossing, and the return trip? How would they survive as a group for more than 2000 years? Even at a very slow population increase rate, one single couple alone would evolve into an enormous population during such a long period. It is difficult to imagine galley slaves rowing across the Atlantic (square sails spread). Conceivably, one would question what happened to the Phoenicians and Carthaginians that stayed in the Mediterranean. Is it probable that half of the Mediterranean population descended from them?

Phoenicians were in the Western Hemisphere hundreds of years before Christ...a stone found in Brazil in 1872...The Instituto Historico do Rio de Janeiro...letter signed by Joaquim Alves da Costa...Ladislau Netto...Bernardo da Silva Ramos...Armando Cortesão...they are all partial to the Phoenician discovery of America.[15] However, Samuel Eliot Morison states that:*...There are still advocates for this...*[Phoenician discovery of America] *before 146 B.C...Investigation failed to locate either the stone or Senhor da Costa.*[16]

Barry Fell, in his book *America B.C.*, shows the possibility of Iberian Phoenicians coming to America, but his detractors state that the *common rat did not reach America until the time of Columbus.* [This would prove]*... that there was no settlement from the ancient Mediterranean, since any decked ships must have carried rats.*[17] What about the Portuguese? What is today Portugal was once home to the Phoenicians. There are many vestiges in the various Phoenician ruins which provide solid proof that they lived there for a long time. It is also possible that the Portuguese may have brought the Phoenician inscribed stone to Brazil, since so many are available in Portugal.

As for the Welsh theory, it has been subjected to study, and those who favor a Welsh-Melungeon link would benefit from the letter written by John Sevier. It reports a meeting with Chief Oconostota in 1782 about a possible Welsh people. However, Sevier wrote another report two years later about the finding of:*...reddish-brown complexion people...who were neither Negro nor Indian, but claimed to be Portuguese.*[18] If there were any connection between the Welsh and his finding, most likely he would have mentioned it.

Tri-Racial, a Melungeon Orthodox View

Kennedy mentions in his book: *...the theory that the Melungeons are a simple "Tri-racial isolate," in this particular case the progeny of a few eighteenth-century whites, escaped slaves, and Native Americans. While there is undoubtedly some Native American and African influence in at least some, if not all, Melungeon populations, it is far more complex....*[19]

With their appearance remaining Mediterranean, their claim of origin, coupled with the small number of black slaves living in the Appalachians at that time, it is most difficult to accept that they would add up to a tri-racial. Complex indeed: *...Burnett (1889) apparently originated this view which describes the Melungeons as a Tri-racial hybrid of Europeans, Blacks and Indians. Dromgoole in 1891 claimed to recognize Cherokee, African, English, and Portuguese surnames in the group.*[20] Again the anthropologists Pollitzer and Brown (1969) stated: *Their findings were in line with those expected of a Caucasoid population, with little evidence of Negroid or Amerindian influence.*[21] There are a small number of Melungeons with black and/or Indian appearance, but the majority are Mediterranean looking. The latter agrees with these findings. Also, the occasional Asiatic or Oriental appearance does not add up to a tri-racial group.

Portuguese Gypsy

Another possible origin is the Indian Gypsy. Due to political and social upheaval in the Kashmiri region about A.D. 1,000, a large group left India. They traveled to Europe and later to America. Their population throughout the world is believed to be about 15 million, with an estimated two million in the U.S., eight million in India, and five million in Europe. In Portugal there are no exact numbers, but it is estimated at 80,000.

They arrived in Portugal in the 1500's after having been in Romania, Hungary, Bulgaria and Greece. Prior to their arrival in Portugal, the Gypsies came to the Iberian Peninsula and settled in Andalucia, Spain. They were also subjected to the Inquisition persecution, just like the Moors and Jews. In 1526 they were expelled from Portugal, and reentry was forbidden. During the 16th century, Portugal deported Gypsies to its colonies in Africa, and later to Brazil and India.[22] In the 19th century the Portuguese government arrested them or any who led a nomadic life style. At the end of the 20th century they are still marginalized by the society in which they live, and accused of many crimes.[23]

Did they come to America at an early period? If so, when? There are no signs of any connection with the Melungeons, except for their Mediterranean and East Indian appearance. It is unlikely that there is a relation, mainly due to the type of life that the Gypsy people lead. They are mostly merchants who work in outdoor markets. They are a nomadic people and seldom establish roots in the area where they live temporarily.

The Melungeons and other groups of people that settled early on the North America continent do not necessarily possess these characteristics, however it is possible that they may have come and isolated individuals then joined the Melungeons at an early date.

Portuguese Sephardim Jews and Ethnic Diversity—1643

There is an interesting theory that was brought to light as early as January 1971. Because of its potential, it could shed greater light if developed further.[24] It may have been possible that the enterprising Jews organized some form of transportation to America: *The role of the Jews in the slave trade is confirmed in Cape Verde, but it is essential to realize that they were only brokers.*[25] It is known that during the 1600's they went to Holland and Brazil, and then from Brazil to the U.S. They may not be the ancestors of the Melungeons, but Portuguese Jews were in this country in the 1600's and may have played a role in the coming of some people that the English would later call Melungeons. Dixon Merritt does a comparison between the Jews and the Melungeons:...*as a body they were as concrete as the Jews, and their descendants are still to be found.*[26]

Another possible way for the Portuguese Jews to have left Portugal was on one or more of the many vessels that sailed to India. This presented a way of escaping the Inquisition. Were they part of a group that wound up on the shores of America, later separated and spread to more populated areas? Legally they could not leave Portugal for India, but: *Officials of the India House in Lisbon and in Goa accepted bribes in return for allocating places on vessels.*[27]

Richard Lobban presented a paper at the University of Massachusetts-Dartmouth on February 11, 1996, about the Jews in Cape Verde and on the Guinea Coast. It reads that: *King Manuel I made reference to a group of lançados—to throw out— on the Senegambian coast; most of these were Portuguese Jews who had been deported...They were usually fugitive Portuguese settlers...following conviction for some political crime as was the case for the Jews following the full scale Portuguese Inquisition in 1536.*[28] This confirms that Portuguese Jews and others did leave Portugal for different areas of the world in ships that may or may not have arrived at their planned destinations.

With the expelling of all non-Catholics from the Iberian Peninsula, once again the Jews went to other parts of the world such as North Africa, the Middle East and Holland. Many of the Jews who left may have emigrated to North Africa, bringing with them Hebrew and other languages they picked up. Bernard Weisberger wrote *A Nation of Immigrants* and remarked on the variety of peoples that came to America and helped bring on the revolution.[29]

John Smith wrote of the presence of other nationalities in subsequent British settlements, such as the 1608 colony with people who came from Poland and Germany: *...as for hiring the Poles and Dutchmen...*[30] By 1643 a lot of traveling was done all along the east coast and it is possible that some of the people found in New Amsterdam—Novum Belgium, Nieuw Netherland, later New York City— may have come from the Carolinas and Virginia. Isaac Jogues, a French Jesuit missionary visiting in New Amsterdam wrote in 1643: *On the Island of Manhatte, and in its environs, there may well be 400 or 500 men of different sects and nations: the director general told me that there were men of eighteen different languages.*[31] Bernard Weisberger adds:... *which probably included Mediterranean and North African dialects and the Hebrew of a small settlement of Sephardic Jews.*[32] The English established the first colony in 1607—Jamestown, not too far away—and 36 years later, there were that number and variety of people. Is it possible that in such a short period, so many and different people settled in New York? Or were they a result of groups of people moving there from other parts of the country, groups that arrived in North America much earlier?

French Theory—1690

A fairly large English community was already in place in South Virginia and North Carolina, and the only French settlement reported in 1700 was near the Santee River. Lawson writes that: *The first Place we design'd for, was Santee River, on which there is a Colony of French Protestants.*[33] Bonnie Ball also writes: *Some of the Indians of Robin* [Robeson] *County have stated that the French immigrants settled the area as early as 1690, and they (the French) came in contact with a mixed race they named "Mero" (Melungeons).*[34] The name *Mero* certainly does not sound much like Melungeon, and this is quite far from East Tennessee. However, the name *Mero* pops up once in a while.

Dr. Celestin Pierre Cambiaire wrote in 1933 about the Melungeons: *They have dark complexion, black hair, brown eyes... their English is the English of two centuries ago.* [The author did not provide the source for this information] *Their names are typically English, they claim Portuguese ancestry...there is nothing to justify that claim...The French came into Tennessee a long time before the English. Some French traders or trappers must have given the name Melangeon.*[35]

In the 1930's the Melungeons spoke just like most mountain people, and to a French person that would naturally sound like the English of the 1700's, which by then was no longer Elizabethan English. The Melungeons may not be able to prove their Portuguese ancestry, but did Dr. Cambiaire do enough research to prove otherwise? There was no large French settlement in Tennessee, and traders or trappers did not stay long enough to put such a long lasting label on a group of people. It is also strange to find that Dr. Cambiaire is the only writer that spelled the word *Melungeon* in a French way—*Melangeon*—to justify the French origin *Mélange.* As for the French theory of the Melungeons being French Huguenots, there is no such indication. If there were, they would follow the various French settlements all the way up to Canada or Louisiana, which were claimed by French explorer Robert Cavalier for France in 1682. However, we should not discard the fact that many fleeing the Inquisition were received by the Huguenots in France.

The Moors were included, and later emigrated to South Carolina with the French Huguenots.

Moor/Muslim Slaves Called Mulangos Sent to Madeira and Brazil

There is yet another possibility presented by Kennedy: *Of even greater significance than the "pardo" question, is the little-known fact that the sixteenth-century South American Portuguese employed large numbers of Muslim/Moorish laborers who called themselves "mulangos."* [36]

Regarding the use of the term *mulangos*, as a rule that name is not known in Brazil, unless it is connected with the African name given to the whites—*Melungo.* Furthermore, there are no records of the Portuguese employing large numbers of North African Moors there. It is, however, possible that the Spaniards may have had Moors in other countries of South America.

The name mulango is the name of a plant from which a reddish oil is extracted. This name is used in East Africa as well as in India. However there is another similar word, *Mulambo*, that means a piece of cloth or rag with which the natives dress themselves below the waist. It may be used in a derogatory manner, as: *...someone that stopped being a man and became a human thing.*[37] I don't think there is a connection with the name Mulango. *Mucamba* means young black girl, and *Mucambo* means fugitive slave settlement.[38] *Mulamba* is a fruit in East Africa, and *Mulambe* is a tree in West Africa. *Mazombo* is a child born in Brazil of European parents.[39]

The article quoted by Kennedy refers mainly to black Muslims seeking to escape enslavement in Brazil. There is still the possibility for the usage of the name *malungo* long time ago with the same meaning as described in Chapter I.

T. B. Irving of the Mother Mosque Foundation in Cedar Rapids, Iowa, does an excellent job in portraying the lives of the Muslim Black slaves. However, the word *mulango* must have been of limited use in the *quilombos* or fugitive slave settlements, because it does not appear in any of the Brazilian dictionaries or encyclopedias consulted.

The book *The Master and Slaves* by Freyre goes into a deep study of the slaves in Brazil, and is also a good source of information on this subject.

It is important to note that the article in question refers to a later time frame: *This African styled community lasted from approximately 1630 to 1697...The Mali movement bears the focal date of 1835.*[40] This almost certainly rules out any connection with the Melungeons or other groups that may have shown up in the Southeast. After the 17th century, it would have been difficult.

Irving confirms that some Portuguese words have their roots in Arabic. Such words may start with **al** and end with **la**. As for being *Muslim/Moorish* laborers, the writer refers to Bartolomeu Las Casas, a Spanish bishop in Mexico, when he: *...suggested the importation of enslaved Africans to the new* [Spanish South America] *colonies...specially the Muslims, who he called "Moors".*[41] The Portuguese never called the Blacks from west or east Africa Moors, except the ones from the Arabian area and the Far East. Again, it is important to differentiate between Spain and Portugal in South America:

These were often West Africans but also Berbers/Moors captured during battle in the Mediterranean.[42] As mentioned elsewhere in this book, the Portuguese did not battle the Berbers/Moors in the Mediterranean. Most battles were inland, in the 15th century. Although no specific origin of Black or Muslim slaves seems to be on record, most of the slaves came from West Africa.

There were limited wars involving the Portuguese and the Turks in the Mediterranean. If any were captured, the number must have been small, such as in the battle of 1501 against the Turks in Mers-el-Quibir which failed.[43] Another was in 1535, as part of Carlos V's fleet in the Tunis operation.

What about Berber slaves in Madeira? Again Kennedy: *Since 1432, the Portuguese had regularly used captured Berbers as slave labor for the sugar plantations on the island of Madeira.*[44]

These were replaced before 1500 by black slaves from Africa, and other slaves from the Canary Islands. The Madeirans eventually asked the Portuguese king to send them to other colonies. Phillips wrote: *Following the first contact with the Americas, there was a voluntary emigration of Moors from Spain, Portugal and North Africa to the Canaries.*[45] These Portuguese and Spaniards settled there and, probably later on, emigrated again to the Caribbean islands where their descendants still remain today. Many whites in the former Spanish Caribbean islands trace their ancestry to the Canary Islands. Also, it has been said that the Canary Islands were a source of indentured servants in colonial America.

Captured Berber slaves were used only in the early 15th century on Madeira sugar plantations, and by the 1500's there were very few. The earlier slaves were from the Canary Islands, as in 1439 when a priest owned a female slave.[46]

However, in the 15th century, João Esmeraldo had 80 slaves and among them, men and women Moors, Mulattos, Negros and others also from the Canaries. Esmeraldo's sugar plantation produced 20,000 *arrobas* [47] per year, being one of the largest farms at the time. [48]

In the 15th century there were white and Black slaves. Even a Jew by the name Mordofay was given to the queen as a slave, but the Jewish community in Évora raised enough funds to pay for his freedom.[49]

Irving stated: *Is it too much to suppose that as the Portuguese developed* [Madeira sugar plantations] *similar plantations in Brazil they also imported captured Berber laborers to accomplish the same tasks there?* [50] During the early 16th century, most immigrants in Brazil were too poor to afford slaves, the record shows. Only in the late 16th and the 17th century were slaves brought in in large quantities.[51]

One other possibility is the freeing of Moors by the Portuguese and Spanish in North America. According to Kennedy: *These people, usually captured in skirmishes with the Portuguese or Spanish in the Mediterranean, had been transported to South America for forced labor purposes....One can easily understand the Portuguese and Spanish rationale for freeing such unwanted "settlers" on North American shores, as opposed to their own territories: it was one more headache for their English adversaries to deal with.*[52]

As slaves they were a valuable commodity. Why let them go then? If the intention was to cause headaches to the English, did that happen?

Indeed, history records that these South American "Melungeons" almost invariably Portuguese and on more than one occasion were freed on distant, uninviting shores by their Portuguese captors. In these cases they were generally referred to as emancipados (that is, freed captives).[53]

It would hardly be possible for the Portuguese to free any Moor or Turk slaves captured in the Mediterranean wars, first because they did not have them, and second, if they had, they were too valuable to let go without compensation. However, the Spaniards may have had some, but again, the same rule applies in regard to their value.

Pardos in the Spanish Military? To Brazil?

The connection made by Kennedy with South America warrants further study: *Although it may be pure coincidence, the darker-skinned Spanish and Portuguese recruits assigned to Brazil and the Caribbean during this same time period were known as "Pardos," a different classification from either "Negroes" or "Mulattos," both categories utilized by the Spanish military.*[54]

The name *Pardo* was used from the 17th century until recently to describe the Brazilian soldiers. Today that is no longer the case. *Pardo* in Portuguese means someone with a darker skin or a color that blends with darkness.

There is a Portuguese proverb *à noite todos os gatos são pardos* or, "at night all cats are *Pardos*," meaning that you can't distinguish their color. The Spanish were confined mostly to the Caribbean, central and southwest America. No significant number of Spaniards is known to have gone to Brazil. The Spanish military did not go to Brazil, not even during the early 1600's when the crowns of Spain and Portugal were united. They were busy with the American southeast, Mexico and Peru.

Across the Atlantic before Columbus

Kennedy suggests in his book that others before Columbus may have been in the West Indies: *Are we, then, to assume that the seafaring Moors and Berbers could not have also made such navigational "errors," ending up by accident or design in the New World? Historians have generally discounted the notion, but I suspect the same old North European prejudices have influenced such dogmatically rigid thinking.*[55] He also quotes the following: *...and according to historian John Dyson, in 1504, during his fourth voyage, Columbus himself...made an extraordinary find on the island of Guadeloupe. In a native hut was an iron pot and the stern post of a European ship, too heavy and distant to be that of the wrecked Santa Maria. All who saw it thought it could only have come from the Canaries, proof that at least one ship had made it across the Atlantic before Columbus.*[56]

This may be disputed, as Columbus and his son Fernando repeated that the natives from the Antilles *did not have any kind of iron objects...*[Fernando writes what his father's men]—*not Columbus himself*—found so marvelous, was the finding of a *cassuelo de hierro*, some kind of frying pan with handle.

He further explains that: *...must have been caused by the pebbles and silex being of a shine iron color...and only some one with little common sense would think it was iron... and since then no one has found anything made out of iron, among those people.*[57]

The preceding is what Mascarenhas Barreto found on the original documents by Fernando Colón, Columbus' son.

The same author does not mention the stern post. There is no evidence that the Moors or Berbers had the knowledge or the navigational capabilities of long voyages in the 15th or 16th century. However, it is indeed possible that a vessel may be pushed by the winds and currents to the U.S. East Coast. Would the people have survived? Would they have had the provisions for such an ocean crossing? If so, did they bring their women on board? Muslims?

South Carolina Moors—Dark Genes—French Huguenots

Henry Coppee's book, *Conquest of Spain by the Arab-Moors,* alludes to another possible source for the Melungeons: *...It has been asserted that, when the Moors were driven out, thousands took refuge in the south of France, who, afterwards abhorring the Roman Catholic persecutions, became Huguenots* (Lutherans) *and that of these many emigrated at a later day to South Carolina...and the great tide rushed in from Protestant Europe...*[58]

This is possible, of course. Many other groups who emigrated to the New World may have mixed with groups already here in the 17th or 18th century. However, the Moors of southern Spain would not have anything to do with the Portuguese.

Columbus had Moors, Arabs, Jews and Portuguese Sailors

Henry Coppee brings to our attention a little known fact: *Christopher Columbus' fleet was fitted out in the little port of Palos, which had lately been a Moorish port; his sailors many of them with Moorish blood in their veins.*[59] It was learned in 1989, through Boris Feinman of Palm Beach County Community College in Florida, that Columbus also had six Jews—*conversos*—aboard his first voyage. Feinman created a visual display that documents the contributions of Jews to American history from 1492 to 1865—from the voyage of Columbus to the end of the Civil War— which has been displayed all over the U.S.[60] Also, Jane Gerber, in her book *The Jews of Spain,* provides six identifiable Jews as part of Columbus's expedition.[61]

Rabbi Levinger's book *History of the Jews in the U.S.* teaches that five or six Jews were part of the 120 men on Columbus' first voyage.[62] He also states that Columbus was of Jewish blood, and claimed to be Christian. Although the name Colombo was common in northern Italy, in Spain he was always and still is known as *Colon.* There was in fact a family by that name of Jewish blood.

To bolster that theory, we should note that Columbus always wrote in Spanish or Latin, but never in Italian or Genoese. Mascarenhas Barreto wrote a book about Columbus that describes him as being a Jewish descendant, and that may explain the secrecy that shrouded his early life.[63] On the other hand, and according to Spanish history, the sailors in Columbus' first trip were mostly from Andalucia.[64]

From the original crew list, there is at least one member from Portugal, João Areias, native of Tavira, Algarve, Portugal. The list also shows many names with Portuguese characteristics, but translated to Spanish with no birthplace shown.[65]

According to recent discoveries, Evelyn Orr—a Melungeon researcher—informs that Arabs were also part of the crew, according to Beverlee Mehdi. In this same book, the author writes that: *...the Arab geographer al-Sherif, eight adventurers sailed from Lisbon, Portugal, trying to discover what was beyond the "Sea of*

Fig. 16—Evelyn Orr

Darkness" the Arab name for the Atlantic. It is said that they landed in South America.[66] These Arabs in Portugal were probably the ancestors of the Portuguese Navigators.

The Turkish-Ottoman Empire and the Melungeon-Turk Connection

The Ottoman Empire played an important role in the world, mostly in the East, but since it controlled vast portions of the Mediterranean, and with their constant wars with Spain and other eastern Mediterranean countries, it is possible that their people may have played an important role in the Melungeon make-up. There are many Melungeon descendants who believe their ancestors were Turks. It is therefore important for the reader to know a little about the Ottoman Empire.

Also, it is important to underline the fact that this book is not concerned with who was the victor, but only if any Turks were made captives, including women or children. Also, if they were transported to the U.S.—willing or not.

The Ottoman Empire was created by Turkish tribes in Anatolia and lasted from the decline of the Byzantine Empire in the 14th century until the establishment of Turkey as a republic in 1922.

The first period of Ottoman history, from 1300 to 1481, was one of almost continuous expansion through war, alliance and outright purchase of territory. In 1453 Constantinople was taken, and in subsequent years Morea, Trebizond, Bosnia, Albania, the Crimea and other areas were conquered or annexed. Under Selim I (1512-20), Ottoman expansion resumed.

His defeat of the Mamelukes in 1516-17 doubled the size of the empire at a stroke by adding to it Syria, Palestine, Egypt and Algeria. The reign of his son Süleyman I (1520-66), known in Europe as *the Magnificent*, was a golden age of Ottoman power and grandeur.

He conquered Hungary from the Habsburgs, annexed Tripoli, extended the empire southeastward through Mesopotamia to the Persian Gulf, and made the Ottoman navy dominant in the eastern Mediterranean.

Although they were often at war with the West, it was common to see Ottoman Empire trading ships flying Christian, Islamic or Judaic symbols when they were carrying mixed nationalities. Many of the merchants were also Jews.[67]

Süleyman himself overran Iraq, and even challenged Portuguese dominion of the Indian Ocean from his bases in Suez and Basra. The Ottomans began to spread their empire from a corner of Anatolia, and during the 17th century, when Turkish expansion was at its peak, the Ottoman Empire reached into central Europe to include what is now Hungary and Romania and most of the other present-day Balkan states. It also included what is now Syria, Iraq, Israel, Egypt and north Africa as far west as Algeria.

Morocco is the only north African country where the Portuguese conquered some of the towns. Because of its lack of natural harbors, its rugged mountainous interior, and its distance throughout its history from imperial centers in the east,

Fig. 17—Map of Europe and North Africa, 16ᵗʰ Century. (Hammond Historical Atlas.)

Morocco remained relatively isolated until the early 20th century. The Ottoman Empire did not reach that far west—Algeria being the westernmost country—and no battles of consequence were fought against the Portuguese. They did have an encounter with a Portuguese fleet of 30 Caravels and other ships, possibly a total of 70, on June 15, 1501, to fight against the Turks in aid of Venice.

The Portuguese were supposed to conquer Mazalquibir, the Oran defense castle, which they were unable to do. They finally returned to Lisbon on December 25.[68] Later, another fleet of 1500 men, led by the Portuguese Prince Luis as part of an alliance with Spain against the Turks, went to Tunis in 1535. The Portuguese officially maintained neutrality so as not to anger the Turks in India. By doing this, they were hoping that helping Spain against Barbarossa would alleviate the military pressure of the Moors in north Africa.

However, the Red Sea and the Indian Ocean saw quite a bit of action between the Turks and the Portuguese. Most Red Sea actions were primarily to investigate or spoil Turkish naval preparations. By the time the Turks arrived in India, the Portuguese were already firmly settled.[69]

Let us take a look at the map showing northwest Africa and the south of Portugal. The area controlled by the Ottoman Empire was called the Barbary States. We can see that the Turks did not come that far west. Also, we must make a distinction between Turks and Moors or Berbers, although any non-Christian in the Mediterranean was given the generic Moor name. The Hadrami chroniclers on Portuguese activities reveal several battles, one in the Islamic year 908—Common Era or Christian year 1502-03. When the battle took place, the Portuguese captured seven vessels and took some prisoners.[70]

Whenever prisoners were taken, very often they were exchanged or ransomed. In 1517: *...some of the Franks went to the port of Aden...the Emir Mardjān gave them water...and ransomed some prisoners from them.*[71]

The author R. B. Sergeant mentions Batticalá (modern Bhatkal): ...as *one of the*

Fig. 18—Ruth Johnson during a visit to Turkey's city of Cesme with a plaque saying: "This forest area is arranged in memory of the people of Cesme, later named Melungeon, who were taken away to America by Portuguese people in the 16th Century." Brent Kennedy and other Melungeons were part of a group of Melungeons who visited Turkey at the invitation of the Government and Universities.

most important ports of Kanara [Portuguese Canará] *and must have been well known at least to all the Gulf Arabs as it was a great center of horse trade.*[In 1529-30, arrived on this port a Portuguese vessel with Muslim prisoners,[72] and in the following year a ship with families is mentioned]...*with their children and women, and Salmăn'să children and servants, on board.*[73]

A Turkish gun (1530-31) is preserved to this day in the Tower of London, with Arab inscriptions. One of them reads, *Entering into the land of India, Portugal* (Burtukăl) *the* accursed, in Cairo the preserved, year 937 H. (A.D. 1530-31).[74]

Turkish Influence in the West

For the first time: *Turkish influence and the Ottoman Empire was to be extended, in 1578 to Morocco. Here the Sheriff of Fez* [town where Henry the Navigator's brother Fernando died in prison under the most horrible conditions many years before] *called for the aid of the Turks against the Portuguese, who landed a large force in support of the pretender. This was granted with alacrity, for fear of Spanish cooperation with Portugal and a great battle was won against the Portuguese at Alcazarquivir in which their King Sebastian was killed, together with the pretender and a quarter of their army. Thus started the decline of Portugal, of which Philip speedily took advantage by its armed occupation.*[75] Let us keep that in mind when we look into the possibility of the Turks being the major component of the Melungeon people. Kennedy maintains: *Moorish and Turkish naval heroes soon evolved, most notably two dark-skinned, red-haired Moorish brothers...*[one of them]*...was known to Europeans as Barbarossa, literally "Redbeard." From the very early 1500's until almost 1546...Barbarossa fought the Spanish at every opportunity along the North African coast. The Spanish and Portuguese continued to wage naval warfare against the unrelenting Moors and Ottoman (Turkish) Empire well into the 1600's, with both sides filling their galleys with oarsmen captured from each other.*[76] Barbarossa's activities were mostly in the Mediterranean, although there was limited Moor or Turkish piracy and French corsair action along the Portuguese coast. The

Moors avoided the area because the Portuguese king had implemented a coast guard fleet between the Azores and the continent to protect the Indian fleet returning from India loaded with spices. The French did it mostly to challenge the Portuguese and Spanish closed-seas policy.

The pirate Berbers used Argel and Tunis as their nest, and from this point they attacked southern Europe, which they did also in 1530 from Tripoli. Dragut, a Turkish pirate, had previously conquered that city.

Dragut captured men and women and later demanded high ransoms. However most of the young women wound up in harems.

Fig. 19—Girl from Turkey holding "The Forgotten Portuguese Book"

Pirate ships, French, English, Turks, and others from Argelia, managed to assault 220 Portuguese ships returning from India and Brazil between 1549 and 1550.[77]

Moors and Turks Freed by the Portuguese

Kennedy reveals yet another possibility: *And, of course, if Drake could have deposited Moors and Turks off our shores, might there not have been other, more obscure incidences of this nature? Emancipados freed by the Portuguese themselves, for example? Undoubtedly there were.*[78] First, we have to accept the possibility of Drake having dropped them off on our shores. Second, we have to question how the *emancipados*—if there were any—got here. On the other hand, if the Turks were galley slaves, they were an expensive commodity to let go that easily. Also, most *emancipados,* or new Christians—Cristãos novos—were Jews. The Moors in Portugal had already been absorbed by the Portuguese community at large by the 15th and 16th centuries. Finally, Portugal did not have any quantity of Turkish captives to speak of in the 16th century. Let us keep in mind that Portugal's major problem was the small size of its population.

The only way the Portuguese could have Turkish slaves would be the result of battles fought in the Indian Ocean. If the Portuguese had Turkish prisoners, they would not have sent them all the way from the Indian Ocean to Brazil. Instead, they would have traded them for Portuguese prisoners, and the Muslims had many.

What happened to the supposedly captured Turks? David Beers Quinn offers a possible answer: *The only trace we find of the passengers is of negotiations to send home some 100 ex-galley slaves to the Turkish dominions.*[79]

We should not rule out the possibility of these Moors, Muslims or Turks having been captured galley slaves at the Battle of LePanto, where the Ottoman Empire had a tremendous loss. Portugal was also involved as an ally in this battle. Again, a separation between the Spanish and Portuguese must be made. The Portuguese did not wage naval warfare against the Turks in the Mediterranean. A possible connection with the Turks is viable, but only if we take into consideration that the Ottoman Empire ruled most Mediterranean countries, except for the northwest coast of Africa, where Portugal was most active. It is questionable whether everyone under the Ottoman Empire should be considered a Turk.

Turkish slaves were men only, and if they intermarried with Indian women, the Melungeons would have a different look. This may, however, be the origin of the Lumbees or other Indian tribes of North Carolina such as the Powatans, Croatans, or others.

Portugal was involved only with the Moors or Berbers of Northwest Africa, and records show that, when attacked by the Portuguese, they were never helped by the Turks or asked for their help, with one exception in 1578. No record of large numbers of Turks made prisoners by Portugal in the 16th century was found in Portuguese history books. The slaves used in Madeira came from Morocco and the Canary Islands in the 15th century.

Most likely Kennedy is referring to Spanish, not Portuguese, battles. As for oarsmen captured by the Portuguese, most battles with the Moors were inland. However, the Portuguese did battle the Turks in the Indian Ocean, quite far from the Mediterranean. That may be the best connection between the Portuguese and the Turks.

The Turk Name and Portuguese-Captured Algerians

Kennedy makes a possible connection with the Berbers: *Even without Drake it is an established fact that the sixteenth-century Spanish and Portuguese regularly used captured Algerians (probably North African Berbers) as galley slaves for both their Mediterranean and New World seafaring endeavors.*[80]

Again, we have to assume that Kennedy is talking about the Spanish and not the Portuguese, as they did not normally get that far east, with the exceptions mentioned above. However, the Portuguese did bring to Portugal Berber slaves captured along the West African coast, mostly in the 15th century.

As for the name *Turk*, it was discovered through consultation with more than one history professor and older people that the English used to call anyone who spoke a foreign language, or whose culture could not be recognized or understood, a Turk. Similarly the Brazilians and Mexicans call the Americans or anyone who does not speak like a native, a *gringo*.

Francisco Coronado, on his famous expedition to Mexico in 1542, had an encounter with an Indian slave called Turk: *...He had been led there by an Indian Turk...and saw that they have been deceived by the Turk...and with Ysopete. The Turk was taken along in chains.*[81]

This was not a connection with the Turks. Apparently, what happened was that when the Spaniards saw that particular Indian, due to his unusual appearance or because he looked like one, they called him *Turk*.[82] He is believed to be an Indian from the Pawnee tribe.[83] However, some Melungeon families stated that their ancestors have said that they were Turks.

The Ottoman Empire in the 15th and 16th centuries controlled most of the Mediterranean, as well as Persia and parts of India, before the Portuguese arrived. They could have played a part also, but I doubt that the Turks could have been the main element according to the studies made so far.

See the chart at the end of this chapter for the Turkish activities during that period, and their possible interaction with the Portuguese. Within these parameters, it was established that the Melungeons' ancestors could be any one of the following nationalities: Spanish, Portuguese, Turkish or from any of the countries in the Far East, such as India.

Turkish may mean any native of the countries controlled by the Ottoman Empire, including all of the eastern Mediterranean and north Africa, except the westernmost part.

Galley Slaves and the Battle of LePanto—1571

A galley was a large seagoing vessel propelled primarily by oars. The Egyptians, Cretans and other ancient peoples used sail-equipped galleys for both war and commerce. Though the advent of the lateen (fore-and-aft) sail and the stern rudder rendered the galley obsolete for commerce, it retained its military importance into the 16th century. It played a leading role at the Battle of LePanto [84] in the eastern Mediterranean.

Rowing in the galleys, particularly those belonging to the Ottoman Empire that sailed the Mediterranean, was another form of brutal slave labor. Tens of thousands of Slavs, victims of Crimean Tartar slave raids, first suffered a hellish existence in the Crimea itself, and then ended their days rowing on Ottoman triremes.[85]

Portugal did not have many galley-type vessels in terms of the 16th century, except in the Indian Ocean.

Also, galleys were used in the Battle of LePanto, which was fought between allied Christian forces and the Ottoman Turks. The Venetians formed an alliance with Pope Pius V and Felipe II of Spain (May 25, 1571). Felipe sent his half brother, Don Juan of Austria, to command the allied forces.

On October 7, 1571, the Battle in the Gulf of LePanto near Corinth, off the coast of Greece, ended in defeat for an Ottoman fleet of 240 galleys.

The maritime league of 212 Spanish, Venetian, Genoese and Maltese ships lost about 5,000 oarsmen and soldiers, but it captured 130 vessels with their stores and provisions.

They also took 4,000 prisoners, freed 12,000 Christian galley slaves and killed 25,000 Turks. This story may give credit to Drake's capture in 1586, but not from the Portuguese—perhaps from the Spaniards. They were the ones that had the Turkish captives, not the Portuguese.

It is possible that Spain may have taken some of these Turkish galley slaves to the Caribbean Islands. Therefore, the same slaves that Drake captured 15 years later from the Spaniards were taken back to England and left with others on the shores of Virginia or the Carolinas. Subsequently they could have met with the

Portuguese, who were already there, as well as other settlers and the Indians, thereby becoming part of the Melungeons.

Would the Spaniards hold them for 15 years? If so, they would be older. Would they take unconverted Muslims to the New World? On the other hand, Manuel da Costa Fontes, while working on his doctoral dissertation at the University of California on Portuguese folk ballads in North America and other Portuguese folk traditions, found an extremely rare ballad remembered by the Portuguese in North America about the Battle of LePanto.

He discovered a fairly complete version in California (1970), and on January 22, 1978, Maria Soares de Sousa, a native of the island of Santa Maria, Azores, recited the following fragment in Portuguese, in Stoughton, Massachusetts:[86]

A peça de D. João era de bronze e rendia;
foi deitada à meia noite p'ra defender sua Turquia
Era tanta a sangueira que pelos embornais corria;
eram tantos os corpos n'agua qu'as anauas entorpeciam.

The translation in English:
Dom João's piece of artillery was of bronze
and it worked plenty;
It was fired at midnight in order to defend* his Turkey.
There was so much blood that it flowed through the supper holes;
there were so many corpses in the water that they hindered the ships.
* should read attack

One should ask, why should such a ballad survive to these times? Did the Turks actually bring it over and pass it along to the Portuguese? Perhaps some of the Portuguese soldiers involved in that battle brought it over to North America. It certainly must have been quite popular to survive four centuries. It also points to a possible Azorean connection.

Portuguese Defeat in Morocco and the Decline—1578

On June 24, 1578, a fleet with 940 sails and 24,000 men departed Lisbon, arriving in Morocco on July 7.[87] The biggest defeat in Portuguese history happened on August 4, when the young, stubborn and inexperienced king of Portugal, Sebastião, was killed and his army annihilated at Ksar el Kebir (*Alcacer Quibir*) in northwest Africa. Here, he and many young Portuguese noblemen—who were as foolish as their king—died or were made prisoners. With him also died a Moorish king and two Moorish princes. He went to battle not heeding the advice of Spanish King Felipe II and the Pope. Just before the battle began, he stubbornly refused to listen to reason as to the best way to wage the war, using proper military positions. That was called the *Battle of the Kings*. The Portuguese noblemen who did not die were made prisoners. This defeat marked the beginning of the fall of the short-lived Portuguese Empire and its supremacy throughout the world.

From that date on, the Portuguese were hard-pressed to exchange whatever Arab, Moorish or Turkish prisoners they may have had for the many young Portuguese noblemen dying in Moorish prisons. It is hard to understand how the Turks or Moors got to Brazil, and for them to be captured or freed by Drake.

Turkish Name *Rëis* and the Map

In 1929, at an Istanbul palace in Turkey, a map dated 1513 appeared showing North and South America as well as the Caribbean.[88] This map was drawn on a gazelle hide by Piri Rëis, a Gallipoli-born Turkish Admiral.[89]

Admiral Rëis was appointed by the Ottomans; he assisted them in suppressing Turkish revolts in central and southern Anatolia (1526), and enjoyed the favor of Sultan Süleyman I the Magnificent. In 1551, a fleet of 30 units under the command of Rëis left the Straits of Mecca, and was sent to overtake Mascate, but failed and took refuge in Bassorah.[90] Later he was beheaded in Cairo, because he fled the Portuguese:...*and abandoned his fleet to the enemy.*[91]

The area drawn on the map was well known by the Portuguese of that time. See Chapter VII, Figure 58, 1502 Cantino map.[92, 93]

The Portuguese Women and the Turks in India

The Portuguese fought many battles in the Indian Ocean against the Turks, such as the Battle of Hormuz (Ormuz) in 1507, Goa in 1510, and Malacca in 1516. The towns of Ormuz and Malacca were held until 1650 when the Turks, Persians and Malayans took it back with the help of the British, Dutch and French.

The Indian Ocean and the Arabian, or Red, Sea was the stage for many battles between Moors—non-Catholics in India—as well as Turks and the Portuguese: ...*here he landed troops on the Island of Diu and, armed with a number of huge cannons which had been dragged across the isthmus of Suez, laid siege to its Portuguese fortress. The soldiers of the garrison with the aid of their women folk, resisted with courage...defeating the Turks.*[94]

Blacks from Cape Verde—Turks

If Drake's release is one of the keys to help find the Melungeons' or other groups' ancestry, then research should be directed to the National Archives *Torre do Tombo* in Portugal for Cape Verde, *Archivo General de Indias* in Seville and *Archivo General de Simancas*, both in Spain, for Turk slaves. There are records of almost every person taken to the West Indies by Spain in the 16th and 17th centuries, including slaves, Turks and other nationalities.

According to records of the 16th century, Turkish slaves were very valuable, and families brought them in small numbers (one or two per family) to the New World as servants. One final point is the distinction between Turks and Moors.

In 1548, Jeronimo Butaca had a Turkish slave.[95] Portugal and Spain classified most Muslims as Moors: *It is not altogether clear whether our sources systematically distinguish between Turks and Moors.*[96]

The Portuguese-Turk-Melungeon Connection

The Turkish connection with the Melungeons and the Portuguese would be more acceptable if they had originated from Portugal or the Azores after having lived there for many years as Muslims. The Portuguese kings, before 1531, did allow the practice of the Muslim religion much in the same way as the Moors allowed practice of the Christian religion when they invaded the Iberian Peninsula. The Mediterranean trade with Portuguese ports would also justify the presence of Turks, either fleeing the Ottoman Empire or just doing business in Portugal.

Many persons wrongly assume that the Portuguese fought most battles in the Mediterranean and North Africa, which is not the case. The capture of Turks or Moors in the Mediterranean by the Portuguese has been mentioned; however it is more likely that this would have been in the Red Sea or the Indian Ocean. In this area of the world, the Portuguese and the Turks often faced each other in warlike manner, and called each other by specific names. The Portuguese in India were called *Franks* and the Turks *Rümï* or *Rumes*. All others were called Moors. The word *Frank* in Portuguese is *Firango* or *Franguês*, which derives from *Fring,* meaning Europe, in the Persian language.[97] The presence of Turks in North America in the 16th century, directly from the Middle East to America, it is highly unlikely. However, if one takes into consideration the encounters between the Portuguese and the Turkish (Ottoman Empire) in the Far East, the Arabian Sea, and the Indian Ocean, then it is quite possible that Turks or their direct descendants were in Portuguese caravels going to or coming from India. Through shipwrecks or other causes, these ships could very well wind up on the U.S. east coast seashores.

The government of Turkey, town officials and scholars, along with Turkish National TV and newspapers, have been giving the Melungeons very much attention. Brent Kennedy, with many others, has visited Turkey several times. The Gowen Research Foundation published a report of the tour written by Col. Carroll Heard Goyne, Jr. in the April 1997 issue of their newsletter.[98]

The following is a chart showing the battles fought since Portugal achieved her nationhood in 1143. The chart shows that most battles were fought in the Far East. The Turks were involved there, and very often they were taken captive along with their women and children. Also, the Turks took Portuguese and their families as prisoners. See notes below.

Chart of Battles Between the Portuguese Navy and Turks, Moors

M	D	Y	Captain	Location	Nations Involved
7	15	1180	Fuas Roupinho	Cape Espichel	Moors, N. Africa
10	17	1182	Fuas Roupinho	Ceuta	Moors, N. Africa
7		1341	Pessanha	Ceuta	Moors, N. Africa
9		1469	King Afonso V	Portuguese Coast [99]	French Corsair, Colombo
8	31	1476	Pêro de Ataide	St. Maria -Lagos	Genoa [100]
10/12		1502	Vasco da Gama	Mt. Deli	Mecca, Calicut, Cairo
12	31	1502	João da Nova (2-1-1503)	Cannanore	Mecca, Calicut
10/12		1504	Lopo Soares de Albergaria	Pandarane	Turks, Mecca
7	24	1504	Garcia de Melo	Larache	Moors, Pirates, N.Africa
10	18	1505	Francisco de Almeida	Onor	Mecca, Onor
11		1505	João Homem	Coulão	Mecca, Coulão
9	27	1507	Afonso de Albuquerque	Ormuz	Turks Ormuz, Oman
3	24	1508	Pêro Barreto	Chaul	Turks, Mecca
5		1508	Rui Soares	Sea of Arabia	Turks, Mecca
2	3	1509	Francisco de Almeida	Diu	Turks
3		1510	Antão de Nogueira	Sea of Arabia	Mecca, Cambaia
6		1510	Antonio de Noronha	Mandovi - Goa	Turks - Narsinga
1		1511	Jorge Botelho	Calicut	Mecca
6	24	1511	Afonso de Albuquerque	Isle of Polvoreira	Mecca
4		1517	Lopo Soares de Albergaria	Jeddah, Red Sea	Turks - Mecca
		1520	Vasco Fernandes César	Alcacer Ceguer, Africa	Moors, Pirates
3	8	1520	Miguel da Silva	Ceuta, NW Africa	Moors, Pirates
7/9		1520	João & Aires Coelho	Tangier, NW Africa	Moors, Pirates
10		1521	Vasco Fernandes César	Strait of Gibraltar	Moors and English
3		1521	Diogo Fernandes de Beja	Diu-Arabian Sea	Turks
3		1521	Simão Martins	Dabul-NW India	Turks
7	27	1521	Antonio Correia	Barem-Persian Gulf	Turks - Persia
9		1521	Nuno Fernandes Macedo	Diu-NW India	Turks
11		1522	Manuel de Sousa Tavares	Ormuz	Turks - Persia
7	14	1535	Antonio de Saldanha	Tunis	Turks[101]
		1550	Gonçalo Vaz	Aden Gulf - Red Sea	Turks
		1551	Luis Figueira	Assab Bay - Red Sea	Turkish Pirate Cafar[102]
		1552	Inacio Nunes Gato	Alcalá - N. Africa	Turks - Argel[102]
		1552	Antão de Noronha	Ormuz- Red Sea	Turks - Mecca[102]
		1553	Pêro de Ataide	Ormuz- Red Sea	Turks - Piri Reis[103]
		1554	Fernando de Meneses	Oman Gulf	Turks - Mecca[104]
		1555	Pedro da Cunha	Carvoeira, Algarve	Turks - Argel

The previous chart shown is part of a much larger chart compiled by the author from information available in documents and books, such as the five-volume collection of the *Batalhas e Combates da Marinha Portuguese* by Saturnino Monteiro and published by the Portuguese Navy Library in Lisbon.

This chart shows only the battles involving the Moors and, more specifically, the Turks or the Ottoman Empire, up to the first half of the 16th century. It should be noted that prisoners were made on both sides, and the Portuguese won and lost many battles. Also, sometimes Muslim women and children traveling to and from Mecca were made captive. The same happened when Portuguese ships were captured with families aboard. The name *Moor* was originally connected with the people of northwest Africa, in the area of Morocco.

That same name was later extended to all Muslims anywhere in the world, in the Ottoman Empire, India, Indochina, Indonesia and most of the lands in the eastern Indian Ocean.

Notes

[1] The Melungeons by N. Brent Kennedy, pp. 94-95.
[2] Atlantis, Dwelling Place of the Gods by Henriette Mertz, p. 54.
[3] The Mongrel Virginias by Arthur Estabrook, p. 182.
[4] Ibid, p. 189.
[5] The Melungeons by N. Brent Kennedy, p. 124.
[6] The Spanish, Portuguese Languages by William J. Entwistle, p. 61-62.
[7] The Melungeons by Eloy J. Gallegos, p. 137, Villagra Press, Knoxville, TN, 1997.
[8] Fomento Rural e Emigração by Oliveira Martins, p. 34.
[9] The Melungeons by Eloy J. Gallegos, p. 137, Villagra Press, Knoxville, TN, 1997.
[10] Whiteside Mountain by Robert Zahner, p. 116
[11] The Melungeons by N. Brent Kennedy, p. 82.
[12] Fleeing Jews... by Cyrus H. Gordon, Arkansas Gazette, Oct. 19, 1970.
[13] The Melungeons by N. Brent Kennedy, p. 82.
[14] The Melungeons by Bonnie Ball, p. 67.
[15] Ibid, p. 69.
[16] European Discovery of America by Samuel Elliot Morison, p. 11.
[17] The Melungeons and Other Mestee Groups by Mike Nassau (McGlothlen), p. 171.
[18] The Melungeons by Jean Patterson Bible, p. 86, "To date this letter has not been found."
[19] The Melungeons by N. Brent Kennedy, pp. 81-84.
[20] Ibid, p. 127.
[21] Ibid.
[22] Bury Me Standing by Isabel Fonseca, pp. 215, 216.
[23] RTP TV Program Reporter, 1996.
[24] Theory...Melungeons...from Jewish origin by Cyrus H. Gordon, Argosy Magazine, 1/1971.
[25] Jews in Cape Verde and on the Guinea Coast by Richard Lobban.
[26] History of Tennessee and Tennesseans by Hale & Merrit, p. 180, Vol. 1.
[27] Men under Stress: The Social Environment...Carreira da India by A.J.R. Russell-Wood, p. 25.
[28] Jews in Cape Verde and on the Guinea Coast by Richard Lobban.
[29] A Nation of Immigrants by Bernard A. Weisberger (American Heritage).
[30] Makers of America by Wayne Moquin, p. 73. (The True Travels by John Smith).
[31] Ibid, p. 85.
[32] A Nation of Immigrants by Bernard A. Weisberger. (American Heritage).
[33] A New Voyage to Carolina by John Lawson (Hugh Lefler), p. 14.
[34] The Melungeons by Bonnie Ball, p. 55.
[35] East Tennessee...Ballads by Celestin Pierre Cambiaire, p. ix.
[36] The Melungeons by N. Brent Kennedy, p.106.
[37] Dicionario da Lingua Portuguesa by Antonio Morais e Silva, Vol. 7, p. 84.
[38] The Masters and the Slaves by Gilberto Freyre, p. 491.
[39] Dicionario Brasileiro da Lingua Portuguesa, Vol. 2, p. 30.
[40] King Zumbi... by T.B. Irving, p. 404 (Amer. J. Islamic S. Sciences, 9:3 Fall 1992).
[41] Ibid, p. 399 (Amer. J. Islamic S. Sciences, 9:3 Fall 1992).
[42] The Melungeons by N. Brent Kennedy, p. 106.
[43] Portugal nos Mares by Oliveira Martins, p. 72.
[44] The Melungeons by N. Brent Kennedy, p. 113.
[45] The Worlds of Columbus by William D. Phillips, p. 60.
[46] Economia Mundial by Vitorino Magalhães Godinho, p. 521.
[47] *Arroba* is a metric measure of weight equal to 33 lbs. 20,000 *arrobas* equals 660,000 lbs.
[48] Saudades da Terra by Gaspar Frutuoso, p. 124.

Notes (Cont.)

[49] Economia Mundial by Vitorino Magalhães Godinho, p. 521.

[50] The Melungeons by N. Brent Kennedy, p. 113; King Zumbi... Irving 9/3 Fall 1992, 399.

[51] Portuguese settlement...by William Freitas, Portuguese Heritage, December 1993, p. 22.

[52] The Melungeons by N. Brent Kennedy , p. 111.

[53] Ibid.

[54] Ibid, p. 106.

[55] Ibid, p. 114.

[56] Columbus: For Gold, God, and Glory by John Dyson, p. 188.

[57] Cristovão Colombo by Mascarenhas Barreto, p. 576.

[58] History of the Conquest of Spain by the Arab-Moors by Henry Coppee, vol. 2, 1881, pp. 445-46.

[59] Ibid.

[60] Letter by John Townsend, Center for Multi-Cultural Affairs.

[61] The Jews of Spain by Jane Gerber, p. xix.

[62] History of the Jews in the U.S. by Rabbi Lee J. Levinger, p. 28-34.

[63] The Portuguese Columbus by Mascarenhas Barreto.

[64] Historia de España, Historia 16, p. 492.

[65] The Log of Christopher Columbus by Robert H. Fuson, p. 225.

[66] Arabs in America by Beverly Mehdi, p. 1.

[67] 16th and 17th centuries.

[68] Portugal nos Mares by Oliveira Martins, p. 72.

[69] The Portuguese off the South Arabian Coast by R. B. Serjeant, p. 18.

[70] Ibid, p. 43; [71] Ibid, p. 51; [72] Ibid, p. 55.

[73] Ibid, p. 56.

[74] Ibid, Appendix I.

[75] The Ottoman Centuries, by Lord Kinross, 1977, New York: Morrow Quill, p. 273.

[76] The Melungeons by Brent Kennedy, pp. 102-103.

[77] As Berlengas e os Piratas by José de Almeida Santos, p. 14.

[78] The Melungeons by Brent Kennedy, p. 112.

[79] The Roanoke Voyages by David Beers Quinn, vol. 1, p. 254.

[80] The Melungeons by Brent Kennedy, p. 112.

[81] Makers of America by Wayne Moquin, p. 5 (Encyclopedia Britannica).

[82] Spanish Explorers of the Southern United States by Theodore H. Lewis, p. 313.

[83] Os Portugueses no Descobrimentos dos Estados Unidos by Jaime Cortesão, p. 28.

[84] Historia de España, Historia 16, p. 507.

[85] 1994 by Encyclopedia Britannica.

[86] Study of the Portuguese Ballad by Manuel da Costa Fontes, pp. 126, 136.

[87] Historia de Portugal by Joaquim Verissimo Serrão, Vol. III, p. 76.

[88] The Ottoman Centuries, by Lord Kinross, 1977, New York: Morrow Quill, p. 245.

[89] National Geographic Magazine, Geographica page, March 1994.

[90] Dicionario de Historia de Portugal, Vol. III, by Joel Serrão, p. 499.

[91] The Ottoman Centuries, by Lord Kinross, 1977, New York: Morrow Quill, p. 245.

[92] Reis is a very common name in Portugal; Lisbon, the capital, alone has more than 150 Reis names in its telephone book. In Portuguese the name does not have a symbol over the letter e.

[93] Brent Kennedy, report to the Gowen Foundation, 1995.

[94] The Ottoman Centuries, by Lord Kinross, 1977, New York: Morrow Quill, p. 244.

[95] Economia Mundial by Vitorino Magalhães Godinho, p. 547.

[96] Turks, Moors, Blacks...by David B. Quinn (Terrae Incognitae 14, 1982, p. 104).

[97] Os Portugueses na India by Agostinho de Carvalho, p. 99.

[98] Gowen Research Foundation Newsletter by Col. Carrol Heard Goyne, Jr., April 1997.

[99] Culam or Colombo was made prisoner, worked later for Portugal.

Notes (Cont.)ᵛ

[100] In this battle, all ships were destroyed by fire, 800 Genoese died, 500 French and 500 Portuguese. According to tradition, it was here that Columbus saved his life by holding onto the wreckage. *Colombo o Velho* (The Old), was the Captain on one of the Portuguese vessels and presumably Columbus' relative.

[101] A fleet of Spanish, Portuguese and others attacked Tunis to free that city from Barbarossa, also known as Red or Blue Beard, who had an army mostly of Berber soldiers. The allied navy freed the city and 20,000 Christian prisoners. No record of Turkish or Muslim prisoners taken. Later Barbarossa recovered from the defeat and attacked Mallorca, captured a loaded Portuguese ship, and took more than 6,000 prisoners. Portuguese women and children captured.

[102] Prisoners, later exchanged.

[103] As a result of this campaign, Süleyman had Piri Rëis executed.

[104] End of the Ottoman Empire expansion in the Far East.

Fig. 20—Map of the Indian Ocean.

Chapter IV

Portuguese Ancestry Follows—to the 19th & 20th Centuries
Portuguese—"Portyghee" or "Portoogais" or "Pokiki"

Just like Kennedy, the author faces the task of proving that the Melungeons were or were not of Portuguese ancestry. There are many claims, but: *Believing the claim and proving it, however, were two different matters....solving a three-hundred-year-old mystery in order to know my family's ethnic roots...Did we indeed have Portuguese roots? If we didn't, why in the world would our people have come up with such a strange heritage? Why not English? Or Irish? Or even Spanish? Why Portuguese, arguably the least believable of all? No, there had to be a basis for the claim.*[1]

Again, it has been documented that:*...the Melungeons claim Portuguese ancestry.*[2] The name *Portyghee* has been popularized by English speaking people in several forms and may be connected with the Melungeons. *...the earliest encountered Melungeons, regardless of their geographical dispersion, invariably claimed to be "Portyghee." Not "Portuguese" but "Portyghee," the way native Iberians or captured Moors would have pronounced it.*[3] Kennedy also writes:*...some of whom were born in the eighteenth century—claiming a Portuguese ancestry. Why such a consistent clamor over the years to be Portuguese if there was indeed no Portuguese ancestry?*[4] Many Melungeons consistently mention the Portuguese: *Among the other ancestries involved in having melungeon ancestry is the Portuguese. Early Melungeons told those who ran into them that they were "Portygee."*[5] The name is known world wide as written in a November 1927 article by the National Geographic Magazine: *All over the world one finds the Portygee sailor and fishermmen.*[6]

In every English-speaking country, Portuguese immigrants are called *Portyghee,* short for Portuguese, and it is very often misspelled as *Portugee* or *Portugese.* In Hawaii they are called *Pokiki.* Any name that distorts the original one can often be considered derogatory in nature for any group. The same applies to the Portuguese when they are called *Portygee* or similar sounding names.[7] The Portuguese ethnic group is not the only one—every nationality or race has a derogatory version of its name, no matter how intelligent, rich or poor it is.

The way Iberian or captive Moors pronounce Portuguese is *Portoogais* and not *Portyghee,* which is how an English-speaking person pronounces it today in every Portuguese-American community in the United States. On the other hand, Kennedy is correct that if the Portuguese are talking to an English-speaking person, then they will say *Portyghee.* Legend or reality—Bonnie Ball wrote: *One son, Andy Brown, also lived in Ab County* (Virginia)*; he married in 1794 and died in 1801, leaving five children. Three of these were married in Ab County after 1822. Later the entire family went west, and the only trace of them ever found was in a County in Illinois in 1848, where a son was recognized as "prominent citizen and grocer."...There was legend that the Browns were Portuguese but the researchers failed to uncover any factual supporting information.*[8] They may or may not have been Portuguese, but this proves that not all the Melungeons stayed in the mountains, and many of them left in search of better opportunities, as soon as it was safe: *...those who stuck with it* [school]...*they often became successful business or professional people. He cited one in particular who is in charge of the city water department in a large town in Florida with over a hundred workers under his supervision—Dungannon, Virginia resident.*[9] Insofar as the Portuguese are concerned, many are in the grocery business, some of them with supermarket chains, not only in America, but also in Brazil, Venezuela and other countries.

The Furman collection has a number of articles written by McDonald Furman as well as others published at the end of the 19th century and the beginning of the 20th. The New York Evening Post of September 11, 1897: *A Strange Tennessee People... Some of them claim to be Portuguese blood...* The Chicago Record of 1900, also publishes an article with the tittle *They are copper colored-Tennessee People who claim to be descended from Portuguese Colony had trouble in Proving they were not Africans.* The New York Post of 1902, states that: ...*The theory most accepted in regard to all the "Malungeons" however is that they are descended from Portuguese. Some support for the idea is found in the departure of numbers of Portuguese colonists for the Western World in the seventeenth century, Several such ventures are recorded of the year 1664.* Page 145 Chapter IV of the Furman Collection.

A Man Named Portugal—1671

The following story may indicate Portuguese ancestry and others. In September 1671, *Thomas Batts, Thomas Wood, and Robert Fallows...accompanied with Penecute*[10] *a great man of the Apomatack Indians and Jack Weson, formerly a servant to Major General Wood, with five horses...who served as their guide...We hence sent back a horse belonging to Mr. Thomas Wood, which was tired, by a Portugal.*[11] Why the name Portugal? The author knows several Portuguese with the surname Portugal, however he does not know anyone of any other nationality with that surname. Was he employed by the explorers?

Rich, Dark and Portuguese—1745

Sometimes a wrong impression is given that the Melungeons, just because they stayed in the mountains, had never amounted to anything. It is not true, because many left the mountains. Just as many emigrants left their countries and succeeded, so did the Melungeons. The following may be just one example with a possible connection between a Robinson from Robeson County—home of the Lumbees and Melungeons—and another Robinson from Virginia.

A public records Office in London states that on: *Apr. 26, 1745, to John Robinson et al 100,000 acres on Green Briar N.W. & West of Cow Pasture [river] and new foundling (partly surveyed).*[12] In 1942 a 93-year-old neighbor of the Robinson family also stated: *The Robinsons were rich people who lived at Castlewood. They were dark and said to be Portuguese.*[13]

Claim Portuguese Heritage to Be Safe

The usage of the name Portyghee as a possible ancestry is mentioned by Kennedy, but: *And here is yet another, more political reason for the Melungeons to claim a Portuguese heritage: the Portuguese, unlike the Spanish, were at least occasional allies with the English. Drake himself made use of a Portuguese navigator. It would not take a genius to recognize the wisdom of claiming to be "Portyghee" rather than "Spanish" when encountering Englishmen in the Appalachians.[14] Portuguese or not, it would have been the smartest "politically correct" heritage for either group to claim given the circumstances of the times.[15]*

That may be possible, but can a lie survive 400 years? Possibly, or even more. On the other hand, Drake was not sparing Portugal, or the Portuguese either, when he attacked Algarve. There was no love lost between Drake and the Portuguese, and that is why when he attacked Portugal in 1589, he was defeated. As far as the English were concerned, being Portuguese was just the same as being Spanish, both being considered the enemy. They had not forgotten that the Invincible Armada was made up of many of Portuguese ships and soldiers who departed from Lisbon, Portugal, to attack England.

Lungeons Silver Smelters and Brandy—1810

According to Melungeon names on Hawkins County tax list: *By 1810 it was certain that a Colony of dark skinned people inhabited the ridgeland near the Clinch River.[16]* In the same year, simple coincidences may point to clues that could result in the solving of a mystery. For example, genealogist Delores Sanders of Houston, Texas, informed Kennedy of the Melungeons' involvement with silver in Baxter County, Arkansas: *Major Jacob Wolf...Father of Baxter County...established his famous trading post...in 1810...In search of fortune and adventure...Jacob Mooney...of McMinnville, Tennessee...four slaves and four other men.... The four other men who had come with Mooney were men of mystery—referred by old-timers as "Lungeons." They were neither Negro or Indian and in later years Jacob Mooney was ostracized for living with those "foreigners."* [Notice that there was a difference—four men were slaves]. *Could these men have been Melungeons—the mysterious people of the hills of Tennessee who have recently been identified as being Mediterranean possibly of Jewish lineage, and who lived in America prior to Columbus' discovery of the "new world"?...improvised a smelter to convert the silver ore into bars...Mooney...started down river...They carried silver.[17]*

Working with precious metals is a tradition inherited from the Moors, and it is important to note that in 1554, Lisbon had 430 jewelry stores selling gold and silver artifacts, and they must have had plenty of craftsmen to supply the demand.[18] Not only did they have silver, but also:...*lead, furs, wild honey and brandy.* Brandy? Brandy is a southern European alcoholic beverage and: *It seems that Ned, the colored overseer, had discovered that a refreshing brandy could be distilled from the paw-paw fruit.[19]* Hale & Merrit also wrote: *In time they* [Melungeons] *became, almost to a man, distillers of brandy.*[20] It is known that Portuguese immigrants to North America also had their own homemade brandy distilleries for personal consumption. See pages under the heading *Saturday Evening Post 1947* for more on brandy.

The *Guineas* and other Groups—1815

In the northern counties of West Virginia, there existed (1946) a people of mixed race, whose ancestry is shrouded in mystery. They are known locally as *Guineas* although they resent being called that name by outsiders. The area they populated was northern Barbour County and southern Taylor County as well as Garret County. In those counties, the Guinea family names began to appear in 1815. There was the mistaken notion that they were *Guinea Negroes.*

They claimed for many years to descend from one of the Guineas, British, French or Portuguese. The term *Guineas* may stem from the English *pennies,* also called *Guineas,* which circulated in early American history. Also, during the 19th century the term was applied to things or persons of foreign, and uncertain origin. (Regarding terms and names, a reference is made in another chapter, where the name *Turk* was applied in a similar manner.) The Guineas worked in both agriculture and mining.

The family names of the *Guineas* are interestingly close enough to those of the Melungeon population, such as Collins, Kennedy, Male, Miner, Newman, etc. *The Guineas varied in color from white to black, often possessing blue eyes and gray hair, sometimes brother and sisters may range from the blackest Negro to a blonde, blue-eyed, fair skinned person with all the shades in between.* [During the World War II draft] *The Guineas of Taylor County have gone for the most part into the army as whites. Apparently there was some sort of prior agreement among them to register as white.* [21] It was known then that in certain counties, military draft registration was refused based on skin color. Like one other group described as Portuguese, later in this book, which had similar problems during WW II.

In addition to the Guineas, there are also the Wesorts of southern Maryland, and the Croatans of North Carolina who later became the Lumbees. Also, there were the West Hills that were rather heavily into bootlegging. In the early census records, the Guinea family names were registered under the *free colored* or *mulatto* categories. Interestingly, there were:... *one or two cases of Portuguese inter-marriage with the Males,* [there is the theory that] *Guinea origins traces them back to lost followers of Hernando de Soto.*[22]

Pure Portuguese and Melongos—1820

When written records are not available, writers very often rely on oral information. Bonnie Ball provides some interesting details about an interview: *A few years ago Mr. G. M. French Jr. A native of southwestern Virginia who lives in Cheverly, Maryland, sent me his notes from an interview he had with one of the oldest residents of the Dunganon area of Scott County, Virginia, who lived on Copper Ridge. The old timer was also known as "Uncle Washington Osborn." In the interview, he said that the Melungeons began their migration to that part of Scott County,*

Virginia, and neighboring Wise County, about 1820..."Uncle Washington Osborne also said that the first Collinses that came to his community were white. He mention one Melungeon "Uncle Poke Gibson" who came from Letcher County, about 1820, and claimed to be "Portuguese Indian"...Mr. Osborne referred to the Melungeons as "Melongo" which he defined as pure Portuguese..."The Bollings, who are numerous in Scott and Wise County...Another name associated with the "Melungo tribe was Lucas...He thought they were descended from the "Portuguese-Indians"...Another name Mr. Osborne connected to Melungeons was Moore. ...they came...as early as 1807...He claimed Ethan was one-third Portuguese Indian.[23] It is possible that some may have mixed with the Indians. Others simply took advantage of the special treatment and advantages that were being given to the Indians, thus claiming ancestry. Insofar as the word Melongo is concerned, it is definitely Portuguese. The correct spelling is "Melungo."

Education and Wilson County—1827-30

It was believed that, in fact, most Melungeons were illiterate, and that their children did not like to attend school. In the 19th century that was common all over the world, not because the children did not like it, but because there were not enough schools and teachers: *Not only did many Melungeons grow up to be illiterate but their Scotch-Irish neighbors as well.*[24] In fact, if we consider the period of the early 1800's, it is not surprising. Andrew Johnson, the 17th president, could neither read nor write. His wife taught him after their marriage in 1827. He was the only president who never spent a single day in a schoolroom.[25]

Furthering the issue of schooling:*...another problem that has made the Melungeon path a thorny one is that, until desegregation was legally decreed, they have almost consistently, refused to attend any school except those of the white children...authorities often tried to force them to attend Negro schools because of their dark coloring. For the most part, when this happened, the parents either refused to let their children attend school at all, or whole communities would move to towns or counties where they would be accepted without question in the white schools.*[26] Illiteracy may have played a part in the beginning, leaving people speaking broken or Elizabethan English when found by the first explorers. Isolation may be the explanation, but it is likely to be the case of colloquial speech.

Later and according to Dixon Merritt, one of the authors of *A History of Tennessee and Tennesseans*: *...a Colony of Melungeons was imported to Wilson County about 1830 to work for a lumber mill...*[27]

According to personal interviews and local records, a similar situation may have occurred in Gaston, North Carolina when a Portuguese group was hired to work on the Roanoke canal, during the early 1800's.

Also the year 1830 was:*...an active time for Melungeon families acquiring land in the Newman's Ridge area,*[28] according to the Hawkins County Registrar's Office.

Among the early Melungeon settlers: *...were at least ten persons who saw service in the America Revolution,*[29] according to the list which constituted only a fraction of names.

Discriminatory Laws and Free Persons of Color

The history of Tennessee records Miss Dromgoole's question to John A. McKinney, past chairman of the committee of the Constitutional Convention of 1834. Did he know the meaning of "Free Persons of Color?"—to which he replied: *...if it meant anything it meant Melungeon.*[30] In the same year, a discriminatory law was passed that made life much harder for the Melungeons and other groups in the same circumstances. In the following year, North Carolina amended its 1776 Constitution: *No free Negro, free mulatto, or free person of mixed blood descending from Negro ancestors to the 4th generation shall vote for the Senate or the House of Commons.* From this wording a vote was denied to all people considered FPC. At the time, much was written, and according to Jean Patterson Bible, James Aswell was the author of the following passage: *The fact that the Melungeons occupied rich farmlands which God had clearly intended as a reward for Scotch-Irish righteousness and enterprise called the newcomers. They made up their minds to oust the squatters on the Promised Land. Of course the Melungeons could have been picked off one by one from ambush, but that method was far too slow. An added disadvantage lay in the fact that the Melungeons would have been more than their match at bushwhacking. So, with fine Scotch-Irish canniness, the settlers passed the law.*

It stated, this law, that in the State of Tennessee no free persons of color—meaning Melungeon—could vote or hold public office. Furthermore, no free person of color could bear witness in court against a white man. In a word, the Melungeons were made legally helpless in any legal dispute involving a white man. If a white man claimed a Melungeon's property, the victim had no recourse...Suddenly found that the strangers they had allowed to settle among them in overwhelming numbers were, cowbird like, pushing them out. Nevertheless, they fought tooth and nail to hold what they had. It was useless. They were driven up the ridges to land too high and poor to arouse the cupidity of the victors...[31]

Then came the Civil War, which presented an opportunity for the Melungeon revenge, and causing terror to the whites. They served honorably also in the Revolutionary War, some with distinction, and in every war in which the U.S. has been involved.

Kennedy describes this classification imposed on the Melungeons, in the following statements: *They and we were "free persons of color," or simply "FPC"...Neither White, Black, Mulatto, nor Indian,...as numerous writers have so often stated, "nobody at all."* [32] It can be understood as applicable to his own family:

Melungeons into any of the then four available legal categories (White, Indian, Negro, or Mulatto), the Scotch-Irish cleverly deployed a new term: "free persons of color," and used it to strip the Melungeons of their lands, their right to be represented in court, their right to vote, and their right to public education. One sweep of the judicial pen, the simple arbitrary assignment of the letters "FPC" (or "FC" to which it was sometimes shortened) alongside one's name in the federal census. [33] The white settlers in those days would take advantage of minorities, perhaps something still alive in current America: *When the Melungeons countered that they were Portyghee, and thus fellow Europeans who should be immune to such a law...* "*FPC*" *soon gave way to* "*Mulatto*" *as census takers lost patience with those Melungeons seeking to hold on to their lands. On several of the old census records one can see the term* "*Port.*" *crossed through and* "*mulatto*" *written in its stead. In any event, census takers eventually settled in on the terms* "*FPC,*" "*FC,*" *or* "*mulatto*" *to describe any person of darker complexion, regardless of their ethnic origin.* [34]

We should not discount the fact that by the 18th and 19th centuries, miscegenation occurred between free Blacks or slaves and Indians as well as other races, thereby producing the Mulatto and Mestizo. It is possible that some groups may be darker than others with the natural gravitation towards the Blacks, Indians or other minority. However the Melungeons claim that they were:*... never slaves, and until 1834 enjoyed all the rights of citizenship...* [35] Just like other groups, the Melungeons tried to maintain social boundaries between themselves and the blacks, due to discriminatory practices, according to Professor Paredes, in the case of the Creeks of Alabama. [36] Dromgoole in a very poetic manner adds: "*Unenviable as is the condition of the slave, unlovely as slavery in all its aspects, bitter as is the draught the slave is doomed to drink, nevertheless, his condition is better than that of the 'free man of color' in the midst of a community of white men with whom he has no interest, no fellow-feeling and no equality.*" [37]

Still, the Melungeons were able to endure all that and survive.

The Mulatto Class, Two Races and the National Census—1850

Kennedy describes the census taker: *... "white," which meant only "pure" northern Europeans, or "black," which meant Blacks, Mulattos, Indians, Jews, Arabs, Asians, and so forth, or anyone with as much as one-sixteenth so-called "nonwhite" blood. Intended to make the Appalachian census taker's task a simpler one.* [38] *From that point onward, the Melungeons became officially a mixture of White, Indian, and Black, or in the reputed words of one nineteenth century Tennessee senator, a "Portuguese nigger."* [39]

While research was being done on the Melungeons, a reporter of a small southeast town newspaper was interviewed, and, in discussing discrimination, he mentioned that it is still very much alive, but in a subtle manner. In another instance, while in Florida, a typical looking Scotsman was asked if he knew what a Melungeon was. His answer: *Blue eyed nigger.* This was in 1995.

One of the reasons that may have caused the eventual disintegration of the Melungeon group as Portuguese—if they were, in fact, Portuguese—was, and still is, the easy acceptance of other peoples and races by the Portuguese. Mrs. Bible adds: *From 1850 on, national census includes state of birth...None of the Melungeons listed was born in Tennessee before 1800...* [That meant the Melungeon families were already established in North Carolina and Virginia in the 1700's before they were pushed out by discriminatory laws]...*No one listed was born in*

Tennessee before 1799...One Gipson wife, 70 years of age, was born in South Carolina—1729.[40] That may also prove that the Melungeons came to the mountains much later and originated on the East Coast.

John Netherland of Tennessee—1859

The Melungeons also had friends in high places: *Col. John Netherland of Hawkins County, Tennessee...1859...restored the right of citizenship for the Melungeons...and their gratitude was manifested towards him in every way as long as he lived.*[41] His daughter Eliza N. Heiskell wrote an affectionate article about the Melungeons later in 1914. The contents were totally different from the unfair and generalized description by Will Allen Dromgoole in 1891.

Melungeons from Portugal and Judge Shepherd in 1872

This story is so fascinating that it merits full reproduction from Jean Patterson Bible's book. It certainly would make a first-class story for a Hollywood movie. It tells how a young attorney, Lewis Shepherd, won a case based on the theory that the Melungeons were of Carthaginian or Phoenician origin, having emigrated from Portugal. (See Appendix "F" for the full story.) Portuguese, Phoenicians and Carthaginians are definitely people with common ancestors.

Coincidence of Typical Portuguese Names and Roots—1888

Names are difficult to prove ancestry, but as Bonnie Ball tells us in her book:... *in 1888...two of their children, Antonio and Dean, were later listed as "white"...in 1902, Ulysses and Helena Jones—he Indian and black— she Indian and white were both given a marriage license as white...*[42] *She* [Dromgoole] *added that a Portuguese named Denham arrived "from somewhere" and married another Collins daughter...*[Dromgoole also lists] *...common surnames as Gorven, Gibbens, Bragans or Brogan...*[among the Melungeons] [43] The name Bragans is a derivative of Braganza or Bragança, to be exact, the same as the Portuguese royal family; and Antonio and Helena are very common first names, but then the same happens with other Latin nations, except that the Portuguese write Helena with an H, as opposed to the Spanish *Elena*.

Swan Burnett—Note on the Melungeons in 1889—Portuguese and Proud

Swan Burnett, a medical doctor in Washington, D.C., born in 1847, wrote that he heard the name *Melungeon* as a child, which had: *...a ponderous and inhuman sound as to associate them...with giants and ogres...They resented the appellation Melungeon, given to them by common consent by the whites, and proudly called themselves Portuguese.*[44] The phrase *proud and Portuguese* was also mentioned in an article published in the *Boston Traveler* on June 13, 1889: *They have not recently* *married with Negroes or Indians...the "more thoughtful" people there was a "disposition" to give credence to the Melungeons' claim that they were a distinct race. A few inclined toward the Portuguese theory...*[45] One of the reasons that they may not have married Negroes or Indians was because they had plenty of women within their group.

The Portuguese, scattered all over the world since the 1500's, have intermarried with other races. They did not have Portuguese women with them, and were encouraged to marry the local natives in order to establish a better Portuguese hold. This point may also serve as an indication that the Melungeons arrived here with their wives, and children of perhaps mixed races. Further discussion on the topic appears later in this book.

It is likely that since the 1800's, or even prior to that date, Melungeons have mixed with Blacks. It is not uncommon to see a person with a black appearance claiming Melungeon ancestry.

It is reasonable to accept why the Melungeons did not want to be classified as Blacks; probably they were not, and if they already had Black ancestry, they had nothing to gain. Just like the Creeks of Alabama, they did whatever they could to distance themselves from the Blacks, so as not to be identified with a minority that was being discriminated against.

Texas County, Missouri—Court awards Portuguese ancestry in 1889

Laura Spencer was kind to provide us the following story by email: *James Henderson Hall, born abt 1825 in Bedford County, Tennessee. He married Sarah D (believe middle name to be Dora) Collier in Pottersville, Howell County, Missouri on Aug. 15, 1855. Children born to this union were William Perry Hall born June 22, 1855, Nancy A Hall born July 1859, John Thomas Hall born Dec 1, 1867, Grant Hall born ????, James Henderson "Jim" Hall born Aug 21, 1869. Family says that Henderson was Chickamaugua Cherokee, but when the family was enumerated as "colored" on a census, Henderson took the state to court and claimed "Portuguese" heritage in 1889. The case was a hot topic around Howell County and a change of venue was granted. He produced affidavits from several older members of the Hall tribe, all stating they were Portuguese. He did win his case, and the Hall children were allowed to attend school again.*

Will Allen Dromgoole's *Boston Arena* articles in 1891

Judging from her articles, it appears that Dromgoole—a novelist and poet—knew little of life outside the big cities. Her description of people living in the mountains in 1890 does not take into account all the amenities that she took for granted. Dromgoole was originally from Nashville and had worked in New York when she came to Sneedville to work on her articles. Sixty years later, (1950) Edward T. Price wrote: *...The County* [Hancock] *has no telephone exchange, but* *one or two long-distance lines have been recently installed...Thus the inaccessibility of this area.*[46] What would Miss Dromgoole have said if she had visited them in 1950? Would she have blamed the Melungeons for the lack of progress in the county? They were, after all, a minority. On the positive side, her report may have brought to the public's attention one of the very few documents that describe the life of the Melungeons in the 1890's, as well as their possible beginnings.

Her comments were derogatory, and were meant for headlines in the *Boston Arena*. She did not take into consideration that life was not so kind to the Melungeons. In her article, Miss Dromgoole wrote: *"The Malungeon Tree..."* adding to the Portuguese claim of ancestry: *The tree at last began to put forth branches, or rather...English (white), Portuguese, and African ...by claiming to have married Portuguese, there really being a Portuguese branch among the tribes. ...The Portuguese branch was for a long time a riddle...It has at last been...traced to one Denham, a Portuguese who married a Collins woman.*[47]

The name Denham as written is not Portuguese; however it may derive from *Dinho* a short form of *Godinho*. The combination of the letters **"nh"** is very common in Portuguese. It produces the same sound as the English word *onions*.

What is rather strange in her articles is that Dromgoole mentions the Portuguese quite often, and does not establish a parallel with the Portuguese community in New England, which by 1890 was quite noticeable, especially in the fishing industry. By that time also, the first Cape Verdeans, black Portuguese, employed by the whaling industry had arrived, a factor which may have caused the Melungeons to start dropping their Portuguese designation.

Small, Shapely Hands and Feet

She [Dromgoole] *calls the hands of the Melungeon women "shapely" and adds that their feet were likewise, despite the fact they often travel barefoot over rough mountain paths.*[48] Dromgoole also mentions: *They follow the body to the grave, sometimes for miles, afoot, in single file.*[49] As for walking single file to the cemetery, that was true in Portugal quite some years ago. Most of the time it was because the path was so narrow that only one person at a time could follow the path without getting scratched by the thorny briars.

Going Barefoot, Single File, to the Cemetery

Jean Patterson Bible quoted a letter by Mr. Grohse: *I have seen some women go barefooted with a good pair of shoes hanging over their shoulders...walking single file all the way to the cemetery.*[50] During the early 1940's in Portugal it was common to see women in the countryside doing exactly that, mostly on Sundays, which was quite natural within the Portuguese culture.[51] During the week, they would go barefoot, but with their legs covered from the ankles to the knees by a wool woven sleeve. This protected them from both the thorns of the briars and from the cold.

The reason they went barefoot most of the time was to divert irrigation water through small channels in the fields using hoes and their feet to better distribute the water. Being barefoot all week, they had a hard time wearing shoes on Sunday, as they felt very uncomfortable. Consequently, they just took them off, and hung them around their necks or over their shoulders. As a custom, the Melungeons follow:... *the casket to the cemetery and observe a year's mourning.*[52] It is still a custom in some villages in Portugal to do exactly that. Another aspect associated with their dead is the fact the Melungeons never cremated the body. They always buried it. Cremation is not readily accepted in Portugal.

Cemeteries, Little Houses over the Graves

Miss Dromgoole also mentioned a strange custom when she visited their cemetery: *...they build a kind of floorless house above each separate grave...The graveyard presents the appearance of a diminutive town, or settlement, and is kept with great nicety and care.*[53]

Fig. 21—Old Cemetery in New Orleans

The present day cemeteries in Portugal still show some graves with a cupola above, mostly in marble as a Portuguese tradition with very elaborate mausoleums. Kennedy's comments are worth quoting:

Fig. 22—Melungeon Cemetery in Sneedville (1996 Photo by the author)

One can only imagine the Scot-Irish as they encountered these improbably dark-skinned mountaineers speaking broken English, claiming a Mediterranean heritage, placing southern European cupolas over the graves of their dead, sporting English surnames, practicing Christianity...[54] *Melungeon burial customs also seem to have a remarkable fascination... Today there are few remaining... paint their house or*

Fig. 23—Cemetery in Portugal showing similar cupolas or little houses

Fig. 24—A funeral in the countryside of Portugal in the early 1960's

their grave shelter, the latter always took precedence.[55] [See pictures on this page]
...and their cemeteries look like miniature villages.[56] This is certainly a tradition with the Portuguese, and sometimes the little house turns into a marble mausoleum.

That is an equally common practice in the South Mediterranean region. Also interesting is the fact that in New Orleans, where the water level is high, a similar type of grave is used.

Therefore, the logical reason for burying the cadavers above ground is to protect them from water or to prevent them from coming out of the ground under water pressure.

Melungeon graves sometimes have small wooden houses built over them, which has reminded some observers of a similar trait among Eskimo members of the Russian Orthodox Church.[57]

This was mentioned by Louise Davis in 1963 and again by Saundra Keyes Ivey in her dissertation of 1976. Why look for the Russian Orthodox Church or the Eskimos? Such an exotic comparison when there are closer comparisons much nearer to home. One needs only to visit a New Orleans cemetery.

Fig. 25—For Life and Death

In the Minho northern province of Portugal there are still little houses called <u>Espigueiros or Caixão</u> in Portuguese. They are built of stone with a door and two crosses, and sit on pillars above ground to protect the contents from rodents.

Just as in life, the same shape and type of construction is used in death.

The Christian Cross as a Religious Symbol, and Indian Religion

Bonnie Ball writes about Dromgoole's experience with the Melungeons: *She described many facets of Melungeon life, some of which she thought might have indicated a Latin origin...was puzzled by an unusual veneration for the Christian cross in view of the fact that most other people who lived in the area, if religious at all, were more inclined toward the "shouting," emotional type of Protestantism, seldom using the cross as a symbol in their services.*[58] The veneration of the cross is also true with the Portuguese. In the small villages in Portugal during the early 1940's, it was common to see the cross in every pathway at a crossroads—and some still do—in a niche, or sometimes with a religious icon. Parents, as a matter of course, would get some kind of a cross made out of wood—or gold if they could afford it—and put them around the necks of their children to protect them from evil. *The Melungeons were never adherents of the Indian religion and rites, but adhered to the Christian religion. The cross was ever held by them* [Melungeons] *to be a sacred symbol.*[59] This fact would rule out Muslim or Jewish ancestry, however, they may already have been Christianized prior to coming to America. If so, they would have been free to practice whatever faith they had. We could also speculate that only Christian groups were found, which does not preclude the presence of Jewish, Muslim or Hindu groups.

History of Tennessee and the Tennesseans—1912

Mrs. Eliza N. Eiskell of Memphis wrote in an article published in the Arkansas Gazette: *...They have had no poet or seer to preserve their history...*[60] This was very unfortunate, but when fighting to survive, keeping track of your ancestry is not necessarily the first priority.

The following description was furnished in 1912 by Col. W. A. Henderson, president of the Tennessee Historical Society, to be included in the history of Tennessee and Tennesseans as a description of the Melungeons in the 19th century: *The Melungeons are a peculiar people living in the mountains of east Tennessee, western North Carolina, southwest Virginia and eastern Kentucky...They have swarthy complexion, straight black hair, black or gray eyes...and are not tall but heavy set...*[61] The description certainly matches a large body of the Portuguese population. When the Melungeons faced hard times and discrimination, and their name was derogatory, their only key to survival was the family, and joining others with similar problems: *...they wrote to a prominent citizen of upper East Tennessee, asking for information on the Melungeons. The answer to their letter came promptly with the statement that "We have no such a race. Our citizens are civilized people and believe in earning their living by the sweat of their brow, and are far superior to those who try to disgrace them by placing the fictitious name of 'Melungeon' upon them."* [62] Although that was back in the 19th century, this is still happening in this century.

The *Handbook of American Indians* speaking of the Croatan Indians: *Across the South Carolina are found a people evidently of similar origin, designated "Redbones." In portions of North Carolina and East Tennessee are found the so-called Melungeons or "Portuguese," apparently an offshoot of the Croatan proper, and in Delaware are found the "Moors."* [63]

This just reinforces the fact that the Melungeons were widespread, with the possible conclusion that some went west to the mountains and others stayed closer to the East Coast. As for the Moors, they form a part of the Portuguese ancestry. Later in this book, the author will discuss his experiences as a stranger trying to research the Melungeons. There are still many people, government officials, who do not want to talk about or cooperate with the research. Also, the descendants of the Melungeon people avoid interviews or get very nervous.

School, Only With the Blacks, and Migration to a Better Life

Bonnie Ball on schools: *After the Civil War the Wins* [Melungeon related group] *were given a chance to attend the schools for blacks, but not for whites.* [64]

The Portuguese are generally not known as a racist people. As a minority, they surely would not have survived around the world if they were.

In a racist and segregated society, if they were Portuguese, why should their children be forced to attend the black schools? They were a little darker, and were refused schooling in white schools then, and also in this century, as will be described later in this book. Bonnie Ball states that: *The Melungeons...migrated...to southeastern Kentucky and Blountstown, Florida, just West of Tallahassee. It is also possible that some went westward to the Ozarks. Their numbers are estimated to be between five and ten thousand, and they have a high birth rate.* [65]

That is the reason for them to come to this continent in the first place. They did migrate, and most of them had success. Their success helped to build this great country. Should the spirit of adventure, ambition and a desire for a better life disappear, we would be sensing the eve of destruction.

Ability to Survive and Make a Living on Water

Means of livelihood: *In earlier years riverboat carriage...Physique:...Their stoic endurance of out-of-doors life is notable...History:...Some believe they are derived from the Croatans; others say they come from the Portuguese...*

They appeared in Tennessee after the American Revolution. [66] *...There are also indications that some of these qualities* [The unusual endurance to a hardy, outdoor existence] *may have come from Portuguese and Moorish ancestors...* [67]

Portugal does not have many natural resources; the landscape is mountainous and not very fertile, and the plains of the South rely on rain, which is very irregular. The water was always a provider, and since remote times they looked to the sea. The riverboat carriage was just another way for their subsistence. As for endurance, the Portuguese immigrants had to endure situations in the early 1950's that even today the poorest do not have to endure.

A true story has been told about Portuguese lumberjacks working in the cold Canadian north, who stayed up all night around a fire to keep warm. The ones who went to sleep found themselves with frostbite in their fingers, toes and noses and eventually lost them. At one time, one of them thought something was biting his ear, and slapped it with his hand. Part of the ear lobe fell to ground.

As for the women, they took care of the house and children, cooked the meals, and also worked the fields. Some still do. This is slowly disappearing, but if one visits the small villages of Portugal's interior, one will find a semi-primitive but healthy lifestyle still existing, and the women play a big part in it.

Admiral David Farragut,
a Possible Melungeon

*Fig. 26—George Farragut,
father of David Farragut*

Eliza Heiskell, the daughter of John Letherland, also wrote about the Melungeons: *Rankin's Ferry at Chattanooga, Tennessee, was once operated by a family of Melungeons, and that Admiral Farragut, of naval fame during the Civil War, was a Melungeon...The Portuguese tradition seems to persist in connection with the Melungeons much more stronger than even that of the Lost Colony.*[68]

Like the Portuguese, the Melungeons seem to find a way of making a living on or near the water. Worthy of note is the fact that Admiral David Glasgow Farragut was born near the Holston River, 15 miles southwest of Knoxville, Tennessee.[69] This was a traditional Melungeon area. This is again repeated by Jean Patterson Bible, who maintains that Admiral Farragut was possibly of a Portuguese strain: *It is said on good authority that the brave Admiral Farragut was a descendant of a Portuguese of that name who married a poor North Carolina girl.*[70] If he is not a Portuguese descendant, he is not far from it. Aragon was an ally of Portugal against Castille, and Portugal's army fought side by side with Aragon against the Moors. Farragut's biography states that his father was a swarthy man named George Anthony Magen Farragut, born on the island of Minorca of fighting blood. Farragut was directly descended from Don Pedro Farragut, who assisted James I of Aragon in driving the Moors from the Balearic Islands in the 13th century.[71]

Fig. 27—Lieutenant David Glasgow Farragut, U.S. Navy ,from the portrait by William Swain in the Smithsonian Institution, Washington, DC.

Racially Distinct—1934

As for being distinct, Bonnie Ball states in a newspaper article: *Roanoke News, February 25, 1934, Dr. Goodridge Wilson wrote the following: "They are socially and racially distinct from the blacks and white around them, and are not classified as Indians. ...the Melungeons and their ancestors lived since 'time immemorial' [in clusters of crude cabins]...They, themselves, disliked the term 'Melungeon.' The Newman's Ridge contingent prefer to be called 'Portuguese,' claiming descent from a band of Portuguese immigrants who, they say settled Newman's Ridge about the time of the Revolution..."* [72]

One major difference that makes the Portuguese racially distinct from others is that our sea border on the Atlantic was much easier to invade from Northern Europe. The Northwest African people, when going away from the Mediterranean, would also find the Portuguese southern and western coasts easy to reach. The other difference is the fact that while the Portuguese chose Lisbon as their capital, being by the sea on a magnificent harbor of the Tagus River, and able to receive very large vessels, the Spaniards chose Madrid as their capital, much against the Castilians that still today consider Burgos the rightful capital of Spain. Today this may not be important, but in the 15th and 16th centuries, the ocean was the gateway to the world, and the Portuguese had such a gateway in Lisbon. As for being in North America before the American Revolution, it is correct, but may be much earlier, and the Melungeons served in the army, thus taking an active part in it.

In Chapter V the reader will discover more about the Portuguese and their ancestry.

Shy and Mysterious People—1937

The persistent Portuguese ancestry tradition is noted in 1937 by James Aswell in the *Nashville Banner*, when he writes about the East Tennessee mountaineers: *When the first Scotch-Irish settlers from Virginia and North Carolina came pushing over the mountains ...they found ...settlements of shy, mysterious people. They were not Indians... When asked who they were and whence they came, they said they were Portuguese.* [73]

The Portuguese people of today may not be mysterious, but they are shy on the average, when put into an unfamiliar and hostile environment.

The Melungeons may have mixed with the Indians, according to extensive studies made.

Childbirth a Minor Event—1940

The Melungeon women's endurance is described thusly: *As a rule childbirth was a minor event with Melungeon women. The day that Marindy discovered she was in labor, she rushed outside and called a neighbor who in turn called my mother...with neither a physician nor mid-wife available, the child was borne before my mother reached the shack....By the time Marindy's husband arrived from work that day, Marindy and her baby were sleeping comfortably....The young mother, likely as not, resumed her household chores the following morning.*[74]
This probably happened in the 1940's. One story has been told of a woman in a small Portuguese village giving birth all alone while working out in the fields, and bringing her baby home, carrying the baby on one arm and the sickle hanging from the shoulder. Another tale is of an employee woman in old Alentejo giving birth in the fields while engaged in manual weeding and harvest work. After a while, she resumed work, leaving the baby in some tree shadow, afraid of being fired. Another story happened in Rio de Janeiro, Brazil in the early 1950's, and was common with Portuguese women. Right after giving birth, only a couple of days later, the mother came home. She not only did her normal house chores, cooked the meals, bought the groceries—without any means of transportation—and took care of the baby, but she also worked as a seamstress to supplement her husband's income. Water was a problem in Rio de Janeiro, and very often the mother had to carry it in pails, not only for household consumption, but also to wash the baby's diapers. This is what it takes to survive, with the Portuguese or the Melungeons, and they knew how to do it.

Eating Habits

The culture of a people is often identified by their food, as written by Bonnie Ball: *...while the men were logging or clearing new ground, the women and children were often seen gathering a fuzzy green plant that grew along clear streams. They called it "bear's lettuce", and ate it raw with salt. They also picked pails full of wild "sallet" (greens). This consisted of poke, narrow dock* [buckwheat family], *crow's foot, cress, lamb's quarter, and many other plants that were known to be edible. They cooked them with a piece of salt bacon, and ate them with a hard corn pone usually baked in a Dutch oven in the open fireplace, or in a small step stove. Corn meal mush was one of their favorite cold weather foods....watched Jassie preparing their evening meal. This consisted of stirring mush in a big black metal pot, using a wooden spade.*[75] In Portuguese villages, women customarily gather various greens from their gardens. Also they may go to a nearby creek and collect greens that grow near the water for the family meal. It is also interesting to note the usage of a black pot and wooden spade by the author's own grandmother.
The wooden spade had another purpose, and that was to discipline the less behaved children by a not so gentle strike on their behind. Finally, the corn meal or stirring mush—*papas de milho* in Portuguese—certainly was one of the children's favorites, with a spoonful of sugar in the center of the plate, which would melt like caramel.

Garlic and Spicy

Another example of a food connection: *It is strong and hot. This sort of ties them to the Latin people, who are fond of onions, garlic, and red peppers.*[76]

The Portuguese are fond of spices. They discovered the sea-route to India just to get them. The Azoreans are especially fond of spicy foods, and this may be a possible connection between the Melungeon and the Portuguese. These Atlantic islands played an important role during the age of discoveries, to include later navigation to and from the Americas. Of course the Portuguese Azoreans are not the only ones that appreciate spicy foods.

Portuguese Ancestry and Record Keeping

Jean Patterson Bible mentions in her book an interview with an important citizen who has lived for many years in Hancock County and has known Melungeons all her life. She shares the following:

I have reached the conclusion that, if they once knew where they came from, after the discrimination practices started, they just didn't talk about it, didn't use the word, Melungeon;...thus did not pass the information on to their offspring...It is only when one's belly is full and the chill is turned away that one can turn to thoughts of other things...Hence, in my opinion, no one traced ancestry or kept records.[77] This has not changed today in many nations of the world, where starvation and disease are a daily occurrence.

First, people must survive in a society where they have to compete for jobs. Next is an education for their children, and later for themselves, as well as other less important matters such as keeping genealogical records.

Who cares about ancestry, if one is hungry, cold and sick? Record keeping in most of Europe did not start until the 15th or 16th century, when the churches were given the task of recording all births and deaths in a book. The royalty, nobility and wealthy could do it. They had their own chapels and priests that did all the writing and record keeping. The common people were not even allowed to learn how to read and write, unless one was a monk, a priest or a seminarian.

Bonnie Ball ends her book with the following conclusion related to the Melungeon ancestry: *It is reasonable almost beyond doubt that the Melungeons had English ancestry...According to historians, the Croatans had some previous white mixture, which would likely have been Spanish or Portuguese...Blue Ridge and Piedmont tribes...They could have been extensions of the Maryland and Delaware groups, who, in some instances, also claim Portuguese ancestry. Is there a Portuguese ancestry? As I see it, Portuguese ancestry is likely; all the older Melungeons have claimed it. Nevertheless, the Portuguese theory has been too long-standing and consistent to ignore.*[78]

Mildred Haun tells of a Melungeon who lived in a smoke house near her grandmother's Hamblen County farm in 1942 and: *...claimed they* [the Melungeons] *were in this country before any other race.*[79]

Discrimination well into the 20th Century—1912-46
Most Present-day Portuguese have Negro Characteristics?

Between 1912 and 1946, Dr. Walker Ashley Plecker was Virginia's Registrar of vital statistics, and very instrumental in creating a two-class people—White and Black. The following did happen not long ago: *Dr. Walker Ashley ("W. A.") Plecker, as late as 20 August 1942 in a letter from the state of Virginia's medical registrar, to the Tennessee state librarian and archivist, Mrs. John Trotwood Moore...Plecker was upholding Virginia's anti-miscegenation laws which prohibited marriages between Melungeons and "whites."...Melungeons who...are now causing trouble in Virginia by their claims of Indian descent, with the privilege of intermarrying into the white race...In that class we include the Melungeons of Tennessee.*[80] Just recently, Kennedy made available a copy of a letter dated August 5, 1930, addressed to Mr. J. P. Kelly in Virginia. The contents show clearly Plecker's problem in accepting the Melungeons.[81]

Shirley McLeRoy described Dr. Plecker as the most outspoken proponent of the anti-miscegenation law of 1942. He became a one-man campaign: *Plecker undertook to erase the state's contemporary Indian heritage, which he felt had been so substantially diluted with negro blood that few Indians still existed...those of Indian blood were described officially as free negros or free coloreds.*[82]

Mrs. John Trotwood Moore, Virginia state librarian and archivist, wrote a letter to Dr. W. A. Plecker that refers to early settlers in South Carolina who migrated from Portugal and later moved to Tennessee about the time of the Revolutionary War.[83] The Virginia doctor in his answer, went so far as to compare the physical appearance of the Portuguese to the African Blacks. He wrote that: *It is a historical fact, well known to those who have investigated, that at one time there were many African slaves in Portugal.* [Here's what Dr. Plecker wrote about Portugal:] *Today there are no true negroes there but their blood shows in the color and racial characteristics of a large part of the Portuguese population of the present day. That mixture, even if it could be shown, would be far from constituting these people white.*[84] According to Plecker therefore, being of Portuguese heritage was meaningless because the Portuguese population had the color and racial characteristics of the Negro.[85]

Dr. Plecker most likely has never been to Portugal and his knowledge of the Portuguese people was obviously quite limited. It is possible that the Portuguese have Negroid blood. After all, they interacted much with Africans. Many Portuguese who went to the previous Portuguese-African colonies married black women, and some of their offspring came to Portugal. Still, that did not alter the appearance of the majority of the Portuguese population.

Saturday Evening Post—1947

In William L. Worden's article titled "Sons of the Legend" in the October 18, 1947 *Saturday Evening Post*, there are many photographs of the Melungeon people of that time. The writer spells Melungeon with an **a**, as *Malungeon*, the same as written by Dromgoole at the end of the 19th century. He also notes Dromgoole's remarks. He describes them as:... *thin-lipped, rather like Indians, but not quite like them...they have some Latin characteristics...the daughters of these people are very often lovely, soft and feminine, in striking contrast to the bony appearance of most mountain women.*[86] The Melungeons were already settled when:... *the first yankee and Scotch-Irish mountain men drifted down the Clinch River...they found in the rich farmland of the Clinch Valley a strange people already settled. They were dark, tall, not exactly like Indians, certainly not at all like the escaped Negroes...There are in Rogersville a few tall, olive skinned people...the young women often remarkably beautiful.*[87]

Worden also quotes Dromgoole as describing a common factor with the Portuguese: ...*the Malungeons commonly made and drank brandy rather than whisky.*[88] Worden challenges several of Dromgoole's theories, and declarations.

The Portuguese in general appreciate brandy, or what they call *água ardente* (fire water). Most commonly they make it out of grapes, as well as any fruits, such as plums, figs, berries, etc. Some Portuguese immigrants to Canada made brandy in their basements, and had their own homemade distilleries. The brandy was a by-product of their annual wine-making routine, which was and still is illegal. Presently they still do it every year during the fall. After making wine in their cellars at home, they proceed with making brandy from *grape-bagasse,* the pulp left over from the wine-making process. Bonnie Ball also writes: *In time they became, almost to a man, distillers of brandy.*[89] Is this a coincidence?

Fig. 28—Modern homemade brandy distillery

Edward T. Price—1950

Dr. Price presented a paper on racially mixed blood groups. One of them is the Carmel Indians, perhaps the only ones found in Ohio. Their surnames and lifestyle characteristics are similar to the Melungeons': *Few, if any, really look like Indians...The country people are quick to point out their differences in language.*[90] He considers the presence of both Indian and Negro, and draws a connection between this group and the Melungeons of Eastern Tennessee.[91]

The writer discounts the *persistent rumor* of Portuguese descent and name derivation, but does not present a plausible explanation for what he calls a rumor and the resemblance of many Portuguese names. Dr. Price also says that the word *Melunge,* deriving from the French *mélange:* ...*seems equally unlikely.*[92]

Precious Metal Craftsman and Claim to Be Portuguese—1963

Louise Davis wrote an article in the *Nashville Tennessean*, quoting the late Mildred Haun:... *as saying that she had always heard of Melungeon skill with gold and silver...and accepted as a fact, that they were especially good at making jewelry from gold, and they were the best silver-bullet makers when there were witches in the country.*[93]

It is still an accepted fact that the Portuguese are very skilled with jewelry. Anyone visiting downtown Lisbon will see many jewelry stores with elaborate jewelry. In fact, the two most famous streets in Lisbon are called *Rua do Ouro* (Gold Street) and *Rua da Prata* (Silver Street).

Their skill is also very visible in a popular souvenir made out of gold wire filigree in the form of a 15th century Portuguese caravel. This is one of the most popular souvenirs sold in Portugal. No one knows its beginnings for certain.

They are available in pure gold, but most are just plated. This type of work, and other jewelry craftsmanship, is common in Portugal today, but long ago was only used by the aristocracy. Kennedy adds a very interesting and more recent finding related to precious metals:...*the colonists at Santa Elena included metallurgists and others whose primary task was to reconnoiter for precious metals, and to refine and work them once found. The Moors of Spain, Portugal, and North Africa were known for their metalworking, having in fact taught the art to the Iberians in the first place. The Melungeons have long been known for their silver-smelting abilities, as well as metalworking in general.*[94]

The Jews were skilled in this art, and Gil Vicente (ca.1465-1536), a noted Portuguese lyric poet, was also a famous goldsmith.

Pollitzer and Brown—1969

The September 1969 issue of *Human Biology* published a study done by the Department of Anatomy and Anthropology at the University of North Carolina at Chapel Hill. While the study is not conclusive as to the ancestry of the Melungeon people, it does not rule it out either. This survey of demography and genetics was conducted by Drs. William S. Pollitzer and William H. Brown.

The article starts out by describing what was known about the Melungeons at that time. It cites Dr. Price's research in 1950, and

Fig. 29—Portuguese 16th century Caravel crafted in solid gold filigree

affirms that the older people living in Hancock County in 1850 were born chiefly in North Carolina and Virginia.

The description of the Melungeon population is:... *moderately tall...within the Caucasoid range...The general closer similarity of the Melungeons...to the White population is evident.* [a comparative gene frequencies table shows that]...*When English and Portuguese frequencies are used, along with Negro and Indian, the methods agree that Portuguese are the more likely of the two European ancestors and contributed the majority of the genes. The data are well fitted by a 90% Portuguese component, with slight Negro and Indian admixture; they are also fitted by a 94% Portuguese and 6% Indian.*[95]

However, the survey also cautions that due to the similarity in English and Portuguese gene frequencies, no clear resolution is possible as to certain contribution of one or the other: *But all methods do agree that a European element predominates.*[96] The English never recognized them as their own, and if this study points to one or the other, which one is the other?

Portuguese from Nazaré, a Village in Portugal—1970

While in the process of gathering information for her book, Jean Patterson Bible interviewed a president of a local bank. In a photo comparison between the peoples of Tangier, Morocco, and Nazaré, Portugal, the people of Nazaré were chosen as the ones that most resembled the Melungeons: *Back in Sneedville, seated at her desk in the Citizen's Bank...gray-haired and blue eyed Miss Martha Collins, its 74 year old President, said thoughtfully, "Yes, some of my ancestors were Melungeons. We don't know but we think possibly they were descended from Portuguese or*

Fig. 30—On the left Maria Antonia Sousa, born in Nazaré, Portugal. Photo courtesy of Antonio Sousa. and on the right Fig. 31—Nancy Kennedy, Melungeon descendant. Photo courtesy of Dr. N. Brent Kennedy's mother. Note the similarity of the faces, forehead, eyes and nose in these photos.

Spanish from Navarre. Some months later at my home, we looked at slides made in Nazaré, a Portuguese fishing village, and others of scenes and people in Tangier, Morocco. Miss Martha studied the pictures carefully. Then, with typical banker's caution, she said slowly, "They might be, but I just don't know. If anything, the Portuguese look more like the Melungeons I've always known all my life than the people in Tangier." [97]

The people of Nazaré are wed to the sea; this is the reason they claim descent from the Phoenician mariners.[98] A Portuguese government official accepts the possibility of Portuguese ancestry:....*in the words of Press Officer Luis de Sousa at the Portuguese Embassy in Washington, is "quite credible" and "quite convincing."*[99] *...the old Melungeon photos. They would look at home on the wall of working-class household in Beira, the central region of Portugal.*[100]

Tradition Dies Hard

This story may or may not have anything to do with the Portuguese, but it is very tragic and at the same time interesting. It was narrated by Mildred Haun in her book *The Hawk's Done Gone*. The story was told by a grandmother acting as midwife to her daughter, who died in childbirth. In her dying breath she asked her mother to raise her daughter as if she were parentless. Granny raised the illegitimate granddaughter. Her name was Cordia Owens, born June 1, 1902. She was never told that her father was a Melungeon. Cordia was kept mostly around the house and Granny never let her go anywhere. One day, she ran away and got married to a white man. The young couple settled down on a farm. One winter, a Melungeon man stayed over at their farm as a helper. Cordia became pregnant, and when the child was born, Granny's worst fears had been realized—it was Melungeon colored.

Fig. 32—Zulmira Pina of Portugal

Fig. 33—Libby's Mother, a Melungeon

The jealous husband took one look and yelled: *"That is why the devil wanted to stay here!"* thinking that the wife had betrayed him with the Melungeon helper. In a fit of anger, he beat the weakened young wife to death with a stick of wood. Later, as she lay in the makeshift coffin, he seized the whimpering baby, crammed it into the coffin alive with the dead mother and nailed down the lid.[101]

The Book: My Melungeon Heritage and more Traditions

Fig. 34— Martha Collins, a Melungeon descendant. Ex-president of the Sneedville Citizen's Bank Photo of Jean P. Bible

Ruth Johnson has recently written a book which mentions:...*there was going to be a snake-handling* [religious] *meeting...taking up a* [hold] *serpent.*[102] The snakes abound in all wooded and hilly places. They usually feed on rats which destroy crops. There is a tradition in India, and it is called snake charming. The snake charmers perform in public areas with a musical instrument called *The Been.* No one has found out what effect the musical instrument has on the snake, if it is a particular tone or some infrasonic vibration that makes the snake come out of the basket.[103] This could be a connection between the Portuguese and the Melungeons. The Portuguese were in India since 1498, and brought with them women, men and their offspring of mixed marriage with the natives. Ruth also mentions: ...*drinking coffee off the saucer...*The author recalls seeing his grandfather in Portugal doing the same.

Jesse Stuart, the Kentucky novelist, also mentions snake handling in his novel, *Daughter of the Legend.* A recent email to the Foundation mentions that a German "surgeon" name Schoepf who traveled the Appalachian Mountains in 1781-82 made a reference to "mountain Indians" somewhere between Pittsburgh and southwest Virginia who "revered" the rattlesnake and handled it with ease. Schoepf was interested in natural pharmaceuticals and was intrigued by these Indians. Were they really native American Indians?

Melungeon Itinerary to the Mountains

It has been established that the Melungeons did not originate in Tennessee. However, no one is certain from where they came. Edward T. Price studied the Melungeons in 1950. From the maps and description of what he found, it seems that they crossed into Tennessee from Virginia and North Carolina in the late 1700's.

He also tells us that Newman's Ridge in Tennessee was not very good land and possibly the only place where they could settle, since no one else wanted it:. *Though much of the ridge land is unused, the poor pastures and second-growth woods on nearly bare limestone attest the futility of cultivating more of it in the same manner.*[104] That certainly indicates that they originated on the east coast of the Carolinas much before the 1700's, where Portuguese, Spanish, English and French navigators were very active in the 16th century. Jack Goins

Fig. 35—Ruth Johnson, Melungeon descendant from Sneedville.

while writing his book traced Melungeons back to Virginia. He states on page 51 that: *Charles Gibson in 1839 was more than 100 years old. He gave his place of birth as Luisa County, Virginia.*

Skillful in the Trades

Jean Patterson Bible, who has known Melungeons for many years, writes: *They go to Michigan and Ohio mostly, and some of them are very skillful in trades of carpentry and bricklaying. Of the Magoffin County Melungeons, a friend from Gifford, Kentucky, writes...They are clannish through necessity but warm up to anyone who will treat them fairly and without prejudice...most of them are very skillful in trades of carpentry and bricklaying.*[105]

In Portugal, during the 1940's, education past grade four was available only to the wealthy people. There was the option of being accepted into a Catholic seminary, and then dropping out before taking the final vows. But even that was limited to a chosen few. The only other choice was to learn a trade, which they started doing at a very young age. That was the only way parents were able to give their offspring a means for making a living.

This resulted in the Portuguese being skillful in the trades and sought after all over the world as good prospective immigrants. Not all immigrants were skilled workers, but most of them were hard-working people of the land and sea.

Navarra, Varr, Vardy and Irish Wake

Based on a letter written by J.G. Rhea, Louise Davis wrote : *Navarrah* [a common Melungeon name] *opened a mineral springs resort long ago...health resort...*[106] One of the favorite vacations for the older Portuguese in Portugal is to spend a few weeks or months at a health resort, usually near a spring called *Termas de Verão*. Later Jean Patterson Bible wrote a story she heard from someone who made a study of Appalachian folkways: *The wakes, in particular the gathering of the "clan" in the home to sit up with the dead for several nights before the burial, are definitely Irish in origin rather than Melungeon.*[107]

This may have an Irish origin, but it is also a Portuguese tradition that is slowly dying out. In rural areas, it is still customary to sit up all night with relatives and friends of the dead, doing what the Portuguese call a *velorio*, or in other words, sit up with the deceased. Also we should not forget that the Portuguese also descend from the Celts, and some of their culture may have been appropriated by the people living in what is today Portugal.

Navarrah or *Navarro* is an important name in Portuguese, besides being common among the Melungeons. It should be noted that Moses Navarro, a Portuguese Jew, arrived in Pernambuco, Brazil, in a fleet of Jews from Portugal.[108]

European Looking and a Group Too Large to Ignore

European looking people who were Christian to boot, a new heritage had to be invented. Never mind that from the earliest encounters the Melungeons seemed to know who they were and that their claim of origin was a nonexotic, easily verifiable one.[109] Why would the English be interested in verifying the origin of the Melungeons? If they were Portuguese or any other nationality, it would be embarrassing, since it was assumed that whoever got there first claimed the land for their king or nation. This is unfortunately true, and while research for this book was being done on a small southeast town's history where the Portuguese—or people officially registered as Portuguese—were part of the town's history, but were simply classified as: *...and others*. Adalino Cabral, Ph.D. shared a known fact in an interview: *There is the case of the Cape Verdeans in Massachusetts (in the 1970's) being classified as "Others," when racial status was officially (requested from public schools) for State purposes. Today, the minority classification includes, Black, Hispanic, Asian...Cape Verdean.* It is very interesting what just a few people can accomplish in a matter of human reproduction. Kennedy wrote: *...professional historians have generally ignored them, even though they numbered in the thousands. Today their descendants undoubtedly exceed 200,000 individuals, perhaps far more, but most are unaware that they carry Melungeon blood.*[110]

Geneticist Nassau (McGlothlen) stated: *One European, African or mulatto...could leave a very disproportionate number of descendants...So if five shipwrecked sailors were adopted by a village of a hundred Indians, in two generations the village would probably be 25 or 30% European rather than 5%.*[111]

Genetic Diseases—Joseph-Machado, Sarcoidosis and others

There are several genetic diseases known to be found most commonly in Mediterranean people: *Thalassemia,* a rare blood disorder; *Sarcoidosis,* a respiratory disease; *Machado-Joseph Syndrome*, which attacks the central nervous system; *Familial Mediterranean Fever (FMF)*, a degenerative disease of the kidneys; and

Paramyloidosis, or foot disease as it is popularly known, which shows up as slurred speech, and weakness in the arms and legs. There is also another one known as *Guillan-Barre Syndrome,* which is the most common cause of acute generalized paralysis. This disease is not genetic and not particular to any segment of the population, but it is known to affect Portuguese people.[119] Kennedy, before he wrote his book, contracted Sarcoidosis. Its causes are unknown, but it can be debilitating, crippling, suffocating, and even blinding to its victims. A sizable percentage of the cases result in death. Because of this event in his life, Kennedy was compelled to take up the quest for his origins and the very essence of who his people were and are. Later he was also diagnosed with Familial Mediterranean Fever (FMF). Machado-Joseph's disease (MJD) is also found among the Portuguese immigrants in New England as well as those in California. Dr. Jorge Sequeiros, who heads the Institute for Study of Genetic diseases in Porto, Portugal in the research of this disease, stated in an interview that Sarcoidosis was not a genetic disease. There are, however, many who do not share his view.

Melungeon descendants show a heavy propensity toward such Mediterranean diseases as Thalassemia, familial Mediterranean fever, and sarcoidosis.[113] Sarcoidosis and thalassemia, also called Mediterranean anemia, are common in Portugal, Italy, and Greece.

The cause is unknown...genetic factors are important...occurs predominantly between the ages of 20 and 40...and Sephardic Jewish ancestry and is rare in other ethnic backgrounds.[114]

While in Lisbon, Portugal doing research for this book at the *Instituto Nacional de Saude* (The National Health Institute), the author obtained information about the Portuguese population genetic diseases. Doctor Odete Rodrigues was kind enough to offer a copy of an article published in the *Medical Journal of Genetics* in 1993. This article deals with hereditary anemias in Portugal, and was the result of a study made by five Portuguese doctors and three Portuguese institutions, and shows the relevant historical events related to thalassemia.

The predominance of carriers of thalassemia is in the southern province of Alto Alentejo, which agrees with the information given above: *In fact the four commonest Mediterranean β thalassemia mutations are found in the Portuguese.*[115] It also connects this disease with African slaves brought in the 15th century and later, as well as with Phoenicians, Romans and Moslems (Moors). The facts stated above are sufficient enough to not dismiss outright the Melungeon claim of Portuguese ancestry, and it presents a strong case for a Mediterranean connection.

Skin Darker than the Portuguese

Traditionally Melungeons were not accepted as Portuguese, because of the color of their skin: *But a skin darker than the English perceived the Portuguese should possess, as well as the use of both English surnames and Elizabethan English language, have historically been cited as evidence against this theory.*[116]

That may be possible, but the English knew that the Portuguese were darker than themselves. On May 31, 1662, Charles II of England married Catherine of Braganza, a Portuguese princess. After the royal marriage, John Evelyn, a 17th century author, wrote in a diary he had kept since he was 6 years old, of the Portuguese ladies-in-waiting for Queen Catherine: *...they are swarthy and olive skinned.*[117] These same words were used later to describe the Melungeons.

The women from Alentejo—a southern Portuguese province—are affectionately called *trigueirinhas* or *trigueiras*, which means swarthy, brown, brunette. It is a derivative of the Portuguese word *trigo* for wheat.

Portuguese Presence on the East Coast and the Same Portuguese Origin

Kennedy also presents one possibility of shipwrecked Portuguese sailors, and mentions what is mostly accepted in North America as a limited Portuguese presence: *Furthermore, it has generally been thought that there was only a minimal Portuguese presence along our southeastern coast, yet another factor arguing against a Portuguese heritage.*[117] The presence of the Portuguese may not have been as numerous as the Spaniards, but certainly was larger than the English or any other European nation in the first half of the 16th century: *...the individual pockets of these people dwelled, the same Portuguese origin was consistently offered to explain their existence.*[119] *Nevertheless, even the skeptics have admitted the difficulty in dismissing outright the possible Portuguese link, primarily due to the early, widespread nature of these claims among even the most widely separated Melungeon settlements, and seeming cultural and linguistic evidences.*[120]

With no easy means of communication, this is quite an accomplishment. With Portugal having the oceans full of caravels, you may also have different groups from various parts of the world being discovered and explored by the Portuguese. Some of these people may or may not be from continental Portugal and may be the result of miscegenation with natives from the most diverse regions. That may also explain why some groups may be different from the others, while claiming to be Portuguese. (See Chapter VII and Chapter VIII for a detailed description of the Portuguese presence in North America.)

Spoke Arabic or Berber at Home and Moor Mass Immigration

A language survives for a while, as long as it is spoken at home. Experience has shown that after just two or three generations, it disappears when the people are exposed to another language in everyday life. Kennedy explains a possible Arabic connection with the Melungeons: *Following the Reconquest about 1200 A.D., an uneasy truce was observed, during which time the Spanish and Portuguese Moors did their best to blend in with their Hispanic neighbors. In greater numbers they intermarried, converted to Christianity, adopted Spanish and Portuguese names, kept a low profile, and generally spoke Arabic or Berber only in the home.*[121] This could be true in southern Spain, but not in Portugal. The end of the reconquest for Portugal was in the 1200's, and by the 1500's the Moors had been absorbed by the Portuguese population.

It only takes as little as one generation to lose the language of your ancestors. This can be proven today, by the most recent immigrant arrivals in America. Entwistle state that: *Portugal had no Moors on its soil in the 15th century...and at that time, Spain still had to reduce the Moslem remnant in Granada.*[122] [Mass immigration took place after the]*...first five years after the fall of Granada...large numbers of its inhabitants...emigrated and settled in...Tunis, Alexandria and elsewhere in North Africa...*[123] [Kennedy mentions the Canary Islands]*...Large numbers of Christianized Moriscoes were permitted to emigrate to the Canary Islands.*[124] This happened much later, in the 16th century. Again, this mass emigration may be true for southern Spain, but not for Portugal, as there was no such mass immigration of the Moors in the 15th or 16th century. That could point to the Spanish Moors, but how did they get to America? Why the Portuguese names? By the time the English met them, there was no war with Spain, and no reason to be afraid of telling the truth to the English. That happened at least one or two generations later. On the other hand, there was a large movement of the Portuguese population in the 16th century, due to the establishment of settlements in Africa, Brazil and India.

Portuguese Name Used by the Jews

Jane S. Gerber, in her well-written book *The Jews of Spain*, describes in detail the Sephardic experience of most Spanish Jews. The Portuguese Jews are also described. The amalgamation of Portuguese and Spanish Jews into one may not reflect the reality as it was known then: *Even among themselves, the conversos in Lisbon, Madrid, or Seville referred to each other as "Portuguese," or "Men of the Nation" and the term "Portuguese" became synonymous with "Jew" or "Judaizer" not only in Spain but wherever these Portuguese New Christians went in western Europe.*[125]

Even after they moved to other countries such as Holland and later to America, they carried their nationality and the Portuguese name with them. According to the same author: [The Jews]*...even as dutifully continued to keep the minute books of their congregation in Portuguese well into 18th century.*[126] *In western Europe, the smaller branch of the Sephardic family was primarily crypto-Jewish and Portuguese speaking.*[127]

There is another fact to which the writer may be referring. It relates to a period after 1580, when King Felipe II of Spain was also King Filipe I of Portugal. Many of the Jews who were forced to Christian conversion in Portugal began to settle in Spain, its colonies, and elsewhere: *There were enough in number for the word "Portuguese" to become almost synonymous with "Jew" in Spain as well as Spanish America.*[128] If that was the case, they were actually Portuguese Jews emigrating to Spain. The hypothetical time frame for the Melungeons' arrival points to the early 1500's. During the middle and late 1600's, it is unlikely that a group of people would arrive and go unnoticed for more than one hundred years.

As for the term *Men of the Nation*, it is believed that it was applied to Jews of all nations, not just of Portugal. Men of the Nation probably meant *The Jewish Nation* within the country or nation in which they settled. It appears to have been used like that throughout the world. Their petition to the Dutch West India Company to be accepted by the governor of New Amsterdam states: *Your Honors...Should also please consider that many of the Jewish Nation are principal shareholders...and many of their Nation have also lost immense and great capital in its shares and obligations.*[129]

Leo Pap also mentions: *The term "gente da nação" or "men of the nation" in Portuguese, was also used by emigrants from the Azores, referring to other Portuguese from continental Portugal or others that had returned from America.*[130] It is obvious that the term does not necessarily apply only to Jews. When the crowns of Portugal and Spain united in 1580, many Portuguese Jews fled to Spain to escape the Portuguese Inquisition, and for a while they were ignored by the Spanish Inquisition. Also, it was much easier to travel to Spain then. In that group were also the descendants of the Spanish Jews who were expelled from Spain in 1492. By then, they considered themselves Portuguese whenever they went to Europe and the Americas. The term *Portuguese* is not accepted by some historians to mean what it actually says. If people of the Jewish faith in America considered themselves Americans, then why not consider those from Portugal to be Portuguese?

Isaac Amoreiras Bitton, a native of Portugal, himself a Jew, emigrated to America in 1959. He was recently interviewed for a Spielberg documentary about the Nazi Holocaust. He is now a successful businessman in Chicago, and an American. He is proud of his Portuguese roots. His success and recognition will raise the esteem level of all Portuguese spread throughout the United States. As far as the possible relationship with the Melungeons or any other early group of settlers, it is known

that the Portuguese Jews arrived at a very early date and also participated in the making of America.[131]

Grape Arbor

Kennedy remembers his youth: *She raised chickens, and grapes, and blackberries which I can still see hanging from the long demolished grape arbors. In the summer, the thick growth of vines made Granny's little vineyard a jungle fantasy land.*[132] The grape arbor—*latada* in Portuguese—is very common in northern Portugal. It is there that most grapes that produce the famous *vinho verde* are grown. They form huge grape arbors, which are also

Fig. 36—Grape arbor in Patton Valley, NC. Helen Patton, one of the descendants of early pioneers in the area, is a lively and active octogenarian who has answered many questions about the mountains, their people and culture.

seen in Madeira and Azores Islands beside steep hills, and seem to be present in mostly mountainous areas. Portuguese from the Azores living in southern New England use the grape arbor method to adorn their houses.

Names that may indicate Portuguese Origin

...Melungeon given names from the earliest known encounters are strikingly Mediterranean when compared to the Scotch-Irish neighbors: Louisa, Helena, Navarrh, Salena, Salvadore, Mahala, Alonso, Sylvester, Eulalia, Elvas, and Canara were names present among the earliest-known Melungeons. "Canara," unknown among other Anglo Appalachian families, is especially intriguing.[133] The name Canara will be studied further, as it may provide a very important clue to solving the Melungeon mystery. As a result of the ongoing research, a logical and acceptable explanation will eventually be found: *The name "Canaira" (pronounced the same as Canara) has been in my family at least since the 1700's. It is the name of a village in northern Portugal,...and Canara was a family tradition well before any of our family could have read about the Santa Elena Colony or even randomly selected "Canaira" from a map of Portugal.*[134]

It would be much harder if the name originated from another part of the world.

By the 17th century, the Portuguese had originated an empire

Fig. 37—A typical Grape Arbor in Portugal in the Mountain area

upon which the sun did not set. Elvas is the name of a town located in the province of Alentejo in southeastern Portugal. *(Yes, Elvis Presley had North Carolina roots; his family left western North Carolina in the early 1800's.)*[135] In Appendix A, see more details about the Portuguese and Melungeon names that may have some connection.

Blood Analysis and Melungeon Comparison—1990

The Pollitzer and Brown survey of 1969 was widespread news. More recently, in 1990, James L. Guthrie made a comparison of gene distribution of the Melungeons and those of worldwide populations. The results were published in the *Tennessee Anthropologist*, Spring 1990, and the following are some of the conclusions: *Worldwide gene frequency distributions in five major blood group systems were*

Fig, 38—Canara Nash, ca. 1910
Dr. N. Brent Kennedy's great-uncle.

searched for similarity to those of the Melungeons. Calculations of the Mean Measure of Divergence (MMD) identified populations from the Mediterranean region and those of coastal Europe that do not differ significantly from the Melungeons. All others, including Amerindians, differ widely... Guthrie adds: *...These results are consistent with the Melungeon tradition that they are Portuguese, and are in substantial agreement with the findings of Pollitzer and Brown, whose 1969 data provided the basis for the present calculations...*[136]

[And concludes]...*their overall findings caused them to favor a predominantly Portuguese ancestry over English ancestry for the Melungeons...The Portuguese match closely by themselves, probably because of early incorporation of a Black component*

Fig. 39—Family Portrait taken in Portugal ca. 1900.
The author's ancestors Great Grand Parents.

Fig. 40, 41, 42—On the left and the right are Portuguese soldiers ca. 1900. The one in the center is Canara Nash, Kennedy's Melungeon great-uncle Note the similarity of these young men's noses, eyes and cheeks.[132]

into Mediterranean populations.[137] It is known that it did happen in the 15th century. Also, the comparison mentions some other countries with which the Portuguese had contact, such as Arabia, India and Turkey.[138]

Portuguese and Cherokee

The author was also told that in the beginning of this century when the Cherokees were being given land and other benefits, many of the people that lived with them nearby also apply as Cherokee Indians; however, they were refused because some of the applicants wrote on their applications that they were part Cherokee and part Portuguese. Because of that, their applications were refused.

Attempts were made to contact someone from the Cherokee tribe to get more information. Nothing else was available than what has been written in books sold at the Heritage Museum, which did not help this research. However, the connection between the Cherokees and the Portuguese pops up once in a while.[139]

Dromgoole also mentions: *The Malungeons believe themselves to be of Cherokee and Portuguese extraction.*[140] *...the master of the house, who claims to be an Indian, and who, without a doubt, possesses Indian blood...boast largely of his Cherokee grandfather...*[141]

Portuguese Vessels in Jamestown Bay—1655

Evelyn Orr, a member of our Advisory Council, has obtained information contained in the McDonald Furman papers which she has been researching for a number of years. The following is her contribution to the research of Melungeon ancestry:

Phase In Ethnology—Washington Post, 1901. This is a 1901 news report defining the Portuguese settlements along the Atlantic Coast. It includes anthropologist James Mooney's "look" into their origins. Mooney was an anthropologist with the Bureau of Ethnology, Smithsonian Institute, Washington, DC. The following is quoted from a news clipping in the Charles McDonald Furman Papers in the South Carolina Library, University of South Carolina, Columbia, SC.

"*Mr. James Mooney, who has just returned from Indian Territory, where he has been making a study of the Kiowa tribe for the Bureau of Ethnology, has also during his career as an anthropologist, done considerable work in the way of investigating the Portuguese settlements along the Atlantic coast of the United States, a subject about which less is known than most any other phase of the modern ethnology of America.*

"*All along the southern coast there are scattered bands of curious people, whose appearance, color, and hair seems to indicate a cross of mixture of the Indian, the white and the Negro. Such, for example, are the Pamunkeys of Virginia, the Croatans Indians of the Carolina, the Melungeons of Tennessee, and numerous other peoples who in the days of slavery were regarded as free Negro and were frequently hunted down and enslaved. Since the war they have tried hard by act of Legislature and otherwise to establish their Indian Ancestry.*

"*Where ever these people are found there also will the traveler or investigator passing through their region encounter the tradition of Portuguese blood or descent, and many have often wondered how these people came to have such a tradition or, in view of their ignorance, how they came to even know the name of Portugal or the Portuguese.*

"*The explanation is, however, far simpler than one might imagine. In the first place, the Portuguese have always been a seagoing people, and according to Mr. Mooney, who has looked up the subject, the early records of Virginia and the Carolinas contain notices of Portuguese ships having gone to wreck on the coasts of the States and of the crews settling down and marrying with the Indians and mulattoes.*

"*Moreover, there are records of Portuguese ships having sailed into Jamestown Bay as early as 1655, and since then there has been more or less settlement of Portuguese fishermen and sailors from Maine to Florida. Now it has been the history of the Portuguese race that where ever they settled they mixed in with the darker peoples forming the aboriginal population of the countries occupied by Portuguese settlers, and this is the reason and cause of the Portuguese admixture among the tribes along the coast of the United States.*

"*In further proof of this he calls attention to the case of a colony of Portuguese fishermen who settled on the coast of Massachusetts a few years ago. The settlers have nothing whatever to do with them, but are intermarrying and intermixing among and with the small remnants of the Narragansett Indians who have survived down to the present day. In short, it has been the history of the Portuguese that where they settled along the Atlantic coast they have intermixed and intermarried among the remnants of the Indians tribes that were once the sole proprietors of that region.*"

Some notes on the scientific research of James Mooney. In his correspondence with McDonald Furman in 1897, he stated: "*He felt that the Croatans, Redbones, Melungeons, Moors, and Portuguese were all local names for 'mixed blood' races along the Atlantic seaboard.. [Mooney] It would be worth while for local investigators to go into the subject systematically.*" This never happened in detail, thus there is continued scientific interest today.

More of Mooney's comments in the 1907: *Handbook of American Indians North of Mexico* reveal his sincerity based on racial views of his time. Yet, his uncertainty to judge these people as fact should be noted. He reveals his awareness that other "races" were along our shores by mentioning the:...*"stray seamen of Latin races from coasting vessels from the West Indies or Brazilian trade, and the Portuguese."* In recent decades, Mooney's early "scientific" views regarding races besides the early Northern European, such as Negro slave and Indian heritage, has been neglected by many researchers. The 2000's research will reveal various complicated "mixes" among some very diverse visitors to the early Atlantic Seaboard. This may give us a broader view of the multiculture (melting pot) in the American Colonies.

Melungeons and the Internet

Modern communications has enabled many Melungeons to trace their ancestry with the help of the computer and the Internet, plus the Unions organized by the Melungeon Heritage Association, and workshops. The following are some emails received attesting to Portuguese ancestry. Last names and email addresses are not shown to protect their privacy.

Erica, looking for a possible Ohio Valley link, says: *Some families (ex. Fontz) lay a claim to a **Portuguese** heritage as well—and find themselves breaking the mold with their practice of the Catholic religion.* Fontz is a variation of the Portuguese name, Fontes.

From Mike in Iowa: *State of Tennessee Maury County...testimony that he said Thomas Hall is entitled to all privileges of a free citizen. Thomas Hall grandfather on his father side was a **portagee**.* This was written in 1835.

From J.A.W. T. to Mr. McDonald Furman: *My Dear Sir...The question on your mind...Of course the people of "mixed breed," that we have among us in Malborough are not known as "Redbones" and not until recently have been called "Croatans," a name which some of them are now adopting. For generations, they have claimed to have been of "**Portuguese**" extraction. For a while the white people have thought them mulattos.*

From Sherla A.: *They lived in a small town near Cadillac, MI...My grandmother always said we were part Indian, but she didn't know how much or what kind. However in her later years, her brother told us that they were **Portuguese**.*

From Rick G.: *William Goings, Sr. was the illegitimate son of John Harmon (born c.a. 1730), a native of Portugal, and Elizabeth Goings regarded as white woman.*

From David Hunt, Supervisor, Educational Programs in Buena Park, California: *My name is David Hunt, descendant of a group of people known as the Melungeon Indians. My ancestors were Portuguese who shipwrecked down in Cape Hatteras, N. Carolina during the early 1700's, 1734 approximately.*

Linda Baggott added: *Pappy as everyone calls him, is an educational tour guide at the theme park who reflects the heritage of many ethnic families that helped* build the old west and what it is today. Mr. Hunt descendant of the **Portuguese/** *Melungeon Indians talks about his ancestors from Newman Ridge, Tennessee, and how he has continued to follow the sunset as his mother and father had advised him.Today he tells the story of the mountainous native American people to our children whom we bring to the park for an educational adventure.*

From Jack Goins: *I have a book almost completed on the Melungeons, hopefully it will be the first book written by a descendant who can prove it. I don't think the Melungeons were Redbones.*

*My hunch is the real Melungeons who came to Newman Ridge circa 1790's from around the New River. They moved to the New River in 1767 from the Flatt River in NC. I trace individual families to their original homeland in VA, using the nationality they claimed to be, which was **Portuguee** and Indian.* His book has been completed and on page 48 states: *Most descendants of Zachariah Minor claim he was of Indian and Portuguese descent. This claim can be substantiated on some Federal Census records of Hancock County, TN where the enumerator wrote the word Portuguese.* Page 90: *Zachariah told his grandson Thurman Hurd to always be proud of his Portuguese ancestors, so obviously this was presented in his illegal voting trial in 1748.*

From Arlee Gowen: REDBONES IN TEXAS. A question was put as to the possible Melungeon/Redbone connection relating George Orr and the Ashworth family: *Should not these leads be explored for possible Redbone/Melungeon connections? The Ashworths immigrated to Louisiana from South Carolina in 1799. The Ashworths were classified as "free blacks" and were land and slave owners. "There is considerable doubt, however, that they were of black origin, as their features were apparently Caucasian. Thomas Jefferson Russell, writing in 1910, suggested that they were of **Portuguese**-Moorish descent.*

From Kathy in Atlanta: *...This family—Ashe, Wilkes, Beaty, Baty, Batey, ...— which has been listed as white in later years, had been shown as "M" earlier on. In discussing this with a fellow researcher, he said that they looked like Melungeons rather than Mulatos...The Georgia Archives has the material...I favored Kennedy and could not understand why they would all call themselves **Portuguese** if they were not.*

From the Gowen Research Foundation's Electronic Newsletter, March 2000, Volume 3, No. 3 and sent by Mike Landwehr West Des Moines: *A number of years ago, as I searched for information about my g-g-g-grandfather, Thomas Hall, who lived at one time in Tennessee, I ran across the following document that I thought might be of interest to those of you with Melungeon ancestry. The document was apparently filed originally in Maury County, Tennessee, on September 19, 1835. The copy I found was filed with deed records in Oregon County, Missouri, in February of 1850. I believe that it was filed in Oregon County by Thomas Hall soon after he moved to Oregon County. The purpose of his filing is made clear by the document. To my knowledge, I am not related to this Thomas Hall. The document reads as follows: "State of Tennessee Maury County this day personally appeared before me James L Crawford one of the Justice of the Peace in and for said County Thomas Hall and made proof of private testimony that he said Thomas Hall is* *entitled to all the privileges of a free citizen Thomas Hall great grand father on his father side was a **Portagee** and his great grand father on his mothers side was an englishman and Thomas Hall grand father on his fathers side was of the **Portugee** descent and his grand father on his mothers side was an irishman and his own father was of the **Portagee** decent and his mother was a white american woman sworn to and subscribed before me this 19 day of September 1835."*

Also from the same newsletter: *George D. Blakey also gives us an insight into the character of William Morriss in his writings for the "Russellville, Kentucky Newspaper Series," article number 54: "I remember several very worthy, old colored people who were early settlers in and about Russellville. There was the Morris family. who I believe claim to be of the **Portuguese** race, born free. The old man and his little family were very clever people, and at one time owned a good farm and several slaves living three miles east of town." We have already stated the arrival of Morris, Goins, Portee, Bird and other families claiming to be Egyptian and **Portuguese**.*

Another email with the following has an interesting story: *The attempt by these people to evade a racial stigma and its consequences in the culture of the United States two centuries ago is understandable. An article found in the Marion, Kentucky library reveals, "They went away but a few days after, they returned for marriage. The woman swore that she had (Negro) blood in her, which she did. Just before they started, the man cut a vein and she drank some of his blood. She had his blood in her." Finley has certainly provided a clear insight into the lives of the tax protestors from South Carolina. Somewhere more documentation exists, perhaps in courthouse basements, in dimly lit archives, in yellowing ship records or in musty private journals that will validate the claims of "**Portuguese** and Egyptian" descent.*

From Gowen Research Foundation's Newsletter, Feb. 2000: *Evelyn Portee Allen provided her family history relating that John and Harriet Portee came to Illinois from North Carolina by wagon train at the time of the "Trail of Tears" and that they were Cherokee Indians. Included was a picture of John and Harriet Portee and their family. They were light complexioned people, some with very fine European/**Portuguese** features and some resembling Indians.*

February 1999 Newsletter by Anna Goings Friedman, Jaymie Friedman Frederick and Helen Bonnie Moore: *One of the questions we must ask ourselves is: Did they learn a lesson from the Turks of Sumter County, South Carolina? The Turks represented themselves as being citizens of Turkey and therefore not "Black/FPC." In Logan County Kentucky our group represented themselves as **Portuguese** and Egyptian. Some Melungeons had a legitimate claim to a Portuguese ancestry, their ancestors having arrived in Jamestown, Virginia in 1619 from Portuguese Angola. In contrast to colonization efforts of the British, the French and the Dutch, the Portuguese did not plant colonies.*

They organized each territory as a state in the Portuguese nation, and the inhabitants of each became citizens of Portugal.

From Kay B: *My Bolton family records state they were **Portuguese**, Spaniard & German... My Boltons are Melungeons.*

Notes

1 The Melungeons by N. Brent Kennedy, p. 93.
2 The Melungeons by Byron Stinson, American History Illustrated, Nov. 1973, p. 41.
3 The Melungeons by N. Brent Kennedy, p. 121. 4 Ibid, pp. 106, 107.
5 Nancy Sparks email of Aug. 5, 1999.
6 Pathfinder to the East by J.R. Hildebrand, National Geographic Society, Nov. 1927, p. 510.
7 Portuguese Enclaves, The Invisible Minority by M. Estellie Smith, p. 83.
8 The Mclungcons by Bonnie Ball, p. 45.
9 The Melungeons by Jean Patterson Bible, pp. 59, 60.
10 Annals of Virginia 1746-1786 by Lewis Preston Summers, pp. 1-2.
11 Early Travels in the Tennessee Country by Samuel Cole Williams, pp. 28-29.
12 Greenbrier Pioneers…by Ruth Woods Dayton, p. 16.
13 Pioneer Recollections of Virginia by Elihu Jasper Sutherland, p. 167-169.
14 The Melungeons…by Edward T. Price, p. 269.
15 The Melungeons by Brent Kennedy, p. xviii.
16 Melungeons: The Vanishing Colony of Newman's Ridge by Henry R. Price, p. 11.
17 The History of Baxter County, Arkansas, (Mountain Home AR, 1972), pp. 5-6.
18 Dicionario da Historia de Portugal by Joel Serrão, V. 6, p. 687.
19 The History of Baxter County, Arkansas, (Mountain Home AR, 1972), p. 6.
20 History of Tennessee and Tennesseans by W. T. Hale and Dixon L. Merritt, p. 182.
21 Mixed Bloods of the Upper Monongahela, WV by William H. Gilbert Jr., p. 5. 22 Ibid, p. 11.
23 The Melungeons by Bonnie Ball, p. 76-77.
24 The Melungeons by Jean Patterson Bible, p. 57.
25 The Presidents of the United States by John & Alice Durant, p. 137.
26 The Melungeons by Jean Patterson Bible, p. 59.
27 The Mystery of the Melungeons by Louise Davies, p. 11 (Nashville Tennessean, 9/23, 1963).
28 Melungeons: The Vanishing Colonoy of Newman's Ridge by Henry R. Price, p. 16.
29 Ibid, p. 17.
30 History of Tennessee and Tennesseans by W. T. Hale and Dixon L. Merritt, p. 182.
31 The Melungeons by Jean Patterson Bible, p. 38, (James Aswell, Lost Tribes of Tennessee).
32 The Melungeons by N. Brent Kennedy, p. 5. 33 Ibid, p.12. 34 Ibid, p.13.
35 The Malungeons by Will Allen Dromgoole, p. 469 (Boston Arena 1891).
36 Eastern Creek Indian Identity by J. Anthony Paredes, p. 65.
37 The Malungeons by Will Allen Dromgoole, p. 471 (Boston Arena 1891).
38 The Melungeons by N. Brent Kennedy, p. 13; 39 Ibid, p.15.
40 The Melungeons by Jean Patterson Bible, p. 26-28.
41 History of Tennessee and Tennesseans by Hale & Merrit, p. 180, Vol. 1.
42 The Melungeons by Bonnie Ball, p. 52; 43 Ibid, p. 72.
44 Note on the Melungeons by Swan M. Burnett, p. 347 (American Anthropologist, Vol. II, 1889).
45 The Melungeons by Bonnie Ball, pp. 67-68.
46 The Melungeons: a mixed blood-strain…by Edward T. Price, p. 259.
47 The Malungeon Tree…by Will Allen Dromgoole, pp. 748-749 (Arena, June 1891).
48 Ibid, (Arena, March 1891) p. 473.—The author remembers his grandmother's feet, so small and shapely, except for the open skin cracks—sometimes bleeding—on her heels from walking barefoot all day on the not so smooth paths and ways. His mother used to send him every summer to his grandparents, and one of the first things he did was to get rid of the shoes, and go barefoot. The main reason was that his mother could not afford to buy him shoes as he was growing, with the result that sometimes he had to wear the same shoes for

Notes (Cont.)

two years, and after one year, they were tight, so tight that his two toes in both feet grew on top of each other. But it certainly was comfortable to go barefoot. The only problem was that his feet were not used to it, and by the end of the summer, his toes and nails were in pretty bad shape. His cousins used to go barefoot all the time, and would laugh at him when he carelessly hit a protruding root of a pine tree on the narrow path that they walked. They somehow were able to detect with their toes anything on the ground, before walking over it.

[49] The Malungeons by Will Allen Dromgoole, p. 478 (Arena, 1891); [50] Ibid, p. 106.

[51] Among the author's recollections as a child, when spending the summers with his grandparents at the small village where he was born, was seeing women going barefooted with a good pair of shoes hanging over their shoulders, mostly on Sundays, which was quite natural.

[52] The Mystery of the Melungeons by Louise Davis, p. 11 (Tennessean Magazine, 9/22, 1963).

[53] The Malungeons by Will Allen Dromgoole, p. 478 (Boston Arena 1891).

[54] The Melungeons by Brent Kennedy, p. 12.

[55] The Melungeons by Jean Patterson Bible, p. 107.

[56] The Mystery of the Melungeons by Louise Davis, p. 11 (Nashville Tennesseean, 9/29/1963).

[57] The Melungeons and Mestee Groups by Mike McGlothlen, p. 44.

[58] The Melungeons by Bonnie Ball, p. 69.

[59] History of Tennessee and the Tennesseeans by Hale & Merritt, p. 180.

[60] Strange People of East Tennessee by Eliza N. Eiskel, Arkansas Gazette, Jan.14, 1914.

[61] History of Tennessee and Tennesseans by Hale & Merritt, Vol. 1, p. 184; [62] Ibid, p. 6.

[63] Handbook of the American Indians by Frederick Webb Hodge, Part 1, p. 365.

[64] The Melungeons by Bonnie Ball, p. 51.

[65] Ibid, p. 61. [66] Ibid, pp. 62-63.

[67] Ibid, p. 96 [68] Arkansas Gazette, January 14, 1914 by Eliza N. Heiskel.

[69] David Farragut by Charles Lee Lewis, V. 1, p. 1.

[70] The Melungeons by Bonnie Ball , p. 111; Hale & Merritt, p. 185.

[71] David Farragut by Charles Lee Lewis, V. 1, p. 1.

[72] The Melungeons by Bonnie Ball, pp. 74-75.

[73] Ibid, pp.8-9 (James Aswell, "Lost Tribes of Tennessee…").

[74] The Melungeons by Bonnie Ball, p. 89.

[75] Ibid, pp. 84-85. [76] Ibid, p. 93.

[77] The Melungeons by Jean Patterson Bible, p. 5.

[78] The Melungeons by Bonnie Ball, pp. 95, 96.

[79] The Mystery of the Melungeons by Louise Davis, p. 11 (Nashville Tennesseean, 9/29/1963).

[80] The Melungeons by N. Brent Kennedy, p. 87.

[81] Letter dated August 5th 1930 from Dr. W.A. Plecker to J. P. Kelly.

[82] Strangers in Their Midst by Shirley McLeRoy, p. 14.

[83] Letter by Evelyn Orr of the Melungeon Research Committee. Also see note 79.

[84] The Melungeons by N. Brent Kennedy, pp. 86-87.

[85] Ibid

[86] Sons of the Legend by William L. Worden, p. 29 (Saturday Evening Post, Oct.18, 1947).

[87] Ibid. [88] Ibid, p. 130.

[89] The Melungeons by Bonnie Ball, p. 70.

[90] Mixed-Blood Strain…by Edward T. Price, p. 281 (Ohio Journal of Science, No. 6).

[91] Ibid, p. 288. [92] Ibid, p. 269.

[93] The Mystery of the Melungeons by Louise Davis, p. 11 (Nashville Tennesseean 9/29/1963).

[94] The Melungeons by N. Brent Kennedy, p. 128.

[95] Survey of Demography…by Pollitzer and Brown, pp. 389-399 (Human Biology, Sept. 1969).

Notes (Cont.)

[96] Ibid.

[97] The Melungeons, by Jean Patterson Bible, p. 2.

[98] National Geographic Magazine by Howard La Fay, October 1965, p. 477.

[99] The Melungeons by N. Brent Kennedy, p. 119.

[100] Charlotte Observer by Bruce Henderson, 15 Aug. 1993, p. 8A.

[101] The Hawk's Done Gone by Mildred Haun, p. 97, 111.

[102] My Melungeon Heritage by Ruth Johnson, p. 42.

[103] Email by Goan Dr. Jose Colaço, dated July 31, 1999.

[104] The Melungeons: a mixed-blood strain…by Edward T. Price, p. 259.

[105] The Melungeons, by Jean Patterson Bible, p. 31; [106] Ibid.

[107] The Melungeons by Jean Patterson Bible, p. 106.

[108] Farewell España by Haward M. Sachar, p. 352.

[109] The Melungeons by Brent Kennedy, p. xiv. [110] Ibid, p. xv.

[111] Mike McGlothlen, document dated March 1997.

[112] New England Journal of Medicine, April 23, 1992, Vol. 326, No. 17, pp. 1130-1136.

[113] The Melungeons by Brent Kennedy, p. 128.

[114] Merck Manual of Diagnosis and Therapy by Robert Berkow, MD, p. 260.

[115] Medical Journal of Genetics in 1993; 30:235-239.

[116] The Melungeons by Brent Kennedy, p. 83.

[117] Catherine of Braganza by Manuel Andrade e Sousa, p. 50.

[118] The Melungeons by Brent Kennedy, p. 83. [119] Ibid, p. 10. [120] Ibid, p. 83.

[121] The Melungeons by Brent Kennedy, p. 101.

[122] The Spanish, Portuguese language by William J. Entwistle, p. 2.

[123] Moors in Spain and Portugal by Jan Read, p. 220.

[124] The Melungeons by Brent Kennedy, p. 103.

[125] The Jews of Spain by Jane S. Gerber, p. 188.

[126] Ibid, p. 209. [127] Ibid, p. 146.

[128] O Sacrificio de Isaac by Manuel da Costa Fontes, p. 58.

[129] The Jews in America, by Max I. Dimont, pp. 38-39.

[130] The Portuguese-Americans by Leo Pap, p. 157.

[131] Mundo Português pp. 28-29, September 1996. Mr. Bitton and the author were raised in the same area of Lisbon—Amoreiras—but never met. Despite the fact that he is a Jew and the author a Catholic, they still have their common roots in Portugal.

[132] The Portuguese-Americans by Leo Pap, p. 51.

[133] The Melungeons by Brent Kennedy, p. 121.

[134] Ibid. [135] Ibid, p. 122.

[136] Melungeons…Gene Distributions by James L. Guthrie, p. 13 (Tennessee Anthropologist).

[137] Ibid, p. 17. [138] Ibid, p. 18.

[139] Cherokee is located in the mountains of Western North Carolina.

[140] The Malungeons by Will Allen Dromgoole, p. 479.

[141] Ibid, p. 477.

Chapter V—Part II
Origins of Portugal, Lusitania—The Make-up of Its People
Brief History to the 15th Century

*God gave the Portuguese a small land for their birthplace,
but all the world to die in.*[1]

The Melungeons and other groups have been traditionally connected with the Portuguese people because of oral information transmitted from generation to generation, and second, due to a Mediterranean, African or Oriental appearance.

This and the following chapters will describe the origins of the Portuguese people, their history and presence in North America and throughout the world. That knowledge will help the reader to better relate what has been written about the Melungeons, and provide the basis for a conclusion where the Portuguese connection is concerned. The following is a poem by Portugal's Poet Camões:

> *In Portuguese...*   *Eis aqui, quasi cume da cabeça
> De Europa toda, o Reino Lusitano,
> Onde a terra se acaba e o mar começa
> E onde o Febo repousa no oceano.*

> *In English...*   *Behold her seated here, both head and key
> of Europe all, the Lusitanian queen;
> where endeth land and where beginneth sea;
> where Phoebus goeth down in ocean green.*

OS Lusíadas by Luis Vaz de Camões iii 20[2]

There is a traditional saying that truly describes the fate of the many Portuguese spread out all over the world. It may also be translated as: *God gave the Portuguese a small country as a cradle, but all the world as their graveyard.*[3]

It may seem that this book is overly biased towards the Portuguese ancestry, but in order to understand the Melungeon odyssey and their possible Portuguese ancestry, some basic Portuguese history would help. The Melungeons should have their place in history, in much the same way as the Portuguese, who so often are completely forgotten.

Unfortunately, there is very little published in English, and whatever is written most often represents a distorted view of the facts and ignores many others much more important. But as Kennedy said in his book, the winners write the History. This does not help when you try to research the Melungeons.

A.J.R. Russell-Wood wrote in his book *A World on the Move: Portugal is a province of Spain, isn't? The capital of Brazil is Buenos Aires, They speak Spanish in Brazil, very few people speak Portuguese because it is a Spanish dialect. Such*

Fig. 43—Historian Professor José Hermano Saraiva, talking about a tree that it is believed to be more than 800 years old. It requires a group of nine persons holding hands to embrace its circumference. It is located in the province of Alentejo. From RTP TV.

statements testify to the ignorance concerning the Portuguese-speaking world... Laborers in the field of Latin American history are resigned to textbooks purporting to be histories of Spain and Portugal in the New World, only to discover that the Portuguese part has about the same ratio to the Spanish as has the visible part of an iceberg to the bulk under water, namely one ninth... How is it that every school boy of the English speaking world can rattle off the names of Cortes, Pizarro, [Hernando] de Soto, Cabeza de Vaca, Balboa, Ponce de Leon and others of their ilk? And yet, when questioned about the pantheon of Portuguese explorers, that selfsame schoolboy would be hard pressed to name one other than the anglicized and inappropriately named Henry the Navigator.

[In order to better understand the resilience of the Portuguese people, we should place them:]...*within the broader framework not only of a Portuguese age of discoveries, but also of the global nature of the Portuguese series of initiatives; secondly, to emphasize the sheer dynamic of the Portuguese enterprise which transcended the limitations of individuals and constraints of time and space.* [4]

It has been said: Portugal is the country that has contributed most to Geographic knowledge of the Globe, as in the course of one century she discovered and explored nearly two-thirds of the inhabited Earth.

The Beginning of Human Population in Portugal

According to a National Geographic Map published in May 1998, the European Continent and the North American Continent were still connected 237 millions

years ago by a land-bridge at what is now Portugal. See the illustration below within the square mark. It is interesting to note that the westernmost point of Europe is in Portugal at about the same location as marked in the map.

About 40,000 years ago, Homo Sapiens emerged from the Neanderthal man. Later, the Chancelade man appeared, who did not look much different from the average

Mediterranean man of today, still living in Europe.[5] A Chancelade skeleton, human fossil remains, were discovered in a rock shelter at Chancelade in southwestern France in 1888. The skeleton was found in a curled posture—an indication of a deliberate burial—below the lower Magdalenian occupation floors of the shelter; it is assumed to be of Magdalenian age (about 17,000

Fig. 44—Dolmen found in Barrocal near Evora, Alentejo.

years old). It could be predicted that the last Neanderthal survivors would have been those inhabiting Europe's Far West: Portugal in the Iberian Peninsula.

Rupestrian type engravings have recently (1995) been discovered in a place called Foz Côa when in the process of building a dam. Paintings and engravings of the rupestrian style were made in rocks about 18,000 years ago. A movement headed by João Crisóstomo started in the U.S. to save the engravings. In 1996 the newly elected government agreed to stop the construction of the dam. Experts have placed the age of those engravings between 10,000 and 27,000 years old. See illustration in Fig. 45.

Dolmen, or *Anta* in Portuguese, is a monument used in funerals or burial traditions during the Neolithic and Bronze Ages. It consists of two or three large stones standing with another one sitting on top forming a sort of bridge, which it was believed would protect the dead buried below ground. They were considered to be collective tombs which the communities used to bury their dead together with their belongings. These are found in the southern province of Alentejo in Portugal, and is probably why the megalithic culture seems to have had its center in Alentejo by the neolithic epoch. Also found are several Megaliths or "standing stones." : *By 3500 BC funerary monuments were prominent in the landscapes of Alentejo (Portugal).*[6]

It has been said that the

Fig. 45—Foz Coa engravings stamp. Portuguese Post Office.

Fig. 46—Skeleton of a Child

Portuguese Megaliths are some of the most beautiful in Europe. In western Europe, the Dolmens are the first examples of the powerful constructive genius of early men. This culture sprang up in the Iberian Peninsula about 6,000 years ago. This was about the same time as farming and domestication of animals began in the Middle East and North Africa: *Ax factories and flint mines were secured by mining in Portugal.* [7] Also about 4,000 years ago during the "Iron Age," highly interesting flowering plants appeared in the southwest of the Iberian peninsula. Across the Ocean in North Salem, New York there is a 90 ton dolmen, which according to Barry Fell is the largest Celtiberian dolmen yet discovered as stated in page 133 of his book *America B.C.*

If we take into consideration that the last ice age occurred about 10,000 years ago, we could assume that Portugal, the western portion of the Iberian Peninsula, could present the best climatic conditions for vegetation, animal and human survival earlier than in Northern Europe.

Physical Anthropology

There is further justification for early human inhabitation in Portugal.: *In 1999 paleoanthropological publications presented new fossil data that might necessitate the rewriting of standard textbook interpretations of hominid evolution. From Portugal came skeletal evidence.* [8]

Lagar Velho, Leiria is the locale where scientists found a skeleton of a child buried between 24,000 and 25,000 years ago. Assumed to have lived during the Paleolithic Superior period, the skeleton reveals marks of both the Neanderthal and the Modern man. [9] That Portuguese specimen of a four-year-old child is considered spectacular by scientists and proves that the geographical area where Portugal is today located lent itself to early development of the human being for climatic reasons. Being near the ocean also presented logical reasons to explore the sea as a means of survival.

Celtics, Carthaginians, Phoenicians, Greeks, Jews, Romans, Suevis, Allans, Vandals, Visigoths, Berbers and Moors
Ancestors of the Portuguese Population

Portugal's people are made up of many races, such as the Celtics, Carthaginians, Phoenicians, Greeks, Jews, Romans, Suevis, Allans, Vandals, Visigoths, Berbers and Moors. Before the Celtics, it is believed that the Lusitanos were a mixture of Indo-European people from different origins, such as the Indi-Arian, Tracians, Ilirios and Celtics. Five thousand years ago, the Greeks named the area which comprises Portugal and Spain, *Iberos,* which means "most-western" or "where the sun sets." See Appendix B for explanation of A.D. and B.C.

After the last invasion of the Moors (A.D. 711), up through the present day, no other people has had an influence on the physical makeup of the Portuguese, except for the little difference that the Crusaders may have made in the 12th and 13th centuries. Not even the black slaves brought in during the 15th and 16th centuries made much difference; naturally that means that some of the Portuguese have negroid blood, as well as that of other races.

The Moors and the Berbers had been in Portugal for at least four centuries, and by the 1500's they were Portuguese, just as the descendants of the English who arrived in America in the 1600's are Americans today.

What it really means is that the Portuguese people's appearance has not changed much for many centuries.

There is a difference, however, between the North and the South of Portugal. It is easy to find fair skin, blond or red hair, and blue eyes in the North, and dark skin, black hair, and brown eyes in the South, where the Moors stayed the longest. The Arabs never fully conquered the northern provinces.

Francisco Antonio Doria, a genealogist from Brazil, describes it in an email: *What about the Germanic peoples that settled in the Peninsula before and after the Romans? Celts, Franks, Vandals, Visigoths, Suevi, etc.? We can still see the remains of this racial melting pot when we go to the North of Portugal. Those (lots of pretty) blond girls with green eyes still astonish me. But you are right about one thing: We can not predict our child's color of the eyes and hair. My sister has black eyes (very dark brown). I have blue eyes. My wife has green eyes. Our son has brown and green eyes. And we all have different hair!*

The Berbers and the Moors marked the end of invasions into what is known today as Portugal, until the 1800's, when Napoleon's army invaded Portugal and Spain. However they did not stay long or had any impact, except for the destruction and death caused to the population.

Now let us review the origins of Portugal and its people. In order to better understand the variety and composition of the Portuguese population, the reader should know what peoples inhabited what is today Portugal, taking into consideration that this is the oldest country in Europe, having maintained its geographic borders for more than 800 years.

Starting with the Iberians, believed to be the original people or the natives of the Iberian Peninsula, Portugal was invaded, conquered and settled by a variety of races in the following order.

Celts and Celtiberians

The Celtics, also called Gauls, Galicians, Gaelic, who spoke the ancient Irish language. The Celtics were barbarian tribes widespread in transalpine Europe and the Iberian Peninsula (Spain and Portugal).

Celtic originates from the Greek word *Keltoi,* and refers to tribes of people that shared a common language and culture. It means secret people. There are nine Celtic areas in Europe, but only two are considered Celtic: Ireland and Portugal. The other areas are: Brittany, Cornwall, Galicia, the Isle of Man, Northern Italy, Scotland and Wales. For more information, see the web site www.celtic.net.

This race formed the Celtiberians, tribes of mixed Iberian and Celtic stock, from the 3rd century B.C. onward: *This could provide a partial explanation for the Welsh as a possible origin of the Melungeons.*[10] The Celts' presence and influence extended from the North Sea to the Mediterranean, and from the Black Sea to the westernmost point in Europe located in Sintra, Portugal.[11] Tras-os-Montes' landscape, typical dances, kilts, etc. look like the Highlands of Scotland, and Minho is just like many regions of France. In other words, this is mainly a Celtic country.

The Phoenicians

The Phoenicians were originally from an ancient region corresponding to modern Lebanon and adjoining parts of modern Syria and Israel. Its inhabitants, the Phoenicians, were notable merchants, traders and colonizers of the Mediterranean in the 1st millennium BC. One of its chief cities was Berot (modern Beirut).

It is not certain what the Phoenicians called themselves in their own language; it appears to have been KenaZani (Akkadian: Kinahna), *Canaanites.* In Hebrew the word *KenaZani* has the secondary meaning of merchant, a term that well characterizes the Phoenicians.[12]

Just recently in 1995, during excavations for a high-rise apartment building, a Phoenician village was discovered across from Lisbon, the Portuguese capital, on the south shore of the Tagus River. It is the largest ever found on the Iberian Peninsula.[13]

The Carthaginians

The Carthaginians' interest in the Atlantic coast of Morocco was stimulated by the more prosaic attraction of the abundant fish. Himilco's voyage was also known to the Greeks and Romans. He sailed north along the Atlantic coast of Portugal, Spain and France, and reached the territory of the Oestrymnides, a tribe living in Brittany. Carthage, a great city of antiquity, was traditionally founded on the north coast of Africa by the Phoenicians of Tyre in 814 B.C., and is now a residential suburb of the city of Tunis. Its Phoenician name means New Town.[14]

The Carthaginian invasion has assumed historic importance for the Iberian Peninsula, as it supplied their army, the Celtiberian infantry and the superb Andalucian cavalry, which helped their General Hannibal devastate Italy.[15]

The Greeks—600 B.C.

The Greek presence in the Iberian Peninsula is known to have begun in the 7th century B.C., when a Greek navy merchant named *Kolaios* returned to Greece with a rich cargo of precious metals. These voyages were followed by others, and in order to protect them, the Greeks founded numerous colonies along the Portuguese Atlantic coast. They also founded the French city of Marseilles (Massalia) in 600 B.C. The Carthaginians retaliated, and after battles in 530 B.C., the Greeks found the Straits of Gibraltar closed to them, and that was the end of their presence in the peninsula.

The Greek presence gave a powerful stimulus to start the formation of the Iberian culture during the 5th century B.C. The colonies were absorbed by the natives, but they also left magnificent temples and statues.[16] Signs of their occupation have been found in the past in Portugal, most recently near Tavira-Algarve. Greek coins and utensils of this same time period were also found.[17]

There is a tradition that the name of the Portuguese capital, Lisbon, stems from the name Ulysses (Odysseus), or from Olisipo, which is a Greek legend of a hero during the Trojan War and the famous wooden horse of Troy. The Greek poet Homer recounts Odysseus' adventures in his epic poems *The Odyssey* and *The Iliad*.[18]

The Jews in Portugal

There have been Jews in Portugal since probably 2000 B.C. Most likely they were not called Jews. They kept coming with the Greeks, and the Phoenicians. According to legend, the first Jews came to the Iberian Peninsula at the time of Nebuchadnezzar, king of the Chaldeans, in the 6th century B.C. or even earlier, at the time of Solomon, who reigned in Israel from 974 BC to 937 BC. While these hypotheses may lie in the legendary domain, it has been ascertained that the Jewish presence in Iberia preceded and accompanied that of the Romans. From the 5th century onward, the Jews reinforced their position and remained active in peninsular society during the Visigoth and Muslim occupations.

The oldest written document which proves the existence of the Jews in Portugal, dates from the third century A.D. A tombstone of a Jew from the 5th century A.D. was found in Espiche, Lagos, Algarve (Etnografia Portuguesa, by Leite de Vasconcelos, Lisboa, 1958, vol. IV).

When the kingdom of Portugal was formed in the 12th century, there were already a number of important Jewish communities in several cities reconquered by the Christians. These included the flourishing commune in Santarem, which was discovered by the first king of Portugal, Afonso Henriques (1139-1185). Generally speaking, Portuguese Jews enjoyed the protection of the crown during the first dynasty.[19] We know therefore that Jews had settled in what is known today as Portugal and Spain as early as the first century A.D. during its occupation by the Romans. They were later persecuted by Reccard, the Visigoth king, also forcing them to embrace Christianity. These Jews would later become the Portuguese Jews and part of the so-called Sephardic Jews of Spain and Portugal.

Sepharad—Portugal and Spain—the endless or western land, was chosen by King Solomon for the source of gold and silver 900 years before Christ to be used in the construction of the Jerusalem temple. He sent his 12th son, Azer, and it is believed that they may have brought the cult of the holy spirit, which was spread mostly in the Ribatejo and Beiras area.

This may have been the result of the formation of a society to help the Jews, by King Solomon, wherever they happened to be living. There is also an interesting aspect of the Portuguese Holy Queen Isabel. She was never canonized by the Portuguese people or by the Christians. She was, however, considered a Saint by the secret Portuguese Jews, the marranos, in analogy with the Jewish Queen Ester of Babylon who was chosen for the King's harem for her beauty, and since she was a daughter of the Jews, naturally protected the Jews from persecution.[20]

In the 1400's there were approximately 30,000 Jews in Portugal, a number which doubled when the Spanish Catholic Kings expelled them from Spain. In turn, they sought refuge in Portugal as well as in other parts of Europe and North Africa. Many that could not pay for their passage were reduced to slavery.[21]

It is important that a separation be made between the Jews of Portugal and the Jews of Spain. Although they were both Sephardim, each group had its own culture and language. The same happened with Jews all over the world. Their religion is what binds them together, not necessarily the culture or the language.

Isaac Abrabanel, a well known Jewish leader, worked with his father for King Afonso V, and in 1471 when the Portuguese conquered Arzila, 250 Moroccan Jews were captured and brought in as slaves. Abrabanel traveled to the countryside to redeem these North-African Jews.[22] His father was the treasurer for Prince Fernando [23] who died in Fez, Morocco, as a captive of the Moors. Prince Fernando was the brother of Henry the Navigator.

King Manuel I was one of the most sympathetic kings to his Jewish subjects, and when he succeeded João II in 1495, one of his first acts was to free those slaves. However, when this same king decided to marry Isabel, daughter of the Spanish king, he had to agree to have them expelled, which he did, giving ten months for the Jews to leave Portugal.

King Manuel I valued their contribution and did not want to lose so many productive subjects. He took several measures to prevent their departure. When 20,000 individuals were gathered together to board the vessels, he ordered everyone not professing the Catholic faith to come and assemble in the main square in Lisbon, and from the balcony had the bishop baptize everyone with a single blessing. After that, the king told the people that they were all Catholics and could go home. Only seven or eight found the strength to resist baptism.[24] When the Spanish princess arrived to marry the King, everyone in Portugal was officially Christian. King Manuel, whom some exiles called the *Holy King* and the *Jewish King* in their chronicles,[25] did as much as he could to protect the Jews, hoping that they would eventually assimilate and become Christians. In 1497 the King also forbade all inquiries concerning the religious beliefs of those who accepted Christianity in the following 20 years, and in April 1512 he extended the period of grace until 1534. In this manner, assimilation of the Jews in Portugal began.[26]

About 1590, Portuguese Jews emigrated to Hamburg in Germany. They were considered educated and rich and contributed greatly to the wealth of that city which reached its golden era between 1660 and 1780. In 1999 an exposition took place at the Hamburg City Hall that was named "The Jerusalem of the North-Sephardic Jews."

Today there are still plenty of signs of their early stay. In 1985, construction in the Portuguese city of Tomar, near the Tomar Synagogue, uncovered the locale where the purification would take place. This was called the *mikev*. This synagogue is one of the oldest in Portugal, and is believed to date back to the 15th century.

The Jews may have played a very important part in the period of the discoveries. Portuguese history shows that they were often appointed to very important places within the government. An interesting note: The Portuguese people in 1995 elected Jorge Sampaio, a Jew, for the highest elected office in the nation, president of the Portuguese Republic. What would the Inquisition say about that?

The Romans, the Lusitanos and Lusitania—100 B.C.-A.D. 200

The Romans had a great impact in Portugal that is still being felt today. The Portuguese language, along with many others, derives from Latin. Also, vestiges of the administrative and law system still remain, along with plenty of Roman ruin sites all over Portugal. Some of the most recent ones that the author became aware of, unfortunately are not open to the public except once or twice a year.

These are underground swimming pools and Roman baths located right in the center of downtown Lisbon, and accessible through a manhole located where two major streets, *Rua da Conceição* and *Rua Augusta,* intersect. There are however and nearby an underground museum showing other Romans ruins well preserved.

Other famous ruins are located in Conimbriga as well as in many other locations. The two major Portuguese cities date back to Roman times: Porto—Portus Cale, Portugal's name origin—and Lisbon (Olisipo). Porto was originally a Roman settlement.

Lusus is a mythical name connected with the first settler of the westernmost part of the Iberian Peninsula, and *Luso* or *Lusitano* today means born in the province Lusitania, of the Roman Empire, which was located more or less where Portugal is today. Today it is synonymous with Portuguese.

A Portuguese-American is called a Luso-Americano in Portuguese. The Lusitanos fought hard against the Romans under the leadership of Viriato before they gave up their independence. It took the Roman Empire many decades, with their mighty army, to subjugate the Lusitanos (Portuguese).

The word Lusitano derives from Lusitania (lux + tania) lux=light and tania=land or land of the sunshine.

Suevi, Suebi, Swabians, Vandals, Alanis—A.D. 409, Visigoths—A.D. 456

Suevi or Suebi were Germanic people. The Suevis came from a Suevi Kingdom in Bavaria and Switzerland, ancestors of the Swabians. The Suevi kings of Galiza and Lusitania were Chavarrico, Theodomiro in 558, Ariamiro who died in 583, and Eburico who lasted until the end of the sixth century. Endeca chased Eburico—who was a child—and sent him to the Dume convent—Dume is near Braga. Then the Goth King Leovigildo, the tutor of Eburico, took power after chasing Endeca. They made their defeated opponents cut their hair—not head! Hair!—so that they couldn't be leaders any more! Endeca ordered the cutting of the hair of Prince Eburico, and King Leovigildo made a hair cut to Endeca. It seems that the Goths, Suevi, Vandals, and Alani never cut their hair. That was the supreme punishment. A prince whose hair was cut could never become a king! Leovigildo united Lusitania and Galicia to his "Gothic" kingdom, ending the Suevi Dynasty.

The Vandals, another Germanic group, came about the same time. They maintained a kingdom in North Africa from A.D. 429 to A.D. 533, and captured Rome in 455. Because of the way they damaged Rome, the name Vandal was adopted to mean destruction.

Another Germanic tribe, the Alanis, who were a nomadic pastoral people from a region northeast of the Black Sea, invaded the Iberian Peninsula, and later crossed into Africa with the Vandals.

The Visigoths were a Germanic religious people that drove out the Vandals and set up an independent kingdom in the Iberian Peninsula, until destroyed by the Muslims in A.D. 711. The Visigoths and Suebis did not have the same effect during their colonizing period as the Romans and later the Arabs.

Arabs and Berbers—A.D. 711-A.D. 1143

The last major invasion of the Iberian Peninsula was accomplished by the Arabs, Berbers, and Moors. They stayed in Portugal for a little more than 400 years, and left behind much of their advanced civilization. The conquering Arabs did not care what religion their subjects professed, so long as unbelievers paid a special tax.

In 710 an Arab-Berber army set out for the Iberian Peninsula and defeated King Roderick in 711, then raided into and through the Iberian Peninsula, and ruled in the name of the Umayyad caliph.

The Berbers are a Caucasoid people and indigenous to North Africa, largely scattered in tribes across Morocco, a territory comprising the western portion of Algeria, Tunisia, Libya and Egypt, which in classical times constituted the Roman province of Mauretania. Despite Roman colonization of the area and an invasion by the Arabs in the 7th century A.D., rural Berber tribes remained relatively autonomous until the 12th century, when invading Bedouin Arabs wrecked the Berbers' peasant economy and converted many of the settled tribes to nomads. Almoravids, a confederation of Saharan Berber tribes, built an empire in the Muslim Iberian Peninsula during the 11th and 12th centuries.

The Moors themselves never used that term. They were Arabs from Damascus and Medina, leading armies of North African Berber converts.

Most married into Spanish and Visigoth families, or took fair-skinned Galician slaves as wives; they brought no women with them.

From this heady mix of race and culture sprang the Moorish civilization that would last 900 years in Spain and 500 in Portugal.[27]

The Muslims never became a majority throughout their 700-year Andalusian presence. Non-Muslims entered into the Muslim realm as Mozarabs—Christians who had adopted the language and manners, rather than the faith, of the Arabs. Given essentially the same administrative arrangements, the Iberian Christian population was later restored to dominance.

Reconquest of the Iberian Peninsula

Although the traditional beginning of the *Reconquista* goes back to ca. 718, when the Christian Asturians opposed the Moors at the Battle of Covadonga, the impulse toward reconquest was not strong during the first three centuries of Muslim hegemony.

It was in the 11th century, when Moorish unity broke down and the Christian kingdoms of northern Spain began to be affected by an aggressive anti-Muslim crusading spirit, that the movement began in earnest.

A series of wars followed, and by the mid-13th century most of the peninsula had been subjected to Christian rule, though the continued existence of a Moorish enclave around Granada in southern Spain served to keep the spirit of the *Reconquista* alive until the end of the 15th century.

Many historians believe that subsequent Spanish emphasis on religious uniformity, evidenced by the strong influence of the Inquisition and the expulsion of people of Moorish and Jewish descent, can be traced back to this crusading struggle of the Middle Ages, with the help of adventurers of Germanic origin.

County of Portugal—1096, Origin of Portugal—1143

From the Frank aristocracy came the knights Raimundo and Henrique, to help Afonso VI of Leon and Castille. These two married his daughters, and the County of Portucale was given to Henrique of Bologne. This county eventually would become the kingdom of Portugal. Henrique married Teresa, born around 1091. The word *Portucale* appeared for the first time in A.D. 954. Right after the reconquest movement, simultaneously initiated from the north and the east, the kingdoms of Leon and Navarra were united. This last one was divided into three other kingdoms: Navarra, Castille and Leon. Later on, the County of Portugal separated from Leon. The word Leon derives from the Latin *legione*, a Roman legion that stationed in the area. In time, Castille and Leon, through union and conquest, managed to get the remaining peninsular kingdoms, including Granada in the late 15th century. Afonso Henriques, son of Henrique, eventually made Portugal an independent kingdom, and the Portuguese monarchy was constituted in 1143 with Afonso Henriques as the first king. The kingdom enlarged quickly at the expense of the Moors, through the conquest of Alentejo and Algarve, thus expelling them from Lusitania, the Roman province that became Portugal.

It is interesting to note that one of the ways used by the Moors to get accepted in the Iberian Peninsula was the same one utilized by the first Portuguese king, Afonso Henriques, and that was to secure consent for the use of their own religion and marriage between both races, a strategy which apparently has worked well in the last eight centuries.[28]

The reconquest of Portugal ended in the 1200's and most of the Moors accepted the new way of life, which after all did not change much. However, eventually and gradually, most accepted Catholicism, and the Portuguese also took advantage of their more advanced civilization. The Portuguese king was most interested in keeping the towns and villages with the people, but there were not enough Portuguese, and that was the biggest problem in centuries to come. By the 1400's and 1500's, Portugal's Moors were for the most part nonexistent. After living in Portugal, they became and felt Portuguese. It has been said that the Portuguese did not have a feeling of nationality. This is not true, and as Professor Saraiva, a Portuguese historian, stated: *At the time when the Portuguese had to affirm their nationality, they changed their military patron from Santiago, which was Spanish, to Saint George. The Portuguese did not want to have the same Patron Saint as the Spanish.*[29]

First Portuguese Naval Battle and End of the Reconquest—1180

It took place in 1180, when Knight Fuas Roupinho defeated the Moors in a naval battle off Cabo Espichel and chased them all the way to Algarve and to Ceuta. The fleet consisted of about 20 galleys and some other smaller transportation boats. They had 150 oarsmen and 40 soldiers, 6 sailors, all under the command of four or five officers.[30]

Algarve was the last area to be reconquered, but the Arab population that lived there stayed in Faro, Loulé and Silves, as the others had done in Lisbon, following the rule since the reconquest of Toledo that put an end to the extermination of the Muslim people.[31]

Portuguese Merchant Navy and the Sargasso Sea—1254

Such a navy existed already in 1254. There are documents indicating important coastal traffic under the reign of King Fernando (1345-1383), which show that the sea was an important part of the Portuguese life and economy.[32]

At the very beginning of the 13ᵗʰ century, Portuguese merchants had already found their way to England, and had judged it worth while, for the sake of trading with that country... [Early commercial ties with England are apparent, as is the presence of Portuguese there. Bartholomew of Portugal is one of four Portuguese citizens of that country already established in London in the year 1220, according to a royal order of the king of England, and to another in 1208] *Considering the hard struggle for independence from which the Portuguese kingdom had but recently emerged.*[33] The tuna fishery in Algarve, an industry engaged in since Roman times, was one of the many industries that King Fernando protected. He also gave free lumber to anyone who would build a ship larger than 100 tons, and exempted other construction materials from taxes.[34] The people of Lisbon and Porto made an actual treaty with King Edward III of England in 1353.

Between the 13th and 14th centuries, possible sporadic discovery voyages were made, but without continuity or persistence.[35]

Due to insufficient documentation, some historians admit that by the 1450's, the Portuguese had reached or at least seen some of the Antilles, the American and Brazilian northeast, Newfoundland and Greenland. During those voyages they discovered the western part of the Azorean islands, having reached without a doubt the Sargasso Sea and gathered information to draw a complete map with precise winds and the Atlantic currents.[36]

The Sargasso Sea or Gulf Sea Weed (Berry Sea) is part of the North Atlantic Ocean west of the Azores and east of the West Indies and located approximately between 20° and 35° North latitude. The Bermuda Islands are within the northwestern portion of the sea. It is the calm center of the clockwise-turning subtropical gyre that dominates the North Atlantic. It is bounded on the west and north by the Gulf Stream and on the south by the North Equatorial Current.[37]

Early Discoveries and Naval Construction—1336-1456

A joint effort between the Portuguese and the Genoese may have taken place around 1336, when the Genoese Admiral Emanuel Pezagno may have been contracted by King Diniz to sail the Atlantic with Portuguese ships, discovering the *Fortunate Isles,* or Canary Islands. Also, Lanzarotto Malocello was probably with the admiral. From that date on, these islands began to be represented for the first time on Genoese and Mediterranean charts, such as the one of Angelino Dalorto (Dulcert).

There is a text attributed to the Italian writer Giovanni Bocaccio that speaks of a voyage to these islands in 1341 by *other Hispanics,* which appears to refer to the Portuguese. Also, the Portuguese King Afonso IV wrote a letter to the Pope making territorial claims to the islands.[38]

Between 1385 and 1456, out of a total of 46 ships engaged in the maritime trade between Portugal, England and Flanders, 83% were owned by the Portuguese.[39] We can easily see that the Portuguese, by the time discoveries started in the 15th century, were well prepared for high sea navigation and could very well have been on the east coast of North America, as some historians claim.

From the 12th century on, there was much trade between Portugal and Bristol, England:...*ships left the Bristol channel for Portugal, where they took on salt, and then sailed for Icelandic waters to fish, returned to Portugal to sell this fish and to buy wine, oil, and salt, and finally returned with this cargo to Bristol.*[40]

Portugal-England Alliance and Elizabethan English—1386

Portugal has the oldest alliance in the world with England, which dates back to May 9, 1386, and is known as the Treaty of Windsor. There are enough facts to conclude that the Portuguese Navy was instrumental in the defense of the British Isles in the 14th century.

Peter Russell, in his book *The English intervention in Spain and Portugal,* writes about the presence of Portuguese "fighters" to help the defense of southern England: *One tangible piece of evidence of the value of the Alliance to England had been the presence in English waters, since 1387, of a squadron of Portuguese galleys. This seems to have consisted of six vessels under the command of João's capitão do mar, Afonso Furtado. The squadron had evidently been based on Southhampton. ... in 1394, Portugal was the only power of military importance in western Europe to appear as an ally of England.* [41]

King João I of Portugal married an English princess, Philippa of Lancaster (1387), sister of Henry IV, King of England, who introduced various English habits into Portugal. Out of this marriage, four sons and a daughter were born, one of their most famous sons being Infante D. Henrique—Henry the Navigator. They all spoke English, and this language was widely used in the Portuguese court. The heavy trade with England carried well into the 16th and 17th centuries.

Catherine of Gaunt, Phillipa's sister, married King Juan II of Castile, which helped to maintain peace between Castile and Portugal for a while. Keeping with a tradition of close ties between Portugal and England, Charles II of England married a Portuguese princess, Catherine of Braganza, who also introduced Portuguese habits into England, such as the famous tea time, and furniture from India. The New York borough of Queens was named after her. Therefore it is safe to assume that during the reign of Queen Elizabeth I of England (1558-1603), people involved in navigation would have acquired English speaking habits of the time. [42]

Taking all of the above into consideration, still it is hard to believe that the Portuguese brought with them enough Elizabethan English speaking habits that would survive for one hundred years without any contact with the English. The author is inclined to rule out that they (Melungeons) were the only ones who spoke Elizabethan English when they were found by early explorers.

There is also a remote possibility that even one survivor of the Lost Roanoke Colony taught enough English to a Melungeon or Portuguese that eventually would have been used by the group. John Lawson, in a passage related to language learning, wrote in the 1700's:...*being of a French-man's Opinion, how that an English Wife teaches her Husband more English in one Night, than a School Master in a week.*

Portuguese and Spanish Inquisition—1391-1492

Jane Gerber, in her book *The Jews of Spain,* writes that after the Black Death in 1348, which wiped out almost a fifth of Europe's population, many German towns had expelled Jews or destroyed their communities—expulsion from Germany began earlier after the 12th century [43]—and the Spanish Jews were refused entry in many countries:...*in 1391 the Spanish persecution overwhelmed the Sephardim* [44] and, prior to that the Portuguese kings—1325/1383—protected the Jews. Apparently they had a relevant position in public finances.[45] King João I (1385-1433) pursued the same policy after winning the war against Castile. Professor Viera stated that the 1391 pogrom in Spain was not motivated by kings, who often protected the Jews. It was motivated by a Spanish preacher, Ferran Martinez. For further research in this time period and related to the Inquisition, Professor Viera also suggests studies by Henry Kamen and Phillippe Wolff: *The Inquisition was just established in Castile when Columbus arrived in Spain (1484)*—Cecil Roth gives 1482—[46] and the Inquisition was instituted in Portugal in 1536 for no apparent reason, except for the pressure put on João III of Portugal by Spanish monarchs who wanted his son to marry one of their daughters. Since Jews and Moors not converted were practically nonexistent, and the Muslims had already been absorbed by the Christian community, they did not constitute a major problem. The Portuguese King João III used it as an excuse to exercise more power and terror. The Jews were a relatively small group—just before the 1500's probably 30,000—and the Moors were a much smaller minority.[47] As for anti-Moor activities in Portugal, we must again make a separation between what was happening in Spain and Portugal, which would be similar to events in Northern Spain, where the Berbers and Moors had already assimilated with the Spaniards after they had been there for almost eight centuries. The expulsion of the free Muslims was more a hypothetical measure than anything else, as most had been absorbed by the Christian community.[48] Also in Portugal, the Moors and Berbers in the 15th and 16th centuries were integrated into the culture and language of the Portuguese since the 1200's. There were not many genuine Moors or Berbers at that time in Portugal, with the exception of the ones captured in the conquest of some Northwest African Moorish towns, and who were used mainly for prisoner exchanges.

The monarchs of Spain expelled the Moors and Jews from Spain after conquering Granada, the last stronghold of the Arabs in the Iberian Peninsula. That caused many people to find a way out of Spain, and later out of Portugal. It has been suggested that the Melungeons may have been part of that group.

Kennedy quotes Major Arthur Griffiths (inspector of prisons in Great Britain):... *the Portuguese Kings João III, Sebastião, and Felipe II were engaging in the same anti-Moor activities in Portugal. In fact, Portugal's Inquisition was far more vicious than Spain's.*[49] Major Griffiths does maintain that: *Autos de Fé* (Acts of Faith) *were frequent, and on a scale hardly known in Spain, though the records are fragmentary.*[50] Out of well over 200 pages, the author dedicates only 12 pages to the Inquisition in Portugal, and a few about an execution of an Englishman who attacked the cardinal archbishop while he was raising the host during a celebration of mass. A serious study after the first quarter of the 16th century in Portugal shows that the economic situation, famine and disease, more than the Inquisition, prompted many people to look elsewhere for survival at any risk.

That part—Inquisition—of the Portuguese history was bad, and no matter how small or large its actions were, it should not be considered unimportant. On the other hand, records show that it was not nearly as terrible as Spain's.

Now, as for Portugal's Inquisition being:...*far more vicious than Spain's*, let us look at the statistics. In the Inquisition Courts of Lisbon, Évora and Coimbra, 50 persons were condemned to death and executed in a public square between the years 1540 and 1609, according to Antonio Joaquim Moreira and described in his book *Historia dos Principais Actos e Procedimentos da Inquisição em Portugal.*[51] During the same period, 5,000 persons were executed in Spain, 70% of them having been Moors and Jews. *Between 1530 and 1609, the Inquisition in Valencia had dealt with more than five thousand cases, an average of sixty a year.*[52] Portugal at the end of the 16th century had a population of about 1.5 million compared to Spain's 8 million, or less than 20%. That means while Portugal executed one for every 30,000 population, Spain executed almost twenty as many for the same population ratio. To have some idea of European population at that time, England's population was between three and four million.[53]

Although Spain's numbers were higher than Portugal's, those were dark years in the Iberian Peninsula. Professor Manuel Fontes of Kent State University in Ohio wrote: *Without minimizing the horror, these sordid activities must be evaluated within the context of the time. To a great extent, Portugal and Spain avoided the witch hunts and the religious wars that brought death to many thousands in Europe...A couple of examples of what was happening elsewhere will suffice to place the two Iberian Inquisitions in perspective. In England, nearly 1,000 individuals were executed for witchcraft between the reign of Elizabeth I (1558) and the Act of 1736. In Southwestern Germany, at least 3,229 persons were executed as witches between 1561 and 1670. Concerning religious conflict during the same period, one only has to remember the numerous victims of the Reformation. A good example is the massacre of St. Bartholomew on August 24, 1572, when Catholics put to death at least 2,000 Huguenots in Paris alone. Thousands more were butchered as the massacre spread throughout the country. Other examples could be brought forth, but these are more than enough to show that the times were at least as cruel elsewhere in Europe.*[54] In this century due to the Holocaust, much has been written about the Jews and their plight. An historian and genealogist stated that: *Not so many Jews were killed in Portugal by the Inquisition. I am sure that the Titanic killed much more people in a couple of hours, than the Inquisition killed Jews (in Portugal) in 300 years.*

The Inquisition not only persecuted Moors and Jews but also the Lutherans. On September 14, 1559, 23 were executed, and 13 more on April 24, 1562.[55]

Notes

[1] Padre Antonio Vieira, 1640, Portuguese Missionary.
[2] Camões is Portugal's poet born before England's Shakespeare.
[3] National Geographic Magazine, November 1992 by Merle Severy.
[4] A World on the Move by A.J.R. Russell-Wood, pp. 4-6.
[5] Paisagens Arqueologicas de Évora, by Jorge de Oliveira, p. 54.
[6] Encyclopedia Britannica, Vol. 28, p. 19, 1993.
[7] Encyclopedia Britannica, Vol. 26, p. 51, 1993.
[8] Encyclopedia Britannica, p. 133, 2000 Yearbook.
[9] Menino de Leiria, Luso-Americano, July 28, 1999, p. 30.
[10] The Melungeons by Bonnie Ball, p. 31.
[11] National Geographic Magazine by Merle Severy, p. 558 (May 1977).
[12] Encyclopedia Britannica (1994).
[13] Luso-Americano Newspaper, Newark, NJ.
[14] Encyclopedia Britannica, 1993.
[15] Historia da Civilização Iberica, by Oliveira Martins, pp. 57-58.
[16] Dicionario de Historia de Portugal, by Joel Serrão, Vol. III, p. 154.
[17] The Portuguese Post, May 14, 1996.
[18] Microsoft Encarta 96 Encyclopedia CD-Rom.
[19] The Jews in Portugal by ICEP, p. 2.
[20] See page 15, of the Cidade de Tomar newspaper
"A Coroa dos Tabuleiros de Tomar" May 14th 1999.
[21] Historia da Origem e…Inquisição by Alexandre Herculano, pp. 67-69.
[22] The Jews of Spain by Jane Gerber, p. xxi.
[23] Historia de Portugal by Damião Peres, p. 656.
[24] Historia da Origem e…Inquisição by Alexandre Herculano, pp. 76-77.
[25] Historia dos Judeus in Portugal by Meyer Kayserling, p. 132.
[26] O Sacrificio de Isaac by Manuel da Costa Fontes, pp. 58-59.
[27] National Geographic Magazine, July 1988, p. 88.
[28] Historia da Civilização Iberica, by Oliveira Martins, p. 163.
[29] Interview with Professor Saraiva, July 1995.
[30] Correio da Manhã, 26 June 1995, by Antonio Pires, p. 2.
[31] Fomento Rural e Emigração by Oliveira Martins, p. 24.
[32] Portugal nos Mares by Oliveira Martins, p. 23.
[33] The Commercial Relations of England and Portugal by Shillington & Chapman, p. 25.
[34] Fomento Rural e Emigração by Oliveira Martins, p. 83.
[35] Historia de Portugal by Oliveira Marques, Vol. I, p. 244.
[36] Ibid, Vol. I, p. 264-7.
[37] Grolier Encyclopedia, 1995.
[38] Portugal and the Discovery of the Atlantic by Alfredo Pinheiro Marques, pp. 22-23.
[39] The Portuguese Seaborne Empire by Charles R. Boxer, p. 7.
[40] A Future to Inherit by David Biggs, p. 7.
[41] The English Intervention in Spain and Portugal by Peter Russell, pp. 527, 547
[42] The author recalls, as a young teenager after World War II in Lisbon which was constantly visited by the U.S. Navy, when we all tried to mimic the English language to get along better with the many sailors showing up all over Lisbon. As all teenage boys of that time, we were very jealous of them, sincc the girls would fall head over heels every time they would see the American sailors.
[43] David Viera 2/26/97 document.
[44] The Jews of Spain by Jane Gerber, pp. xii, 138, 139.
[45] Historia de Portugal by Oliveira Marques, Vol. I, p. 222.
[46] The Jews of Spain by Jane Gerber, p. xvi.
[47] Historia de Portugal by Oliveira Marques, pp. 289-290.
[48] Ibid, p. 367.

Notes (Cont.)

[49] The Melungeons by Brent Kennedy, p. 102.
[50] In Spanish Prisons by Arthur Griffiths, p. 113.
[51] Historia de Portugal by Joaquim Verissimo Serrão, p. 267.
[52] Ecclesia Militans by Miroslav Hroch / Anna Skýbová, p. 126.
[53] Historia de España, Historia 16, p. 507.
[54] O Sacrificio de Isaac by Manuel da Costa Fontes, pp. 59, 60.
[55] Ecclesia Militans by Miroslav Hroch / Anna Skýbová, p. 110.

*Fig. 47—Map of Portugal, the Westernmost European Nation,
and the one closest to the United States.*

Chapter VI

The Beginning of the Age of Discovery

*Enough for us that the hidden half of the Globe is brought to light,
and the Portuguese daily go farther beyond the equator.
Thus shores unknown will soon become accessible; for one in emulation of
another sets forth in labours and mighty perils.*[1]

The Discoveries period is the one most likely responsible for bringing the Melungeon ancestors to America. Since the Portuguese were the ones to pioneer navigation and discoveries of new lands, it is only proper to dedicate this Chapter to that time frame, and to how the Portuguese had the means to bring their people to this Continent, and other races with a different ethnic background.

Nau São Rafael 1498

Fig. 48—Ship of Discovery, Portuguese caravel of the 15th Century [2]
Painting of the model used by Vasco da Gama

Action on the Sea and Reaction to the Land

Genoa was, in the 13th century, the most active maritime power. It is known that in 1291 two Genoese galleys commanded by the Vivaldi brothers, with two Franciscan friars on board, sailed into the Atlantic and disappeared forever without the slightest trace, although between 1292 and 1304 several expeditions were sent from Genoa in search of them.

The next great expedition into the Atlantic was Portuguese; it sailed from Lisbon in 1336, probably under the command of the Genoese Lanzarotto Malocello, then a Portuguese subject serving Portugal. He succeeded, and these expeditions were followed by others from Castile.[3]

After that, Portugal became the Atlantic sea power in the early 15th century.[4] The exploits and influence, through four centuries of Europe's first great maritime empire, at their peak virtually girdled the earth.[5]

The caravel—diminutive of *caravos*—as the name implies, originated with the caravos, ships used by the Arabs since ancient times. Prince Henry's shipbuilders produced the famous caravel, which combined some of the cargo capacity features of the Arab caravos with the maneuverability of the Douro River caravels. It is interesting to note that Prince Henry was born in Porto by the Douro River.

When it was recognized that on long trips the Latin caravels had to use round sails to take advantage of the winds in different directions, the round caravel was created in Portugal at the beginning of the 16th century. It was extensively used on the routes to India as part of the armed fleet.

Besides the caravels, Prince Henry also had seamen that later in 1622 were described by Richard Hawkins, a contemporary Englishman and a competent judge: *...the Spaniards and Portingals doe exceed all that I have seene, I meane for their care, which is chiefest in navigation. And I wish in this, and in all their workes of Discipline and reformation, we should follow their examples...In every Ship of moment...whilst they Navigate, the Pilot...never depart, day or night, from the sight of the Compass.*[6]

If the Melungeons and other groups were Portuguese as they said they were, first the Portuguese presence on the East Coast must be proven, which apparently is not hard to do—as we shall see.

Not everyone knows the extent of the Portuguese presence on the East Coast. Well, it is quite substantial, and their contribution to this continent's development has been recognized throughout the years. However, some writers state that there is little concrete evidence of Portuguese activity in northeastern North America between the 1520's and the 1560's. Based on that, Kennedy mentions on page 83 of his book: *...it has generally been thought that there was a only a minimal Portuguese presence along the southeastern coast.* Yes, he is correct if we consider only those who arrived under the Portuguese flag.

Historians cannot ignore that the Portuguese were the closest Europeans to North America. The trip actually takes less than two weeks from the Azores on a 16th century caravel, with good weather, according to Quinn: *For a long time they had the capabilities, as well as the know-how of safely navigating in open oceans. ...For from the said Azores to the said Canada is not more than 400 leagues.*[7]

Not all historians agree that the Portuguese were great and courageous navigators. Fernand Braudel, writer of *The Mediterranean and the Mediterranean World in the Age of Philip II,* dedicated just a few paragraphs to the Portuguese: *...how the*

Portuguese, at the beginning of the 15th century, tackled the immense problem of navigation in the high seas, in the Atlantic, which was entirely new to them.[8]

Yes, the Atlantic was new to them, but it was new to everyone. On the other hand, it is known that the Portuguese merchant marine were in Flanders and the British Isles as early as the 13th century. How did they get there? Was the Atlantic really new to the Portuguese, when more than half of their nation borders on the ocean? *A position that deprived her of the cream of Mediterranean trade.*[9] How did the fishermen make their livelihood? Just fishing within sight of the coast? Why would the Portuguese venture out in the open seas?

Very simple. There is such a thing as survival, and when it comes to surviving you do whatever it takes. Portugal had nowhere to go but to the sea. What about the other European kingdoms? First of all, they had fertile agricultural lands, which are scarce in Portugal, and when the numerous small kingdoms wanted to enlarge their empires, all they had to do was to invade nearby lands.

Dr. Braudel goes on to repeat the words of Georg Friederici, a German writer: *...the Portuguese discoverers, following the endless African coast line, that in the lifetime of Henry the Navigator they were primarily timid and fearful coast-huggers, with no spirit of adventure.*[10] The world is full of injustices, and this is a typical example. Major powers of the world and their scholars not only ignored the Portuguese, but also laid on them derogatory epithets.

How did the Portuguese venture on the high seas being so *timid and fearful*? If timid and fearful people were able to do it, what happened to the others that we assume were courageous? My answer is to look at the results: The courageous followed the timid and fearful to the places discovered by the Portuguese.

Fortunately, there are other historians that do justice to the Portuguese, such as the five professors from four major universities who wrote the book *A History of the Western World—Ancient Times to 1715.* They made reference to the *...Technical Superiority of the Portuguese—The Portuguese were first. A maritime people, whose interest in European affairs was never great, their eyes were turned naturally to the sea. They were also a crusading people, hard-bitten fighters who had won back their land from the Moors.*[11]

Most Portuguese do agree that they were the worst business people in the world. At one time they had most major markets and lost them. As a matter of fact, they should go into the *Guinness Book of Records* for that.

Henry the Navigator (Infante D. Henrique) in his Lifetime

At the time of Prince Henry, and in the 1300 years since the Roman geographer Claudius Ptolomeu (ca. A.D. 73-151) of Alexandria, knowledge of the world did not advance much. Europe's northern people touched Iceland, Greenland, Labrador and possibly New York. All these voyages had no method, or were not followed, and their scientific value, if any, was lost.[12]

The love of adventure manifested in seeking new scenes beyond the wide seas, became for two or three generations an absorbing passion with multitudes. Nowhere was this spirit more prevalent or more fruitful than in Portugal. To her sons must be given the credit of having taken the lead in the maritime discovery of the period, and foremost among them must be ranked Prince Henry, the Navigator.[13]

Fig. 49—Henry the Navigator and Prince João, later King João II, who said No! to Christopher Columbus. Contemporary portrait. Courtesy of the Biblioteca Nacional, Lisbon, Portugal

Prince Henry the Navigator is a term coined in the 18th century. Infante D. Henrique, in Portuguese, was born in the city of Porto on March 4, 1394, and died on November 13, 1460. During this period, very important events took place. The following are just some of them that may have opened the oceans for the presence in North America of the Melungeons or other groups.

While the Portuguese prepared for their first venture in North Africa, much secrecy was involved, and it almost failed due to the fact that Portuguese Queen Filipa— Henry's mother—had a Black Jew as a servant who saw a letter revealing the expedition to Ceuta, supposedly a very well kept secret. The conquering of Ceuta on Aug. 21, 1415, was the beginning of the march from west to east. That expedition used 240 ships—27 galleys triremes, 63 round transport boats and 120 others— 50,000 men of which 30,000 were oarsmen and soldiers. There also was a boat loaded with armed soldiers which moved fast with the vigorous impulse of the oarsmen. Henry's purpose was to gather more information about the Far East and the caravans arriving there with precious and rare merchandise from India, China, etc. Apparently in that battle there was no mention of the capture of Moors as slaves.

One of the best sources of information that Henry had was his brother Pedro, duke of Coimbra, who traveled extensively in Europe. From 1425 to 1428, he spent much time traveling throughout Europe. The first visit was to Castile's King Juan II, his cousin. After that, England, where he intervened with success in a conflict between John de Gaunt and his uncle the Duke of Gloucester. Then he went to Bruges, Cologne, Vienna, Hungary, Romania, Venice, Florence, Rome, Catalonia and Aragon.

He stayed for a long while in the Italian Peninsula, because that area of the Mediterranean had intense relations with the Arab world. Here Prince Pedro visited the naval yards and casually gathered important information on the construction of ships, which he passed along to Henry.

There were plenty of myths about islands having been discovered by the Phoenicians and others that may be taken seriously according to the evidence presented, such as the Antilles, Seven Cities, etc.[14] The first Portuguese settlement attempt was on Madeira island, which almost failed in the beginning but prospered later on with vine plants that came from Chipre Island and sugar cane from Sicily.

It was not until 1435 that the Portuguese navigators first met black people, south of Cape Bojador, off Northeast Africa.

Henry's father, King João I, died and his son Duarte was crowned. During that same period, it was in Portugal that the Jews found relative security, in spite of the friction and disagreements. At the time King Duarte was crowned, the Jewish community was distributed throughout Portugal and had reached large proportions, a nation within a nation.

Antão Gonçalves captured ten Berbers in the East Sahara in 1441, with various tones of skin color, both darker and lighter. Out of these, one seemed to be a noble Berber. His name was Adahu.

He spoke Arabic and appeared to be a well traveled man with much knowledge. They were taken to Portugal, and Henry obtained valuable information. That Berber later arranged, for himself and two more, a return trip to the Sahara, with the promise that he would give in exchange ten black slaves.

In 1443 the first shipment of black slaves arrived in Portugal from Africa, south of the Sahara desert. After that, village was thrown against village, kingdom against kingdom, on a ferocious hunting for slaves by the black chiefs that lasted several centuries.

In 1445, wealthy navigators wanted to equip ships and, on their own, sail across the sea in search of fortune. The art of navigation was well known, even by the fishermen that would venture much further south—Rio de Ouro—to fill their nets. *Not only the adventurers wanted to go on Maritime voyages, but also many others, just for the honor of serving under Henry the Navigator.*[15]

The Berbers of the Sahara region would eagerly await the arrival of the Portuguese caravels. On one of the voyages they climbed aboard the ships in groups, where they spent all day having fun.

That did not last long due to Gomes Pires, who having been cheated by one of the Berbers, threw all of them out, captured 80, and brought them to Portugal.[16] That was the only capture of Berbers known. Would their descendants emigrate to America later in the 16th century?

During that period, Diogo Gomes, (1440-84) a Portuguese explorer, was sent by Prince Henry about 1456 to investigate the West African coast.

The so-called *Catalan Atlas* of 1375 was made for the King of Aragon by Abraham Cresques, a Jew of Palma on Mayorca working for the king. As the persecution of the Jews resumed in Aragon late in the 14th century, Abraham's son Jehuda, who was carrying on his father's work, was forced to emigrate. *Accepting the invitation of Prince Henry, he took refuge in Portugal, where he helped the Portuguese prepare the maps for their overseas discoveries.*[17]

This Jew must be the same one mentioned by Oliveira Martins, a 19th century Portuguese historian. In his book *Portugal nos Mares* the name is spelled differently, *Jafuda*. He had such a reputation and credit as a cosmographer that he was known as the Compasses' Jew or *o Judeu das Bússolas*.

Later on he changed his name to Jaime Ribes due to persecution in Aragon against the Jews, and he may be the one that later taught at the primitive Sagres School of Navigation with Prince Henry the Navigator.[18]

The techniques for marking latitudes were developed by the Portuguese in the 15th century by mariners sailing down the coast of Africa.

Between 1419 and 1433, about 20 sea exploratory voyages were made by the Portuguese, and for many of them no records have been found of their discoveries.

Due to the scarcity of human and material resources, the Portuguese King João II left the western explorations up to private enterprise, according to Ribeiro of the Portuguese Navy: *Only the African Coast explorations were made at the expense of the Crown.*[19]

That may also explain the privately financed trips of which no records were made.

Portuguese Secrecy of Navigation—Portuguese Navigators

Bonnie Ball writes: *It is not beyond the realm of possibility that some Portuguese sailors could in fact be ancestors of the Melungeons, for their unrecorded explorations could have easily reached into North America.*[20]

The breach of secrecy, passing secrets to Spain or to any other nation, was punishable by death, and that was a deterrent.[21] Unfortunately, not keeping records did not help the historians, but did help the Portuguese then, as it took many years for other European nations to accomplish the same as the Portuguese did around the world. Oliveira Martins states that in 1531 and during the reigning of King João III, the silence of the best pilots was paid a high price, and the indiscretion of the cartographers could result in severe punishment or even execution.[22]

Fernand Braudel notes that King João II ordered the Portuguese pilot who told him that it was possible to get back from the coast of Mina with any ship in good condition, to remain silent under threat of imprisonment.[23] However, Morison does not give much credit to this alleged secrecy by the Portuguese, thus discounting any early discoveries by the Portuguese navigators based on oral history. But, on the other hand, he fully credits Cabot's discovery of Newfoundland under the English flag, based solely on oral versions of his voyage. Anderson & Higgs, two Canadian historians in their book *A Future to Inherit* stated on page seven that: *He* [Morison] *has particularly distinguished himself in denying the Portuguese claim to a place in the forefront of the discoveries in the Northwest Atlantic.*

It was this secrecy that enabled King João II to sign the Treaty of Tordesilles, which proved to be advantageous to Portugal. During King Manuel I's reign, the death penalty was established for anyone divulging navigation secrets.[24]

Although hard proof may not be available, the oldest sources available demonstrate that astronomical navigation was invented and developed by the Portuguese in the late 15th century: *Again to some extent this has been created by the existence of policies of secrecy.*[25]

Skelton points out that Portuguese maps went to: *...humanist Konrad Peutinger (1465-1547) who had particular opportunities for collecting in Portugal.*[26]

Allied to secrecy and stealing is also the destruction of many documents, to the point that the Portuguese do not even know the precise date of the death of Camões, Portugal's great epic poet (some time between 1579 and 1580) nor the location of his tomb[27] Moura wrote: *Not a single manuscript with his own handwriting has survived...*[28] Camões was well known by his contemporaries, famous throughout Europe, and his epic poems were translated and published. It is therefore not surprising that documentation proving the Portuguese discoveries is also not available. Historian Morison does not accept the Portuguese policy of secrecy as an excuse for not having records, and states that the secrecy was to protect Portugal, but apparently ended up benefiting Spain, England and France, as it would be very hard to keep secrets in the 15th century. However, secrecy existed then and still does today in practically every country. There are spies and counter spies and double agents. Back then it was no different.

Holland also benefited in no small way, as stated in the *History of the Western World—Ancient Times to 1715*: *...The Portuguese tended to be closed with the secrets of navigation on the sea road to the Indies, secrets which they patiently accumulated over nearly two centuries of exploration. Fortunately for the Dutch, a Netherlander, Jan Huyghen van Linschoten, who had spent six years with the Portuguese in India, published a very informative book of sailing directions. Equipped with this guide, in 1595 a Dutch expedition...*[29]

Russell Miller in his book *The East Indiamen,* adds: *Until its publication in 1596, information about the Orient had been sparse and details of Portuguese trade there a well kept secret.*[30]

There is one factor, however that historians sometimes forget: In the 15th century illiteracy was common among most fishermen, sailors, and possibly some of the early navigators. Only a select few could read or write. How could they keep records if they could not write? That was the best secret, except sailors did a lot of gossiping, and that is why the oral stories told throughout the centuries should not be completely disregarded.

In order to help solve the problem, according to one chronicle, a Captain decided to tie a bundle of garlic over one side of the ship and a handful of onions over the other. Then the pilot would shout to the helmsmen:*...onion your helm* or *Garlic your helm.*[31] Louis André Vigneras, a professor at George Washington University makes this point quite clear: *The armada de Sancho de Archiniea, bringing in supplies and reinforcements from Spain, finally reached St. Augustine on June 20 (1566). With this fleet came a man who would play a leading role...He was Domingo Fernández, a pilot in whom the Spanish general placed implicit trust. Although an **illiterate** man who could not even sign his own name, Fernández must have been a first class pilot...And since Fernández was one of the few pilots who knew the coast of Florida...he acted more or less as (piloto mayor).*[32]

João Rocha Pinto, in his book about ship log books, concludes that there were no log books during the major part of the 16th century, and that only after 1530 do we start seeing an attempt to record the daily navigation. Some narratives were written, but there was far from a daily record of the voyages. Only towards the end of the 16th century did the daily practice of recording the magnetic needle deviation of the latitude and longitude evolve.[33]

The passage of Neville Williams' book *Great Lives,* about Drake, shows that secrecy existed and the Portuguese were not the only ones to keep their plans secret.[34] Francis Drake did not reveal to his crew in advance the full purpose of his voyages or his intention to sail into the Pacific. He gave his colleague officers on board the bare information necessary to conduct the ship to the next port.[35] Some historians, such as Morison, still do not believe that the Portuguese had a strong policy of secrecy during the early period of the discoveries.[36]

Portuguese Navigators Working for other Countries

During the times of Portuguese discoveries, at least 68 Portuguese navigators worked for Spain—25 for France, six for England and one for Holland.[37] Patterson said: *Giving due recognition to the presence of other nations on the field, however, enough has been adduced to show that the Portuguese occupied a prominent, I think I may say the foremost, place in the exploration of the north-east coast of America in the 16th century.*[38] Another historian also wrote that the Portuguese did indeed play a major but unheralded role in the Spanish expeditions.

The number of Portuguese navigators that worked for Portugal is definitely much greater. These were the registered ones, but it is believed that there were many more. However, Portugal also had foreign men working in the navy, but mostly cartographers or astrónomers.

In 1457, the Venetian Alvise Ca' da Mosto (Cadamosto), envoy of the Portuguese Prince Henry the Navigator, explored the Ziguinchor harbor, a river-port town, in southwestern Senegal, lying along the Casamance River. He also discovered the river Gambia in 1455, and the Senegal in 1457.[39] He said when he saw the first caravel that it was the best ship on the sea, and there was not a place where it could not navigate. Another foreign navigator, Amerigo Vespucci—later he lent his name to the North and South American continents—worked for Portugal in 1501-02, and helped to explore the South American coast of Brazil before he went to work for Spain in 1503.[40] Also, several Spanish sailors joined the Portuguese expeditions of Pedro Álvares Cabral to Brazil and India.[41]

During an interview with professor and Portuguese historian Dr. Saraiva, he stated that Queen Isabel of Castile was known to have said that the best nanny she knew was the king of Portugal, because he raised the gentlemen (fidalgos) from little children and would give them to her when they were already grown up.[42] This was true, as Portuguese men were and still are fond of Spanish women; many Portuguese nobles would go to Spain, and eventually marry there.

Discovery of Madeira Island—1424

These islands off North Africa's Atlantic coast may have been visited by Arabs and others before the Portuguese, but no attempt was ever made to claim or settle them. There is a legend about the main island, Madeira, known by Madeirans, which may have been started and perpetuated by the English. The legend has its beginnings in England, when a couple in love did not have the approval of their parents. They decided to run away in a boat with a small crew, and due to a storm, landed in Madeira. Later the young maiden died, was buried, and an inscription made on the tombstone. Her lover died shortly after and the crew left the island to tell the story. As in all legends, there are no dates. The name of the Englishman was Machin, and the lady was Anna de Harfet.[43] There is today a place in Madeira called Machico. There are, however, other stories, such as one about a merchant also called Machico who conducted business in Portuguese ports during the 1370s.[44]

Whoever had been there provided information for Prince Henry's later discovery. By 1417 or 1419 the Portuguese navigators João Gonçalves Zarco, Tristão Vaz Teixeira and Bartolomeu Perestrelo may have landed there. The names of the islands derived from the Latin, such as *legname* (wood) for the main island. The others, Porto Santo and Desertas, did not need translation.

After arriving in Porto Santo, the Portuguese planted crops. However in the beginning this turned out to be a complete failure, due to a rabbit. Apparently someone gave Bartolomeu Perestrelo a pregnant rabbit as he was leaving Portugal. During the voyage little rabbits were born, and later on arrival he let them loose on the island. Naturally the rabbits proliferated and ate all the crops. But, as tradition has it, the first female and male children born on the island were named Adam and Eve.[45] Later, slaves from the Canary Islands provided a large part of the population.[46]

Pizzigano Map—1424

There is cartographic evidence that the Portuguese were in Newfoundland before August 22nd 1424, according to the Venetian Zuanne Pizzigano's nautical chart. He may have been Venetian, but the names he used were Portuguese. Dr. Manuel Luciano da Silva describes it in detail in his book *The True Antilles*. This nautical chart represents a Venetian adaptation of a Portuguese cartographic design that made its way to Italy, documenting real discoveries in the west made by the Portuguese at this early stage.[47] This opinion is shared by the Portuguese historian Armando Cortesão and by Lieutenant-Commander Avelino Teixeira da Mota: ...who wrote: *we are convinced...which in this chart lie westward of the Azores...visited by unknown Portuguese at an early date, probably just before 1424*.[48] This view is not necessarily shared by all historians. On this same map, a note appears in the middle of the Atlantic, calling the area the Sargasso Sea—knowledge obtained from the Portuguese, thus indicating they had been much farther west, and possibly close to the North American continent.

Dr. Silva has discovered that the actual latitudinal position of the Antilles on the Pizzigano map places them in approximately the same location as Newfoundland and Nova Scotia in Canada. There are also Portuguese names on the same map.[49] The Pizzigano map, now in the University of Minnesota library, was studied by historian Armando Cortesão in 1950. The Portuguese presence in the Antilles is confirmed by the reputed discovery of the Soviet historian Tspernick in 1959, of a letter from King Fernando and Queen Isabel of Spain which states that Columbus knew of the existence of land in the Antilles before starting out on his voyage, because he had heard about this from a sailor, Alonzo Sanches, who had mapped the Antilles. A study of this map may be read in Vol. II of *Historia da Cartografia Portuguesa* by Armando Cortesão.

A Portuguese by the name of Dualmo, if we are to believe the British historian A. Davies, sailed from the Azores in 1487 and discovered America five years ahead of Columbus.[50] Also, with Prince Henry's encouragement, at least one enterprising navigator seems to have reached the Maritime Provinces of Canada around 1424.

Unfortunately we do not know his name, but the Pizzigano map gives us the cartographic evidence of his visit.[51]

The historian Samuel Eliot Morison calls the isles drawn on this map *The Fabulous Antilles Group,* and dismisses: [the]...*discoveries because the names appeared only on Italian, Spanish, or other maps but never on a Portuguese map.*[52] Again, secrecy would have been one reason for not recording lands discovered in maps, such as the Antilles. One should ask, what does Morison mean by an Italian map in the 15th century, since there was no such country as Italy? Probably he means one of the Republics in the Italian Peninsula. If so, the words were most likely in Latin. In the 15th century, there was no abundance of maps showing the exact position of continents, much less countries or islands. However with all the secrecy, the earliest map showing the East Coast of North America was made in Portugal, as we shall see in the following pages.

Professor Morison not only rejected Dr. Cortesão's conclusions, but he also had some harsh words for the Portuguese University of Coimbra.[53]

Discovery of the Azores—1427-32

These islands were the westernmost known place in the Atlantic, and historians point to 1427 as a possible early date of their discovery by Diogo de Silves. The most cited date of discovery is August 14, 1432, by Gonçalo Velho Cabral, however there is no documentary proof. The actual distance between the Azores as the most westward landfall and the North American Continent was unknown at that time. The Azores were the most important stop, first for the Portuguese when exploring the west coast of Africa, next for the Spaniards when going to or returning from the West Indies, and later for the English privateers awaiting the return of the Spanish galleons laden with treasure. Many battles were fought off the Azores, and in one that took place off Flores Island in 1591, Grenville, an English vice-admiral at the time, was killed and his vessel *Revenge* sank in a storm on the way to Cadiz as a Spanish prize.[54] Also, *Pedro de Valdez* (or Pedro Menéndes de Aviles, the founder of St. Augustine) *was defeated in the Battle of Salga on July 25th 1581, when attempting to invade Terceira Island.* [55]

Portuguese in Labrador and Newfoundland—1452-74

History, in order to be believed, must have solid proof of written records plus other archaeological or anthropological findings, which sometimes are obtained with basis on oral traditions. The explorers had their names recorded for posterity. However, the true pioneers of discovery in eastern North America were very often the fishermen, from whom the navigators received information brought back from their fishing trips. Their knowledge was considered valuable news to the navigators. John Bartlet Brebner wrote about the European fishermen of Newfoundland: *These nameless men, Portuguese, Basques, Bretons and Englishmen, were the really consistent maintainers of European contact with north-eastern North America, rather than the explorers who from time to time got their names recorded in documents of state.*[56] Right after the settlement of the Azores, the fever of discovery filled the minds of many seamen, who asked the king to grant them special advantages of lands or islands that they eventually would discover. Based on obscure and imprecise information in various documents, some historians believe that Portuguese navigators arrived in Newfoundland, or at least nearby waters, shortly after 1450, and certainly before 1480. This affirmation is extremely bold after reading the documentation.[57] The above commentary was written by Luis de Albuquerque in a book by Maria da Graça Pericão. He may be right, but after some investigation, no proof has been presented one way or the other. This historian also said that there was no such thing as a Navigation School of Sagres.[58] Well, it all depends upon what was considered a school in the 15th century. Did it have a large building and a faculty, staff, professors, etc. such as the University of Coimbra in those days? Most likely not. But what would you call a place where learned men met to discuss and to learn from each other, as well as to teach those around them? The Greek philosopher Plato taught in a garden called Academus, and his pupil Aristotle started a school of logic, metaphysics, etc., in a garden called Lyceum. Should we say that those schools never existed?

Based on Chapter IX of the *Historia de Colon* (Italian translation), written by Columbus' son Fernando Colon, and Chapter XIII of the *Historia de las Indias* by Las Casas, a voyage was made to the banks of Newfoundland by the Portuguese Diogo de Teive and the Spanish Pero Vasquez de la Frontera.[59]

Columbus's son Fernando wrote that his father collected information in Portugal about an island 200 leagues from the Azores and Canaries, and that some Portuguese sailors were pushed there by a storm, but afterwards could not get back since they did not know the way.[60]

It is possible that voyages to Canada were made by Álvaro Martins Homem and João Vaz Corte Real, but nothing was ever recorded, except that a letter by the Princess Dona Brites refers to a voyage made in 1472 or 1474.[61]

Another Terceiran, João Fernandes, called *o Lavrador* from his occupation as a farmer or small landowner, went on a voyage of exploration to the north in 1492 (or 1499) together with one Pedro de Barcelos. It has been surmised, chiefly from maps showing the Land of Labrador, that Fernandes discovered what is now known as Labrador; but closer investigation suggests that the land he visited is present-day Greenland.[62] Secrecy is one of the reasons presented; however, historians scorn that. The distance from Azores is rather close, and fishermen were known to venture out to sea for long periods of time in search of good fishing, which the banks of Newfoundland provided.

Bartolomeu Dias and Cape of Good Hope—1488

Four years before Columbus' first voyage, Dias, a Portuguese navigator, rounded the Cape of Good Hope in South Africa. That may have nothing to do with the presence of the Portuguese on the U.S. East Coast but, as we will discover later, it does present us with an interesting possibility.

The traffic of caravels for the following 50 years was so heavy that vessels almost bumped into each other, and many disappeared without a trace, never reaching their chartered destinations.

Later in 1500, Dias' caravel was lost in the same area, when going to India as part of the Cabral fleet.[63]

Columbus in America—1467-92

When the grandchildren of famous Portuguese navigators were already sailing, Christopher Columbus, of questionable Genovese birth, crossed the Atlantic

Fig. 50—This is considered as the only authentic Columbus portrait 1507-15. Courtesy of Biblioteca Nacional, Madrid.

and landed in the West Indies. Skelton points out that:...*before 1500 Portugal had a hydrographic office charged with the custody and correction of sea charts.*[64]

Certainly it must have been easy for Columbus to attain the sea navigation knowledge he needed.

He derived much of his nautical knowledge and interests from the Portuguese.

Historian Samuel Eliot Morison, a much cited author, states with conviction: *...without the preliminary work of the Portuguese, the...Voyage of Columbus could not have attained its object.*[65]

Rev. George Patterson, on his presentation to the Royal Society of Canada in 1890 said: *There is no reason to believe that it was in these explorations that Columbus was led to those conclusions, which issued in the discovery of America, he was in Portugal from 1470 to 1484, during which time he made several voyages to the coast of Guinea in the Portuguese service.*[66]

A famous Norwegian historian and seafarer, Thor Heyerdahl, claimed that Columbus arrived in America in 1467, and not in 1492.[67]

He goes on to say that archive studies show that Columbus was in America long before he discovered it, on a Danish-Portuguese expedition to the Davis Strait in 1467.

This Norwegian researcher, who gained fame for his daring 1947 trans-Pacific voyage aboard a flimsy raft, said that Columbus did not accidentally stumble onto the American continent while looking for India, as most

Fig. 51—Columbus' Signature

historians believe. Instead, he knew exactly where to sail because he previously traveled with a Danish-Portuguese expedition to Greenland as a teenage crew member.

To his credit, it can be said that at that time (1448-1481), Portuguese King Afonso V was trying to reach East India using the northern route, and negotiated with the Danish King Christian for a joint venture.

Portuguese association with Danish and English exploration is well known. Close relationships between Portugal and Denmark in the 15th century were a result of royal marriages, and to the visit of Prince Pedro—brother of Henry the Navigator— to Denmark in 1426, after evidently hearing reports of expeditions to Greenland.

The Portuguese king supplied ships and crews, and the Danish king supplied two Norwegians, Didrick Pining and Hans Pothorst.

João Vaz Corte Real was made viceroy of whatever they would discover. The narration of this voyage is a brief one because of Portugal's reluctance to publicize their discoveries, and so this adventure was so shrouded in secrecy that its discoveries were not made known.[68]

Armando Cortesão stated: *...beside Pinzón in Castile, there was in Portugal many that were convinced of the existence of such lands (America) and had even already been there.*[69]

That only proves that the Portuguese knew for a long time where America was, except no one was interested in this continent.

Fig. 52—Vasco da Gama, portrait painting. Courtesy of the Museu Nacional de Arte Antiga, Portugal.

Their aim was to reach India or the Far East.

We have to draw a similar parallel: The Chinese knew where Europe was in the 15th century and how to get there, they also had the resources to make the voyage, and they did not do it because they were not interested and: *...deliberately turned their backs on maritime expansion before the end of the 15th century.*[70]

The original narrative of Columbus' third voyage tells us that he arrived at Porto Santo on Thursday, June 7th, 1498, where he stopped to take on wood, water and supplies and to hear mass.

Next Columbus arrived in Madeira on Sunday, June 10, and was very well received in Funchal with much rejoicing, because he was well known there, having been a: *...citizen thereof during some time.*[71]

Vasco da Gama—Sea Route to India—1498

Six years after Columbus discovered America, trying to get to India or the Far East—without ever getting there—the Portuguese found the sea route to India, quickly establishing a profitable trade. Vasco da Gama's fleet was composed of four caravels and 160 men, all well chosen as the best sailors that Portugal had, many of them nobles.

Vasco da Gama departed on July 9, 1497 and arrived in Calicut in May 1498. His ships cruised uncharted seas for 4,500 miles, a voyage of 96 days, without a glimpse of land. Columbus had sailed for 3,500 miles after he left the Canaries, when he sighted the Bahamas.[72] *Gama's 23,800 mile voyage to India and back stands unique in navigation history.*[73]

A contemporary narration mentions the effects of s*curvy*, without knowing at the time that it could be cured just by eating fresh fruits. Not until the 18th century were the two connected by Captain James Cook. Dr. Luciano da Silva has also written a medical article about Camões and scurvy.

Vasco da Gama's discovery may not be related to the U.S. East Coast, but, as we will find later in one of the next chapters, it may have something to do with the subject being researched.

Fig. 53—Painting by José Velloso Salgado, Sociedade de Geografia de Lisboa, depicting Vasco da Gama at the Court of the Zamorin of Calicut in India.

Also in this same year, Duarte Pacheco Pereira may have reached Florida.[74] The following year the Spaniard Alonso de Ojeda, accompanied by the Florentine

Amerigo Vespucci, sailed to the mouth of the Orinoco and explored the coast of Venezuela. It is interesting to note that Vasco da Gama's route to India brought his fleet quite close to Brazil; hence, he may already have known of the existence of lands to the west.

A poem from the Lusiadas. *This masterpiece of Camões, one of the world's greatest epic poems, is the finest monument to Vasco da Gama's genius.*[75]

> Nor less of pomp the Lusitanian shows
> When, with his gallant retinue, advance
> The Armada's boats, midway to welcome those
> Of the Melindan on the bay's expense
> Clad in the vogue of Spain, Da Gama goes
> All but the cloak, a gorgeous robe of France,
> The web Venetian satin, and the dye
> A glorious crimson that delights the eye.[76]

Fig. 54—*Pedro Álvares Cabral as depicted in an 18th century engraving* [70]

Pedro Álvares Cabral in Brazil by Accident—1500 ?

The discovery of Brazil by accident has been one lie perpetuated by less informed writers. Here is what Charles Ralph Boxer says in his book *The Portuguese Seaborne Empire: ...during three years the Portuguese were making secret voyages in the south Atlantic in order to familiarize themselves with the sailing conditions there.*[77]

Cabral explored well over a thousand miles of the Brazilian sea coast, a fact that demonstrates he had previous knowledge of the area. This fact was reported by Venetian diplomats, in conflict with the veiled letter that King Manuel I sent to the Pope.[78]

Kennedy, probably due to an oversight, wrote in his book: *Renowned Portuguese explorer Pedro Álvares Cabral discovered Brazil in 1500 by accident. Rounding the southern tip of Africa and heading northward on his return to Portugal, Cabral made a miscalculation that took him farther west than he intended. Where the South American and African continents are at their closest, Cabral unexpectedly "bumped" into Brazil.*[79] Actually, he landed in Brazil when he was heading southward on the way to Africa.

Fig. 55—Andrea Bianco map of 1448

The not very well known Andrea Bianco Map of 1448 clearly shows that the Portuguese already knew about the existence of land to the west of Africa, and the distance from Guinea to the north coast of South America. The map on Fig. 55 shows the distance to be 1,500 miles to the west. Also notice the Amazon river mouth. There are reasons to believe that Diogo de Teive was there, and informed Bianco and Antonio Leme in 1471.

As a matter of interest, it should also be noted that Antonio Galvão wrote a book in 1550, translated into English in 1601, and reprinted in 1862 with notes by Admiral Bethune. Galvão states that in 1428 in Venice, Prince Pedro—brother of Henry the Navigator—received a world map that supposedly showed the African and South American continents. In 1447, Andrea Bianco, a Venetian cartographer working for Fra Mauro, was in Lisbon on the way to London. While in London he made a nine-page atlas based on information obtained in Portugal. That same information may have been related to a 1447 voyage that was reported in Galvão's book. The Bianco atlas shows a large island located 1,500 miles west of Cape Verde, which in itself is amazing, taking into consideration that it was in error by only 20 miles.[80]

This map, or a copy, was later (ca. 1480) in the hands of Pero Vaz da Cunha, the Bisagudo. It was also referred to in a letter sent by Mestre João, physician to King Manuel I of Portugal, from the coast of Brazil in 1500.[81] The following are some of the contemporary chronicles about Portuguese voyages, first in Portuguese, followed by a translation in English: [in Portuguese] *Porem, tendo-se perdido tambem o piloto, este acontecimento nautico revela-nos que as viagens de retirada da Costa da Guiné, seguindo em largo arco a rota indirecta, já em 1446 não eram misterio...confirmação de aquele mar de baga da Carta de Bianco datada de 1436, já fora descoberta dos mareantes portugueses por essa época.* [In English] *However, the pilot got lost and this nautical event reveals that the voyages from the Guinea coast, following in an indirect large arch, already in 1446 were not a mystery...confirming that sea of baga on Bianco's map dated 1436, already had been a discovery of Portuguese seamen of that time.*[82]

As for Cabral's accidental discovery, that he *unexpectedly "bumped" into Brazil*, it is a well known fact that he was not the first Portuguese navigator to arrive in Brazil. Others preceded him. Kennedy quotes Zvi Dor-Ner rather differently due to the generally accepted belief about Cabral's discovery.

Here is how Zvi Dor-Ner describes Cabral's landing on the coast of Brazil: *In 1500 the Portuguese explorer Pedro Álvares Cabral, who had been following Vasco da Gama's route to India via Africa's Cape of Good Hope, swung far to the west after rounding the bulge of Africa and became the first person in recorded history to land on the coast of Brazil.*[83] The book *Civilization in the West* written by Christopher Brinton from Harvard University and Robert Lee Wolf from the University of Rochester, notes: *It may be that this was not accidental as it seems.*[84] By 1500 the Spanish were well launched in exploration, and Columbus' voyages were well known. In 1493, after Columbus' first voyage, Pope Alexander VI had granted to Spain all lands south and west of a north-south line drawn in the Atlantic between the Azores and the Cape Verde Islands.

In 1494, the Portuguese, by the Treaty of Tordesilles with Spain, succeeded in having this line moved 270 leagues farther west. Thus Brazil fell into the sphere of the Portuguese, who may have known about it all along, and who only announced their landing there after Cabral's voyage. *In any case, it was now determined that Brazil alone in Latin America would be Portuguese; everything else lay on the Spanish side of the line.*[85]

There is, however, a little known fact: In the 18th century, Uruguay was located on the Portuguese side, but later was exchanged by the Portuguese for Amazons, which was on the Spanish side. Because of that, Uruguay's language is Spanish and the Amazons', Portuguese.

Duarte Pacheco Pereira, Portuguese sea captain and explorer, may have discovered Brazil in 1498, two years before Pedro Álvares Cabral explored the Brazilian coast. Because of his military exploits in India, the poet Camões called him Aquiles Lusitano (the Portuguese Achilles).

The only indication that he may have been in Brazil in 1498 is his writing of the *Esmeraldo situ orbis,* where he states that the king had ordered him to discover the western part beyond the great ocean.[86]

Pacheco Pereira, reared at the Portuguese court, was an educated man, serving as a squire to King João II. He became an expert cartographer as well as a pilot and shipmaster. He explored the coast of Africa in 1488, returning with Bartolomeu Dias, who had discovered the Cape of Good Hope.

Pereira sailed with Dias in 1500 on the voyage during which Cabral claimed Brazil for the king of Portugal. In 1504 Pacheco Pereira helped defend the Portuguese trading station at Cochin, India, against attacks by the ruler of Calicut. With about 200 Portuguese, Pereira successfully held off armies that numbered well over 20,000 men.

Returning to Portugal in 1505, Pereira received many honors. He collected his log books and charts and wrote a valuable account of Portuguese exploration— published in modern editions in 1892 and 1903.

He was appointed governor of São Jorge da Mina but fell into disgrace when enemies reported that he had embezzled official funds. He was exonerated, but he died shortly thereafter in poverty.

The narrative of the third voyage of Columbus in 1498 reads that Columbus said: *...he wished to go south...and that he wishes to see what was the idea of King João II of Portugal, who said that there was mainland to the south.*[87] This and other facts should not be ignored when establishing what the Portuguese discovered.

Much has been written about the discovery of Brazil; however, the end is still not in sight, with more information being unveiled as time passes. One example of this is Chapter V of Jaime Cortesão's book *Os Descobrimentos Portugueses*.

Cortesão and his brother, Dr. Armando Cortesão, are history professors and have to their credit many books. American historian Samuel Eliot Morison has also referred to their books, not necessarily always agreeing with them. One of the chapters, *Viagens pré-cabralinas ao Brasil* or *Voyages pre-Cabral to Brazil* in English, caught the author's attention and presented a different story. When Martin Afonso de Sousa, working for Spain in 1531, was on the way to Argentina, he anchored in Cananeia (state of São Paulo) and met a man in exile (*degredado*) that history would call the Bachelor of Cananeia. Pêro Lopes mentioned this man in the exploration's log book as having been in Brazil for a good 30 years.

If this was the case, he had lived there since 1501. This does not seem to make sense; and then, to make matters worse, Diogo Garcia, a Portuguese pilot also working for Spain, wrote in Spanish about events in 1527: *E aqui fuímos a tomar refresco en San Vicente, que está en 20 grados e alli vive un Bachieller y unos yernos suyos mucho tiempo ha que ha bien treinta años.*[88] In English: *...here we went to have refreshment in San Vicente, which is at 20 degrees, and there lives a Bachelor and his sons-in-law for a long time, a good thirty years.* In 1530, when Diogo Garcia returned to Andalucia, Spain, he referred to the arrival of the *Bachelor of Cananeia* in 1497 or 1500. The expression *bien treinta años,* a good thirty years, must mean more than thirty.

Rui Diaz de Guzmán qualifies the Bachelor as a Portuguese gentleman or *Fidalgo* and calls him Duarte Pires in his book *La Argentina,* written in 1612. Then, by chance, a document dated April 24, 1499 was found that mentions a certain exiled Bachelor and no other name. The common designation is *Bachelor* and *exiled,* which led Dr. Cortesão to believe that it was the same person. The reference is part of a long will by Álvaro de Caminha, Captain of São Tomé Island, off west Africa, which also describes the colonization of that isle, in which Jewish babies took part, sent there by King João II.[89]

By this document it can be concluded that a depository of exiled persons existed on the island. At least 65 names are mentioned.

The same document mentions the Bachelor and the way his belongings should be disposed of, without mentioning that he was dead, but rather that he was absent from the island. It is assumed with certainty that the Bachelor was the same person being mentioned both in Africa and in South America. But if that was the case, how did he get to Cananeia?

Admiral Gago Coutinho, another famous Portuguese—historian and pilot—admitted that Bartolomeu Dias was one of the discoverers of Brazil. This navigator was the first European to go around the tip of South Africa in 1488, opening the Portuguese sea route to India.

Bartolomeu Dias was on São Tomé Island, and left towards the end of 1497. Is this the same Bartolomeu Dias, or was there another navigator with the same name who took the Bachelor to Cananeia? Another Portuguese already mentioned had the same task, that is, to go from São Tomé to explore the Brazilian coast in 1498.[90]

This fact enforces the previous assumption—and Cortesão believes—that the Bachelor of São Tomé left that island at the end of the 15th century in a caravel commanded by Bartolomeu Dias. We should not overlook the fact that, in order to reach the southern tip of Africa, any sailing ship must sail west towards South America to catch the proper winds and currents going in a southeasterly direction. Trade winds and currents—Brazilian current—were the cause of many shipwrecks. Bartolomeu Dias knew that in 1488, and Duarte Pacheco knew it in 1498.

1498-1998—500 Years Later

In 1998, Portugal celebrated the 500-year anniversary of the Discovery of the Sea Route to India. Lisbon was chosen as the site for the World Expo in 1998. The theme was The Oceans, thus remembering their contribution to mankind by making it possible for the convergence of cultures from all over the world.

Vasco da Gama's discoveries raised his native Portugal to the apex of wealth and power among the nations of Europe.

Notes

[1] The Discoverers by Daniel J. Borstin, p. 145 (by Peter Martyr d'Anghiera in 1493).

[2] Model of a Caravel Nau São Rafael of the "Museu da Marinha de Lisboa."

[3] Portvgaliae Monvmenta Cartografica by Armando Cortesão, pp. xxv-xxix.

[4] The European Discovery of America by Samuel Eliot Morison, p. 94.

[5] The Portuguese Seaborne Empire by Charles R. Boxer, front cover.

[6] Portuguese Roteiros by C.R. Boxer, p. 185.

[7] Newfoundland from Fisheries to Colony by David Beers Quinn, p. 183.

[8] The Mediterranean World by Fernand Braudel, p. 108.

[9] The Colonial Experience by David Hawke, p. 8.

[10] The Mediterranean World by Fernand Braudel, p. 108.

[11] A History of the Western World by Clough, Garsoian, Hicks, Brandenburg & Gay, p. 367.

[12] Infante D. Henrique e sua época by Mario Domingues, p. 19.

[13] The Portuguese in the NE Coast of America by Rev. George Patterson, p. 127.

[14] Infante D. Henrique e sua época by Mario Domingues, p. 154.

[15] Ibid, p. 276, first edition.

[16] Ibid, pp. 67, 70, 82, 88, 120, 133, 206-331.

[17] The Discoverers by Daniel J. Boorstin, p. 150.

[18] Historia de Portugal by Oliveira Marques, Vol. I, p. 264-267.

[19] Colombo em Portugal, Marinha Portuguesa, p. 15.

[20] The Melungeons by Bonnie Ball, p. 29; Aug. 22, 1937, Nashville Banner, James Aswell.

[21] Interview with Professor José Hermano Saraiva, July 1995.

[22] Portugal nos Mares by Oliveira Martins, p. 280-281.

[23] The Structures of Everyday Life by Fernand Braudel, p. 412.

[24] Historia da Expansão Portuguesa no Mundo by Antonio Baião, p. 19.

[25] Portugal and the Discovery of the Atlantic by Alfredo Pinheiro Marques, p. 80.

[26] Maps by R. A. Skelton, p. 41.

[27] June 10, 1580 has been established as Portugal's National Day. The Visconde de Juromenha discovered in a document found in the Torre do Tombo (Portuguese National Archives) that Luis Vaz de Camões, died on that date. Some historians still dispute it.

Notes (Cont.)

[28] Luis de Camões by Vasco Graça Moura, p. 17.

[29] A History of the Western World by Clough, Garsoian, Hicks, Brandenburg & Gay, pp. 452-453.

[30] The East Indiamen by Russell Miller, p. 26.

[31] National Geographic Magazine, November 1927, p. 511.

[32] A Spanish Discovery of North Carolina by L. A. Vigneras, p. 403.

[33] Houve diários de bordo durante os séculos XV e XVI? by João Rocha Pinto, pp. 404-416.

[34] Great Lives, Sir Francis Drake by Neville Williams, p. 88.

[35] Sir Francis Drake revived by Philip Nichols, Harvard Classics, Vol. 33

[36] The European Discovery of America by Samuel Eliot Morison, p. 102.

[37] Felisberto Roliz, Legends and Notes in Maps.

[38] Portuguese in North America by Rev. George Patterson, p. 162.

[39] Encyclopedia Britannica, 1993, Vol. 2, p. 271.

[40] Historia de España, Historia 16, p. 537.

[41] Knight of the Americas by Miguel Albornoz, p. 14.

[42] Interview with Professor José Hermano Saraiva, July 1995.

[43] As Saudades da Terra by Gaspar Frutuoso, p. 4.

[44] Portugal and the Discovery of the Atlantic by Alfredo Pinheiro Marques, pp. 33-34.

[45] Ibid, p. 38.

[46] Os Escravos no Arquipelago da Madeira by Alberto Vieira, p. 48.

[47] Portugal and the Discovery of the Atlantic by Alfredo Pinheiro Marques, p. 50.

[48] Portvgaliae Monvmenta Cartografica by Armando Cortesão, p. xxxiii.

[49] The True Antilles by Dr. Manuel Luciano da Silva, p. 6.

[50] The Portuguese Americans by Leo Pap, p. 3.

[51] Anomalies in Archaeology by W. David Crocket, p. 129.

[52] The European Discovery of America by Samuel Eliot Morison, p. 102.

[53] Historia da cartografia Portuguesa by Armando Cortesão, pp. 129-130.

[54] The Sea Dogs by Neville Williams, p. 203.

[55] Azores Island a History by James H. Guill, Vol. 5, p. 329.

[56] The Explorers of North America by John Bartlet Brebner, p. 114.

[57] The Discovery of Florida by Maria da Graça Pericão.

[58] National Geographic Magazine, November 1992, p. 92, by Merle Severy.

[59] A Viagem de Diogo de Teive…de la Frontera ao Banco da Terra Nova by Jaime Cortesão, p. 5.

[60] Historia da cartografia Portuguesa by Armando Cortesão, pp. 129-130.

[61] Portuguese Pilgrims by Dr. Manuel Luciano da Silva, p. 28.

[62] The Portuguese-Americans by Leo Pap, p. 4.

[63] Historia de Portugal by Oliveira Marques, p. 104, Vol. II.

[64] Maps by R. A. Skelton, p. 40.

[65] Portuguese voyages to America in the 15th century by Samuel Eliot Morison, p. 5.

[66] Portuguese in North America by Rev. George Patterson, p. 127.

[67] Associated Press News Release, Summer of 1995.

[68] Anomalies in Archaeology by W. David Crocket, p. 132.

[69] Cartografia e Cartógrafos Portugueses dos séculos 15 e 16 by Armando Cortesão, p. 230.

[70] The British Empire by Gerald S. Graham, p. 12.

[71] The Northmen, Columbus and Cabot by Edward Bourne, p. 320.

Notes (Cont.)

[72] National Geographic Magazine, Nov. 1927, p. 516;   [73] Ibid, p. 507.

[74] Historia de Portugal by Joaquim Verissimo Serrão, V. III, p. 110.

[75] National Geographic Magazine, Nov. 1927, p. 550.

[76] Ibid, p. 531; Os Lusiadas by Luis Vaz de Camões, canto II, strophe 97.

[77] The Portuguese Seaborne Empire by Charles R. Boxer, p. 36.

[78] Historia de Portugal by Damião Peres, p. 598.

[79] The Melungeons by Brent Kennedy, p. 114.

[80] Historia de Portugal by Damião Peres, pp. 591-592.

[81] Geographic Journal, London, February 1887, by Jaime Batalha Reis as per email from Francisco Antonio Doria from Rio de Janeiro, Brazil.

[82] Monumenta Henricina Vol. XI, pp. 235-236; Vol. IX, p. 145, Coimbra, 1970.

[83] Columbus and the Age of Discovery, by Zvi Dor-Ner, p. 300, 1991.

[84] Civilization in the West by Christopher & Brinton, Wolff, p. 293;   [85] Ibid.

[86] Historia de Portugal by Damião Peres, p. 596.

[87] The Northmen, Columbus and Cabot by Olson and Bourne, p. 326.

[88] Os Descobrimentos Portugueses by Jaime Cortesão, p. 64.

[89] Crónica d'el Rey D. João I by Rui de Pina, p. 1019.

[90] Os Descobrimentos Portugueses by Jaime Cortesão, p. 67.

Fig. 56—16th Century astrolabe. Lisbon Maritime Museum. The Portuguese were the first sailors to use the astrolabe, a device for taking the altitudes of celestial bodies, as a navigational instrument.

Fig. 57—Tratado da Esfera, used later by Portuguese kings as a symbol of discoveries around the world. Guia Nautico de Evora, c. 1516.

Armillary Sphere, used since the 16th century in the center of the Portuguese flag, including the present one.

Chapter VII

Portuguese Presence in North America—15th and 16th Centuries

This chapter shows the presence of Portuguese people in North America, and therefore the very likely possibility that the Melungeons and other groups have Portuguese ancestry—either directly, or indirectly through intermarriage with other races, cultures and ethnic backgrounds. See Appendix B, Part II for the early presence of settlers from the Iberian Peninsula to North America, according to archaeologists.

In writing the past as far as the light of history will allow, Rev. George Patterson, said more than 100 years ago to the Royal Society of Canada: *Our work has been like that of the scientist, who seeks to picture the life of a by-gone era by means of a few imperfect fossils, or like that of a trapper tracing the course of the passing creature by the faint pressure of the falling leaves, the broken twig, or some other sign equally trifling.* [1]

Colonizing Process and Portuguese Methods

The first attempts by the Portuguese at colonizing were done by leaving domestic animals—such as pigs, cows and poultry—on the islands to be used later as a means of survival. Contrary to popular belief, the Portuguese were more concerned with trade than with conquest,[2] and it is reasonable to understand why.

Prince Henry adopted the method of releasing livestock in newly discovered places, in order to establish a claim of sovereignty, as well as to resupply ships. He started that in Porto Santo, Madeira, Azores, and so on, and it became an established practice.

Grace Anderson and David Higgs, two Canadian Professors, wrote that according to a document dated January 1568 which spoke of a land: *...where cattle were said to have been released in Sable Island orPrince Edward Island in Canada...*[French explorer]*...Breton Marquis de la Roche put down settlers who found cattle.* [Historian Marc Lescarbot, stated in 1608] *...the cattle had been released by a nobleman of the time of Francis I.* [Samuel de Champlain also found cattle on the island during his voyage of 1613] *...and stated that they have been left by the Portuguese.*[3]

Portuguese records show that in their colonizing process, Portugal actually encouraged their people to marry and mix with the natives, because they just did not have a large enough population to settle the immense world that they were discovering. Therefore, they relied on later generations to keep the colonies for Portugal, which was the last colonial power to give them independence. William Freitas, Ph.D., professor at Stanford University, wrote that: *...the Portuguese settlement was family oriented.*[4] In 1550 the king promoted importing settlers to Brazil from the Azores, but he preferred married couples.[5]

The Portuguese were and still are known as one of the peoples that adapt well to the culture of the society where they live.

The society that developed in the colonies was, in its evolution, less protected by consciousness of race, which was practically: ...*non existent in the cosmopolitan and plastic-minded Portuguese.*[6] It may be an exaggeration to say that there was not racial discrimination at all, but it is true that the Portuguese were more liberal in this respect than the Dutch, the English or the French colonizers.[7]

The result is that presently, there many white Portuguese who proudly call themselves Angolans, Mozambiqueans, East Indians, Chinese and others. They have told the author that they will be willing to return to Africa as soon as the war ends and the political situation is settled. They may be white, but have a strong nationalistic feeling of the African nation where they were born. A few years ago, on a visit to Macau, off the China mainland, the author spoke with a few people born in Macau having an Oriental appearance. When asked about Portugal, they replied that they were sorry they could not speak Portuguese well or at all, but they treasure their Portuguese Citizenship in their place of birth, although they have never been in Portugal.

Naturally, and due to miscegenation, you'll be able to find a Portuguese outside Portugal with different skin color and appearance.

Merchant Navy and Marine Traffic—1500's

There were already wealthy owners of fishing fleets at the beginning of the 16th century, and in 1518-19, overseas commerce represented 68% of the crown's income.[8] The New Christians, as the people forced to convert, primarily from Judaism, were called, formed for the most part a middle class of merchants and capitalists. As such, they had access to the ships and commercial expeditions, which they financed on their own or via the Portuguese crown. While studying emigration patterns of the Portuguese, let us keep in mind that during the beginning of the 16th century, a strong possibility was being developed for the union of the crowns of Portugal and Spain in the same manner as Castille had united with Aragon in the previous century. Such a union had been the dream of kings of both Portugal and Castille since the 13th century. In order for that to happen, quite a few marriages were arranged. First the Portuguese King Manuel I married Isabel, then he married Maria, also of Castille, and his third marriage was with her niece Leonor, all of them Spanish princesses. After that, the Spanish King Carlos I married the Portuguese Princess Isabel, and out of that marriage was born Prince Felipe, who eventually would inherit the Portuguese crown and become Filipe I of Portugal and Felipe II of Spain.

All of these marriages worried the people, as they meant that eventually Portugal would be governed by a Spanish king, if the Portuguese king did not provide an heir to the throne. That nationalistic fear, coupled with the risk of being persecuted by the recently installed Inquisition, could be another reason to seek refuge in another land, even at a great danger. This new religious organization was given great support by King João III, and following his death, by his son, King Sebastião.

The prospect of an Iberian union led to several concordance laws between Portugal and Spain in 1568, with which the people of the south province of Algarve did not agree. In 1563, there were regular maritime commercial routes between the Americas, India, Portugal and Spain, and some of these shipping enterprises were using unregistered Portuguese boats, both in Lisbon and Algarve. How many ships were contracted by unscrupulous businessmen with unknown destinations? Who knows? It is known for example, that a Portuguese caravel was sent from Seville and, when returning from Peru with 100,000 ducats in gold and silver, was taken by the French. Merchant capitalists controlled part of the Portuguese marine traffic and performed relevant acts in the Portuguese enterprises developed by the crown. Between 1497 and 1692 a total of 806 ships left from Portugal to India and only 425 returned, and that was only the recorded traffic.[9]

Foundation of Spain—1500's

Any Portuguese in America is confronted with the constant confusion by many persons that Portugal is part of Spain. Fletcher states it better: *Spain as a term for the whole peninsular land mass between the Pyrenees and the Straits of Gibraltar is open to objection that it will inevitably suggest the modern state of Spain and thereby exclude the area covered by modern Portugal...Castille...was a modest County by the year 1000 of the kingdom of Leon...*[10] just like Portugal in 1096 AD. It was not until the beginning of the 16th century that the Spanish Monarchy was founded as a nation much like the one we know today. The union of Castille and Aragon, caused by the marriage of Fernando and Isabel, was just a simple dynastic union and not a true national union. The territories had the same kings. Each had its own institutions, currency and customs, just like any independent territory. Only in 1556 was King Felipe II able to reign over Spain, after his brief marriage with Mary Tudor, Queen of England.[11]

Portuguese in Canada—Newfoundland and Corte Real—Maine

Fifty years ago, Admiral Samuel E. Morison (1887-1976) wrote that for the first quarter of the 16th century: *...Newfoundland was in fact an outlying transatlantic province of the great and growing Portuguese empire.*[12] Another historian described the early discovery of Florida: *Alberto Cantino, the Italian agent who reported the return of the Corte Real ships to Lisbon (1501).* [13]

There has been considerable debate on the question of the earliest Portuguese crossing to North America. One Portuguese author has argued that the honor of the first landfall in North America after the Norsemen should go to the Portuguese.[14] It has been claimed that in 1452, acting on the orders of Prince Henry of Portugal, Diogo de Teive set out from Lisbon with a Spanish pilot to explore far into the Atlantic. The results of this expedition were known to Christopher Columbus and to a member of the Pinzón family.

Bartolomé de las Casas, a 16th century historian, stated that the Portuguese had made voyages to the American shoreline 40 years before Columbus.

Meanwhile, Diogo de Teive in 1452, João Vaz Corte Real in 1471 and Álvaro

Martins Homem in 1473 had already made voyages to the West, trying in vain to discover a sea-route to India. Due to the secrecy imposed by the Portuguese king on navigation, very little was recorded—also due to the fact that there was rarely anything interesting to record, as most of the time they found nothing but icebergs and frozen wasteland. The best evidence of the trip to Canada, which may have departed from Norway or Denmark and probably took place in 1472, is seen in a globe made in 1492 by Martin Behaim—known in Portugal as Martinho de Boémia—a German Jewish geographer.

In the early 1470's, João Vaz Corte Real and some Danes visited Greenland and probably Labrador. Anderson/Higgs, in their book *Future to Inherit,* cites Oleson: *All in all, there can be little doubt that the two Portuguese visited Greenland, Labrador and Hudson Bay.*[15] For this he received a captaincy in the Azores Islands as a reward for having made a voyage to Newfoundland—*Land of the Cod Fish*— and the younger Corte Real explored the coast of Labrador.

The historian Samuel Eliot Morison dismisses Corte Real's trip because the alleged discovery was based on a statement by Gaspar Frutuoso (born in 1522) in the *Saudades da Terra* (which Morison translates incorrectly as *Souvenirs of the Land*; it more nearly means *Longings for Home*), because he was a notoriously unreliable collector of gossip.[16]

Probes into the Atlantic continued with Fernão Teles de Meneses and Fernão Dulmo from the Azores, as well as Afonso do Estreito from Madeira.

In support of the argument for early exploration of the North American shoreline, one can point to the large numbers of Portuguese names that survive on the Atlantic coast in anglicized form.[17] João's son Gaspar Corte Real also traveled deep into the Atlantic, and during one of the trips, he sailed south as far as Florida and received several benefits from King Manuel I. This Portuguese navigator made the first authenticated European landing on the northern continent of the Western Hemisphere, in 1500-1501. On a second expedition, and while looking for a passage to the Pacific Ocean, they came upon a river, and very disappointed, exclaimed repeatedly, *Cá-nada,* meaning in Portuguese: there was nothing. The words caught the attention of the natives, and were remembered and repeated by them when they saw other Europeans, such as Jacques Cartier in 1534.[18] This story may not be true; however it is a folk tradition with the fishermen from long ago, and the author has heard it said in Portugal many times since he was a child.

Patterson wrote in 1890: *...and this seems to indicate that the Portuguese had entered the River St. Lawrence before Cartier, and frequented at least its mouth for such points had become well known and their names established.*[19] *And here we may say that there is a strong reason to believe that the name Canada itself was derived from the Portuguese....The view commonly held is, that it is a modification of the Indian word Kanata, signifying a village or cluster of dwellings, and that the French mistook the natives pointing to their village as Kanata, and they supposed they meant the country. This we do not think likely, and besides, from his vocabulary of Indian words, we know that Cartier did not mistake the meaning of this one. But the word pronounced Canáda is pure Portuguese.*[20] The word in Portuguese meant the same in the 15th century as it means today—a double palisade in a river that indicates the passage or crossing; also a narrow path in the fields, or an old walled road. *The Portuguese having ascended the river St. Lawrence, either persuaded themselves that it was a channel...Cartier, on his 2nd voyage...one of the tribes up the river, told him that there began the great river...the highway to Canada...that the farther it went the narrower it became and that there...Canada...the fresh water began.*[21]

Parkman in 1865 writes that the name Canada has been a point of discussion: It is appended to the journal of Cartier's second voyage as a name of a town or a village. Lescarbot affirms that Canada is simply an Indian proper name, of which it is vain to seek a meaning. Well, this is possible, but the fact remains that most Indian names had a meaning, and *Canada* did not, which means that it will remain: *...a point of discussion.*[22]

For further information, see Dr. John E. Manahan's report at the University of Virginia under the title *Peter Francisco, Virginia Giant of the Revolution*, where he goes into detail relating to the origin of the name Canada and that of the St. Lawrence River, *Rio São Lourenço* in Portuguese.[23]

The last expedition by the Corte Real brothers was in 1500-1501. Gaspar did not return. The same happened with his brother Miguel. Patterson wrote: *Kohl says that comparing this map* (Cantino) *with the present map of Newfoundland, "we must come to the conclusion that Corte Real entered and explored nearly every bay and gulf on the east coast of Newfoundland.*[24] Can we assume that being in the northeast, he also would have gone south to Maine and New England? There are some vestiges that suggest Miguel was in New England. Such as the inscriptions found on a rock near Dighton, MA, which have been the cause for some controversy.

Dr. Luciano da Silva has studied these inscriptions, together with other scientists, and concluded that the name Miguel Corte Real and the date 1511 were inscribed in the stone. Professor Edmund Burke Delabarre of Brown University made an exhaustive study of the so-called Dighton Rock, and was able to detect recognizable European inscriptions on its surface, such as the date 1511. It remained for Joseph Damasco Fragoso, a language instructor at New York University in 1951, to recognize the existence of four crosses of the Order of Christ on the rock. Dr. Silva has also pointed out that the Newport Tower's eight arches bear a definite resemblance to the Castle of Tomar in Portugal, built by the Knights Templar, who later became the Order of Christ.

David Biggs and Grace Anderson, in their 1976 book, *A Future to Inherit*, mention that it is probably safe to discount the theory put forward by Delabarre. It is also possible that these two writers did not read Dr. Silva's book, published in 1974, which goes into detail on Delabarre's theories and adds new discoveries.

Scandinavian researcher Jorgen D. Simeonson said that the Newport Tower could have been built by French, Italians, Spanish, Portuguese or Dutch, and concluded that it was probably built between 1492 and 1620, which indicates Corte Real's date of 1511 is the right place at the right time.

There is still another mystery, about Fort Ninigret. William B. Goodwin concluded in 1932 that it was Dutch in origin, mainly because of some blue pottery with the letter *R* inscribed on it. He believes that this was the initial of Isaac de Rasier, secretary of the Dutch Indies. However, experts told him that the pottery was Spanish in origin.

Again, Dr. Silva points out that many think of Portugal as being part of Spain and do not know that Portugal has a long tradition of blue and white pottery. The Portuguese royal flag's colors are blue and white, and Dr. Silva also notes the *R* might well have been a part of Miguel Corte Real's name. All the discoveries, as mentioned before, were protected by secrecy, which makes it harder to find any documents, and the few made were destroyed by fires or earthquakes, or taken by the Spaniards during the 60 years of their domination, and later during the French invasion by Napoleon's forces. All the diaries, books, letters and route maps were destroyed. As if this were not enough, the Inquisition burned many, suspecting that some of them were subversive material against the Church. The earthquake of 1755 in Lisbon, the most severe in modern times and felt throughout western Europe, is a perfect example of what catastrophic occurrences can do to documents, books, etc. This quake killed more than 50,000 in Lisbon, and 10,000 in Morocco. The 70,000-book library in the King's palace, which included an extensive collection of rare books handwritten before the invention of the printing press, was lost. More than 200 priceless paintings, including works by Ruben, Corregio and Titian, were destroyed. Maps and charts of the world, made by Portuguese seamen over centuries of exploration, were gone forever. For decades, writers from Voltaire to Holmes lamented the loss of Lisbon.

Another problem surfaced in a letter from King Afonso V dated October 22, 1443, who complained that navigators' records had been haphazard and slovenly, according to Borstin: *...not marked accurately on sailing charts...except as it pleased the men who made them.*[25] No wonder historians have a hard time writing who did what and when. And that is why Samuel Eliot Morison concludes that there is lack of evidence of a Portuguese discovery of America. On the other hand, the same writer gives other non-Portuguese navigators credit for their achievements without clear evidence.

Were the Portuguese the first colonists? O. Louis Mazzatenta of the National Geographic Society wrote about a tower near Cape Cod commemorating the Pilgrims' first landing in 1620, and a conversation with a Portuguese-American sailor: *I was told by a Portuguese sailor! When those Pilgrims arrived, we had the harbor all buoyed out for them.*[26]

Cod Fish in Newfoundland

Leo Pap writes about the Portuguese in Canada, and the landmarks left by fishermen: *Reverend George Patterson pointed out on May 28ᵗʰ 1891, in his address before the Royal Society of Canada, each of these rival groups (Basque, Breton, English and Galician) would strive to locate the best fishing grounds, thus in turn contributing to the overall knowledge of the coast. Nevertheless, such extensive onshore commercial activity by other nationalities never challenged Portugal's territorial claims and left little impact on the nomenclature of the east Newfoundland coast, which at every significant landmark remained Portuguese.*[27]

Not much is known of the Portuguese settlers—as distinct from explorers—in the 16th or the first third of the 17th century within the territories now constituting the United States and Canada. However, according to Leo Pap, during that period the Portuguese kept in close contact with the: *...northeastern corner of North America through fishing enterprises.*[28] Apart from starting a cod fishery at Newfoundland in 1502, in which the English were followed by other European nations, much of the exploration of southeastern North America was left to the Spanish.[29]

The name *bacallao,* as most non-Portuguese call the cod fish, is written in Portuguese as *bacalhau* with a sound totally different from the Spanish. Most non-Portuguese people can't pronounce the sound of the letters *lh* and replace them as *ll.* Most often the Spaniards do that. Some historians point to the Basques as the possible originators of the word *bacallao.*[30] While on a trip to Norway, the author asked a fisherman in an outdoor market the name for cod fish. He answered: *Bacallao, and we export a lot of it to Portugal.* He did not know that the author had been born in Portugal.

For centuries, cod fish was a staple food of the Portuguese diet. Salted and dried, it was highly portable and served as an important source of protein. It is also known for its nutritional value. You can ask any Portuguese how many ways there are to cook cod fish, and the answer will be 365, one for each day of the year.

Portuguese Settlements in Canada

João Álvares Fagundes, a nobleman from Viana do Castelo, conducted extensive explorations south and west of Cape Race, Newfoundland, sometime around 1520.[31]

According to *Tratado das Ilhas Novas*, written by Francisco de Sousa in 1570, a company formed in 1521 in Viana do Castelo (home town of Fagundes) was given a grant by the Portuguese king and sent two vessels to Newfoundland waters in order to colonize the territory frequented by the fishermen. This writer's account says that: *Portuguese who came from Viana do Castelo (in northern Portugal) and the Azores to people the New Codfishland, some 60 years ago...the natives were friendly...having lost their ships, the Portuguese stayed there.*[32]

The colonists first settled at what is now Ingonish, a small village on the coast of Cape Breton Island. But after spending a winter there, they moved to another unknown location and built a town of some 80 homes.[33] Pap states: *...up to 400 Portuguese, English, and other European vessels swarmed around Newfoundland every year.*[34] By 1550 the town of Aveiro, Portugal, was sending 150 fishing boats to the Great Banks.

To magnify the presence and influence of the Portuguese in North America in the 16th century, there were places in Canada named Fagundes, as shown in 54 different maps dated between the early 1500's and 1600.[35]

The above may be part of another possible settlement in Nova Scotia by the

Portuguese fisherman who founded St. Peters Colony, but did not survive.

Anthony Parkhurst, an English merchant, would buy salt from the Portuguese, and recorded their activities. In 1578 he reported 50 Portuguese boats, and also encountered Portuguese when he explored the coast of Cape Breton. Later in 1668, Marie l'Incarnacion from Quebec wrote to her son in France of a vessel just arrived with *Portuguese*, Germans and Hollanders. There were also Moorish, *Portuguese* and French women.[36] Cannons of the 16th century have been found nearby which have been a subject of controversy. Archaeologists are still investigating.

During 1562 and 1568 there are records showing initiatives of the Barcelos family in Sable Island and elsewhere. In the Praia da Vitoria papers, the *Arquivo Publico de Angra*, Terceira Island, Azores has a petition and depositions on behalf of Manoel de Barcelos relating to expeditions sent to the Island of Barcelona of São Bardão, which has been identified with Sable Island, although there is a possibility of Barcelos' expeditions to Cape Breton as well. They were found by Manuel C. Baptista de Lima and published by him in a paper titled: *A Ilha Terceira e a colonização do Nordeste do Continente Americano no Seculo XVI*. Also in *Boletim do Instituto Histórico da Ilha Terceira, XVIII (1963), 5'37, app. I-xiii* [and another valuable paper] *Uma tentativa açoriana de colonização da ilha denominada 'Barcellona' no século XVI*, at the *Congresso Internacional da Historia dos Descobrimentos, Actas (6 Vols., Lisboa, 1960-1961),V, p. I, 161-7.*[37]

Again, on March 2, 1567, there was a report of a proposed Portuguese plan for an expedition to Canada. The indications of Portuguese activity with regard to northeastern North America include a suggestion that a fleet was ready to go to Canada by way of the Azores to find a land route to the Pacific. However, Frenchman Pierre de Monluc's recent raid into Madeira had diverted their attention and the expedition was postponed.

John and Sebastian Cabot—1480-97 and 1539-40

Englishmen may have sighted Newfoundland as early as the 1480's, and John Cabot may have clearly delineated eastern Newfoundland, which he thought was Asia, in 1497. Sebastian Cabot's attempt in 1508-09 to get around it by a northwesterly route to reach Asia also failed.[38]

It has been stated by some historians that Cabot's crew was mostly Portuguese, which is not too difficult to believe taking into consideration that by then, Portugal had a surplus of seamen. Dr. Manoel da Silveira Cardozo, a professor at the Catholic University in Washington, D.C., wrote in 1958: *The Pilots in the first English expeditions to the New World were Portuguese, already during King Henry VII.*[39]

In the same manner, that Corte Real's first voyage to Newfoundland in 1474 is questioned by historians, so should Cabot's claim for England be questioned.

While looking at hypothetical discoveries of America, a French writer made an ambitious claim, that America was discovered by a Frenchman in 1488. Apparently Cousin, a navigator of Dieppe, being at sea off the African coast, was forced westward—it is said—by winds and currents to within sight of an unknown shore.

On board was Martin Alonso Pinzón, who later went to Spain, met Columbus, told him of the discovery and joined him on his voyage in 1492.[40]

Although John Cabot—born Giovanno Caboto in Genoa of Venetian Citizenship—is mentioned by the English to have been in Newfoundland before the 1500's, nothing was recorded till June 24, 1540, when he reached Labrador and Nova Scotia, returning to Lisbon, Portugal, on August 6. On this trip he notes vast codfish banks off the coast of Newfoundland. He had previously settled in England, where King Henry VII granted him a patent to search for new lands, since England did not recognize the Tordesilles Treaty between Spain and Portugal.

In his book *Sixteenth Century America*, Carl Ortwin Sauer wrote: *The Cantino map is the earliest known representation of Florida and Florida Strait.*[41] Between

Fig. 58—Planisferio "Cantino" (1502), Biblioteca Nacional, Portugal.
The U.S. East Coast, Florida is shown at the upper left.
Newfoundland is shown to the upper right, purposefully too far east to fall
on the Portuguese side of the Tordesilles Treaty.

the short period of 1492 and 1504, there were 81 overseas expeditions, of which 17 were Portuguese, two French and nine English, all along the North American east coast, from Labrador to Florida and beyond.[42]

Alberto Cantino Map—1502

Anyone who studies cartography knows of the existence of a Portuguese map dated 1502, the so-called Cantino Map—a world chart showing the Portuguese discoveries—after Alberto Cantino, a secret agent working for Ercole d'Este in Lisbon. Ercole was the heir to Duke Borso d'Este of Ferrara on the Italian peninsula.[43] He may have had it purchased in Lisbon, Portugal and then forwarded to Ferrara, according to the following account: *...was sent by Cantino...with a note dated date November 19th 1502, showing that it must have been constructed immediately after the return of the vessels of Gaspar's 2nd voyage. It gives a representation of the coast of the U.S. from Florida northward.*[44] Cantino also states that his report and map reflect what one Captain reported to King Manuel I, according to Fidelino de Figueiredo's book *Estudos da Historia Americana*. This map shows the Florida peninsula and the U.S. East Coast. However, that same writer states that in the late 15th century there were no typical portolan Portuguese charts showing the graduated meridian, or any other indications of astronomical navigation, such as the equator and the two tropics.[45]

On the other hand, the historians say that Florida was discovered by the Spanish explorer Juan Ponce de Leon, who looked for the Fountain of Youth in 1513.

The Portuguese knew where Florida was located before the Spaniards discovered it. Therefore there is a possibility that the Portuguese may have reached Florida according to Cantino's map, before the official discovery by Ponce de Leon in 1513.[46] This map may be considered the most important one in the history of cartography, because it provides the first view of the world as we know it today.

Equally important was the publication in the 15th century of a Latin translation of Ptolemy's *Guide to Geography*, which had been forgotten throughout most of the Middle Ages. Reprinted in 1475, the Geography reached its 7th edition in 1490.

It reappeared in 1507, and the 11th edition, published in Strasbourg in 1513, included new maps. A planisphere was modeled after the Cantino map.[47] Based on that, this map certainly credits the Portuguese with knowledge of the existence of lands to the west.

The Cantino and the Reinel maps give a clear indication that the Portuguese were the early explorers in that region. Pedro Reinel, in the words of Herrera, was a Portuguese pilot of much fame,[48] and the map with his name is preserved in the Royal Library of Munich. The following are names given to places by the Portuguese as shown on these maps dated 1502 and 1505:

Ilha da Fortuna, Fortune—*Ilha da Tormenta*, Cape Tormentine—*Cabo do Marco*, Cape Mark—*Cabo São João*, Cape St. John—*São Pedro*, St. Peter—*Ilha das Aves*, Bird Island—*Cabo das Gamas*, Deer Island—*Cabo da Boaventura*, Bonaventure— *Ilha do Frey Luis*, Freels Island—*Baia de Santa Ciria*, Trinity Bay—*Baia da Conceição*, Conception Bay—*Cabo da Espera*, Cape Speer—*Rio São Francisco,* Cape St. Francis—*Cabo Raso*, Cape Race—*Baixos do medo,* Shoals of Terror— *Portugal cove* and Portuguese cove—*Ilha do Batel*, Battle Island—*Baia Funda*, Bay of Fundy—*Porto do Refugio*, Port Refuge—*Rio dos Jardins*, Jordan River— *Porto Formoso*, Port Joli (French).

Fernão de Magalhães (Magellan)—1519-21

Fernão de Magalhães was born in Saborosa, which is in Vila Real, Tras-os-Montes. After having served the Portuguese King Manuel I, first in Africa and later in India, Magellan went to the King to request some form of recognition, otherwise, he would go to Spain and offer his services. To which the King replied that he did not care, in not so kind a manner.

While in Spain, Magellan married the daughter of an influential Portuguese who controlled the Spanish voyages to the West Indies.[50]

Just as with Columbus, history would repeat itself. That is when Magellan went to Spain and began the first circumnavigation, although he did not complete it. He was killed in the Philippines, and the Spaniard Sebastião del Cano finished it.

Fig. 59—Magellan's signature [49]

With the Magellan fleet, there were 30 Portuguese working for Castile at the time. With him was the Portuguese navigator Estevão Gomes—who later explored the east coast of North America—and his brother-in-law Duarte Barbosa, plus João Lopes de Carvalho, pilot of the vessel *Concepción*, Estevão Dias, and others.[52]

Five of the Spanish vessels had Portuguese pilots.[53] Not only did Magellan give his name to the Strait in South-America, but he also named the Pacific Ocean, due to the calm, stormless waters in which they were able to navigate for 12,000 miles.[54]

On March 6, 1521, Magellan anchored for refreshment and supplies at Guam. There they were greeted by good natured but greedy natives, who swarmed all three ships, on deck and below, promptly removing everything movable. Magellan christened these the Isle of Thieves, now known as the Marianas.[55]

Verrazano in Madeira—1524

Giovanni di Verrazzano of Florence, working for France, departed January 17, 1524 from Madeira Island with 50 men. Quinn stated that some must have been Portuguese.[56] Verrazzano was the first European to sight New York and Narragansett Bay.

Before the Europeans came, the Delaware (or Lenni Lenape) Indians had long occupied the region. Almost a century passed before colonization began, with the arrival in 1609 of the English navigator Henry Hudson, who sent a party to explore Sandy Hook Bay.

BRAZÃO DE FERNÃO DE MAGALHÃES

Fig. 60—Magellan's family crest [51]

The first permanent European settlement was at Bergen (now Jersey City) in 1660.

While France was looking to the New World to establish her colonies, she was at the same time engaged in the corsair and piracy business against Portugal. It has been estimated that in 1540 about 10,000 Portuguese were victims of French piracy, with great loss. As a comparison, Carlos V, the Spanish emperor, received just a little more than the equivalent value in gold from America for the period 1526 to 1530.[57]

Fig. 61—Newport Tower with eight arches

New England and the Portuguese

The presence of the Portuguese on the North American continent may be noticed in many ways.

The existence of a tower constructed out of stone in Rhode Island, called the Newport Tower, is a strange fact. It is believed to have been built by Portuguese navigators in the 16th century. The date was recently confirmed by Danish scientists.

Archaeological Anomalies is the name of a book published in 1994 and written by W. David Crocket. As the name implies, in the archaeological sense something is out of time and place. This book brings up some interesting points and disputes long established theories. The following paragraphs are some of the anomalies mentioned by the author.

The Newport Tower or the *Old Stone Mill in Rhode Island was probably built about 1600 by the State's first Governor Benedict Arnold* [so the sign says. It also tells us of legends that] *...ascribe its erection to Norseman during their supposed visit about 1000 A.D. Governor Arnold might well have adapted an existing struc- ture for this purpose.* [windmill]*...A revolving top of some sort would have had to be built in order for the mechanism to take advantage of the wind directions... The Newport Tower is not perfectly circular...In addition to plastered columns, there is a fireplace in the structure with the interesting feature of an internally built double flue. No miller in his right mind would have allowed a fireplace in his mill.*

In January 1993, a team of Scandinavian researchers led by Danish businessman Jorgen D. Siemonson visited Newport in order to discover, through radiocarbon dating, the age of the Newport Tower's mortar...[and in September of the same year] *...the group announced that the tower could have been built any time between 1450 and 1700, but probably before Newport was settled by the British*[and after taking careful measurements used in its construction] *...announced that the unit of measurement used in its construction was not the British foot but rather the ell, from Central and Southern Europe.* [Crocket does ask the question:] *Does that eliminate the possibility that it was the work of the Vikings?* [58]

Dr. Manuel Luciano da Silva, also of Rhode Island (Bristol), stated in an interview to the reporter James A. Merolla that the dates of the samples taken by the Scandinavian scientists were between 1500 and 1650, plus or minus 50 years, which could place them anywhere between 1450 and 1700, as stated above by Mr. Crocket. These dates would coincide with Dr. Silva's long documented theory that the tower was built sometime in the early 16th century, the peak century for Portuguese exploration around the world. [59]

Pap also wrote: *Proceeding south the first Europeans to set foot on New England were Portuguese.*[60] However, larger settlements did not occur until the 1800's, when the whaling industry attracted many Portuguese fishermen from the Azores and the Cape Verde Islands. Actually, most of the 200,000 who emigrated to the United States in the late 1800's settled in southeastern New England, where to this day they still live and form an important part of this area of the U.S.

In 1699 Isaac da Costa, a Huguenot (Lutheran) of Portuguese ancestry, arrived in Boston from England. Benjamin Franklin da Costa, a clergyman and writer born in 1831, was one of his descendants.

Portuguese Navigator Estevão Gomes—1525

Next we have Estevão Gomes, a pilot who in 1519 navigated under Fernão de Magalhães—already mentioned—and had been in the East Indies. Gomes was appointed by Emperor Charles V to find a northwest passage to India, but failed in his mission. Nonetheless he did important exploring. [61]

He left La Coruña at the end of 1524 or early 1525 and steered for Newfoundland, then sailed on to Nova Scotia, and down North American coast, perhaps as far as Cape May or even beyond Chesapeake Bay. Later research done by Louis André Vigneras proved that Gomes sailed from Florida to Newfoundland, which makes sense since that was the way most navigation was done, to take advantage of the winds and currents. A few months earlier, Verrazano, working for France, also made the voyage in a south-north direction.[62]

On his course, Gomes charted the coastline of Maine, Massachusetts, Connecticut, New York, Manhattan (Hudson River), New Jersey and Delaware. Henry Hudson is credited with the discovery of the Hudson River in 1609. The Portuguese cartographers Diogo Ribeiro and Chaves drew the official sailing chart. [63]

There is a Spanish map made in 1529 showing the area as *Tiera de Estevã Gomez* (Land of Estevão Gomes), which includes a brief description of the navigator's accomplishments. To the northeast, the Map also shows *Tiera Nova de Corte Real*, and *Tierra del Labrador*, referring to voyages made by Portuguese navigators and explorers. It is assumed by many historians that Gomes went all the way to Florida— or started from Florida all the way to New England—charting the complete East Coast. We can conclude and without a doubt that the Portuguese knew the East Coast, including the state of Virginia. Recently a monument was erected in Bangor, Maine by the river shore, a place visited by Estevão Gomes as proposed by Edmund Dinis of New Bedford.

Cabeza de Vaca expedition into the Southeast and California—1527-42

Portuguese were also part of this expedition. The original narrative by Alvar Nuñez Cabeza de Vaca, spells Cabeza as the Portuguese do, Cabeça with a ç instead of a *z*. The island of Malhado[64]—presumably Galveston Island or Vellasco—is also spelled in Portuguese with the *lh* instead of *ll* as it would be written in Spanish. As spoken, the resemblance is less evident than in written form.[65] Malhado, when pronounced as Portuguese *Mal olhado,* has almost the same sound and means a superstitious curse by someone on a place or person, and also misfortune or ill fate. In the same narrative he mentions: *These men were excellent swimmers. One of them was Álvaro Fernandes, a Portuguese sailor and carpenter...*[66] This same name is mentioned again in the Hernando de Soto expedition as the possible author of the narrative by the Gentleman of Elvas. Could it be the same person? It is also interesting that when Cabeza de Vaca met the natives, he was told by signs that there were men like them nearby. Apparently they were the crew from an earlier expedition in November 1528 whose boat was shipwrecked. As part of this expedition there was also an Arabian Black called Estevanico, a native of Azamor, a Moroccan town conquered by the Portuguese in 1513 and later abandoned by King João III in 1541. The author also quotes Fernão Alves de Castanheda as the source of some of the information published in his book.[67] After his adventure in the Southeast, Cabeça de Vaca returned to Spain, leaving Havana with a Spanish galleon loaded with silver and gold. When near the island of Corvo, Azores, he was attacked by the French that had already seized a caravel carrying a cargo of slaves. A Portuguese fleet of nine ships, under the command of Diogo da Silveira, returning from India laden with spices, managed to rescue him and his ship, arriving in Lisbon on 1537.

Portuguese Soldiers on Hernando de Soto Expedition of 1539-41

The latest biography of Hernando de Soto was written by David Ewing Duncan, who refers to the explorer as Hernando de Soto or Soto and not the anglicized version *de Soto*.[68]

The author's middle name is Sousa, but is connected to the first name by *de*; so that the last name of Manuel de Sousa would be Sousa not *de Sousa*. On many of his personal documents, very often, the middle name is switched from Sousa to DeSousa, which is not correct. The author will also always refer to *Soto* or Hernando de Soto, rather than *de Soto*.

Fig. 62—List of Portuguese with Hernando de Soto's expedition. Notice the name Joam in Portuguese.

The Spanish conquistador Hernando de Soto was probably the first European to enter southern Appalachia in 1539-40. At least 100 of the 600 men who disembarked with him in 1539 were Portuguese. The ship commanded by André de Vasconcellos, one of the larger ones among the six carrying the expeditionary force, was entirely

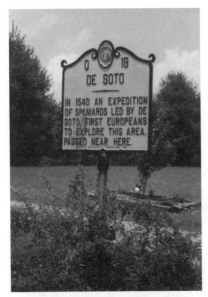

Fig. 63—Plaque in Hiwassee, NC marking the area Hernando de Soto explored nearby.

filled with Portuguese.[69]

Writer Miguel Albornoz describes Hernando de Soto as a man who explored the area of ten states of the union: Florida, Georgia, Alabama, South Carolina, North Carolina, Tennessee, Mississippi, Arkansas, Louisiana and Texas. This area was the property of warlike, proud Indian nations, that were hostile toward white men well into the 19th century. Albornoz wrote that: *...it took the might of fully equipped modern armies to overcome decisively the resistance of tribes that three centuries earlier, a man had tried to subdue with only a thousand brave Spanish and Portuguese soldiers mounted on 350 horses.*[70] Elvas' book states that: *In the temple of Cofitachequi, Hernando de Soto...also found a variety of European items including a knife or dirk, glass beads, rosaries, and Biscayan axes.*[71] All members of the expedition agreed that these materials must have originated from Ayllon's 1526 expedition.[72] That also points to a European presence of Basques, and possibly Portuguese, near the North Carolina mountains.

Hernando de Soto's information, gathered by the Roosevelt-appointed Swanton Commission in 1938, is based on a book titled *The narrative of a Gentleman of Elvas.* Álvaro Fernandes was probably the writer of this first recording of the discovery and navigation of the Mississippi River.[73] Historian Theodore H. Lewis, honorary member of the Mississippi Historical Society, wrote about this book:

Fig. 64—A plaque in Highlands, NC honoring Hernando de Soto

Nevertheless, when the narrative is considered as a whole, it is decidedly the best full account that has been handed down to us.[74] The name of the book is *Hardships suffered by Governor Fernando de Soto and certain Portuguese gentlemen during the discovery of the Province of Florida. Now newly set forth by a Gentleman of Elvas.*[75] The name in Portuguese is *Relação verdadeira dos trabalhos que o Governador D. Fernando de Soto e certos fidalgos Portugueses passaram no descobrimento da província da*

Florida. James Alexander Robertson translated this book from the Portuguese original in 1933. Only two originals still exist, one in London and another one in Lisbon, Portugal. This book was used extensively by the Hernando de Soto Swanton Research Commission, and it should be subjected to a deeper study by a Portuguese scholar that could relate the writings to the Melungeons or other groups.

The *Spanish Explorers* book describes in several pages the presence of Portuguese men during the expedition: *From Elvas went André de Vasconcelos, Fernan Pegado* [and others] *...they went to the residence of the Governor.*[76] Notice the difference: *...the Portuguese turned out in polished armor, and the Castillians very showily* [de Soto did not find it proper, so he ordered another review] *...to which the Portuguese came as at first... the Castilians were in a very sorry and rusty shirts of mail.*[77]

Many of Hernando de Soto's former companions in arms went with him, several from Seville, and a number of Portuguese led by André de Vasconcelos. *The Gentleman from Elvas* gives a lively picture of this gathering of adventurous souls for the new enterprise. He tells us that the Portuguese, among whom he was of course numbered, left Elvas (the city) on January 15: *...Two more Portuguese have been added...*[78] *...In the above enumeration are included at least 19 Portuguese,*

probably more, and who entered mainly through the province of Badajoz...One of the Berbers also remained behind as they were passing through the Appalachian mountains and was perhaps the one who is said by Elvas to have married the Lady of Cofitachequi, though he states this man was a slave of André de Vasconcellos,...the leading man in the Portuguese contingent.[79] *...Álvaro Afonso, João Álvares de Valverde, Abião Lopes, Gavião Lopes, Manuel de Torres, Simão Rodrigues do Marão, Mem Roiz Pereira, Domingo Sardinha, Fernão Pegado, Estevão Pegado, Antonio Martins Segurado, etc.*[80, 81] The above proves again that there were plenty of Portuguese and also some Berbers or Moors on the east coast of the North American continent. There is the calculation that at least 100 Portuguese soldiers occupied one of the larger of the six ships.[82] Besides Elvas, there is also another narrative by Rangel,

Fig. 65—The Front Page of the Gentleman of Elvas' Book

Hernando de Soto's secretary. *A. Oviedo, Historia General,* first published in 1981, includes the narrative of Rodrigo Ranjel, who wrote a day by day account of their activities. Ranjel's original document is not known to have survived, *and the degree to which Oviedo modified the text is unknown.*[83] It should be noted that the Gentleman of Elvas, unlike Rangel, does not put himself forward, but rather was so modest that he referred to himself only once—while on a march through Florida, on the occasion of the deaths of some relatives while at Aminoya. Ranjel's translation closely follows the original book written by the Portuguese Gentleman of Elvas, which has survived.

Another book about Florida was published in Lisbon, Portugal in 1605, titled *La Florida del Inca,* which was later translated with notes by Sylvia Hilton, and published in 1982 and 1986.[84]

who tried to defend himself, they killed immediately in that place, and Juan Ortiz they seized by the hands and led to their chief, Ucita. The men in the brigantine refused to land and [f. xxiiii, v] made for the open sea and returned to the island of Cuba. Ucita ordered Juan Ortiz to be bound hand and foot on a grill laid on top of four stakes/. He ordered a fire to be kindled under him in order to burn him there. The chief's daughter asked him not to kill him /, saying that a single Christian could

Fig. 66—Translation of a story similar to Pocahontas written in 1540 by The Gentleman of Elvas.

Pocahontas, John Smith and the Gentleman of Elvas

While doing the research for this book, the author obtained a copy, No. 354 of the original book, translated and transcribed by James Robertson in 1933. The Gentleman of Elvas, or Álvaro Fernandes, was a Portuguese nobleman who joined the Hernando de Soto expedition along with 30 other Portuguese.

While crossing the Southeast, he wrote a book describing the journey. One of the few survivors, when he returned to Portugal, his book was printed and a copy made its way to the Spanish archives in 1544. Later, in 1557, this book was published in the Portuguese city of Évora, and another copy went to London but published under a different name.

That same book was used by the first English settlers to find their way around, and also to make them aware of the different Indian nations in the New World. Thirteen editions were made of the original, and one was given to the first English settlers when they came to America. Translations were also made in French and Dutch. The book narrates an interesting story about an Indian girl named Ulele who saved a Spanish captain named Ortiz from being killed. The story happened more than 60 years before John Smith set foot on American soil.

All the many attempts by the English to settle Virginia in the 16th century failed. On the other hand, by the middle of the 16th century, well before Roanoke, the Portuguese were already settled in several parts of the world, and were exporting sugar, spices, etc., to Europe—much of it to England.

John Smith was born in Willoughby, Lincolnshire, England in 1580 and died in London, June 1631. He was an English explorer, and the principal founder of the first permanent English settlement in North America at Jamestown, Virginia, in

fiseram ao largo τ ſe toznarã perſ
a rlbaᴅe Cuba.IƷo Ɑcita mãdou
atar a Ʒoam oztiᴣᴅc pes τ mãos
ſobze quatro eſtacas encimaᴏbũa
barra,τᴅebaixolbe mandouacen
derſogo pera que alli ſe queimaſſe
τ bũa ſuafilbalbe rogou que bonã
mataſſe,q̃ bum ſoo cbziſtão nã lbe

*Fig. 67—Pocahontas story in the
original Portuguese as written in 1540*

1607. At the age of 20, his adventuresome spirit found an outlet in the war against the Turks, being fought in Hungary. In one of his narratives, he describes how he was about to be put to death, then saved when the chief's 13-year-old daughter, Pocahontas, threw herself between him and his executioners.

John Smith's writings include *The General History of Virginia, New England, and the Summer Isles (1624); The True Travels, Adventures and Observations of Captain John Smith in Europe, Asia, Africa and America (1630).*

The following is the original story told by *The Gentleman from Elvas* of an occurrence in Florida, which is very similar to the one told by John Smith 60 years later. It was translated by James Alexander Robertson in 1933: *...many Indians came...seized them...The other man who tried to defend himself, they killed...and Juan Ortiz they seized by the hands and led to their chief Ucita...Ucita ordered Juan Ortiz to be bound hand and foot on a grill laid on top of four stakes. He ordered a fire to be kindled under him in order to burn him there. The chief's daughter asked him not to kill him saying that a single Christian could not do him any ill or good, and that it would be more to his honor to hold him captive. Ucita granted this and ordered him taken care of and as soon as he was well, gave him charge of guarding the temple, for at night the wolves would carry the corpses from inside it...One night the wolves carried off from him the corpse of a child, the son of one of the principal Indians. Going after it, he threw a club which struck the wolf carrying the body, which finding itself wounded abandoned it and went off to die nearby. He not knowing what he had done as it was night, returned to the Temple. At daybreak, when he found the body of the child gone, he became very sad. As soon as Ucita learned of it, he determined to have him killed. He sent along the trail where he said the wolves had gone and they found the boy's corpse and farther on the dead wolf. Whereupon Ucita was greatly pleased with the Christian and at the watch he had kept in the Temple, and thenceforward showed him great honor....another chief...Mocoço...came and burned the town...Juan Ortiz learned from the girl...that her father had determined to sacrifice him the next day; and she told him that she should go to Mocoço,...At night since he did not know the way, the Indian woman went a half a league from the town and put him on it.*[85]

Juan Ortiz after many years and tribulations, finally met Governor Hernando de Soto. On July 10, 1995, the Associated Press released a story that was picked by major newspapers all over North-America, which stated that John Smith read the Elvas book and made up the story. I do not think Disney's director of the movie

Fig. 68—The Discovery of the Mississippi by Hernando de Soto,AD 1541, romanticized on a large canvas (144" x 216") by William H. Powell, 1853, hangs in the rotunda of the U.S. Capitol. Courtesy, architect of the Capitol.

Pocahontas read the book. The Portuguese newspaper Luso-Americano of New Jersey published an article by the author also about this book. Unfortunately, very few people know about it, including the Portuguese, and that book, if read carefully, should give us more clues about the Portuguese in the Southeast.

Don Juan Oñate had Portuguese Soldiers

Early Spanish and Portuguese New World settlers were of a varied ethnic mix, not only in the Southeast but elsewhere. For example, Don Juan de Oñate himself was Basque and a number of his soldiers were Portuguese.[86]

The Basque whaling industry was well known in the late 1560's, according to an article written by James A. Tuck and published in the *National Geographic Magazine* of July 1985. The Basques' early presence in the New World had been recognized by a few scholars. It remained for historical geographer Selma Huxley Barkham to reveal the scope of their operation.[87]

The finding of a Basque galleon off the coast of Labrador provided all the proof needed. Their crew, most likely, included many Portuguese whalers. Centuries later, the Portuguese became part of the American whaling industry. Only the Basques had shown no urge towards expansion,[88, 89] so their presence may be limited to the fishing industry and a few other isolated incidents, except for their presence in Newfoundland as whalers.[90]

Portuguese in Peru and Mexico

It is well known that the Portuguese were the first Europeans in the Pacific Ocean. Aleixo Garcia was the first Portuguese to contact the Inca Empire, between 1521 and 1525. He was shipwrecked during one of the Spanish expeditions to Argentina, with a few of his compatriots. Coming from Santa Catarina (Brazil), he climbed to the Andes in Bolivia, heading an army of *Chiriguanos* Indians, and was the first European to set foot in the empire of the Incas—years before Francisco Pizarro. The omission of Aleixo Garcia from the history books has been an injustice, according to the American Charles E. Nowell.

Even the Spanish discoverer Alvar Nuñez Cabeza de Vaca, who explored Paraguay and the southern United States, wrote years later: *...the old timers said that Garcia, the Portuguese, made war in those lands with many Indians and having with him only five Christians.* Another *conquistador,* and one of the first, was Lope Martin Pereira, accompanied by Frei Pedro Português or Frei Pedro dos Algarves, the founder of the church of San Francisco in Cuzco in 1534. In this same city appears Ximon Português in the list of the founders.

João Fernandes is another possible Portuguese admiral of Pedro Alvarado's fleet, mentioned by him as one of the two Portuguese pilots who arrived in 1532, when he wrote to Emperor Carlos V. Genes de Mafra was designated as the master pilot by Alvarado.[91] The other probable pilot was Gonçalo da Costa. Gaspar Rico is the name of another Portuguese master pilot with the Spanish fleet, under the command of Rui Lopes de Villalobos.[92]

Many Portuguese Jews went to Brazil and to other South American countries; along with them went Catholic and non-Catholic Portuguese running away from the Inquisition, and more likely for economic reasons. Thousands of Portuguese arrived in Peru from Portugal or Brazil and gradually settled in Mexico, Peru and La Plata.

Portuguese merchants and capital reached relevant importance that could not be ignored, contributing 35% annually in silver to the Spanish treasury in 1635. However, by the first quarter of the 17th century, the Spanish colonists and the Inquisition, using Judaism and other excuses, started to persecute them. Gonçalo de Reparaz, a well known historian, describes the Portuguese presence in Peru: *...the streets of Lima were full of them...*[The Portuguese not only preferred the mines, commerce and navigation, but also did not disdain]*...agriculture...In 1571 we found five Lusitanos in the Andes, near Lima.* [James Lockhard also said:]*...they were numerous in the farming and gardening...overwhelming predominant in this role...Portuguese sailors occupied prominent places in the Pacific navigation.* [The Portuguese dominated commerce so much that the Castilians believed that in order to succeed they had to associate themselves with the Portuguese.] *The well to do people trusted them and loaned money, they were the Lords of the Land, they were honest and paid the interest punctually.*[93]

All the above can be confirmed by reading the index of 68 legal documents in the archives of Lima, Peru, in which several Portuguese are mentioned.[94]

If the Portuguese were in Peru during the 16th and 17th centuries, and in such large numbers, actively participating in the making of that nation, why is it so hard for many historians to believe that the Portuguese were also in North America, a place much closer to Portugal than Peru?

Who would think that the Portuguese had anything to do with Mexico? Well, Cortês, the founder of Mexico, had Portuguese in his expedition. Bernal Diaz del Castilho noted that the name Castillo Blanco was given by Portuguese, due to the fact that the locals reminded them of Castelo Branco in Portugal. After conquering Mexico, other Portuguese came, and one of them was an architect responsible for the only signs of the *Manuelino* style in New Spain.[95]

Portuguese in the Southwest—1541/1543

One group of a Spanish expedition led by Francisco Vasquez de Coronado pushed into Arizona and discovered the Grand Canyon in September 1540. In April 1541, Coronado led his army across northern Texas into Oklahoma and Arkansas, and then with a smaller group he pushed north into Kansas, reaching close to the Nebraska border in July.

From the muster roll records it appears that there were five Portuguese among Coronado's men. One of them, the soldier André do Campo, was with friar Juan de Padilla when the latter was killed by hostile Indians at Quivira; but André himself escaped, reaching New Spain from Panuco.[96]

Later, in 1542-1543, another Portuguese navigator, again working for Spain, for the first time reached California, which he carefully explored all the way to the Bay of San Francisco. His name was João Rodrigues Cabrilho. Antonio Herrera y Tordesillas, Chief of the Indies and Chronicler of the Crown of Castille in 1612 describes him as: *Portuguese, a person very skilled in matters of the sea...* See Bibliography under Herrera. Cabrillo or Cabrilho was born in the north of Portugal in a place called Lapela, Cabril, near the city of Montalegre, province of Trás-os-Montes. His name is well known by the Portuguese living in the United States, who hold an yearly Festival in his honor in California, with a "Cabrilho state holiday" on September 28. Recently, Cabrillo—as he is known in the U.S.—was honored by the U.S. Postal Service with the issuance of a commemorative stamp. According to some scholars, Cabrilho's place of birth has not been definitely established.

Portuguese Navigator and Drake—1555

On 15 Nov. 1555, the fleet sailed from Plymouth. The Portuguese pilot, Nuno da Silva, who had 15 years navigational experience, noted with a practiced eye: *Drake's ship is very stout and very strong.* [Neville Williams wrote that] *More important than the capture of the Mary was the acquisition of her pilot, Nuno da Silva, whom Drake pressed into his service. He was a most experienced navigator and the English captain was fascinated by his collection of charts and nautical instruments. Nuno was to stay aboard the Pelican, where he was honorably treated, feeding at the captain's table for some 15 months. By now Drake had divulged to his officers that he intended to sail into the Pacific, and the Portuguese pilot caught the adventurous spirit of his captor to travel into the new discovered parts of the world.* [97]

Nuno's experience in the South Atlantic was considerable, and once they reached the South American coast, he displayed detailed knowledge.

Another Portuguese is mentioned as having worked for Drake. Pedro Sanchez made the following deposition in Havana after Drake ransacked San Domingo and Cartagena in 1585: *Their admiral is a Portuguese and is called Don Francisco Dragon; and all the pilots are Portuguese and Genoese, and the ships' masters also, all well acquainted with this course and the ports of Indies.* [98]

If the English had at their service Portuguese and other foreigners, it is reasonable to assume that some or most of the early immigrants, such as the colonists of the Lost Roanoke Colony and later colonies, were Portuguese or other nationalities.

Portuguese Pilot in Virginia—1560

Quinn wrote: *Simão Fernandes—a Portuguese pilot—had guided them skillfully to their destination, where he had apparently been previously on a Spanish expedition in the 1560's.* [99]

John Lawson, the first Carolina historian, wrote in 1700: *The Indians, which were the Inhabitants of America, when the Spaniards and other Europeans discover'd the several parts of this Country.* [100] The only other Europeans in the early 1500's that visited the U.S. east coast were the Portuguese. The French came in the 2nd half of the century, as did the English.

Was Pardo a Portuguese Explorer?—1565

In Chapter I, the possibility that *Juan Pardo* was a Portuguese working for Spain in the 16th century was mentioned by Kennedy, according to information given to him by historian and researcher Eloy Gallegos. The author decided to do his own investigation, and to establish whether he was or was not Portuguese. Since *Pardo* is not a common Portuguese name—there are only two Pardos listed in the 1996 Lisbon telephone directory—a visit to the Portuguese National Archives *Torre do Tombo,* with the help of Pedro Penteado, one of the archivists, produced some results.

He was able to ascertain that during the reign of King João III (1521-1557), one Pardo was mentioned several times in the *Chancelarias de D. João III* (chancellery or king's official documents), recorded when he applied for official licenses and/or permissions. The time period is about ten years prior to the Pardo's presence in the Southeast (1565-1570).

A coincidence is worth mentioning. This Pardo was born in the city of Aveiro, a traditional place for Portuguese seaman, explorers and navigators. The Pardo's

Fig. 69—The King of Portugal João II, his name written as Juan in Tordesilles

name and dates can be seen on the original documents of the 1500's. Seeing is not the same as reading, because it is very difficult to read much more than his name.

Only an expert reader trained in Paleography is able to do it properly.

The illustrations show the name of the Portuguese King João II written in Spanish (Juan) on the famous Treaty of Tordesilles, and on the same document written later by Portuguese. The Pardo from Aveiro was written as *Joam Pardo,* not Juan as in Spanish. When researching the North Carolina archives in Raleigh for the document signed by Pardo when he explored the Southeast in 1565-69 for Spain, it could not be found.

Fig. 70—The name of the Portuguese King João II as written in Portugal on the Treaty of Tordesilles (1494)

However there is a transcription of the original in Spanish written by Charles Hudson of *The Pardo Relation* written and signed by Pardo.[101]

On this document several words are written in Portuguese. In some places a word is written in Spanish, and the some word in other parts of the text is written in Portuguese. We caution the reader for the possibility of a mixture of the Galician language. But then again the Galician language was much closer

Fig. 71—Juan Pardo signature, notice the symbol on the left over the third letter

to Portuguese after the 15th century.[102] The same does not happen with the documents written by Juan la Bandera (Vandera), the notary that wrote the narration for most of the expedition. The original document, *Bandera Relacion* dated April 1st, 1569, does state that he is a native of *quenca "natural de la ciudad de quenca...rreyno de España."*[103] Most likely the name *quenca* applies to the modern city of Cuenca in Spain. The name *Juan* in Portugal during the 15th and 16th centuries was written as *Yoam, Yoao, Joa'o* or *Joam,* but never *Juan.* Unfortunately the above does not help the Portuguese theory, although it may show close links to Portugal. Another document states that Pardo is a resident of Seville.[104]

After investigating in the *Archivo General de Indias* in Seville with the help of one of the archivists, the author was able to obtain a copy of Pardo's signature as he signed in one of Bandera's documents. The author found it interesting that the name as signed does not look like Juan, and does show what looks like the character ~ over the vowel *a* as in Portuguese *ã.* [105] See Fig. 71.

David Henige, Ph. D. recently published his viewpoint about Brent Kennedy's book, *The Melungeons, The Resurrection of a Proud People,* as a critical analysis.

Dr. Henige is rather unfair with his strong criticism in his viewpoint towards Dr. Kennedy. The author recognizes that he is not qualified as a scholar to analyze or criticize either Henige's or Kennedy's work, but in all fairness, certain points mentioned by Henige should be brought to the attention of the reader.

1. *...the ease with which one language is picked up and another one discarded...*[106] A closer analysis in the different ethnic immigrant communities would prove exactly that, they drop their native languages in favor of the English language, which becomes their primary language for the sake of survival.

2. *...claim that Pardo signed his name as "João" rather than Juan.*[107] Pardo's nationality has not been proven yet, however extensive research has shown that it is far from proving whether he is Spanish or Portuguese and wrote his name one way or the other. It points however that the name Juan was signed both ways, the Portuguese and the Spanish way. Let us keep in mind that the Portuguese are mistaken by many as being Spanish.

3. *...of the nearly 80 men listed, not one...is shown with a Portuguese birthplace.*[108] Well, yes there is at least one shown and his name is Antonio Pereira, son of Blas Pereira and Ana Carneira, a native of Porto, a city in the north of Portugal. This is established in documents dated 1566, 1A-A12-5-4/12,3-4 1566. Again, more research is needed.

Spanish Confirms Portuguese Settled in Newfoundland

Pedro Menéndez de Aviles—the founder of St. Augustine in Florida—who in 1566 ordered an expedition to the Carolinas, had Antonio Pereira, a native of Porto, listed as one of the Portuguese members of the forces.[109] Aviles, in 1568, considered the Portuguese to have colonized Terra Nova two to three years before. The evidence of Pedro Menéndez de Aviles was given before the inquisitor Juan de Ovando during the course of inquiries being made at Fuenterrabia.

The following are some excerpts from the inquiries transcribed by Quinn: [Avilez stated that] on the coasts of Florida and Terra Nova, which are in his charge] *The Portuguese fortified in Terra Nova and Florida... and the discovery of which has been made...two years ago (1566)...the Portuguese settled after he had taken possession of that land in the name of his majesty and fought the Huguenots [Lutherans]. And it is said they have fortified more than two hundred leagues inland from the conquest of that discovery.*

[Again and according to Quinn] *These certain persons, inhabitants of Fuenterrabia, who were with them, speaking in the presence of Don Juan de Acuña.* [Aviles said]: *...that the French had told him there in San Sebastian that they had seen colonies of Portuguese in Florida, each village of very big Indians, and their company have entered by way of Tierra Nova which he understands to be a branch of the sea between the land of Florida. And this he had given to the Royal Council* *of the Indies. It appears that unless they are beaten out of there...they are certain to fortify themselves there, to go later from there, especially in view of the ease with which they can be supplied from the Azores (which are King of Portugal's) and from which the sailing time in good weather is twelve to fifteen days.* [110]

There is also a story about a Biscayan sailing with a French Pirate ship that was shipwrecked, and the Biscayan was rescued by a Portuguese vessel. [111]

Another isolated incident also confirms an early Portuguese presence in Canada, when Tomás André was brought before the Aveiro (a fishing town in north Portugal) judge for having an English passport dated August 17, 1583, and related to fishing in Newfoundland. All the above indicates, in sum, that the Portuguese knew well the northeastern coast of the North American continent since the late 1400's.

Portuguese Helped the Spaniards in Florida—Corte Real—1567-1574

During the first half of the 16th century, French corsair activity made itself felt near the Portuguese coast. The following is a sample of correspondence in which the presence of Portuguese in America was mentioned.

A Frenchman, M. de Fourquevaux, wrote a letter to Queen Catherine de Medicis. This letter was part of documents between him and the king of France, Charles IX.

I am assured, Madame, that they will not be in the aforesaid country [Portugal] so enthusiastic nor so ardent as to set out their army against the said (Algerians) pirates, as they were recently against the late Captain Monluc—Pierre de Monluc who had attacked Madeira in revenge for Portuguese help to Spain in Florida—; and I am informed that if it had not been for the Madeira alarm a little while ago throughout all the islands subject to the King of Portugal, a fleet which is set for the Azores would have gone to Terre Neuve, to take possession of the land and people in the Grand Bay of Canada (The Strait of Belle Isle). [112]

Kennedy, in a letter to CNN (Cable News Network) also gives a good indication of the Portuguese presence: *...following examples already uncovered from the Archives by Dr. Lyon and Dr. DePratter: Portuguese seaman Juan Fernández de Cea (João Fernandes de Ceia) was given permission by the Spanish to sail to Florida and dig for treasure (January 26, 1568). 50 Portuguese farmers from the Azores accompanied Pedro Menéndez de Aviles to Florida (January 26, 1573) and 100 Portuguese farmers accompanied Menéndez from the port of Bayona to Florida. (July 13, 1573).* [113]

Domingos Fernandes, a Portuguese, piloted a Spanish ship into an opening in the Outer Banks. A native of Terceira, Azores, he may be the same, or a relative of Simão Fernandes.

In 1582, when Portugal was under the Spanish crown, Richard Hakluyt was completing his book about the discovery of America. He picked up from Antonio Castillo, the Spaniard who was representing Portugal at the English court, some rather vague information about a voyage up the Labrador coast by Vasques Eanes Corte Real. In 1574 it was said that he had reached a northern latitude of some 58°.

Also, from Cardinal D. Henrique, Vasques received confirmation of the Newfoundland charter granted to Manoel Corte Real on July 12, 1574, by King Sebastião who had died in 1578. All that took some legal shape, when a royal permission was received on May 4, 1567, to appoint a governor with legal qualifications to administer the proposed (or actual?) Portuguese settlement.[114] Also in 1574, there was a Portuguese attempt by Eanes Corte Real, who had been on a Labrador voyage, to find a northwest passage from the island of Terceira in the Azores.[115]

Defeat in Alcacer-Quibir (Ksar el Kebir) and the Union—1578-80

On August 4, 1578, Portuguese King Sebastião was defeated by the Moors at the battle of Alcacer-Quibir. In this battle, the Moors were helped for the first time by the Turks (Ottoman Empire).

The Portuguese king died in that battle, along with many Portuguese nobles, and two other Moorish kings.

This defeat marked the beginning of the fall of the short lived Portuguese Empire and its supremacy throughout the world, which led to the 60-year union of the Portuguese and Spanish kingdoms by Felipe II of Spain, the Portuguese king's uncle.

In 1580, Felipe II of Spain became Filipe I of Portugal. He was the son of Princess Isabel of Portugal, and the grandson of the Portuguese King Manuel I.

Many historians erroneously write that the King of Spain conquered Portugal in 1580. According to established monarchy laws, and with agreements previously made between the monarchs of Spain and Portugal, if one of the kingdoms did not have a direct descendant, whoever survived would reign over both crowns.

Due to family ties, Felipe was the natural heir to the Portuguese crown. Felipe II of Spain was also the son of the Emperor Carlos V of Austria and Germany.

For centuries it was the dream of both Portuguese and Spanish kings to unite the two kingdoms.

Many times the king of Portugal had the opportunity to also become the king of Spain. Had that happened, Portugal and Spain would ironically have become one country. But Castille waited too long, and the spirit of nationhood settled in Portugal after the 13th century.

During the period of Portuguese and Spanish union, many Portuguese navigators were in North America under the Spanish flag.

One of them was Vincente Gonçalves, a pilot sent by Pedro Menéndez de Aviles to reconnoiter Chesapeake Bay in May 1588.[116] Later, in 1593, a large contingent of Portuguese soldiers arrived in San Juan, Puerto Rico.

Filipe I gave them orders to sail from Lisbon. Many of the men brought their wives, and others married on the island. From these men descend many Puerto Rican families.

Portuguese in New Mexico—1596

Portuguese soldiers were among Don Juan de Oñate's group of colonists going to settle New Mexico. Unfortunately, life was not very kind to two of them. Two Spanish brothers, Juan and Matias Rodriguéz, convinced João Gonçalves and Manuel Português—two Portuguese, unhappy with Oñate—to leave New Mexico, which they did by taking their horses and some food with them. They were later caught and were executed, after being seized through trickery, as their captors had previously promised their lives would be spared.

However, they realized later that they were going to be executed and begged to be allowed to confess to a priest. That last request was denied. They were beheaded and had their hands chopped off.

The Spanish brothers were permitted to escape as they were friends of one of their captors.[117] After the war with Mexico, one of the first chronicles of the area in the 17th century was written by Benevides Memorial, a Portuguese friar from the Azorean St. Michael Island.[118]

One of the distinguished family names in New Mexico is Chaves. Manuel Antonio Chaves, son of Julian Chaves and Maria Luz Garcia, was born on October 18, 1818. He became famous in the battles with hostile Navajo, Ute and Apache Indians, earning the name of *El Leoncito* or The Little Lion. There is an indication that he was of Portuguese ancestry.[119]

The name can be traced back to the Portuguese city Chaves in Portugal. The spelling of the name in Portuguese ends with an *s* and in Spanish with a *z*.

There is a small city in New Mexico called *Chaves*.

Manuel Brazil is another Portuguese, found in New Mexico as a cattle rancher during the years 1870 to 1880. He was also a commissioner in Roberts County, but is better remembered as the man responsible for the capture of Billy the Kid, a well known outlaw of the western frontier.[120] Brazil was born in Rosais, São Jorge, Azores in 1850 as Manuel Silvestre Brazil and may have arrived in the U.S. when he was a teenager.[121]

Portuguese Navigators, Soldiers and Explorers of the North American East Coast Before Sir Walter Raleigh—1587

The following chart shows just a few of those who explored the coast of North America before the first attempt to establish an English colony. There are many more to be added as research continues.

1470-02 João Vaz Corte Real, Newfoundland
1492-05 João Fernandes Labrador and Pedro Barcelos in Newfoundland and Labrador
1500-01 Gaspar Corte Real, Greenland and Canadian coast
1519-21 João Álvaro Fagundes, Greenland and Canadian coast
1525   Estevão Gomes, East Coast, from Newfoundland to Chesapeake Bay and possibly Florida.
1540   André de Vasconcelos and at least 30 Portuguese soldiers took part in Hernando de Soto's expedition to the Southeast.
1555   Nuno da Silva, captured by Drake and later worked as a pilot in his South American expedition
1568   João Fernandes de Ceia to Florida
1578   Manuel and Vasques Corte Real to Labrador and Newfoundland
1585   Don Francisco Dragon, an admiral with Drake

Portuguese Navigators in 15th and 16th century North America.

Portuguese Log Book Value

Charles Boxer, who wrote Portuguese *Roteiros* (logbooks, 1500-1700), mentions the ones kept by João de Castro in 1538: *...because the needle of the compass varied on board ship...* [when moved from one place to another, he concluded that this was due to the fact that it had been placed near a cannon, and that the iron attracted the needle to itself and made it move. That was] *...noted 128 years before it was vaguely suggested by Denis of Dieppe.* [122]

Raleigh paid £60 (English Pounds)—a colossal price in those days—for an original *Roteiro* or logbook written by the Portuguese navigator João de Castro about the Red Sea, showing that he appreciated and valued Castro's talents.[123]

* * *

Rulers of Portugal to 1580
Portuguese Dynasty Chart

Dynasty of Burgundy

Afonso Henriques	1128-1185	Sancho I	1185-1211
Afonso II	1211-1223	Sancho II	1223-1248
Afonso III (a)	1248-1279	Dinis	1279-1325
Afonso IV	1325-1357	Pedro I	1357-1367
Fernando	1367-1383	Leonor Teles (c)	1383-1385

Dynasty of Avis

João I	1385-1343	Duarte	1433-1438
Afonso V (b)	1438-1481	João II	1481-1495
Manuel I	1495-1521	João III	1521-1557
Sebastião	1557-1578	Henrique	1578-1580

(a) Regent until 1248   (b) Prince Pedro, Regent until 1448   (c) Regent

See Page 358 for Rulers of Portugal from 1580 to 1910
and Page 382 for the list of Presidents of the
Portuguese Republic from 1910 to 2001.

Notes

[1] The Portuguese in North-America by Rev. George Patterson, DD, p. 127. Section II, 1890
[2] Christians and Spices by John Correia Afonso, p. 33.
[3] A Future to Inherit by David Biggs, p. 9, and Portuguese in North America by Patterson, p. 166
[4] Portuguese Heritage, December 1993, p. 22.
[5] Historia da Lingua Portuguesa by Serafim da Silva Neto, p. 421.
[6] The Masters and the Slaves by Gilberto Freyre, p. 3.
[7] Christians and Spices by John Correia Afonso, p. 34.
[8] Infante D. Henrique, Mario Domingues, p. 8.
[9] Portugal nos Mares, Oliveira Martins, p. 37.
[10] Moorish Spain by Richard Fletcher, p. 9.
[11] Historia de España by Joseph Perez, 1986, p. 479, 480.
[12] João Alvares Fagundes by Richard Goertz, p. 116. Canadian Ethnic Studies, 33. No. 2, 1991.
[13] Sixteenth Century America by Carl Ortwin Sauer, p. 25.
[14] A Future to Inherit by David Higgs, p. 4 (Jaime Cortesão, Viagem de Diogo Teive, 1933).
[15] Ibid (Early voyages and Northern Approaches by Trggvi Oleson, p. 119, Tor. 1963).

Notes (Cont.)

[16] The European Discovery of America by Samuel Eliot Morison, p. 93.

[17] A Future to Inherit by David Higgs, p. 5.

[18] The Portuguese in America by Manoel da Silveira Cardozo, p. 4.

[19] Portuguese in America by Rev. George Patterson, p. 137.

[20] Ibid, p. 138.

[21] Ibid, p. 139 (Discovery of Maine).

[22] Pioneers of France in the New World by Francis Parkman, p. 205.

[23] Peter Francisco by William Arthur Moon, p. 52.

[24] Portuguese in America by Rev. George Patterson, p. 138.

[25] The Discoveries by Daniel J. Borstin, p. 162.

[26] Little Portugal by O. Louis Mazzatenta, p. 90-107.
    (National Geographic Magazine, Jan. 1975).

[27] João Alvares Fagundes by Richard Goertz, p. 118.
    Canadian Ethnic Studies, 33. No. 2, 1991.

[28] The Portuguese Americans by Leo Pap, p. 8.

[29] Set Fair for Roanoke by David Quinn, p. 13.

[30] Pioneers of France in the New World by Francis Parkman, p. 192.

[31] The Portuguese-Americans by Leo Pap, p. 5.

[32] A Future to Inherit by David Higgs, p. 8 (Trato das Novas Ilhas by
    Francisco de Sousa).

[33] The Portuguese-Americans by Leo Pap, p. 9.

[34] Ibid, p. 8.

[35] João Alvares Fagundes by Richard Goertz, p. 127-128.

[36] A Future to Inherit by David Higgs, p. 8.

[37] Newfoundland, from Fisheries to Colony by David Beers Quinn, p. 183.

[38] Set Fair for Roanoke by David Quinn, p. 12.

[39] Boletim do Instituto Historica, Presença de Portugal…E. U. by
    Manoel da Silveira Cardozo, p. 9.

[40] Pioneers of France in the New World by Francis Parkman, pp. 189-190.

[41] Sixteenth Century America by Carl Ortwin Sauer, p. 25.

[42] O nome de América, Cartografia, by João Vidago, p. 9 (Harrise pp. 662-700).

[43] Maps by R. A. Skelton, pp. 39-40.

[44] The Portuguese in America by Rev. George Patterson, p. 136.

[45] Portugal and the Discovery of the Atlantic by Alfredo Pinheiro Marques, p. 77.

[46] Historia de Portugal by Joaquim Verissimo Serrão, Vol. III, p. 110.

[47] Pioneers of Ocean Exploration by Luis de Albuquerque, p. 13.

[48] Portuguese in America by Rev. George Patterson, p. 140.

[49] Historia de España by Joseph Perez, 1986, p. 479, 480.

[50] The Discoverers by Daniel J. Boorstin, p. 260.

[51] Historia de Portugal by Damião Peres, Vol. III, p. 601.

[52] Historia de Portugal, Vol. III, by Joaquim Verissimo Serrão, p. 30.

Notes (Cont.)

[53] Os Pioneiros Portugueses by Dr. Luciano da Silva, p. 55.

[54] Historia de Portugal by Damião Peres, Vol. III, p. 600.

[55] The Discoverers by Daniel J. Boorstin, p. 265.

[56] North American Discoveries by David Quinn, p. 59.

[57] O Essencial sobre o corso e pirataria by Ana Maria Pereira Ferreira, p. 35.

[58] Anomalies in Archaeology by W. David Crocket, pp. 1, 4, 5, 10

[59] The East Bay Window by James A. Merolla, Section B, December 22, 1993.

[60] The Portuguese-Americans by Leo Pap, p. 5.

[61] Ibid, p. 5.

[62] The Voyage of Esteban Gómez…by L.A. Vigneras, pp. 25-28
    (Terrae Incognitae, 1976 Vol.II).

[63] Sixteenth Century America by Carl Ortwin Sauer, p. 64.

[64] Spanish Explorers in the Southern States by Frederick W. Hodge, pp. 12, 57.

[65] The Spanish, Portuguese Languages by William J. Entwistle, p. 282.

[66] Spanish Explorers in the Southern States by Frederick W. Hodge, p. 49.

[67] Ibid, p. 126.

[68] Hernando de Soto by David Ewing Duncan, p. xx.

[69] The Portuguese-Americans by Leo Pap, p. 241, Jaime Cortesão, p. 43-44.

[70] Knight of the Americas by Miguel Albornoz, p. 351,
    also Swanton's Final Report.

[71] The Gentleman of Elvas, p. 65.

[72] The Forgotten Centuries by Charles Hudson, p. 100.

[73] The Portuguese-Americans by Leo Pap, p. 6.

[74] Spanish Explorers in the Southern States by Theodore H. Lewis, p. 130.

[75] Final Report of the United States de Soto Commission by Swanton, p. 4.

[76] Spanish Explorers in the Southern States by Theodore H. Lewis, pp. 137-138.

[77] Ibid, p. 139.

[78] Final Report of the United States de Soto Commission by Swanton, p. 82.

[79] Ibid, p. 82, 83, 85.

[80] Spanish Explorers of the Southwest States by J. F. Jameson, p. 138.

[81] Final Report of the United States de Soto Commission by
    John R. Swanton, p. 350.

[82] Os Portugueses no Descobrimento dos E. Unidos by Jaime Cortesão, p. 48.

[83] The Forgotten Centuries by Charles Hudson, p. 100.

[84] Ibid.

[85] The True Relation of the Fidalgo of Elvas, pp. 39-46 Chapter IX.

[86] The Melungeons by N. Brent Kennedy, p.107; The Last Conquistador
    by Marc Simmons.

[87] National Geographic Magazine, July 1985, p. 41.

[88] Ibid, pp. 41-71.

Notes (Cont.)

[89] The Spanish, Portuguese Languages by William J. Entwistle, p. 5.

[90] National Geographic Society, July 1985, pp. 41-71.

[91] Os Portugueses no Vice-Reinado do Peru, by Gonçalo de Reparaz, pp. 9-11.

[92] Os Portugueses no Descobrimento dos Estados Unidos by Jaime Cortesão, p. 64.

[93] Historia de Portugal by A.H. de Oliveira Marques, Vol.II, pp. 171-172.

[94] Os Portugueses no Vice-Reinado do Peru, by Conçalo de Reparaz, p. 41.

[95] Boletim do Instituto Historica, Presença de Portugal...E. U. by Manoel da Silveira Cardozo, p. 10.

[96] Spanish Explorers in the Southern States by J. F. Jameson, p. 385.

[97] Great Lives, Sir Francis Drake by Neville Williams, p. 88.

[98] Further English Voyages to Spanish America, 1583-1594 by Irene A. Wright, p. 212. Cf. Document No. 35. Encl. No. 2.

[99] North American Discovery by David Quinn, p. 200.

[100] A New Voyage to Carolina by John Lawson (Hugh Lefler), p. 172.

[101] The Juan Pardo Explorations by Charles Hudson, pp. 305-310.

[102] Gran Enciclopedia Gallega by Silverio Canada, Vol. 18, pp. 104-105.

[103] Archivo General de Indias in Seville, signature Santo Domingo, p. 224.

[104] Catholic Historical Review, Vol. LI, 3, Oct. 1965 by Michael V. Gannon, p. 340.

[105] Archivo General de Indias, Patronato 19, ramo 22, year 1566.

[106] The Melungeons became a race by David Henige. Appalachian Journal, Spring 1998, p. 273.

[107] Ibid, pp. 274.

[108] Ibid, pp. 275.

[109] A Spanish Discovery of North Carolina by L. A. Vigneras, p. 410.

[110] Newfoundland, from Fishery to Colony by David Beers Quinn, p. 186.

[111] The Spanish Jesuit Mission in Virginia by Lewis and Albert Loomie, p. 20.

[112] Newfoundland, from Fishery to Colony by David Beers Quinn, p. 185.

[113] N. Brent Kennedy letter to Victor Marques of CNN (March 2, 1995).

[114] Newfoundland, from Fisheries to Colony by David Beers Quinn, p. 185.

[115] Ibid, p. 187.

[116] North American Discovery by David Beers Quinn, p. 178.

[117] The Last Conquistador by Marc Simmons (1991), p. 119-21.

[118] Boletim do Instituto Historica, Presença de Portugal...by Manoel da Silveira Cardozo, p. 10.

[119] The Little Lion of the Southwest by Marc Simmons, pp. 1-11.

[120] Luso-Americano, Jan.13, 1993—Manuel Brazil by Geoffrey Gomes, p. 2.

[121] Ibid, Apr. 6, 1994—Manuel Brazil by Geoffrey Gomes.

[122] Portuguese Roteiros by C. R. Boxer, pp. 174/5 (Mariner's Mirror, April 1974).

[122] Ibid

Chapter VIII

Portuguese Presence after the 16th Century in North America

*If we are on a river shore and looking at the other, we must think, that a raft
or a bridge existed there, in order that the conquerors' army could cross.
The historian's logic and imagination,
allows him to put the bridge or the raft in his chronicles.* [1]

To Emigrate, the Destiny for the Portuguese
A Poem to the Emigrant, Portuguese or any Other [2]

Portuguese	English
Ao deixar a minha terra	When I left my country
Eu pensei que navegar	I thought that navigate
Era só partir para longe	Was only to leave for far away
E um dia regressar	And one day to return
Ao chegar à nova terra	Arriving at the new world
Quiz fazer dali meu lar	I wanted to make my home there
Estrangeiro eu fui para sempre	But foreign forever I was
Nunca tive o meu lugar	Never had I my place
Quem somos nós	Who are we
Em frente ao mar	Facing the sea
Com sonhos loucos	With crazy dreams
De navegar	To navigate
Quem somos nós	Who are we
Em frente ao cais	Facing the sea
Com sonhos loucos	With crazy dreams
Voltar atraz	To go back
Um Natal que eu não esqueço	A Christmas I'll never forget
Regressei ao meu país	As I returned to my country
Cada amigo que eu conheço	Each friend that I meet
Me abraça e me diz	Embraced me and told me
Que eu deixei de ser quem era	I, no longer was the same
E que estranho o meu falar	So strange is my talking
Emigrante eu fui p'ra sempre	Emigrant I was forever
Já não tenho mais um lar	No longer had a home [3]

This chapter portrays the known Portuguese immigrations to North America in a broad manner. It does not, by any means, replace other books that study this aspect in detail. However, it may show a possible migration of Melungeons or other groups, from or to areas where larger groups of Portuguese were known to be established.

Immigrants from Portugal

Judge Shepherd in his eloquent oratory about the celebrated Melungeon case, stated that the immediate source of Melungeon origin stemmed from a group of immigrants from Portugal. [4] Adalino Cabral wrote a paragraph as to the global impact of the Portuguese: *No European people has been longer in the New World or more continuously than the Portuguese. Perhaps this is the way it was meant to be. After all, they have proportionally furnished more emigrants to the Western World than any nation of Europe (with the possible exception of England). Having established the first of the modern empires, and on virtually all continents of the world, this errant race, not content with the enormity of its own geographical space, also emigrated to lands under the control of other sovereignties.*

They emigrated to English-speaking nations (United States, Canada, England, Australia, South Africa...) and, in each of them, the Portuguese have been affected by the dominant language, having no alternative but to employ a mixture of linguistic phenomena borrowing or Portinglês. [5]

Geoffrey Gomes, of the California State University at Hayward, wrote about one Portuguese immigrant that no one knew about, and goes on to say: *...that Portuguese immigrants have been more integrated into the American experience than previously thought. Clearly, a Portuguese presence is to be found beyond the traditional geographical focal points...It makes one wonder, however, how many more like him remain to be rediscovered and salvaged from the obscurity to which they have been relegated.* [6]

Ellis Island tourist information states that 120,725 Portuguese immigrants were processed through that center before it was closed down. This number exceeds that of people from Denmark, Spain, Belgium and France.

Portuguese Emigration from the Azores and North of Portugal

A study made in the 19th century pointed to Minho, Beira Alta and the Azores as the areas from which most of the Portuguese were coming. Between the period of 1860 and 1888, a total of 113,280 came from Minho (north), 70,890 from Beira Alta (north central), 60,088 from the Azores, and 23,202 from the Madeira Islands, while from the rest of Portugal only 23,134 emigrated.

Portuguese Women Immigrated in the 1600's

The Dutch, by establishing New Amsterdam (New York), put a colonial wedge between the English colonies and New England. The first settlers came in 1623, and in 1643, Father Isaac Jogues, a French Jesuit missionary, arrived. In 1646, Father Jogues wrote a letter describing the colony: *...for there are in the Colony besides the Calvinists, Catholics, English Puritans...it is near this river that a gold mine is reported to have been found...*[7]

Leo Pap wrote: *...and...it turned out that his hostess...was a Portuguese Catholic woman...*That there were one or several Portuguese residents in New York at that time is also indicated, for instance, by the old marriage records of the Dutch Church.[8]

Much earlier, Portuguese women according to Freitas: *...endured heat, disease, snakes, jaguars, fierce Corsair and Indian attacks, and French and Dutch invasions.*[9]

Portuguese Jews in America—1621

Due to the fact that the Jews were one of the peoples most displaced in the 15th and 16th centuries, there are indications that they travelled by whatever means available to various parts of the world. It is known that many, disguised as Christians and through bribery, obtained passage in caravels bound to India and Brazil to escape the Inquisition. Their presence is noted in South America in the early 16th century, and then in North America in the early 17th century. It is therefore possible that some Portuguese Jews arrived on the North-America's East Coast during the early 16th century and later moved north.

Most likely, they were joined by other *cristãos novos* (new Christians) who formed their own group, either based on family ties or race, which did not follow the Jews. It is important to know the pattern of Jewish migration to establish a possible Melungeon connection.

The earliest date recorded for the presence of Jews in America is 1621, with an Elias Legardo as a probable Portuguese Jew, being noted in Virginia. Before that, it is also known that in May of 1549 a ship loaded with fugitives from Portugal had arrived in Ragusa (Dubrovnik, Croatia) and Syria, as well as European Turkey. These cities daily received Portuguese families looking for some religious freedom, as written by Herculano: *...given to them by half Islamic tolerance.*[10] In one group of Jewish refugees were João Migueis and his brother, and their aunt Beatriz Mendes, a Portuguese Jewess lady later known as Gracia Nasi — born in Lisbon, Portugal in 1510, died in 1569 — who became one of the most influential women in the Ottoman world and organized the largest underground railroad out of Portugal.

Those vessels were loaded with *fugitives*. Did they all go to Europe, or did some of them go to the New World, like the Pilgrims?

The Portuguese Jews played an important role in the development of the countries discovered by Portugal. Gilberto Freyre, a well known Brazilian writer and social anthropologist, tells us in his classic book *The Master and the Slaves* (translated into English by Samuel Putnam from the original *Casa Grande & Senzala* and published by the University of California Press): *As for the Jew, there is evidence to the effect that he was one of the most active agents in the winning of a market for the sugar producers of Brazil.*[11] In 1636, Jews were arriving not only from Portugal and Spain, but also from Italy, Turkey, North Africa and the Netherlands.[12]

In 1507, Portugal decreed that all Jews be allowed to leave Portugal, and trade or buy property anywhere in the world. So they went to the Ottoman Empire, Brazil, Holland and the Dutch colonies. The descendants of these Jews came to settle in the American Colonies. [13] The date of the first arrival is not known, but there had been Portuguese Jews in the Colonies as early as 1621, as already mentioned. The next date on record is 1634, of Mathias de Sousa in Maryland.

The new and modern view is that American Judaism began in May 1654 with the arrival of the first Portuguese Jews from Recife, Brazil. Just as it can be held that American history began at Jamestown and that this experience set the framework for future American history, so it can be demonstrated that the Portuguese Jews and their successor immigrants in the Colonial period set the framework for a new Jewish history. [14] The age of the Sephardim Jews in America is considered to be from 1621 to 1776. [15]

Francis Salvador was a prominent patriot of the Revolutionary War in South Carolina, and appears in history as early as 1732. He was related to a wealthy family of Portuguese Jews in England, and cousin to Mrs. Mendes da Costa. While in South Carolina, he was held in such esteem that he was elected to that state's General Assembly. He died August 1st 1776, while on an expedition against the English and Indians. Other names, such as David Nunes Cardozo and Isaac N. Cardoso, also fought in a militia company of Charleston, South Carolina. [16]

Collectively, the American Jews are one of the most remarkable groups in the world. A society of 6 million Jews has attained the highest economic, educational and social levels in Jewish history, and enjoyed a degree of freedom never attained by Jews in any country, in any civilization, in any age, as stated by Dimont: *...including the kingdoms of Judah and Israel in ancient days, and the state of Israel today.* [17]

All Sephardic Jews are from Portugal and Spain, or of Portuguese and Spanish ancestry. They were viewed by the British as *Portugals*, and were a puzzle to them, after New Amsterdam was taken over by England and renamed New York in 1664. The Portuguese Jews always kept their Portuguese names after arriving in America. They were persecuted during the Inquisition, but did not change their names, while others that were not persecuted, quickly changed. [18]

They kept not only their Portuguese names, but also the language. In Surinam, where many Portuguese Jews settled before coming to America, their slaves adopted the Portuguese language, and went on speaking broken Portuguese. [19] In Newport, Rhode Island, the Jews contributed to the city's commercial prosperity early in the 18th century, when trade sprang up between Portugal, the West Indies and Newport. Among them were many Portuguese. The great earthquake of Portugal in 1755 brought additional Jewish settlers. [20]

Founding of the Virginia Colony and the Portuguese—1621-49

This colony was founded by respected members of the Anglican church. Many of the early settlers in Virginia were rich English merchants, and their wish in England was to become country gentlemen. This was rather difficult to achieve in England, so Virginia became their *Little England*, and although Jews were not allowed to settle in this colony, Portuguese Jews did trickle in as early as 1621, according to some sources. Those of Sephardic origin married into some of the finest of Virginia's transplanted gentry.[21] In 1649, Virginia already had an English population of 15,000 plus Black slaves.[22] Also, in 1645, Portuguese Madeira wine was already being sold in Boston.

In Richmond, Virginia, the Synagogue Beth Abrabah was founded by Portuguese and Spanish Sephardic Jews, according to its Rabbi Lawrence A. Schlesinger.

Maryland and Rhode Island—1654-58

There are records of a colony of Spanish and Portuguese Jews arriving from Recife, Brazil. The Portuguese Jews were called the Portuguese Nation.[23]

Among the varied mix of settlers in that Colony was Dr. Jacob Lumbrozo, who arrived from Portugal in 1656. There were Portuguese Jewish settlers in Newport as early as 1658. Tombstones in the first Jewish cemetery in Newport are still intact, the earliest dating from 1677.

The Touro Synagogue was built in 1763, and still stands. According to Humberto Carreiro of Bristol, Israel is the correct name, and was changed to Touro in 1820 due to large contributions by Abraham Touro. In 1947, President Harry Truman proclaimed this synagogue a historic monument due to the fact that it has never been remodeled. One of the families of the Newport Jewish community was the Aaron Lopes family, who arrived from Portugal in 1752.[24] In 1655, the Portuguese Jews were excluded from serving in the military when Peter Stuyvesant was preparing for a military expedition against New Sweden. Not only were they not allowed to serve, but they had to pay a special tax.[25]

New York—1655-1730

The first official (not necessarily the oldest) Jewish synagogue, Shearith Israel, was built on Wall Street, and David Mendes Machado, a native of Lisbon, became the rabbi. Still in existence, this congregation founded in 1728 is now located on Central Park West. The earliest minutes and accounts of the Congregation Shearith Israel—now the Spanish-Portuguese Synagogue on Central Park West, New York—were written in the Portuguese language.[26] In 1655 this same congregation is recorded to have petitioned the local authorities for the right to establish a Jewish cemetery in the city. A small part of that cemetery, located near New York's Chatham Square, still exists. Portuguese names can be found amongst the wills filed between 1665 and 1796 in the surrogate's Office of the County of New York—names like Marques, Pinheiro, Nunes, Fernandes, Machado, Pacheco da Silva, and others.[27]

Isaac Mendes Seixas, a Portuguese Jew, arrived in New York from Portugal in 1730. His son Benjamin Mendes Seixas, of New York and Newport, was one of the founders of the New York Stock Exchange. Carlos Seixas, the Portuguese harpsichord baroque musician, may have been related.

Benjamin Nathan Cardozo, born 1870 in New York City of Portuguese ancestry, was named to the Supreme Court of the United States.

First Mailman was Portuguese—1693

Portuguese names appear in French-Canadian legal records in 1698, and 1693 Montreal judicial archives show that Pedro da Silva, from Lisbon, was paid 20 sols for the transport of a bundle of letters from Montreal to Quebec City. This was the first known mail service between the two cities.

When he was 33 years old, Pedro da Silva married a 17-year-old French-Canadian and had at least two daughters and seven sons. His sons had large families and just the three of them had 45 children. Jean had 17, Dominique 15 and Nicolas 13.

The name Silva, Sylva or Dasilva is to be found in North America in the 19th and 20th centuries. [28] The town Sylva, North Carolina is located in an area where the Melungeons were known to have settled.

Savannah, Georgia—1733

Fig. 72—Synagogue in Savannah, GA.

Diogo Ribeiro Nunes, a physician, was born in 1668 in Beira Alta, Portugal. He practiced medicine in Lisbon until he was arrested and his property seized in 1703 by the Inquisition for speaking up in favor of Judaism. In 1726 he and his family escaped to England where his name was changed to the Hebrew name Samuel. He came to Georgia in 1732 with a group of Jews. When he arrived in 1733, he found people dying of an epidemic. Nunes took charge and brought the epidemic under control. This action may have saved the struggling infant colony from a serious epidemic. Oglethorpe gave Nunes and other Jewish settlers plots of land, however these were later abandoned due to Jenkin's War which threatened Georgia with a possible takeover from Florida. [29]

The Sephardic Jews still remembered vividly the Portuguese and Spanish Inquisitions, so they left to New York. Nunes and his sons returned later, and his sons were known to have lived in Savannah.

There is a synagogue in Savannah where the Portuguese Jews were active participants, well before the Revolutionary War, in 1733. It is the third oldest in the U.S., and is built using a Gothic architectural style, very unusual for a synagogue. The original Portuguese Jews did profess Catholicism to escape death by burning, but reverted to the Jewish faith as soon as they arrived in the U.S. The history of this synagogue shows that the original Jews were Portuguese Sephardim.

Abraham de Lyon, who was a vintner in Portugal before coming to the United States, began growing grapes in Georgia in 1737.

New England—1740-1900

New England has been the traditional place of choice for the Portuguese immigrant since the early times of settlement. Unfortunately, there are very few non-English records available to document the presence of the Portuguese in this area of North America. However, if a serious search is done, much more can be found, and the areas to be investigated are in Holland, Belgium and France. There are a wealth of documents out there waiting to be found. Naturally you must be fluent in one of three languages—Flemish, Dutch or French—and have paleographic reading knowledge of the 16th century. It is not impossible, and it can be done.

Aaron Lopes, baptized as a Catholic, fled Portugal in the early 1740's. He settled in Newport, Rhode Island, where he openly professed Judaism. He became one of the wealthiest merchants and shippers of his day, building the whaling industry, and owning at one time about 30 ships. Lopes was one of the founders of the Touro Synagogue in Newport.

José Dias, a Portuguese who settled on Martha's Vineyard, served in the American Revolutionary War. He was captured by the British and died in their custody in 1781. Moses Seixas, who died in 1809, was the grand master of the Masonic Order of Rhode Island, and cashier of the Bank of R.I. Also in Rhode Island, James Lucena began the manufacture of Castile soap about 1769.

Antone S. Sylvia, a native of the Azores, arrived in New Bedford, Massachusetts in 1855 at the age of 15. He began as a clerk in the Joseph Frazer Whaling Outfitting Co. in New Bedford, and in 1862 became the sole proprietor of the business and a millionaire.

The presence of the Portuguese mariners made itself well known from the beginning of the 19th century to the following century. Names like George A. M. Brier (Silva), George M. Chase, Henry Clay, Francis J. Sylvia, Manuel King Sylvia and many more. A book titled *They Ploughed the Seas* by Pat Amaral provides a wealth of information about the Portuguese presence in New England during the early 19th century. It should be known that most of the Portuguese there were born in the Azores Islands, and many of them became ship owners, master mariners and whaling masters, such as John E. Simmons, born in Faial. [30]

In the second half of the 19th century, an industrialist named William Madison Wood became famous in the textile industry. Both his mills and his mansions were frequently the subject of books and press articles. [31]

The US Revolution and the First Census—1779-90

After the Declaration of Independence, the crew of one of the earliest American warships, *Bonhomme Richard*, under the command of John Paul Jones, a founder of the American Navy, consisted primarily of Portuguese. By the 18th century, American ships traveled regularly between New England, Portugal and the Caribbean. These ships brought in the Madeira wine so much appreciated by George Washington. [32] The Portuguese wine from Madeira was the preferred wine during Colonial America. It was imported directly from Madeira and was not taxed. One fact not very well known is that the famous Boston Tea Party revolt was started because of a shipment of 100 barrels of Madeira wine ordered by John Hancock. The first three U.S. Presidents, George Washington, John Adams and Thomas Jefferson, all liked Madeira wine.

It was the favored drink of George Washington and of Benjamin Franklin, who drank half a liter per day. The Declaration of Independence was toasted with Madeira wine in 1776, as well as when President Washington was inaugurated. During his first year of the presidency, Thomas Jefferson bought approximately 2,000 liters to entertain his guests at the White House. [33]

Salvador Fidalgo, a Portuguese navigator, discovered a stretch of the Pacific coast south of Alaska. [34] He also explored the coasts of Alaska and British Columbia, as well as Puget Sound in the 1790's.

There are records dating back to the colonial period that point to an already fairly large Portuguese population in the United States. The study made in 1920 was based on Portuguese family names existing in 1790, when the first census was taken. At that time it was shown that the population of Portuguese origin was estimated at 24,000. [35]

Pennsylvania, Portuguese from Lisbon, 1769-1805

While searching for possible Portuguese Melungeon roots, other Portuguese groups, who may or may not be connected with the Melungeons, were discovered. The following pages describe a particularly interesting group that also suffered discrimination until very recently.

Leo Pap mentions the possibility that they may have come from Pennsylvania. This is doubtful, however. There are records of a group coming into Pennsylvania from Lisbon, Portugal, but it is not connected with the group or groups discussed in this book.

By the 18th century, communication and transportation were much easier, compared to the 16th and 17th centuries. From 1794 to 1799, Portugal already had a diplomatic mission headed by Cipriano Ferreira.[36] Later, the Abbot José Correia da Serra was the Portuguese diplomat (1816-1820) in the U.S., representing Portugal during the Thomas Jefferson administration (1801-1820). That was before the Portuguese government recognized American independence. Portugal, being an old ally of England, was under pressure not to recognize it. Portugal, however, was one of the first three nations, along with France and Holland, to do so on February 15th 1783. During a 4th of July 1999 celebration in Lisbon, the US Ambassador to Portugal pointed out in his address that in addition to 223 years of independence of the United States…Portugal was the first neutral country to recognize the independence of the U.S.

Fig. 73—Association Booklet
Courtesy Antonio Matinho

When the American Revolution started, Portugal was governed by one its fiercest dictators, Prime Minister Marquis of Pombal, whose iron fisted government in time of crisis benefited the people and the nation. He, however, sided with Great Britain in some of the measures taken.

On Sept. 10th 1813, a major U.S. naval victory took place in the War of 1812, ensuring U.S. control over Lake Erie. Commandant Oliver Perry's fleet of nine ships engaged six British warships. Portuguese names were found on the muster roll, and since Perry was living in Newport, Rhode Island at the time, it is only natural that he would pick up Portuguese settlers and seamen living there.

Later in the 19th century, we encounter signs of a very well organized Portuguese community in Erie, Pennsylvania. An organization called the Holy Trinity Portuguese Association was founded in 1874. The name indicates that it was a religious association; however, the Portuguese usually form an organization that serves as a social as well as a religious gathering. Jacob Mendez da Costa, a Medical doctor of Portuguese and Spanish ancestry, studied at Jefferson Medical College in 1849, where in 1872 he was elected professor. He was active in the foundation of the Pathological Society in 1857, serving as its first secretary. Costa also has to his credit several medical writings.[37]

Fig. 74—Peter Francisco in 1828 painting.
Courtesy Virginia State Library

Peter Francisco
The Portuguese Patriot—1765

Peter Francisco, born Pedro Francisco in Azores, was kidnapped, presumably by Moorish pirates, from his home on Terceira Island, and left on a dock in Virginia in 1765 when he was approximately 5 years old.

He grew up to be a giant of a man who served the American Revolution with fierce pride and performed outstanding feats of strength and heroism. [38] To appreciate better his tremendous contribution to the American Revolution, note the words of General George Washington: *Without him we would have lost two battles, perhaps the War, and with it our freedom. He was truly a One-Man-Army.* [39] Dr. John Manahan reported to the University of Virginia under the title *Peter Francisco, Virginia Giant of the Revolution*—a lengthy document from which comes the following quote: *He (Peter Francisco) was of a dark complexion, with black eyes...* [40] Again this color description is similar to the one given to the Melungeons. Francisco was known to have fought in various northern battles and is reputed to have slain 11 British in one battle, and captured an 1,100 pound cannon, turning it on the enemy.

"Abbot" José Correia da Serra and Thomas Jefferson's Monticello

Fig. 75—The "Abbot" José Correia da Serra room

The third President of the U.S., Thomas Jefferson, took 25 years to build his dream house, Monticello. The room used by *abade* José Francisco Correia da Serra (1750-1823) was recently refurbished. It was inaugurated on June 18th 1995, after a restoration project financed by the Foundation for Luso-American Development (FLAD).

Correia da Serra was known to the American President's family as *abade—abbot* in English—because of his original Portuguese title. President Jefferson is known to have invited Correia da Serra to give his opinion of the Philadelphia University articles and by-laws. [41] He was also a scientist, botanist, polyglot and founder of the Portuguese Sciences Academy.

To be admired is the meticulous work done to restore the room. The highlight of the room is an 18th century Portuguese Arraiolos rug that was donated by FLAD, previously restored in the *Arte Antiga* museum in Lisbon. Correia da

Fig.76—"Abbot" José C. da Serra, painting at the Academia das Ciencias de Lisboa.

Serra was a university professor in the U.S. and, after being introduced into the circle of enlightened individuals with whom President Jefferson enjoyed spending time, Correia da Serra won the President's respect and friendship.

He lived in the U.S. until 1820, the year he returned to Portugal where he spent the last three years of his life. By that time he had been Jefferson's guest in Monticello on numerous occasions, accepting the President's repeated invitation to: ...*come and make yourself at home.* [42]

Dr. Manuel Luciano da Silva, an historian and researcher of the Portuguese in America, was awarded the Peter Francisco Medal on November 4, 1995. During this event, it was mentioned that Humberto Carreiro discovered that Monticello, the famous home of President Thomas Jefferson in Virginia, had been the property of a Portuguese Jewish family, Machado Philips Levy, who saved Monticello from destruction.

The Azoreans in Trinidad & Tobago—1834

Our research department about Portuguese in America and their participation in the making of the Americas has come across the drama of a group of Azoreans who left their homeland to look for a better life in Trinidad and Tobago. Some of them paid the ultimate price, their lives.

The following are transcriptions of documents found: Sir George Hill, Governor of Trinidad to the Right Honourable Thomas Spring Rice. Trinidad, 20 July 1834 (an abstract): *Gov. Hill reports that on 15 July the British Schooner "Watchful" arrived in Trinidad from "Fayal" with "44 of the natives of that place by previous engagement," to work as indentured field laborers, or "in any manner most advantageous to the employer for a period of 3 years in return for which they are to receive 6 dollars per month wages, a piece of land for their own use and cultivation, and to be provisioned...until their lands are productive."* One half of their wages were to be retained until the laborer's passage had been paid for, the amount per person being 60 dollars. The report states that the laborers had been *"accordingly taken as apprentices by some of the planters."* It also states that *"these people have been accustomed to work in the field in their own climate and will be able to withstand the sun heat here—they are looked upon as a very valuable acquisition to an Island such as this"* and it was expected that such laborers would render the island *"the most valuable of His Majesty's West India colonies."* Because of the reputation of the Azoreans as good workers, planters were desirous of engaging a larger number of them.

Petition, to the Governor of Trinidad in 1835: *The humble Petition of the undersigned subjects of the Crown of Portugal respectfully sheweth that with many others of their countrymen, they were induced by certain evil disposed persons, under false pretences, to quit their native country, Fayal, to become agricultural labourers in this Colony. Of the whole number thus cajoled, one third only are still in existence. The rest have fallen victims to the unhealthiness of the climate or to the cruelties of the slavery system to which we, equally with the unfortunate blacks, have been subjected. For let speculators in human blood deny it as they will, the awful calamity which has occurred among our countrymen, in so short a period as ten months, must have resulted from one or the other of these fatal causes, or from both combined.*

Men, women and children, have suffered the greatest misery and oppression on the several estates where they have been forced to work far beyond their strength by coercion of the whip, without proper shelter at night or adequate food during the day. The consolation of religion has been denied them in the hours of sickness and death; whilst the bodies of the miserable victims of avarice have been thrown into holes and ditches without Christian burial.

The cries of the fatherless children and widows have been loud in the land, but there was no response from Christian charity to soften their grief, no arm of justice to relieve them from the hands of oppressors. Few are they who are left to tell their tale of woe. Your Excellency has often been apprised of these truths but our sufferings are unheeded. We have been advised that an appeal to the Governor General for the information of His Britannic Majesty's Government would be attended to, but we hope Your Excellency will obviate the necessity for such an appeal by mercifully acceding to the prayer of your humble petitioners; which is that Your Excellency will be pleased to collect together the few Portuguese labourers yet in existence in this Colony; That you will humanely relieve their immediate and pressing wants, particularly those of the poor and helpless orphans; and that you will cause them to be transported back to their native country. Rosa Constancia (who has lost her husband and three children). Felicia Perpetua de Castro (who has lost her husband and one child). Maria Constancia (who has lost two children).

Mariana Francisca (who has lost four children). Josef Francisco Macieda (who has lost his wife and four children). Antonio Francisco Dabla (who has lost two children). Anna Perpetua (the mother of seven children). Francisco de Utro Perreira (whose wife and four children are at Fayal) and 28 others.

A Petition from Josef da Costa, a Portuguese, To the Lieutenant Governor of Trinidad in 1835: *The humble Petition of Josef da Costa, free Portuguese by birth, but now an apprenticed labourer, states That he came to Trinidad on certain conditions and sailed from Fayal on 31st October 1834. He and 27 others were clandestinely landed on the north coast, 15 days after their arrival, were carried to Mr. Graham's estate at Chaguanas. There they remained two months where they worked with the negroes in the fields. The consequence was that they all fell sick and many died. The Petitioner and his wife were, through the humanity of Mr Graham, removed to town and placed in Marie Ursula's hospital where his unhappy wife died. After this, his services were bought by one Mr. Lock and he was sent down the coast where he was badly treated and, when unable to work as the negroes did, cruelly beaten. To escape from this misery, he left the estate on the 18th of the present month, and is now lying in town in the last stages of misery and starvation. He humbly implores that his case be inquired into; Josef da Costa. Witness; A. Shaw.*[43]

Portuguese in Virginia & Washington, D.C.

One of the most famous Americans was born in Washington, D.C., on November 6, 1854, and his name was John Philip Sousa, son of the Portuguese João António Sousa and Austrian Maria Elizabeth Trinkaus.[44]

He grew up to become the famous march composer of *Stars and Stripes Forever*. In 1987, President Ronald Reagan approved a law proposed by Tony Coelho, a Congressman from California, that made *Stars and Stripes Forever* the official march of the United States.

In Virginia, it is interesting to find the existence of a large thoroughfare, "Portugee Road," which is not far from the Richmond airport.

During an interview with Isabel Paul of the Enrico County Library, she stated that the name Portugee dates to the early 1800's, however in 1887 it was called White Oak Swampy Road, and before that it was called New Road, a name given to any road where the naming presented a problem. Isabel could not tell the author the exact date when the road was finally named Portugee. The 1978 issue of the Enrico County Historical, page 44, had additional

Fig. 77—Sign near Richmond, VA. by Linda Aguiar

information on naming of roads.

Fig. 78—John Philip Sousa

After some more research, the author came across Dr. Lewis Manarin—a member of the Enrico Historical Society—whom he interviewed. The author was told of a legend dating back to the late 1700's and early 1800's, that in the neighborhood there was a Portuguese settlement, and the road now called Portugee Road led to it.

Later the settlement was abandoned and the name disappeared, to show up 50 years later. Dr. Lewis Manarin also mentioned Jim Walthal, whom the author later had the opportunity to talk with, and the result is an amazing story.

Mr. James B. Walthal was kind enough to provide the author with the information related to his relatives.

His great grandfather, José Vieira Ramos, came to this country in the 1830's under amazing circumstances.

Before proceeding with his story, let us review Portugal's situation in the early 1800's. France's Napoleon had just made a pact with Russia in 1807, which left him free to turn against Britain, Sweden and Portugal. Spain had been Napoleon's ally since 1796. He then summoned Portugal to close all ports to the British and declared war on Britain.

A French army of 30,000 crossed Spain and invaded Portugal, while the Portuguese royal family fled to Brazil, which later proved to be the beginning of the independence process for the largest South American country, then a Portuguese colony.

While in Portugal, the Napoleonic forces occupied Porto (Oporto), a northern city, and also other places in Portugal.

The war with France lasted until 1814, and during that time, Jim's grandfather, as a very young man, apparently fought against Napoleon's army during the occupation and later when retreating under pressure of the Portuguese and British allied army. The part of the Napoleonic wars fought in Portugal and Spain contributed considerably to Napoleon's eventual downfall.

After that, José Vieira Ramos returned to his native Azores, where he got himself involved in some kind of rebellion against the government. The details are rather sketchy.

He, together with other participants in the rebellion, were put aboard a ship and deported to another island, presumably Tarrafal in Cabo Verde, the favorite place for the Portuguese government's political prisoners.

He knew what was in store for him and his companions, and they together mutinied and took over the ship's command, forcing it to go west towards the American east coast, and landing in southeast Virginia.

The American government considered them refugees and gave them some land as a place of settlement near what is today Portugee Road in the suburbs of Richmond, Virginia. Some of them stayed for awhile, and others moved to the city, including Jim's great-grandfather, who met a Virginian lady, married, and had children whom he encouraged to learn music.

One of the children was Manly Burrows Ramos, a name borrowed from one of the Baptist ministers, whom he held in high regard. Manly was Jim's grandfather and the father of Alice Ramos, the mother of Jim.

One of the offspring became a pharmacist, another a school teacher, and so on. José Ramos Vieira was naturalized as an American citizen in 1836, one of the earliest, and joined the Baptist Church, where he was held in the highest respect. When he died in 1895, he was the oldest member of the Baptist Church.

Emma Lazarus—1849-1887

Reader's Digest published an article about *The Statue of Liberty*. In it the ancestors of poet Emma Lazarus — author of the poem *The New Colossus* — were described as having emigrated from Portugal in 1649 among the first Portuguese Jews to settle in what is today New York. [45] Emma was born on July 22, 1849 and died on Nov. 19, 1887. The poem, *The New Colossus*:

Not like the brazen giant of Greek fame,
With conquering limbs astride
from land to land;
Here at our sea-washed, sunset-gates shall stand

A mighty woman with a torch, whose flame
Is the imprisoned lightning and her name
Mother of Exiles.

From her beacon-hand
Glows worldwide welcome,
her mild eyes command

The air bridged harbor that twin-cities frame.
Keep, ancient lands, your storied pomp!

With silent lips. "Give me your tired, your poor,
Your huddled masses yearning to breathe free,
The wretched refuse of your teeming shore;

Send these, the homeless, tempest-tost to me,
I lift my lamp beside the golden door!

Fig. 79—Emma Lazarus, a Portuguese Sephardic Jewish Poet, a niece of the Supreme Court Justice, Benjamin, Cardozo, also a Sephardic Jew.

Fig. 80—Portrait of President Lincoln by Chicago photographer Alexander Hesler, taken in Springfield June 3, 1860. One of the few photographs showing Lincoln without a beard.[46]

Portuguese in Illinois and President Lincoln—1846

The state of Illinois received a group of Portuguese in 1846 under unique circumstances.

Robert Reid Kalley, a medical doctor and Protestant English missionary on his way to the Orient, stopped in Madeira, and due to his wife's illness he had to stay. While there he was able to convert a number of Madeirans.

After a while, the Catholic clergy became hostile. A few years later, this group left Madeira Island and went to the British West Indies and Trinidad to work on a plantation. Due to climate and work conditions they did not adapt well, and the first group of 130 eventually wound up in Springfield, Illinois after overcoming quite a number of problems. The number of Portuguese who left Madeira is calculated at over 2,000.

Although they found work conditions unbearable in Trinidad, [47] they were good workers, which is reflected in a favorable report on them by the governor that sparked the beginning of the emigration to Bermuda of many Portuguese.

Other groups also went to Jacksonville, Illinois and for the next few years many more of the original group joined them. Many of the traditions no longer exist, except for a place still called the Portuguese Hill and a few typically Portuguese family names. Abraham Lincoln, who later became President, also lived in Springfield, and a member of his household staff was Frances Affonsa, one of a Portuguese refugee group from Madeira. Manuel de Fraita (Freitas), another Portuguese that Frances liked, would come to visit Frances at Lincoln's place and they had supper together. It is believed they got married.

President Abraham Lincoln, a Melungeon Descendant?

Anyone reading President Abraham Lincoln's biography would see good indications that his mother, Nancy Hanks, may have descended from Melungeons.

The sixteenth President of the United States was born on February 12th, 1809, in a log cabin in a backwoods farm of Kentucky, near a place called Hodgenville in what is now Lauren County. Samuel Lincoln, the President's ancestor, emigrated to Massachusetts in 1638.

Later, his grandson Abraham Lincoln crossed the mountains from Virginia and settled in Kentucky. His son Thomas Lincoln worked under Joseph Hanks learning carpentry, and later married Joseph's niece Nancy, who gave birth to Abraham Lincoln, and 50 years later would be nominated for President.

Not much is known of his mother, except that she was the illegitimate daughter of a Virginia planter and a woman called Lucy Hanks. [48] Abraham Lincoln said of his mother, "I owe everything that I am to her," explaining further, that he inherited from her, *the mental qualities which distinguished him from the house of Lincoln.* [49]

From the above, and also from Nancy's physical features, it is possible to assume she is of Melungeon descent. It is also written that her name was Nancy Sparrows Hank, and that her mother was Lucy. Studying Lincoln's genealogy on his mother's side is a monumental task, as many doubts are presented along the way. No clear decision has been reached by the historians, or at least their opinion is not unanimous. [50] Also, the description of Nancy Hanks adds another common factor: *Her dark skin, dark brown hair, keen little gray eyes, outstanding forehead...*[51] As to the description of his father Tom Lincoln, it is somewhat similar to his son Abraham, according to Carl Sandburg: *As Tom Lincoln came to his full growth he was about 5 feet, nine inches tall...His dark hazel eyes...coarse black hair.* [52]

Portuguese and Moor—According to Abraham Lincoln

Further research into President Lincoln's life reveals a connection with dark complexioned people and the Portuguese. While working as a lawyer in Springfield, he accepted a case from a Portuguese called Dungey. The name written in Portuguese, *Dungue*, is not very common, and may indicate that in the 1850's, Dungey's past generations had already been established. The name may have originated from *Godinho*, a Portuguese name.

As to the Portuguese Dungey's case, this was the result of him being called a *negro* by his brother-in-law, named Spencer. It was a crime under Illinois laws then for a white to marry a *negro;* therefore, the words were slanderous and Dungey had Lincoln bring a slander suit in which Spencer stated that Dungey was that: *Black Bill is a negro and it will be easily proved if called for.*

[Lincoln, when addressing the jury, accused Spencer of having called Dungey a *nigger* and argued:] *Gentlemen of the jury, my client is not a negro, though it is not a crime to be a negro—no crime to be borne with a black skin. But my client is not a negro. His skin may not be as white as ours, but I say he is not a negro, though he may be a Moor. Not only had Spencer called Dungey a nigger but he had followed it up with adding a nigger married to a white woman.* [53] The jury gave a verdict of $600.00 to the Portuguese.

When reading *Alex Stewart, Portrait of a Pioneer* by John Rice Irwin, the founder and director of the Museum of Appalachia in Norris, Tennessee, it is interesting to note what he wrote: *...when I enrolled in Lincoln Memorial University in Harrogate, Tennessee, a small college in full view of Cumberland Gap. Abraham Lincoln had suggested the college be built to educate the mountain people, the majority of whom had remained loyal to the Union throughout the Civil War.* [54] There are indications that well known figures may be Melungeon descendants. Since Kennedy's book was published, a number of personalities have come forward and shown interest in Melungeon genealogy.

Court rules changes from African Black to Portuguese White

Race status changes were allegedly common in the 19th Century in the United States, mostly in the South. It was generally accepted that if a person were not pure White, he or she would be considered Negro. Several groups were affected by this. In particular, reference is made to the Melungeons and the Portuguese. This matter was the cause of many social concerns. The major dilemma was that the individual in question would not be accepted in his or her community as a White, Negro or Indian person. The issue eventually required legal action. Of several court cases on the subject, two in particular rose to fame—one defended by President Abraham Lincoln in 1850 (Dungey vs. Spencer) just mentioned, and another by Lewis Shepherd who later became a Judge in 1872 (Bolton vs. Williams & Divine). See Appendix F. Because dark-complexioned people were considered *Negroes*, unfortunately their human rights were considerably curtailed. There is another case of one called John Griffin whose race status was changed from that of African descent *Negro* to Portuguese descent White. Records shows that: *John Griffin was released from being placed on the Negro list, and hereafter he will be listed as a white man, proof being made to the satisfaction of the court that he was of Portuguese descent instead of African descent.* [55] Although *Griffin* is a popularly accepted spelling, the name is also seen—among others—in the forms of *Griffith* and *Griffie*. These name variations are also used by Melungeons.

Portuguese in Hawaii

Of more than one million people living in Hawaii, 20 percent have Portuguese blood. [56] It is not hard to believe that a Portuguese may have been its discoverer. English historians record Captain James Cook as the discoverer of the islands in 1778, however, other historians refer to Juan Gaetano (João Caetano), who was a Portuguese navigator working for Spain, as the discoverer in 1555. Hawaiian traditions tell of the arrival of mysterious foreigners who remained and intermarried. [57] Felix and Senecal wrote that: *In 1527, Fernando Cortez, the conqueror of Mexico,*

Fig. 81—Lusitana Street in Honolulu, Hawaii

dispatched a fleet of three vessels to the Spice Islands (the Moluccas) by way of Guam and the Philippines...and two ships disappeared [58] which reinforces the Hawaiian oral traditions of a shipwreck about the same time. In 1542, the Spanish sent another fleet with João Caetano as chief navigator.

Jean de La Perouse, the famous navigator who followed Captain Cook to Hawaii in the 1780's, was convinced that Caetano had discovered Hawaii, and wrote of the voyage as follows: *It appears certain that these islands were discovered for the first time by Caetano in 1542.* [59]

After Caetano's voyage, the Spanish produced a number of charts indicating a group of several large islands known to them as *Isla de Mesa*. After some debate, it was assumed to be the same group seen by Caetano. Honolulu Professor A. Mouritz also concluded that a relationship existed with Caetano's discovery.

Captain Cook, the official discoverer, asked if the Spanish knew the location of Hawaii, why did they not make use of the islands to provision their ships? The answer again is secrecy, also given by the Portuguese to justify the lack of detailed information about their discoveries. We know that in late 16th century the Spanish were at war with the English who were also already navigating in the Pacific. It is natural to assume that the Spanish did not want the enemy to know the location of any islands in the Pacific, and strict orders were issued to avoid any mention of the *Isla de Mesa* group.

Eventually the charts fell into the British hands, possibly in the 1740's, 30 years before Captain Cook arrived in Hawaii in January 1778. [60]

It is hard to believe that, with so many Portuguese and Spaniards sailing the Pacific Ocean since the beginning of the 16th century, the islands would await discovery by Europeans for more than 200 years. Magellan and many others sailed the Pacific in the early 1500's. Portuguese were living in the islands as early as 1794, however the earliest Portuguese visitor was John Elliot de Castro, of whom details are available. He first arrived there in 1814 [61] and later became Secretary of Foreign Affairs to King Kamehamea (1790-1818). Portuguese emigration did not occur in great numbers until the late 19th century. Between 1878 and 1899, approximately 11,937 Portuguese immigrants landed in Hawaii, most of them after a lengthy voyage of more than three months. [62]

After the overthrow of the monarchy, three of 18 delegates to the Constitutional Convention were Portuguese, and two out of six from the Oahu District were also Portuguese. Between 1909 and 1929 no less than 31 members of the territorial legislature were ethnically Portuguese.

Jacinto Pereira, known as Jason Perry, was born in Faial, Azores, in 1826. One of the most distinguished among the early Portuguese in Hawaii, he served as a consular agent and was instrumental in getting the Hawaiian authorities to recruit laborers from Madeira. By 1913, it is estimated that just from the Azores Islands, around 10,000 had settled in Hawaii, officially known as the: ...*sister islands to the Azores.* [63] Manuel Pico was described in a Hawaiian newspaper as of the Portuguese Islands and not having skin as white as English or Americans, similar to how the Melungeons were described in the 19th century.

Fernando dos Santos, editor of the Portuguese-American newspaper *Luso-Americano,* wrote a book titled *The Portuguese in Hawaii* based on many interviews

Fig. 82—Mausoleum—Proud members of the New Lusitanos Benevolent Association inspect their new society tomb in the Girod Street Cemetery on the day of its dedication in October 1859. The tomb was decorated with black velvet panels trimmed with silver. Tomb designed by N.J. de Pouilly. Courtesy Leonard V.

with Portuguese descendants in Hawaii, providing a picture of the Portuguese making of the youngest American state.

The four-string ukelele that most people believe to be native to Hawaii, is of Portuguese origin. It was brought over by the Portuguese emigrants when a large percentage of Madeirans emigrated to Hawaii in the 19th century. Today it is a symbol of Hawaiian music. In continental Portugal it is called the *cavaquinho* or *braguinha,* with possible origins in the Portuguese city of Braga. This musical instrument is very popular in the north of Portugal and in the Madeira Islands.

The name ukelele means *jumping flea* in Hawaiian. King Kalakaua became fond of the original *braguinha* and started the trend. Three Madeira immigrants, Augusto Dias, José do Espirito Santo and Manuel Nunes, set up a business to manufacture the instrument in Honolulu. It was produced in Hawaii by a Portuguese between 1877 and 1878, and Arthur Godfrey made it very popular through television. [64] In an interview Mariano Rego, an Azorean musician, said that the braguinha was brought into Hawaii by an immigrant from Madeira by the name Barbosa. Also from Hawaii, the steel guitar evolved from the Portuguese *viola* or guitar when a native Hawaiian boy got the idea of using his pocket knife to get a special sound effect.

Fig. 83—New Orleans Mausoleum of a Portuguese family.
Photo courtesy Ilidio Pereira

Portuguese in Louisiana

In a New Orleans cemetery, a Delaney family tombstone has several Portuguese names. The earliest ones are D.N. Manuel Pereira, dated 1837; Teodoso Pereira, 1841; Maria Joaquina Pereira in 1849; and others with more recent dates.

In August 1853, the Portuguese Beneficence Society celebrated its fifth year with 430 members. The Portuguese had one of the best halls in New Orleans, and in 1891, 1892 and 1893 the Knights of Joy Parade, as well as New Year's Eve events were held there. [65]

Several associations were formed, such as the Portuguese Benevolent Society in 1857, the Portuguese Society in 1855, the Portuguese Benevolent Association in 1870, the Lusitano Benevolent Society in 1848, and the New Lusitanos Benevolent Association after that. On Delacroix Island, Louisiana, lived a group of people called *The Islenos* who in the 1970's were still speaking 18th century Spanish brought to Louisiana by their ancestors as reported by John R. Kemp: *Linguistic studies have found the presence of Portuguese, French and English...* [66]

That may also indicate the presence of the Portuguese at an early period.

Portuguese in Nevada and the West

It is known that during the latter half of the 18th century, a group of emigrants from Madeira, as part of an exodus that began in the 1840's from Funchal, eventually wound up on the Midwestern frontier.

First to California at the time of the gold rush, beginning in 1849, came thousands of Azoreans, Madeirans and Cape Verdeans, who also made their way to Hawaii. This restless population of the 1850's and 1860's, now in California's Sierra Nevada, came down to Nevada, Oregon, Washington, Idaho and the South Dakota Black Hills.

It is in Nevada that in 1853 some Portuguese surnames are recognized. Solomon Nunes de Carvalho, a Sephardic Jew, David Nunes and Sara d'Azevedo, a Jewess. The greatest part of Virginia City's population was foreign born, and among them were some Portuguese. The Surrey County of 1875 census lists 109 males born in Portugal. Seventy five percent were miners, including one woman, which was extremely rare. The same data indicates that many Portuguese appear to have preferred to operate small businesses, such as grocery stores, restaurants and others. [67] Donald Warrin has made extensive studies in this area together with Geoffrey Gomes. They authored a book about the Old West which is to be published in 2001 by Arthur H. Clark publishing house.

Portuguese in California, Arizona, Oregon

The presence of Portuguese in California goes back to the 16th century, with explorers and navigators already mentioned. Later, in the 18th century, José Manuel Machado was placed in command of the Presidio at the San Diego Mission in 1769. In the 19th century, Antonio José Rocha, also known as Don Antonio Rocha, settled in Los Angeles in 1815.

Rocha was born in Minho, Portugal, on January 18th 1790, and died in 1837. His peasant background, as well as the tragic consequences of the Napoleonic Wars, combined to obscure all but scattered bits of information. However, it is assumed that he may have embarked in Madeira aboard the Canadian schooner *Columbia*, bound for Monterey, California, where he arrived in November of 1814. Later he married Maria Josefa and had several children. [68] His son, Antonio José Rocha, served as the district judge of Balboa, 1868-1873.

Also, there was a Portuguese in the Spanish army stationed at the Presidio in Santa Barbara (1798-99). His name was José Antonio de Azevedo, he was a native of Lisbon, Portugal. [69]

It is interesting to note that at just about the same time, we have other Portuguese arriving in Virginia, also as a consequence of the Napoleonic Wars mentioned earlier. Rocha built his house, which later was sold to the municipality and became the first City-County Municipal building of Los Angeles. There is still another: Carlos Pedro Diogo Andrade also arrived in California shortly after 1825 and moved to Sacramento in 1846.

These are not the only ones. Francisco José da Silva and João Soito Freitas, both from the Azores, are but a few of the many Portuguese who went to California in the early 1800's. Some of them drifted north to Oregon and into the Rocky Mountain territories. [70]

Captain Antonio Mendes, said to have been the first person to navigate the Sacramento River, arrived in San Francisco in 1853. He was born in Terceira, Azores, and joined the crew of a whaling expedition bound for the China Sea.

He tried his hand at mining, then bought some ships and, later in life, farmed in Sutter County. Professor Eduardo Mayone Dias has made extensive studies about the Portuguese presence in California.

Joseph King is another Portuguese who stuboroly stayed in his Arizona ranch during the Apache war and John A. Pereira was the first Mayor of John Day city in Oregon.

Also in Arizona, there are two Portuguese Clubs, one in Yuma and the other in Tucson, both founded by Carmelina Rio-Borroz, which founded the first Portuguese Club in Vancouver, Washongton State.

Portuguese in Wyoming

John *Portugee* Phillips was born in 1832 as Manuel Filipe Cardoso in Pico, Azores. Leo Pap, in his well researched book *The Portuguese-Americans,* describes an interesting part of his life where he became a sort of Paul Revere of the West. While working at Fort Kearney, along the Bozeman Trail in Wyoming, Phillips volunteered to break through the siege lines to seek help at the next fort, where he arrived on December 25, 1866. This meant riding 240 miles through hostile territory, in freezing snow, which earned him special praise in Congress. That almost impossible task was called a much greater feat than the famous ride of Paul Revere. [71] He died in Cheyenne at age 51. He was depicted in a John Wayne movie some years back without credit to the rider as Portuguese.

Antonio Monteiro, was another Portuguese in the Rocky Mountains in the 1830's. He worked for John Jacob Astor's American Fur Company in the fur trade business, with Spaniards and French. Born in the city of Porto, Portugal, he was the son of José Soares Monteiro and Ana Maria Manuel Monteiro.

Monteiro commanded a 50-man expedition into Crow Indian country, and it was in this expedition that he made his most significant contribution to the history of the Western frontier by establishing a trading post in Powder River, which consisted of a cluster of cabins that came to be known as Portuguese houses. [72]

Portuguese in Idaho

Gold also attracted the Portuguese to this state, and in 1862 there are records of Portuguese being in the gold mines of Idaho and the rush to Boise. Bancroft stated in his works: *...Late in the summer of 1862, the opinion of old miners that a rich deposit would be found...finding to be rich for fifteen miles...While encamped...they* *were fired upon by some Shoshones who had hung upon their trail for several days. Grimes, Wilson, Splawn and the Portuguese pursue the attacking party...Grimes was shot...the eleven returned to Walla Walla...bringing with them...between $4,000 and $5,000 in gold-dust...*[73]

The names of the four Portuguese miners are unknown, as is that of another Englishman also with the group.Thome Luis de Freitas was a large land owner in this state as well as a playwright. Like in every State, there is also a portuguese Community in Buhl, Idaho.

Portuguese in Missouri

The Portuguese may have arrived there in 1803 when a Portuguese Jew by the name Salomão Barbosa accompanied the famous Lewis and Clark explorations to the West as a cartographer. Also, a priest named Father Himalaya was contracted as a scientist by the U.S. armed forces, and some inventions have been attributed to him. Later, in 1904, when the World's Fair was held in St. Louis, Portugal had a pavilion there. The grandson of the director for the Portuguese exhibit still lives in St. Louis, and owns a gallery called Gomes Gallery. Manuel Luis da Ponte, who had a weekly radio talk show in St. Louis when the author visited that city while doing the research for this book, provided the above information. [74]

Antonio Monteiro, a fur trader, also came to Missouri and returned in 1839-40 to Wyoming, but later moved to northern New Mexico where he married and had two children. His presence in this state was noticed until 1845.

Portuguese in the Bermudas

It is rather difficult to talk about Portuguese and Spanish navigators without mentioning the Bermuda Islands. After all, situated in the Atlantic Ocean, they are about 570 miles (900 km) east of Cape Hatteras (North Carolina), an area where navigation activity has occurred since the early 1500's .

The Spanish navigator Fernández de Oviedo sailed close to the islands in 1515, and attributed their discovery to his countryman Juan de Bermúdez, probably between 1503 and 1511. In 1612, Bermuda was included in the third charter of the Virginia Company, and 60 English settlers were sent to colonize the islands. Indian and African slaves were transported to Bermuda beginning in 1616, and soon the slave population outnumbered the white settlers.

There is an inscription on a rock that marks one of the intrusions by Portuguese navigators into the overseas dominions of Castille.

The story relates to a Portuguese merchant ship that left Santo Domingo with its men and shipwrecked off Bermuda in 1543, but all the men were able to save themselves. [75] They stayed there for 60 days and left a mark with a Portuguese Cross of Christ, the letters *JR,* and the date 1543.

About three-fifths of the population are descended from African slaves brought to Bermuda before Britain outlawed the slave trade in 1807. Whites include the

British and descendants of Portuguese laborers from Madeira and the Azores who went to Bermuda in the mid-19th century. English is the major and official language, but some Portuguese is also spoken. It is believed that between 15 and 20 percent of the population has Portuguese ancestry. The Portuguese population is estimated between 3,000 and 5,000.

The Portuguese do participate actively in the social and political life of the islands. Trevor Monis is a member of the Bermuda Parliament (1996) and is one of four already in the House of Assembly. The others are Ernest DeCouto, Harry Soares, Clarence Terceira. [76] There is also a very active portuguese Club (Vasco da Gama) in Hamilton.

The Virginian-Pilot FEATUI
and
The Portsmouth Star
SEC'

Century-Old Stigma Remains

'Portuguese' Youngsters Segregated in Carolina

Fig. 84—Article title about the Portuguese in 1958

North Carolina—Searching for Roots in 20th Century
Gaston, Northampton County, N.C. near the Virginia Border—1958

The next illustration is the title—from not so long ago—of an article that occupied the full center page of the Virginia newspaper *The Virginian Pilot* on January 26, 1958. The article was written by Luther J. Carter, and was accompanied by three large photographs depicting the school and a group of Portuguese children playing. The following is a transcription of the article in its entirety, so that the reader can make a proper judgment of the circumstances of these *Portuguese* people, as they were classified.

JACKSON, N.C.—A tiny group of "Portuguese" children occupies a narrow, forsaken middle zone in Northampton County's Segregated school system.

Eighteen pupils, aged 6 to 16, attend the Bethany School, a one classroom cinder-block building tucked away in a pine grove in the County's northwest corner just below Emporia, VA.

The shabbily clad children come from widely scattered homes in Gaston township, some of them walking six miles to reach the school.

These innocents bear a stigma imprinted at least 100 years ago. The approximately 16 "Portuguese" families now living in the County are further

Fig. 85—These "Portuguese" children are delighted with themselves, like chil-dren anywhere. But what of the future, as fugitive students and citizens apart?

isolated from their white and Negro neighbors by a 35 year old legislative act creating for them the separate school.

Why? For one thing, there is a widely held belief among the county's white residents that these people are descendants of Northerners who mingled with five Negroes in pre-Civil War days, with some intermarriage taking place.

The origin of these people, and how they came to be known as Portuguese is obscure. Apparently illiterate, just as some still are today, they left little or no records relating to their history. Hearsay, speculation, unsubstantiated theories are all that is left.

The hard lot of the present day "Portuguese" is easy enough to document, however. Unwilling to associate with the Negroes, and generally unwanted by the whites, their tradition of ill luck and ignorance is being perpetuated. Only those who leave the County appear to have a chance to escape this curious web of circumstance.

Strange Blend—The Bethany School is a strange blend of the modern and antiquated. Built several years ago to replace an older building that burned, its *front consists largely of glass and steel framing, and, inside, modern circular light fixtures hang above the rows of desks.*

Against the rear wall there is a pot-bellied coal stove. Behind the building one sees a hand operated water pump and privy.

The teacher, Miss Osceola T. Crew, a slim, white-haired spinster who 17 years ago went to the school after the superintendent asked her if she wanted to do some "mission work," occupies a role that has all but vanished in American education.

Fig. 86—The building where the Portuguese School classes were held in 1958 for the segregated Portuguese children is still standing. Shown in the photo is Mr. Tom Willey.

The grades are from the first through the eighth and she teaches them all. In nearly every grade the children vary one to three years in age, and most are over

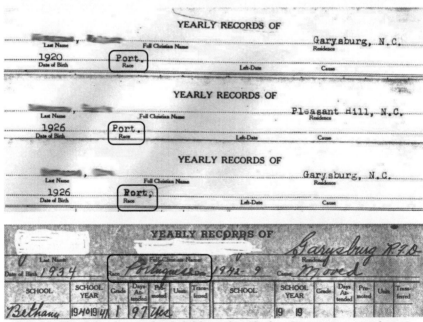

Fig. 87, 88—School records of children classified as Portuguese race born in the 1920's. See word "Port." circled. Names have been covered for privacy.

Fig. 89—The sign today means what it says.

age for their grade. One third-grader, a 15-year-old child has recently had a brain tumor removed, Miss Crew described as "almost a mental case."

Slow Progress—The other children, she says, are of average ability, with a few above average. Their progress is slow because of poor attendance.

State Law fixes the public school year 180 days. Miss Crew estimates that, on the average, her pupils are in class somewhere around 100 days.

Various reasons are given for this. She says most of the children come from farm homes whose "economic condition is terrible." In the spring and fall the parents want the children to help with the crops.

Normally attendance is best in mid-winter, but when a reporter visited the school recently one third of the class was absent. "Hog killing time," Miss Crew explained...

Hog killing time. Something typical of Portugal; a very special time in rural communities of the mainland and with islanders of yesteryear, when complete families, neighbors and friends gather together in, sometimes, a few days feast. This is still an important event today with the Portuguese people.

The fact that the County operates no school bus for these children contributes to the bad attendance, particularly in inclement weather. Miss Crew picks up some of the pupils each morning, but others must walk.

Fig. 90—Northampton County Courthouse in 1995

Another explanation, which appears especially important where the older children are concerned, is indifference. Some of the pupils regard the Bethany School as an academic dead end. The County provides no high school education for the Portuguese. They are not allowed to attend the white schools and do not wish to attend the Negro schools.

How it Happened—*How did this came about? Judge W.H.S. Burgwyn of Woodland, who has served in both the state House of Representatives and Senate, caused to be passed by the 1923 session of the General Assembly a Law stating "that the people known as 'Portuguese' shall have a separate school from the white and colored schools...."*

Two years later, the Assembly enacted a Law permitting the same people to register themselves as "Portuguese" on the voter registration books.

Burgwyn hazily recalled the 1923 school Law, but when first asked about the registration Law he drew a blank. His best recollection was that he introduced the school bill at the request of the Portuguese. The County school officials were in accord with the proposal but did not originate it.

"I don't know why they call themselves Portuguese," Burgwyn says, then indicates he introduced the bills chiefly out of sympathy.

A Forlorn Group—*"I had a distinct belief that they were not Negroes," he explains. "I just thought they were a forlorn group of people. They were not accepted by white people and they didn't want to associate with Negroes."*

Many were "blue-eyed and sandy-haired," he remembers and bore names that were not of English origin. (However pupils now attending the Bethany School have such names as Bass, Scott, Peters, Turner, and Hobbs.)

Before the enactment of special school Law the Portuguese apparently did not send their children to school at all or sent them to a private school. Miss Crew has heard that Bethany Mission Church (now the Bethany Methodist Church where the Portuguese still go) and a private school were organized during the decades immediately after the turn of the century.

Has no Illusions—*N. L. Turner, a pleasant easy going man, has been superintendent of County schools for 19 years. He has no illusions about the quality of education provided the Portuguese but seems to see no way of giving them something better. He thinks that consolidating the Bethany School with white schools wouldn't work "The white folks just never accepted them here," he remarks. A step towards consolidation might be to admit pupils finishing Bethany to the white school at Gaston. But not long ago a girl who wanted to enter this school was rejected. For such a pupil the County will offer to pay only $25 a month towards his room and board if he wants to attend high school in another community.*

Some pupils have done this and been readily accepted by white schools. Rarely one is rebuffed. Asked about the lack of school bus service for the Bethany pupils, 'Turner replies, "They never asked for any. The fact is that they're so scattered you couldn't get them."

The poor attendance of the pupils, coupled with the fact that there is no high school for them, raises the question of the enforcement of the compulsory attendance Law. ''The Law is not enforced," Turner says without hesitation. ''It is not enforced anywhere, not in this County or anywhere else." He believes the regular attendance of pupils is virtually impossible without the cooperation of parents and suggests that cooperation of Bethany families is often lacking.

What about the future? What's to become of the Portuguese?

With the air of one who prefers to let history run a free course, Turner replies, "It'll take care of itself. There aren't half as many of them now as when I first came here. They'll eventually go away. Some will marry colored, others will marry white." Meanwhile, Miss Crew works patiently with her pupils. She teaches them

Fig. 91—Copy of the article published in the Portuguese newspaper Diario de Noticias

about DaGama, Magellan, the other great Portuguese explorers. "I try to give them a sense of pride," she says.

Meanwhile in Portugal

Human Dignity and Respect for Someone else's Name

That was the title of the article—translated into English—in the largest Portuguese newspaper *Diario de Noticias* out of Lisbon, Portugal, on March 11, 1958. Apparently it was referring to the previous article published by *The Virginian Pilot*. This newspaper was considered to be the official voice of the Portuguese government, a dictatorship under Salazar at the time, and in this article it was demanding that the American government—North Carolina—would cease to call this people Portuguese. It goes on to repeat much of the *Virginian Pilot* article, translated into Portuguese.

Sunday Herald

43rd YEAR—NO. 57   ROANOKE RAPIDS, N. C., SUNDAY, MARCH 2, 1958   5c DAILY; 10c SUNDAY

Northampton's Portuguese
Go Elsewhere For Higher Education

Fig. 92—Roanoke newspaper March 3, 1958

An official from the Embassy of Portugal in Washington named Bernardo Teixeira, press and cultural affairs attaché, visited the area in March 1958 and reported that the families in question *"were all completely white, related to each other, with Anglo surnames; they claimed to have been in Northampton County since the construction of the Roanoke Rapids Canal, c. 1820, when their allegedly Portuguese ancestors came from Pennsylvania or from Portugal to work on the canal; and they have been locally described as 'Portygee,' never as Croatan or Melungeon, as far back as at least 100 years."*

It is reported, according to the records of Pennsylvania Colony from 1727 to the Revolution, that there were some Portuguese. Scattered lists of immigrants landing at Philadelphia from Lisbon or Amsterdam between 1769 and 1805 include a number of Portuguese names, some undoubtedly belonging to persons of Jewish descent. [77]

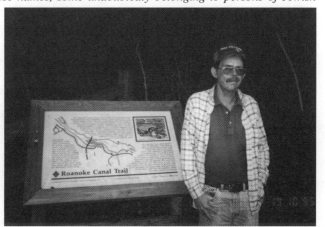

The Portuguese newspaper ends the article with a veiled threat, stating that only a few miles away, in Norfolk, is the (NATO) North Atlantic Treaty Organization headquarters, of which Portugal was and still is a member, and if nothing is done about it, the Portuguese voice would be heard in protest.

Fig. 93—Glenn Scott beside the plaque describing the historical Roanoke canal and honoring the Portuguese immigrants who built it.

Roanoke Rapids—March 2, 1958

The Portuguese from Gaston were again in the news. This time the *Sunday Herald* of Roanoke Rapids featured a front page story with the title *Northampton's Portuguese Go Elsewhere For Higher Education.* Dick Kern wrote the story that describes the education problem with the *Portuguese Community* in the County of Northampton. His remarks are interesting: *Many veteran public officials admit it is one of the most unique situations in the state, if not the nation. The people are registered on election books as Portuguese, but still are not accepted for what they are by many people who often call them resentful names.* [78]

* * *

Gaston, NC

The author did visit the Gaston area in North Carolina and, while searching for anyone that could help, he met Reverend Simpson from the United Methodist Church, who pointed him to Mr. Willey. At the time, he found that there are still a number of families living in the area, known to be descendants of Portuguese left over from a much larger group. These people do not want to talk about it due to discrimination suffered that ended just recently. The local people feel guilty about it, and they are quick to point out that *we are all united now.* Even during the second world war they were refused service in the armed forces and had to move to a different county.

They, just like the Melungeons, do not speak Portuguese or keep any Portuguese culture, and use English names such as Turner, Bass, Scott and Hobbs. They were there in the early 1800's and worked on the Roanoke River waterways canal, having moved from the mountains.

On researching at the local library and the few historical records available, the author found that the Roanoke waterway was constructed by several groups of people who provided labor. However, the description terminated with...*and others*, probably referring to persons that the historians did not want to name by group.

Fig. 94—Portuguese Embassy letter

The Gaston Portuguese children of 1958 as adults

Later the author returned to Gaston and talked with Glenn Scott, one of the descendants of the Portuguese families living in the area for almost two hundred years. After the first few words of introduction, the author told him that he was Portuguese. That seemed to have had an impact, as from that moment on, he was much more friendly and communicative.

Someone told him that their ancestors may have came from Brazil, Pennsylvania or the mountains looking for work, and established themselves in the area after the building of the Roanoke canal was completed.

Scott offered the author a tour of the area. The place where the canal was built is a beautiful trail to visit and enjoy. It is not likely that this group originated from Brazil or Pennsylvania, unless they belonged to one of the groups in the Pennsylvania mountains.

If Gaston's Portuguese came from Pennsylvania, it is hard to believe that they would have lost all signs of Portuguese culture, including all surnames, since the 1800's, a time when communications and regular travel between Portugal and the U.S. were frequent. An official Portuguese diplomat was already in place. Also, while doing research for this book, the author spoke with descendants of Portuguese immigrants who arrived in 1830, and who still remembered their ancestry and family names.

CHAPTER 602

AN ACT TO PROVIDE SEPARATE SCHOOLS FOR THAT RACE OF PEOPLE IN GASTON TOWNSHIP, NORTHAMPTON COUNTY, KNOWN AS THE "PORTUGUESE."

The General Assembly of North Carolina do enact:

Separate school. SECTION 1. That the race of people known as "Portuguese" in Gaston Township, Northampton County, shall have a separate

Proviso: school building. school from the white or colored schools in said county: *Provided,* said Portuguese shall furnish a suitable building situate in Gaston Township for said school, said building to be approved by the county board of education for said county of Northampton.

Teachers supplied. SEC. 2. That after said building shall have been provided as aforesaid, the board of education for Northampton County is hereby 687
empowered and directed to provide teachers for said school for said race, and said teacher or teachers shall be paid as other Payment of teachers in said county are paid without extra tax on said race teachers. of people, except as they may vote same upon themselves. The Teachers of teachers of said school shall be either of the said race known as Portuguese or Portuguese or white persons, as in the discretion of the board of white race. education for Northampton County it may deem proper.

SEC. 3. This act shall be in force from and after June fifteenth,. When act effective. one thousand nine hundred and twenty-three.

Ratified this the 6th day of March, A.D. 1923.

Fig. 95—Record as ratified on March 6, 1923.

Baldomiro Soares is one of many persons who has been assisting in this research, obtained a copy of a letter—now a historic document—addressed to the Portuguese Consulate in Philadelphia from the Portuguese Embassy in Washington, testifying to the truth of this incident with the following message to (in Portuguese):

AFTERNOON SESSION

SENATE CHAMBER,
MONDAY, March 5, 1923.

The Senate meets pursuant to recess, and is called to order by Honorable W. B. Cooper, Lieutenant-Governor.

The President names Senator Woodson as a member of the commission to investigate as to the advisability of renovating the Canova statue of Washington.

Upon motion of Senator Woodson, S. B. 1182, A bill to repeal subsection 7 of section 5151 of the Consolidated Statutes, relating to Confederate pensions, and providing for an appropriation of $500,000 for additional pensions, is taken from the Committee on Pensions and referred to the Committee on Appropriations.

Passes its second and third readings and is ordered enrolled.

S. B. 1463, H. B. 1661, A bill to provide separate schools for that race of people in Gaston Township, Northampton County, known as "Portuguese."

Passes its second and third readings and is ordered enrolled. (CHAPTER 602)

Fig. 96—Record as passed on March 5, 1923.

Exmo. Sr. Vice-Consul de Portugal em Philadelphia.

Para conhecimento desse posto, comunico a V. Exa. que de acordo com instruções do Ministério dos Negocios Estrangeiros, fui recebido pelo Secretário de Estado Assistente dos Negócios Europeus junto do qual protestei pelo facto de a legislação do estado da Carolina do Norte designar por "portugueses" um grupo de pessoas, de vaga origem portuguesa, segregadas, e portanto consideradas como cidadãos de 2ª classe, residentes na cidade de Gaston. Instei por que fosse posto termo a tão lamentável abuso que não podemos tolerar, e tão ofensivo é do brio nacional português.

Junto remeto a V. Exa. uma fotocópia do artigo de fundo que o Diario de Noticias, de Lisboa, de 11 de Março último publicou sobre o assunto.

A Bem da Nação, [79]
(signature not legible).

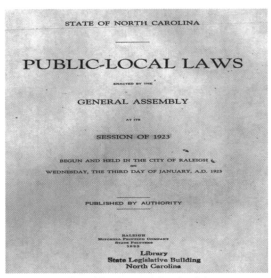

STATE OF NORTH CAROLINA

PUBLIC-LOCAL LAWS

ENACTED BY THE

GENERAL ASSEMBLY

AT ITS

SESSION OF 1923

BEGUN AND HELD IN THE CITY OF RALEIGH
ON
WEDNESDAY, THE THIRD DAY OF JANUARY, A.D. 1923

PUBLISHED BY AUTHORITY

RALEIGH
MITCHELL PRINTING COMPANY
STATE PRINTERS
1923
Library
State Legislative Building
North Carolina

*Fig. 97—Record Book of the
NC General Assembly of 1923.*

The English translation:
*Mr. Vice-Consul of
Portugal in Philadelphia:
For your information and
according to instructions
received from the Ministry of
Foreign Affairs, I was
received by the Assistant
Secretary of European
Affairs, and protested the
fact that the legislation of the
State of North Carolina has
designated as "Portuguese"
a group of persons, of vague
portuguese origin,
segregated, thus considered
as second class citizens,
residents in the city of
Gaston.
I insisted that this
intolerable abuse be terminated, and so offensive it is to Portuguese national pride.
Enclosed find a copy of the article as published by the "Diario de Noticias" of
Lisbon, dated March 11th last. For the Good of the Nation....*

The Embassy letter and other documents are now part of the history of the
Portuguese making of America.

Roanoke Canal Built by Portuguese immigrants

The Roanoke Canal contains some of the most impressive and best preserved
early 19th century canal construction in the nation. Begun before 1819 and completed
in 1823, the Roanoke canal was built as the North Carolina segment of the ambitious
Roanoke navigation system designed to connect the Blue Ridge mountains of
Virginia with Norfolk, over a distance of 400 miles.

The canal was constructed by hand and has an aqueduct built of local granite that
spans 30 feet in a single arch. It is one of the area's most impressive engineering
accomplishments.

According to local tradition, it was built by Portuguese immigrants, many of
whom remained in the area. It is interesting to note that this construction was built
to connect the Blue Ridge Mountains to the seacoast by water. The Blue Ridge
Mountains are the home of many Melungeons. Presently, part of the remaining
aqueduct is located near Gaston, where many families known as the Portuguese
still live. There is a plaque, in a simple way, which does honor the Portuguese.

One Section of the aqueduct Built by Portuguese in the early 1800's

Fig 98—Glenn Scott and the aqueduct built by his Portuguese ancestors
Research at the Raleigh archives of North Carolina produced a copy of the General Assembly laws passed in 1923, as shown in Figures 79 and 80. They were there in the early 1800's and worked on the Roanoke River waterways canal, having moved from the mountains.

Luther J. Carter was the journalist who wrote the story about the Portuguese from Gaston, and now, almost 38 years later, he still remembers the article vividly. He could not add any more than what was published. However, he said that the Portuguese government did send a protest note to the State Department.

The governor of North Carolina, in order to appease the Portuguese government, called the Portuguese ambassador in Washington and sent him a gift with the emblem of North Carolina (Tar Heel).

Robert Mason, then the editor of the *Virginian Pilot,* also followed the story. The author contacted Mason. He remembers the article, the meeting with Bernardo Teixeira, and the fact that he began to rage and criticize the Americans and North Carolina—while having coffee at a restaurant—for the conditions that they forced the *Portuguese* people to endure. At that time, Mason warned him, *if you don't shut up, I will call the waiter and tell him that you're Portuguese, and I am sure that he'll throw you out of this restaurant.* Mason also recalls that he was for the most part interested in the young Portuguese girls. *"Well, they were good-looking too, I can add,"* said Mason. The Portuguese diplomat also mentioned that these people reminded him of people from the Azores Islands. Later, Teixeira became quite upset for getting a traffic ticket from the local police. In a later interview, Mason added that he believes that these Portuguese people are connected with the Melungeons and also the possible shipwrecks off the coast of North Carolina.

In the next Chapter we shall see how the Portuguese may have been responsible for bringing such a variety of people into many parts of the world.

Portuguese in every State of the Union

According to Adalino Cabral, Ph.D. there are Portugese in every one of the 50 States. See the last volume of his 1985 dissertation. The State that had the least amount of Portuguese was North Dakota as per the 1980 Census.

Notes

[1] La España del siglo X, Fray Justo Perez del Urbel, p. 12.
[2] Roberto Leal and Márcia Lúcia, CD.
[3] Translation by Melissa Mira Knippel.
[4] Memoirs of Judge Lewis Shepherd, 1915, p. 87-88.
[5] Portinglês, Vol. 4, p. 1348, by Adalino Cabral.
[6] UPEC, Summer 1988 issue, Antonio Monteiro by Geoffrey L. Gomes, p. 7.
[7] Makers of America by Wayne Moquin, p. 85.
[8] The Portuguese-Americans by Leo Pap, p. 9.
[9] Portuguese Settlement, by William Freitas, Ph.D., Portuguese Heritage, 12/1993, p. 22.
[10] Historia da Inquisição em Portugal by Alexandre Herculano, pp. 98-99.
[11] The Master and the Slaves by Gilberto Freyre, p. xii.
[12] Farewell España by Howard M. Sachar, p. 352.
[13] The Jews in America by Max I. Dimont, p. 28.
[14] Ibid, p. 11-12.
[15] The Jews in America in Colonial and Revolutionary times by Leon Huhner, pp. 16-31.
[16] The Jews of South Carolina by Leon Huhner, p. 50-51.
[17] The Jews in America by Max I. Dimont, p. 240.
[18] Boletim do Inst. Historica, Presença de Portugal, by Manoel da Silveira Cardozo, p. 11.
[19] Historia da Lingua Portuguesa by Serafim da Silva Neto, p. 528.
[20] The Jews of Newport by Hugh Huhner, pp. 4-6.
[21] Ibid, p. 49.
[22] Makers of America by Wayne Moquin, p. 85.
[23] Ibid, p. 91.
[24] The Portuguese-Americans by Leo Pap, p. 44, 1752 as per Humberto S. Carreiro's letter 3/10/2000.
[25] The Makers of America by Wayne Moquin, p. 127.
[26] The Portuguese-Americans by Leo Pap, pp. 10-11; [27] Ibid.
[28] A Future to Inherit by David Gibbs, p. 19.

Notes (Cont.)

[29] Dictionary of Georgia Biography edited by Kenneth Coleman & Charles Stephen Gurr, Vol. II, pp. 754, 755.

[30] They Ploughed the Seas by Pat Amaral, pp. 132-133.

[31] Mills, Mansions and Mergers in 1858 by Edward G. Roddy.

[32] Boletim do Instituto Historica, Presença de Portugal...by Manoel da Silveira Cardozo, p. 12.

[33] Relações entre Portugal e os Estados Unidos, p. 69, FLAD, Lisboa, 1997.

[34] The Portuguese in America Chronology by Manoel da Silveira Cardozo, p. 20 (Geoffrey Gomes from the University of California in Hayward states that he may have been Spanish, according to an email received by the author).

[35] The Portuguese-Americans by Leo Pap, pp.15-20.

[36] Luso-Americano, Nov. 22, 1996, p. 14.

[37] Dictionary of American Biography by Allen Johnson, Vol. V, p. 24.

[38] Peter Francisco by William Arthur Moon, cover painting.

[39] America's Great Soldier (Esquire Magazine, March 1942) by Robert Buckner.

[40] Peter Francisco by William Arthur Moon, p. 52.

[41] Dicionario de História de Portugal, Vol. V, p. 540.

[42] FLAD Newsletter, August 1993, p. 8.

[43] Truths from the West Indies by Captain Studholme Hodgson (19th Regiment of Foot), 1838. Historical Society of Trinidad and Tobago. Publications no. 796 and 797. We thank Augusta Elmwood for the kind help in providing the information.

[44] Encyclopedia Britannica, Vol. 20, p. 953 (1967 edition).

[45] Our Fair Lady: The Statue of Liberty, Reader's Digest, July 1986, pp. 191-197.

[46] Abraham Lincoln by Carl Sandburg, p. 159.

[47] The Portuguese Immigrants by Leo Pap, pp. 23-24.

[48] In the Footsteps of the Lincolns by Ida M. Tarbell, p. 82.

[49] Abraham Lincoln by Lord Charnwood, p. 6.

[50] In the Footsteps of the Lincolns by Ida M. Tarbel, p. 84.

[51] The Prairie Years by Carl Sandburg, Vol. II, p. 52.

[52] Ibid, Vol. I, p. 13.

[53] Ibid, Vol. I, p. 6-7.

[54] Alex Stewart Portrait of a Pioneer by John Rice Irwin, p. 12.

[55] Clay County Records (Kentucky St. Archives, Frankfort) p. 35, Order Book, Volume I (4/24, 1855-1/30, 1869).

[56] The Portuguese in Hawaii by Fernando dos Santos, p. 5.

[57] The Portuguese Immigrants by Carlos Almeida, UPEC, p. 14.

[58] The Portuguese in Hawaii by John Henry Felix and Peter F. Senecal, p. 150.

[59] Ibid, p. 151; [60] Ibid, pp. 153-154.

[61] The Portuguese-Americans by Leo Pap, p 31; [62] Ibid, pp. 14, 15.

[63] Azores Islands a History by James H. Guill, Vol. 5, p. 651; [64] Ibid, p. 18.

Notes (Cont.)

[65] New Orleans Public Library Documents.
[66] New Orleans Times Picayune of July 5, by John R. Kemp.
[67] Portuguese Immigrants in Nevada by Donald Warrin, UPEC Life, 1989.
[68] California History, 9/1987, El Portuguese by Eduardo M. Dias &
    David E. Bertão, p. 188.
[69] Geoffrey Gomes, California State University at Hayward.
[70] The Portuguese Americans by Leo Pap, p. 30.
[71] Ibid.
[72] UPEC, Summer 1988 issue, Antonio Monteiro… by Geoffrey L. Gomes, p. 6-8.
[73] The Works of Hubert Howe Bancroft, Vol. XXXI, p. 259.
[74] Interview with Manuel da Ponte in April 1996.
[75] Eprigrafia Portuguesa by João Vidago, p. 174 (Oviedo Y Valdés p. 577).
[76] Luso-Americano, 4/10/96, p. 6-7.
[77] Portuguese-Americans by Leo Pap, p. 242-243.
[78] Northampton's Portuguese… by Dick Kern (Sunday Herald,
    March 2nd 1958, f. page).
[79] Embassy of Portugal letter dated 1958.

Chapter IX

Portugal Leads the Way to New Worlds

Animals leave nothing, people leave history

Before we get to the final chapter and the conclusion, we first must explain how such a small country was able to bring such different people to so many parts of the world at a time when global navigation was still in its infancy. Portugal is the only modern national state to reach its present size by the 13th century, and the first to lead the way in the attempt to reach the Far East by water. Her good location and her seamen, trained in the school established by Infante D. Henrique (Henry the Navigator, 1394-1460), provided ideal conditions. The poverty of her people— unable to buy high-priced luxuries—and her desire to expand territorially, as well as a holdover of the crusading spirit, were major reasons for her enterprising spirit. The route sought was around the tip of southern Africa, and success was finally achieved when Vasco da Gama reached India in 1498.[1] That single event was to affect the world in an unforeseen way.

Portugal began its overseas expansion in 1415, establishing colonies in the 1500's (Goa, Damão e Diu), and in other parts of the world.[2]

There has been some controversy by historians and scholars about the existence of the Sagres school for navigation in the 15th century. They doubt that possibility. Well, they may be right, if they refer to the Sagres school in the same manner as the modern naval learning institutions we know today. Most likely it did not have elaborate buildings or a proper faculty—but the first school known to men was just a few bench seats in a park.

The Portuguese Sea Route to East India

The discovery of America, and of a passage to the East Indies by way of the Cape of Good Hope, are the two greatest and most important events recorded in the history of mankind.[3] The reader probably will be thinking, what has East India to do with the Melungeons or the Portuguese in North America? As it will be shown, it may have the most logical explanation for the origin and arrival time of the people—who later would form the Melungeons and other groups—on the North American continent.

As we read in the previous chapter, Bartolomeu Dias rounded the southern tip of Africa in 1488, which he called the Cape of Good Hope, *Cabo da Boa Esperança*, and also Cape of Storms or *Cabo das Tormentas*.

He accomplished that nearly five years before Columbus made his first landfall in the Caribbean, in what he thought were the East Indies.

Ten years later, Vasco da Gama, following the Bartolomeu Dias route, found the seaway to India. He was to die in that same area when he was part of Cabral's fleet to India. The Portuguese discovered what Columbus was seeking: The fabled East

Indies. They also chartered new sea-lanes halfway around the globe to Japan.[4] The Portuguese, by their discoveries, not only extended the limits of the world known to Europe, but contributed greatly to its more accurate representation.

At the end of the 15th century, the introduction of a scale of latitudes was made, and in 1502 the Cantino map was already showing the Portuguese discovery of India.[5] Also shown on that same map are the Caribbean and Florida.

The Search for India by Land—1487

Pero da Covilhã and Afonso Paiva, of Portuguese Jewish origin, traveled to India by land. On the way they separated. Covilhã did get to India, and on the way back to Portugal he met emissaries from the Portuguese King, ordering him to go back and get more information. It is not known if Covilhã's letter ever got to Portugal, but if it did, the king would have known then that the shortest way to India by sea would be to follow the African coast to the south, turn north and east.

This information was kept secret and may have been the basis for Portuguese King João II's rejection of the Columbus proposal.

It is unfortunate that this record was ignored when Anthony Weller wrote an article about the Travelin' Man, Thomas Coryat (1577-1617), which incorrectly stated that he was the first European to reach India since Alexander the Great. The Portuguese again were forgotten.[6]

The Portuguese in East India—1498

Trade, not conquest, attracted the Portuguese to India, and the 16th century brought two factors into Indian history: the *Mughuls* who came by land, and the Portuguese by sea. *These two carried India into a new age.*[7]

Vasco da Gama, a Portuguese navigator, found a sea route to India in 1498, and from that date, Portugal changed drastically during a golden age that lasted only fifty years. During that time, trade, traveling and emigration were very heavy to the Far East.

Later, in 1540, Vasco da Gama's son, with an armed force, kept the Turks on alert over a period of 15 years.[8]

Right from the beginning, the Portuguese government was involved in fostering mixed marriages of Portuguese and East Indians. According to royal plans, actual official intermarriages began in Goa by 1509. Each couple was granted a substantial subsidy or dowry in money, which rapidly increased the number of weddings.

In three or four years, more than 500 marriages took place, mostly in Goa, but a few in Cannanore and Cochin also.[9] Duarte Pacheco Pereira became famous for his defense of the Cambalaan Pass against the Calicut's rajá during the beginning of Portuguese settlement in Canará (modern Karnataka).[10]

The intermarriages of Portuguese with the natives were common all over the Far East, as well as in Africa and Brazil.

In India, these intermarriages meant improved status to Muslim women, and the descendants of these marriages are still today all over the East, with Portuguese names and Portuguese words embedded in their speech.[11]

Out of one of these mixed marriages came Manuel Godinho de Heredia, who was no longer a pure-blooded Portuguese. His father, João de Heredia, married Helena Vassiva, daughter of the King of Supa, João Tubinanga.

Manuel was therefore a mixture of Malay and Portuguese, and became famous for having claimed the discovery of the Isle of Gold in 1601, later called Australia. Only in 1606 did the Dutch ship *Het Duifken* reach this continent, claiming its discovery.[12]

Malacca and Malaysia—1509

The Portuguese arrived in Malaysia in 1509, occupied it for two years, and controlled it for 130. The Dutch defeated the Portuguese in 1641, however, they were not able to erase all vestiges of the Portuguese presence. Today there is still a dialect derived from Portuguese and the Catholic religion. The *Portugis,* as they are called in Malacca, still have folkloric dances which are predominantly Portuguese, such as the *Vira* and *corridinho.*[13]

The Moluccas Sea and the Moluccas (Maluku) Islands, today part of Indonesia, were originally named by the Portuguese as *Ilhas Malucas* in 1511, and were also known as the Spice Islands. A film documentary presented by PBS-TV with the title *Ring of Fire*, demonstrates vividly the Portuguese presence on these remote islands, during a festival on the Aru and Garuda islands. The Portuguese were the first Westerners to be seen by the natives. Echoes of the past are seen in a Portuguese soldier's helmet of the 16th century used as a symbol, and having Portuguese fado music in the background sung by Amalia Rodrigues.[14]

North Carolina, Graveyard of the Atlantic

David Stick wrote a book about shipwrecks in the Outer Banks of North Carolina. Although he was not able to find any records of early shipwrecks, he presents us with an impressive story of many ships lost in that area, starting with the Spanish brigantine of the fleet under the command of Lucas Vasquez de Ayllon in 1526, en route to Cape Fear in the Spanish colony of Chicora.[15] In order for the reader to better understand that part of the North Carolina coast, let us read what David Stick wrote: *You can stand on Cape Point at Hatteras on a stormy day and watch two oceans come together in an awesome display of savage fury...the northbound Gulf Stream and the cold currents coming down from the Arctic run head-on into each other...Seafaring men call it the Graveyard of the Atlantic.*[16]

It is important to note that not only ships bound to the West Indies or the American coast met their final destination at the graveyard. Stick goes on to say: *...Ships of many nationalities, of almost every shape and size, bound to and from the ports of Europe, Africa, and even Asia.*[17] [The reason for so many vessels lost is due to the fact that this section of the North Carolina coast extends out into the sea from the South Carolina coast to Cape Hatteras] *...the past history and the present day life* *of the entire coast of N.C. are closely integrated with shipwrecks.*[18]*...there are entire villages today populated with descendants of shipwrecked mariners.*[19]

Verrazano reported to the King of France that he explored the Outer Banks (North Carolina) and landed on the coast in 1524 at a latitude of 34°—approximately the same as the Portuguese Madeira Islands—just above Cape Fear.[20] In this same area there were at least two known shipwrecks, in 1559 and 1564.[21]

Shipwrecked Portuguese Caravels

The East India trade book records written by Luis de Figueiredo Falcão show that between 1497 and 1692 a total of 806 ships left Portugal on their way to India and only 425 returned. Out of the 381 ships that did not return, 285 stayed in India, 20 ran aground, 6 burned, 4 were captured by enemy forces or pirates and 66 were lost or shipwrecked. The maritime connection from Lisbon to the Far East between 1497 and 1580 was by 620 ships with an average of six to seven ships per year. However, in 1505 the fleet was comprised of 28 caravels, and during the early 16th century, each fleet had 14 to 15 ships.[22]

From 1495 to 1578, 100 ships were lost by accident, shipwreck or piracy. The larger losses occurred in the early 1500's on the returning trips, as these were the most dangerous. The size of each ship was about 500 to 600 tons with a crew of 123 persons, or an average of 175 including passengers.[23]

On the same note, in 1591, of the 22 ships that left for India, only two returned to Portugal.[24] Pedro Álvares Cabral, the official discoverer of Brazil, departed Lisbon, Portugal on March 15, 1500, with a Calicut, India destination. Cabral commanded a fleet of 13 ships in 1500, and fewer than half arrived in India. The first one to disappear, without anybody ever knowing how, was the one commanded by Vasco de Atayde when he was off the Cape Verde Islands, south of the Canary Islands and in the same latitude as the Caribbean Sea, thus subjected to the equatorial currents, which could erroneously bring ships to the East Coast instead of South America, the original destination. Refer to the map, Fig. 100 in this chapter.

After passing the Canary Islands and Cape Verde, going in a westerly direction, the ship separated from the fleet and was never found.[25] Where did this ship go?

Carlos de Passos wrote that there were 27 shipwrecks lost due to storms, and 12 to other causes in a period of 122 years. But many more occurred without anyone ever having any knowledge. Only after 1527 did narratives start to appear, and before that all is ignored, though the shipwrecks did happen.[26]

Bernardo Gomes de Brito, author of the book *The Tragic History of the Sea,* published in the 18th century, describes the losses of Portuguese ships on the voyage to or from India, while the west coast of India was under the rule of Portugal.[27]

These are very interesting facts. Where did these vessels go or where were they shipwrecked? On the way to India, or on the way to Portugal?

In either direction it is very easy to be pushed in a westerly direction, by currents or by winds, towards the North American continent.

Could some of the ships have made their way to the east seacoast of America, either intentionally or forced by forces of nature, before or after rounding the Cape of Good Hope in South Africa? The fleets to India always left Lisbon in March for the 18-month round trip. If they left later, they could not take advantage of the southeast winds in order to arrive in India by September.

Fig. 99—Map of the Atlantic Ocean, showing winds and currents.[28]

On the return trip from India, the fleet would leave in January, and no later than February 15.

If during the many regular voyages, any one of the southbound ships was forced westward by winds and currents after passing the Canary Islands, or on the return trip from India while approaching the equator, they would arrive on the U.S. East Coast during late spring—shipwrecked, mutinied, pirated or looking for lands to the west, known to exist. That time of arrival would give the settlers plenty of time to prepare for the winter, thus guaranteeing their survival, which the English were not able to do untill almost a hundred years later.

Illustration Fig. 99 above shows how the winds and currents affected the caravels. It also shows that as soon as a sailing vessel rounds the Cape of Good Hope, it will be pushed by these same winds and currents. The wind is an important factor, and in this case it is the southeast trade winds that would prevail, pushing the vessels towards the west and the north of Brazil and the equator. As they get near the equator, the south equatorial ocean currents also give them a push, again to the northwest.

Once they pass the equator, the north equatorial currents will do the rest of the job by getting the ships into the Gulf Stream, towards the U.S. East Coast and Cape Hatteras—the easternmost point before the Gulf Stream again pushes them towards the east in a clockwise direction. The same situation occurs on the way south past the Canary Islands, when the ships are naturally pushed west towards the Caribbean. If their destination is India or Brazil, then the vessels must negotiate the most difficult part of their voyage before they reach the equator, according to Commander Malhão Pereira of the *Sagres*, a Portuguese navy school windjammer. See Fig. 100 and details about the 1996 Conference in this chapter.

We can conclude without a doubt that it is very easy for a caravel to wind up on the shores of the U.S. East Coast, either going to India or Brazil, or on the return trip. These trade winds and currents brought Columbus to America, as well as all later navigators. The author's question: would it be possible for the Portuguese

Fig. 100—General circulation of the surface currents in the south Atlantic.

ships to wind up on the U.S. East Coast? Let us also keep in mind that most of the losses and shipwrecks occurred on the return trip.Or could the passengers have demanded that they be taken to America, which they knew about? Also, life in India may not have been the land of milk and honey that the Portuguese expected. Naturally, if that was the case, then they and everyone else on board immediately became outlaws and avoided contact with anyone, taking refuge anywhere.

On the previous page it was shown how a sailing vessel could wind up on the east coast of the North American Continent. The illustration above shows the winds and currents of the South Atlantic in more detail.

At the IV Portuguese Navy Academy Symposium held on November 1996, Commander Malhão Pereira gave a conference about Vasco da Gama and sailing navigation. In this conference, he made it very clear how a caravel, if not properly navigated, could wind up in the Caribbean or on the U.S. east coast.

This is the most logical explanation, that some of the many Portuguese ships lost or shipwrecked could bring Portuguese and their families to America, either from Portugal or from the Far East, and including natives from that region.

José Manuel Malhão Pereira is a well experienced high seas navigator, and is "Comandante de Mar e Guerra" of the Portuguese Navy.

He is also the author of a book about sailing titled *Manobrar é Preciso*, published in Portugal. The title means "*to maneuver is a precise science*" and is attributed to a Roman General before the Common Era who wrote it in Latin: *nauigare necessi uiuere non necessi.*

Commander Pereira participated in the 1992 ocean *Regata*, commanding the Portuguese Navy school ship *Sagres,* along with major nations and their tall ships.

Fig. 101—Map of Western India showing a native boy from Goa [33]

Shipwrecked with Women and Children

One of the most tragic stories of the sea is the shipwreck of the galleon *S. João* in 1552 off the East African coast. Manuel de Sousa Sepulveda, the Captain, his wife, and children all perished, along with many slaves and servants, in very tragic circumstances.[29] Another tragic story is the shipwreck of the *Garça,* described in one of the Hakluyt Societyworks: *Francisco Barreto, the captain of the ship, and all the other officers, seeing the state she was in and that there was nothing else to do but abandone her, they agreed to trans-ship to the Aguia the women and children and other useless mouths in the first place....decided to make a muster of all in his ship, so as to organize and accommodate them in the best way; and he found that they amounted to 1,037 souls, between gentlemen, soldiers, seamen, slaves, women and children.*[30]

In 1537, captain and ship owner Duarte Tristão, with his vessel *São Miguel,* departed from Mozambique on the return trip to Portugal loaded with riches, and disappeared without a trace.[31] These events point to the fact that complete families traveled in those days. Portuguese nobles took their families with them, as well as an enormous number of people on one ship alone.

See Appendix E for a chart of known Portuguese shipwrecks.

English and French Corsairs

Not only shipwrecks prevented many vessels from arriving safely in Portugal; corsairs and pirates also awaited the Spanish and Portuguese galleons loaded with riches on their return home.

During the first half of the 16th century, the French corsairs were very active in attacking Portuguese ships off Portugal's coast and the islands. The third quarter of the 1500's saw plenty of action by English corsairs, Drake being the most famous.

Out of five ships that left Goa, India on January 10, 1592, only one arrived safely in Lisbon on July 17, 1592. The second, *Bom Jesus,* having as captain Manuel de Sousa Coutinho, with his wife, many nobles, soldiers, sailors and slaves, shipwrecked off the east Africa coast with no survivors.

The third, *São Bernardo,* disappeared without a trace. The fourth was beached and burned on Flores Island by its crew to avoid being captured by the English. The English were still able to salvage part of the cargo.

The fifth, *Madre de Deus*, commanded by Fernão Mendonça Furtado, was attacked by a large English fleet of corsairs and captured after a fierce battle. It had aboard almost 600 persons, including women, children and slaves.[32]

John Burrough, who was in command of the squadron, gave orders for the *Madre de Deus* to proceed to Dartmouth, where it caused great admiration.

Russell Miller described it: *Pandemonium broke loose in England's Dartmouth harbor...when the Madre de Deus...dropped anchor...She was the biggest ship anyone in Elizabethan England ever seen...She stretched 165 feet in length, and had a beam of 47 feet and a burden of nearly 1600 tons—about three times the capacity of the largest English ships. Her seven decks...were studded with 32 brass guns...Chests were crammed with gold and silver coins, flawless pearls, amber, jewelry set with large diamonds and vials of precious musk...425 tons of pepper, 45 tons of cloves, 35 tons of cinnamon...*[33] and much more, including cochineal, mace, nutmeg, benjamim (an aromatic substance) and ebony.

This is an example of the many battles fought on the high seas by the Portuguese, causing eventual loss of many lives and the capture by the enemy of Portuguese and Indian nobles for ransom.

Did the English capture and take any of them to England? Did they later come to America as part of Jamestown Colony, to be established in 1607?

Portuguese Emigration to and from India

Emigrant families from Portugal going to India, and others returning home with their relatives—some of them from mixed marriages, as encouraged by the Portuguese government—were good candidates for arrival in North

Fig. 102—Map of Western India, showing Karnataka, formerly Canará

America instead of their chartered destination. Afonso de Albuquerque thought that it was necessary to create, in a place so far from Portugal, a strong and solid nucleus of roots, and to achieve that he promoted the marriage of good women and clean men. To those in mixed marriages he conceded favors, giving a home, land, cattle and a horse to start life. Later, in 1529, there were already more than a thousand children, sons and daughters of Portuguese, in Goa. These people from Goa were later called Goans, a name still used by everyone born there.

That did not happen just in India, but also in Abyssinia (modern Ethiopia) when in 1646, Pedro Barreto de uw wrote that he found a thousand men, children and grandchildren of 400 Portuguese, from when Cristovão da Gama passed by the area with their women, children and their elders more than 100 years before.[34]

The list of 54 weddings shows that 25 women were Moors from India—possibly Turkish—five were from Canará, and the rest from Malabar, Java, Burma and nearby lands.[35] In India, after the marriages, there were two classes among the European population, the *casados* (married) and soldiers.

According to historians of the 16th century, India was absorbing the better part of 8,000 men per year, and it is possible that its Portuguese population would have thus been reduced to less than half from the 16th century to the next.[36]

Fidelino de Figueiredo wrote that each India-bound ship transported an average of 250 persons. Between 1497 and 1527, the first 30 years of the Portuguese Empire in the Far East, 320 vessels departed to India and transported 80,000 persons, including soldiers and passengers.[37]

By 1570 there were 16,000 Portuguese in India.[38] In 1589, Paulo de Lima—a Portuguese captain—departed from Goa in India with a caravel loaded with spices and slaves. He had with him his wife and servants. Also aboard were many passengers, soldiers returning…and women.[39] It is also a fact that more than 10,000 men disappeared or died at sea. And to confirm that, Boxer also writes: …*during the 16th century approximately 2,400 people left Portugal yearly overseas, the great majority of them being able bodied and unmarried young men, bound for golden Goa, and…few of them returned.*[40]

Boxer and according to Lucena, describes what life was like aboard the ships going to India: …*what thing is an India nau* [ship] *put to sea on sails with 600, 800 and sometimes more than 1000 inside herself, men, women, little boys, free, slaves, nobles, common people, merchants, soldiers and sea people. Someone that compared it to a large village, was not exaggerating.*[41]

There is another fact that should not be ignored: the Portuguese Jews also signed up in many ships going to India, secretly, to avoid the Inquisition: *During the 17th century the Portuguese Jewish Diaspora stretched rapidly from the Ottoman Empire to Goa on the Indian subcontinent, from Denmark and Northern Germany all the way to Brazil and the islands of the Caribbean. Though so widely scattered, its members retained their identity as Portuguese Jews, seeing themselves as citizens of a nation uniquely heroic and tragic past.*[42] Would they have any advantage by identifying themselves as Portuguese if they were not? Why not Spanish or another nationality?

*Fig. 103—Photo of a Melungeon child and Melungeon young man taken by
Doris Ulmann in the 1920's. Used with special permission from the Berea
College and the Doris Ulmann Foundation.*

The major emigration movements from the Azores were registered around the
16th century, towards Africa and India.[43] From the above information, we know that
complete families traveled between Portugal and India, which means they could
settle and survive wherever they would go. Also, a large Portuguese population
was traveling. Many vessels were not arriving at their destinations, and no one ever
heard of them again. The trend established long ago continued into the 18th century,
when it was recorded that many orphan girls went to India.[44] In any event, the
Portuguese were the first Europeans to establish themselves in India, and the last

ones to leave: *Four and half centuries were to pass between the conquest of Goa and the lowering of the Portuguese flag in that territory in 1961.*[45]

Rejected in India

Kennedy brings to our attention a possible fact that may help make the connection when he wrote: *Streams of escaping or exiled Moors made their way abroad, and historical records even depict a shipload of these hapless people seeking asylum in India, vainly claiming to be "sunburned Portuguese" in an effort to explain their ruddy complexions. However, the Catholic friar at Bombay, upon hearing their plea, knew better and denied them entry.*[46]

A further study of his source tells us that in 1589, the religious order of the Franciscans was still admitting *mestiços* as novices in Goa (India), though they had been ordered not to by their superiors in Portugal. Only 50 years later, a determined attempt was made by the European born Franciscans friars at Goa to prevent any Creole from holding office. The Creoles later defeated this order, and Friar Miguel da Purificação, who had been born near Bombay, argued that the many dark-complexioned Portuguese who came out to India were in reality Mulattos and contaminated with Negro blood: *...although they allege that they got sunburnt during the voyage.* [47] From this we have to assume two things, one that they indeed were accepted in India, and two, that the problem was only in the fact that these dark Portuguese were not being allowed to hold office within the Catholic Church, and he was referring exclusively to the friars. Furthermore, this occurred in the early 17th century, many years after Drake's famous Roanoke rescue and the massive expulsion of Moors from Spain, which occurred in the late 15th and early 16th centuries.

If we add to this the fact that a trip from the Mediterranean to India would be quite costly, just for food and water alone, it is difficult to believe that this ship would have made it all the way to India, without Portuguese knowledge or authorization. This fact may not be important, but it may point to the many missionaries in East Africa who were looking for positions in India, and these missionaries were definitely a mixture of African, Portuguese and Indian, thus explaining the dark complexion, which you find today in many Portuguese living in Portugal and elsewhere, who descend from East Indian families.

Portuguese East India Men and Women

From the above, we may also have overlooked another aspect, and that is the possibility of East Indians, living in some of the Portuguese colonies in India, and having already intermarried with local people, produced a new generation of Indian-Portuguese.

Fernão Vaz Dourado was a famous cartographer born during the early 1500's in India of an Indian mother, and he produced many atlases often known as the Vaz Dourado type.[48]

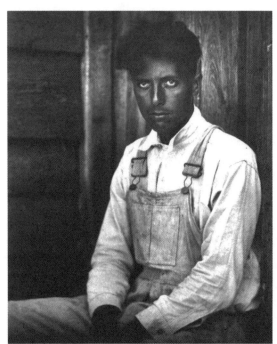

Fig. 104—Photo of a Melungeon young man taken by Doris Ulmann in the Appalachians ca. 1930. Used with special permission from the Berea College and the Doris Ulmann Foundation.

The classification of Moors (to all the Muslims) by the Portuguese may have brought the same name to the North American East Coast, to anyone originating from any of the areas controlled by the Ottoman Empire.[49]

Let us look further into this possibility and read what William H. Gilbert, Jr., a well known anthropologist, wrote in his book *Peoples of India* about racial types of this nation: *The physical types of the people of India show a wide range in all the characteristic features of skin color, nose and head form, hair, and stature...The color of the skin ranges from dead black...to the ivory skin of the Kashmiri beauty and the wheat color of the higher casts of upper India....A third element in the racial typology of India is a strain similar to the Mediterranean peoples of southern Europe.*[50]

This may provide us with a connection, but it also may add confusion to the already confused puzzle, as Gilbert adds the next paragraph:

A fourth racial type is a generally reminiscent of the Nordic type of Europe, except that the complexion is more brunet. Its traits include long-headedness; a tall stature; a long face; prominent, narrow nose; usually straight hair, with body and head hair well developed; and occasional light eyes or hair. Among the Kaffirs and the Pathans, the skin color of this type is mainly a rosy white tint, and an appreciable number possess gray-blue eyes and chestnut hair.[51]

This description adds strength to a possible connection to the Melungeons, if we recall the first encounters of the English with Indians in 1584 and John Lawson with the Hatteras in 1700.

James Adair wrote in his thesis: *Doubtless the idea that the Carolina natives were backward cousins of the people of Bombay and Calcutta influenced, to a certain extent, many of the old descriptions of their dress and ornaments.*[52] The parallel this writer established with the East Indians is quite interesting.

We found another connection with the East Indians in 1635 on a land grant to

Fig. 105—Cas Goins, daughter Gladys Goins, wife Ritter Jane Sergen and son Homer Goins, a Melungeon family in the early 1900's. Photos Courtesy of Pat Rice, Shepperdsville Kentucky.

George Menifye in which he is compensated for paying the transportation of at least one East Indian by the name of Tony or Anthony.[53] Most likely these East Indians were brought by Portuguese to Europe and then found their way to England.

See Appendix D for a chart showing the marriages of Portuguese men and East Indian women.

Canará Melungeon Name

The name Canará may help to put the puzzle together. As mentioned in Chapter IV, Kennedy revealed to us in his book that his great uncle's name was Canara Nash, and this name was common among the earliest Melungeon families.

Battles took place in 1509, involving many nationalities, between Muslims and Portuguese, and among them was a very confused population with their junks—a type of boat used in the far east—from Diu on the Gujerât, and from Calicut (Kalikodu) on the Canará.[54]

Kennedy, a Melungeon descendant, also has darker skin and blue eyes, as well as some Mediterranean and East Indian resemblance. He himself said that he was often mistaken as a Turk when he visited Turkey for the first time. Let us keep in mind that the Turks (Ottoman Empire) were very active in India during the 16th century. Also, the name Canara is mentioned again in similar circumstances by Charles R. Boxer.[55]

Another coincidence shows up when you look at an older map of India and verify that there is a large area in northwest India named Canará by the Portuguese, and later named Karnataka. This area is located near Goa, which the Portuguese actively visited since 1498 when Vasco da Gama found the sea route to India, and held until 1961. Karnataka, or Canará (Kannara in English), is rather large and divided into north and south regions, each with their own language, called Canarês or Canarim, and Goa also had its own language, Konkani—India as of 1979 had approximately 1650 languages. It is known as a land of seafarers even today. The name Canarim was erroneously applied by the Portuguese to the people of Goa.[56] Fig. 102 shows the area of Karnataka, and to the north, the cities where the Portuguese built their empire of the Indias. (Goa, Damão and Diu.) Bombay was also part of the Portuguese Empire, but it was given to King Charles II as the dowry of the Portuguese Princess Catarina de Bragança. Also notice the artist's conception of a typical Christian boy native to Goa. His face denotes a Mediterranean resemblance and would be quite at home in any Portuguese village. All of the above describe the Portuguese connection of the name Canará (Karnataka), the English, and the people from India.

Let us keep in mind that Portuguese families, of both mixed and unmixed marriages, were traveling back and forth on a regular basis betwee n Portugal and India. If they wound up on the North American east coast, that would explain the variety among the Melungeon groups and others that may have separated and formed other communities mixed with the local Indians, such as the Lumbees.

Also, the cover page of the National Geographic Magazine of June 1985 gives another example of a Far East face with red-brown color and striking greenish-blue eyes, of a girl refugee from Afghanistan, not far from the west coast of India. Since we are looking at strange coincidences, the name Kannada (a corruption of the name Karnataka) is the name for a large area of India and sounds just like Canada. The Portuguese were the early explorers and settlers in both places.

Portuguese in Australia

The writer W.A. Richardson stated that: *The Dutch in 1606, and English in 1770, have long been known to have reached Australia. However, for more than two centuries a debate has been going on about other Europeans who may have preceded them.*[57] Noel Grove wrote: *Portuguese, Spanish and French voyages into the Pacific and Indian Oceans may have brought explorers close to Australia in the early 1500's.*[58] Yes, the Portuguese were there at an early date, but the French and Spaniards came much later.

Between 1500 and 1550, there were no Spanish or French explorers in the Pacific or Indian Oceans, except for the Portuguese navigator Magalhães (Magellan) in 1520 working for Spain. Now let us examine the facts.

The Dauphin or Harleian map shows inscriptions on the apparent continent (Java-la-Grande) Australia south of Indonesia that derived from Portuguese sources. The presumption was that some Portuguese mariners were really the first Europeans to reach Australia. Numerous writers have upheld and elaborated upon this theory. Apparently the case for an early Portuguese discovery of Australia rests entirely on imagined resemblance between the continent of Java-la-Grande on the Dieppe map

Fig. 106—Cas Goins, a Melungeon c. 1945
Photos Courtesy of Pat Rice,
Shepperdsville Kentucky.

and Australia. According to Richardson, despite this similarity, it does not provide any evidence of a Portuguese discovery whatsoever. He justifies this by going into great detail about how words were written and pronounced in 16th century, giving an example of the English *Queenborough* sounding just like the Portuguese *Coimbra*.

The only argument left is to use some logic. The Portuguese were in Indonesia and Sumatra—known in the 16th century as *Taprobana*, a name made famous by the Portuguese national poet Camões—which is close to Australia, and used native pilots whenever possible. This is confirmed by Richardson, who does not agree with Kenneth McIntire and Ian McKiggan—the two strongest advocates of the Portuguese discovery—when he states that: *The Spaniards, French, Dutch and English did their best to lay hands on charts made by the Portuguese, using bribery, subversion or capture.*[59] This is understandable since the Cantino map of 1502, made in Portugal, had the most cartographic information of the world at the time.

The Portuguese conquered Malacca and were in the Moluccas in the 16th century. The distance from these islands to the north or west coast of Australia is only a few hundred miles. Timor, which is very close to Australia, was visited by the Portuguese in 1514 and became active in the third quarter of the 16th century with the presence of missionaries.

Timor was part of Portugal until 1975, when Indonesia annexed it. Their people did not accept the annexation and have been rebelling for the last 20 years. Their leaders, Dr. José Ramos Horta and Bishop Carlos Filipe Ximenes Belo, have recently been awarded the Nobel Peace Prize for their activities.

In 1999, a referendum was held in Timor, with the overwhelming majority voting in favor of total independence from Indonesia. This was followed by death and almost total destruction of Timor. The United Nations and international outcry forced the eventual removal of the Indonesian armed forces.

Australia, being so close, played a major role in the peace keeping efforts; Portugal and many nations followed with help and started the major task of rebuilding a small nation.

Is it possible that the Portuguese and the area's native pilots did not know about Australia? Most likely they did, but since there was no immediate trading value, it was ignored. Manuel Godinho de Heredia—half Malay—claimed the discovery of the Isle of Gold, later called Australia, in 1601.

Let us remember that Portugal and Spain had previously signed the Tordesilles Treaty, which would enable Spain to claim ownership of Australia. So why tell the world about new lands that Portugal could not claim under the treaty?

Just recently (1996) a Portuguese silver coin from the 16th century was found on a beach near Melbourne, Australia. The Australian State Museum in Victoria has confirmed the coin's country of origin and its date; however, coin experts disagree. One other 15th century coin has also been found and is now awaiting confirmation from experts in Portugal. Some Portuguese historians, including Admiral Gago Coutinho, believe that Gomes de Sequeira discovered York Peninsula in Australia and spent some months there living in peace with the natives. This conclusion is based on the Gastaldi map published in 1554.[60]

Gomes de Sequeira was away from his base for eight months, and the question is, where did he spend the winter of 1525? He visited New Guinea, which is approximately 100 miles from Cape York in Australia.

He also recorded the discovery of a large island inhabited by Pacific natives. We should keep in mind that discussions were under way as to whom the Spice Islands belonged—Portugal or Spain. The argument was settled when Portugal bought them. Later it was discovered that they were on the Portuguese side of the Tordesilles Treaty. So Portugal had paid for what was already hers.

For more information about Australia, consult the following books: *Chance Discovery of Australia and New Zealand by Portuguese and Spanish Navigators between 1521 and 1528,* Palmerston North, 1983 by Roger Hervé; *Secret Discovery of Australia* by K. G. McIntyre, London 1977; *The Portuguese Expedition to Bass Strait in AD 1522*, Journal of Australian Studies, June 1977.

Asiatic and Oriental Appearance

Dr. Edward T. Price, in his doctoral dissertation on mixed-blood groups, published in 1951, wrote: *An Oriental appearance is occasionally attributed to them,* [Melungeons] *but they are commonly thought to be of at least partly Portuguese descent.*[61] Louise Davis of the Nashville *Tennessean* describes Mrs. Bell, a Melungeon lady, after an interview: *...her skin had the red-brown color of an Asiatic.*[62] Is this a coincidence? In the mountains of Tennessee? Again she writes that the *Encyclopedia Americana* states: *Chinese sailors were known to have made their way to Portugal and intermarried with the Portuguese, and the slightly Oriental strain is one of the clues to the occasional slant eyes and silky skin of some of the Melungeons.*[63] Arthur Estabrook writes in 1926: *...in Ad County, Virginia* *there is a group of "red skinned people" who have considered themselves white.*[64] The Asiatic appearance, with its varied colors, is possible and easy to explain, if we interject the Portuguese element and the fact that they were on the Arabian coast and throughout Asia during the early 16th century, with the consequent miscegenation well documented and recorded. In 1952, North Callahan wrote: *...Colony of strange people with dark complexions of a reddish-brown hue was found in the upper Smokies.*[65] Bonnie Ball, a teacher who taught the Melungeon offspring, wrote of her own personal experience and knowledge: *Their skin was dark and oily, showing more of a coppery color than of, say, Ethiopians or darker members of the white race.*[66]*...They* [Melungeons] *had a noticeable red color that was constant throughout their family...*[67] Again: *She* [Melungeon student] *was very dark, with dark eyes and drooping eyelids; however, her nose and mouth were more oriental than Caucasian or Ethiopian.*[68] Jean Patterson Bible, on their possible ancestry, also writes: *The most likely tradition of the Asiatic or European strain in the Melungeon heritage, according to a majority of Melungeons, and one shared by a number of early and later Tennessee historians is that of Spanish and/or Portuguese mixed with Indians.* [69] An Oriental appearance is not common with the Portuguese, but you can still find looks that may resemble the Oriental. This explains the discrimination that the Melungeons had to suffer because of the color of their skin, and it also points to an origin.

Henry Price, an attorney in Rogersville, Tennessee, wrote about the Melungeons in 1971 as someone that lived with the Melungeons and studied them for 25 years: *As a rule the young men are quite handsome and the young girls are strikingly beautiful. The latter...might suggest Eurasian and Polynesian ancestry.*[70]

Speaking of Asiatic appearance, the ethnologist Mooney cited a reference made by Barton in 1797 relating to white people and also to moon-eyed people. This is rather interesting and should not be ignored: *There is a dim but persistence tradition of a strange white race preceding the Cherokee... The Cheerake* [old spelling, also CHALAQUE written for the first time by the Gentleman of Elvas, later written by the French as CHARAQUI] *tell us that when they first arrived in the country which they first inhabit, they found it possessed by certain 'moon-eyed people' who could not see in the day time...He* [Barton in 1797] *seems to consider them an albino race. Haywood, twenty six years later, says that the invading Cherokee found "white people" near the head of the* [river] *Little Tennessee.*[71]

It can be concluded that there is a long road ahead before the early history of America can be completely known.

Portuguese in Japan and China—Portuguese Language in the Far East

The Portuguese arrived on the southeast coast of China in 1513 and were considered no threat. After a period of hostilities and clandestine trade, the Canton provincial governor signed a treaty in 1550. Eventually the Portuguese were allowed to set up shop in Macau, where they stayed until the end of 1999 when it was peacefully handed over to China, making Portugal the longest standing colonial power in the Far East. In 1543, the Portuguese Antonio Peixoto, Antonio da Mota and Francisco Zeimoto were the first Europeans to arrive in Japan, and Europe's first major port in Japan, the city of Nagasaki, was founded in 1570 by the Portuguese seeking a harbor for their ships.[72] In the following century (1660), Portuguese navigators went from Japan to Lisbon by way of the Arctic.

In 1544, on the way to Japan, Portuguese explorer Fernão Mendes Pinto discovered and named Formosa[73]—meaning *beautiful*—the island of Taiwan off the Chinese mainland, as well as the Formosa Straits. The origin of the Chinese name Taiwan is not known. Some of the small islands (Penghu Islands) are also known as the islands of the *Pescadores*, a Portuguese name. In Indonesia the *Flores* Island name was also given by the Portuguese.

The Portuguese also visited Thailand, Cambodia and Vietnam. It was here near the Mekong River where the Portuguese epic poet Luís Vaz de Camões shipwrecked when he was returning from China, in the 16th century.

The Portuguese language is the fifth most spoken language in the world, after Mandarin Chinese, English, Hindi and Spanish. It is also the third European language ahead of German and Italian, as well as one of the oldest in Europe, with a rich literary tradition. It is the official language in seven independent countries, and is spoken by 200 million people. English is, however, the most widely spoken language in the world, and considered to be the current *lingua franca*.

The spreading of the Portuguese language began in 1430 in the Azores and Madeira islands, 100 years before the first attempt to populate Brazil. In 1551, the English Winham visited Guinea, and the King of Benim spoke Portuguese to the English, a language that he had learned in infancy. The importance given to the Portuguese language is not surprising, if we take into consideration that Portugal was the only country in Europe that spoke only one language as stated by David Hawke: ...*a linguistic unity absent elsewhere in Europe.*[74]

This is just to show the expansion of the Portuguese language in the world, and according to Barreto, it is a: ...*fact that Portuguese today has more words of Asian, African and Amerindian origin than any other European Language...*[75] It is one result of the far-reaching dialogue between civilizations, in which the Portuguese were the pioneers.[76] Between the 16th and 18th centuries, the Portuguese language in creole versions was used as the international language of the Orient and along the African coast.

In 1658 the Dutch governor, Van Goens, decreed that it would be forbidden for the slaves to speak Portuguese among themselves, with the Dutch, or with foreigners.[77]

He tried in vain to stop its use in Ceylon (modern Sri Lanka) and Java. Even the Danish and English missionaries preached in Portuguese right up to the dawn of the 19th century. In order for the French priests to be understood, they had an interpreter repeating the sermon aloud in Portuguese. In South Africa, Portuguese was the second language during the 17th and 18th centuries, and it is not surprising to find words of Portuguese origin in the Dutch, French and English languages.

See Appendix F for a glossary of words with Portuguese roots used in Japan.

Notes

[1] Colonial America by Oscar Theodore Barck, Jr., p. 3.

[2] The Melungeons by Bonnie Ball, p. 29.

[3] The Conquest of Paradise by Kirkpatrick Sale, p. 3 (Adam Smith).

[4] National Geographic Magazine by Merle Severy, p. 57, November 1992.

[5] Christian and Spices by John Correia Afonso, p. 33.

[6] Travelin' Man by Anthony Weller, Sky Magazine, April 1999, p. 15.

[7] History of India by Romila Thapar, 1974, p. 336.

[8] The Ottoman Centuries, by Lord Kinross, 1977, NY Morrow Quill, p. 246.

[9] History of Portugal by Oliveira Marques, p. 249-250.

[10] Portugal nos Mares by Oliveira Martins, p. 270.

[11] National Geographic Magazine by Merle Severy, p. 79 (November 1992).

[12] Portugal nos Mares by Oliveira Martins, p. 151-153.

[13] Lusa News Agency by Brian Oneil, Luso-Americano, April 25, 1995.

[14] Ring of Fire by Lorne and Lawrence Blair (PBS TV), VHS tape.

[15] Graveyard of the Atlantic by David Stick, p. 5.

[16] Ibid, p. 1; [17] Ibid, p. 2; [18] Ibid, p. 3; [19] Ibid, p. 4.

[20] The Outer Banks of North Carolina by David Stick, p. 13.

[21] Ibid, pp. 13, 14.

[22] Historia de Portugal by Joaquim Verissimo Serrão, Vol. III, pp. 159-162.

[23] Historia de Portugal by Oliveira Martins, p. 299.

[24] Os Navios de Vasco da Gama by João Brás de Oliveira, p. 14.

[25] Historia de Portugal by Joaquim Verissimo Serrão, Vol. III, p. 102.

[26] Navegação Portuguesa dos Séculos XV e XVII by Carlos de Passos, pp. 10-11.

[27] Portuguese Voyages by Charles David Ley, p. xviii.

[28] Map by Navy Commander Malhão Pereira, presented at the Marine Academy.

[29] Historia Tragico-Maritima by Bernardino Gomes de Brito (Damião Peres), pp. 23-39.

[30] The Tragic History of the Sea by Father Manoel Barradas (C. R. Boxer), pp. 40-43.

[31] Peregrinação by Fernão Mendes Pinto, p. 22.

[32] Batalhas e Combates da Marinha Portuguesa by Saturnino Monteiro, pp. 269-272.

[33] The East Indiamen by Russell Miller, p. 8.

[34] Historia da Lingua Portuguesa by Serafim da Silva Neto, p. 518.

[35] Ibid, pp. 534-535.

[36] Fomento Rural e Emigração by Oliveira Martins, p. 32.

[37] Estudos de Historia Americana by Fidelino de Figueiredo, p. 21.

[38] Fomento Rural e Emigração by Oliveira Martins, p. 32.

Notes (Cont.)

39 Ibid, p. 291.

40 The Portuguese Seaborne Empire by Charles R. Boxer, p. 52.

41 Historia da Vida do Padre Francisco Xavier by João de Lucena, Vol. 1, p. 44.

42 The Jews of Spain by Jane S. Gerber, pp. 188-189.

43 Portuguese Immigrants by Carlos Almeida, UPEC, p. 4.

44 Historia da Lingua Portuguesa by Serafim da Silva Neto, p. 533.

45 Christians and Spices by John Correia Afonso, p. 34.

46 The Melungeons by Brent Kennedy, p. 103.

47 The Portuguese Seaborne Empire by Charles R. Boxer, p. 253.

48 Japan in Early Portuguese Maps by Alfredo Pinheiro Marques, p. 15.

49 The Portuguese Seaborne Empire by Charles R. Boxer, p. 44.

50 Peoples of India by William H. Gilbert, Jr., p. 17.

51 Ibid, pp. 17-18.

52 The Red Carolinians by Chapman J. Milling, pp. 7-8.

53 Cavaliers and Pioneers by Nell Marion Nugent, pp. 24, 54.

54 Historia de Portugal by Oliveira Martins, p. 231, 286, 288.

55 The Portuguese Seaborne Empire by Charles R. Boxer, p. 41.

56 Glossário Luso-Asiático by Sebastião Rudolfo Delgado, pp. 196-197.

57 The Portuguese Discovery of Australia by W. A. Richardson, p. 5.

58 Atlas of World History by Noel Grove, p. 173, National Geographic Society.

59 The Portuguese Discovery of Australia by W. A. Richardson, p. 12.

60 Onde Teria Invernado Gomes de Sequeira em 1525 by Gago Coutinho, p. 1525.

61 The Melungeons by Bonnie Ball, p. 8, Edward Price,
   Geographical Review, Vol. 41.

62 Mystery of the Melungeons by Louise Davis, p. 11
   (Nashville Tennesseean 9/29/1963).

63 Ibid.

64 Mongrel Virginias by Arthur H. Estabrook, 182.

65 Smoky Mountain Country by North Callahan, p. 162.

66 The Melungeons by Bonnie Ball, p. v.

67 Ibid, p. 56; 68 Ibid, p. 89.

69 The Melungeons by Jean Patterson Bible, p. 93.

70 Melungeons: The Vanishing Colony of Newman's Ridge by Henry R. Price, p. 1.

71 History, Myths, and Sacred Formulas of the Cherokees by James Mooney, p. 22.

72 National Geographic Magazine by Merle Severy, p. 90 (November 1992).

73 Portugal nos Mares by Oliveira Marques, p. 316.

74 The Colonial Experience by David Hawke, p. 8.

75 The Dawn of a New Age by Luis Filipe Barreto, p. 7 (The Courier, Unesco, 1989/4).

76 Historia da Lingua Portuguesa by Serafim da Silva Neto, pp. 421, 514-518.

77 Ibid.

Chapter X

Conclusion

Portuguese, Melungeon and/or other Groups' Connections and Roots

From hypothesis to hypothesis, the truth eventually will be found[1]

The author explored certain areas using logic and facts, but conclusions sometimes came thanks to intuition. The following are three guidelines established to set the hypothesis and arrive at a logical conclusion:

First, a time frame between 1500 and 1600 was established for the arrival of a group of people that would be known later as the Melungeons, Portuguese or any other name. Earlier or later arrivals were ruled out. If they arrived before Columbus, a totally different set of circumstances would have to be considered, and would be so speculative—almost as complex as trying to find the origin of the native American Indian. If they came later than 1600, they would have had contacts with the many settlers that arrived after Jamestown. The English or other explorers did not seem to have encountered any recent arrivals. The groups said to be found were already established.

For the time frame being considered, the earliest Spanish voyages to the American Southeast occurred in the period of 1521-1526. French and Spanish colonial activities materialized only in the 1560's. The Frenchman Jean Ribault learned of tales about the Southeast that Lucas Vásquez de Ayllón had spread in 1523.[2] During that time period, there was not much movement by Europeans, other than the Portuguese or the Spanish. The English, French and Dutch became active in voyages to the North American continent during the latter part of the 16th century and after. The Spanish failed in their early attempt at settling in South Carolina, and the English failed in Roanoke Colony, North Carolina as well as later on in Jamestown. Only the pilgrims that arrived from England in 1620 aboard the Mayflower—after staying in Holland for some time—were able to succeed. By then the Portuguese had been exporting sugar and other products to Europe from the colonies for 100 years.

One strong factor for the possible survival of a Portuguese group in the early 1500's is the fact that they crossed with so many different races right in their own country, due to invasions as described in Chapter V. According to Freyre and climate studies by Beringer, it has been shown that the Portuguese acclimatize themselves in various parts of the world better: *...than almost all the other European races,*[3] and the Portuguese race appears to be endowed with a temperament that permits it to adapt itself much easier than other races to climates that are: *...different from that of the mother country.*[4]

Second, their nationality or place of origin ought to be established, as well as their means of arrival, and not necessarily their race. Therefore, if they were Moors, Berbers, Jews or others that came from Spain, and had been there for several generations, they would be considered Spaniards. The same would apply to Portuguese nationals. If these parameters were not established, it would be very difficult to come up with sensible answers. How could anyone be considered Carthaginian, Phoenician, Greek, Roman, Gothic, Moorish or Berber if they all came from the European continent, except the African Black slaves, who arrived at a later date. It has been established that they were not Black or American Indian when they were first met by the English, or possibly the French.

The Iberian Peninsula was invaded by different races of people, and the makeup of the Portuguese people naturally reflects a bit of everyone that lived in Portugal for a long period.

As stated, the Melungeons or any other group claiming Portuguese ancestry were made up of more than one component, but they started out with a major component that may have been responsible for their presence in America. There is no such thing as pure Melungeon, European, African or another race, nowadays; all Americans are made up of many races, not necessarily a melting pot, but a mosaic of cultures. We have to rule out the English, French or other Northern European countries, as well as the small Italian republics of the time. As for being Spanish, it has been shown in Chapter III that this is unlikely.

Third, it was assumed that in order for a group to survive over such a long period of time, and still hold onto its own identity and physical appearance, men and women would have to be part of the equation in the same manner as Black slaves from Africa. If just black male slaves had been brought in, then we would not have today the beautiful black skin of the slave descendants. Therefore, male slaves or soldiers were ruled out, although, if they were in the U.S., most likely they intermarried with female native Indians, Blacks or any others. Naturally, in this case their offspring would carry their genes to the present.

Preliminary calculations assumed that the Melungeons may have started out with only 200 persons. If that was the case, the group has been able to survive over 14 generations, with many thousands still living today according to Kennedy.

How Important was it to be White?

In Elizabethan times, the need to be white was so great that even Queen Elizabeth covered her face generously with a white powder made of lead. Since everyone wanted to have a white face, they often risked their very lives, due to the corrosive action of the lead that penetrated the skin.[5]

The color of one's skin was important then, and it still plays an important part in some segments of society. Colleen McCullough, author of the well known and famous book, *The Thorn Birds,* wrote:[6]

Safely hidden in the last row of desks, Meggie dared to glance sideways at the little girl sitting next to her. A gap-toothed grin met her frightened gaze, huge black eyes staring roundly out of a dark slightly shiny face. She fascinated Meggie, used to fairness and freckles, for even Frank with his dark eyes and hair had a fair white skin. So Meggie ended in thinking her deskmate the most beautiful creature she had ever seen... [Later Meggie's parents commented]: *'I don't think it is such a good idea to be too thick with the Dagos,' they muttered sharing the British community's instinctive mistrust of any dark or Mediterranean people. 'Dagos are dirty, Meggie girl, they don't wash too often,' he explained lamely, wilting under the look of hurt reproach Meggie gave them.*

This is a fictitious story of the early 20th century, but in real life it was also true.

Why Would the Portuguese Emigrate in the 16th Century?

Would the Portuguese emigrate as settlers to North America willingly? Possibly, because conditions since the 1540's aggravated at a steady pace and many families went in search of better living conditions, or just to survive. In the 16th century they did emigrate to Africa, Brazil and India. Why not to the North American continent? After all, it was much closer. The basic reason for emigration was probably always economical first, then religious or political as the second most important consideration.

After the first golden years of the 1500's, the economic situation was terrible. The establishment of the Inquisition did not help matters. Lisbon was visited with plagues and earthquakes during that time, but they proved easier to face than the cost of 50 years of glory. Literally half the nation's population had vanished in pursuit of wealth in the new colonies.

King Sebastião came to power in 1566 and, in the same year, the copper coin was reduced to 1/3 its value, a cruel but needed measure because the English had taken all the silver and gold. The business people, who had increased to a large number after the discoveries, knew in advance and paid all debts. The poor people got caught with 2/3 less money. Many hanged themselves, and if that was not enough, the bubonic plague came with full force.

During the time when the plague was at its height (July and August of 1569), 700 persons died daily in Lisbon alone. There were no places for burying the dead. Huge ditches were dug and the bodies thrown in fifty at a time. It was a fast and fatal disease. More than one third of Lisbon's population succumbed to the plague— approximately 40,000 people.

Then there was the great disaster of Alcacer-Quibir (1578) in North Africa, plus the consequent Iberian union of both crowns in 1580. Life got much worse when Felipe II of Spain became Filipe I of Portugal. He was the son of Princess Isabel of Portugal and the grandson of the Portuguese King Manuel I, as well as the son of the Emperor Carlos V. England, previously an ally, became an enemy of great proportions.

The high level of emigration registered in the 16th century coincided with a period of catastrophes suffered by the Portuguese,[7] as well as the prospect of an Iberian union which brought several concordance laws between Portugal and Spain. These laws faced heavy opposition from the people of Algarve in 1568. Prior to that, in 1563, there were already regular maritime commercial routes between the Americas, India, Portugal and Spain. To add more confusion for the historian and researcher, some of these shipping enterprises were using Portuguese boats without registration, both in Lisbon and Algarve, with no records ever made of their activities.

This union [Portugal and Spain] was accepted by most Portuguese business people and large land owners. They now could import and export to Spain duty free. To make things more palatable, the Spanish king promised complete autonomy, with separate language and control, as part of a kingdom united to Spain. As time went by, subsequent Spanish kings did not keep Felipe's promises and eventually caused the Portuguese to revolt in 1640, when their total independence was restored.

Ever since Portugal expelled the Moors in the 1200's from what is now her present territory, it had nowhere to expand, and therefore always looked to the seas as the new frontier. First it conquered some cities in Morocco. That did not prove very advantageous. The cost of keeping these towns was far greater than the economic benefit. The existence of the North American continent had been well known since the early 1500's, and the people dreamed of rich lands on the other side of the Atlantic. The large quantities of silver, gold and diamonds arriving in Portugal actually impoverished the people.[8] The merchant marine, which was a crown monopoly, was then in the hands of businessmen without scruples. Many times, anarchy was the dominant power. It is not certain whether the Portuguese left Portugal proper or the islands with America as a known destination. However, they certainly left by the thousands for Africa, Brazil and India.

The Return of the Navigators

The first thing Columbus did when he returned from his voyage to America was to visit the Portuguese King João II. Both Columbus and his crew spoke of many wonders. The same happened earlier when other navigators returned from Africa, thereby starting a wave of settlers to new places recently discovered.

After Columbus, Portuguese navigators returned from India, Brazil and other locales. Later, Portuguese navigators and explorers found themselves employed by other nations. This was the case with Spain, with navigators such as Fernão de Magalhães (Magellan), Estevão Gomes, João Rodrigues Cabrilho and many others.

During the first half of the 16th century, economic conditions deteriorated to the point that emigration was the only way out even for what remained of the middle class. Portugal verified a typical contradiction of the Portuguese history: A country with a lack of skilled labor was supplying other countries with their best resource, their people. Those were the prevalent conditions at the time, causing many to emigrate.

The news was tempting not only from Africa, Brazil, South and Central Americas, but also later from the North American east coast, from Newfoundland to Florida.

Pardo may have recruited Portuguese soldiers and their families to settle the Spanish colony of Santa Elena. He already had Portuguese soldiers in his service. Would it be possible for entire Portuguese families to emigrate without leaving any record of their departure? It may be possible, because many of the records, books and notes were destroyed by fires and earthquakes, burned by the Inquisition, removed by the Spaniards during their occupation, or later destroyed by Napoleon's invading army. There is also another possibility, which is still evident presently: emigrate illegally and fill caravels with families that gave all their savings to dishonest businessmen looking for a quick profit. The emigrants arriving on American soil did not have to pay taxes to the crown or abide by any Portuguese laws if they had left illegally.

Meanwhile, Felipe II of Spain took advantage of the strong Portuguese navy remaining from the discovery period, and decided to invade England with the *Invincible Armada.* It turned out to be a great loss for Spain, and even more so for Portugal. The Portuguese had paid dearly for their king's foolishness ten years earlier in Alcacer-Quibir.

Before the 17th Century, Caravels with Non-Anglo Settlers to the East Coast

We can assume that the Portuguese people—formerly Moors, Berbers, etc.— had plenty of information about the New World, and with all the economic woes, religious persecution, and epidemics, why not emigrate to America. After all, everyone in search of a better life was emigrating to Africa and Brazil, where they had news of the inhospitable climate with fevers and death. Knowing about the malarial and fever stricken tropical coasts of Africa and Asia, it is possible that they would attempt emigration to North America.

The information reaching Portugal was that the area of Virginia and North Carolina had a temperate climate with fertile soil, so why not try it? Well…a possible theory, but not proven. One of the concerns for many before they left was how to return. That did not seem to be a problem.

The prospective settlers were aware of the regular shipping routes between Africa, Brazil, Central America and South America, as they spoke to many who returned from that part of the world. They knew about the Spanish attempts to settle the east coast during the early 1500's, and later the Santa Elena colony. If these Portuguese settlers were in Santa Elena at the time it was being destroyed and abandoned, would they move to St. Augustine? Maybe not, because they were also aware that a Spanish king and his army had invaded Portugal and, not being Spanish, they could have chosen to search for safer and more productive areas. Then, add the fact that there was talk of gold and jewels in the mountains.

The English and Indian attacks may also have been a contributing factor for moving towards the higher grounds away from the coast. There is still a question that some Melungeons and other groups of early settlers did not necessarily look Mediterranean or Portuguese. If so, how and when did they arrive in America? A possible explanation may be the description by A.J.R. Russell-Wood of the life aboard one of the ships in the *Carreira da India* [Indian Route]: *As the voyage progressed the crew became a floating United Nations with disregard for race or religion: slave and free blacks from Brazil and so-called Kaffirs (Port. Cafres) from east Africa, whose presence was sometimes essential to the continuation of a voyage: Chinese, Javanese, and Indians forcibly recruited in the ports of the Indian Ocean.*[9] It may very well be possible for one of these ships to have arrived in America at an early date.

João de Lucena, a 16th century Jesuit priest and chronicler, wrote of the life of St. Francis Xavier. St. Francis was born in Pamplona, Navarra—a name very familiar with the Melungeons—Spain in 1497 as Francisco Jasso Xavier and died in China on Dec. 2, 1552. He served as an evangelist for Portuguese King João III from 1541 until his death. For his work, the Catholic Church later made him a saint. Lucena describes what life was like aboard the ships going to India: ...*what thing is an India nau* [ship] *put to sea on sails with 600, 800 and sometimes more than 1000 inside herself, men, women, little boys, free, slaves, nobles, common people, merchants, soldiers and sea people. Someone that compared it to a large village, was not exaggerating.*[10] Lucena also describes a trip to India in 1531 in a similar manner. It may very well be possible for one of these ships to have arrived in America at an early date.

The story of the Jesuits aboard the vessels on the Indian route between 1541 and 1598 tells us of the main points in the voyages according to Lucena: ...*religious life, distractions, fights, heat, diseases, accidents and presence of women.*[11]

The Azores Connection

The Azores' population was originally partially made up of some people from Flanders. Not only do the Azoreans have common English and Flemish names, there is also an area called the *Bretanha* located in *São Miguel,* the largest of the nine island archipelago. In the north of France there is a province with the same name, Brittany. Foreign surnames are common in the Azores, such as Morrisons, LaBescat, Bettencourt, etc. Also, on Faial Island there is an area called Flamengos which originated with the Flemish from Flanders. Holland, Belgium and France share what used to be called Flanders in Europe.

Portugal's relations with Flanders date from the beginning of the Portuguese monarchy. Teresa, the daughter of the first Portuguese King Afonso Henriques, married the Flemish Count Filipe I and later adopted the name Matilde in her new country.[12] These relations were reinforced into an alliance with Flanders in the 14th and 15th centuries due to the marriage of the Portuguese princess, Isabel of Portugal, to the King of Flanders, Philip the Good. Isabel was the sister of Henry the Navigator. Because Flanders was going through hard times, such as war—death, destruction, hunger and disease, ran rampant. Isabel requested that her brother settle the displaced Flemish in his island ventures, such as on his new found Azores. This was about the mid-15th century, however according to Guill: *A voyage from Portugal to Flanders to obtain settlers was no easy matter....combined Portuguese and Flemish fleet that carried Isabel to Flanders in 1429, left Cascais on October 17, and arrived at Sluis on Christmas day, December 25.*[13]

The Azores were rediscovered on Aug. 14/15, 1432 when the Portuguese arrived at an island later called *Santa Maria*, because it was Saint Maria's day. At that time, Prince Henry ordered sheep and goats released to provide food for later expeditions. Later, Moorish prisoners captured in the Moorean wars were used for work there as well as in the Madeira Islands. Also, settlers from Flanders, Artois and Picardy, sent by Philip the Good, as well as Flemish people, were entering the service of Henry the Navigator. It should be noted that it is not uncommon to find blue eyes and blonde hair among the Azoreans. *União Portuguesa do Estado da California*, Portuguese Union of the State of California, published a book, *Portuguese Immigrants,* which states: *The popular feast of St. Mark, "Festa dos Cornos," celebrated on the 25th of April of each year in Faial and other islands, is another of the few testimonies of the Flemish presence, not to mention the blue eyes and blond hair adorning the Azoreans.*[14]

Dr. James H. Guill, author of the book *A History of the Azores Islands*, knows about the Melungeons, and has for the last 45 years researched every possible aspect of the Azorean people. He maintains that there is a record of a certain captain leaving the Azores to go to the continent to pick up settlers, but one or two voyages never ended. He's of the opinion that some of the Melungeons are descendants of people who came from the Azores. In his book he states that: *...One such voyage to the Azores from Flanders may not have turned north to the islands at the correct time to reach the islands. One voyage may have neared the coast of North America, turned north, and encountered what is now the North Carolina coast. When colonization of this region was begun nearly two centuries later, the colonists encountered a European group calling themselves Melungeons and identifying with the Portuguese.*[15]

The Azores' Portuguese Islands are only 1,200 miles from Newfoundland and less than twicw that from New York. Portugal has the closest European point to the U.S. and Canadá. The Azorean islands of Corvo and Flores are situated at 36° 55' N. latitude—the same as New York—and 24° 46' W. longitude, while the closest point in the United Kingdom or Ireland is at 52° N. latitude and 10° W. longitude. Newfoundland is located at 48° N. latitude and 53° W. longitude. It is not very hard to imagine determined Azoreans reaching North America without much difficulty, planned voluntarily and/or by forces of nature.

As a matter of record, it is known that 50 Portuguese farmers from the Azores were contracted by Pedro Menéndez de Aviles to Florida on January 26, 1573. And on July 13, 1573, 100 more Portuguese farmers followed.[16]

Azores to America in a Small Boat

Not long ago, in 1951, Victor Caetano, a married man living on São Miguel Island was talking to his friend, a single man engaged to be married. He asked him: *Do you want go to America?* The other answered: *When? Tonight? How?*

No! Victor replied: *...in a boat that we are going to build.* So they did, evading the authorities and their families by saying that they were building the boat for someone and being paid for it.

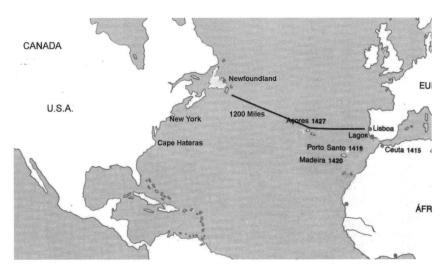

Fig. 107—Map of the North Atlantic showing Portugal on the east and the USA on the west. Notice the distance from the Azores Islands.

The boat was made of cheap lumber and measured approximately 15 feet. When the "vessel" was completed, the two men gathered some provisions and a fishing rod, and set out to sea at 1:00 AM. The following morning, the wife and family went to the police, who in turn set out on a wide search towards the west—the direction of the American coast.

After many hours of searching, they found some signs of boat wreckage and assumed that the two men had drowned. Meanwhile, the adventurers, instead of going west, had gone north, thus avoiding the police. Later they turned west, and after a couple of weeks of rowing and sailing, they were spotted by a Greek cargo ship that offered to rescue them.

They refused, saying: ...*We're going to America*. The Greek Captain informed Portugal, and left them out in the ocean. A few days later a storm hit, damaging the small sail and mast.

By then they were starving and suffering from exposure. Not giving up, they went on, eating raw fish. Already near the U.S. east coast of New England, they were spotted by the Coast Guard, which rescued them. The single man met a cousin and married her, and obtained legal status.

The married man went to Washington, D.C., and made a petition to remain in the U.S. He was refused and was told that he was going to be deported. He said: *You may deport me, but when I get back to the Azores, I will build a bigger boat and return.*[17] After much public interest, he was finally allowed legal status. A mini-series movie was made out of the story and is available on videocassette from Henda Records. The following is the title and description in Portuguese: *O Barco e o Sonho, a partir do conto homónimo de Manuel Ferreira e do depoimento de Victor Caetano. O relato ficcionado das aventuras vividas por dois açorianos que na decada de 50 rumaram num barco à vela em direcção dos Estados Unidos*. The translation in Portuguese: *The Boat and the Dream*, from the story written by Manuel Ferreira, as told by Victor Caetano. He writes about two Azoreans who in the 50's sailed in a boat to the U.S.

Nature has proven that anything put into the North Atlantic Ocean will eventually travel in a clockwise manner. To attest to that fact, just recently Life magazine reported that a bottle covered a distance of 2,286 miles between Massachusetts and the Azores Island of *Terceira*.

Those facts are presented as evidence just to show that it was not hard for any Portuguese person to come to America from the Azores as early as the 15th century.

The favorable winds and currents would bring them in with very little effort on their part, contrary to Admiral Morison's conclusion that it would be unlikely, in the early period of navigation, for boats to reach Newfoundland from the Azores.[18]

Coincidences? Hypothesis?

In the beginning, some questions related to the Melungeons were presented. Not all the answers were found. However, some coincidences shown are hard to ignore. It is up to you, the reader, to draw your own conclusions after evaluating the evidence presented. Here are some facts which point towards Portuguese ancestry as an answer:

1. The origin of the name Melungeon is Portuguese.
2. The Portuguese knew that America existed and where it was.
3. The Melungeons always affirmed that they were Portuguese.
4. The Melungeons had physical characteristics similar to those of the Portuguese.
5. The English considered them Portuguese.
6. The census registered the Melungeons as Portuguese.
7. Declarations by their ancestors pointed to a Portuguese origin.
8. They were considered Portuguese by the courts and the laws.
9. Some of the original names point to a Portuguese origin.
10. Since the Portuguese were emigrating to Africa, Brazil and India, they would also have come to North America.
11. There were regular means of transportation between Portugal, Spain, and the New World.
12. The Melungeons, as well as the Portuguese, were precious metals craftsmen.
13. The Portuguese name survived to our days among the Melungeons.
14. Portuguese farmers were brought in by Pedro Menéndez in 1573.
15. What other modern language has names still in use that are very similar to Melungeon, such as Melungo, Mulango, Malange? Only the Portuguese language has these names still in the dictionary.

Portuguese Ancestry Claims

1. *The older Melungeons always claimed positively that they were Portuguese.*[19]
2. *And yet, no matter how distant their settlements lay from one another, they invariably claimed to be Portuguese.*[20] *I assumed the Melungeons were telling the truth, that is, that they were indeed Portuguese.*[21]
3. *They called themselves Portuguese and were found in the regions mentioned by our first pioneers of civilization there. They must come of some Colony emanating from Portugal.*[22]
4. *The present day Melungeons claim to be of Portuguese descent.*[23]
5. *The most plausible theory seems to be the theory which holds that the Melungeons are of Portuguese extraction. This theory is verified by the Melungeons who from early dates have claimed to be Portuguese.*[24]
6. *Burnett (1889)...who considered themselves of Portuguese extraction.*[25]
7. *Possibly they...descended from Portuguese or Spanish...*[26]
8. *[B]ut when all the racial ethnic theories failed, the people* [Melungeons] *themselves still maintained they were Portuguese.*[27]

The above are just a few examples of the many Portuguese ancestry claims. There are many more. At the time this book is being written, excavations are being conducted by archaeologists who may come up with new discoveries, on a site believed to be the place where Pardo built one of his forts.

Archaeologists and anthropologists may indeed provide many answers. They are in the ground. Time will tell, as long as the "digging" does not stop.

For now, this book may not give solid proof that the major component of the Melungeon people was Portuguese. However, all indications are that the Portuguese were early European settlers, if not the first ones. Although some of the Melungeons may have originated outside Portugal proper, they were Portuguese by nationality. The Melungeons may have come from continental Portugal, the Azores, Madeira, or other Atlantic islands, Africa, Brazil or the Far East. All of these places, or parts of them, were Portuguese territories and under the Portuguese flag.

Before concluding, it is most appropriate to let the reader see an email received by the author from Francisco Antonio Doria, a historian, researcher and genealogist born in Brazil and living in Rio de Janeiro: *We are all mongrels, both in Portugal and in Brazil. A huge melting pot. That's why we have the privilege of being related to Prophet Muhammad (since almost everybody in Portugal is descended from Abunazar Lovesendes, lord of Maya in the 10th century); of being close kin of St. Anthony (through Paio Soares Romeu, in the 12th century) and to many, uncountably many Jews who lived in Portugal from unnamed times on. Oh, of course we have lots of African blood, mixed up with a Berber strain...I look like an Amerindian; my daughter & youngest son are blond. The advantage of being a mongrel is that you can never predict your children's hair color. My mother in law is blue-eyed from Oporto, very white skin; my father used to joke with her and call her Frau Bertha, which of course she didn't understand, as she speaks no language but Portuguese.*

This is the only logical explanation of why the Melungeons are so diverse in physical appearance. Perhaps DNA [**d** (eoxyribo) **n** (ucleic) **a** (cid)] will bring us closer to the truth.

There is still ongoing research on the "Y" chromosome which is passed only from father to son. The population of a South African village that claims ancient Jewish descent has recently been tested. Ten percent of the men tested may descend from a single "Y" chromosome as far back as 3,000 years ago, which according to the Bible is the time period when the prophet Abraham lived.[28]

Portuguese Historians

Professor and author José Hermano Saraiva, Ph.D. is a well known historian and a great communicator who has many books to his credit. He also has a weekly program about the History of Portugal on the Portuguese TV network, RTP. During an interview with the author, and after he read portions of Kennedy's book, Professor Saraiva requested a copy, which Kennedy sent. His final comment was, *it is very important that the subject should be studied.* He leans heavily on the Azores theory, and stated that a number of ships left the islands or the continent and were never again heard from. He also mentioned that in the Azores, Santa Maria Island, Bay of Cré, 150 meters from the Chapel of the Angels, are buried some 16th century cannons that marked the locale where Columbus landed in 1493 when returning from his first voyage. It is also interesting that *Historia Concisa de Portugal,* a book written by Professor Saraiva, has been translated into the Chinese language. He also told the author that no writer has ever attempted to write Columbus' life story prior to his arrival in Portugal, or even while he was in Portugal. That should be done in order to shed more light on his accomplishments, as well as possible earlier navigations.

Professor and author Artur Teodoro de Matos, Ph.D. president (1996) of Damião de Gois Institute at the Torre do Tombo in Lisbon, stated in an interview that he also was interested in the subject, and he recommended that it should be studied further. Professor Matos lived in the Far East for a number of years.

*Fig. 108—Professor
Saraiva and the Author*

Notes

[1] Historia da Civilização Iberica, Oliveira Martins, p. 41.

[2] New Andalucia by Paul E. Hoffman, p. ix.

[3] The Masters and the Slaves by Gilberto Freyre, p. 9.

[4] Ibid, Studies by Emile Béringer of the Climate…Pernambuco.

[5] Correio da Manhã, 2 July 1995, p. 27.

[6] Thorn Birds by Colleen McCullough, pp. 27, 32 (also a movie).

[7] Fomento Rural e Emigração by Oliveira Martins, p. 172.

[8] Historia da Civilização Iberica, Oliveira Martins, p. 270.

[9] Men Under Stress: The Social Environment…the Carreira da India by A.J.R. Russell-Wood, p. 23.

[10] História da vida do Padre Francisco de Xavier by Padre João de Lucena, p. 44.

[11] As Relações de Viagens dos Jesuitas na Carreira das Naus da India by José Wicki, p. 8.

[12] Historia de Portugal by Damião Peres, p. 641.

[13] Azores Islands, A History by James H. Guill, Vol. 5, p. 141.

[14] Portuguese Immigrants by Carlos Almeida, UPEC, p. 1.

[15] Azores Islands, A History by James H. Guill, Vol. 5, p. 141.

[16] N. Brent Kennedy letter to Victor Marques of CNN.

[17] Interview with Mariano Rego from Toronto.

[18] A Future to Inherit by Anderson and Higgs, p. 7.

[19] The Melungeons by Bonnie Ball, p. vi.

[20] The Melungeons by N. Brent Kennedy, pp. 11-12.

[21] Ibid, p. 93.

[22] History of Tennessee by Hale and Merrit, pp. 180, 181.

[23] Smoky Mountain Country by North Callahan, p. 162.

[24] The Treatment of the Melungeon by Jacqueline Daniel Burks, p. 23.

[25] Genetics in the Melungeons…by Pollitzer and Brown, p. 388 (Human Biology, Sept. 1969).

[26] The Melungeons by Jean P. Bible, p. 2 (Martha Collins, Sneedville Bank President).

[27] Atlantis, Dwelling Place of the Gods by Henriette Mertz, p. 58.

[28] 60 Minutes, CBS TV program of April 18th 2000.

Appendix A
Common Surnames, Places and Portinglês[1] Words
(Evidence that may indicate Melungeon and other group connections)
Names Used in the Appalachian Mountains and throughout North America

The following is a list of surnames used by people of Portuguese ancestry, including the Melungeons, and other groups of people that may be connected with the Portuguese. All of these may be coincidental, but are worth considering. Some of them belong to the Santa Elena settlers.[2] Others are the result of the author's literary research and personal interviews.

English/Melungeon	Portuguese	English/Melungeon	Portuguese
A		Barber	Barbeiro
Abreau	Abreu	Barber	Barbosa
Acevedo	Azevedo, Azevada	Barbera	Barbeiro
Adams	Adão	Barbour	Barbeiro
Adkins		Barcelles	Barcelos
Agatha	Agata, Agueda	Barcels	Barcelos
Aguir	Aguiar	Barker	Barqueiro
Alberta	Alberta	Barnes	
Alexander	Alexandre	Barrett	Barreto
Allen	Alem	Barrios	Barros
Allmond	Nogueira	Barry	Barrios
Almeda, Alameda	Almeida	Bass	
Alvas	Alves	Battle Island	Batel
Alvernez	Alvernaz	Bean	Feijão
Amadas	Amada, Almada	Beckler	
Amador	Amador	Bedgood	
Ambrose	Ambrózio	Bell	Bela
Andrada	Andrade	Benavidez	Benevides
Andrew(s)	Andrade, André	Benevedes	Benevides
Antone (1)	Antonio	Benito	Bonito
Aprizio	Aparicio	Bennet	Bernardo
Aquina	Joaquina	Bennet	Bonito
Aragon	Aragão	Bennitt	Bonito
Arauz, Aravio	Araujo	Berberia	Bebereia
Arez, Ares	Aires	Bernal	Bernardo
Arlee, Arleen	Arline	Bernard	Bernardo
Armitta, Arminda	Arminda	Berne	Bernardo
Arude	Arruda	Berry	Morango
Ascucena	Acucena	Bertain	Bertão
Ashworth		Bettencourt	Bethencourt
Athayede	Ataide	Beverly	
August	Augusto	Biana	Viana
Augustina	Agostinho	Biggs	
Ayres	Aires	Blacksmith	Ferreiro
B		Bodge	Borges
Bacalieu (Canada)	Bacalhau	Bollen, Bolin, Bolton	Volta
Badby		Bolling, Boulden	
Bairos	Barros	Boone	
Baldwin	Ballduino	Bordges	Borges

English/Melungeon	Portuguese	English/Melungeon	Portuguese
Borge	Borges	Cardoza	Cardoso
Borling, Bowlen		Carero	Carreiro
Boteilho	Botelho	Carmel	Carmo, Caramelo
Botela	Botelho	Carrico, Carico	Carriço
Bothelo	Botelho	Carrier	Carreiro
Bowling, Bowlin		Carriere, Carrieiro	Carreiro
Bowman		Casar	Casar
Brabosam	Barbosa	Casemero	Casimiro
Bradby		Casteel, Steel	Castilho
Bragans	Bragança	Catania	Caetano
Brager	Braga	Caton	Caetano
Bragg	Braga	Catrina	Catarina
Brandon	Brandão	Catrino	Catarino
Branham		Catten	Caetano
Brass	Brás	Caudill	Caudilho
Braveboy	Bravo	Cayton	Caetano
Braze	Brás	Celia	Celia
Breyner	Breyner	Chambers	Camara
Brier	Silva	Chapman	
Brewington	Census (Portuguese)	Chavis, Chavers	Chaves
Brigman		Chula (Georgia)	Chula
Brogan	Bragança	Cintron	Sintra
Brooks	Ribeiro	Clark	
Brown, Browne	Abrão	Clay	Barros
Brown	Brum	Clement	Clemente
Brun	Brum	Clementine	Clementina
Bruym	Brum	Cloud	
Bulcan	Bulcão	Coal, Cole, Coles	Calero
Bullion	Bulhão	Codeglio	Cordeiro
Bulscamp	Bulcão	Codina	Codinha
Bunch		Coffey	Café
Buran	Beirão	Coit	Couto
Burgess	Borges	Coite	Couto
Burrows	Barros	Coleman	
Burton		Colings	
Bush	Bucho	Colley	
Butler, Buttler, Butters		Collier, Colyer	
Buxton		Collingsworth	
Byrd		Collins	Colina
C		Concealor	
Caldero	Caldeira(o)	Conception (Canada)	Conceição
Calloe	Calhau	Consalues	
Cambra	Camara	Conselah	
Camello	Camilo	Constant	Constantino
Cameron	Camara	Conti	Conde
Camp	Campos	Cook, Cooke	
Campbell		Coone	Cunha
Canara	Canará	Cooper	
Canara	Caneiro(a)	Corea, Corey	Correia
Canary	Canário	Corria, Corry	Correia
Cantal	Quental	Cory, Corey	Correia
Carder, Carter	Carda	Costello	Castelo

English/Melungeon	Portuguese	English/Melungeon	Portuguese
Costmore		Doodes	
Cotman		Doolin	do Lino
Counsellor	Conselheiro	Dorinda	Dorinda
Counts	Condes	Dorton	
Covarelli	Carvalho	Doyle	
Cox, Coxe	Cocho, Coxo	Driggers	Drummond
Cravalho	Carvalho	Driggus, Driggues	Rodrigues
Crémaillière (Canada)	Caramelo	Duart	Duarte
Crews	Cruz	Dungey	Dungue
Criel, Creeley	Criela	Dye	
Cross	Cruz	**E**	
Croston		Eanos, Eanes, Eannes	Enos, Eanes
Crow	Corvo	Edna	Edna
Cubans	Cubano	Efreginia	Virginia
Cumba	Macumba	Elvis	Elvas
Cumbo		Ely	Elias
Cumbow		Emery	Amaral
Curry	Correia	Emmerich	Americo
Custalow	Castelo	Enes, Ennes, Ennis	Eanes, Enos, Ennes
D		Enos	Inácio
Dalton		Epps	
Dambrosio	de Ambrósio	Escubar	Escobar
Damera	de Amaral	Espindola	Espinola
Damin	Damião	Espindula	Espinola
Damos	Dámaso	Espingula	Espinola
Daniels	Daniel	Estevo	Esteves
Dare		Eulalia	Eulalia
Daveiro	de Aveiro	Evans	Ivo
Davilla	de Avila, D'Avila	**F**	
Davis	David	Fabian	Fabião, Fabiano
Day(s)	Dias	Fabritius	Fabricio
Deas	Dias	Facha	Focha
Debrum	de Brum	Fanal, Fanais, Fenais	Fire, beaches
Decost	da Costa	Fantes	Fontes
Dews, deDews	Deus, de Deus	Farilham, Canada	Farelhão
DeFrates	de Frades	Farres, Farris	Ferro
DeFreytas	de Freitas	Felis, Feliso	Félix
Delima	de Lima	Felix	Seles
Delp	Delfim	Fellow	Fialho
Deluz	da Luz	Fellows	Félix
Demello	de Meio	Fereria	Ferreira
Demings	Domingues	Fermeuse, Canada	Formoso
Denham, Denhan	Dinho, Godinho	Ferris, Ferry	Ferreira, Faria
Dennis	Deniz	Fields, Fielder	Campos
Dennis	Dinis	Fields	Fialho
DeRoos	da Rosa, Rose	Figeroid	Figueiredo
Dial, Dial, Dick	Dalia	Figueredo	Figueiredo
Diaz	Dias	Fisher	Ficher
Dimenco	Domingues	Fletcher	
Domings	Domingues	Flora	Florinda
Dominico	Domingos	Florest	Flores
Dondrado	da Andrade	Fontz	Fontes

English/Melungeon	Portuguese	English/Melungeon	Portuguese
Foster	Faustino	Gowin(s), Gowine	
Frager, Frega	Fraga	Gowing, Gown	
Forger	Fraga	Gowne, Gowyn	
Fragouzo	Fragoso	Gowyne, Goyen	
Francis	Francisco	Goyne, Goyenne	
Frates, Fratis	Freitas	Grace	Graça
Fratus, Freates	Freitas	Gracia	Garcia
Frazer	Freitas (5)	Graham	
Freels (Canada)	Frey Luis	Grants	
Freeman		Greaves	Graves
French	Francês	Green, Greene	Verde
Fretard	Freitas	Griffin, Griffie, Griffith	
Fundy (Canada)	Funda	Groom	
G		Grawl, Graul, Growall	
Gallagher	Galego	Guyn, Gwin, Gwinn	
Gallant	Galante	**H**	
Games	Gomes	Haires	Aires
Gann		Hale	
Garland		Hall	Sales
Garrett	Garret	Hambricks	
Gaspari	Gaspar	Hammond	
Gasper	Gaspar	Hanks	
Gawen, Gawne		Harmon	
Gawin		Harris	
George	Jorge	Harvey, Harvie	
Geravazo	Gerevásio	Hatcher	
Gerevas	Gerevásio	Hawkes	
Gerie, Gerry, Jerry	Geraldo, Geraldina	Head	
Gibbens		Helen	Helena
Gibbs		Henas	Ignacio
Gibson, Gipson		Hendrick	Henriques
Gier	Aguiar	Henry	Henriques
Gill	Gil	Herma (3)	Herminia
Goain, Goane	Goeses	Hill Monte	
Goains, Goen, Goene	Gois	Hillman	Ilma
Goan	Goa	Hines	Enos
Goens, Goine, Going	Goes	Hogge	
Goff		Hoimes	Homem
Goings, Goune	Goios	Holloway	
Goins, Goin, Goines	Góis, Goiás	Holmes, Hoimes	Homem, Homen
Gonsaloo	Gonçalo	Homen	Homem
Gonsalos	Gonçalves	Hope	Esperança
Gonsela, Gonsolve	Gonçalo	Hopkins	
Goodman		Howe	
Gormes, Gormus	Gomes	Hunt	
Gorven(s)		Hyatt	
Gouen		**I**	
Gouvea	Gouveia	Ingles	Inglês
Govea, Gouvim	Gouveia, Govio	**J**	
Gowain, Gowans		Jacinth(o)	Jacinto
Gowan, Gowane		Jacintho	Jacinto
Gowen, Gowene		Jacquin	Joaquim

English/Melungeon	Portuguese	English/Melungeon	Portuguese
James	Joackin	Lonzo	Alonso
James	Jaime	Lopes	Lopes
Janes	Yanes (old Port.)	Lorentz	Lourenço
Jaques	Joaquim	Louis	Luis
Jardine	Jardim	Lowry	Louro
Jarvis	Gerevásio	Lucas, Lucus	Lucas
Jason	Jacinto	Lucido	Lucindo
Javier	Xavier	Lucinda	Lucinda
Jerome	Jerônimo	Lula	Lula
Jess	Jacinto, José	Lunardi	Leonardo
Joackin	Joaquim	Lyon	Leão
Joanes	Annes, Eanes	**M**	
Joe King	Joaquim	Maddox	Matos
Johnson		Madruegh	Madruga
Jones		Mae	Mãe
Jordan	Jordão	Mageilan	Magalhães
Joyce		Maggard	Magro
Juditha	Judite	Major	Major
Judy	Juvenalia	Male, Mayle	Mala
K		Maloney	Malhou
Kardoza	Cardoso	Manhan	Manhã
Katen, Katon, Katten	Caetano	Maral	Amaral
Keith, Keyes, Keys	Chaves	Marcial	Maciel, Marcia
Kennedy	Canadei	Marciel	Marcelo
King	Reis	Maciei	Macieira
Kiser		Markes	Marques
Korie	Correia	Marks	Marques
Kuite	Couto, Coito	Marreis	Marisco
L		Marshall, Marsh	Machado
Labrador (Canada)	Lavrador	Martin	Martins
Laborde	Labuto (a)	Mateas	Matias
Lamb	Cordeiro	Mathias	Matias
Langston		Mathews	Mateus
Lasie		Matoza	Moitoso
Lavada	Levada	Matteri	Medeiros
Lawrence	Lourenço	Mattes	Matos, Mattos
Lawson		Mayle	Melo
Lazarus	Lazaro	McCiel	Maciel
Le Blanc		Meadows	Medeiros
Lela	Lila	Mederios	Medeiros
Lema	Lima	Medero	Medeiros
Lenard	Leonardo	Medrows	Medeiros
Levada	de Oliveira	Megre	Magro
Levin	Levinho	Meilow	Meio
Leviner		Mell	Mel
Lewis	Luiz	Melli	Amelia
Light	Luz	Mellow, Mellon	Melo
Limas	Lima	Mendoes	Mendes
Limon	Lima	Meniz	Moniz, Menezes
Linn	Lino	Menze	Mendes
Lisbon	Lisboa	Meyers	Maio
Locklear	LaBescat	Mihil	Miguel

English/Melungeon	Portuguese	English/Melungeon	Portuguese
Milee	Miles	Nursmith	Nascimento
Milier	Meio	**O**	
Miller	Melo	Oak	Carvalho
Millhouse	Meio	Oakes	Carvalho
Millhouse	Azinheira	Oaktree	Carvalho
Minalda	Miralda	Oberia	Iberia
Minard	Minar	Odell	Odelia
Miner	Mineiro	Olive	Oliveira
Miner	Minervina	Oliveaira	Oliveira
Minor	Menor	Oliver	Oliveira
Moitoz	Moitoso	Ormond(e)	Ormonde
Moluccas (Indon.)	Maluco	Orr	
Molungo	Melungo	Osborn	Osverno
Molyns	Molino(a)	Oxendine	
Monez	Moniz	**P**	
Monice	Moniz	Pachao	Paixão
Monize	Moniz	Pacincia	Paciencia
Montero	Monteiro	Page	
Moones	Moniz	Paine	Pena
Moore	Moreno	Paiz	Pais
Moore	Moura	Palacioz	Palacio
Morley		Pareira	Pereira
Morris	Morais	Pariera	Pereira
Morrison	Morrison	Pashotte	Peixoto
Morton	Martinho	Passus	Passos
Motoza	Moitoso	Patrick	Patricio
Mowra	Moura	Patterson	Patrão
Mozingo	Mouzinho	Pavon	Pavão
Mull	Moules	Peacock	Pavão
Mullins	Molino(a)	Peary	Pereira
Munice	Moniz	Perkins	
Munice	Moniz	Perlrins	Pery
Muniz, Moniz	Moniz	Perreira	Pereira
Mure	Moura	Perry	Pereira
Mursh		Perry	Peres, Pires
Myer, Mayer	Maia	Peters	Pita
N		Peters	Pedro
Nash (Nasi for Jews)	Nasce	Pettingalle	Portugal
Navarrah	Navarro(e)	Phelps	Filipe
Nelson	Nelson	Philips	Filipe
Nettie	Neto	Phipps	Filipe
Nevas	Neves	Pidgeon	Pombo
Nevis	Neves	Pimental	Pimentel
Newman		Pinder	Prinder
Niccans	Nicas	Pine	Pinheiro
Nicholas, Nichols	Nicola	Piver	Paiva
Nobriga	Nóbrega	Polly	Paulo
Noel	Noel	Portees, Portes	Portas
Nora	Nora	Portz	Portes, Sasportes
Norager	Nóbrega	Powell	Paulo
Norberg	Nóbrega	Powers	
Norris		Prairie, Prara	Pereira
Noyer	Noia	Prince	Principe

English/Melungeon	Portuguese	English/Melungeon	Portuguese
Pritchard		Sedalia (NC)	Cidalia
Pruitt		Seles	Félix
Q		Semas	Simas
Qates	Aveia	Semerteen	São Martinho
Quail	Coelho	Senram	Serrão
R		Sequira	Sequeira
Race (Canada)	Raso	Sexton	Sacristão
Rames	Ramos	Shavis	Chaves
Ramey	Rama	Shephard, Shepherd	Pastor
Rangel	Rangeis	Shephered	Pastor
Raphael	Rafael	Schire	Xira
Rapoza	Raposo	Shavis	Chaves
Rasnick		Short, Shortt	Curto
Raymund	Raimundo	Silvay	Silveira
Raymus	Ramos	Silver	Silva
Reaves, Reece, Reese	Rios	Sílveria	Silveira
Reposa	Raposo	Silvey	Silva
Revels, Reeves		Silvia	Silva
Reyes, Reies	Reis	Silvia, Sylvia	Silveira
Richardene (4)	Ricarda	Simmons	Simões, Semião
Richards	Ricardo	Simon	Simão
Richardson		Simons	Simas
Ries, Rivers	Reis, Rivas	Sims	Simas
Rivers	Ribeiro	Sizemore	
Roach, Roark	Rocha	Smith	Ferreiro(a)
Robertson, Robinson	Roberto	Smith	Semedo
Roby	Rubim	Snow	Neves
Roche, Roca	Rocha, Roça	Soiza, Souza, Suza	Sousa, Dasouza
Roderick, Roderigo	Rodrigues	Soeza, Soza, Suizer	Sousa, deSousa
Roderick, Rodiriguez	Rodrigues	Solomone	Salomão
Rodgers	Rogério	Spair, Spear (Canada)	Espera
Rodrick	Rodrigues	Spencer	
Rogers	Rodrigues	Springs	Fontes
Rogers	Rogério	St. John Harbor	São João
Rose, Rouze	Rosa	Stallard	
Ross	Roça	Stanley	
Russell, Rossie	Rossa, Russa	Stanton	Eustacio
S		Star	Estrela
Sales	Sales	Statua	Eustacio
Salvadore	Salvador	Steel	Aço, Ferro
Salvo (NC)	Salvo	Stevens	Esteves
Sammons	Simão	Stewart	
Sampson	Sansão	Stitt	
Sands	Areias	Stone	Pedreira, Pedras
Sappers	Serpa	Strother	
Sawyer		Stuve	Esteves
Scares	Sequeira	Sudeley	Sodré
Schmidt	Ferreiro(a)	Suares	Soares
Scott	Chicote	Sumar (Su(o)mer)	Sumares, Somares
Seamas	Simas	Supriano	Cipriano
Sears	Soares	Swartz	Soares
Sears	Soares	Swartz, Sowa	Soares
Secara	Sequeira	Swayze	Soares

English/Melungeon	Portuguese	English/Melungeon	Portuguese
Swears	Soares	Videll	Vidal
Sweat, Sweats, Swett		Viery	Vieira
Swindall		Vincent	Vicente
Sylva	Silva, Sylva	Viola (TN)	Viola
Sylvester	Silvestre	**W**	
Sylvia	Silva	Wager (Wedge)	Cunha
T		Walter	Valtério
Tacheira	Teixeira	Ware	
Tacherra	Teixeira	Washburn	
Tally		Watts	
Tarves, Tarvis	Tavares	Weaver	Uiva
Tash	Teixeira	Wedge	Cunha
Tavare	Tavares	White	Alves
Taveres	Tavares	White	Branco
Tavis	Tavares	Whited	
Taylor		Wilkins	
Teichera	Teixeira	William(s)	Guilherme
Terry	Terra	Williamson	
Teewen	Teves	Willis	
Texeira, Texieira	Teixeira	Wisby	
Thieal	Faial	Wise	
Thomas (2)	Tomaz	Wolf	Lobo
Tobias	Tobias	Wood(s)	Matos, Madeira
Tolliver		**X**	
Tormentine (Canada)	Tormentinha	Xaviel	Xavier
Tosta, Tosti	Toste	**Y**	
Towers	Torres	Young	Novo
Travers	Tavares	**Z**	
Travis	Tavares	Zachery	Zacarias
Trigeiro	Trigueiro	Zina	Zina
Trinidad	Trindade	Zorro	Raposa
Tuppance		Zulema	Zulmira
Turley			
Turner			
U			
Ulveira, Dulveira	Oliveira, de Oliveira		
V			
Valadon	Valadão		
Valentine	Valentim		
Valine	Valim		
Van de Olm	Dulmo		
Vardy, Verry	Vieira		
Vargen	Vargas		
Varum	Varum		
Vass	Vaz		
Vera, Viera, Vierra	Vieira		
Veriato	Viriato		
Verstraeten	Estrada		
Vey	Veigas		
Viator	Vieira		
Vicars, Viccars, Vicker	Vigario		
Vidalia	Vidalia, Vitalia		

(1) Anntoin, Antin, Antoine, Anton, Antone, Antonello, Antoney, Antoni, Antonin, Antonino, Antonius, Antons, Antony, Antuwan, Antwahn, Antwohn, Antwon, Antwuan, Toney, Toni, Tony.

(2) Tam, Tamas, Tamhas, Thom, Toma, Thomason, Thomson, Thompson, Tom, Tomaso, Tomasso, Tomasz, Tome, Tomek, Tomey, Tomie, Tomislaw, Tomkin, Tomlin, Tommaso, Tommey, Tommie, Tommy.

(3) Herminia, Hermione, Erma, Hermia, Hermina, Hermine,

(4) Ricarda, Richanda, Richarda, Richardella, Richardene, Richardette, Richardina, Richardyne, Richel, Richela, Richele, Richella, Richelle, Richenda, Richenza, Richette, Rchia, Richilene, Richina, Richmal, Richmalle.

(5) de Freitas, deFreitas, Fraites, Fratas, Fratus, Fraytas, Fraytus,Freites, Freitaz, Freytas, Freytes, Freytez, Freytus

Translation Table of Names used in this Book
Foreign name chart

Portuguese	English	Spanish	Others
Abade	Abbot		
Afonso		Alfonso	Affonso
Alcacer, Quibir	Alcazarquibir		Ksar el Kibir
Álvares		Alvarez	
Bragança		Braganza	
Cabrilho		Cabrillo	
Canara	Karnatka		Kannara
Castanheda		Castañeda	
Colombo	Columbus	Colon	
Coração	Curaçao		
Diogo		Diego	
Estevão		Esteban	
Fernandes		Fernandez	
Fernando	Fernando	Hernando	Fernão, Ferdinand
Filipe	Phillip	Felipe	
Góis	Goins	Goys	Goes
Gomes		Gomez	
Gonçalves		Gonzalves	
Henrique	Henry	Enrique	Anrique
João, Joa'o	John	Juan	Joam, Yoao
Lisboa	Lisbon	Lisboa	Olissipo
Lopes		Lopez	
Macau	Macao		
Magalhães	Magellan		
Mendes		Menendez	Mendez
Mendonça		Mendonza	
Nunes		Nunez	
Pedro	Peter	Pedro	
Porto	Oporto		
Rodrigues		Rodriguez	
Salsaparrilha	Sarsaparilla	Zarzaparrilla	
Sebastião	Sebastian	Sebastian	
Simão	Simon		
Tejo	Tagus		
Viriato	Viriatus		

Góis

*Fig. 109 —Gois
Family Crest*

DAMIANVS A GOES

Fig. 110—Damião de Gois

Gois, Goios, Goes, Gowens, Goins, Gomes, Goans, Goa

The Góis family was a family of nobles in the Portuguese royal court. The County of Goes is located 135 miles north of Lisbon, and D. Anian Estrada, a lord from Asturias, founded and populated it in the 11th century. Estrada was a friend of Count Henry of Burgundy, the father of Portugal's first king. Asturias was the last Christian kingdom to remain when the Arabs invaded the Iberian Peninsula.

Gonçalo Gois was a knight in the 12th century who fought for the first Portuguese king, Afonso Henriques. Brites de Gois was grandmother of Filipa Perestrelo, the wife of Christopher Colon (Columbus). There were family ties with Columbus which lasted for many generations.

Jorge de Portugal, grandson of Rodrigo Afonso de Melo and Isabel de Meneses, married Isabel Colon de Toledo, Columbus granddaughter.[39]

Another famous Gois was Damião de Gois, written as *Damianvs A Goes* in the 16th century. He was born in Alenquer in 1502 and died in 1574. He was a royal historian, humanist and famous writer who in 1538 married a Dutch noble, Joana Van Hargen; in his time he was one of the very few who had a friendship with Saint Ignatius of Loyola and with Martin Luther—a very unusual combination. Gois was also persecuted by the Inquisition due to his book, which was published in 1541 and banned by the Inquisition. Later he was appointed *guarda-mor* (director) of the Torre do Tombo (Portuguese National Archives).[40] See a contemporary 1546 engraving of Gois on this page. (Biblioteca Nacional, Lisbon, Portugal.)

Bento de Gois was a famous missionary in the 16th century. Goiás or Goyaz is an area of Brazil explored in 1592, mainly because of the existence of gold. Today, Brasilia, the capital of Brazil, and the *Distrito Federal* are located in that region. The capital of the Brazilian State of Goiás is called Goiânia. Some of the many variations of the name Goins were submitted by the Gowens Foundation, for which the author is grateful. According to Edward Price, the name Goins: *...seems to be a peculiar marker of...mixed bloods...Further, Goins is an unusual name; though many whites are named Goins, it occurred with much greater frequency among* *free colored persons in 1830...(2.8 per thousand) than among the population at large in 1790...The Goins name arrived in Virginia as Gowen, one "Tho: Gowen" having been listed as a passenger on the Globe in 1635.*[41]

Price further states that: *...a phenomenon as the Goins family must have a definite story behind it, but has it made its way into the records?* For anyone interested in finding the origin of certain names with possible Azorean connections, the author recommends the book by James H. Guill, *Azores Islands, A History.* It has over 2,000 names with their derivations and family origins.

Portinglês is the language of Portuguese-speaking people in selected English-speaking communities. For the most extensive glossary of Portinglês, or English words as spoken by the Portuguese in America, see *Portinglês* by Adalino Cabral, Ph.D., four volumes, published in 1985 by University Microfilms International, 300 N. Zebb Road, Ann Arbor, MI 48106. This work represents a dissertation for the partial fulfillment of the requirements for the degree of doctor of philosophy.

Also see Leo Pap's *Portuguese American Speech* published in 1949 by Columbia University, New York and the Portuguese Continental Union, Boston, MA.

Portuguese Sounds and a Very Important Name

As stated at the beginning of this appendix, the coincidences are so overwhelming that they should not be ignored. For some they may be farfetched, but for many who lived and still live in the Southeast, these coincidences make sense.

From an academic point of view they may not be accepted, but the many people interviewed would like to see it in print. It has been said that some names may have a Celtic, Irish or English origin.

That may be possible, if one takes into consideration that the Celtic people at one time controlled most of Europe. However, the names or coincidences are very much alive today in Portugal, and have been for hundreds of years, as well as in many parts of the North-American Continent.

The name MAE is rather intriguing, as it has meant "mother" in Portuguese for many centuries. The word in Spanish is *Madre,* and no other language uses this name. The spelling of mother in Portuguese is *Mãe,* or *Mae* without the tilde. An interesting coincidence is related to this name. Many families in the Southeast use the middle name Mae, as in Billy Mae, Lillie Mae, Effie Mae, Ollie Mae, Dollie Mae, Lucy Mae, Mae West, Pearl Bailey Mae, Rita Mae, etc. It is also interesting that these names belong to families that claimed Portuguese ancestry and live in North Carolina, connected or not with the Melungeons. Mae Jamison is the name of the first American of African ancestry to travel in space, and she was born in the Southeast. Another name with a famous connection is Minnie Mae Presley, the grandmother of Elvis Presley.

The author has researched the origins of the word Mãe, and the results are rather unusual. It was found in the following: *Cronica D. João III, Cap. 51-f400,* by

Francisco D'Andrada, 1786, introductory page 363-364; *Lusiadas, Canto IV—26*; *Primeiro Cerco de Diu, Francisco de Andrade, Vol. XI, F 89*; *Cronica do Imperador Clarimundo, Vol. III, Ch. 2—f25. Irmão da Imperatriz sua Mãy.* Evolution of the word by Adriano Capelli in *Dizionario de abbreviature latin ed italiane, Milano 1912.* Also see: *Dicionario Etimologico da Lingua Portuguesa* by José Pedro Machado, Vol. 4, M-P, 3rd. Ed. Livros Horizonte, p. 18.

There is also the theory that the word MAE may have originated in Ireland The author found that not a single Mae surname existed in the Ireland telephone directory. In the United Kingdom, two names were found: Andrew Mae of Spring Groke 32, Thomhill, Cardiff, U.K. and C. Mae of Throston Gnge. Lane 250, Hartlepool, Cleveland, U.K. The source for Ireland was the Enterprise Ireland Phone Directory.

Just a final thought: which word does a baby learn first and forget last? The answer is Mom, Mother, or Mãe in Portuguese.

There are many Portuguese sounds that, when words are combined, can produce the same sound as an English word or name. An old Portuguese lady in her late nineties, still enjoying full mental faculties, has a special way of doing that, since she does not speak English. Only one problem, she sometimes finds a humorous way in the translation, for example, *Kentucky.* She finds it easy to remember if she says in Portuguese *quente aqui* or *hot here*; Cherokee, *cheira aqui;* Cincinnati, *se ensina a ti;* and so on.

Another coincidence in Portuguese sounds was found in Dromgoole's article. This writer, who lived with the Melungeons for a short period to study them, refers to their behavior and a refusal by some people to employ them as servants: ...*their ignorance of defiance of the difference between **meum** and **tuum**...they expect remuneration for the slightest service...*[42]

These are Latin words and mean *mine* and *yours*. In Portuguese they are written very similarly—*meu* and *teu*—and in order to add a nasal sound at the end of the word, the letter m is added. This would be the way an English-speaking person would pronounce *mine* and *yours* in Portuguese. These same words in Spanish are written as *mio* and *tuyo,* which are different.

Why did Dromgoole use Latin words? My understanding is that the writer is referring to a possible selfish attitude: Not knowing the difference between what belongs to them and what belongs to others, which in certain conditions may not be justifiable but may be explainable. These words and sounds may be irrelevant, but other less probable similarities have been used when establishing connections with other groups.

English Surnames and the Name Change Game

One of the first things many immigrants face when arriving in America is a likely change of their name. Columbus is the most famous name change in history. In the books written about the Melungeons, the fact is mentioned that most had English surnames, which is not surprising when one knows that Columbus' real name was, and still is, in the Spanish-speaking world *Colón*. But very few people know him by that name in North America.

The name Colombo in Italian and Portuguese means pigeon, and it is hard to believe that he would be called that. Name change happens and is perpetuated, just like in Columbus' case. Did the name originate in Genoa?

Fig.111—Christopher Columbus' name as written by the Pope, 11

If Genoa was indeed the place of Columbus' birth, it hardly registers on his soul. Nowhere does he refer to the home in which he was born or the way he spent a single moment of his early years. Kirkpatrick Sale wrote: *Nowhere, also, does he use a word or phrase of substance in any Italian dialect including Genoese.* [43] Indeed, it is hard to see how, even assuming Genoese birth, one could really construe Colón as an Italian, if one can even talk about such a thing as Italy in the 15th century. The language he used in writing his letters and papers was Spanish,[44] not Genoese, Italian or Latin. No document was ever found written in Italian, not even the ones he wrote to *Italians* or his personal papers such as expenses, etc.[45] Some less informed writers blame this on the fact that Genoa did not have a written language, and it was for the most part a dialect, or that Columbus could neither read nor write his native language when he left Genoa at 24. One could hardly believe that, since was Genoa one of the most important republics of the Mediterranean. And how could Columbus become the well-educated man portrayed in history? But that is another story. When he arrived in Spain he was considered a Portuguese citizen, and the Spaniards later made him a Spanish citizen—not formally—and his name was forever bound to Portugal and Spain.

Dr. Luciano da Silva, a medical doctor and Portuguese history researcher, has found some very interesting information in Rome: A document written by Pope Alexander VI on the 3rd and 4th days of May, 1493, clearly names Columbus as Colon, and not as Colombo, as shown and provided by Dr. Silva, to whom we owe a great deal for this discovery. The name Columbus is Latin for Colombo. Why would the pope write *Colon* when the primary language of the Catholic church was Latin? And why would

Fig. 112—Christopher Columbus' name as written by the Pope, 31

the Spaniards call him *Colon* if Latin in the 16th century was still a very common language taught in Spanish colleges? Since the Pope was born in Jativa, Spain in 1431, some may give that as the reason, but then why just *Colon*? What about his first name? Why was it written in Latin?

Rui de Pina, a Portuguese writer and contemporary of Columbus, does call him *Christovam Colombo*[46] once in his chronicles, and that is where most Portuguese historians explain or justify his name. However Pina was also known to write what the king liked to read, and Pina did not like Columbus. Did he change his name on purpose? The name Colombo, or pigeon, could be considered derogatory, which would not fit well. The only reason the name Columbus is mentioned is to show how easy it is to change a name, and not to prove that Columbus was or was not Portuguese. According to scholars, there is not enough documentary proof available of his birth place.

Is it possible that the names of the Melungeons were quickly changed by the first English clerks in charge, due to the language, speech, inability to spell, illiteracy? Or the desire to conceal their non-Anglo origin, as still happens in this century with Portuguese and other immigrants? A nickname was and still is very common. Very often the illiterate families were registered by their family nicknames.[47] Another very common way, still in practice, is the naming of a person by his place of birth, origin or length of stay. The name Portugal or Brazil is used as a surname in many Portuguese areas, as well as in Brazil. The surname *Mira,* if one wants to give it a glorious origin, came from *Mira Ceti,* the first variable star, acquiring the Latin name *Miraculous* in the 17th century. However, that may not be the origin. Most persons with the surname Mira trace their origins to a village called Mira, from where most fled after the French Napoleonic invasion of Portugal. The name in Spanish means *look* and it is not regularly used as a surname in Spain.

There is also a common misconception among some scholars that all Latin families name their offspring by a saint's name, which is not always the case.

Anglicizing the names was done not only to be safe, but to survive in a culturally different society, where one must do whatever is necessary. As the proverb goes:

When in Rome, do as the Romans do.

Lisbon, the Capital of Portugal—The name in the USA

There are at least 37 communities in the United States that bear some form of the name of Lisbon, Portugal's city and cultural center. These places are located in 26 eastern states. New York or Lisbon? In 1672, in pirating a 16th century image of Lisbon, a French publisher simply relabeled the streets and landmarks, presenting it as a faithful depiction of New Amsterdam, later called New York City. C. L. Jollain, 1672, Vol. 20, p. 3.

Portuguese Names That May Indicate Melungeon Connections—Canara

Fig. 113—Caneiro village in Portugal.

Many people in the old days took the name of the town as their second name. When the Ourem town historian was interviewed, he did confirm that the little village of Caneiro had a history of people emigrating to the U.S., back as far as the 17th century. Many people carried that name as their surname, and some with that name were interviewed.

This small village is located near the

Fig.114—11ᵗʰ Century Ourem Castle near Caneiro

Castle of Ourem, originally built by the Moors and conquered by the Christians in 1136. Also nearby there is another village called Canhardo. That name can easily sound like Canara in English.

The names Caneiro and Caneira are common in Portugal. There are at least 20 other villages in Portugal with that name, as well as others in Spain, but not as many. It may not have anything to do with the Melungeons, but since they have a tradition of Moorish ancestry, and Portugal is full of stories and legends about the Moors, it is appropriate to mention one of them.

In a town not far from Ourem, called Figueiró dos Vinhos, it is known that as early as the end of the 8ᵗʰ century AD, Guesto Ansures rescued six noble maidens who were being taken by the Moors to Abderrhamen, King of Córdova. Every year 100 girls were sent to swell his harem, in accordance with tribute agreed on with Maregato, the eighth king of Leon. This feat succeeded in breaking forever that infamous pact. Also, one of the most popular stories in Portugal still being told is about the *Princesa Moura Encantada* or enchanted Moorish princess, who would take a man with her to paradise.

Southeast Towns and Portuguese Names

Fig. 115—Sylva in North Carolina

Vidalia, famous for its sweet onions; Vitalia, Lula, Alto, Mendes, near Glenville south of Claxton; Portal near Statesboro, all are in Georgia and are also well known Portuguese names. Dona is another one previously given to today's Blackwater village in Lee County, Virginia. In this area lived a settlement of Melungeons, and it is believed to mean that a large tract of land was given to an heir (female).[48] The name *dona* is a Portuguese noun, and means *owner*. It is also used as a title when addressing an older woman, usually

Fig. 116—Typical sign advertising Country Ham for sale at a roadside in North Carolina.

married or widowed. It originates from the Latin word Domina, meaning "lady of the house." The word is also used in Spain as a title, but not as commonly, and is written as *doña*. The word *owner* in Spanish is written as *dueña*.

Another strange coincidence is the name of a town in the mountains of Western North Carolina in Jackson County, where Portuguese explorers passed as part of the expeditions of Hernando de Soto in 1540 and Juan Pardo in 1567. It is an area where Melungeons used to live, and a traditional Cherokee area. Further inquiry into the town name's history shows it as having originated from a Danish itinerant who passed by in the 1800's. Well that may be so, but the name Sylva is not a Danish name, a fact confirmed by the Danish Embassy in Washington through Arcindo dos Santos, a Portuguese married to a Danish lady. He also informed us that there is not a single Sylva in the telephone book for Copenhagen, the Danish capital. There are, however, a few Silvas, but they are Portuguese families living in Denmark. *Silva* or *silvado* is the Portuguese name for a thorny bramble fruit-bearing bush that gives wild berries, also called multiflorous rose, found in abundance in the same area. It is found in northern temperate regions of both the Old and New Worlds. The farmers took advantage of their rapid spreading and used them as fences to keep animals in and people out.

According to the *Hernando de Soto Commission's* report on the most likely route followed by the Spanish explorer in 1540, a major town named Cale was visited by the expedition, which happens to be in the area of the present-day city Ocala in Florida. The original name of Portugal was *Portus Cale*.[49] Also, one of the original Timucuan related groups was called Cale or Ocale; however some of these names may have been generated by Spaniards or Portuguese, such as the group called a Spanish name, Agua Dulce, or Sweetwater in English.[50]

In all fairness, place names or surnames can be misleading, and one has to be careful when establishing a definite connection.

Foods in the Southeast That May Indicate Portuguese Origin

For many years the author noticed the similarity of foods used in North Carolina to those of his own culture in Portugal, such as turnip greens, collard greens, kale, black-eyed peas, country ham, etc. His wife is the one who brought it to his attention. That prompted him to inquire with the local folk and asked if they knew where this type of food came from. The answer was: ...*the slaves brought it in.* According to sources describing the origin of foods, such as the Encyclopedia Britannica and others, these foods are classified as of Mediterranean origin, and do not grow in hot or tropical climates, as we know all slaves came from.

It is possible that the Spaniards brought some, but their impact in the Southeast was mostly in Florida, and this type of food is not common there. The way country ham is prepared is in much the same way as the Portuguese and the Spaniards prepare it today. Since pork meat is mentioned, let us keep in mind that the Muslims do not eat it and it is also very hard to find it in Turkey, according to a Portuguese industrialist who does business on a regular basis in Turkey. Also, his Turkish customers do not eat pork or their derivatives when visiting Portugal.

It is also very interesting that only in the Southeast U.S. are you able to find a chains of restaurant serving turnip greens with ham and black eye pea salad. The restaurants are the *Cracker Barrel* and the *Black-Eyed Pea,* as well as others less well known. Some of the most popular foods in the Southeast are also part of typical Portuguese eating habits, more so in the countryside than in the city. They are mostly vegetables, easy to grow and take care of. The way turnips and other vegetables are cultivated, and the time of the year—usually planted at the end of the summer—makes them able to survive the first fall frost, providing food for the winter.

Another coincidence mentioned by Lawson, the first historian of North Carolina: *I am not a judge of the different sorts of Quinces, which they call...Portugal...The Chestnut-Tree of Carolina...The Nut is smaller than those from Portugal, but sweeter.*[51] Two typically Portuguese fruits are mentioned here. One is Quince—marmelo in Portuguese—*marmelo* derives from the Latin word melimelus and is produced by a small tree. Its origins are from East Asia and it was brought into the Mediterranean 4,000 years ago. The Greeks attributed a mythological meaning to its flower as the sacred symbol of Aphrodite, the goddess of love. Later the Romans called her Venus. The fruit is mostly used to make marmalade in Portugal, thus its name in English. The question is, if the quince came from East Asia via the Mediterranean, how did it get here at such an early date? Both of these fruits grow wild in milder climates with very little care, and are vital to pioneer survival. If the Portuguese arrived here at an early date, they would find fruits such as the quince and chestnut very similar to the ones found in Portugal. They are not used exclusively by the Portuguese—they are also used by other folks—but it is interesting to note.

Portuguese Food Connection

England and Japan are both fond of deep-fried fish and batter-coated fish: Fish and chips and tempura. Both countries picked up the recipe from Portuguese visitors in the 16th and 17th centuries. The Portuguese merchants introduced tempura to Japan because of their habit of eating fried fish during religious holidays that required abstinence from meat. Deep frying has been the standard for many centuries, and appears in 13th century books. The Portuguese Jews fleeing the Inquisition brought batter-fried fish to England. *Jewish fried fish* was originally served cold. Small fried fish, such as sardines, is still eaten cold in Portugal both in the morning and throughout the day as a snack. President Thomas Jefferson also developed a taste for it. In 1860, Irish immigrants introduced the fried potato to London.

Typically Portuguese Foods

English	Portuguese
Mustard greens, sprouts, broccoli rabe	Grêlos
Turnip greens	Nabiças
Galician cabbage, collard greens, kale	Couve Galega or Portuguesa
Cured, salted country ham	Presunto
Black-eyed pea or cowpea	Feijão Frade
Green peas used in England since 1514	Ervilhas
Chick peas	Grão de bico
Corn meal, grits	Papas de milho
Rabbit	Coelho
Sarsaparilla	Salsaparrilha

Collard Greens—Kale is a non-heading leaf vegetable that is eaten as a cooked green and is an excellent source of minerals and the vitamins A and C. One of the oldest cultivated vegetables, kale closely resembles wild cabbage and may be the ancestor of all the common cabbage crops. It is hardy in cold weather—in fact, its flavor is improved after it has been touched by frost. Kale is grown in the Southern U.S. in every season except summer, and in the North as a spring and fall crop. The reason collard and kale are being mentioned is due to the fact that the Portuguese use them in large quantities. Collard is, however, the one used in what is considered the national soup, called caldo verde or green soup. This soup is made using potatoes, shredded collard, onions, olive oil and one slice of Portuguese sausage or *chouriço*. According to Dr. Luciano da Silva, a physician, this soup prevents cancer of the colon due to its fiber content.

A story related to kale and collard is interesting enough to repeat, and we will leave it up to the reader to draw any conclusions. During a multi-cultural festival in Florida, a Portuguese group—Portuguese-American Cultural Society—was serving their own style of food. However, the ladies selling the food were not able to sell the Portuguese soup, which was being called collard soup. Then one of the Portuguese ladies changed the sign to say kale soup and, amazingly enough, the soup started to sell and it was a success. Why?

Sarsaparilla [52] is one of the roots that the Melungeons used as a tonic. They also gathered it and sold it. It was used as an aromatic flavoring agent to mask the taste of medicines, in root beer and other carbonated beverages. This root is well known in Portugal and Spain, often used as a tea. The spelling in Portuguese is Salsaparrilha and in Spanish, Zarzaparrilla.

Turnip Greens—Turnips originated in middle and eastern Asia, and by cultivation spread throughout the temperate zone. The foliage turnip does not produce an enlarged root, but only a profusion of leaves which are used as a pot-herb. A variety called Seven Top is widely grown in the southern United States. Cultivation started in England in 1724, mostly for feeding stock. Turnips afforded large quantities for winter feeding.[53] Henry R. Price is quoted to have written: *During the summer the Melungeons grow several root crops: turnips and potatoes are favorites.*[54] Bartram wrote that in 1775, Dr. B. S. Barton, vice-president of the American Philosophical Society, told him about the Creek and Cherokee diet: *Turnips, parsnips, salads...they have no knowledge of.*[55]

Of the cultivated greens, collards are probably the most nutritious, though turnip greens are the most popular throughout the region. Kale and mustard greens have their own advocates; preference varies by region, turnips being a hardy biennial plant cultivated both for its fleshy roots and its tender growing tops.

Young turnip roots are used raw in salads or as appetizers, and the young leaves may be cooked and served. The fully grown roots are also cooked and served as whole or mashed vegetables in stews. Also used by the Portuguese is a vegetable called broccoli raab or broccoli rabe—Grêlos in Portuguese. It is a vegetable plant related to the turnip and grown for its pungent leafy shoots. Calcium is plentiful in nature in leafy green vegetables, such as turnips and collard greens, and about 50 Old World species, including Portuguese cabbage.[56]

Turnips in England—After the two Whig factions were reconciled in 1720, Townshend became president of the Privy Council and (in 1721) secretary of state. Townshend earned his nickname Turnip Townshend for his contribution to the development of the use of turnips in crop rotation. Greek and Roman farming techniques are known from contemporary textbooks that have survived, and methods were dictated to some degree by the Mediterranean climate and by the contours of the area. The majority of the crops cultivated today on the Mediterranean coast were known at that time in England, but some were not very popular.

The olive, the vine and fruit trees were grown, as were turnips and radishes. The Arabs had introduced sugar cane and rice to some parts of southern Europe. The voyagers to North America returned with corn (maize), tobacco and the turkey. South America supplied the potato, cocoa, quinine, and some vegetable drugs, while coffee, tea and indigo came from the Orient.

The history of vegetables is imprecise, though familiar types, including the radish, turnip and onion, are known to have been in cultivation from early times.[57]

Corn or Maize, Corn Meal, Stirring Mush, Grits—Corn, a cultigen that was grown in Mexico as early as 5000 B.C., first showed up in the southeastern U.S. at about A.D. 200, but for hundreds of years it was only a minor part of the diet.[58] The Portuguese may have been the first Europeans to recognize its value, and were planting it in Portugal as well as other parts of the globe in the early 16th century. They were the first to bring corn to Europe, and it is on record that it was being planted in 1500 in Portugal and was taken to China in the early 1500's. It is therefore possible that corn meal would have been brought over by the first European settlers, where grits originated.

Black-eyed pea, or cowpea, is one annual plant within the pea family. In other countries they are commonly known as China bean, or black-eyed bean. The plants are believed to be native to India and the Middle East, but in early times they were cultivated in China. In the southern United States, the cowpea or black-eyed pea is grown extensively.[59] In Portuguese they are called friar's beans, because the Jesuit friars brought them from the Far East, according to tradition.

Portuguese Quilting—Quilt

Manta de retalhos in Portuguese is used as a bedcover. I remember it more as a necessity than an art or choice as it is now known in the Southeast.

The author°s aunt, a dressmaker, was constantly asked by the local folk for the small pieces of leftover cloth.

His grandmother used to spend the evenings making a quilt out of these small pieces of cloth, by the light of a kerosene lamp, to be used as a bedcover and to keep everyone warm during the cold winter nights.

Quilting is an ancient tradition, and using a quilt as a bedspread is an extremely old custom, referred to in the earliest written sources, for example, the Bible. It is believed to have originated in the Middle East. In his book, Kennedy mentioned a possible connection between the Melungeons and the Turkish tradition of quilt-making with very elaborate designs.

All that, may not mean anything, but this and other bits of customs or culture that have survived over the years are very interesting and worthwhile to keep in mind.

Music and Folklore Dance in the Southeast—Square Dance—Baile Mandado

There is one type of folk dance that is still being performed in the south of Portugal, and only there, and it is called Baile Mandado. In North America it is a variation of a square dance called out by a singer.

This dance, and variations of it, are very popular, mostly in the Blue Ridge and Appalachian mountains. The similarity is due to the fact that the steps of both dances are called out by a man, usually the director of the group.

The singing calls made by the caller give instructions for couples to perform a variety of movements, and are all based on a smooth, shuffling walk. So far I have not found any other dances in the world performed the same way.

Here's how the square dance came to be. In colonial days, European dances were taught in the cities with figures or movement called spontaneously as the dance progressed.

Although the dancers would have to learn the figures just prior to the dance— taught by the caller—they could be put together by the caller in any sequence on the spot.

This method of dancing provides an interesting and spontaneous competition or challenge between the caller and the dancers, with the caller trying to fool the

Fig. 117—Portuguese Folk Dance Group from Faro, Algarve

dancers—who were daydreaming or flirting—while keeping the dance flowing, and the dancers trying to execute the calls without a break in rhythmic step or motion.[60,61]

The square dance is also said to have derived from the European quadrille—a four-couple square dance—and seems to have been more common during the early 1700's[62] in the Appalachian Mountains. In Portugal it had its origins in Algarve, the south of Portugal. According to the Faro group director, it is also called the mountain quadrille or Quadrilha Montanheira in Portuguese, and it is one of the oldest traditional dances.

The caller in Portuguese is called the mandador, and the dancers are subject to his orders. The quadrille was very fashionable in the late 18th and 19th centuries, and was performed by English aristocrats in 1815, and in elite Parisian ballrooms.[63] The city of Waynesville, located in the mountains of western North Carolina, is the American capital of folklore dance. Every year in July it holds a Folklore Festival—Folkmoot—with the participation of about 12 countries worldwide. In 1994, a group of folklore dancers from Faro in the south of Portugal participated with great success, and again in 1996, another group from the north of Portugal—Grupo Folclorico da Santa Marta do Portuzelo—performed.

By the way, neither the author or his wife was brought up in the U.S. However, they always liked most types of country music. This may be because Portugal has a national song or music style called Fado, meaning fate.

The lyrics tell a story—a sad one most of the times—and it is thought to have derived from the Moors, another reminder of one of the many things that Portugal inherited while occupied by the Arabs for four centuries.

Country music songs tell a folk story and also, most of the time, its a sad one, too. Also, it has been said that Ireland is the origin of country music. If so, that reinforces the fact that the Portuguese and Irish people may have common roots, since both had the Celts as common ancestors.

A Good-bye with Flowers

During this research and while interviewing many Melungeon descendants, they stated that the Melungeon had an old custom with flowers which Jess Stuart mentions: *...It was an old custom to give flowers to a departing guest.*[64] This is also a tradition with the Portuguese which is slowly disappearing. Naturally, one may say that it is also common with other nationalities, but other nationalities may not have so many other shared coincidences.

The Portuguese Water Dog

Without the Portuguese Water Dog in their ancestries, there would be no modern Poodle, no Irish Water Spaniel, no Kerry Blue Terrier, no Labrador Retriever, no Curly Coated Retriever and no Newfoundland...perhaps no Puli. The fisherman's dog left his mark on all these breeds in various ways.[65]

This is quite a statement on behalf of the Portuguese Water Dog. The reader should ask, what does that have to do with The Portuguese Making of America? There are at least two reasons. Most persons who live in the Appalachian Mountains know that mountain people are hunters. Hunting is part of their culture, and when hunting season is on, only that matters—everything else is unimportant.

Dogs are very precious for the hunter and it is known that they pay many thousands of dollars for a single dog because it becomes the most reliable help the hunter can count on. It is also known that one of the dogs Appalachian hunters, including the Melungeons, use most often is the Portuguese water dog, if they can afford one. The following explains why a water dog would be used in the mountains where rivers and lakes are found.

There are many theories of ancestry for these herding dogs. One is that these long coated water dogs grew up with the prehistoric civilizations of shellfish eaters in Portugal and Spain, known as the Iberians. It is a certainty that this breed existed in fishing villages all along the coast of Portugal.

The dog was taught to herd fish into a net. He retrieved lost tackle and nets. The dog also acted as a courier, from boat to boat. Our ancestors were great fisherman. By the middle of the 1300's, they fished off the coasts of Iceland and Newfoundland. These dogs went with the fishermen.. In the fog of these cold climates, the dog rode in the bow of the boat to alert other boats of his position. These dogs assisted the fisherman in every way.

He usually sat in the bow of the boat so that he could see everything. Seeing a school of fish, he would bark. If a fish escaped the net, he would jump into the water to catch it. If sharks were in the vicinity, he refused to jump. The fisherman had learned not to force his dog into the water. And amazingly, the dog knew how to relieve himself on ropes that hung over the side of the boat, standing on three legs or when squatting. Not too long ago the Portuguese Water Dog teetered on the brink of extinction. His traditional employment disappeared and many of his most loyal supporters in his native land died or stopped using dogs.

His comeback is an inspiring success story—a success that came about because enough determined dog fanciers cared about preserving a breed that is fascinating by itself and is also ancestor to an amazing number of our favorite pure breeds.

The dog looks something like a large poodle.

The dogs are black with a round head. Some dogs have white paws, and a few have white chests, but most of the pictures of these pedigree dogs are black. Some have wavy hair, and others curly hair. This dog through the centuries was similar to a hunting dog, except that the Water Dog worked every day of the year. These dogs went out with their owners in very fragile boats, and they surely had a great deal of courage. The dog had to have the instinct to chase and retrieve fish that the fisherman had lost. The dog had to recognize danger—mostly the danger of sharks.

The fishermen knew that when the dog went to the bottom of the boat with his tail between his legs, sharks were near. And when the dog returned to his place of work, this was a signal that the sharks were gone. How did the dogs know sharks were near? They had extremely good vision and probably could smell the sharks. But whatever, the dogs knew when sharks were near.

The dogs were given a daily portion of fish, and were generally well cared for. If a fisherman abused a dog, the dog was given to someone else. On larger vessels, a fisherman could forfeit his salary for a time for mistreating a dog. The older dogs were trained as leader dogs, and on board the vessels they trained the younger dogs. The dog was well paid for his work, dining well on fish.

He had a good place to sleep. Fishermen grew to love their dogs and these dogs became a part of the crew. Some of the other things the dogs could do was to haul the fishing nets as draft dogs. They could carry mail from boat to boat in waterproof pouches.

They guarded the catch when it was being unloaded. When the boats were out of the water, most of the dogs stayed aboard to guard them. While the fishermen mended their nets, these dogs headed to the homes in the village to bring back lunch pails. In the early 20th century the dog's work began to diminish and so did his numbers. Later the dog was only found in the southern province of Algarve. What a wonderful dog! Some of us had ancestors who fished the waters off the coast of Portugal—fished them with these brave dogs.

Another interesting fact about these dogs is that they have webbed feet. Over the years, they've developed a skin between their toes, which helps them swim. These water dogs were dying out until Vasco Bensaude became interested. He lived in Benfica and was already breeding Irish Wolfhounds, Cocker Spaniels and Clumber Spaniels.

He had kennels and employed a kennel master and trainers. Bensaude was told of a magnificent dog owned by a retired fisherman in the Algarve. This dog was called *Leão* and there are various stories as to how Bensaude was able to buy this dog. In time he was able to acquire *Leão*, and the renaissance of the Portuguese Water Dog began. *Leão* soon adapted to his new home, and enjoyed riding in cars.

Every now and then *Leão* would run away and he was found at the home of his former master. In time *Leão* became famous.

He was noted for his intelligence, his affection and his temperamental, almost moody nature. Some people who knew him said he should have been born a human. They said the only problem was that he had four legs and couldn't talk.

He could break ice with his teeth. He would dive even in the winter. He dove for bricks. His favorite water toy, however, was a hard rubber ball.

Leão and a Cocker Spaniel lived together in Vasco Bensaude's home in Lisbon. If the door to a bathroom was left open, *Leão* would walk in, turn on the water faucet in the tub and lie in the water. *Leão* is the dog upon which the standard for Portuguese Water Dogs was based.

He was born in 1931 and died in 1942. He had the title of C.B.—Dual (Working-Trial-Show Champion) *Leão*.

He was buried under a magnolia tree in Soeiros. I believe this is the only breed of dog to have webbed feet. However, German Shorthair Pointers have webbed feet according to Joanne de Oliveira Schechter. Through the Internet, Eloise Cadinha contributed the above information.

The reader is also invited to visit the following websites to obtain more details: www.pwdca.org and www.cpc.pt.

Money in History

Many readers researching their ancestors have requested information on the value and names of the Portuguese currency in times past. The following is just a sample to give an idea of what was like.

Before the present currency called "escudo" the unit was the real (plural reis or reais) and the sign $ was used to separate the thousands. So one real would be written $001 and mil reis (one thousand reis) 1$000.

There was also the "cruzado." Its value was $400 (four hundred reis). After that it came the "tostão" valuing $100 (one hundred reis). For large amounts there was the "conto" meaning "one million" so "one conto de reis" would be 1.000$000 (one million reis). Coroa is 5 "tostões" = 1/2 escudo = 500 réis

After the republic (1910) the real was abolished and it was created the escudo. One escudo equals 1$000 (one thousand reis) and that's why we use the sign $ separating the escudos from the centavos as the escudo was divided in 100 centavos. So 1 tostão was 10 centavos and was written $10.

One escudo (the first was in silver) is 100 réis. Twenty reis is a vintem. "Pataca" is still the currency in Macau and was also in Brazil there was an old silver coin with 320 reis value. A popular expression is still used today "meia pataca" to designate something with no or very little value.

Money values in 1498: Arroba of Sugar (34 lbs.-+) 350 reais.

Salaries in Madeira (1518-1520):

1. Mayor in Funchal 12$000;
2. Councilman: 100$000;
3. Clerk in Calheta: 24$000;
4. Judge in Funchal: 40$000;
5. Vicar in Funchal: 31$100 + 2 arrobas of sugar;
6. Vicar in Ribeira Brava: 7$800;
7. Cathedral Sexton: 5$000;
8. Church Treasurer in Calheta: 2$000;
9. Customs Clerk: 2$000.

In 2002 the Portuguese escudo will be replaced by the Euro, the European currency. Presently in Brazil the currency is the Real, but it was also called in the past Cruzeiro and Cruzado.

Notes

1 Portinglês Dictionary of Words spoken by Portuguese by
   Adalino Cabral, Ph.D.
2 The Melungeons by N. Brent Kennedy, p. 122.
3 Names found in the early enumeration of Melungeon families.
4 Captain Philip Amadas, voyage of 1584, The Roanoke Voyages by David B.
   Quinn, Vol. 1, p. 91.
5 Found in the Azores
6 Common in the Azores Islands, and found on the telephone list of Sneedville,
   where many Melungeons live or lived.
7 Ibid.
8 Ibid.
9 Ibid.
10 Ibid.
11 Ibid.
12 Names found in the early enumeration of Melungeon families; 13 Ibid.
14 Found in the Azores; 15 Ibid.
16 Elvis Presley's family had roots in North Carolina in the early 1800's.
17 Elvas Hall was the name of a Melungeon. Elvas is the name of a large city
   in the south of Portugal, as well as the place where The Gentleman of Elvas,
   the writer of the first book about the Southeast, was born.
18 Names found in the early enumeration of Melungeon families.
19 Caneiro is the name of a village near Ourem, as well as the name of 20 other
   villages in Portugal, and a common surname. Brent Kennedy's great-uncle's
   name was Canara, which when pronounced in English has the same sound
   as in Portuguese.
20 Found in the Azores.
21 Ibid.
22 Names found in the early enumeration of Melungeon families.
23 Found in the Azores.
24 Names found in the early enumeration of Melungeon families.
25 See section under Gois.
26 Found in the Azores
27 Name of a town in Georgia.
28 Names found in the early enumeration of Melungeon families.
29 Found in the Azores.
30 Ibid.
31 Ibid.
32 Ibid.
33 Ibid.
34 Ibid.
35 Ibid.

Notes (Cont.)

[36] Silva or Sylva is a very common name in Portugal, and among the Portuguese in all Portuguese-American communities. It has been on the North-American continent at least since the 1600's.

[37] Gonçalo Silvestre was a soldier and commander—also a noble of the Hernando de Soto expedition in the southeast, including North Carolina.

[38] Vidalia is a town in Georgia famous for its sweet onions.

[39] Azores Islands A History by James H. Guill, Vol. 5, p. 163.

[40] Um Humanista Português, Damião de Gois by Aubrey F. G. Bell, pp. 15-27.

[41] Racial Mixtures in Eastern United States by Edward T. Price, p. 150, Los Angeles S. College

[42] The Malungeons by Will Allen Dromgoole, p. 474 (Arena, 1891).

[43] The Conquest of Paradise by Kirkpatrick Sale, p. 53.

[44] Historia da Civilização Ibérica by Oliveira Martins, p. 247.

[45] Cartografia e Cartógrafos Portugueses dos séculos 15 e 16 by Armando Cortesão, p. 199.

[46] Crónicas d'el Rey D. João II by Rui de Pina, p. 1016.

[47] The Portuguese-Americans by Leo Pap, pp. 206-207.

[48] N. Brent Kennedy, letter to the author.

[49] Atlantis Dwelling place of the Gods by Henriette Mertz, pp. 35-56.

[50] The Forgotten Centuries by Charles Hudson & Carmen Chaves Tesser, p. 28.

[51] A New Voyage to Carolina by John Lawson (Hugh Lefler), p. 107.

[52] The Melungeons by Edward T. Price, p. 4 (Geographical Review, April 1951).

[53] Encyclopedia Britannica, book 22, page 414.

[54] Melungeon Treatment… by Jacqueline Daniel Burks, p. 39.

[55] The Indians of the Southeastern U.S. by John R. Swanton. 1946, p. 286.

[56] Southern Cooking by Bill Neal, p. 79.

[57] Encyclopedia Britannica, 1994 edition.

[58] The Forgotten Centuries by Charles Hudson, p. 7.

[59] Encyclopedia Britannica, 1994 edition.

[60] Southern Appalachian Square Dance by Frank X. Bonner, p. 29.

[61] The Discovery of the Dance by A. S. Barnes, p. 117.

[62] Random House Dictionary, 1983.

[63] Encyclopedia Britannica, 1993.

[64] Daughter of the Legend by Jesse Stuart, p. 226.

[65] The Complete Portuguese Water Dog by Kathryn Braund and Dayanne Farrell Miller.

Part I

In Chapter V, there is a summary of the beginnings of Portugal and the makeup of the Portuguese from the early invaders to the 12th century. Part I of this appendix shows a more detailed description and presents the more important events that affected Portugal and the Portuguese. Part II gives the chronology of events and information available related to the Melungeons after the 15th century, as well as to Portuguese or other groups that may or may not be connected.

The Ancient and Modern World Calendars

Before reading the following chronology, it is appropriate to mention a few words about the dates and the calendar used.

The dates listed, which may not necessarily be correct, are based on the western calendar. Apparently Pope John I asked monk *Dionisio Pequeno* or *Dinosio Exiguo*, who was a specialist in mathematics and astronomy, to calculate the Easter date, in order to end the irregularities of the celebration. During the study he arrived at the conclusion that Jesus Christ would have been born in the year 753 of the Roman calendar, which was used later to establish the Christian era. Based on the Bible, Christ was born when Herod was the king of *Judea*, and *Herod*'s death is calculated in the year 750 of the Roman calendar.

Let us keep in mind that the Christian calendar is also called the Gregorian calendar due to a reform made in the 16th century (1572) by Pope *Gregory XIII*, also famous for *St. Bartholomew's* Massacre of Protestants. This calendar was adopted by all Catholic countries in Europe, and later by others under western influence. The Eastern Orthodox Church did not accept the change and still keeps the Julian calendar for its own calculation of Easter. As for the United States, it was not until 1752 that England and America made the change; therefore all dates of events in the U.S. prior to that are based on the *Julian* calendar, which means that George Washington's birthday, which fell on February 11, 1732, old style, became February 22, 1732, new style.[1]

The Chinese revolution of 1911 brought a reform which introduced the calendar of the West alongside the traditional Chinese calendar. In 1929 the Soviet Union, aiming to dissolve the Christian year, replaced the Gregorian calendar with a revolutionary calendar. The week was to have 5 days, 4 for work, the fifth free, and each month would consist of six weeks. The extra days needed to make up each year's complement of 365 or 366 days would be holidays. By 1940 the Soviet Union had returned to the familiar Gregorian calendar.

The years get rather complicated when you take into account other civilizations. For example, the Jewish calendar that corresponds to the Christian year of 2001 is 5761, changing to 5761 on September 18. With all the scientific advances, the Jewish people know that this is arbitrary, as it was instituted between 200 and 600 AD, and it was thought to correspond to the creation of the world as described in the Bible approximately 4,000 years before.

The Islamic year in 2000 is 1420 of the Muslim era, changing to a new year in May. The new year is based on new phases of the moon and starts when Mohammed, the founder of the Islamic religion, ran away from Mecca to Medina in the actual Saudi Arabia, which was in the year 622 of the Christian era. (An Islamic year has only 354 or 355 days, compared to the Gregorian year's 365 or 366 days.)

While in most of the world it is 2000, the Chinese are living in the year 4697 under the sign of the Golden Dragon, and will change again between January 21 and February 21 to the year 4698. The Chinese new year is celebrated during the second new moon, and is not associated with any special cultural event. It is only an indication of the number of years since they decided to officially keep track of the count. The lunar Chinese year is divided into 12 months of 29 or 30 days and adjusted to the solar year, with the introduction of another six months cyclically.[2]

The seven day week dates back to Roman times and remains a proving witness to the early powers of astrology. The days are named after the planets as they were known in Rome 2,000 years ago. English and Italian: Sunday (Sun, Domenica); Monday (Moon, Lunedi); Tuesday (Mars, Martedi); Wednesday (Mercury, Mercolodi); Thursday (Jupiter, Giovedi); Friday (Venus, Venerdi) and Saturday (Saturn, Sabato).

When people tried to extinguish ancient idolatry, they replaced the planetary names with simple numbers. So the Quakers call their days First Day, Second Day and so on up to the Seventh Day. In modern Israel, too, the days of the week are given ordinal numbers, and the only other country in Europe and the world to use a similar method is Portugal, with the exception of Sunday and Saturday which they kept as the ancient Domenica and Sabbath.

The most common date abbreviations used are: BC for Before Christ and AD for Anno Domini (Year of the Lord), however non-Christians also use CE as Common Era and BCE as Before the Common Era.

Summary of Facts in Chronological Order
Related to Portuguese History before the Christian Common Era[3]

40,000   *Homo Sapiens* emerges from the Neanderthal man.[4]

27,000   Child's skeleton found in Leiria, Portugal.

18,000   Paintings and engravings made in rocks, rupestrian style in Foz Coa. See the book by Antonio Faustino de Carvalho, Côa Valley, Rock Art.

15,000   Paleolithic cultures in western Portugal.

4000   Iberians, the name given to a people that inhabited the Iberian Peninsula, is a name of Greek origin, which along with Algarve (Arabic), and Sephardic (Judaic) means *land of the West.*

3200   First writing: Sumerians keep records in cuneiform symbols on clay tablets.

2750   Tyre is founded by mariners on the east coast of the Mediterranean and begins its rise as a great Phoenician sea power. The Greek historian Heredotus will say in 450 B.C. that Tyre was founded 2,300 years ago.

1424   Egyptian king Thutmose IV forms alliances with Babylon and leads military expeditions into Phoenicia.

1000   Phoenicians, Greeks, Carthaginians.

814   Carthage is founded in North Africa by refugee Phoenician colonists.

776   Greek's first recorded Olympic Games.

700   Phoenician colonists plant olive trees in the Iberian Peninsula. Celtic migrations begin.

698   Greek colonization of the Mediterranean. In the next two centuries they will be motivated primarily by a need to find new sources of food as Greece's population expands.

600   Celtic people settle on the Iberian Peninsula and form the Celtiberians. Not long ago, similar signs of Celtic culture could be found in both Portuguese and Irish fishing villages.

562   The Phoenician city Tyre falls to Nebuchadnezzar II after a 16 month siege.

520   Phoenician city island of Tyre has a population of 25,000; Old Tyre on the mainland is even larger.

418   Athenian forces crush Carthage.

408   *Orestes* by Euripides, who continues the theme of his 413 B.C. tragedy *Electra by Sophocles;* Euripides dies two years later in Macedonia at the age of 77.

300   Carthage in North Africa gains economic ascendancy in the Mediterranean by trading in slaves and silver from the Iberian Peninsula. Celtiberians inhabit an area around the Tagus River. Today, the Portuguese capital Lisbon is located where this river meets the Atlantic Ocean.

280   The king of Syria loses control of Phoenicia to Macedonian's Ptolemy II.

195   Celtiberians submit to Romans; total submission in 133 B.C. However, Viriato and his successor Sertorio, the first Portuguese heroes, fought lengthy battles against several Roman generals.

161 Lusitania, a Roman province, approximately comprised the area that is now Portugal. The Roman Galba, vexed by the bravery of the Lusitanians— natives of Portugal—ordered the massacre of 30,000. One of the survivors, Viriato, led a revolt against Rome and defeated five Roman generals in succession, forcing the last one to sign a peace treaty.
Some historians stated that the war between the Lusitanos and the Romans lasted from 153 B.C. and 80 B.C., with Viriato followed by Sertorio, who at one time took refuge in Mauritania.

AD or Christian Era, also known as CE, Common Era

146 After a long blockade, Carthage falls to Roman legions led by Scipio Aemilianus in six days and nights of house-to-house fighting. Some 900 Roman deserters torch the Temple of Aesculapius and choose death by fire rather than execution.
Hasdrubal surrenders his garrison, and his wife contemptuously throws herself and her children into the flames of the temple. The city's ashes are plowed under, its environs become the Roman province of Africa and the Third Punic War is ended.

409 Suevis-Suebis settle in the north of Portugal and form a kingdom with the Portuguese city of Braga as their capital. The Allans invade the Iberian Peninsula and settle in the center of Portugal. The Vandals also invade and settle in the north of Portugal and the south of Spain. Later the Suevis occupy the center of Portugal, forming with the Visigoths the two independent kingdoms of the Iberian Peninsula, till A.D. 585 when the Visigoths dominate the entire peninsula.

416 More Visigoths invade the Iberian Peninsula and one group settles in the center of Spain.

439 October 29—Carthage falls to the Vandals, who have been led by Genseric. He makes Carthage his capital.

448 Suevi King Rechiar comes to the throne as a Catholic.

456 Suevis attack the Romans in Tarraconensis but are defeated by the Visigoths under Theodoric II, as described by the Bishop Hydatius of Chaves, a Portuguese city. This was the end of the Suevic kingdom.

The Islamic Era
Portugal from the 6ᵗʰ Century to the 16ᵗʰ Century

622   Mohammed goes from Mecca to Medina in modern Saudi Arabia after having received revelations later recorded in the Koran.To the north: the Suevi Kingdom; to the south and east: the West Gothic Kingdom. From 622 AD to 700 AD, this same kingdom governed the area where Portugal is today located, as well as part of Spain.

697   Carthage is destroyed by the Arabs, ending Byzantine rule in North Africa forever.

711   North African Arabs, Moors and Berbers invade the Iberian Peninsula.

739   The reconquest of the Iberian Peninsula begins, due to the expansion of the kingdom of Asturias and its union with the Cantabric kingdom.

755   Political constitution of the County of Leon; independence of the Arabs; independence of Navarre.

757   Kingdom of Asturias under Alphonso I began the reconquest of the Iberian Peninsula from the Arabs.

863   Separation and independence of the County of Galicia.

885   Galicia submits again to Leon.

967   Independent County of Castile is formed.

1073   Alphonso VI of Leon conquers Castile.

1099   Death of El Cid. Rodrigo Diaz de Bivar, or Rui Dias de Bivar, married Jimena Dias de Las Asturias. Her family later took the name Meneses, as an Azorean family.[5]

1109   The County of Portugal is formed and given to Henry of Bologne. In this same year the kingdom of Aragon absorbs the kingdoms of Leon and Castile.

1143   Constitution of the Portuguese monarchy and foundation of the Kingdom of Portugal.

1147   Santarem and Lisbon are reconquered from the Moors by the Portuguese. May 23—Portuguese ships sailed for Brittany in France for the Crusades.

1180   First naval battle won by the Portuguese against the Berbers.

1250   Portugal expels the last Arab settlement from Portugal.

1254   Seeding of the Leiria forest by King Dinis. It was already being planned to build boats, looking out to sea. Later, this forest provided the lumber to build the caravels of discovery. Later, King Dinis authorized merchants to create an insurance exchange due to maritime development in Portugal.

1276   Portuguese friar Pedro Julião is elected pope and is named João XXI.

1291   The Genoese Vivaldi brothers attempt to reach the wealth of India by crossing the Atlantic. The attempt fails and the Vivaldis are lost at sea.

1308   Commercial treaty between Portugal and England.

1311   Extinction of the Order of the Templars and creation of the Order of Christ. This would have an effect on Portuguese discovery, as Prince Henry would later be given this order and its wealth.

1314   King Dinis nominates Nuno Fernandes Cogominho as admiral-in-chief. On his death, King Dinis called the Genoese Emanuel Pezagno to organize and command the royal fleet. He stayed in Portugal and his family—the *Peçanhas*—held the title of Admiral of Portugal for generations.

1325   King Dinis dies and King Afonso IV becomes king of Portugal.

1336   Canary Islands expedition ordered by the Portuguese king. They show up on the chart drawn by Angelino Dalorto, Dulcorot or Dulcert. These islands proved to be of extreme importance for later navigation, including Columbus' first voyage to America. In a letter, King Afonso IV claims Portugal's right to the Canaries.

1346   The Catalan Jaume Ferrer attempts a voyage along the African coast and fails to return, another example of the difficulties encountered by Mediterranean sailors to navigate the Atlantic.

1357   King Afonso IV dies and Pedro I is crowned king of Portugal.

1367   King Pedro I dies and is succeeded by Fernando.

1372   Treaty between the king of Portugal and the duke of Lancaster. The following year this treaty is confirmed by the kings of Portugal and England as the Treaty of Westminster.

1383 Portuguese win a decisive victory against Castille in the famous battle of Aljubarrota, where 5,000 Portuguese defeated the Castilian army of 30,000, and affirm their nationality.

1386 Alliance between England and Portugal. Portugal has the oldest alliance in the world with England, which dates back to May 9th 1386, and is known as the Treaty of Windsor. The following year, King João I marries Filipa, daughter of the duke of Lancaster.

1394 Henry the Navigator is born on March 4th in the city of Porto.

Portugal and the World in the 15th and 16th Centuries
Conquests and Discoveries

1415 August 21st—Portuguese conquer Ceuta in Morocco, and a new vessel called *the barinel* was used for the first time.

1417 Madeira Islands, off North Africa's Atlantic coast, may have been visited by Arabs and others. By 1419 Portuguese navigators João Gonçalves Zarco, Tristão Vaz Teixeira and Bartolomeu Teixeira landed there.

1419 Prince Pedro embarks on what appears to be a voyage of tourism; however it was a secret mission to obtain information for his brother Henry the Navigator, which he later uses on his voyages of discovery.

1422 Caesar's era ends and Christian era begins.

1425 Portugal wrests the Canary Islands from Castile. Settlement of the Madeira Islands begins. Sugar cane from Sicily and vines from Cyprus are planted.

1427 Azores' possible early date of discovery by Diogo de Silves.

1432 Azores Islands rediscovered August 14, 1432 by Gonçalo Velho Cabral.

1433 King João I dies and his son Duarte succeeds him. Africa's Cape Bojador, south of the Canary Islands, is rounded by Portuguese navigator Gil Eanes.

1437 Portuguese are defeated by the Moors when trying to conquer Tangiers in Morocco. Prince Fernando is kept prisoner and dies there while awaiting the ransom demanded by Sala-ben-Sala.

1438 King Duarte dies and Prince Afonso, his heir, is still a child. Prince Pedro assumes the regency of the kingdom till 1446, when King Afonso V takes over the government of Portugal. He marries Prince Pedro's daughter in 1447.

1443   African slaves are introduced into Portugal, sold to Portuguese explorers in exchange for goods, by other blacks. The black brokers became the major traders.

1444   Portuguese explorer Nuno Tristão reaches Senegal.

1445   Portuguese explorer Diniz Dias rounds Cape Verde and 25 caravels per year trade between Africa and Portugal.

1448   Possible birth of Cristóbal Colón (Christopher Columbus).

1449   Prince Pedro, brother of Henry the Navigator, falls victim to the intrigue and the ambitions of the ducal house of Braganza. He may have been responsible for valuable information gathered while traveling throughout Europe and given to Henry.

1450   Flemish nobleman Josue Van den Berg, who served under Prince Henry, begins to colonize Terceira Island, Azores.[7]

1452   Diogo de Teive may have visited Newfoundland, as written in 1571 by Fernando Colombo, Christopher Columbus' son, in Venice.

1453   The Turks (Ottoman Empire) conquer Constantinople (modern Istanbul). This event marks the end of the Byzantine Empire and of the European crusades against Islam. Coffee is also introduced by the Turks.

1456   Diogo Gomes arrives at Guinea-Bissau, on the East African coast, and sugar from Madeira reaches Bristol, giving many Englishmen their first taste of the sweetener.

1458   Portuguese conquer Alcacer Seguer in Morocco.

1460   Henry the Navigator dies in Sagres on November 13.

1462   Portuguese begin settlement of Santiago Island, Cape Verde, with blacks from Guinea and Moors from Morocco.

1471   Tangiers and Arzile in northwest Africa fall to the Portuguese, who have earlier taken Casablanca. Tangiers is given to England in the 17th century as the dowry of Portuguese Princess Catherine of Braganza when she marries English King Charles II.

1472   Portuguese navigator Fernão Pó discovers the Islands of São Tomé, Prince, Cameroon off the West African coast.

1475-6 Columbus arrives in Portugal[10] when he is approximately 24 or 25 years old, fifty years after the Portuguese initiated the conquest of the Atlantic. To understand his isolated adventure, it is important to be aware of the geographic discoveries made by the Portuguese between 1419 and 1542, from the Atlantic isles to Japan.

Sugar from Madeira is exported to Europe in large quantities as news arrives from France in this and in following years.

1479 Columbus marries the Portuguese lady Filipa Moniz de Perestrelo, daughter of the navigator Bartolomeu Perestrelo.[11] He lived ten years in Portugal. His mother-in-law gives him charts and other documents that belonged to her late husband. He also travels the Portuguese routes to Guinea and the western Atlantic, gathering information about Portuguese discoveries. Birth of Diogo Colón in Madeira, Columbus's son.

1481 King Afonso V dies and João II is proclaimed as king.

1480 Convention between Castile and Portugal on how to treat the Berbers and the Moors.

1482-3 Portuguese in Malange, Africa. Diogo Cão's expedition, ordered by King João II, discovers most of Angola, including the area of Malange.[12]

1483 Martin Luther is born on November 10. He later inspires the reform of Christianity in the 16th century against the Catholic Church.

1484 Portuguese explorer Diogo Cão discovers the Congo River in West Africa. Inquisition is established in Castile.

1484-6 Columbus leaves Portugal to go to Spain and offers his services to the Spanish monarchs, after the Portuguese King João II turned him down. When he arrives in Castile, he is considered Portuguese. It is recorded that he was more fluent in Portuguese than he was in Castilian. In 1486 the Portuguese occupy Azamour in Morocco.

1487 Portuguese navigator Bartolomeu Dias rounds Africa's southern tip, later called the Cape of Good Hope.

1488 Fernando Colón, son of Columbus and a Spanish woman, is born in Córdova. King João II sends an enigmatic letter to Columbus in Spain, promising him that he would be welcome and his services recognized.

1489 The Portuguese king renews the alliance with the British, reconfirming the Treaty of Windsor.

1490 Portuguese explorers convert the Congo Empire to Christianity.

1492 The Catholic monarchs complete the unification of Spain by conquering Granada, the last Islamic kingdom on the Iberian Peninsula. The Jews are expelled from Spain. German Behaim, a resident of Portugal, builds his famous globe on which he registers the progress of Portuguese discoveries.

1495 King João II dies and Manuel, the duke of Beja, is crowned king of Portugal.

1496 Expulsion from Spain of Moors and Jews who refuse Baptism.

1497 After 10 years of inactivity, the Portuguese start their exploratory trips again. This period was used to carefully study all the knowledge obtained until then as to winds and currents. The years following the voyages were carefully planned and had preassigned destinations. In July, Vasco da Gama sails from Lisbon on the way to India.

1498 Portuguese explorer-scientist Duarte Pacheco Pereira is sent on a secret expedition and touches the South American coast. This information is later used by the Portuguese to send Pedro Álvares Cabral and officially discover Brazil in 1500. Portuguese navigator Vasco da Gama discovers the sea route to India, establishing a trade route between Europe and India, bypassing the Venetian middlemen.

1499 Spanish navigators Alonso de Ojeda, Diego de Lepe and Vicente Yanes Pinzón, with Amerigo Vespucci, sail the northern coast of South America while working for Spain. Already in Brazilian territory, they found a cross, presumably left there by Duarte Pacheco Pereira.

1500 Rediscovery of Brazil by Portuguese navigator Pedro Álvares Gouveia, later known as Cabral. The date of the first discovery was kept secret due to the negotiated treaties with Spain.

1501 Portugal sends a fleet to help Venice against the Turks,[14] and in 1502 corn is planted in Portugal for the first time.

1503 Fernando de Noronha discovers the islands that later receive his name.

1505 Sri Lanka (Ceylon), off the coast of India, is discovered by the Portuguese Lourenço d'Almeida.

1506 Tristão da Cunha, Portuguese navigator, finds islands in the south Atlantic that will later bear his name.

1507   Portuguese colonize Mozambique in East Africa, where the word *Melungo* appears to have originated. The Portuguese capture Zafi in Morocco and begin commerce in captive Moors, Berbers and Jews. Many were women, all are called white slaves. Almeida da Cunha discovers Madagascar.

1509   Portuguese explorer Diogo Álvares Correia establishes the first European settlement in Brazil near Porto Seguro.

1511   First Portuguese expedition to the Pacific and Malacca.

1512   A Portuguese caravel reaches Guangzhou (Canton). The first European ship lands in China. Diogo Garcia discovers *Rio da Prata.*

1514   Green peas come into use in England.

1516   Duarte Coelho discovers Cochin China (modern Vietnam) and Fernão Peres de Andrade arrives in China.

1517   Fernão Andrade and Tomé Pires land in China, and the Portuguese plant maize there.

1518   Portuguese King Manuel I requests the pope to elevate the Congo Prince D. Henrique to bishop of Utica. He becomes the first black Christian Bishop.

1521   King Manuel I dies, and João III succeeds him. Princess Isabel of Portugal marries Carlos V of Spain.

1522   Magellan's ships and crews return to Seville after accomplishing the first circumnavigation of the world.

1524   Probable birthdate of the Portuguese poet, Luis Vaz de Camões, writer of the epic poem, *The Lusiads.* Vasco da Gama dies and is buried in Cochin, India. The first book published in India is published in Cochin in 1577, while under Portuguese rule.

1526   The first English ships explore the African Guinea coast.

1529   Chinese orange is introduced to Europe by Portuguese.

1530   Plan to colonize Brazil by the Portuguese.

1531   Earthquake in Lisbon. Papal request to establish the Inquisition in Portugal.

1536   Pedro Nunes (1502-1578), a Portuguese mathematician, invents the nonius for graduating instruments, used by Pierre Vernier in 1631 and by William Oughtred in 1630 for the slide rule, a primitive analog computer. Oceans navigation treaty signed between France and Portugal. Inquisition is put into operation in Portugal, more than three centuries after it was established in France, Aragon and northern Italy.[18] First *auto de fé* occurs in 1540.

1542-3 Lourenço Marques discovers bay and river in East Africa that later receive his name, which changes to Maputo after Mozambique's independence.

1543   Portuguese Antonio Peixoto, Antonio da Mota and Francisco Zeimoto are the first Europeans to arrive in Japan. Princess Maria of Portugal marries Prince Felipe, future King Felipe I of Spain.

1544   Fernão Mendes Pinto discovers and names Formosa (Taiwan).

1547   A law is passed in Portugal to register every ship going to Brazil.

1549   Settlement of São Salvador, Baía, Brazil.

1550's Mass emigration from the island of São Tomé to Brazil.

1553   Turks siege Ormuz, a Portuguese territory in India.

1556   Founding of Portuguese settlements in Japan.[19]

1557   King João III dies and his grandson Sebastião succeeds him. The peninsula of Macau, off the China coast near Hong Kong, is ceded by China and later settled by Portuguese.

1558   A Portuguese caravel is sent from Seville and in 1558 is captured by the French when returning from Peru with 100,000 gold and silver ducats.

1559   The first executions in an *auto de fé* took place in Seville.

1564   William Shakespeare is born. Later he is associated with the term "Elizabethan language."

1566   Great plague in many Portuguese cities causes thousands of deaths.[20]

1567   Portugal approves a law that forbids new Christians to leave for overseas territories or colonies.

1568   The Portuguese ambassador in London, England, presents a complaint against clandestine English navigation in overseas territories.

1570 City of Nagasaki is founded in Japan by Portuguese seeking a harbor for their ships.

1571 Oct. 7—The Battle of Lepanto, in the Gulf of LePanto near Corinth, ends in defeat for an Ottoman fleet of 240 galleys.

1572 The epic poem *The Lusiads* by Luis de Camões is published.
Massacre of Protestants in Paris on St. Bartholomew's Day.
Pope Gregory XIII asked the Jesuit Clavius to examine calendar proposals.
In February 1582 he wrote the papal bull for the Gregorian calendar, which made slight changes to the Julian calendar..

1576 French pirates attack Santa Maria Island, Azores.
Brazilian population reaches 57,000.

1577 Renewed law to forbid new Christians—recent converts to Catholicism—to leave for the colonies.

1578-9 August 4—Portugal's King Sebastião is killed and his army annihilated at Alcacer Quibir in northwest Africa. Luis Vaz de Camões, the greatest Portuguese poet, dies on June 10.

1580 Union of the Portuguese and Spanish crowns. Felipe II of Spain becomes Filipe I of Portugal. He is the son of Princess Isabel of Portugal and the grandson of the Portuguese king Manuel I. Felipe II of Spain is also the son of Emperor Carlos V of Austria and Germany.

1582 Catholic Europe adopts the Gregorian calendar, which was ten days behind the Julian calendar.

1583 Francis Drake attacks Brazil.

1587 Francis Drake attacks the Portuguese province of Algarve in the south, sacks and burns Sagres.
February 8—Catholic Mary Queen of Scots is executed.

1588 May 27—Felipe II, king of Castile, invades England to terminate Elizabeth I's reign.[21] The fleet of 200 ships and 20,000 soldiers leaves Lisbon, Portugal. Many Portuguese soldiers and ships are forced to participate, since Portugal was governed at that time by the king of Spain. The Portuguese people pay a very high price for this defeat, since their soldiers and ships took a larger and disproportionate part in this Armada. On July 30, the Spanish Invincible Armada is defeated, a turning point in Elizabethan England. English privateers attack Brazilian ports.

1589   Drake attacks Lisbon and fails. England tries to free Portugal from Spain. João da Gama sails from Macau, China, across the Pacific, making the first recorded voyage by a Portuguese ship.

1594-5   Englishman Francis Drake attacks and sacks the Brazilian city of Recife.

1598   King Felipe II of Spain dies and is succeeded by Felipe III.

1601   Manuel Godinho de Heredia, born in Portuguese East India of a Portuguese father and an Indian mother, claims to have discovered Australia.

1617   Moors attack Porto Santo, one of the Madeira Islands, and capture almost all of the population.

1622   Turks (Persians) unite with the English against the Portuguese and capture the city of Ormuz. Moors and Turks raid the Algarve coast.

1640   Dec. 1—Portugal regains total independence from Spain.

1646   William Shakespeare dies on April 23.

1654   Portugal recovers the Brazilian territory held by the Dutch.

1660   Portuguese navigators sail from Japan to Lisbon by way of the Arctic.

1662   May 31—Catherine of Braganza, daughter of Portuguese King João IV, marries Charles II of England.

1697   July 18—Portuguese missionary Antonio Vieira dies, aged 88 years old.

1717   Portuguese fleet, at the request of pope Clement XI, defends Venice and Corfu against a Turkish armada, defeating it, thus preventing it from becoming part of the Ottoman Empire.

1752   Great Britain adopts the new style Gregorian Calendar; Sweden adopts it in 1753.

1755   Earthquake in Lisbon destroys the city and kills thousands.

1807   November—Napoleon invades Portugal. The Portuguese royal family flees to Brazil.

1814   French Napoleon's armed forces are expelled from Portugal.

1822   Sept. 7—Brazil declares independence from Portugal by Portuguese Prince Pedro, later called Emperor Pedro I. Independence is achieved almost peacefully, as the result of his father Prince João, later Portuguese King João VI, having moved to Brazil after Portugal was invaded by the Napoleonic army. When Prince João arrived he forms the united kingdom of Portugal and Brazil.

Part II
European Settlers, Melungeons and other Groups
Chronology in North America—Early Explorations of North America

The history of the North American continent is still under study. Revelations made by two archaeologists at a 1999 conference in Santa Fé, New Mexico, shed some light onto what may have been the earliest European settlers to North America. Before proceeding with the chronology of the Portuguese presence in North America, it may be worth considering the following contribution received in 1999 from Lionel Holmes, an author from California: According to a report by the Associated Press, the first inhabitants of this continent may have crossed the Atlantic Ocean more than 18,000 years ago from Europe's Iberian Peninsula. This is at odds with the the long-held notion the continent's first settlers came across a land bridge from Asia to Alaska some 13,500 years ago. Since this is a radical departure from what is known, it is of value to present it herein with a rather long explanation.

Two prominent archeologists, Dennis Stanford and Bruce Bradley, say North America's first inhabitants may have crossed the icy Atlantic Ocean some 18,000 years ago from Europe's Iberian Peninsula (now Spain, Portugal, and Southwestern France). Belonging to a group known as the Solutreans, these pre-modern explorers are believed to have originally settled the Eastern Seaboard, according to the researchers. Over the next six millennia, their hunting and gathering culture may have spread as far as the American deserts and Canadian tundra, and perhaps into South America.

According to the AP's Joseph B. Verrengia, this new theory clouds the Asian Land Bridge theory. Archeologists say some nomads almost certainly made their way into Alaska and found an ice-free highway via the land bridge down into the continent some 13,500 years ago. Their culture has been named Clovis for their distinctive weapons that have been found in digs nationwide. Clovis points are among the oldest tools discovered in North America, and have often been found with the remains of Ice Age animals. The Clovis people attached these points to lances or spears and probably hunted animals in groups.

Stanford and Bradley concede the Solutreans may not have been the only paleo-explorers to reach the Western Hemisphere. But judging by their distinctive style of projectile points and other clues in the archeological record, they may have been the first settlers who brought to North America what, until now, has been considered the Clovis culture. "There is very little in Clovis—in fact, nothing—that is not found in Solutrea," said Stanford, who is anthropology curator at the Smithsonian Institution. "Their blades are virtually indistinguishable." Stanford and Bradley, an independent researcher from Cortez, Colorado, offered their stunning reinterpretation of the standard settlement theory at the archeology conference in Santa Fe. The meeting was devoted to re-examining Clovis research seven decades after it was accepted as historical bedrock.

Other scientists say the Solutrean alternative is such a radical departure that it might take years to adequately evaluate. Stanford and Bradley's new explanation, they noted, is based primarily on comparisons of projectile points and other artifacts already discovered on both sides of the Atlantic. No unequivocal Solutrean settlement remains have been found in North America, they said. Researchers who believe Clovis and the Bering Sea land-bridge theory is outdated point to sites at Monte Verde, Chile as well as Pennsylvania, Virginia and South Carolina as being settled in 12,500 BC to 16,000 BC. But Clovis defenders say many artifacts from those digs are so crude that they may be rocks that have broken naturally rather than actual stone tools fashioned by prehistoric hands.

Still, observers said, the older Solutrean projectile points from Europe and the more recent Clovis points from the Americas closely resemble each other. That's what makes the new "Out of Iberia" theory so tantalizing. "There is no question about it," Kent State University archeologist Kenneth Tankersley said. "There are only two places in the world and two times that this technology appears—Solutrean and Clovis." How seafaring Solutreans could have arrived in North America is unknown. Based on his knowledge of modern native cultures above the Arctic Circle, Stanford said it is not farfetched to imagine Solutreans sailing to the New World in skin boats. With a strong current and favorable weather, the trip might have taken as little as three weeks, he calculated. By this time in prehistory, he said, South Pacific islanders had been sailing open waters for at least 20,000 years.

Additionally, no one has proven that the Irish Brendan Monks of 8th century Ireland did not sail in a series of voyages in ox hide covered boats to the "promised land." Or that his ancient navigation documents in Latin were just a legend. In 1976, Irish exploring expert Tim Severin researched and duplicated the voyage with National Geographic support. As documented in the 1976 book "The Brendan Voyage" by Tim Severin, they proved that Brendan's ships could have made a series of such trips, eventually landing on the shores of North America. We ask scholars to take a look at the possibility of either the Irish or "others" making it here by the 15-16th centuries.

1000   Calusa, a tribe of 20,000 hunters, mound building Indians in Florida, were the third most numerous after the Timucuans and Appalachees. The name Miami originates with the Calusa "Mayaimi."

1424   Chart of Zuanne Pizzigano. There is cartographic evidence that the Portuguese were in Newfoundland before August 22nd 1424, according to the Venetian cartographer and his nautical chart.[6] This map is part of a collection of 60,000 old and rare manuscripts belonging to Sir Thomas Phillips of London.

1448-81 Portuguese-Danish expeditions. Portuguese King D. Afonso V and the Danish King Christian I of Denmark and Norway agree to make joint expeditions to the West between 1448 and 1481.

1467   Columbus sees America at 16. Famous Norwegian historian and seafarer Thor Heyerdhal claimed that Columbus first arrived in America in 1467 and not 1492, while traveling with a Danish-Portuguese expedition to Greenland as a teenage crew member.[8] See 1448.

1470-2 João Vaz Corte Real, possible presence in Newfoundland.[9]

1473 Álvaro Martins Homem, possible presence in Newfoundland.

1474 João Vaz Corte Real makes a voyage to the "Land of the Cod Fish" and the younger Corte Real explores the coast of Labrador.

1484 Possible voyage of Columbus to the Antilles for Portugal. Death of Columbus' wife Filipa Moniz Perestrelo.

1492 In October, Columbus arrives on the Antilles island of Watling—Saint Salvador—thus discovering America. Pedro de Barcelos and João Fernandes Labrador, sailing from the Azores, discovered a peninsula on the northeast coast of North America which they named Labrador. They also explored the east coast of Canada in the same area.

1493 Feb. 13—Columbus stops in the Azores Islands on his return to Spain from America, and then went to Lisbon on March 4th. The Portuguese were the first to know of his discovery.
May 4—Pope Alexander VI establishes a line of demarcation between Portugal and Spain for dominion over the lands discovered. West of the line belongs to Spain and East of the line belongs to Portugal.

1494 The Treaty of Tordesilles, signed in June, divides the globe between Spain and Portugal as established in the previous year by Pope Alexander VI, giving Portugal almost 1,000 more miles to the west.

1494 To 1500, Gaspar Corte Real goes to Newfoundland to look for his father who disappeared on a previous trip. On one of these trips, Gaspar contoured the coast of Florida.

1496 Columbus returns to Spain without managing to find India. He has exhausted his human and material resources. Doubts are beginning to set in about him and his plans.

1497 Between the years 1497 and 1692, a total of 806 ships left Portugal, and of these, only 425 returned. This was the activity registered.[13] June 24—John Cabot, born Giovanno Caboto in Genoa, of Venetian citizenship, reaches Labrador and Nova Scotia, returning to Lisbon, Portugal, on August 6. No records exist for these voyages.

1498 John Cabot and his son Sebastian coast Newfoundland and Nova Scotia; no records were kept. Possible voyages to Greenland and the North Atlantic by João Fernandes Lavrador, a Portuguese from the Azores.

1500-25 Portuguese vessels on voyages to or from India and Brazil are shipwrecked or lost at unknown sites. At least 11 of them are recorded. Some of the caravels carried complete families.

1500   Columbus is arrested and sent back to Spain. He still is able to make another voyage at his own expense in 1502-1504. Gaspar Corte Real, a Portuguese navigator, makes the first authenticated European landing on the northern continent of the Western Hemisphere.

1502   Miguel Corte Real goes to the northeast coast of North America to look for his brother Gaspar. He does not return, but left an inscription on Dighton Rock.[15] See 1511. Also, Cape Race, Newfoundland, is shown on a Portuguese chart as *Cabo Raso*. Alberto Cantino map clearly shows Greenland and North America as well as the Florida peninsula.

1507   Christopher Columbus dies.

1510   European explorers probe the east coast of North America to a point north of Savannah.

1511   Miguel Corte Real may have left a message on Dighton Rock, with this date and the Portuguese coat of arms, according to declarations in 1926 by Professor Delabarre of Brown University.

1512   The Newfoundland cod banks provide fish for Portuguese, English, French and Dutch vessels, which dry the catch there for shipment back to Europe.

1513   Ponce de Leon rediscovers Florida while looking for the Fountain of Youth.

1519   The dollar has its origin in the "thaler" minted in Bohemia. Fernão de Magalhães (Magellan), who has accomplished many expeditions for the Portuguese king Manuel I, both in Africa and the Orient, leaves Portugal to offer his services to Spain.

1520   Magellan, a Portuguese navigator working for Spain, rounds the straits of the southern tip of South America and stops in Guam, Marianas Isles. Álvaro Fernandes, also a Portuguese, is on Pánfilo de Narvaéz's expedition to the coast of Mexico.

1521   Aleixo Garcia crosses the South American continent from the Atlantic to Paraguay before many famed explorers. He is killed by the Indians in 1525. The colony of St. Peters in Nova Scotia, Canada, is founded by Portuguese fishermen and João Fagundes de Viana. There are eight Portuguese in the Spanish forces when Hernan Cortez conquers the Aztec capital, future Mexico City.

1524-5 Estevão Gomes, a Portuguese navigator who took part in the Magellan expedition, is chartered by Emperor Carlos V to find a northwest passage to India, but fails. He does, however, explore the east coast of North America from Florida to Newfoundland, including Chesapeake Bay. There are maps in the archives of Seville showing the entire U.S. East Coast with that date and his name. He also discovers Manhattan, New York and the Hudson River. Henry Hudson is credited with its discovery in 1609.

1526 July—the Ayllon fleet departs from Spain with six ships carrying some 500 souls: men, women, children, soldiers, priests and the first black slaves to reach American shores. Many ships are lost and only 150 people return.[22] Lucas Vásquez de Ayllón leads the first settlement attempt on the South Carolina coast.

1527 English ship sails along the coast from Labrador to Florida and the West Indies, but nothing follows.[16] French ships sail in Mozambican waters, East Africa, where the name Melungeon or Melungo is used by the black people when calling whites.

1528 Pánfilo de Narvaéz lands at Tampa Bay with 400 men.[23]

1533 French pirates in Brazil. Portuguese pilot Martim da Costa, working for the Spanish fleet of Fernando de Grialva, discovers lower California.[17]

1539-40 Hernando de Soto, the Spanish *conquistador,* lands at Tampa Bay with 600 men—many of them Portuguese—in ten ships. He was probably the first European to enter southern Appalachia. Fernando Colon, Columbus' son, dies. The narratives he wrote about his father will be referred to later by many historians.

1540 The Gentleman of Elvas writes a book about the Southeast. The well known and cited book, *Gentleman of Elvas,* is written by Álvaro Fernandes, a Portuguese nobleman who joined the Hernando de Soto expedition along with 30 other Portuguese.

1541 May 21—Hernando de Soto dies and is buried in the Mississippi. The survivors make it to Mexico, including a few Portuguese .

1542/3 September 28—California is discovered by the Portuguese navigator João Rodrigues Cabrilho, working for Spain. Antonio Correa, another Portuguese, is Cabrilho's shipmaster.[24] João Caetano, a Portuguese navigator working for Spain, may have discovered some of the Hawaiian Islands.

1544   A copy of the book written by the Portuguese Gentleman of Elvas arrives in Spain, the first book about the American Southeast.

1545   Brazil's first confirmed export of sugar. Luis de Góis is the first to take tobacco leaves to Europe. Jean Nicot, the French ambassador in Lisbon, takes a few leaves to France. The word *nicotine* derives from the ambassador's family name.

1550's   It was told to the Englishman in 1584 that a Spanish ship had, in fact, been wrecked on the Outer Banks and some of her men rescued by the Secotian Indians. The survivors had patched two boats together from the wreck and set southward, but shortly afterward the boats were found cast away along the shore and it was presumed that all drowned.[25]

1555   Possible discovery of the Hawaiian Islands by João Caetano, a Portuguese working for Spain. History names Captain John Cook as the discoverer in 1778.

1557   The Gentleman of Elvas' book is published in the Portuguese city of Évora. That year or before, copies found their way to London, England, and to Spain.[26]

1558   Henrique Garcês, a Portuguese from Porto, discovers mercury in Peru, increasing production of silver greatly.

1559   Spanish colonists arrive in South Carolina and try to settle. Two years later they are forced to leave.

1560   Simão Fernandes, a Portuguese pilot, navigates the East Coast, Virginia and the Carolinas as part of a Spanish expedition.

1562   French Protestants called Huguenots land near Jacksonville, Florida.

1563   Regular maritime routes are established between America and the Indies, with many unregistered Portuguese ships from Lisbon and Algarve.

1565   The Spanish establish St. Augustine in Florida and Menéndez is given the right to bring 500 Negro slaves to Florida.

1566   Early in the year, Menéndez builds a fort on Parris Island, the first of four that would stand there, and the first structure of Santa Elena. In July, a troop of 250 men under Captain Juan Pardo arrives from Spain.[27]

1567   Juan Pardo reaches the Tennessee Valley. Sergeant Hernando Moyano de Morales writes a letter to Santa Elena.

1568   March 2—Pardo returns to Santa Elena, bringing sacks filled with sorely needed corn and a description of the interior as good for bread and wine and all kinds of livestock. That hope brings settlers to Santa Elena. January 26—Spanish permit Portuguese Seaman Juan Fernández de Cea (João Fernandes de Ceia) to sail to Florida and dig for treasure.

1569   Two caravels unload 193 emigrants, farmers and their families. By October, the little capital—Santa Elena—numbers 327 souls.

1570   A Spanish mission to Chesapeake Bay ends when an Indian convert leads an attack.

1578-9   Simão Fernandes serves as a master under Raleigh in the *Falcon*, as an experienced pilot.[28]

1581   Spain's King Felipe II sends black slaves to his Florida colony of St. Augustine. They are the first blacks to land in North America.

1584   July—Simão Fernandes, a Portuguese navigator, leads an expedition to North America under the command of Philip Amadas and Arthur Barlowe. The first colonists arrive in Roanoke, Virginia.[29] This colony is named after England's virgin queen.

1585   Raleigh sends a new expedition to Virginia under the command of his cousin, Sir Richard Grenville. Colonel Ralph Lane leads the expedition, with John White and Thomas Harriot having special responsibilities. Simão Fernandes is the chief pilot and master of the ship that leaves 107 men at the colony.[30] Drake's armada sails from Plymouth on September 12, with 25 ships and 2,300 soldiers and mariners. He attacks Vigo in Spain, the island of Santiago in Portuguese Cape Verde.

1586   May 28—Drake sacks and burns St. Augustine. Drake arrives in Roanoke and may have deposited slaves previously released from Cartagena and Santo Domingo: Turks, blacks, etc. A few days later he departs with the colonists.

1587   John White lands 150 settlers, including 17 women, in the Virginia colony—what later is to be called the lost Roanoke Colony. *All contact with the Lost Colonists…is lacking from 1587 to at least 1603* (15 years).[31]

1607   May 14—Jamestown, Virginia is founded by colonists from England under Captain John Smith. After three years, only 150 of the 900 survived. American history refers to Jamestown as the first colony of European settlers. It is assumed that the settlers planted tobacco and had the first slaves in North America, which actually only happened after 1619.[32] A fire almost destroyed the settlement and later it had to be abandoned. The last population census of 1624 showed 183 persons.

1609   Translation of the Elvas book, written by the Portuguese Álvaro Fernandes, the Gentleman of Elvas. This book is published in London under a different title, as an incentive to English discovery and an aid to *our enterprise on foot* namely the settlement of Virginia. Two years later it is reissued.

1611   Authorized (King James I) version of the Bible is published. The original English used (Elizabethan) is still being spoken today in the Appalachian Mountains area.

1619   The first 20 black slaves arrive in the Virginia colony, brought over by a Dutch privateer for sale, *who are now wonderfully encreased.*[33]

1620   November 11/21—after a voyage of 65 days, the *Mayflower* arrives in Cap Cod and anchors in Provincetown with more than 100 passengers. These are English Puritans, Pilgrims from Holland, where they had gone in 1607. They established the first permanent New England colony on Plymouth Bay, 37 miles (60 km) southeast of Boston.

1625   Second translation, in English, of the book written about the Southeast travels of Hernando de Soto, by the Portuguese Gentleman of Elvas.

1626   Manhattan is purchased from the Indians for 60 guilders. (24 US$).

1642   Jews sail from Holland to Brazil.

1643   Isaac Jogues, a French Jesuit missionary visiting New Amsterdam, says he heard 18 languages spoken in that seaport town, which probably included Hebrew, Mediterranean and North African dialects and a small settlement of Sephardic Jews.

1649   Black laborers in Virginia colony still number about 300.

1654   First encounters with Melungeons. French and English explorers in the Southern Appalachians reported encounters with dark-skinned, brown- and blue-eyed, European-featured people.

1663 Founding of what would later be called the State of North Carolina. English King Charles II issues a charter that establishes Carolina as a proprietary colony.[34] The northern part of the Carolina colony is known as Albemarle until 1691, when it is renamed North Carolina. Parts of this state will later form the State of Tennessee, which after the American Revolution caused serious problems for the State of South Carolina.

1664 New Amsterdam is taken from the Dutch by 300 English soldiers and becomes New York.

1669 John Lederer leads an expedition across the Piedmont plateau to ascend the Blue Ridge Mountains, followed by more in 1670. In one of those expeditions he reports a town of bearded men.

1671 Small English party penetrates the Ohio River watershed beyond the Blue Ridge Mountains. A man named Portugal works for Thomas Wood. Black population in Virginia is less than 5%. By 1715 it will be 24%.

1673 April 1673 to August 22, 1674—White, hairy people wearing clothes and performing a Catholic religious ritual are found by James Needham and Gabriel Arthur.[35]

1683 An English shipwreck off the Africa east coast will contribute to exploration of the region. A Portuguese survivor of a wreck 42 years earlier is met. He was married to an Amapondo woman.

1685 Translation and printing of the book by the Gentleman of Elvas into French, and then translated back into English in 1686 and reissued in 1687, 1699.[36]

1700 Boston ships 50,000 quintals of dried cod fish to market, most to Bilbao, Porto and Lisboa.

1701 Louisiana becomes a province of Spain.

1705 Virginia act declares *who shall not bear office in this country*, no Negro, Mulatto or Indian.[37]

1709-45 John Lawson encounters a people that he calls the Hatteras Indians—later called the Lumbees, that are different from the other Indians. Lawson is told legends about their ancestors from the coast of North Carolina. Among the families he encounters, many of them are of *Portuguese* origin, according to their legends.

1712 North Carolina and South Carolina formed by a division of the Carolina Colony, founded in 1663.

1716   A company of Virginia colonists crosses the Blue Ridge Mountains under the leadership of Alexander Spotswood.

1718   Great Scots-Irish immigration to America begins.

1733   Savannah, Georgia—Sephardim Portuguese Jews and others build a synagogue, the third oldest in the U.S., using a Gothic architectural style.

1740-1810 Height of slave trade: 60,000 Africans a year are enslaved and shipped to the Americas.

1745   April 26th—a land grant of 100,000 acres is made to *John Robinson...*[38] *...They were rich, dark, and said to be Portuguese.*[39]

1750   March 5/6—Dr. Thomas Walker sets out on his tour of the land to be surveyed with companions and finds a possible route used by the Melungeons to the East Tennessee Mountains, the Cumberland Gap.[40]

1751   Benjamin Franklin discovers the electrical nature of lightning.

1763   Spain trades Florida to England for Cuba. British splits La Florida into colonies of East and West Florida.

1767   Daniel Boone is on his way to Kentucky through the Cumberland Gap.

1769   Virginia's colonists defy King George III's decree of 1763 and establish the first pioneer settlement at Watauga, in upper east Tennessee.[41]

1773   December—Boston Tea Party. Colonists demand independence.

1776   Declaration of Independence is signed on July 4, followed by the American Revolution.

1782   Spanish forces complete their conquest of Florida from the British.

1783   Florida is given back to Spain by England under the Versailles Treaty. Portugal recognizes U.S. Independence and signs friendship treaty.

1784   John Sevier organizes State of Franklin and finds a dark-skinned, reddish-brown complexioned people supposedly of Moorish descent, who are neither Indian or Negro, but have fine European features, and claim to be Portuguese.[42]

1789   George Washington is elected the first U.S. President, to govern until 1797. North Carolina cedes the territories to a state later called Tennessee.

1790   Census takers' guide says: *Identify all free whites over the age of 16 and slaves.* This may have been the beginning of the term FPC—Free Persons of Color. They try to identify people such as the Melungeons.[43]

1794   Founding of the City of Toronto in Ontario, Canada. Portuguese would have been part of it.

1795   Spain creates Florida's current boundaries. National census shows that there are 973 free persons who were neither white, Indian nor black.

1796   The State of Tennessee is founded from the failed State of Franklin. Melungeon people have already been established there.
Translation to Dutch of the Portuguese book by the Gentleman of Elvas.

1797   Tradition of a strange white race preceding the Cherokee in Tennessee.[44]

1803   The United States purchases the Louisiana Territory from Napoleon.

1807   Melungeons with names like Lucas, Osborne and Moore may have come into southwest Virginia.

1809/12 New printing of the book by the Gentleman of Elvas.

1810   Jacob Mooney arrives in Baxter County, Arkansas, with four dark-skinned men assisting him, who could not be categorized as Negro, Indian, or white. They are simply *Lungeons.*[45]

1814   João Elliot d'Castro becomes secretary to the king of Hawaii.

1819   Spain sells Florida to the U.S. under the Transcontinental Treaty.

1820   Building of the aqueduct Roanoke Canal by a group called Portuguese.

1834   Citizenship Rights—The Tennessee Constitution states that only free white men 21 and over can vote and bear arms. This could easily exclude the Melungeons and other groups not considered white at a given time and place.[46] John A. McKinney, of Hawkins County, is chairman of the Committee of the Constitutional Convention, and declares that a *free person of color,* if it meant anything, meant Melungeon.[47]

1835   Citizenship Rights—The North Carolina Constitution amendment to the previous one of 1776, states that: *no free negro, free mulatto, or free person of mixed blood descending from Negro ancestors to the 4th generation shall vote for the Senate or the House of Commons.*
1835-1842 Second Seminole war in Florida

1840   Oct. 7—*The Whig*, Tennessee newspaper, mentions *Melungeons*.

1845   Florida is admitted to the Union as the 27th State.

1846-50   New printing of the book by the Gentleman of Elvas.

1848   September 6—*Knoxville Register* article mentions the *Melungens*.

1849   March 31—Littell's Living Age reprints the same article.

1859   Col. John Netherland's efforts restore the citizenship of the Melungeon people and he runs for Governor.

1860   Jupiter Lighthouse, oldest landmark in Palm Beach County, Florida.

1861   Abraham Lincoln is elected President and the Civil War begins in April. Through 1865 the Civil War devastates Florida: of 15,000 soldiers, one-third die.

1872   The Celebrated Melungeon Case—Phoenicians, Carthaginians and Portuguese. Judge Lewis Shepherd writes in his memoirs that the Melungeons descended from the Phoenicians, Carthaginians and Portuguese, or descendants of them from the southern coast of Portugal.

1877   St. Anthony Portuguese Benevolent Society is formed in Hawaii.

1884   New printing of the book by the Gentleman of Elvas, and again in 1890.[48]

1886   New printing of the book by the Gentleman of Elvas in New York by Buckingham Smith.[49]

1885   Discriminatory Law—If a white man wants to marry a dark girl he can get a license, but a dark man cannot get a license to marry a white girl. That is much more difficult.

1887   *History of East Tennessee*—This book discusses Newman's Ridge and the people who occupied it.[50]

1888   Ethnologist James Mooney writes about a strange white race preceding the Cherokee in the Tennessee area. Mooney corresponds with McDonald Furman in South Carolina about the Redbones and his interest in their heritage.[51]

1889 Swan M. Burnett writes *Notes on the Melungeons.*[52] April 13 or June 13—*Boston Traveler* article about the Melungeons.

1891 Will Allen Dromgoole writes about *The Malungeons*. This derogatory report leaves a legacy that the Melungeons have to endure for many years to come.[53]

1897 May 25th, The Melungeons by McDonald Furman. Furman Collection, SC Library.

1899 *American Anthropologist*, vol. 2, publishes *A note on the Melungeons.*

1904-5 New printing of the book by the Gentleman of Elvas in New York and in London.

1912 January 12—*Arkansas Gazette*, article by Mrs. Eliza N. Heiskell, of Memphis about the Melungeons. October 12—*Nashville Banner* article about the Melungeons. December—*The Melungeons* by Paul Converse, *Southern Collegian*. Col. W. A. Henderson, president of the Tennessee Historical Society and member of the Tennessee bar, gives a description of the Melungeons.

1913 *History of Tennessee and Tennesseans* by W. T. Hale and Dixon L. Merritt is published, describing the Melungeons.

1915 Judge Lewis publishes his memoirs.[54] The Celebrated Melungeon Case that took place in 1872 garnered wide public interest, especially after Judge Shepherd published his autobiography, which described his involvement in a judicial process related to the romantic case of a Melungeon family and their descendants.
North Carolina Supreme Court holds hearings on the case: Croaton Indian School of Pembroke, N.C. vs. Three Goins Families regarding Indian qualifications for school admission. Melungeon, Redbone and Croaton Indian names appeared for these citizens of North and South Carolina in the late 1800's who might want entrance to this school.[55]

1922 New printing in New York of the book by the Gentleman of Elvas.

1923 North Carolina State House of Representatives and Senate, General Assembly pass a law stating "*...that the people known as Portuguese shall have a separate school from the white and colored schools...*"
July 29—*The Knoxville Journal and Tribune* publishes a Melungeon article titled: *Melungeons, Mystery Race...after South Carolina Hegira.*

1924   August 3—*Nashville Banner*, Melungeon article by Douglas Anderson
Virginia enacts the racial integrity law, known as the one blood drop law.

1925   The General Assembly of the State of North Carolina enacts a law
permitting *the people known as Portuguese to register themselves as
Portuguese* on the voter registration books.

1929   Portuguese Indian—Mary Killen Hollyfield, descendant of Betsy Reeves,
remembers that in 1929, the Reeves were known as having come from
Portugal.

1933   New English translation by James Robertson of the book written by the
Portuguese Gentleman of Elvas.

1936   June 21—*Chattanooga Sunday Times-Magazine*, Melungeon article.
Congress creates a seven-member Hernando de Soto Expedition
Commission. *Final report of the Swanton Commission* by John R. Swanton
of Smithsonian Anthropology was largely based on the book titled *The
narrative of a Gentleman of Elvas*.

1937   August 22—*Nashville Banner* publishes "Lost Tribes of Tennessee
Mountain" by James Aswell.

1939   N.L. Turner is nominated superintendent of Northhampton County Schools,
NC, including the Bethany School in Gaston, a separate school for
Portuguese. *Tennessee Guide*, NY—*The Melungeons in Oakdale*, p. 362.

1940   Legacy from Dr. W. A. Plecker. There were only two classes of people,
white (northern European) and "Colored" (those with 1/16 or more black,
Indian, Asian, or southern European heritage). Dec. 1—*Louisville Courier*,
Melungeons article by Woodson Knight.

1941   Miss Osceola T. Crew, a teacher, is appointed by the Northhampton School
superintendent to teach grades one through eight at the Portuguese School
in Gaston as "mission work." James Aswell publishes book *God Bless the
Devil*, Melungeon stories.

1942   Mrs. John Trotwod Moore, Virginia state librarian and archivist, writes a
letter to Dr. W. A. Plecker that refers to early settlers in South Carolina
who migrated from Portugal about the time of the Revolutionary War and
later moved to Tennessee.[56]

1944   May—*America's Mysterious Race* by Bonnie Ball (Read).

1945   July 29—*Baltimore Sun* publishes article by L.F. Addington, "Mountain Melungeons." April—*Southern Literary Messenger* publishes *Who are the Melungeons. American Journal of Sociology* includes the article "Goins and Melungeons," Vol. 51.

1947   October 18—*Saturday Evening Post*, "Sons of the Legend."

1949   March—*Association of American Geographer Annals* of East Tennessee Melungeons, publishes "Mixed Blood Strain."

1951   April—Edward Price's doctoral dissertation on mixed-blood groups notes that they (Melungeons) were attributed an Oriental appearance, but in reality, he thinks that the Melungeons were of Portuguese ancestry, or at least partially.[57] Geographical Review XLI-2.

1958   January 26—"Century-Old Stigma Remains—Portuguese Youngsters Segregated in Carolina," a full page article written by Luther J. Carter is published in *The Virginian Pilot—The Portsmouth Star*. Sunday, March 2—*Sunday Herald* of Roanoke Rapids features a story about the Portuguese of Northhampton County (Gaston). October 10—*Knoxville Sentinel* article, "East Tennessee Melungeons have a past clouded in myth."

1957   *Eugenics Quarterly*, "American Tri-Racial Isolates."

1959   August—*Tennessee Conservationist*—"Mystery People of Tennessee."

1960   Bonnie Ball writes for the Ross County Historical Society paper read at Chillicothe, Ohio. Also writes several articles in the 60's.

1963   September 22-29—*Nashville Tennessean*, "The Mystery of the Melungeons" by Louise Davis.[58]
June 21—*Chattanooga Sunday Times*, "Romance of the Melungeons."

1964   November 26—*Knoxville News-Sentinel* publishes Melungeon article.

1965   August—Graduate thesis about the Melungeons by Phillis Barr, East Tennessee State University, Department of English Faculty.

1965-6   Dr. William S. Politzer and Dr. William Brown, University of North Carolina: Health survey of Melungeons in Hancock County.

1966   October 30—*Baltimore Sun*, article by Mary Conelly.
March 10—*Knoxville News-Sentinel*, "Strolling" and Melungeons.
June 12—*Knoxville News*, article "Olive Skinned Hancock Countians."

1967   August—*Tennessee Conservationist*, article about the Melungeons.

1968   Mildred Haun writes "Melungeon Colored." Dec. 1—*Knoxville News* writes "New outdoor drama on Melungeons" by Willard Yarbrough.

1969   First performance of the Melungeon outdoor drama "Walk towards the Sunset" by Kermit Hunter is staged at Sneedville, Tennessee, and runs until 1976. Bonnie Ball's first edition of *The Melungeons*.
          June 26—*Life Magazine,* John Futterman writes "The Mystery of the Newman's Ridge."[59]
          March 30—*Louisville Courier, Journal and Times Magazine* editorial about "The Melungeons."
          The Melungeons, their Origin and Kin by Bonnie Ball.
          Human Biology by Pollitzer & Brown, Genetics and Melungeons.

1970   November 11—*Chicago Tribune*: "Melungeons, Tennessee Mystery."
          October 19—*Knoxville Journal*: article about the Melungeons.
          July—*Tennessee Conservationist*: article about the Melungeons.
          November 30—*Chattanooga Times*: article by Mouzon Peters.

1971   January—*Argosy Magazine*, "Melungeons came from Jewish origin."
          June 27—"Drama of the Melungeons," *Grit*, Family Section.
          August 10—*New York Times,* "Mysterious Hill Folk Vanishing."
          September 5—"The Last of the Melungeons," *Kingsport Times-News.*
          Nov. 7—*Johnson City Chronicle*, "Melungeons" by Johnnie Neal Smith.

1972   Spring issue of the *Tennessee Valley Historical Review*: Reprints article by Louise Davis.
          April 19—*Knoxville News*, "Melungeon Drama."

1973   November—*American History Illustrated*: Stinson, Byron writes about the Melungeons.[60]

1975   Jean Patterson Bible publishes a book, *The Melungeons Yesterday and Today*. April—Saundra Keyes Ivey's dissertation "Oral, Printed, and Popular Traditions" related to the Melungeons of Hancock County, Tennessee for a Ph.D. degree in Philosophy at Indiana University.
          September 25—*Knoxville Journal*, "Melungeons" by Juanita Glenn.

1981   Leo Pap of New York State University publishes his book *The Portuguese Americans*, mentioning Melungeons on pages 13-14 and 241-2.

1983   From Newman's Ridge, TN to Southeast Kentucky highlands, trail of Portuguese-English mixed clans.[61]

1988   March—*National Geographic Magazine* publishes an article about Santa Elena Island by Joseph Judge. Possible origin of the Melungeons.

1989   Shepperd's Satellite TV transmits program about the Melungeons.

1990   The spring issue, Vol. XV, p. 1, of *Tennessee Anthropologist* includes an article by Dr. James Guthrie about Melungeons: "Comparison of Gene Frequency."

1991   July/August—*Blue Ridge Magazine* article about the Melungeons, "Who Are These Mysterious People."

1992   July/August—*Blue Ridge Magazine*: "The Melungeon Mystery Solved." December 6—*Kingsport Times*: Melungeons subject of study by Barbara Watson.

1993   Dr. James H. Guill publishes *History of the Azores* and mentions the Melungeons on page 141.
July 7—*Atlanta Constitution*: Article by Chris Wohlwend, "Mystery of the Melungeons."
July 12—*The News & Observer* of Raleigh, N.C. "The Mystery of Virginia's Melungeons" by Chris Wohlwend, Cox News Service.
August 15—*The Charlotte Observer* "Melungeons in the New World" by Bruce Anderson. First presentation of the Book-Document, *Melungeons and other Mestee Groups* by Mike McGlothlen.
November 1—*Tuscaloosa News Alabama*: Story about "Melungeon Ancestry."

1994   June—*The State Magazine*: Article by Billy Arthur, "The Melungeons."
February—Kennedy publishes his book *The Resurrection of a Proud People*. *Portuguese RTP TV* transmits a program about the Melungeon people. Virginia TV channel transmits a program about the Melungeons with Greg Wallace of WCYB-TV, Bristol Virginia. *New England Cable TV* transmits Melungeon program with Dr. Manuel Luciano da Silva, from the series "Portuguese Around Us."

1995   *Luso-Americano* of Newark, NJ, the largest Portuguese-language newspaper outside Portugal, publishes a series of seven articles about the Melungeons, written by the author.
Portuguese RTP TV transmits a second program about the Melungeon people, with more extensive interviews.
May and December—Trip to Turkey by Kennedy as a guest of the Turkish Government for further research on the Melungeon people.
Dec. 7—Article about the Melungeons by Bryon Crawford in the *Transylvania Times* of Brevard, NC.

1996   Production of the play *Peter Pan* featuring an interracial cast, in which the pirates are played as Melungeons. May 28—*Kingsport Times-News* "Melungeon Museum," and on October 26, "Melungeons and Turks, A Key to Mystery" by Brad Lifford.
September—Gowen Research Foundation, Lubbock, Texas, publishes Melungeon origin research articles, and family histories of Gowen, Goin, Goyne and other spellings showing clearly Portuguese origin.

1997   April 14—*The Wall Street Journal*: "Appalachian Clan and Web Sites." July 27—*Richmond Times* "(People) Blurring Boundaries" by Rex Bowman about the Melungeon First Union.

1998   June 14—*Canada's Toronto Star:* Article "Appalachia's Genetic Mystery."

1999   June—*The Tennessean*: "More people tracing roots to Melungeons."

2000   May 18—Third Union of the Melungeons in Wise, Virginia.
May 30—"Beneath Myth, Melungeons Find Root of Oppression," *Washington Post*, Page A01
July 24/31—*U.S. News & World Report*, "Maybe DNA will do" by Nancy Shute

Brief History of Slavery

This book would not be complete without mentioning the subject of slavery. Most likely some of the early settlers, Melungeons and others, did intermarry and live with slaves, many times helping them to obtain their freedom. It is natural that we should look, very briefly, into their history.

From the beginning, the truth, or what is known of the truth, is being stated whether it is politically correct or not. Therefore, the subject of slavery must be brought up, although many tried to avoid it.

Professor John T. Strunk of Harriman, Tennessee, informed the author that one of his students, Bret Wright, believed to be a Melungeon descendant, came from Hancock County. Wright told Mr. Strunk that he recalled stories his grandfather had told him, and that there was a dispute over a slave or the question of slavery and so his branch of the family left Hancock County because of the feud. According to Mr. Strunk, most of the Melungeons and their descendants who came to Bazeltown near Harriman intermarried with blacks, and the ones who settled in Rhea County near Dayton intermarried with whites. He also stated that most of the Melungeons that came to Harriman were named Goins. Although they intermarried with blacks, many retain a Mediterranean appearance, with gray eyes, olive complexion, light brown or dark blond hair and freckles.

The above illustrates the fact that Melungeons did live and interact with slaves. It also helps the long established traditions stated in this book.

What about the Portuguese and the slaves? Famous Brazilian historian and sociologist Gilberto Freyre, writer of the critically acclaimed book *The Masters and the Slaves*, went into gruesome detail about slavery in Brazil, but he also said: *Although the Portuguese have been portrayed as the evil or the inventor of black slavery from Africa to the Americas, they were the only ones to treat the slaves on equal footing as other whites.* In Brazil, the use of the black slave was due to the Brazilian Indian's inability to work as a slave. Also, in the early 16th century the Spanish tried unsuccessfully to subjugate and enslave the native populations of the West Indies, without result.

Yes, the Portuguese were one of the European countries to start the slave trade and, even seen in the context of the times, it was not justifiable, at least the type of treatment dispensed to slaves. But the Portuguese were not alone, and not necessarily the worst offenders. Charles R. Boxer, famous historian, wrote: *The Portuguese empire might be moribund, decaying, corrupt, but, at least, it was far from racial prejudice.*[62] In another study made about the Jews in Cape Verde, Richard Lobban wrote: *It is essential to realize that the Portuguese were only brokers within a system...Moreover for those engaged in finger pointing...we must not forget African participation...The celebrated ancient African empires of Ghana, Mali...were all built upon the slave export business as much as the plantations* [of the] *south in the USA.* [There were also Muslims and Jews involved as brokers] *For those who single out Jews in this sorry traffic in humans, it must also be recalled that African Muslims were earlier into the trade across Sahara, down the Nile and in the Indian Ocean; it is in those regions of Muslim Africa that this cruel trade still continues to the very present.*[63]

We should also note that African slaves contributed to the building of Brazil and: *...small farmers and artisans could move up more easily in Brazilian society than they could in the southern (and northern) United States....Mulattos found more chances for education in Brazil than did their counterparts elsewhere.*[64]

Most of the black population of North America is in the U.S., where 29,986,060 blacks were counted by the 1990 census; Canadian blacks numbered less than 1 percent of the population (170,340). Almost all these people are descendants of Africans brought to the New World as slaves between 1501, when Spain first permitted African slavery in its colonies, and 1808, when the U.S. banned the importation of new slaves.[65]

In chronological order, the following paragraphs point out some of the more important events in slavery that culminated with its abolition.

Slavery in the British Isles at an early date: *Slavery existed in Britain when history commenced the records of that island. It was there found in a state and condition predicated upon the same causes by which its existence is now continued and perpetuated in Africa.*[66] Although abundantly practiced there and widespread in the ancient Mediterranean world, it had nearly died out in medieval Europe. It was revived by the Portuguese in Prince Henry's time, beginning with the enslavement of Berbers in 1442.

1433—To the surprise of the people waiting for the caravels to arrive in 1433, Gil Eanes, a Portuguese navigator, brought the first captured slaves from the Canary Islands.[67]

In 1441 Antão Gonçalves captured ten Berbers in the East Sahara, and out of these, one seemed to be a noble Berber. His name was Adahu.

He spoke Arabic and seems to have been a well traveled man with much knowledge.

They were taken to Portugal, and after questioning, Prince Henry obtained valuable information. But it was not until 1443 that the first African slaves arrived in Lagos, Algarve in the south of Portugal, brought in also by Antão Gonçalves.

Some could be considered white and handsome, others swarthy and still others quite black.[68] Zurara, a contemporary chronicler and eyewitness of the first European episode of the African slave trade, wrote this painful glimpse.

He (Zurara) insisted, however, that they were treated with kindness, and no difference was made between them and the freeborn servants of Portugal.[69]

There was regular commercial maritime between Venice and Morocco in the 15th century to transport and deal with commercial goods and slaves.[70]

During the 1450's an average of 700 to 800 slaves entered Europe annually through the Algarve and Lisbon. The coast of Guinea proved a better slave market than any land previously visited by the Portuguese.

While some captives came as a result of direct incursions inland by the Portuguese, most of them were regularly purchased from Muslim traders and the *Negros* themselves.

Slaves could be exchanged for cloth or other merchandise, which the Portuguese often acquired from Morocco, again, by legal trade.

From Portugal, a great number, the majority perhaps, were then profitably sold to Castille, Aragon and other European countries, only a part being employed in the sugar plantations (as well as other agricultural or domestic jobs) of Madeira.[71]

Writers of the 15th and 16th centuries exaggerated the number of slaves in Portugal. The number in Lisbon never exceeded 5,000.[72]

The Portuguese could obtain slaves on the Moroccan coast, but it was dangerous. The Moors were excellent fighters and had an efficient military organization that stopped the attempts of slavery. *It would be necessary for the Portuguese to control vast portions of the hinterland, which they were never able to accomplish.*[73]

1471—Conquest of Arzila and the Jewish Slaves—In the 1400's there were approximately 30,000 Jews in Portugal, which doubled when the Catholic Kings expelled them from Spain, and they in turn sought refuge in Portugal, others parts of Europe, and North Africa. Many that could not pay for their passage were reduced to slavery.[74] Isaac Abrabanel, a well known Jewish leader, worked with his father for King Afonso V and in 1471, when the Portuguese conquered Arzila, 250 Moroccan Jews were captured and brought in as slaves. Abrabanel traveled to the countryside to redeem these North-African Jews.[75] His father was the treasurer for Prince Fernando, who died in Fez, Morocco, as a captive of the Moors.

1492—Blacks in the Americas—African immigration to the Americas may have begun before European exploration of the region. Blacks sailed with Christopher Columbus even on his first voyage in 1492, and the earliest Spanish and Portuguese explorers were likewise accompanied by blacks—Africans who had been born and reared in Ibéria. In the following four centuries, millions of immigrants from sub-Africa were brought to the New World as slaves.

Most of the earliest black immigrants to the Americas were natives of Spain and Portugal, men such as Pedro Alonso Niño, a navigator who accompanied Columbus on his first voyage, and the black colonists who helped Nicolás de Ovando form the first Spanish settlement on Hispaniola or Española (Haiti) in 1502.

1498—When the Portuguese arrived in India, slavery was everywhere, more predominant in the Islamic north. The slavery had several origins: by birth, by insolvency and in payment of debt, captive in war, some selling themselves and their family in cases of extreme necessity, etc.[76]

1501—Spain introduced African slaves in Hispaniola or Española (Haiti). The first importation of blacks to the New World.

1505—Portuguese King Manuel I, in answer to a request made by the people of Madeira, ordered all slaves from the Canaries to be expelled, except the ones skilled in the sugar industry, which declined after that.[77]

1518—By 1518, the demand for slaves in the Spanish New World was so great that King Charles I of Spain sanctioned the direct transport of slaves from Africa to the American colonies. The slave trade was controlled by the crown, which sold the right to import slaves (*asiento*) to entrepreneurs.

Black slaves in Spain (about 50,000) were considered a deluxe status for well-off families, and very few worked in the fields or in production. Their condition was not the worst. They worked mostly in domestic chores. The Moorish slaves in Spain, after conversion to Catholicism, worked in the fields, constituting cheap and competent labor but hated by the old Christians, as they suspected complicity with the Berbers.[78] As an example of non-discriminatory practices against blacks, in 1518 Portuguese King Manuel I requests the pope to elevate the Congo Prince D. Henrique to Bishop of Utica. He becomes the first black Christian bishop.

1562—Sir John Hawkins was considered to be the father of the English slave trade. He had been to the coast of Guinea, where he bought and kidnapped a cargo of slaves.[79] In 1562-63, John Hawkins' first slave-trading voyage on behalf of a syndicate of London merchants was so profitable that a more prestigious group, including Queen Elizabeth I, provided the money for a second expedition. Soon Drake joined up with his kinsmen, the Hawkinses of Plymouth, ship owners and seamen. In the late 1560's Drake accompanied John Hawkins as he ranged the

West African coast gathering slaves to take across the Atlantic.[80] English Admiral John Hawkins led trading ventures that often began with a stop on the coast of Guinea (West Africa) to capture *negro* slaves. Hawkins embarked on his second voyage to the West Indies in 1564. After exchanging his cargo of slaves for the rich produce of the islands, he went on to explore the Florida coast.[81]

1565—Pedro Menéndez de Aviles of Spain was given the right to import 500 Negro slaves into Florida.

1606—A law was passed in India to forbid the importation of female slaves or others less than 16 years old. Also, it was said that Moors from India were very intelligent, and with very lively eyes.

1619-20—Counselors called an Assembly of Burgess who, being elected by the people, met the governor and council at Jamestown and stated: ...*About this time the Dutch brought over some negro slaves for sale, who are now wonderfully increased; besides the constant supplies of them imported yearly.*[82]

1663—Permanent settlement of Carolina began in the mid-seventeenth century, and by 1663 it is possible that the Virginians brought a few slaves with them. Meanwhile, events in England assured that North Carolina would become a slave colony.[83]

1761—A law was passed in Portugal to consider all Indians from Brazil free. It abolished slavery within continental Portugal and also gave equal rights to people from India.

1788—A bill designed to restrict the number of slaves carried by each ship, based on the ship's tonnage, was enacted by parliament on June 17, 1788.

1792—Denmark abolished slave trade.

1808—Finally, in 1807, the British Parliament passed an act prohibiting British subjects from engaging in the slave trade after March 1st 1808.

1811—Slave trading was declared a felony punishable by transportation (exile to a penal colony) for all British subjects or foreigners caught trading in British possessions. Britain then assumed most of the responsibility for abolishing the transatlantic slave trade, partly to protect its sugar colonies.

1815—The Treaty of Vienna between Portugal and England abolished slavery north of the equator, and Portugal restricted the slave trade to Brazil.

1817—Spain abandoned trade with Cuba, Puerto Rico and Santo Domingo.

1818—Holland and France abolished the trade.

1831—Brazil agreed to abolish slavery, but trafficking continued until 1851.

1836—In Portugal, a law was passed December 10, 1836 to abolish slavery south of the equator.

1848—The French emancipated their slaves.

1861—Abraham Lincoln was elected President, and the U.S. Civil War began in April. It was fought partly over the issue of slavery. It caused almost 900,000 deaths, and suffering for many more. Eventually the slaves of the Confederacy were declared free by Lincoln in 1863.

1864—The Brazilian Emperor D. Pedro II emancipated the slaves that formed part of his daughter's dowry, and committed the government to end slavery.

1865—Slavery was constitutionally abolished in the United States with the passing of the 13th Amendment.

1888—In Brazil, on May 13, 1888, Isabel, daughter of the Brazilian Emperor D. Pedro II, signed a law to abolish slavery. When she did, she was told that she redeemed a race but lost the throne.

Rulers of Portugal from 1580 to 1910 *

Dynasty of Habsburgs, United Crowns, Portugal & Spain

Filipe I	1580-1598
Filipe II	1598-1621
Filipe III	1621-1640

Dynasty of Bragança

João IV	1640-1656
Afonso VI	1656-1683
Pedro II	1683-1706
João V	1706-1750
José I	1750-1777
Maria I and Pedro III	1777-1786
Maria I	1786-1792
João VI (Regent)	1792-1807
João VI (Brazil)	1807-1821
João VI (Portugal)	1821-1826
Pedro IV (Emperor of Brazil)	1822-1831
Pedro IV (Portugal)	1826-1826
Maria II	1826-1853
Isabel Maria (Regent)	1826-1828
Miguel I	1828-1834
Fernando II (Regent)	1853-1855
Pedro V	1853-1861
Luis I	1861-1889
Carlos I	1889-1908
Manuel II	1908-1910

End of Monarchy	October 5th., 1910

See Page 221 for Rulers of Portugal to 1580 and
Page 382 for the list of Presidents of the
Portuguese Republic from 1910 to 2001.

Notes

[1] The Discoverers by Daniel J. Boorstin, p. 9.
[2] Luso-Americano, February 1996.
[3] Except as noted, Peoples Chronologies by James Trager,
Dicionario de Portugal Vol. I-VI, Historia de Portugal em Datas by
Antonio Simões Rodrigues, The Portuguese in America by
Manoel da Silveira Cardozo, as well as others were used.

Notes (Cont.)

[4] Historia de Portugal by Oliveira Marques, Vol. I, p. 15.
[5] Azores Islands, A History by James H. Guill, Vol. 5, p. 93.
[6] The True Antilles by Dr. Manuel Luciano da Silva, p. 5.
[7] Atlantic Islanders by Francis M. Rogers, 1979.
[8] The Palm Beach Post, June 24, 1995, p. 2A; Luso-Americano, July 26, 1995.
[9] The True Antilles by Dr. Manuel Luciano da Silva, p. 11.
[10] Colombo em Portugal, Marinha Portuguesa, p. 7.
[11] Ibid., p. 14.
[12] Historia de Portugal by Oliveira Marques, p. 5, Vol. II.
[13] Portugal nos Mares by Oliveira Martins, p. 37.
[14] Historia da Civilização Ibérica by Oliveira Martins, p. 83.
[15] The True Antilles by Dr. Manuel Luciano da Silva, p. 11.
[16] Set Fair for Roanoke by David Quinn.
[17] Portugal nos Mares by Oliveira Martins, p. 317.
[18] Columbus by Mascarenhas Barreto, p. 28.
[19] Portugal nos Mares by Oliveira Martins, p. 316.
[20] Historia de Portugal by Oliveira Martins, pp. 340-341.
[21] Dicionario da Historia de Portugal by Joel Serrão, Vol. I, p. 184.
[22] National Geographic Magazine, Joseph Judge, March 1988.
[23] Ibid, March 1988.
[24] The Portuguese-Americans by Leo Pap, p. 7.
[25] Set Fair for Roanoke by David Quinn, p. 12.
[26] Hernando de Soto Commission by John R. Swanson, p. 4.
[27] National Geographic Magazine, Joseph Judge, March 1988.
[28] Set Fair for Roanoke by David Quinn, p. 22.
[29] Ibid, p. 28.
[30] Harvard Classics, Vol. 33, p. 237.
[31] Set Fair for Roanoke by David Quinn, p. 350.
[32] Present State of Virginia by Hugh Jones, p. 67.
[33] The Present State of Virginia by Hugh Jones, p. 64.
[34] Encyclopedia Britannica.
[35] Early Travels in the Tennessee Country by Samuel Cole Williams, pp. 28-29.
[36] de Soto Commission by John R. Swanson, p. 4.
[37] Letter by Evelyn Orr of the Melungeon Research Committee.
[38] Ruth Woods Dayton, Greenbriar Pioneers, Charleston, WV Pub. 1942, p. 16.
[39] Pioneer Recollections of SW Virginia by Elihu Jasper Sutherland, pp. 167-169.
[40] The Melungeons by Jean Patterson Bible, p. 24.
[41] Ibid, p. 25.
[42] Ibid.
[43] Letter by Evelyn Orr of the Melungeon Research Committee.
[44] History, Myths, and Sacred Formulas of the Cherokees by James Mooney, p. 22.
[45] The History of Baxter County, Arkansas, (Mountain Home AR, 1972), pp. 5-6.

Notes (Cont.)

[46] Letter by Evelyn Orr of the Melungeon Research Committee.

[47] History of Tennessee and the Tennesseans by Hale & Merritt, p. 182.

[48] The History of Baxter County, Arkansas, (Mountain Home AR, 1972), pp. 5-6.

[49] Ibid.

[50] The Melungeons by Jean Bible, History of East Tennessee, p. 871.

[51] History, Myths, and Sacred Formulas of the Cherokees by James Mooney, p. 22.

[52] Notes on the Melungeons by Swan M. Burnett, Vol. II, p. 347, American Anthropologist.

[53] The Arena, Vol. 3, March, pp. 470-479.

[54] The Melungeons by Jean Patterson Bible, p. 16.

[55] Letter by Evelyn Orr of the Melungeon Research Committee.

[56] Ibid.

[57] The Melungeons by Jean Patterson Bible, p. 12.

[58] The Mystery of the Melungeons by Louise Davis, p. 11 (Nashville Tennesseean 9/29/1963).

[59] Life Magazine, June 26, 1970, p. 23.

[60] Stinson, Byron, The Melungeons, American History Illustrated, Nov. 1973.

[61] By Norm Isaac for Tennessee Historical Society, Prinit Press, Box 65, Dublin IN 47335 (E. Orr).

[62] The Portuguese Seaborne Empire by Charles R. Boxer, p. xxv.

[63] Jews in Cape Verde and Guinea Coast by Richard Lobban, p. 6.

[64] King Zumbi…by T.B. Irving, p. 408 (Amer. J. Islamic S. Sciences, 9:3 Fall 1992).

[65] Contributed by Franklin W. Knight, Clayborne Carson.

[66] Studies in Slavery by Jackson Warner, p. 67.

[67] Infante D. Henrique e sua época, Mario Domingues, p. 201.

[68] Ibid, pp. 266-267.

[69] The Discoverers by Daniel J. Boorstin, p. 167.

[70] Infante D. Henrique e sua época by Mario Domingues, p. 134.

[71] History of Portugal by Oliveira Marques, Vol. I, pp. 158-159.

[72] Ibid, Vol. I, p. 289.

[73] History of Portugal by Oliveira Marques, Vol. I, p. 274.

[74] Historia da Origem e… Inquisição by Alexandre Herculano, pp. 67-69.

[75] The Jews of Spain by Jane Gerber, p. xxi.

[76] Economia Mundial by Vitorino Magalhães Godinho, p. 547.

[77] Dicionario da Historia de Portugal by Joel Serrao, Vol. II, p. 421.

[78] Historia de España, Historia 16, p. 502.

[79] Pioneers of France in the New World by Francis Parkman, p. 90.

[80] National Geographic Magazine, Drake by Allan Villiers, p. 224.

[81] Annals of America by Clements R. Markham, Vol. 1, p. 6.

[82] The Present State of Virginia by Hugh Jones, pp. 63-64.

[83] History of African Americans in North Carolina by J. Crow, P. Escott, F. Hatley, p. I.

Appendix C

Portuguese Navigators, Explorers and Missionaries
Not directly involved with North America of the 15th, 16th and 17th Centuries
In Alphabetical order by Last Name

Name	Surname	Date	Activity
Antonio de	Abreu	1611	Sumatra with Francisco Serrão
Lopo	Abreu	1504	India
André	Afonso	1526	Captain, Sierra Leoa
Diogo	Afonso	1461	Cape Verde Islands
Mestre Martins	Afonso	1565	Far East voyage by land and sea
Estevão	Afonso	1445	Madeira, East Africa
João	Afonso	1550	Pilot, Cape Verde
Jorge de	Aguiar	1508	India, Tristão da Cunha
Pedro Afonso de	Aguiar	1524	Brazil
Lopo Soares de	Albergaria	1515	India
Fernão Soares de	Albergaria	1552	Navigator to India
Francisco de	Albuquerque	1503	India
Afonso de	Albuquerque	1505	Africa, Brazil to India, and Viceroy
Pero d'	Alenquer	1470	West Africa and Guinea
Francisco de	Almeida	1509	India
Fernão Martins de	Almeida	1503	India
Lourenço de	Almeida	1502	Maldives Islands, India
Francisco	Álvares	1540	Abyssinia
Jorge	Álvares	1513	Southern China
Gonçalo	Álvares	1505	India
Diogo	Álvares	1511	Brazil and Caramuru
Padre. José	Anchieta	1560	Brazil
Pedro de	Andaia	1505	West Africa
Simão Peres de	Andrade	1500	Brazil
Anselmo de	Andrade	1560	First European to enter Tibet
Fernão Peres de	Andrade	1517	China, Canton
Martins	André	1539	Explorer, New Mexico
Pero	Anes	1470	West Africa, Diogo Cão Pilot
Pero de	Astuniga	1486	West Africa
Luis de	Ataíde	1569	India
Pero de	Ataide	1500	Brazil, India
Vasco de	Ataide	1500	Brazil, also with Bartolomeu Dias
João Afonso de	Aveiro	1486	East Africa
Diogo de	Azambuja	1451	East Africa
Simão de	Azevedo	1500	India
Fernando Roiz	Badacas	1502	India
Afonso Gonçalves	Baldaia	1436	North East Africa
Duarte	Barbosa	1500	Commercial Guide, Orient, 1500's
Diogo	Barbosa	1501	Santa Helena Island
Francisco	Barreto	1570	East Africa
Manuel de Campos	Bicudo	1600	Brazil
Simão Afonso	Bisagudo	1521	Far East
Pero Vaz	Bisagudo	1488	West Africa
Gaspar	Bocarro	1606	West Africa
Jorge	Botelho	1515	Malaca
Diogo	Botelho	1535	India
Rui de	Brito	1513	Malaca
Manuel Teles de	Brito	1504	India

Name	Surname	Date	Activity
Pedro Álvares (Gouveia)	Cabral	1500	Official discoverer of Brazil.
Gonçalo Velho	Cabral	1432	Azores
Fernando Álvares	Cabral	1432	Tangier, grandfather of Pedro Álvares Cabral
Luis Alvise	Cadamosto	1445	Genovese, northeast Africa for Portugal
João	Caetano	1555	Possible discoverer of Hawaii
Vasco Rodrigues	Caldas	1561	Brazil
Rui Gonçalves da	Câmara	1474	Azores
Pero Vaz de	Caminha	1500	Brazil
Afonso de	Campos	1601	Northwest Africa
Antonio do	Campo	1502	India
Diogo	Cão	1482	West Africa
Tomás de	Carmona	1502	India
Joao	Carvalho	1519	Pilot with Estevão Gomes
Fernão Alves de	Castanheda	1528	India, historian
Álvaro de	Castro	1547	India
Fernando de	Castro	1424	The Canaries and West Africa
Filipe de	Castro	1504	India
João de	Castro	1546	India, noticed compass magnetic deviation
Nufro de	Chaves	1560	Brazil
Gaspar	Colaço	1550	Merchant in Bolivia
Gonçalo	Coelho	1504	Brazil
Nicolau	Coelho	1500	Brazil, also with Vasco da Gama
Duarte	Coelho	1535	Brazil
João de	Coimbra	1498	With the Vasco da Gama fleet to India
Frei Henrique de	Coimbra	1500	Brazil
Gaspar	Colaço	1550	Bolivia
Aires	Correia	1500	Also with Vasco da Gama to India
Diogo Fernandes	Correia	1550	India
Gonçalo da	Costa	1541	Paraguay, South America with Cabeza de Vaca
Afonso Lopes da	Costa	1504	India
Soeiro da	Costa	1478	East Africa
Vasco	Coutinho	1540	Brazil
Leonel	Coutinho	1504	India
Pero da	Covilhã	1487	West Africa, India by land in 1488
Gaspar de	Cruz	1556	Missionary in China, Hormuz
Brás	Cubas	1550	Brazil
Tristão da	Cunha	1506	S. Atlantic Island that bears his name
Nuno Leitão da	Cunha	1500	India
Francisco	Cunha	1502	India
Rui Nunes da	Cunha	1511	Far East
Bartolomeu	Dias	1488	Round Cape of Good Hope, S. Africa
João	Dias	1520	Magellan's pilot
Dinis	Dias	1439	Northeast Africa, Cape Verde
Diogo	Dias	1506	Madagascar, São Lourenço Island, Brazil
Diogo	Dias	1525	First hospital in Mexico City
Lopo	Dias	1502	India
Pedro	Dias	1500	East Africa, Red Sea
Fernão Vaz	Dourado	1560	Cartographer born in India
Gil	Eanes	1434	Northeast Africa
Heliodoro	Eboanos	1568	Brazil
João	Escobar	1500	Brazil
Pedro	Escobar	1470	West Africa, also with Vasco da Gama
Martim	Esteves	1470	West Africa

Name	Surname	Date	Activity
Antonio de	Faria	1550	India
Gil	Fernandes	1500	India
João	Fernandes	1445	Northeast Africa
Simão	Fernandes	1580	North America
Álvaro	Fernandes	1446	Northwest Africa
Diniz	Fernandes	1450	Northwest Africa
Duarte	Fernandes	1511	Far East
Antonio	Fernandes	1514	East Africa
Gonçalo	Ferreira	1460	Guinea, West Africa
Manuel Pereira	Forjaz	1590	Tried Angola-Mozambique by land
Álvaro de	Freitas	1448	West Africa
Antonio	Galvão	1536	Captain and governor in the Moluccas
Cristovão da	Gama	1541	Somalia, son of Vasco da Gama
Paulo da	Gama	1500	India, brother of Vasco da Gama
Estevão da	Gama	1524	India, son of Vasco da Gama
Vasco da	Gama	1498	Discovered sea route to India
João da	Gama	1589	Sailed across the Pacific
Paulo da	Gama	1498	With Vasco da Gama fleet (Captain) India
Henrique	Garcês	1558	Discovers mercury in Peru
Diogo	Garcia	1506	Indian Ocean island, bears his name
Aleixo	Garcia	1521	Explores South America continent
Álvaro	Gaspar	1540	Explorer, New Mexico
Diogo	Gil	1447	Sea land to Arabia
Frei Bento de	Goes	1603	Mongolia
Pero de	Gois	1536	Brazil
Diogo	Gomes	1447	West Africa
Fernão	Gomes	1455	Guinea, West Africa
Estevão	Gomes	1524	From Newfoundland to Virginia
João	Gomes	1510	North West Africa
Amador	Gonçalves	1543	Bermudas
André	Gonçalves	1502	Brazil with Americo Vespucci
Antão	Gonçalves	1441	Northeast Africa
Gaspar	Gonçalves	1585	India, pilot
Lopo	Gonçalves	1472	East Africa
Jorge	Gonçalves	1448	East Africa
Manuel	Gonçalves	1585	India, master
Diogo	Homem	1500	Cartographer, worked for England, 1500's
Manuel Godinho de	Heredia	1596	Claim discovery of Australia in 1600
Manuel Rodrigues	Homem	1572	East Africa
Álvaro Martins	Homem	1474	Azores
Garcia	Homem	1445	Navigator, East Africa
Lopo	Homem	1500	Cartographer, worked for France, 1500's
Joao	Infante	1487	West Africa
Lançarote de	Lagos	1448	West Africa
Rui de	Lasteneda	1502	India
Jerónimo	Leitão	1585	Brazil
Gaspar de	Lemos	1488	Cape of Good Hope, with Dias
João de	Lisboa	1512	Brazil
Paulo de	Lima	1587	Malacca
Pero	Lobo	1532	Brazil
Padre. Jerónimo	Lobo	1625	East Africa, Abyssinia (Ethiopia)
Duarte	Lopes	1578	Angola, West Africa
Frei Fernando	Lopes	1487	Voyage to the land of Prestes João

Name	Surname	Date	Activity
João	Machado	1500	India
Fernão de	Magalhães	1519	Traveled with Vasco da Gama
Nuno	Manuel	1514	Explored Rio de La Plata in South America
Padre. Luis	Mariano	1624	Discovered Nile waterfalls, Marchinson
Sebastião	Marinho	1582	Brazil
Lourenço	Marques	1542	East Africa, Mozambique
João	Martins	1585	Possible north passage to India
André S.	Martins	1520	Pilot with Magellan
Jorge	Mascarenhas	1517	Discovered the Liew Islands
João de	Mascarenhas	1546	Diu, India
Pedro de	Mascarenhas	1528	India
Gil	Matoso	1502	India
David	Melgueiro	1660	North passage to India for the Dutch
Duarte de	Melo	1518	India
Fernão de	Melo	1499	S. Tomé Island off West Africa
Manuel Afonso de	Melo	1526	India
Fernão de	Mendonça	1585	Admiral, India
Cristovão de	Mendonça	1524	Possible early voyage to Australia
Pero de	Mendonça	1503	India
Duarte de	Meneses	1522	India
Pedro de	Meneses	1415	Ceuta, Morocco
Henrique de	Meneses	1524	India
Jorge de	Meneses	1525	Far East
Álvaro de	Mesquita	1519	Pilots with Estevão Gomes
Antonio de	Miranda	1517	Ambassador to Sião
Antonio	Moniz	1560	India
Belchior Dias	Moreira	1591	Brazil
Antonio de	Mota	1542	Discovers Japan
Luis de	Moura	1500	India
Bernardo	Nasci	1551	Navigator to India
Father Manuel da	Nobrega	1560	Brazil
Antonio de	Noli (Nola)	1456	Cape Verde
Antão de	Noronha	1552	India
Garcia de	Noronha	1511	Brazil
Fernando de (Fernão)	Noronha	1502	Discovered island that bears his name
João da	Nova	1501	Discovered Ascension Island
Francisco de	Novais	1501	India
Paulo Dias	Novais	1575	Kingdom of Angola
Gonçalo	Nunes	1498	With Vasco da Gama fleet to India
João	Nunes	1498	Portuguese Jew, first to set foot in India
Manuel	Nuno	1514	Explored Rio de la Plata
João	Ornelas	1446	Canary Islands
Nicolau	Orta	1507	India to Portugal by land
Padre Pero	Paes, Paez	1617	Discovered Nile river source
Afonso	Paiva	1495	Northwest Africa
Antonio	Peixoto	1506	Far East and Japan
Diogo	Pereira	1541	Far East with Saint Francis Xavier
Duarte Pacheco	Pereira	1498	North coast of Brazil
Diogo	Pereira	1535	Voyage on an 11 feet Boat, India-Portugal
Bartolomeu	Perestrelo	1423	Madeira Islands
João Lopes	Perestrelo	1502	India
Lançarote	Pessanha	1490	Far East
Luis de	Pina	1500	India

Name	Surname	Date	Activity
Simão de	Pina	1488	Cape of Good Hope, South Africa, with Dias
Fernão Mendes	Pinto	1534	Far East
Tomé	Pires	1517	China, apothecary
Diogo	Pires	1502	India
Bernardo	Pires	1524	Brazil
Gomes	Pires	1448	East Africa, Sahara region
Luis	Pires	1500	Brazil
Fernando	Pó	1472	East Africa
Francisco	Proença	1596	Brazil
Pedro Fernandes de	Queiroz	1596	New Guinea, Far East, New Hebrides, 1774
Pero	Rafael	1502	India
João	Ramalho	1522	Brazil
Rodrigues	Ravasco	1504	India
Rodrigo	Rebelo	1486	West Africa
Pero, Pedro	Reinel	1486	West Africa
Jorge	Reinel	1500	Cartographer, worked for Spain
Diogo	Ribeiro	1500	Cartographer, worked for Spain
Afonso	Ribeiro	1512	Brazil
Master	Rodrigo	1480	Physicist, astrolabe, worked royal court
Mem	Rodrigues	1486	West Africa
Fernão	Rodrigues	1503	India
Francisco	Rodrigues	1524	Navigator to Moluccas
Jeronimo Barreto	Rolim	1565	Navigator, India
Salvador Correia de	Sá	1514	Governor Rio de Janeiro, lived 101 years
Mem de	Sá	1560	Brazil
Afonso	Saldanha	1599	Brazil
Antonio	Saldanha	1540	India
Lopo Vaz de	Sampaio	1528	India
João de	Santarem	1470	East Africa
Pêro Fernão de	Sardinha	1547	India
Pantaleão de Sá	Sepulveda	1542	East Africa
Manuel de Sousa	Sepulveda	1560	India and West Africa, captain
Diogo Lopes de	Sequeira	1505	Far East, Malacca
Gomes de	Sequeira	1523	Far East
Rui de	Sequeira	1474	West Africa
João	Serrão	1520	Part of Magellan's crew
Francisco	Serrão	1511	Sumatra with Antonio de Abreu
Aires Gomes da	Silva	1500	Cape of Good Hope
Gonçalo da	Silveira	1500	Southeast Africa
João de	Silveira	1516	Far East
Antonio da	Silveira	1538	India, Diu
Diogo de	Silves	1420	Possible sighting of the Azores Islands
Gonçalo de	Sintra	1444	East Africa
Pero de (Pedro)	Sintra	1461	Northeast Africa
Fernão	Soares	1551	Navigator to India
Brás	Sodré	1502	India
Vicente	Sodré	1502	West Africa with Estevão Gomes
Bras Dias de	Solis	1512	Brazil
Diogo Lopes de	Sousa	1551	Navigator to India
Gonçalo de	Sousa	1490	West Africa
Gabriel Soares de	Sousa	1587	Indians of the Brazilian coast
Pedro Lopes de	Sousa	1532	Brazil
Tomé de	Sousa	1549	Brazil

Name	Surname	Date	Activity
Martins Afonso de	Sousa	1541	India
João Coelho de	Sousa	1580	Brazil
Francisco de	Sousa	1580	Brazil
Belchior de Sousa	Tavares	1529	Explored Euphrates, Tigris Rivers
Diogo de	Teive	1455	West Africa
Pedro	Teixeira	1600	Far East, via Central America
Tristão Vaz	Teixeira	1423	Madeira Islands
Aires	Tinoco	1446	West Africa
João Vaz de	Torres	1606	Far East
Sancho de	Tovar	1501	West Africa, Brazil
Nuno	Tristão	1443	Northeast Africa
Luis Mendes de	Vasconcelos	1502	India
Álvaro	Vasques	1446	Northeast Africa
André	Vaz	1550	India
Pero Vaz da	Veiga	1503	India
Bartolomeu	Velho	1561	Cartographer, worked for France
Gonçalo	Velho	1500	Brazil
Diogo	Veloso	1593	Cambodian ambassador to Philippines
Americo	Vespucci	1502	Genovese, coast of Brazil for Portugal
Padre Antonio	Vieira	1640	Brazil
Master José	Vizinho	1485	Physicist, astrolabe, pupil of Zacuto
Saint Francis	Xavier	1540	Born in Navarra, Spain, Lisbon and India
Abraham Ben Samuel	Zacuto	1480	Astronomer, solar tables used by Columbus
João Coutinho	Zamiro	1502	India
João Gonçalo	Zarco	1423	Madeira Islands
Francisco	Zeimoto	1542	Japan

List of Weddings of Portuguese Men and Native Women in 1529 [1]

Native Wife	Portuguese Man	Wife Origin
Caterina Álvares	AfonsoÁlvares	Guzerate
Felipa Fernandes	Afonso Galego	Malabar
Luzia Fernandes	Afonso de Morales	Moor
Biatriz Nunes	Afonso de Motta	Moor
Caterina Tonso	Afonso Fernandes	Moor
Biatriz Vaz	Afonso Paes	Malabar
Felipa Morena	Afonso Rodrigues	Canarim
Caterina Afonso	Álvaro Pirez	?
Antonia Lopes	Antonio do Rego	Moor
Maria Morena	Antonio Folgado	Moor
Inês Gomes	Bastiam Gomes	Moor
Lucrecia Borges	Bras Gonçalves	Canarim
Lianor Arganosa	Bras Lopes	Malabar
Izabel da Silva	Diogo Correia	Malabar
Cristina Fernandes	Diogo de Laniz	Moor
Maria Lopes	Diogo Lopes	Moor
Margarida Vaz	Domingos Gonçalves	Burma
Vyolante Vaz	Estevão Chaves	Java
Caterina Gonçalves	Fernão Lopes	Moor
Lianor Nunes	Fernão Nunes	Malabar
Cristina de Saa	Francisco de Saa	Moor
Johana Gonçalves	Francisco Fernandes	Jaoa
Isabel Fernandes	Francisco Fernandes	Moor
Isabel Morena	Francisco Tinoco	Canarim
Biatriz Morena	Gonçalo Moreno	Nayra
Felipa Fernandes	Gregorio Fernandes	Moor
Cristina Fernandes	João Carvalho	Malabar
Justa Fernandes	João Fernandes	Moor
Caterina Fernandes	Joham Alvarez	Moor
Joana Diaz	Joham Diaz	Canarim
Maria Fernandes	Joham Gonçalves	Nayra
Branca Gonçalves	Joham Gonçalves	Socotorina
Biatriz Fernandes	Joham Gonçalves	Nayra
Biatriz Lopes	Joham Lopes	Malabar
Izabel Marques	Joham Marquez	Malabar
Maria Fernandes	Joham Nunes	Moor
Caterina Vaz	Joham Nunes Trombeta	Socotorina

[1] Historia da Lingua Portuguesa by Serafim da Silva Neto, p. 534-536

Native Wife	Portuguese Man	Wife Origin
Antonia Fernandes	Joham Vaz	Moor
Lianor Rodrigues	Jorge de Sezimbra	Moor
Caterina de Alboquerque	Jorge Nunes	Moor
Beatriz Fereyra	Lopo Afonso	Moor
Caterina Fernandes	Lourenço Saldanha	Moor
Antonia d'Albuquerque	Manuel Gonçalves	Malabar
Maria da Sylva	Manuel Gonçalves	Moor
Joana de Araujo	Nemo Vaz	Malabar
Marta Diaz	Pero d'Evora	Canarim
Inês de França	Pero de França	Moor
Izabel Fernandes	Pero Fernandes	Malabar
Isabel da Costa	Pero Mendes	Burma
Caterina Vaz	Pero Petro	Moor
Felipa Fernandes	Richarte	Moor
Guiomar Gonçalves	Rodrigo Esturiano	Moor
Filipa Fernandes	Salvador Afonso	Malabar
Briola Vaz	Simão Vaz	Nayra

List of weddings of Far-East Native Women with Portuguese Men

The Classification of Moor is generic. It applies mostly to Muslims, except the Turks, which the Portuguese called Rumes. Also, to most of the India area natives, including the Mollucas, Indonesia, etc.

List of Portuguese Shipwrecked Caravels to 1550

M	D	Y	Captain/Pilot	Vessel	Shipwreck Area
7	8	1497	Gonçalo Nunes	Supply ship	Cape of Good Hope
7	8	1497	Paulo da Gama (2)	S. Rafael (1)	Off East Africa
3	9	1500	Aires Gomes da Silva		Cape of Good Hope
3	9	1500	Bartolomeu Dias		Cape of Good Hope
3	9	1500	Pêro de Ataíde		Near Mozambique
3	9	1500	Pêro Dias		Red Sea
3	9	1500	Sancho de Tovar	Rei	All survived
3	9	1500	Simão de Pina		Site unknown
3	9	1500	Vasco de Ataíde		Site unknown
2	10	1502	Antonio do Campo		Angediva *
2	10	1502	Antonio Fernandes		Sofala
2	10	1502	Brás Sodré	Leitoa a Velha	Curia Maria
2	10	1502	Diogo Fernandes Correia	Borreco	Angediva *
2	10	1502	Pêro de Ataíde		East Africa
2	10	1502	Vicente Sodré	Esmeralda	Curia Maria
4	14	1503	Francisco de Albuquerque	Rainha	Site unknown
4	14	1503	Nicolau Coelho	Faial	Site unknown
4	14	1503	Pero de Ataide	Bate Cabelo ?	Banks of S. Lazaro ?
4	14	1503	Pêro Vaz da Veiga		Cape of Good Hope
4	22	1504	Pero de Mendonça		Near S. Brás
3	21	1505	Lopo Sanches	Nau	Site unknown
3	21	1505	Pêro de Ataíde	Caravel	Outside Lisbon
3	21	1505	Pêro Ferreira Fogaça	Bela	Mozambique
5	18	1505	Francisco de Anaia	S. João	Site unknown
5	18	1505	Pêro Barreto Magalhães	Galega	Bay of Quiloa
3	6	1506	Job Queimado	Job	French captured
3	6	1506	Leonel Coutinho	Leitoa a Velha	Mozambique
3	6	1506	Rui Pereira Coutinho	S. Vicente	Natal
4	13	1507	Fernão Soares	S. Antonio	Site unknown
4	20	1507	João Chanoca	Caravela	Rio Sanagá
4	15	1507	Jorge de Castro	Rumesa	Nazareth
4	13	1507	Rui Cunha	S. João	Site unknown
4	20	1507	Vasco Gomes de Abreu	S. Romão	Santiago
4	11	1508	Jeronimo Teixeira	S. Clara	Polvoreira
4	9	1508	Jorge de Aguiar	S. João	Tristão da Cunha
		1508	Gonçalo de Sousa		Site unknown
3	12	1509	Francisco Sá	S. Vicente	Cananor
3	12	1509	Sebastião de Sousa Elvas	S. Jorge	Cananor
3	16	1510	Manuel da Cunha	S. Roque	Mozambique

M	D	Y	Captain/Pilot	Vessel	Shipwreck Area
3	25	1512	Francisco Nogueira	S. Julião	Angoche
3	14	1513	Francisco Correia	S. Antonio	S. Lázaro Island
3	22	1516	Antonio de Lima	S. Simão	Banks of S. Lazaro
3	22	1516	Francisco Sousa Mancias	N. Sra. da Luz	Banks of S. Lazaro
4	23	1519	Francisco Cunha	S. Antonio	Quiloa
4	23	1519	Luis Gusmão, Castelhano		Brazil
4	23	1519	Manuel de Sousa	S. Antonio	Quiloa
4	5	1521	Duarte de Meneses	S. Jorge	Ilha Terceira
4	23	1522	Pedro de Castelo Branco	Nazaré	Bay of Goa
4	6	1523	Aires da Cunha	S. Miguel	Mozambique
4	9	1524	Cristovão Rosado	Caravela Rosa	Site unknown
4	9	1524	Fernando Monroy	S. Jorge	Melinde Banks
4	9	1524	Francisco Brito	Barbosa	East Africa
4	9	1524	G. Pereira Macherquim	Garça	Site unknown
4	15	1525	Diogo de Melo	Paraiso	Cachopos
4	15	1525	Filipe de Castro	Corpo Santo	Cape Rosalgate
4	8	1526	Francisco de Anaia	N. S. Victoria	Near Lisbon
4	8	1526	Vicente Gil	S. Leão	Returned to port
3	26	1527	Aleixo de Abreu	Bastiana	East Africa
3	26	1527	Manuel de Larcerda	Conceição	East Africa
4	18	1528	Afonso Vaz Zambujo	Ship	Near Mozambique
4	18	1528	Bernardim da Silveira	Galeão	Sofala, East Africa
4	18	1528	João de Freitas	Nau	Canary Islands
4	18	1528	Nuno da Cunha	Rosa	Near Mozambique
		1529	João de Freitas		Cape Verde
4	20	1531	Manuel Macedo	Esperança	Calicut
		1532	Felipe de Castro	Corpo Santo	Cachopo, Barra
		1532	João de Melo e Silva	Conceição	Site unknown
3	4	1533	Francisco de Noronha	S. João	Cape of Good Hope
3	25	1536	Duarte Barreto	S. Miguel	Site unknown
4	6	1538	Bernadim Silveira	Galega	Site unknown
3	24	1539	Pero Lopes de Sousa	S. Cruz	Site unknown
4	7	1541	Martim Afonso Sousa	S. Tiago	Baçaim, R. Cabras
4	7	1541	Martim Afonso Sousa	S. Tiago	Baçaim, R. Cabras
4	4	1542	Baltasar George	Grifo	Terceira, Azores
4	4	1542	Vicente Gil	N. S. da Graça	Melinde
4	19	1544	Simão de Melo	N. S. da Graça	Near Mozambique
3	28	1547	Pedro da Silva	S. Tomé	Angoche
3	3	1549	João Figueira	Burgalesa	Site unknown
5	3	1550	Álvaro de Ataide	S. João	Cape of Good Hope
5	3	1550	Diogo de Noronha	Frol de la Mar	Mazagão
3	20	1551	Jorge de Meneses	Barrileira	Site unknown

M	D	Y	Captain/Pilot	Vessel	Shipwreck Area
3	10	1551	Lopo de Sousa	Biscainha	Site unknown
3	24	1552	Antonio Dias Figueiredo	S. Tiago	Islands unknown
3	24	1552	Antonio Moniz Barreto	Zambuco	Near Goa
3	24	1553	Fernão Álvares Cabral	S. Bento	East Africa, Natal
4	2	1554	Belchior de Sousa	S. Cruz	Site unknown
4	2	1554	Francisco de Gouveia	S. Francisco	Terceira, Azores
4	2	1554	Pedro de Mascarenhas	S. Boaventura	Goa coast
		1555	Francisco Nobre	Algaravia Nova	Pêro de Banhos
		1555	Jacome de Melo	Algaravia Velha	Terceira, Azores
4	30	1557	João Rodrigues Carvalho	Aguia	Mombaça
4	20	1557	Luis Fernandes	S. Maria Barca	East Africa
3	28	1559	D. Constantino	Garça	Site unknown
		1592		Madre de Deus	English Captured

List of Portuguese shipwrecks

The above chart has been compiled from several sources. Portuguese Navy Commander Encarnação Gomes has been instrumental in obtaining most of the information which he has been doing for many years in his series *Subsidios para o Estudo da Carreira das Indias* of the *Anais of the Clube Militar* in Lisbon. Other sources consulted were: Portuguese National Archives *Torre do Tombo*; *Livro da Fazenda* de Luis Figueiredo Falcão; *Livro das Armadas*; Portuguese National Library *Biblioteca Nacional,* and others.

Due to the variety of sources, some of the details may not be correct and sometimes are contradictory. Further research is required to complete the chart, which should be done, at least covering the whole 16th century, not just the Indian route but also to Brazil and Africa. This part of Portuguese history is still to be completed and there is plenty of information available.

Influence of the Portuguese Language in Japan and the World

Monsignor Sebastião Rodolfo Dalgado compiled a list of 47 Oriental languages that have words of Portuguese origin: Concanim, 815; Malaise, 361; Japanese, 78, to name just a few. [1] At a much earlier date, in 1514, Afonso de Albuquerque, the viceroy, wrote to King Manuel I that in Cochin 29 students were registered in school to learn the Portuguese language. [3] Between 500 and 1,000 Portuguese words passed to Oriental cultures, [3] and the opposite as well, e.g., *Chá* in Portuguese is the same in Chinese, and is pronounced like *shah* as it was used in Persia. Just a small example, in Malai …the following words have Portuguese roots, in the order presented: English, Portuguese, Malai: Coast - Costa - Kósta; Potatoes - Batata - Battatas; Wheat - Trigo -Trigu; Lizard - Lagarto - Lagarti; Head - Cabeça - Kembesa; Father - Pay - Pai; Mother - Mai - Mãe; Jeweler - Ourives - Orivis, and so on.[4]

Unfortunately, not enough resources have been provided for a deep study of the Portuguese language. When this is done, then many similarities will be discovered, not only in current usage, but also by natives many years ago.

As a point of interest, the Portuguese language also had an influence on the Japanese language.

The following are just some of the words compiled by Armando Martins Janeira in his book *O Impacto Português sobre a Civilização Japonesa.*

Japanese	Portuguese	English
Amendo	Amendoa	Almond
Amen	Amen	Amen
Anjo	Anjo	Angel
Barsan	Bálsamo	Balm
Baputesuma	Baptismo	Baptism
Kontasu	Contas	Beads of Rosary
Banku	Banco	Bench
Bisukoto	Biscoito	Biscuit
Pan	Pão	Bread
Iruman	Irmão	Brother
Manteka	Manteiga	Butter
Butan	Botão	Button
Kompra	Compra	Buy
Boru	Bolo	Cake
Kappa	Capa	Cape
Katoritu	Católico	Catholic
Karisu	Cálix	Chalice
Kirishtan	Cristão	Christian
Ekirinji	Igreja	Church
Koreijo	Colégio	College

Japanese	Portuguese	English
Kapitan	Capitão	Captain
Kataru	Catarro	Catarrh
Katana	Catana	Catan
Confeto	Confeito	Comfit
Kompasu	Compasso	Compass
Kohismo	Confissão	Confession
Kirismo	Crisma	Confirmation
Karusu	Cruz	Cross
Koppu	Copo	Cup (glass)
Jejun	Jejum	Fasting
Furasuko	Frasco	Flask
Zenerasu	General	General
Jiban	Gibão	Gerkin (short jacket)
Biirodo	Vidro	Glass
Uru	Ouro	Gold
Gomu	Goma	Gum
Abito	Habito	Habit
Inferno	Inferno	Hell
Osuhitari	Hospital	Hospital
Ostiya	Hóstia	Host (religion)
Jaketsu	Jaqueta	Jacket
Zesusu (Zesu)	Jesus	Jesus
Rabirinto	Labirinto	Labyrinth
Reguwa	Légua	League
Karuta	Carta	Letter
Manto	Manto	Mantle
Maruchiru	Mártir	Martyr
Sinnyoro	Senhor	Mister
Banzai	Banzé	Noise
Kurusan	Calção	Pants (gibão)
Paraizo	Paraíso	Paradise
Pisturu	Pistola	Pistol
Pappu	Papa	Pope (pap)
Byôbu	Biombo	Portable partition
Orashyo	Oração	Prayer
Bateren	Padre	Priest
Rõsa	Rosa	Rose
Seito	Santo	Saint
Tentasan	Tentação	Temptation
Arigato	Obrigado	Thank you
Tabako	Tabaco	Tobacco
Taifu	Tufão	Typhoon

Japanese	Portuguese	English
Birodo	Veludo	Velvet
Saya	Saya	Skirt
Shabon	Sabão	Soap
Ranbiki	Alambique	Still

Portuguese and Japanese Words.

There are many more. Naturally, some words are the same in other European languages. But since the Portuguese were the first Europeans, they brought their language with them to Japan and the Orient.[5] They also brought other words used throughout the world, such as Guiné, Guinea; pagode, pagoda; moeda de ouro, moidore; varanda, verandah; cobra, etc.

Influence of the Japanese Language in Portugal

The Portuguese language has also been influenced by Japanese and other Asian languages. The following are just a few examples of the Japanese.

Japanese	Portuguese	English
Banzai	Banzé	Noise
Byôbu	Biombo	Portable partition
Katana	Catana	Catan

Influence of the Portuguese Language on English and the USA

There are at least 38 English words derived from the Portuguese language; the following are just some of them: [6, 7, 8]

English	Portuguese	English	Portuguese	English	Portuguese
Albatross	Albatroz	Firm	Firma	Picaninny[9]	Pequenino
Albino	Albino	Flamingo	Flamengo		
Apricot	Albricoque	Lingo	Lingua	Stagnant	Estagnado
Bagasse	Bagaço[10]	Madeira	Vinho	Tank	Tanque
Caste	Casta	Marmalade	Marmelada	Typhoon	Tufão
Corvette	Corveta	Molasses	Melaço	Yam	Inhame
Fetish	Fetiche	Parasol	Para-sol		

* * *

Portuguese and the Languages of the World

The Portuguese language evolved from spoken Latin in 218 BC. It was highly influenced by German and Arabic during the first millenium and later on by Galician, a language still spoken in a Spanish province north of Portugal.

Also French and English had some influence. Between the 14th and 16th centuries the Portuguese language spread in Asia, Africa, and the Americas.

Portuguese entered its modern phase in the 16th century with the grammar defined Portuguese morphology and sintax.

In 1986, became an official language in the European Union. The Community of Portuguese Speaking Countries (CPLP in Portuguese) was formed in 1996.

Languages spoken by most people around the world:

1. Chinese Mandarin
2. English
3. Spanish
4. Bengali
5. Hindi
6. Portuguese

If you combine Bengali and Hindi, spoken in India & others, then Portuguese is the fifth most spoken language in the world.

It is however the third most spoken European language in the world.

Notes

[1] A Lingua Portuguesa no Mundo by Jorge Morais Barbosa, pp. 148-155.
[2] Historia da Lingua Portuguesa by Serafim da Silva Neto, p. 542.
[3] Luso-Americano, 4-24-1996.
[4] Lingua Portuguesa no Mundo by Jorge Morais e Silva, p. 151.
[5] O Impacto Português sobre a civilização Japonesa by Pedro Canavarro.
[6] Encyclopedia of English by Arthus Zeiger, p. 435, Arco (1959).
[7] Michaels, Dicionario Ilustrado, 27 Edition, (1981).
[8] Lingua Portuguesa no Mundo by Jorge Morais Barbosa, p. 161.
[9] Hawaiian for *small child*.
[10] Pulp of sugar cane or grapes.

* * *

The Celebrated Melungeon Case in 1872 by Judge Shepherd

* * *

The following is an article based on Judge Shepherd memoirs written by Jean Patterson Bible in her book, *The Melungeons, Yesterday and Today*, which is still in print. We thank the author for her permission to use it. Since it endorses some of the theories about the Melungeons, it is appropriate to present it to readers.

* * *

It was in 1872 that a fledgling Chattanooga, Tennessee, lawyer based his case and won a lawsuit on the hitherto almost unheard-of theory that Melungeons were of Carthaginian or Phoenician origin. From this auspicious beginning, the young attorney Lewis Shepherd went on to become a judge and a leading member of the Chattanooga bar.

In 1915 Judge Shepherd published a collection of reminiscences of his legal experiences, entitled *Memoirs of Judge Lewis Shepherd*, which included the "Romantic Account of the Celebrated 'Melungeon' Case." In it, the judge recounts many of the details of the buildup, trial and resolution of the lawsuit that has sometimes been dubbed the "Chattanooga Story" by those who sympathized with the plight of the Melungeons.

During the era in which it took place, the case was probably one of the most publicized of its kind where a decision was rendered favoring a minority group over a white prosecutor. The outcome, the awarding of an inheritance to the daughter of a Melungeon mother and a white father, hinged on Shepherd's successfully establishing his claim that his client was not of Negro blood but was descended from the early Carthaginians.

Had she been proved to have Negro blood, according to the then Tennessee law of miscegenation (Judge Shepherd defined it as the marriage of a white person with one of Negro blood to the sixth degree), the marriage of her parents would have been illegal, leaving her with no claim to her father's property.

The background of the strange true story that reads more like a romantic novel goes back to the early settlement of the Chattanooga area. A wealthy man from Virginia bought a large tract of land in Moccasin Bend, where today the Tennessee River winds its way around Chattanooga, and moved in with his family and slaves. The fertile, river-bottom land soon became a rich and productive farm, so that by the time of the owner's death, he was able to leave each of his three sons a good farm piece.

Two of the brothers never married and, on their deaths, the surviving one inherited their estates. He rented the land, hired out his slaves and went into business in Chattanooga.

In the meantime, his widowed mother remarried and had three daughters by her second husband. Several years later, the surviving brother was stricken with a mental illness that left him temporarily deranged. By 1848, however, he was able to resume his normal schedule, including the management of his extensive holdings. One of the tenants was an elderly Melungeon named Bolton who had served in the War of 1812, joining the army in South Carolina, where he was living at the time.

Bolton had a daughter "famed for her beauty, her grace of manner and modesty. She was a dark brunette. She had a suit of black hair, which was coveted by all the girls who knew her. Her form was petite and yet, withal, was so plump and so well developed as to make her an irresistibly charming young woman.

She was most beautiful of face, and had a rich black eye, in whose depths the sunbeams seemed to gather. When she loosed her locks they fell, almost reaching the ground, and shone in the sunlight, or quivered like the glamour which the full moon throws on the placid water..."

The young man fell in love with her, and the attraction was mutual. They planned to get married but, when the news reached his mother and half-sisters

Fig. 118—Indian Girl from India.
Photo by the author

they strenuously opposed the union, knowing that if it took place, they stood to lose all chance of becoming heirs to the property he had inherited.

They notified the licensing clerk that if he issued the two a marriage license, they would file suit against him, claiming not only that the young man was mentally incompetent but that the girl had Negro blood and such a marriage would be illegal. The alarmed clerk was so impressed by their threats that he refused to grant the Groom-to-be a license when he applied for one several days later.

Not to be outwitted, the young man persuaded two of his friends, Ab Carroll and John Cummings, to accompany him and the girl across the river to Dade County, Georgia, to serve as witnesses. The marriage license was purchased in Trenton, the Dade County seat, duly registered, and the ceremony was performed June 14, 1856, by a local squire at his Dade County home.

The couple returned to the groom's plantation and set up housekeeping. Their first child, a son, died in infancy, and the second, a daughter, was born in the latter part of 1858. When the mother died in childbirth eight days later the bereaved husband was thrown into such a state of shock he never fully recovered.

His mental condition was such that a guardian was appointed to look after him and manage his affairs.

In the meantime, the mother and half-sisters had not been idle. They either coerced or bribed "Aunt Betsy," the child's maternal aunt, into taking her far away and promising never to return. A little later, the aunt took the child, along with the family Bible containing the birth and marriage records, to a small place in Illinois,

75 miles from Cairo. As the time went on, the sad story was almost forgotten by the public. The insane man's guardian continued to manage his various properties until he had built up a fund of many thousand dollars for the estate. But one person had not forgotten. A friend, Samuel Williams, had kept up with the child from the beginning by a secret arrangement with her aunt Betsy to keep him informed as to her welfare.

The historic lawsuit was instituted in 1872 when the man's two surviving half-sisters and the children of the deceased half-sister brought suit in the chancery court, attempting to surcharge and falsify the settlements of the guardianship by the guardian, Mr. Foust. He was charged with mismanagement of the estate, wasting its assets, lending large sums of money to poor people, taking inadequate security from them. In addition, they sought to make him account for assets supposed to be on hand.

The second feature of the suit was that Mr. Foust's ward was an incurable lunatic, and that the complainants were heirs apparent who would certainly inherit the estate. They asked that the present guardianship be revoked and that the ward and his estate be turned over to them, promising to give bond and security that they would provide for his needs. Finally, they asked a decree adjudging them to be heirs apparent. And, for good measure, they also sued Mr. Williams and Col. John Divine, sureties on Mr. Foust's bond as guardian, in order to make good the hoped-for decree.

Now the time had come for Mr. Williams to produce the rightful heir to the estate and to protect her rights. Seeking a trustworthy and competent lawyer, he found that all the experienced ones were already involved in the suit on one side or the other. On the advice of a friend, he consulted Lewis Shepherd, a young attorney just starting out in his profession. Shepherd agreed to take the case, with Mr. Williams acting in the capacity of best friend of the young girl.

The suit they filed for the child came like a bolt out of the blue. They asked that she be adjudged the child and heir apparent of the deranged father, that she be supported and educated out of his estate.

The dismayed opposition promptly labeled the whole thing a "tissue of falsehoods and slanders…a fabrication of old man Williams, and that the girl was an impostor. They even denied her identity as the child of the crazed man, and also denied that he had ever been married to his alleged wife, and claimed that if he had gone through the form of marriage it was void for numerous reasons, and the issue of such marriage was illegitimate."

At that time, young Shepherd produced his trump card, the daughter in person, then nearly 15 years old. He had previously sent Mr. Williams to Illinois to bring her back to Chattanooga, along with the family Bible containing the birth and marriage records.

Proof of the marriage was not difficult to obtain as the magistrate who performed the ceremony and the two witnesses to it were still living. When asked how he remembered the exact date so well, one witness said that it was impressed on his mind because his wife had given birth to a baby girl that same evening, and the date and name were in the family Bible.

The record in the Bible carried to Illinois by aunt Betsy verified the birth of the daughter and the date. As to the father's sanity, the judge ruled that a marriage which was voidable could not be questioned by anyone except one of the parties to the contract and could not be charged collaterally.

But the issue at stake on which the real battle lines were drawn was the allegation that the marriage was void because the mother in the case had sufficient Negro blood that the ceremony could not be legally recognized because of the then Tennessee law against miscegenation.

The opposition brought in a number of old-time Negroes who testified under oath that the Boltons were kinky-headed Negroes, that "the whole bunch of them had kinky hair," just like a Mulatto Negro. They also swore that aunt Betsy and the girl's mother had kinky hair, not knowing that the young girl was at that moment actually in Chattanooga.

The "kinky head" question was settled once and for all with a deposition taken from the girl at Mr. Williams' home. Asked to cut off a lock of her hair, and pin it to the deposition, "she reached up to her topknot and pulled out her old-fashioned tucking comb, and a monstrous mass of coal black hair, as straight as the hair of a horse's tail, fell down to the floor.

It was about four feet long, and perfectly free of a kink or a tendency to curl. She exhibited with her depositions a fair sample of her magnificent suit of hair, which completely destroyed the depositions of the Negroes taken on the other side to prove that the Bolton people were Negroes."

By way of additional proof, Shepherd went back to the Melungeon tradition of Carthaginian ancestry, in an exceedingly eloquent plea even in that period of old-fashioned oratory. In his account in the memoirs of how he developed his defense based on the theory of Carthaginian descent, he says it was satisfactorily established in the proof that the family of this woman was in no way allied to, or connected with, the Negro race; that there was not a feature of herself or ancestry that was at all similar to the distinguishing characteristics or features of the Negro, except that they were of dark color, about the color of a Mulatto.

They had high foreheads; long, straight, black hair; high cheek bones, thin lips, small feet with high insteps and prominent Roman noses, while the features of the Negro and Mulatto were exactly the reverse of these.

In truth, these people belonged to a peculiar race, which settled in East Tennessee at an early day and, in the vernacular of the country, they were known as "Melungeons," and were not even remotely allied to Negroes.

It was proven by tradition amongst these people that they were descendants of the ancient Carthaginians (sic); they were Phoenicians who, after Carthage was conquered by the Romans and became a Roman province, emigrated across the Straits of Gibraltar and settled in Portugal.

They lived for many years and became quite numerous on the southern coast of Portugal, and from thence came the distinguished Venetian general Othello, whom Shakespeare made immortal in his celebrated play "The Moor of Venice."

These were the same people who fought the Romans so bravely and heroically in the Punic Wars, and whose women sacrificed their long black hair to the state to be plaited and twisted into cables with which to fasten their galleys and ships of war to the shore.

About the time of our Revolutionary War, a considerable body of these people crossed the Atlantic and settled on the coast of South Carolina, near the North Carolina line, and they lived amongst the people of Carolina for a number of years. At length, the people of Carolina began to suspect that they were Mulattos or free Negroes, and denied them the privileges usually accorded to white people.

They refused to associate with them on equal terms and would not allow them to send their children to school with white children, and would only admit them to join their churches on the footing of Negroes.

South Carolina had a law taxing free Negroes so much per capita, and a determined effort was made to collect this tax off them. But it was shown in evidence in the trial of this case that they always successfully resisted payment of this tax, as they proved they were not Negroes.

Because of their treatment, they left South Carolina at an early day and wandered across the mountains to Hancock County, East Tennessee...A few families of them drifted away from Hancock into the other counties of East Tennessee, and now and then into the mountainous section of Middle Tennessee.

As proof that Bolton had been consistently regarded as white since his arrival in Hamilton County, it was cited that the old man had been allowed to vote in all elections at a time when Negroes were not, and also to testify in court when a Negro would have been regarded as incompetent to do so.

Moreover, Shepherd added that since the grandfather received a pension for serving in the War of 1812, he was legally considered white, because at the time he enlisted, neither Negroes nor Mulattos were looked on as soldiers and could serve only as teamsters or cooks.

Other evidence included the relating of an incident in the grandfather's life when a white man killed one of his grandchildren. Bolton prosecuted him, but the defendant filed a plea in abatement saying that since Bolton was a Negro, he had no right to prosecute. The jury found the plea not true, that Bolton was not a Negro. The defendant was convicted and sent to the penitentiary.

The chancellor allowed both sides a great deal of time and leeway in arguing the case but, when the final verdict was rendered, it was in favor of the girl. The court judged that she was the heir apparent of her father, entitled to be supported and educated out of his estate, and to inherit it on his death.

Her guardian was instructed to pay for her education and maintenance, and to pay the young lawyer 5,000 dollars for his services (a munificent sum for that time, especially for a beginner in law practice).

The true story of the young Melungeon girl not only had a storybook beginning, it also had a "lived happily ever afterward" ending. When Mr. Williams brought the girl back to Chattanooga, he had promised aunt Betsy that he would bring her back to Chattanooga as soon as she could dispose of her belongings, a promise he carried out. In his memoirs, Judge Shepherd gives a summary of events following the trial.

When Mr. Williams got back to Chattanooga, the girl was nearly 15 years old. She knew nothing about the ways of the world. She was totally ignorant of the prevailing fashions of dress; she did not know what a corset was or how it was worn, whether over or under the dress.

She had spent most of her life in the forests along the banks of the Mississippi, where she and her aunt had made their living by cultivating a small patch with hoes, and by cutting cordwood and selling it to the steamboats which plied up and down the river, and which used wood for fuel.

She knew nothing whatever of the arts of fashionable women in making themselves attractive forms and figures by skillful lacing—she was simply an uncouth, an unsophisticated, unmadeup, natural girl from the backwoods; a girl, withal, possessed of a strikingly beautiful face, and a figure which, by proper development and dress, was capable of being molded into a form that would please the most fastidious. She was very much like her mother, and possessed all the charms and grace she did, but they were undeveloped.

Mr. Williams took her to a milliner and had her provided with a wardrobe suitable to her changed surroundings. She very readily adapted herself to her new surroundings and her new life, out in the midst of civilization. She was kept at the Williams home and sent to school from there for about two years.

She had to be started at the very beginning, but, being ambitious to get education, she studied hard and learned very rapidly, and in the short time of her school days got a very fair and practical education.

She afterwards married her teacher, who was a splendid young man and became one of the leading men in the community, and managed his wife's affairs very successfully and added considerably to her fortune.

At the time of his death, which occurred about 20 years ago, he was a prominent official in the county. The echoes of the outcome of the "Celebrated Melungeon Case" reverberated throughout most of the Melungeon settlements in the Southeast. Undoubtedly it furnished a legal guidepost which affected decisions concerning Melungeons for many years afterward.[1]

Notes

[1] *The Melungeons Yesterday and Today by Jean Patterson Bible*, p. 61

The Presidents of the Portuguese Republic since 1910 *

First Republic (From 1910 to 1926)

1911 - Manuel José Arriaga Bruno da Silveira
1915 - Bernardino Luís Machado Guimarães
1917 - Sidónio Bernardino Cardoso da Silva Pais
1918 - João do Canto e Castro Silva Antunes
1919 - António José de Almeida
1923 - Manuel Teixeira Gomes
1925 - Bernardino Luís Machado Guimarães

Second Republic, also know as "Estado Novo" or New State,
        (From 1926 to 1974)

1928 - António Óscar Fragoso Carmona
1951 - Francisco Higino Craveiro Lopes
1958 - Américo de Deus Rodrigues Tomás

Third Republic (After 1974)

1974 - António Sebastião Ribeiro de Spínola
1974 - Francisco da Costa Gomes
1976 - António dos Santos Ramalho Eanes
1986 - Mário Alberto Nobre Lopes Soares
1996 - Jorge Fernando Branco de Sampaio
2001 - Jorge Fernando Branco de Sampaio, reelected

After October 5th, Portugal was governed by a temporary government led by Teófilo Braga.

The Presidents only came after a new Constitution was ratified and the first President was Manuel José de Arriaga Brum da Silveira from the Azores.

In fact the first President was Manuel de Arriaga who served till 1915 having defeated Bernardino Machado.

However we must take into account that Arriaga was elected, Teofilo Braga was the President of the temporary Government.

This is the reason why is quite normal to consider Teofilo Braga the first President.

* See Page 221 for Rulers of Portugal to 1580 and
Page 358 for Rulers from 1580 to 1910.

Portuguese who contributed in one form or another to the Making of America, prior to the 20th century.
* * *

These are some of the forgotten Portuguese,
shown in alphabetical order by last name, activities and details:
* * *

Frances Affonsa; Cook; 1858; President Lincoln's cook.

Isaac Abrabanel; Jewish Leader; 1471; worked with his father for the Portuguese King Afonso V, redeemed 250 Moroccan Jews.

Carlos Pedro Diogo Andrade; Pioneer; 1825; Amador County, East Sacramento, California.

Laurinda C. Andrade; teacher; 1889; Born in Terceira.

João Areias; Sailor; 1492; member of Columbus' crew on first trip, native of Tavira, Algarve.

Mary Astor; Actress; 1890; Born in Illinois of Madeiran Immigrants.

Duarte Barbosa; Navigator; 1519; Member of Magellan (Magalhães) crew.

Pedro Barcelos; Navigator; 1494; Rediscovered Newfoundland, Greenland.

Bernard Baruch; Politician; U.S. Presidential advisor.

Francisco L. Borges; politician; Connecticut State treasurer.

Family Bettencourt; Soldiers; 1835; fought for freedom of Texas.

Catherine of Braganza; Queen of England; 1640; Borough of Queens, N.Y., married Charles II of England.

Manuel Silveira Brazil; settled in New Mexico 1871, County Commission; Texas, 1908-1914, involved with Billy the Kid.

João Rodrigues (Cabrillo) Cabrilho; Navigator; 1500; discover of California, born in Pamela, "Freguesia de" Cabril, Montalegre, Trás-os-Montes.

André do Campo; Soldier; 1541; Coronado's expedition into Grand Canyon, Texas, Arkansas, Oklahoma, Kansas.

Aaron Nunes Cardozo Amsterdam; 1752; married daughter of Moses Mendes Seixas; parents of Benjamin Cardozo.

Benjamin N. Cardozo; Judge; 1870; U.S. Supreme Court Justice.

Solomon Nunes Carvalho; artist and photographer, worked with Colonel John C. Freemont in the exploration of the west.

Luis de Carvalhal; Explorer; 1579; Texas, married Guiomar Alvares de Rivera, a Jewess native of Lisbon.

João Lopes de Carvalho; Navigator; 1519; Member of Magellan's (Magalhães) crew.

João Elliot de Castro; Pioneer; 1814; early arrival in Mimai, personal physician of King Kamehamea I.

Family Chaves; Soldiers; 1835; fought for freedom of Texas.

João Coelho; Navigator; 1475; possible voyage to West Indies with Frois.

João Cordeiro; Explorer; 1540; with the Hernando de Soto expedition.

Antonio Correia; Shipmaster; 1500; Member of the Cabrilho expedition in California.

João Vaz Corte Real; Navigator; 1474; Possible arrival in North America.

Corte Real; Navigator; 1500; Dighton, Massachussets, first arrival.

Gaspar Corte Real; Navigator; 1500; Colonies of New England, Carolinas 1501-03, from Terceira, Azores.

Miguel Corte Real; Navigator; 1500; Colonies of New England, Carolinas 1501-03, from Terceira, Azores.

Family Cunha (Wager); Fisherman; 1850; Fall River, from Azores.

Estevão Dias; Navigator; 1519; Member of Magellan's (Magalhães) crew.

José Dias; Soldier; 1776. Revolutionary War, Martha's Vineyard, died 1781.

João Estaço; Missionary; 1552; Native of Terceira, Azores, was named bishop of Puebla in Mexico.

Fernão Dualmo/Dulmo; Navigator; 1487; May have discovered the Antilles in 1487, British historian A. Davies.

João Afonso Estreito; Navigator; 1486; May have been in Newfoundland with Dulmo.

Brothers Faleiro; Navigator; 1519; Member of Magellan's (Magalhães) crew.

João Alvares Fagundes; Navigator; 1520; Explored Newfoundland and US East Coast in 1520, from Viana do Castelo.

Bento Fernandes; Explorer; 1540; with the Hernando de Soto expedition.

Álvaro Fernandes; Explorer/writer; 1540; Gentleman of Elvas, wrote the first book about the Southeast, traveled with Hernando de Soto.

Simão Fernandes; Navigator; 1560; Explored U.S. east coast and later was the pilot under Sir William Raleigh.

Bartolomeu Ferrelo; Explorer; 1542; Chief pilot with Cabrilho, discoverer of California.

Mathias Figueira; Doctor; 1853; Founder of American College of Surgeons, born in Madeira.

Peter Francisco; Soldier; 1776; Fought in American Revolution with George Washington.

Estevão Frois; Navigator; 1475; Possible voyage to West Indies with Coelho.

Luis de Góis; Jesuit; 1545; First to take tobacco to Europe from America.

Bento de Góis; Soldier—Missionary; 1580; Born in Vila Franca do Campo, São Miguel Island, Azores.

Estevão Gomes; Navigator; 1525; US East Coast, Virginia also previously with Magellan (Magalhães).

Lewis Gomes; Portuguese Jew; 1707; Sloop Flying Horse.

Marcelino Manuel Graça (Grace); Bishop; 1882; Born in Cape Verde, founder of a large Protestant congregation.

Horta; Explorer; 1540; Southwest U.S.

Portuguese Joe Soldier; 1812; Hero captain fought in the successful Battle of Lake Erie.

João Fernandes Lavrador; Navigator; 1474; Discovered Greenland, Labrador; From Terceira, Azores.

Afonso Gonçalves; Pilot; 1519; Member of Magellan's (Magalhães) crew.

Emma Lazarus; Poet; 1800; Statue of Liberty inscription.

Benjamin Levy; Merchant; 1773; Cofounder of the first Portuguese Jewish settlement in Maryland.

Henrique Lopes; Merchant; 1500; Merchant in caravel captured by English privateers, see Irene Wright's book.

Aaron Lopes; Merchant; 1750; Baptized Catholic, fled Portugal 1740's, Newport, RI, founder of Touro Synagogue.

James Lucena; Manufacturer; Begins the manufacture of Castile soap in Rhode Island.

Jacob Lumbrozo; Physician; 1656; Portuguese Jew, settled in Maryland in 1656, died in 1666.

Abraham de Lyon; Vintner; 1737; Began growing grapes in Georgia in 1737.

David Mendes Machado; Rabbi; 1734; Spanish-Portuguese congregation in New York City.

José Manuel Machado; Soldier; 1769; Commander of the Presidio in San Diego, California.

Fernão de Magalhães; Navigator; 1500; Circumnavigation of the world, crossed into the Pacific Ocean from the Atlantic.

Martim de Magalhães; Navigator; 1519; Member of Magellan's crew.

Isaac Marques; Portuguese Jew; 1707; Sloop *Flying Horse.*

Luis R. Medeiros; School Teacher; 1894; Honolulu, Hawaii, Captain National Guard.

Gracia Mendes; Diplomat; 15??; Jewess born in Lisbon, became famous in the Ottoman Empire where she fled after the Inquisition.

Antonio Mendes; Captain, whaler; 1600; Born Terceira, Azores, first to navigate the Sacramento River.

H. Pereira Mendes; Rabbi; 1724; Shearith Israel.

Tom Mix; Cowboy; 1890; Born in Portugal as Antonio Nunes Pinguelo.

Benjamin Nunes; Soldier, Officer; 1770; Washington's staff, served with General Pulaski.

Joseph Nunes; Portuguese Jew; 1707; Sloop *Flying Horse.*

Pedro Nunes; Cosmographer; 1537; Tables and the "Tratado da Esfera."

Samuel Ribeiro Nunes; Physician; Portuguese Jew arrived in Georgia in 1733.

Pedro Fernandes de Queiroz; Navigator; 1596; Central America to India.

Moses Pacheco; Portuguese Jew; 1658; Arrived from Amsterdam, Newport, RI.

Fernão Pais; Explorer; 1540; Southwest U.S.

John dos Passos, Journalist, poet, novelist of USA Trilogy.

Jacinto (Jason) Pereira (Perry); Consul agent; 1826; Faial, Azores, Hawaii.

John Philips; Hero US West; 1800; Manuel Filipe Cardoso, Pico, Azores.

Isaac Pinto; Economist; Far East explorer.

Jacob & Solomon Pinto; Emigrants; Residents of New Haven, CT, in 1724.

Hill Portuguese Ridgmanites; Soldiers; 1776; Revolutionary war, known by the English colonists.

John Freitas Raposo; Merchant, postmaster; 1882; Island of Kauai, Hawaii. Recruited labor in Madeira.

José Vieira Ramos; Settler; 1830; settled in Virginia, one of the first to receive American citizenship.

Diogo Nunes Ribeiro, Physician, see Samuel Ribeiro Nunes, MD.

Gonçalo Rico Navigator; 1545; Chief pilot with Ruy Lopez de Villalobos, sailed from Mexico to New Guinea.

José Antonio Rocha; Settler; 1815; first owner of Los Angeles City Hall, son of a judge in Balboa, California; 1868-1873.

Nicola Rodrigo; Sailor; 1586; Captured by Thomas Cavendish off the coast of Mexico.

Family Rodrigues; Portuguese Jew; 1624; Virginia 1624.

Gonçalo Rodrigues, Blacksmith; 1519; Magellan's (Magalhães) crew.

Francis Salvador; Politician, soldier; 1770; active in South Carolina during the American Revolution.

Afonso Sanches Navigator; 1452; Possible voyage to West Indies.

Antonio Martins Segurado; Explorer; 1539; with the Hernando de Soto expedition.

Isaac Mendes Seixas; Supporter; 1776; American Revolution, married Rachel Levy; Merchant vessels.

Gershom Seixas; Rabbi; 1770; Shearith Israel, for 50 years, supported the cause from the pulpit.

Abraham Seixas; Patriot; 1800; Colonel, Georgia brigade.

Moses Seixas; Cashier; 1809; Bank of Rhode Island, grand master of the Order of RI.

Abade José Correia da Serra; Diplomat; 1801, Represented Portugal after U.S. Independence, Ambassador to President Thomas Jefferson.

Sebastião Rodrigues Seremenho; Navigator; 1595; Surveyed the California coast.

Francisco José da Silva; Whaler; 1826; Pico Azores; settled in San Francisco.

M. A. Silva; Editor; 1884; Madeira; Portuguese newspaper editor in Hilo, Hawaii.

Hattie Bence Silvia; Teacher; 1899; First woman teacher of Portuguese descent in Fall River.

João Dias Sollis; Navigator, Spain; 1500; Possible voyage to Central America and Brazil.

Matias de Sousa; Settler, emigrant; 1634; Arrived in Maryland, possibly of Jewish descent.

Mae de Sousa; Opera Singer; 1800; Daughter of John de Souza, descendant of Jacksonville pioneers.

John Philip de Sousa; Musician; 1800; Musician, *the March King*.

Antone S. Sylvia; Whaler; 1855; Born Azores, arrived in New Bedford, MA at 15, died a millionaire.

Antone Ferreira Tavares; House representative; 1898; Lawyer, politician.

Diogo de Teive; Navigator; 1452; Azores and possible voyage to West Indies.

Pedro Teixeira; Navigator; 1600; West Indies, Central America to India, discovered Tahiti in 1602.

Lucas Thomas; Politician; 1890; Elected to Hawaii territory's legislature.

Luis Vaz de Torres; Navigator; 1605; Discovered Torres Straits between Australia and New Guinea.

André de Vasconcelos; Explorer; 1540; With the Hernando de Soto expedition.

William Madison Wood; Textile industry; 1858; Son of Portuguese immigrants. Mills, Mansions and Mergers.

✳   ✳   ✳

Distinguished Persons with Portuguese ancestry, by field of endeavor and last name in the 20th Century.

The PAHR Foundation has initiated a data base containing anyone with Portuguese ancestry who has achieved notoriety since the beginning of the 20th century. Our web site has published the names indicated below, however we realize that many names are still missing and others do not deserve the distinction given.

Readers are invited to send names of notable people who may have Portuguese ancestry, and may have contributed to Canada and the United States in the fields of Government, Entertainment, Education, Literature, Science, Media and Business with public recognition by their respective communities.

The following is a tentative list and subject to change. Please send your comments with details to add to the names, or if their inclusion here is appropriate or not, including the ones presented below. (Also send more details of the names shown if you have any additional information.)

Business

Patrick M. de Barros
Mariano S. Bishop
Micahel Botelho
Bernardino Coutinho
Victor do Couto
Evaristo Cruz Sr.
John Henry Felix
Joseph Fernandes
Antonio Frias
Augusto Gomes
Manny Gomes
Teresa S.Ferreira Heinz
Maria Monet
Miguel Monteiro
Robert J. Morgado
William L. Pereira
Joseph Perry, Jr.
Manuel L. Ponte
Maria Isilda Ribeiro
Alfredo dos Santos
Antonio Leal da Silva
Maria Hortencia Silveira
Luis Tormenta

Manuel Viegas
Fred Vierra
William Madison Wood

Canada

Prof.Aida Baptista, PhD.
Tony Dionisio
John Elias
Carlos de Faria, MPP
Christine Ferreira
Prof. Ilda Januario M.Sc.
Manuela Marujo, Ph. D.
Nellie Pedro
Victor M.P. Rosa, Ph. D.
Mario Silva
Prof. Elvino Sousa, Ph.D.
John Sousa
Maria Teresa L. de Sousa
Carlos Teixeira, Eds.
José C.Teixeira, Ph. D.

Education

Dr. David Almeida

Onesimo Almeida, Ph.D.
Joe Alves
Laurinda Andrade
Antonio Jose Carvalho
João C.dos Santos, Ph.D.
Joaquim F. Coelho
Antonio José Costa
Francis A. Dutra
Antone Felix
José M. Figueiredo, Ed.D.
Maria F. Pereira, Ph.D.
Manuel C. Fontes Ph.D.
Florbela M. F. Gomes
Geoffrey L. Gomes
Larry Hanks
Antonio Ladeira, Ph.D.
Maria Rosa Menocal
David Pimentel, Ph.D.
Julio Ramos
Gregory Rocha, Ph. D.
Linda Rodrigues
Francis M Rogers, Ph.D.
Jorge de Sena
Catherine Silvia
Frank Sousa, Ph. D.

Mario Vieira, Ph. D
David John Vieira, Ph. D.

Entertainment

Abilio Oliveira Aguas
Joaquim de Almeida
Dennis Alves
Pat Amaral
Mary Astor, Actress
Carlos Avalon
Raul Benevides
Nuno Bettencourt
Brannon Braga
Mario Carvalho
Art Coelho
Steven Correia
Cindy Silva Costner
Edmund Dinis
Louise Fazenda
Richard Fernandes
Mario Gonçalves
Thomas (Tom) Hanks
Don Ho
Bobby Justin
Emeril Legasse
Francis Madeira
Vanessa Marcil
Fausto Mathias
Carlos de Mattos
Glenn Medeiros
Joe Medeiros
Rod de Medicis
John A. Mendes
Sam Mendes
Carmen Miranda
Susan Neves
Silvia Nevjinsky
Elmar Oliveira
Nathan Oliveira
John R. dos Passos
Harold Peary
Diana Pereira

Steve Perry
Artur Pizarro
Joe Raposo
Stephen Rebello
Gerardo Ribeiro
Carmelyn Rio-Borroz
Eugenio M. Rodrigues
Nicole dos Santos
Daniel Silva
Tom Silva
William Posey Silva
Hattie Bence Silvia
John Philip de Sousa
Steven de Sousa
Danielle Steel
George C. de Sylva
Henry da Sylva
Karen Valentine
Meredith Vieira

Government

Antone Aguiar
Fred Aguiar
John Almeida,
Joseph S. Almeida
Ed Alves
Rosa Alves
Stephen. Alves
Augusto Amador
Annelle Claire Amaral
John Amaral
Curt Andre
Daniel Andrews
William Andrews
Ron Andrade
John M. Arruda
Mary-Jo-Avellar
Clarence Azevedo
William San Bento
Maria Beirão
William Augusto Borba
Lisa Gomes Boscola

Bruce Botelho
Joseph H. de Bragga
Anthony Brazil
Antonio F.D. Cabral
Steven A. Camara
Ben Vieira K Campbell
Benjamin Cardozo
Dennis Cardoza
Arthur A. Carrelas
Elmer de Carvalho
Romeo Cascaes
Raymond C. Coelho
Tony Coelho
Robert Correia
James Manuel Costa
Jim Costa
Michael Costa
Alberto Coutinho
E.H. Christian
Edward Cruz
Tina Cruz (Lawyer)
Arthur F. Desrocher
Eduardo Dias
Jacinto F. Diniz
John Dutra
W. Enos
Joseph L. Faria
Manuel Faria
Armand Fernandes, J.D.
Maria Fernandes
Mary L. Fonseca
Armando Fontoura
Joseph Fortes
Donald P. Freitas
Joseph Freitas, Jr. **
Brian Gomes
Shirley Gomes
Donald Gonçalves
Jane L. Gonsalves
Manuel R. Grova, Jr.
Tom Jardim
Dennis Lawrence
Helena S. Lawrence

Charlene Lima
Fana Lopes
Maria J. Lopes
Nelson Macedo
Michael John Machado
Valdemir Machado
Helen Mathieu
João G. Mattos, Jr.
James P. DeMattos,
Elio Melo
Henry Mello
John F. Melo
Aristide Soua Mendes
Isidro Meneses
Norman Mranda
Tony Monteiro
Paulo E. Moura
Joaquim Nobrega
John B. Nunes **
Manuel Caetano Pacheco
Marc R. Pacheco
Thomas Pacheco
M. Teresa Paiva
Anthony Perry
Victor Pinheiro
Antonio J. Pires
Richard Pombo
Daniel da Ponte
Philip Rivard-Raposo
Maria Reis
Julio F. Rocha
Michael Rodrigues
Antonio A. Rogers
Everett Rogers
George Rogers
Henry Rose
Lehua Fernandes Salling
Alberto Santos
Agostinho Saraiva
Anthony Silva
Manuel Vitorino da Silva
Custodio Silva, Jr.
Fernando Silva

Mario Silva
Milton Silva
William Silva
Frank M. Silvia
Anthony Soares
Robert Sousa
Joseph Sylvia
Cyrus Nils Tavares
Paul J. Tavares
Augusto C. Taveira
Nancy Teixeira
Joseph Theriaga
Patrick Andrade Toomey
Ernest C. Torres
Manuel Valerio
Joe Vas
John Vasconcellos
Adriano S. Veiga, MD
Jennifer Veiga
William Vieira
Carlton Viveiros

Literature

José Brites
Adalino Cabral, Ph.D.
Eduardo M. Dias, Ph. D.
Katherine Vaz, P.h. D.

Media

Xana Antunes
Maria João Baptista
Lionel Rocha Holmes
Vasco S. Jardim
Stuart Marques
Antonio Matinho
João Rocha

Military

Charles Braga
Lt. Colonel MarioCarmo

Lt.Col. John Constantino
Col. Ronald Cruz
James Francis Dias
Ralph Ellis Dias
Mary Ann Faias
Walter Goulart
Alberto S. Leonardo
Roger Machado
Brothers Moraes
Lt.Col. AntonioH.Rebelo
Americo Sardo
H. C. Hank Stackpole II

Religion

Stephen Peter Alencastre
M.Rev.Tod David Brown
Mons. José Cacella
Marcelino Manuel Graça
Rev. William J. Levada
Humberto Medeiros

Science & Medicine

Steve Abrantes
Dr. Roy Almeida
Joseph Amaral, MD,
John Andrews
Angelo Cardoso, Ph. D.
Vitor Cardoso
José Pacheco Correia
Burke Cunha, MD
Gregory Curt, MD
Antonio Damasio, MD
Sebastião Luiz Dias
Carlos Fernandes, MD
David Fernandes, MD
José dos S.Fernandes
Mathias Figueira, MD
Mario Gomes, MD
David Gouveia, M.D.
Abilio da Silva Greaves
Rogerio Lobo, MD

John C. Lobato
Joseph Loureiro, Ph. D.
Ruy V. Lourenço, MD
Ernest J. Moniz, Ph. D.
Paulo Pacheco, MD
David Pereira, MD
Stephen Pereira, MD
Ronald de Pinho, MD
Manuel V. dos Santos
Dr. Angelo T.Silva
Dr. Manuel L. Silva, MD
Milton A. Silveira, Eng.
Rui Soeiro, MD
Caesar Ventura
Dr. Jeffrey Vieira
Gilbert Vincent, Dentist

Sports

Billy Andrade
Wayne Fontes
Rockne Freitas
Kurt Gouveia
Tony Lema
Davey Lopes
Francisco Marcos
Billy Martin
Al Melo
Jim Mello
John Mota
Ticha Penicheiro
Pedro Pinto
Ephraim (Red) Rocha
Henrique Santos
Jose Luis Soares
Fernando V. Ferreira
Jose Violante
Bernie de Viveiros

US Universities

David Almeida, Ph. D.
Maria José Bolina Alves

Onesimo Almeida Ph. D.
Maria Laura Areias
Antonio José S.Carvalho
Nelson F. de Carvalho
Joaquim F. Coelho
Maria Duarte
José Manuel Faria
Manuel C.Fontes, Ph. D.
Florbela M.R. Gomes
Geoffrey L. Gomes
Antonio José C. Ladeira
Maria Rosa Menocal
Maria T. Machado Neves
Rita D. Marinho Ph. D
Maria F. Pereira, Ph.D.
Julio Ramos
Linda Rodrigues, Ph. D.
Ferreira Salgado
Carlos A.Veloso da Silva
João Camilo dos Santos
Ana C.C.Oliveira Sousa
Ronald Sousa
Frank de Sousa

For more information on the above names, visit
our web site at: **www.PortugueseFoundation.org**
or send your comments
by email to: **portugal@dnet.net**

This Bibliography is divided into two sections.

The first section is of published books and is indexed by the author's last name, followed by the name of the book and publishing information.
The second section is of Newspapers, Magazines and other Media, and is indexed by the name of the publication followed by the author's name and date of publication.
* * *

Adams, James Truslow. *Dictionary of American History*. Vol. 3. Scribners, NY (ICGP 1141), 1940.
Afonso, John Correia. *Christian and Spices, The Portuguese in India*. Unesco Courier, Paris, France, April issue, 1989.
Aguiar, João. *A Voz dos Deuses (Memorias de Viriato)*. Perspectivas e Realidades, Lisboa, 1984.
Albornoz, Michael. *De Soto, Knight of the Americas*. Franklin Watts, NY, 1986.
Albuquerque, Luis de. *Alguns casos da India Portuguesa, D. João de Castro*. Alfa, Lisboa, 1989.
Albuquerque, Luis de. *The Courier and the Portuguese Voyages of Discovery*. Unesco, Paris, France, April issue, 1989.
Albuquerque, Luis de. *Dicionario de Historia dos Descobrimentos Portugueses*. Circulo de Leitores, Lisboa, 1994.
Albuquerque, Luis de. *Rutters of India of D. João de Castro*. Inapa, Lisboa, 1988.
Allen, W. C. *History of Halifax County*. Cornhill Co., Boston, 1918.
Almeida, Carlos de. *The Portuguese Immigrants*. União Portuguesa do Estado da California, 1992.
Amaral, Pat. *They Ploughed the Seas*. Valkyrie Press, Inc., 1978.
Anderson-Biggs, Grace M. David. *The Future we Inherit*. McClelland & Stewart, Secretary State of Canada, 1976.
Andrade, Francisco de. *Cronica do Imperador Clarimundo*. Vol. XI, F 89, Vol. III, Ch. 2- f25.
Armstrong, Zella. *Who Discovered America?* Lookout Publishing, Chattanooga, TN, 1950.
Aswell, James & others. *God Bless the Devil, Melungeon Tales*. UNC, Chapel Hill, 1944.
Baganha, Maria Ioannis Benis. *Portuguese Emigration to the United States (1820-1930)*. Garland Publishing, New York, 1990.
Baião, Antonio Blanco. *Historia da Expansão Portuguesa no Mundo, Vol. II*. Atica, Lisboa, 1939.
Bailey, Philip A. *Golden Mirages, Ramona Antonio Joseph, California Prospect*. Acoma, 1971.
Baird, Charles W. DD. *History of the Huguenot Emigration to America*. Dodd, Mead & Co. NY, 1907.
Ball, Bonnie Sage. *America's Mysterious Race*. Vol. XVI, May 64-67. Pick of the Month, 1944.
Ball, Bonnie Sage. *The Melungeons*. Historical Sketches by Historical Society of Southwest Virginia, No. 2, 1966.
Ball, Bonnie Sage. *The Melungeons*. The Overmountain Press, Johnson City, TN, 1969.
Ball, Bonnie Sage. *The Melungeons*. 5th edition 1975.
Ball, Bonnie Sage. *The Melungeons, Origin & Kin*. Author, 1969.
Ball, Bonnie Sage. *Mystery Men of the Mountains*. Negro Digest, 3, Jan 1945, 39-41.
Ball, Bonnie Sage. *Virginia's Mystery Race*. Virginia State Highway Bulletin 2, No. 6, Apr 1945, 2-3.
Ball, Bonnie Sage. *Who are the Melungeons?* Southern Literary Messenger, 3, No. 2 (June 1945), 5-7.
Bancroft, Hubert Howe. *The works of Hubert of...1882-1890, Vols. 18-21*. History Co., San Francisco. 1882.
Barbosa, Jorge Morais. *Lingua Portuguesa no Mundo*. Sociedade Geografia de Lisboa. 1968.
Barck, Oscar Theodore, Jr. *Colonial America*. MacMillan, NY. 1958.
Barr, Phyllis Cox. *The Melungeons of Newman's Ridge*. East Tennessee State University, 1965.
Barreira, Anibal. *Historia de Portugal*. Edições ASA, 1978.
Barreto, Luis Filipe. *Camões & the Portuguese Voyages*. The Courier, Unesco, Paris, France, April issue, 1989.
Barreto, Mascarenhas. *O Português Cristovão Columbo*. Edições Referendo, Lisboa, Portugal, 1988.

Barreto, Mascarenhas. *The Portuguese Columbus.* MacMillan Press London, England, 1992.
Bell, Aubrey F.G. *Damião de Gois, Um Humanista.* Imperio, Lisboa, 1942.
Bensaude. Joaquim. *Roteiro de Flandres e D. João II.* Sociedade Astoria, Lisboa, 1945.
Berkow, Robert. *The (Diagnosis and Therapy)*, Merck Manual, Merck Sharp, Rahway, NJ, 1982.
Berry, Brewton. *Almost White.* MacMillan, NY, 1963.
Bible, Jean Patterson. *The Melungeons Yesterday and Today.* Mountain Press, Signal Mountain, TN, 1975.
Biggs, Captain Walter. *Voyages and Travels, Vol. 33.* Drake's Voyages, Harvard Classics, 1910.
Blackmun, Ora. W. *North Carolina, Its Mountains, Its People to 1880.* Appalachian Consortium Press, Boone, NC, 1977.
Blue, Karen I. *The Lumbee Problem.* Cambridge U.P., NY, 1980.
Boland, Charles Michael. *They all discovered America.* Doubleday, NY, 1961.
Bolton, Herbert E. *The Colonization of North America.* Hafner Publishing Co., NY, 1971.
Bolton, Herbert E. *Spain's Title to Georgia.* Univ. of California Press, Berkeley, 1925.
Boorstin, Daniel J. *The Discoverers.* Vintage, Random House, N.Y., 1985.
Bourne, Edward Gaylord. *Narratives Hernando de Soto.* Rodrigo Rangel, Biedma, Allerton Book Co., NY, 1922.
Bourne, Edward Gaylord. *The Northmen, Columbus and Cabot.* Barnes & Noble, 1959.
Boxer, Charles Ralph. *From Lisbon to Goa.* Variourum Reprints, London, 1984.
Boxer, Charles Ralph. *The Portuguese Seaborne Empire.* Alfred A Knopf, NY, 1969.
Boxer, Charles Ralph. *The Tragic History of the Sea.* The Hakluyt Society, 1967.
Braswell, Peggy Jo Cobb. *The Roanoke Canal.* Halifax County, 1958.
Braudel, Fernand. *The Mediterranean World....* Harper & Row, NY, 1972.
Braudel, Fernand. *The Structures of Everyday Life.* Harper & Row, NY, 1975.
Brazão, Eduardo. *Descobrimentos Portugueses nas Historias do Canada.* Agencia Geral do Ultramar, Lisboa, 1969.
Brazão, Eduardo. *Os Cortes Reais e o Novo Mundo.* Agencia Geral do Ultramar, Lisboa, 1965.
Brebner, John B. *Explorers of North America 1492/1806.* MacMillan New York, 1933.
Brickell, M.D., John. *The Natural History of North Carolina.* Johnson Publishing Co., Murfreesboro, NC.
Brito, Bernardo Gomes & Peres, Damião. *Historia Tragico-Maritima, Vol. I.* Editora do Minho, Barcelos, Portugal, 1942.
Bromwell, William J. *History of Immigration to the U.S.* Arno, NY, 1969.
Brown, Alexander. *Genesis of the United States, Vol. I, p. 337.* Russel & Russel, NY, 1964.
Burks, Jacqueline Daniel, *Treatment of the Melungeons in Gen. Literature....* Tennessee Tech, Masters Thesis, 1972.
Burns, Edward McNall. *World Civilizations.* W. W. Norton & Co., 1955.
Cabral Ph.D., Adalino. *Portinglês.* 4 volumes, Univ. Microfilms Internat'l, Ann Arbor, MI, 1985.
Callahan, North. *Melungeons in Smoky Mountain Country.* Little Brown & Co. Boston, 1952.
Cambiaire Ph.D., Celestine Pierre. *W.V. Mountain Ballads, Last American Pioneer Stand,* London, Mitre Press, 1935.
Camões, Luis Vaz de. *Os Lusiadas.* Imprensa Nacional, Lisboa, 1970.
Canfield, Jack. *Chicken Soup for the Soul* (Mark Victor Hansen), Health Communications, Inc., 1995.
Canto, Ernesto do. *Centenario da Descoberta da America.* Tipografia Ponta Delgada, Açores, 1892.
Capelli, Adriano. *Dizionario de abbreviature latin ed italiane.* Milano 1912.
Cardozo, Manuel da Silveira. *Portuguese in America 590 BC–1974 Chronology.* Oceana Publications, Dobbs Ferry, NY, 1976.
Carvalho, Agostinho de. *Portugueses na India.* Tipografia Rangel, India Portuguesa, 1943.

Carvalho, Antonio Faustino de. *Côa Valley, Rock Art and Prehistory.* Ministerio da Cultura, Lisboa, 1996.

Castanheda, Fernão Lopes de. *Historia Descobrimento Conquista India.* (M.L. Almeida), Lello & Irmão, Porto, 2 Vols. (1979), 1551.

Chagas, Manuel Pinheiro. *Portugueses em Africa, Asia, America e Oceania.* Liv. A.M. Pereira, Lisboa, 1879.

Charnwood, Lord. *Abraham Lincoln.* Pocket Books, Cardinal, 1954.

Christovich, Mary Louise. *New Orleans Architecture.* Pelican Publishing Co., LA, 1989.

Clough & Others, Sheppard B. & Others. *Ancient Times to 1715, A History of the Western World.* D.C. Heath and Company, Boston, 1964.

Cohen, Martin A. *Sephardim in the Americas* (Abraham J. Peck). University of Alabama Press, 1993.

Colaço, Dr. J. A. *St. Francisco Xavier—his life and times.* Internet: jcolaco@bahamas.net. 1996.

Coleman, Kenneth. *Founding a Colony—Colonial Georgia: A History.* University of Georgia Press, Athens, GA.

Coleman, Kenneth & Burr, Charles Stephen. *Dictionary of Georgia Biography.* UNC, Chapel Hill, 1928.

Cool, Linda E. *Lá Muito Longe Para Alem do Mar.* Angra do Heroismo, Açores, 1994.

Coppee, Henry, *History of the Conquest of Spain by...Moors.* Little Brown & Co., Vol. 2, 1881.

Cortesão, Armando. *Cartografia e Cartografos Portugueses, Vol. I.* Seara Nova, Lisboa, 1935.

Cortesão, Armando. *Historia da Cartografia Portuguesa, Vol. I, II.* Junta de Investigações do Ultramar, Lisboa, 1969.

Cortesão, Armando & Mota, Avelino. *Portugaliae Monumenta Cartographica.* Seara Nova, Lisboa, 1960.

Cortesão, Jaime. *Os Descobrimentos Portugueses (2 Vol.).* Arcadia, Portugal, 1958.

Cortesão, Jaime. *Os Portugueses no Descobrimento dos E.U.* Seara Nova, Lisboa, 1949.

Cortesão, Jaime. *Viagem de Diogo de Teive e Pero Vasquez....* Imprensa da Armada, Lisboa, 1933.

Coutinho, Almirante Gago. *Onde teria invernado Gomes de Sequeira em 1525.* Sociedade de Geografia, Seie 58-1/2, Lisboa, 1940.

Crocket, W. David. *Archaeological Anomalies.* Crocket, 1994, Anudsen Publishing Company, Decorah, IA, 1994.

Crow, Escott, Jeffrey J. (Hatley). *African Americans in North Carolina.* N.C. Dept. of Cultural Resources, 1992.

Cumming, William P. *The Discoveries of John Lederer.* U of Virginia Press, Charlottesville, VA, 1958.

Cunha, MªCristina & Fonseca, Luis Adão. *Tratado de Tordesilhas, Diplomacia Luso-Castelhana.* Inapa, Lisboa, 1991.

Dalgado, Sebastião Rodolfo. *Glossario Luso-Asiatico.* Imprensa da Universidade, Coimbra, 1919.

D'Andrada, Francisco. *Cronica D. João III, Cap. 51-f400,* 1786.

Dayton, Ruth Woods. *Greenbriar Pioneers and their homes.* West Virginia Publishing, 1942.

Denton, Gilian, *History of the World.* Dorling Kindersley, 1994.

Dias, Eduardo Mayone. *Coisas da Lusalandia.* Instituo Português Ensino, 1981.

Diez, Mª del Carmen Galbis. *Catalogo de Passageros a Indias.* Archivo General de Indias, Sevilla, 1986.

Dimont, Max I. *The Jews in America.* Simon & Schuster, NY, 1980.

Domingues, Mario. *Camões a sua vida e a sua época.* Romano Torres, 1980.

Domingues, Mario. *Cardeal D. Henrique, o homem, o monarca.* Romano Torres, 1964.

Domingues, Mario. *Infante D. Henrique e sua época.* Romano Torres, 2ª edição, 1957.

Domingues, Mario. *João III, D. e sua época.* Romano Torres, 1960.

Domingues, Mario. *Manuel I, D. e a Epopeia dos Descobrimentos.* Romano Torres,1971.
Donald, David Herbert. *Abraham Lincoln.* Simon & Schuster, 1995.
Dor-Ner, Zvi. *Columbus and the age of discovery.* William Morrow and Co., NY, 1991.
Duncan, David Ewing. *Hernando de Soto.* Crown Publishers, NY, 1995.
Durant, John & Alice. *Presidents of the United States (Andrew Johnson).* Gaché
    Publishing, NY, 1970.
Dutra, Ramiro Carvalho. *Tecnologia de Alimentos no ano 2000.* Inst. Univ. de Trás-os-
    Montes, 1979.
Dyson, John. *Columbus, for Gold, God and Glory.* Simon & Schuster, NY, 1991.
Elder, Pat Spurlock. *The Melungeons: Examining.* Continuity Press, Tennessee, 1999.
Entwistle, W. J. *The Spanish, Portuguese, Catalan and Basque Language.* Faber and
    Faber, London England, 1951.
Estabrook, Arthur Howard & Ivan E./McDougle. *Mongrel Virginians.* Williams and
    Williams, Baltimore, 1926.
Ewen, Charles R. *The Archaeology of Spanish Colonialism in SE United States....*
    Society for Historical Archaeology, 1990.
Falcão, Luis de Figueiredo. *Livro de toda a Fazenda dos Reinos de Portugal.* Imprensa
    Nacional (Original 1607), 1859.
Felix, John Henry. *The Portuguese in Hawaii.* Peter F. Senecal, Honolulu, Author's edition, 1978.
Fell, Barry. *America B. C., Ancient Settlers.* Demeter Press Book, 1977.
Fernandes, Alvaro. *Gentleman of Elvas, Hernando de Soto Travels.* Florida Historical
    Society, 1933.
Ferreira, Ana Maria Pereira. *Essencial sobre o Corso e a Pirataria.* Universidade Nova,
    Lisbon, 1986.
Ferreira, Ana Maria Pereira. *Importação e o Comercio Têxtil...1385-1481.* Universidade
    Nova, Lisbon, 1986.
Ferreira, Ana Maria Pereira. *Problemas Maritimos entre Portugal e França, Sec. XVI.*
    Imprensa Nacional, Lisboa, 1983.
Ferreira, Seomara da Veiga. *Cronica esquecida d'el Rei d. João II.* Imp. Universitaria,
    Edit. Estampa, 1984.
Figueiredo, Fidelino de Sousa. *A Épica Portuguesa no Século XVI.* Imprensa Nacional,
    Lisboa (1987), 1950.
Figueiredo, Fidelino de Sousa. *Estudos de Historia Americana.* Melhoramentos de S.
    Paulo, S. Paulo, Brasil, 1927.
Figueiredo, José de. *Época dos Descobrimentos.* Exposição Cultural em Sevilha,
    Catalogo, 1929.
Fletcher, Richard. *Moorish Spain.* Henry Holt, NY, 1992.
Flores, Joaquim/José. *Ourem, Três Contributos para a sua Historia.* Câmara Municipal
    de Ourem, 1994.
Flores, Maria da Conceição. *Portugueses e o Sião, seculo XVI.* Universidade Nova,
    Lisbon, 1991.
Fonseca, Isabel. *Bury Me Standing, The Gypsies and Their Journey.* Random, Vintage,
    1996.
Fonseca, Luis Adão. *Tratado de Tordesilhas.* Inapa, Lisboa, 1991.
Fontes, Manuel da Costa. *Anti-Christian Jewish Ballad.* University of California Press,
    1994.
Fontes, Manuel da Costa. *Sacrificio de Isaac, Portuguese Oral Tradition.* Journal of
    Folklore Research, Vol. 31-1-3, 1994.
Fontes, Manuel da Costa. *Study of the Ballad.* Folklore Institute, Indiana University,
    1994.
Forsyth, William B. *The Wolf from Scotland.* Anchor Press, Essex, UK 1998.
Frazier, Charles. *Cold Mountain.* Atlantic Monthly Press, NY, 1997.
Freijeiro, Antonio Blanco. *Historia de España.* Historia 16, Informacion, 1986.
French, Laurence & Hornbuckle, Jim. *The Cherokee Perspective.* Appalachian C. Press,
    Boone, NC, 1981.

Freyre, Gilberto & Putnam, Samuel. *The Master and the Slaves*, (Translation). University of California Press, 1986. *Casa Grande & Senzala* em Português.

Frutuoso, Gaspar. *Saudades da Terra (Livro 4, Vol. 1, Livro 2)*. Inst. Cultural Ponta Delgada, Azores, 1991.

Frutuoso, Gaspar & Azevedo, Alvaro Rodrigues. *Saudades da Terra, Historia das Ilhas....* Typ. Funchalense, Funchal, Madeira, 1873.

Funk & Wagnalls. *New Standard Dictionary of the English Language*. Dr. Isaac K. Funk, NY, 1913.

Fuson, Robert H. *The log of Christopher Columbus*. International Marine, Camden, 1992.

Gerber, Jane S. *Jews of Spain, The Sephardic experience*. Free Press, NY, 1992.

Gilbert Jr., William Harlen. *Eastern Cherokees*. AMS, NY, 1978.

Gilbert Jr., William Harlen. *Peoples of India*. Smithsonian, Washington DC, 1944.

Gildemeister, Henrique Eugene. *Local Complexities of Race in the Rural South Carolina*. State University of New York College at Purchase, 1977.

Godinho, Vitorino Magalhães. *Os Descobrimentos e a Economia Mundial Vol. II*. Arcadia, Lx, 1965.

Goertz, Richard. *João Alvares Fagundes, Capitão de Terra Nova, 1521*. Canadian Ethnic Studies Vol. XXXIII, No. 2, 1991.

Goins, Jack. *Melungeons: And other Pioneer Families*. Author jgoins@usit.net, 2000.

Gonçalves, Julio. *Portugueses e o mar das Indias*. Livraria Luso-Espanhola, 1947.

Gowan, Walter. *New Orleans, Yesterday and Today*. LA Univ. Press, 1983.

Graham, Gerald S. *The British Empire*. Thames and Hudson, 1972.

Gregorie, Anne King. *History of Sumter County, SC*. Library Board, 1954.

Griffiths, Arthur. *In Spanish Prisons: Persecution and Punishment*. Dorset Press, NY, 1991.

Grohse, William Paul papers. (Microfilm #501), Tennessee State Library and Archives. *Melungeon family data collected prior to 1989*.

Grove, Noel. *Atlas of the World History by National Geographic Society*. 1997.

Guill Ph.D., James H. *Azores Islands, A History*. Golden Shield Inc., 1993.

Hale, William T. & Merritt, Dixon L. *History of Tennessee and Tennesseans Vol. 1*. Lewis Publishing Co. Chicago, NY, 1913.

Haun, Mildred. *The Hawk's Done Gone, The (Melungeon Colored)*. Vanderbilt Univ. Press, 1968.

Hawke, David. *Colonial Experience*. Bobs Merrill, NY, 1966.

Herculano, Alexandre. *Historia Origem, Estabelecimento Inquisição, Portugal*. Circulo de Leitores, Lisboa, 1982.

Herrera y Tordesillas, Antonio. *Historia General de los Hechos de los Castellanos en las Islas y Tierra Firme del Mar Oceano*. (Madrid 1615), Decada 7, libro 5, capitulo 3.

Higgs, David & Anderson, Grace M. *The Future we Inherit*. McClelland & Stewart, Secretary State of Canada, 1976.

Hodge, Frederick Webb. *Handbook of the American Indian*. 2 Vol., Greenwood Press, 1971.

Hoffman, Paul E. *A New Andalucia and way to the Orient*. Louisiana State Univ. Baton Rouge, 1990.

Hoffman, Paul E. *Spain and Roanoke Voyages*. NC Cultural Dept., Raleigh, 1987.

Hollingsworth, Jess Gentry. *History of Surry County, NC*. W. H. Fisher Co. (Private Printing), 1935.

Hourani, Albert. *History of the Arab people*. Warner Books, 1992.

Hroch/Skybova, Miroslav/Anna. *Ecclesia Militans: The Inquisition*. Dorset Press, NY, 1991.

Hudson, Charles. *The Forgotten Centuries*. Georgia University Press, 1994.

Hudson, Charles M. *The Juan Pardo Expeditions, 1566-1568*. Smithsonian Press, 1990.

Huhner, Leon. *Jews in America in Colonial...Revolutionary....* Gertzs Brothers, 1959.

Huhner, Leon. *The Jews of Newport.* Gertzs Brothers, 1959.
Huhner, Leon. *The Jews of South Carolina.* Gertzs Brothers, 1959.
Huyghe, Patrick. *Columbus was last.* Hyperion, New York, 1992.
Irwin, John Rice. *Portrait of a Pioneer, Alex Stewart.* Schiffer Publishing, West Chester, PA, 1985.
Ivey, Saundra Keyes. *Oral, Printed...Popular Culture, Tradition of the Melungeons.* University Micro Films, Michigan 48106, 1976.
Iyas, Ibn (Mamluk, Egypt). *Rivalry in the Red Sea, Portugal's impact.* Unesco, Courier, Paris, April 1989.
Jackson, Harvey H. & Spalding, Phinizy. *Forty Years of Diversity Essays on Colonial Georgia.* University of Georgia Press, Athens, GA.
Janeira, Armando Martins. *Portugueses no Japão.* Publicações Dom Quixote, Lisboa, 1988.
Johnson, Charles A. *Wise County VA.* Overmountain Press, 1938.
Johnson, Allen & Malone, Dumas. *Dictionary of American Biography.* Vol. 3, 190-191, 396-397; Vol. 5, pp. 24-25; Vol. 17, pp. 407-408, Scribners, 1959.
Johnson, Ruth. *My Melungeon Heritage.* The Overmountain Press, Johnson City, TN 1997.
Jones, Hugh. *The Present State of Virginia.* VA Historical Society, UNC Press, Chapel Hill, 1975.
Jordan, Vern. *The Melungeons Peoples, (Cherokee Country).* Moccasin telegraph Network, 1996.
Kayserling, Meyer. *Historia dos Judeus em Portugal* (Trad. G. B. C. Silva). Livraria Pioneira, São Paulo, Brazil (1971), 1867.
Kegley, F. B. *Virginia Frontier.* SW Virginia Historical Society, Roanoke VA, 1938.
Kennedy, N. Brent. *The Melungeons, The Resurrection of a Proud People.* Mercer Univ. Press, 1994.
Kinross, Lord Patrick Balfour. *The Ottoman Centuries, Rise and Fall.* Morrow Quill Paperbacks, NY, 1977.
Langdon, Barbara Tracy. *The Melungeons, Bibliography.* Dogwood Press, 1998.
Lawson, John & Lefler, Hugh Talmage. *A New Voyage to Carolina, or History of Carolina.* University of NC Press, 1984.
Levenson, Jay A. *Circa 1492.* National Gallery of Art, Yale U. Press, 1991.
Levinger, Ph.D., Rabbi Lee J. *History of the Jews in the United States.* Union of American Hebrew Congregations, 1961.
Lewis, Charles Lee. *David Glasgow Farragut, Vol. I, II.* United States Naval Institute, 1943.
Lewis, Clifford M. & Loomis, Albert. *Spanish Jesuit Mission in Virginia.* U. of NC Press, 1953.
Lewis, Theodore & Hodge, Frederick. *Spanish Explorers of the Southern United States, 1528-1543.* Barnes & Noble, NY, 1959.
Ley, Charles David. *Portuguese Voyages.* J. M. Dent & Sons Ltd. London, 1953.
Lobban, Richard. *Jews in Cape Verde and on the Guinea Coast.* University of Massachusetts, Dartmouth, 1996.
Lopez, Juan Perez. *El Cid, El distierro.* Burgos, Spain, 1979.
Lourenço, Eduardo. *From National Epic to Universal Myth.* Unesco, Courier, Paris, April, 1989.
Lucena, João de. *Historia da Vida do Padre Francisco de Xavier.* Alfa, Lisboa, 1989.
Lyon, Eugene. *The Enterprise of Florida.* University of Florida, Gainesville, 1976.
Machado, José Pedro. *Grande Dicionario da Lingua Portuguesa.* Amigos do Livro Editores, Portugal, 1981.
Machado, José Pedro, *Dicionario Etimologico da Lingua Portuguesa*, Vol. 4, M-P, 3rd. Ed. Livros Horizonte, p. 18.
Mahan, Alfred Thayer. *Admiral Farragut.* Haskell House, NY, 1968.
Manucy, Albert C. *Calendar of the N. C. Spanish Records, 1566-1570.* N. C. State Archives, 1946.

Marcus, Jacob Rader. *The Colonial American Jew, 1492-1776.* Wayne State University, 1970.
Marcus, Jacob Rader. *Early American Jewry, The Jews of NY.* Lopes-Rivera. Jewish Publications Soc. Phil., 2 Vols., 1951.
Markham, Clements R. *The Annals of America (1878 pp. 8-64).* Encyclopaedia Britannica, Vol. 1, 1976.
Marques, A. H. de Oliveira. *Historia de Portugal, Vol. I, II, & III.* Palas Editores, Lisboa, 1982.
Marques, A. H. de Oliveira. *History of Portugal, Vol. I & II.* Columbia University Press, 1972.
Marques, Alfredo Pinheiro. *Guia da Historia dos Descobrimentos.* Bib. Nacional de Lisboa, 1988.
Marques, Alfredo Pinheiro. *Japan in early Portuguese maps.* Unesco, Paris, France, April, 1989.
Marques, Alfredo Pinheiro. *Portugal and the Discovery of the Atlantic.* Imprensa Nacional, 1990.
Martins, Oliveira. *Fomento Rural e Emigração,* 3rd edition. Guimarães Editores, 1994.
Martins, Oliveira. *Historia da Civilização Iberica,* 11th edition. Guimarães Editores, 1994.
Martins, Oliveira. *Historia de Portugal,* 15th edition. Guimarães Editores, 1968.
Martins, Oliveira. *Portugal nos Mares,* Vol. I, 3rd edition; Vol. II, 2nd ed. Guimarães Editores, 1994.
Mason, A. E. W. *The Life of Francis Drake.* Hodge and Stoughton Ltd., 1950.
Matar, Matar. *Turks—Moors & Englishman.* Columbia University, 1999.
Mathews, Warren. *Abraham Was Their Father.* Mercer University Press, 1981.
Matos, Artur Teodoro de. *Na Rota das Indias.* Missão de Macau, 1994.
Mattoso, José. *Historia de Portugal,* 8 Vols. Editorial Estampa, Portugal, 1994.
Maxwell, Hu. *History of Barvour County, West VA Guineas.* McClain Printing Co. Parson, WV, 1968.
Mayer, Henrietta Mello. *Silva Descendants: Portuguese Genealogy.* Stonington, CT, 1978.
McCary, Ben. *Indians of the 17th century Virginia.* University of VA Press, Charlottesville, 1990.
McEvedy, Colin. *Atlas Historico-Geografico.* Difel, Lisboa, 1984.
McGlothlen, Mike. *Melungeons and other Mestee groups.* Author, Gainesville, Florida, 1994.
McLeRoy, Sherrie/William R. *Strangers in their midst, Free Blacks of Amherst Cty.,* VA. Heritage Books, MD 20716, 1993.
McRae, Barbara. *Know Your County.* Franklin Press, NC, 1985.
Mehdi, Beverlee Turner. *Arabs in America.* Oceana Publications, NY, 1978.
Melvin, Richard. *New Thoughts on the DeSoto Expedition in Georgia.* Author, 1978.
Mertz, Henriette. *Atlantis, Dwelling Place of the Gods.* Henriette Mertz, Chicago, 1976.
Messick, Mary Ann. *History of Baxter County.* Mountain Home C. C., 1973.
Midelfort, H. C. Erik. *Witch Hunting in Southwestern Germany, 1562-1684.* Stanford Un. Press, 1972.
Miers, Earl Schenk. *American Story.* Channel Press, Great Neck, NY, 1956.
Miller, Russel. *The East Indiamen.* Time-Life Books, Alexandria, Virginia, 1980.
Milling, Chapman, J. *Red Carolinians.* UNC, Chapel Hill, 1940.
Mira, Manuel. *Melungeons and the Forgottten Portuguese.* PAHRF, Inc., 1995.
Monteiro, Saturnino. *Batalhas e Combates da Marinha Portuguesa.* Vol. 1/5. Sá da Costa, Lx, 1990.
Monumenta Henricina, Vol. XI, pp. 235, 236 and Vol. IX, p. 145. Coimbra, 1970.
Moon, William Arthur. *Peter Francisco, The Portuguese Patriot.* Colonial Publishers, 1980.
Mooney, James (George Ellison). *History, Myths and Sacred Formulas of the Cherokees.*

Bright Mountain Books, Asheville NC, 1992.

Moquin, Wayne. *Makers of America: The First comers, 1536-1800.* Ed Wayne Moquin, 1971.

Moreira, Antonio Joaquim. *Sentenças da Inquisição em Lisboa, Evora e Coimbra.* Imprensa Nacional, Lisboa, 1980.

Moreira, Rafael de Faria D. *Portuguese Art in the Maritime Era.* Unesco, Courier, Paris, April 1989.

Morison, Samuel Eliot. *Admiral of the Ocean Sea.* Little, Brown and Company, 1942.

Morison, Samuel Eliot. *European Discovery of North America.* Oxford Univ. Press, NY, 1971.

Morison, Samuel Eliot. *Journals & other documents, Columbus.* Heritage, NY, 1963.

Morison, Samuel Eliot. *The Oxford History of the American People.* Oxford Univ. Press, NY, 1965.

Morison, Samuel Eliot. *Portuguese Voyages to America, 15th Century.* Octagon Books, NY, 1965.

Morris, Richard B. *Encyclopedia of American History.* Harper & Row, NY, 1961.

Moura, Vasco da Graça. *Luis de Camões, the eventual life and times.* Unesco. The Courier, Japan in early Portuguese maps, April 1989.

Natella, Jr., Arthur A. *The Spanish America 1513-1974 Chronology.* Oceana Publications, NY, 1975.

Neto, Serafim da Silva. *Historia da Lingua Portuguesa.* Presença, Rio de Janeiro, 1979.

Nichols, Philip. *Sir Francis Drake Revived.* Harvard Classics, Vol. 33, 1910.

Nugent, Nell Marion. *Cavaliers and Pioneers.* Genealogical Publishing Co., Baltimore, 1983.

Nunes, E. Borges. *Abreviaturas Paleograficas Portuguesas.* Faculdade de Letras de Lisboa, 1981.

Nunes, E. Borges. *Paleografia Portuguesa, Album.* Faculdade de Letras de Lisboa, 1981.

Nunn, Louise. *Thesis-Comparison of two Indian Groups in North Carolina.* Columbia University, 1933.

Offutt, Chris. *Melungeons from Story.* Suffolk, Ma, 1996.

Oliveira, João Brás de. *Os Navios de Vasco da Gama.* Agencia Geral do Ultramar, Imp. Nac., 1971.

Oliveira, Jorge de. *Paisagens Arqueologicas de Évora.* Camara Municipal de Évora, 1997.

Pap, Leo. *Portuguese Americans.* Portuguese Continental Union, 1981.

Pap, Leo. *The Portuguese in the United States: A Bibliography.* Center for Migration Studies, 1976.

Pardo, João. *Index da Chancelaria de D. João III.* Proprios. L 51, F 82v, 132, 132v—L3, F74v—L12, F74, 1523.

Pardo, Juan. *Archivos General de Indias, Juan La Bandera.* NC State Archives NC 2-31 AI148-2-8, T. 17, 1567.

Paredes, James Anthony. *Indians of the Southeast late 20th Century.* University of Alabama Press, 1992.

Paredes, James Anthony. *Social and Cultural Identity, Eastern Creek….* Southern Anthropological Society, UGA, 1974.

Parkman, Francis. *Pioneers of France in the New World.* S. J. Parkhill & Co., Boston, 1865.

Passos, Carlos de. *Navegação Portuguesa dos Séculos XV e XVI.* Imprensa da Univ., Coimbra, 1917.

Patterson, Rev. George. *Portuguese in North America.* Montreal, 1891.

Perdue, Theda. *Native Carolinians, The Indians of North Carolina.* NC Dept. of Cultural Resources, 1985.

Pereira, A. B. de Bragança. *Portugueses em Diu.* Bastora, India, Tip. Rangel, 1938.

Pereira, Duarte Pacheco. *Esmeraldo de situ orbis, livro I, Capitulo II.* Academia Portuguesa da Historia, Lisboa, 1988.

Peres, Damião. *Historia dos Descobrimentos Portugueses.* Vertente, Porto, 1981.

Peres, Damião. *Historia de Portugal, Vol. III.* Portucalense Editora, 1931.

Pericão, Maria da Graça. *O Descobrimento da Florida*. Alfa, Lisboa, 1989.
Phillips, William D. *The Worlds of Christopher Columbus*. Cambridge Univ. Press, NY, 1992.
Pidal, Ramon Menendez. *Historia de España, Tomo XVIII*. España: Calpe, Madrid, 1966.
Pina, Rui de. *Chronica d'El Rey D. João II* (M. Lopes de Almeida). Lello & Irmão, Porto (1977), 1497.
Pinto, Fernão Mendes. *Peregrinação, Vol. 1*. Imprensa Nacional, Lisboa (1988), 1614.
Pinto, Fernão Mendes & Águas, Neves. *Peregrinação, Vol. 1*. Europa-America, 1989.
Pinto, João Rocha. *Houve Diarios de Bordo...séculos XV e XVI*. Inst. Invest. Cientifica Tropical, Lisboa, 1988.
Powell, William S. *The North Carolina Gazetteer*. University of NC, Chapel Hill, 1968.
Prestage, Edgar. *Descobridores Portugueses*. Edições Gama, Portugal, 1943.
Prestage, Edgar. *Viagens Portuguesas de Descobrimento*. Livraria Portugalia, 1940.
Pretty, Francis. *Sir Francis Drake's Famous Voyage Round the World*. Harvard Classics, Vol. 33, 1910.
Price, Jr., Edward Thomas. *Geographic Analysis of White-Negro-Indian Racial Mix....* Los Angeles State College, 1953.
Price, Jr., Edward Thomas. *Melungeons, Mix Blood Strain of the S. Appalachians*. Doctoral dissertation at University of California, 1950.
Price, Henry R. *Melungeons, The Vanishing Colony of Newman's Ridge*. Hancock County Drama Association, 1971.
Quinn, David Beers. *The First Colonists, Doc. the First English Settlements*. NC Dept. of Cultural Resources, 1982.
Quinn, David Beers. *Newfoundland from Fishery to Colony*. Arno Press, NY, 1979.
Quinn, David Beers. *North America Discovery, 1000-1612*. Univ. of South Carolina Press, 1971.
Quinn, David Beers. *The Roanoke Voyages* (2 Volumes). Dover Publications, New York, 1991.
Quinn, David Beers. *Set Fair for Roanoke*. UNC Press, Chapel Hill and London, 1985.
Ramsey, J. G. M. *Annals of Tennessee, end 18th century*. Walker and James, Charleston, 1853.
Rangel, Rodrigo. *Hernando de Soto, narratives by B. Smith, E. Bourne*. Allerton Books, NY, 1936.
Read, Jan. *The Moors in Spain and Portugal*. Rowman & Littlefield, Totowa NJ, 1974.
Reparaz, Gonçalo de. *Portugueses no Vice-reinado do Peru, XVI/XVII*. Inst. Alta Cultura, 1976.
Ribeiro, Antonio Silva. *Colombo em Portugal*. Marinha Portuguesa, Lisboa, 1992.
Rice, Horace Richard. *The Buffalo Ridge Cherokee*. Bowie, MD, 1995.
Richardson, W. A. R. *Portuguese Discovery of Australia*. National Library of Australia, Albury, NSW, 1989.
Rights, Douglas L. *American Indian in NC*. John F. Blair, 1957.
Ritchie, Jean. *Singing Family of the Cumberlands*. University of Kentucky Press, 1988.
Roberts, J. M. *The Pelican History of the World*. Penguin Books, NY, 1987.
Roddy, Edward G. Mills, *Mansions and Mergers, William M. Wood, 1858*. Merrimack Valley Textile Museum, 1982.
Rodrigues, Antonio Simões. *Historia de Portugal em Datas*. Circulo de Leitores, 1994.
Rogers, F. M. *Portuguese Americans, Harvard Encyclopedia of Ethnic Groups*. Cambridge, MA, 1980.
Rogers, Francis Millet. *Americans of Portuguese Descent*. Sage Pub. Beverly Hills, CA, 1974.
Roth, Cecil A. *History of the Marranos*. Hermon Press, NY, 1974.
Rountree, Helen C. *Pocahontas people, Powatans Indians of Virginia*. University of Oklahoma Press, 1990.
Rountree, Helen C. *Young Pocahontas in the Indian World*. University of Oklahoma Press, 1995.
Russell, Peter. *The English Intervention in Spain and Portugal*. Oxford at the Clarendon

Press, 1955.

Russel-Wood, A. J. R. *Men under stress,social environment carreira da India*. Inst. Investigação Cientifica, Lisboa, 1985.

Russel-Wood, A. J. R. *World on the Move, the Portuguese in Africa*. Carcanet Press Ltd., 1992.

Sachar, Howard. *Farewell España*. Knopf, NY, 1994.

Sale, Kirkpatrick. *Columbus, Conquest of Paradise*. Random House, 1990.

Salley, Jr. Alexander S. *Narratives of Early Carolina*. Charles Scribner's sons, 1911.

Sams, Conway Whittle. *Conquest of Virginia, First attempt (1584 Exped.)*. Keyser-Doherty Norfolk, VA, 1924.

Sandburg, Carl. *Abraham Lincoln, the Prairie Years, Vols. I & II*. Harcourt Brace Jovanovich, Inc, 1970.

Sandburg, Carl. *Abraham Lincoln, the Prairie Years and the War Years*. Harcourt Brace Jovanovich, Inc, 1970.

Sandoval, John S. *Mt. Eden cradle Salt Industry in California*. Mt. Eden Historical Publishers, 1988.

Santos, Fernando dos. *The Portuguese in Hawaii*. Luso-Americano Newspaper, Newark, N. J. 07105, 1996.

Santos, José de Almeida. *As Berlengas e os Piratas*. Academia de Marinha, 1994.

Santos, Robert L. *Azoreans to California*. Alley Cass Publications, Denair CA, 1966.

Saraiva, Antonio José. *Inquisição e Cristãos-Novos*, 5ª edição. Lisbon, Estampa, 1985.

Saraiva, José Hermano. *Historia Concisa de Portugal*. Publicações Europa-America, 1981.

Sauer, Carl Ortwin. *Sixteenth Century North-America*. Univ. of California Press, LA, CA, 1971.

Serjeant, Robert Bertram. *The Portuguese off the South Arabian Coast*. Oxford at the Clarndon Press, 1963.

Serrão, Joaquim Verissimo. *Historia de Portugal, Vol. III* . Verbo, 1978.

Serrão, Joel. *Cronologia geral da Historia de Portugal*. Horizonte, 1973.

Shillington, V. M. (A. B. W. Chapman). *The Commercial Relations of England and Portugal*. Burt Franklin, NY (A. B. Wallis Chapman), 1976.

Silva, Antonio de Morais e. *Grande Dicionario da Lingua Portuguesa, Vol. VI*. Confluência Editora, Portugal, 1954.

Silva, Dr. Manuel Luciano da. *Christopher Columbus name and the Pope*. Author, 1994.

Silva, Dr. Manuel Luciano da. *Columbus was 100% Portuguese*. Author, 1989.

Silva, Dr. Manuel Luciano da. *Os Pioneiros Portugueses e a Pedra de Dighton*. Brasilia Edit., 1974.

Silva, Dr. Manuel Luciano da. *Portuguese Pilgrims and Dighton Rock*. Nelson D. Martins, Bristol, RI, USA, 1971.

Silva, Dr. Manuel Luciano da. *The True Antilles and Rock of Dighton*. Author, 1987.

Simmons, Marc. *Last Conquistador, Juan de Oñate*. University of Oklahoma Press, 1991.

Simmons, Marc. *The Little Lyon of the SW—a life of*. Ohio U. Press, 1983.

Skelton, Raleigh Ashlin. *Maps, Historical Survey*. Hermon Dunlap, Chicago, 1995.

Smith, James Morton. *Seventeenth Century America*. University of North Carolina Press, 1959.

Smith, Captain John. *General History of Virginia (1624)*. London, England.

Smith, Captain John & Sparks, Michael. *History of Virginia or True Relations*. Michael Sparkes, 1624.

Smith, M. Estellie. *Portuguese Enclaves: The Invisible Minority*. Southern Anthropological Society, UGA, 1974.

Sousa, Francisco de. *Tratado das Ilhas Novas*. Typ. Archivo Açores, Ponta Delgada, 1884.

Sousa, Frei Luiz de. *Os Anais de D. João III*. Sá da Costa, Lisboa, 1938.

Sousa, Manuel Andrade e. *Catherine of Braganza*. Edições INAPA, 1994.

South, Stanley. *Discovery of Sta. Elena, Parris Island*. Univ. of SC, Nat. Geographic Society, 1980.

Stapleton, Michael. *Greek and Roman Mythology*. Peter Bedrick Books, Inc. New York,

1986.
Stick, David. *Graveyard of the Atlantic (Shipwrecks of NC)*. University of NC, Chapel Hill, 1968.
Stick, David. *The Outer Banks of North Carolina*. University of NC, Chapel Hill, 1958.
Stick, David. *Roanoke Island, the Beginnings of America*. University of NC, Chapel Hill, 1983.
Stokely, Jim & Cavender, Anthony P. *Encyclopedia of East Tennessee*. Jim Stockley, Jeff D. Johnson Oak Ridge, 1981.
Stuart, Jess. *Daughter of the Legend*. New York, McGraw Hill, 1965.
Summers, Lewis Preston. *Annals of Southwest Virginia*. Summers, Abingdon, Virginia, 1929.
Summers, Lewis Preston. *History of Southwest Virginia*. Overmountain Press, 1989.
Sutherland, Elihu. *Pioneer recollections of Southwest VA*. Mullins Printing, Rt 2, Box 307, 1984.
Sutton, Jessie, *The Heritage of Macon County*. Historical Society, 1987.
Swanton, John R. *De Soto Expedition Commission Final Report*. Smithsonian Institutional Press, 1985.
Tarbel, Ida Minerva. *In the Foot Steps of Lincoln*. Harper Brother, NY, 1924.
Tavares, Maria José Pimenta F. *Os Judeus em Portugal no Século XV*. Universidade Nova, Lisbon, 1982.
Taviani, Paolo Emilio. *Columbus,The Grand Design*. Orbis, London, 1985.
Teague, Michael. *Rota dos Navegadores Portugueses*. Quetzal Editores, Lisboa, Portugal, 1988.
TePaske, John. *Report on the Spanish Records of the NC State Archives*. Duke University, Ellen Z. McGrew, 1980.
Thapar, Romila. *History of India*. Penguin Books, 1966.
Thompson, George Malcom. *Sir Francis Drake*. William Morrow and Co., NY, 1972.
Tindall, George Brown. *America, a Narrative History*. W. W. Norton & Co., 1984.
Trager, James. *Peoples Chronology*. Henry Holt, NY, 1994.
Treen, Maria de Freitas. *The Admiral and his Lady*. Robert Speller, NY, 1989.
Trindade, Maria José Lagos. *Portuguese Emigrations to the US*. 19th century. SHBAI, 1976.
Ulmann, Doris. *Appalachian Photographs*. Jargon Society, KY, 1971.
Urbel, Fray Justo Perez. *La España del Siglo X*. Ediciones Alonso, Madrid, 1983.
Van Sertima, Ivan. *They came before Columbus*. Random House, NY, 1976.
Velho, Alvaro. *Roteiro da 1ª viagem de Vasco da Gama*. A. Geral do Ultramar, Imprensa Nac., 1969.
Vidago, João. *Epigrafia Portuguesa nas Ilhas Bermudas, 1543*. Associação dos Arqueologos Portugueses, 1964.
Vidago, João. *O Nome da América e a Cartografia Portuguesa de 1500*. Revista Ocidente, Volume LXXV, 1968.
Viegas, Valentino. *Cronologia da Revolução de 1383-1385*. Imprensa Universitaria, 1984.
Vieira, Alberto. *Escravos no Arquipelago da Madeira, Sec. XV a XVII*. Centro Est. Hist. do Atlantico, 3 Vols., 1991.
Viera, David J. *Bibliography History of Portuguese Language, Pedagogy*. David J. Viera, 1992.
Vigneras, Louis Andre. *La Busqueda del Paraiso y las Legendarias Islas....* Museo de Colon, Univ. Valladolid, 1976.
Vivente, Antonio Luis. *Portugueses nos E.U.A., Poliitica e Comunidades*. F.L.A.D., Lisboa, 1998.
Wairaven, O. N. *The Melungeons of Oakdale*. Manuscript G. 08 from VVTA Federal Writers' Guide, in McClung Historical Collection, Lawson McGhee Library, Knoxville, TN.
Warner, Jackson. *Studies in Slavery*. Mnemosyne Publishing, Miami, FL, 1851.
Weber, David J. *Spanish Frontier in North America*. Yale University Press, 1992.
Wheeler, Douglas L. *History Dictionary of Portugal*. The Scarecrow Press, Inc. New

Jersey & London, 1993.
Wicki, Joseph. *Relação das Viagens dos Jesuitas, 1541-1598*. Inst. Inv. Cient. Trop. Lisboa, 1985.
Williams, Max R. *History of Jackson County*. Jackson County Historical Association, 1987.
Williams, Neville. *Great Lives Francis Drake*. Weidenfeld and Nicholson, London, 1974.
Williams, Neville. *The Sea Dogs*. MacMillan Publishing Co., Inc., NY, 1975.
Williams, Samuel Cole. *Dawn of the Tennessee Valley and TN History*. Watauga Press, Johnson City, TN, 1937.
Williams, Samuel Cole. *Early Travels in the Tennessee County*. Watauga Press, Johnson City, TN, 1928.
Williamson, Joel, *The New People: Miscegenation and Mulattoes in the United States*. New York: Free Press, 1980.
Wirth, Fremont P. *The Development of America*. American Book Co., 1938.
Wise, Jr., W. Harvey. *Andrew Jackson, Biographical Sketch*. Burt Franklin, NY, 1935.
Witt, E. Carl. *Foot Prints in Northampton*. Northampton County, 1976.
Wolff, Christopher, Brinton. *Civilization in the West*. Prentice-Hall, Inc., NJ, 2nd edition, 1969.
Wolforth, Sandra Knight. *The Portuguese in America*. Florida Atlantic University, 1976.
Wright, Irene A. *Further English Voyages to Spanish America*. Kraus Reprint, Liechtenstein, 1967.
Wright, Louis Booker. *The Atlantic Frontier*. Cornell University Press, 1966.
Wright, Louis Booker. *The Elizabethan's Americans*. Stratford/Avon, 1965.
Wright, Louis Booker. *History & Present St. of VA ed. Robert Beverley of 1705*. University of North Carolina, 1947.
Xavier, Pde. Manuel. *Relações da Carreira da India*. Alfa, Lisboa, 1985.
Zachary, Thomas. *The Melungeons*. Undergraduate thesis, Department of Education, University of Tennessee.
Zielonka, David M. *The Eager Immigrants*. Stipes Publishing Co. Champaign, IL, 1972.
Zuber, Leo, *The Melungeons*. Typewritten Manuscript #G.08, WPA Federal Writers' Guide, McClung Historical Collection, Knoxville, TN.
Zurara, Gomes Eanes da. *Crónica da Guiné (José de Bragança)*. Biblioteca Historica—Serie Ultramarina, 1973.
Zweig, Stephan. *Magellan, Conquerer of the seas*. MacMillan Co. of America, 1938.

Newspapers, Magazines and other Media

American Anthropologist, A note on the Melungeons, Swan M. Burnett & W. H. Holmes, Oct. 1889.
American Anthropologist, The Physical Anthropology and Genetics…, William Pollitzer, Vol. 74, 1972.
American Heritage, First Photograph of Lincoln, Harold Holzer, Feb./Mar. 1994.
American Heritage, Nation of Immigrants, In the News, Bernard A. Weisberger, Feb./Mar. 1994.
American Heritage, Was America Discovered by Columbus? Alvin M. Josephy, Jr., 1955.
American History Guidebook, Chronology, Bobley Publishing, 1975.
American History Illustrated, The Lost Roanoke Colony, Walter Spearman, May 1993.
American History Illustrated, The Melungeons, Byron Stinson, Vol. 8, No. 7, Nov. 1973.
American Journal of Islamic Social Sciences, King Zumbi and the Malé Movement in Brazil, T. B. Irving, 1992.
Annais do Clube Militar, No. 1 to 11, Subsidios para o Estudo da Carreira das Indias, 1989. Cte. Carlos Alberto Encarnação Gomes, 1996.
Appalachian Journal, The Melungeons became a race, David Henige, 25: 3, pp. 270-298.
Appalachian Journal, Origin Traditions of American Racial Isolate, David Henige, 11: 3, pp. 201-213.
Arena, The Malungeons, Will Allen Dromgoole, Vol. 3, March 1891.

Arena, The Malungeons Tree and its Four Branches, Will Allen Dromgoole, Vol. 3, May 1891.
Arkansas Gazette, Fleeing Jews Discovered America Before Columbus, Cyrus Gordon, Oct. 19, 1970.
Arkansas Gazette, Strange people of East Tennessee, Eliza N. Heiskell, Little Rock, AR, Jan. 14, 1914.
Atlanta Constitution, Mystery of the Melungeons, Chris Wohlwend, July 6, 1993.
Atlanta Journal, Native Africans' bones..., Bill Hendrick, p. C7, May 11, 1997.
Baltimore Sunday Sun Magazine, A People With an Unknown Past, Jean P. Bible, June 13, 1971.
Blue Ridge Country, The Melungeons, N. Brent Kennedy, July/Aug. 1992.
Blue Ridge Country, The Melungeons, Joan V. Schroeder, July/Aug. 1991.
Boletim do Instituto, Historia da Ilha Terceira, Presença de Portugal nos E. U. A., Manoel da Silveira Cardozo, Açores, Vol. XVI, 1958.
California History, Don Antonio José Rocha, El Portugues, Eduardo Mayone Dias and David Bertão, Vol. LXVI, No. 3, Sept. 1987.
The Catholic Historical Review, Sebastian Montero: Pioneer American Missionary, Michael V. Gannon Vol. LI, No. 3, Oct. 1965.
Charlotte Observer, Unlocking Melungeon Ancestry, Bruce Henderson, Aug. 15, 1993.
Chattanooga Times, Jews Were First to find America, Assoc. Press, NY, Oct. 19, 1970.
Chattanooga Times Sunday Magazine, A Romance of the Melungeons, T. A. Rogers, June 21, 1936.
Chesopiean Archaeology, The Melungeons of Eastern Tennessee, Thurston L. Willis, Vol. 9, 1971.
Chicago Record, They are Copper Colored, Furman Collection, SC Library, 1900.
Chicago Tribune, Melungeon Colony Fading Away, NY Times News Service, Aug. 19, 1971.
Chicago Tribune, Melungeons: a Tennessee Mystery, Editorial, Nov. 11, 1970.
Cidade de Tomar, A Coroa dos Tabuleiros de Tomar, p. 15, May 14, 1999.
Citizen Tribune, Morristown, TN, Melungeons, Editorial, June 8, 1968.
Coalfield Progress, Melungeon connection to Turkey, Jeff Lester, June 6, 1995.
Correio da Manhã, Relações Luso-Americanas nos anos da Independencia, white skin, Victor Luis Eleuterio, Lisboa, Portugal, 1995.
Diario de Noticias, Lisboa, Dignidade e Respeito, Portugal, Editorial, Mar 11, 1958.
Dictionary of Georgia Biography, ed. by Kenneth Coleman & Charles Stephen Gurr, Vol. II, pp. 754-755.
East Bay Window, Local Historian says Portuguese built Newport Tower, James A. Merolla, Dr. Luciano da Silva, Dec. 22, 1993.
East Tennessee Historical Society Bulletin, The Melungeons, John Fetterman, No. 32, 1960; Louisville Courier-Journal Magazine, March 30, 1969.
Enciclopedia Gallega, Grande, Silverio Cañada, España, Vol. 18, 1974.
Encyclopædia Britannica, Hard Cover Edition and CD 2.0, Chicago, 1993.
Encyclopædia Britannica, Turnips in the Southeast & England, Chicago, Book 22, 1963.
Encyclopædia Britannica, Year Book 2000, Anthropology, Chicago, IL, 2000.
Encyclopedia Judaica, Iberian Downgrade, Suffolk, MA, 1972.
Encyclopedia Judaica, Portugal and the Sephardim, Suffolk, MA, 1972.
Eugenics, Quarterly, American Triracial Isolates, Calvin L. Beale, Vol. 4-4, Dec. 1957.
Figueiró dos Vinhos, Municipal Tourism Office Edition, Turismo Local, 1979.
Fundação Luso-Americana para o Desenvolvimento, Relações entre Portugal e os Estados Unidos, Lisboa, p. 69, 1997.
Geographic Journal, Andrea Bianco Map by Jaime Batalha Reis, Feb. 1887.
Geographical Review, The Melungeons, Edward T. Price, No. 2, April 1951.
Gowen Research Foundation Newsletter, Articles by Evelyn McKinley Orr and M. Ruth Johnson, 1989 to 1996.
Halifax County, Centennial Year Book, County Commissioners, 1958.
Halifax Heritage, Historical Sketches, Weldon High School, 1958.
Hammond Historical Atlas, C. S. Hammond & Co., 1957.
Hancock County Post, Hancock County Land of Mystery (10 page transcript), William P.

Groshe, McClung Historical Coll., July 4, 1968.

Hancock County Post, The Land of Mystery, William Grohse, July 2, 1970.

Human Biology, Survey of Demography, Genetics, Melungeons, William Pollitzer & William H. Brown, Vol. 41, p. 3, Sept. 1969.

O Jornal, New Providence, Melungeons and their claim of Portuguese, Manuel Mira, 1995.

Journal and Tribune, Melungeons: Mystery Race, Associated Press, July 29, 1923.

Journal of Medicine, Genetic, Hereditary anaemias in Portugal, epidemiology…, Martins, Olim, Melo, Magalhães, Rodrigues, 30:235-239, 1993.

Journal Washington, Academy Sciences, Mixed Bloods of the upper Monongahela Valley, WV, William Harlen Gilbert Jr., Vol. 36-1, Jan. 15, 1946.

Journal of Science, Mixed Blood Racial Strain of Carmel, Ohio, Magoffin, KY. Ohio, Edward Thomas Price Jr., Vol. 50, 1950.

Kingsport Times News, The Last of the Melungeons, Editorial, Focus, Sept. 5, 1971.

Kingsport Times News, Melungeon and Turks, A Key to a Mystery, Brad Lifford, Oct. 6, 1996.

Kingsport Times News, Melungeon Line Almost Extinct, John Gamble (UPI), Nov. 26, 1964.

Kingsport Times News, Melungeon Museum, Christopher Schnaars, May 28, 1996.

Kingsport Times News, Melungeons Subject of Study, Barbara Watson, Dec. 6, 1992.

Knoxville News Sentinel, East Tennessee Melungeons Have Past Clouded in Myth, Bill Rawlins, Oct. 10, 1958.

Knoxville News Sentinel, Maligned Mountain Folk, Willard Yarbrough, Jan. 8, 1968.

Knoxville News Sentinel, Mediterranean Scholar's Theory, Associated Press, Oct. 10, 1970.

Knoxville News Sentinel, Melungeon ways are passing, Willard Yarbrough, April 26, 1972.

Knoxville News Sentinel, Mysterious E-T Mountain Clan, John Gamble, Nov. 26, 1964.

Knoxville News Sentinel, Olive-Skinned Hancock Countians, Willard Yarbrough, Jun 10, 1966.

Knoxville Register, Melungeon Drama goes on despite money problems, Editorial, April 19, 1972.

Littel's Living Age, The Melungens, Cornell U. MOA, N° 254, pp. 618-619, March 1849.

Luso Americano, Abade José Correia da Serra, Henrique Mano, Nov. 22, 1996.

Luso Americano, Bermuda Portuguese and Politician Interview, Newark, NJ, 1996.

Luso Americano, The First New York Portuguese, Newark, NJ, April 3, 1996.

Luso Americano, Garrafa com mensagem de NJ Portugal, Franklin Cruz, April 17-19, 1996.

Luso Americano, Livro sobre o Sudeste dos E. U., Manuel Mira, May 31, 1995.

Luso Americano, Melungos, Chamam-se, Manuel Mira, April 15, 1995.

Luso Americano, Menino de Leiria, p. 30, July 28, 1999.

Luso Americano, Manuel Brazil, pioneiro Português no NM e TX, Geoffrey L. Gomes, April 6, 1994.

Luso Americano, Manuel Brazil, um pioneiro Português no NM, Geoffrey L. Gomes, Jan. 13, 1993.

Luso Americano, Presença Portuguesa na India, Fernando G. Rosa, April 24, 1996.

Luso Americano, Sinagoga de Tomar, Magazine, Dec. 1, 1995.

Luso Americano, Various Articles in Portuguese about Columbus, Dr. Luciano da Silva, July 8, 1992.

Macon County, Archaeological report, Industrial Park, Cherokee Village, Susan M. Collins, Dave Moore, Ruth Y. Wetmore, 1977.

Macon County Heritage, The Macon Co. Historical Society, Inc., Delmar Printing, 2nd prt, 1993.

Mare Liberum, Instrumentos de Navegação, José Manuel Malhão Pereira, N° 7, Mar. 1994.

Mare Liberum, Movimento da Carreira da India, Lopes-Frutoso-Guinote, Secs. 16-18, Dec. 1992.

The Mariner's Mirror, Portuguese Roteiros by Charles Ralph Boxer, Society for Nautical Research, London, April 1934.

McClung Historical Society, The Melungeons, Historical Collection, 1968.

McClung Historical Society, The Melungeons at Oakdale, Otho N. Walraven, 1968.

Melungeon Bibliography, University of Tennessee, Knoxville, Reference Library, 1992.

Mountaineer Times, The Melungeon Mystique, Maryann Herberman, Vol. 9 No. 2, Early

Fall 1994.
Mundo Português, Various Issues, Henrique Mano, 1996.
Nashville Banner, What do you know about Malungeons, Douglas Anderson, Aug. 3, 1924.
Nashville Tennesseean, Melungeon Mystery, Louise Davis; also the Magazine, Louise Davis, Sept. 22/29, 1963.
National Genealogical Society Quarterly, Looking at Legends—Lumbee and Melungeon, Virginia Easley DeMarce, Vol. 1, #I, Mar. 1993.
National Genealogical Society Quarterly, The Melungeons, Essay Review, Virginia Easley DeMarce, Ph.D., Vol. 84, p. 2, June 1996.
National Genealogical Society Quarterly, Tri-Racial Isolate Families of the Upper South—A Genealogical Study, Virginia Easley DeMarce, Vol. 80, # I, Mar. 1992.
National Geographic Magazine, Along Afghanistan's Border, June 1985.
National Geographic Magazine, Basque Whaling in America, XVI century, July 1985.
National Geographic Magazine, Celts, Europe's Founders, May 1977.
National Geographic Magazine, Elizabethans in America, Blanch Nettleton Epler, M.D., Dec. 1933.
National Geographic Magazine, Exploring Forgotten Centuries, Joseph Judge, March 1988.
National Geographic Magazine, Fair of the Berber Brides, Carla Hunt, Jan. 1980.
National Geographic Magazine, Long slow death of a Jewish Language, Nov. 1993.
National Geographic Magazine, Moors Ruled Spain, July 1988.
National Geographic Magazine, New England's Little Portugal, O. Louis Mazzatenta, Jan. 1975.
National Geographic Magazine, Portugal at Cross Roads, Oct. 1965.
National Geographic Magazine, Portuguese Sea Route to India, Nov. 1992.
National Geographic Magazine, Sir Francis Drake and John Hawkins, Feb. 1975.
National Geographic Magazine, Turkish portrait of the World in 1513, March 1994.
New England Journal of Medicine, Vol. 326, No. 17, pp. 1130-1136, April 23, 1992.
New Orleans, Portuguese and Associations, Public Library, 1850.
New York Evening Post, People of East Tennessee, Furman Collection, SC Library, 1902.
New York Evening Post, A Strange Tennessee People, Furman Collection, SC Library, 1897.
New York Times, Indians resist integration plan in NC county, Ben Franklin, Sept. 13, 1970.
New York Times, Mysterious Hill Folk Vanishing, Jon Nordheimer, Aug. 10, 1971.
News & Observer (Raleigh, NC), Melungeons, Author finds clues to mysterious origin, Associated Press, Nov. 15, 1995.
News & Observer (Raleigh, NC), The Mystery of Virginia's Melungeons, Chris Wohlwend, Jul. 12, 1993.
News & Observer (Raleigh, NC), Turkish TV and University Study Melungeons, Editor, Nov. 15, 1995.
North Carolina Historical Review, The Acculturation of the Eastern Cherokees, Leonard Bloom, Vol. 19, 1942.
North Carolina Historical Review, The Catawba Nation and its neighbors, Frank G. Speck, Vol. 16, 1939.
North Carolina Historical Review, Spanish Discovery of North Carolina in 1566, L. A. Vigneras, Vol. 46, 1969.
The North Carolina State Magazine, The Melungeons, Arthur Billy, 1994.
The North Carolinian, Orange County Tax List, NC of 1755, William Perry Johnson, Editor, Vol. 1-4, Dec. 1955.
Palm Beach Community College, Center for Multicultural Affairs, West Palm Beach, FL, 1989.
Palm Beach Post, Pocahontas tale, plagiarism, West Palm Beach, FL, July 10, 1995.
PBS TV, Spice Islands, Ring of Fire, by Lorne and Lawrence Blair, VHS Cassette, 1988.
Portuguese Around Us, Melungeons TV Program with Dr. Luciano da Silva, VHS Cassette, 1995.
Portuguese Heritage, Portuguese settlement was family oriented, William Freitas, Ph.D., 1993.
Portuguese Historical/Cultural Society, Portuguese Pioneers in Sacramento, Lionel Holmes, Joseph D'Alessandro, 1977.

Portuguese Post, Greek Presence in Tavira, Newark, NJ, May 14, 1996.
Portuguese Studies Review (ICGP), Portuguese in the US, A Bibliography, David
     Wheeler, David Viera, Geoffrey Gomes, 1995.
RTP TV Portugal, Melungeons TV Program, Mario Crespo, VHS Cassette, 1994.
RTP TV Portugal, Melungeons TV Program, 2nd. program, VHS Cassette, 1995.
Ramsey Privateer Township, The Melungeons, McDonald Furman, SC Library Furman
     Collection, May 25, 1897.
Reader's Digest, Our Fair Lady: The Statue of Liberty, Special Feature, pp. 191-197, July 1986.
Revista de Portugal, Lusismos na União da Africa do Sul, Antonio Barradas, Vol. 6, Nº
     29, Fev. 1945.
Roanoke Rapids Sunday Herald, Northampton's Portuguese go Elsewhere... Front Page,
     Dick Kern, Mar. 2, 1958.
Roanoke (Virginia) Times, First African in Virginia, Mark St. John Erickson, April 24, 1999.
Saturday Evening Post, Sons of the Legend, Terry P. Wilson, William L. Worden, Oct. 18, 1947.
Savannah Synagogue, History of the First Savannah Synagogue, City Tourism Office, 1992.
Shepperds TV Channel, Melungeons, VHS Cassette, 1989.
Sky Magazine, Travelin' Man, Anthony Weller, pp. 13-15.
Smithsonian Institute, Synoptic data, Survival of Indian. Part-Indian Blood E. U. S.,
     William Harlen Gilbert, Jr., 1947.
Sol Português, Portuguese Sun, Toronto, Ontario, Canada, Dec. 12, 1997.
Southern Collegian, The Melungeons, Paul Converse, Dec. 1912.
Southern Cultures, Mixing in the Mountains, John Shelton Reed, Vol. 3, No. 4.
Tennessee Anthropological Association, Bibliography of Tennessee Anthropology,
     Donald Bruce Ball, 1976.
Tennessee Anthropologist Association, Melungeons, Comparisons of Gene Distribution,
     James L. Guthrie, 15/1, Spring 1990.
Tennessee Conservationist, The Mystery People of Tennessee, Swan Burnett & W. H.
     Holmes, Aug. 1959.
Tennessee Historical Quarterly, Andrew Jackson, Citizen of Spain, Robert V. Remini,
     Spring 1995.
Tennessee Valley Historical Review, The Mystery of the Melungeons, Louise Davis,
     Spring 1972.
Terrae Incognitae (Journal), Motives of Portuguese Expansion...Indonesia...16th
     century, John Parker, Vol. 14. pp. 23-39, 1982.
Terrae Incognitae (Journal), Original Sources...Revisionism...Historiography of
     Discovery, John Parker, Vol. 13. pp. 31-34, 1981.
Terrae Incognitae (Journal), Turks, Moors, Blacks and Others in Drake's..., David B.
     Quinn, Vol. XIV, 1986.
Terrae Incognitae (Journal), The Voyage of Esteban Gomez from Florida to the
     Baccalaos, Louis Andre Vigneras, Vol. II, pp. 25-28, 1976.
The Times Picayune Islenos, The fight for survival of a culture, John R. Kemp, 1979.
Transylvania Times, Mysterious Culture winds through Kentucky, Bryon Crawford, p.
     8B, Dec. 7, 1995.
Tuscaloosa (Alabama) News, Historic ancestry explored, solving a folklore mystery,
     Dana Beyerle, Nov. 1, 1993.
UPEC Life, Portuguese Immigrants in Nevada, Donald Warrin, Spring 1989.
UPEC Life, Portuguese...on the Western frontier, Antonio Monteiro, Geoffrey L. Gomes,
     Summer 1988.
US News & World Report, Mysteries of History: DNA, Nancy Shute, July 24, 2000.
Virginian Pilot, Segregated Portuguese Children, Luther J. Carter, Jan. 26, 1958.
Wall Street Journal, Appalachian Clan Mines Web sites for Ancestral Clues, Fred R.
     Bleakley, pp. B1-B5, April 14, 1997.
Washington Post, Beneath Myth, Melungeons Find Roots and Oppression, Carol
     Morello, p. A01, May 30, 2000.
William and Mary Quarterly, articles by Engel Sluiter and John Thornton, April 1997
     and July 1998.